Seeing Anthropology

SEEING ANTHROPOLOGY
Cultural Anthropology through Film

Third
Edition

Karl G. Heider
University of South Carolina

Boston ▪ New York ▪ San Francisco
Mexico City ▪ Montreal ▪ Toronto ▪ London ▪ Madrid ▪ Munich ▪ Paris
Hong Kong ▪ Singapore ▪ Tokyo ▪ Cape Town ▪ Sydney

Series Editor: Jennifer Jacobson
Editorial Assistant: Amy Holborow
Production Editor: Michelle Limoges
Editorial Production Service: P. M. Gordon Associates
Compositor: Omegatype Typography, Inc.
Composition and Prepress Buyer: Linda Cox
Manufacturing Buyer: JoAnne Sweeney
Cover Designer: Linda Knowles

For related titles and support materials, visit our online catalog at www.ablongman.com.

Library of Congress Cataloging-in-Publication Data

Heider, Karl G.
    Seeing anthropology : cultural anthropology through film / Karl G. Heider.—3rd ed.
       p. cm.
    Includes bibliographical references and index.
    ISBN 0-205-38912-0
    1. Motion pictures in ethnology.   2. Ethnology.   3. Indigenous peoples in motion pictures.
  I. Title.

GN347.H46 2004
306—dc21

                                         2003045208

Printed in the United States of America

10 9 8 7 6 5 4 3 2 1   RRD-IN 07 06 05 04 03

CONTENTS

4   Meanings: Language, Symbols, and Art   97

5   Psychology and Culture   133

7   Distribution and Consumption   199

11   Power and Politics

14   Medical Anthropology and the Future   404

PREFACE

This textbook has several specific goals. My first goal, announced in both title and subtitle, is to integrate ethnographic films into the introductory cultural anthropology course. Achieving this goal involves three operations: (1) building each chapter around one film that illustrates the subject of the chapter; (2) making each film suitable for study by introducing the culture that it presents and the particulars of the film and by suggesting setup questions that can be thought about while viewing the film; and (3) giving some overall suggestions in this preface on how to think about ethnographic films as ethnographies, complementary to but different from the usual written ethnographies.

My second goal is to concentrate on a limited number of ideas, illustrated by examples from a few representative cultures, rather than to produce a data dump that includes every fact and every culture in the anthropological literature. I attempt to be inclusive but not exhaustive. Thus there are fourteen focus cultures shown in the films and used as ethnographic examples in the text.

A third, more theoretical goal, is to develop the ideas of eclectic holism, using a biocultural model where appropriate. That is, by drawing out the relationships between cultural features as much as possible and showing interrelationships, interconnections, and cross-influences where they can be found, the book tries to avoid the compartmentalization of factoids, which can turn the study of anthropology into a sort of pursuit of exotic trivia.

A fourth goal, especially toward the end of the book, is to discuss ways in which anthropological approaches and ideas can contribute to public discourse on particular issues and to the solutions of problems in the world.

The book springs out of a deep conviction that anthropology is the most exciting and important social science for our increasingly multicultural lives, and it is my hope that this book will help instructors convey this excitement to their students.

The films are meant to be taken as seriously as the text itself. Just as you read a text differently from the way you read a light novel, so you will need to study these films with a care you would never use for a feature film or a TV sitcom. The words and the images will constantly complement and reinforce each other. For example, in Chapter 1 you read about frogs and ducks in Balinese rice fields, and on film you actually see them. The words intellectualize the creatures, but when the American professor pulls a frog out of the water, you have an image that you will not easily forget.

THE FILMS

The fourteen films that I have matched with the fourteen chapters of this third edition were selected after months of deliberation from a list of several thousand films.

Since 1966, I have been compiling a catalog, *Films for Anthropological Teaching,* published by the American Anthropological Association, and now in its eighth edition (Heider and Hermer, 1995). It includes some 3,000 titles. I have not seen all of these films, but over the years I have seen hundreds of them and have used many in classes of all sorts, experimenting with different ways of presentation. The fourteen presented here are not "the best ethnographic films of all time," whatever that might mean, but I believe they make the best fit for this textbook.

Choosing the Films

I used several criteria in choosing the films: (1) they should be relatively short and relatively didactic, and they should represent a wide range of culture types and world areas; (2) they should be ethnographically accurate and have solid written ethnographic backup; (3) they should be well made and fun to watch; (4) each should contribute to the subject of a particular chapter; and (5) the films should represent, so far as possible, the whole range of human culture types and world areas.

To be sure, many splendid ethnographic films were made in the 1990s, as viewers at the annual Margaret Mead Film Festival and the American Anthropological Association meetings can attest. But it has turned out, somewhat to my surprise, that in many cases the older films spoke better to the subjects of particular chapters. Needless to say, for other sorts of anthropology courses, one would want a different set of films. But here is my reasoning for choosing these particular ones:

The Goddess and the Computer is a particularly dramatic view of anthropological research, which is at once theoretical and applied. J. Stephen Lansing has written two books and several articles on the same subject, and the culture, Bali, is an especially interesting one for a focus culture.

Latah: A Culture-Specific Elaboration of the Startle Reflex, about the startle reflex in Malaysia, is the best illustration I know of what a biocultural model entails, and Ronald Simons's book (1996) expands on his film.

Dead Birds, an early film by Robert Gardner, depicts many aspects of Dani life, including extraordinary scenes of intergroup warfare with bows and arrows and with spears.

Box of Treasures shows the Kwa Kwaka' Wakw (Kwakiutl) of British Columbia as they struggle to preserve their culture—especially language, rituals, and art—in the face of North American consumer culture and its televised spokespersons.

How to Behave (Chuyen Tute) is a completely different sort of film, made by a Vietnamese film crew—not anthropologists at all—who in a way reinvent anthropology as they explore values and personality concepts.

Dani Sweet Potatoes is another short subsistence film. Although it tells mainly of the Dani's sweet potato horticulture, there is a subtext on childrearing.

Appeals to Santiago focuses on the cargo ritual of the Chiapas Maya as it existed in the 1960s, when it was a famous example of how religion and economics were interrelated.

Farm Song was not actually made by an anthropologist, but it shows most effectively the way an extended family functions in rural northern Japan.

The Nuer is a beautiful evocation of some Nuer people and their cattle. It alludes at various points to their social organization, made famous through E. E. Evans-Pritchard's ethnographic writings.

N!ai: The Story of a !Kung Woman is a film by John Marshall that incorporates footage he shot of N!ai, a Ju/'hoansi of the Kalahari Desert, over the years as she matured from a girl to a married woman. It incorporates N!ai's frank accounts of her own sexuality.

The Cows of Dolo Ken Paye builds on the ethnographic research of James L. Gibbs, Jr., as it follows a judicial procedure in a Kpelle village in Liberia.

Eduardo the Healer is about an exuberant cosmopolitan shaman, or curer, on the North Coast of Peru.

Trobriand Cricket: An Ingenious Response to Colonialism is Jerry Leach's film of the people studied by Malinowski long ago, showing how they have ingeniously reacted to colonialism by adapting the staid English game of cricket to their own cultural needs.

House of the Spirit: Perspectives on Cambodian Health Care was made by the American Friends Service Committee to explain Cambodian ideas of health and sickness and to show how important it is to understand the culture when working with Cambodian refugees in the United States.

Using the Short Film Clips

We have provided a videotape or CD-ROM with short clips taken from the ethnographic films. Students can watch and analyze the clips as homework, and instructors can show them in class, leaving plenty of time for discussion. Needless to say, the short clip cannot substitute for seeing the entire film, but it can serve important pedagogical purposes. At first glance this approach may seem like a violation of the integrity of the film. As a filmmaker myself, I am very aware of how much thought goes into editing a film, and how painful it is to discard each precious foot of film. As a teacher, however, I have tested the use of short clips in many class situations (this effort is now greatly facilitated with films on videotape) and I have been converted. Using both clips and complete films allows more flexibility, permits viewers to focus on particularly important sequences, and also lets them see the whole film as intended by the filmmaker. In the future, I think, we will be using clips from films as easily as we take quotations from books. Today, it is still a new idea for many, and I am very interested to hear how people react.

Acquiring the Films

This book is built around films, so it is important to be able to see some or all of them. Most schools already have many films and will want to rent or buy others, whether

Summary of Focus Cultures and Films

Religion	Sociopolitical Organization	Main Ethnographic Information In	Films
Hinduism	Nation (Bali, Indonesia)	Chapter 1	*The Goddess and the Computer*
Islam	Nation (Malaysia)	Chapter 2	*Latah: A Culture-Specific Elaboration of the Startle Reflex*
Animism	Band (Ju/'hoansi)	Chapter 10	*N!ai: The Story of a !Kung Woman*
Animism	Tribe (Dani)	Chapter 3	*Dani Sweet Potatoes* (Chap. 6) *Dead Birds*
Animism, Christianity	Tribe (Kwa KwaKa' Wakw)	Chapter 4	*Box of Treasures*
Mahayana Buddhism, Neo-Confucianism	Nation (Vietnam)	Chapter 8	*How to Behave (Chuyen Tute)*
Roman Catholic	Nation (Mexico)	Chapter 7	*Appeals to Santiago*
Shinto, Mahayana Buddhism	Nation (Japan)	Chapter 8	*Farm Song*
Animism, Christianity	Tribe (Nuer)	Chapter 9	*The Nuer*
Animism, Christianity	Chiefdom (Kpelle)	Chapter 11	*The Cows of Dolo Ken Paye*
Christianity	Nation (Peru)	Chapter 12	*Eduardo the Healer*
Animism, Christianity	Chiefdom (Trobriands)	Chapter 13	*Trobriand Cricket: An Ingenious Response to Colonialism*
Therevada Buddhism	Nation (Cambodia)	Chapter 14	*House of the Spirit: Perspectives on Cambodian Health Care*

on celluloid or in video form. Instructors will perhaps have their own favorites, which they will substitute for some suggested here. The following is a list of the primary North American distributors for each film in this text.

American Friends Service Committee
15 Rutherford Place
New York, NY 10003
212-598-0950   Fax: 212-529-4603

House of the Spirit: Perspectives on Cambodian Health Care

University of California Extension
Center for Media and Independent
  Learning
2000 Center Street, Fourth Floor
Berkeley, CA 94704
510-642-1340   Fax: 510-643-9271
E-mail: dbickley@uclink.berkeley.edu
	Appeals to Santiago
	Dani Sweet Potatoes
	Trobriand Cricket: An Ingenious
	  Response to Colonialism

CRM Films 2215 Farraday Avenue Carlsbad, CA 92008 800-421-0833	*The Nuer*
Documentary Educational Resources 101 Morse Street Watertown, MA 02172 800-569-6621 Fax: 617-926-9519 E-mail: docued@der.org www.der.org/docued	*Box of Treasures* *N!ai: The Story of a !Kung Woman* *The Goddess and the Computer*
First Run/Icarus Films 153 Waverly Place, Sixth Floor New York, NY 10014 800-876-1710 Fax: 212-989-7649 E-mail: frif@echonyc.com	*How to Behave (Chuyen Tute)*
Instructional Support Services Indiana University Bloomington, IN 47405-5901 800-552-8620 Fax: 812-855-8404 E-mail: issmedia@indiana.edu	*Latah: A Culture-Specific Elaboration of* *the Startle Reflex*
Asian Educational Media Service University of Illinois at Urbana–Champaign 805 West Pennsylvania Avenue Urbana, IL 61801 217-265-0642 or 888-828-AEMS Fax: 217-265-0641 E-mail: sibarbou@uiuc.edu	*Farm Song*
Penn State Media Sales 118 Wagner Building University Park, PA 16802 800-770-2111 www.mediasales.psu.edu E-mail: lxm49@psu.edu	*Eduardo the Healer*

Phoenix Films
2349 Chaffee Drive
St. Louis, MO 63146
800-221-1274   Fax: 314-569-2834
E-mail: rdphoenix@aol.com

The Cows of Dolo Ken Paye
Dead Birds

ETHNOGRAPHY IN STONE

At the head of each chapter is a photograph of a bas-relief, carved in stone, from one of the great monuments of Southeast Asia: Borobudur, erected by Buddhists in Central Java around the 9th century C.E. (see Miksic, 1990), and the Angkor complex, built by the Hindu Khmer Kingdom in present-day Cambodia, dating from around the 12th century C.E. (see Giteau, 1976). Most of the images carved on both monuments represent theological, mythological, or dynastic events and accounts. But in the backgrounds of these reliefs one can see a remarkable wealth of everyday life, giving us ethnographic bits of long-gone cultures.

PRESS WATCH: HEADLINE ANTHROPOLOGY

You will find cultural anthropology and its concerns in the daily news, not just tucked away in textbooks like this one. Each chapter begins with newspaper items that reflect the topics of that chapter. As you get into the book, you will catch on to the idea of Headline Anthropology and will recognize anthropological stories in your own reading.

HOLLYWOOD-STYLE ANTHROPOLOGY

This book is built around ethnographic, documentary, nonfiction films, but many fictional feature films grapple with anthropological concepts and problems. At the end of each chapter is a brief introduction to a fiction film (or television episode) that deals with some concept in the chapter. If you are a typical moviegoer or television watcher, you should be able to suggest other titles that also help you in "seeing anthropology."

THE INSTRUCTOR'S MANUAL

The *Instructor's Manual and Test Bank* should be particularly useful for integrating the films into the chapters. The manual has the usual chapter objectives, chapter overviews, lecture topics, discussion topics and research projects, key terms, and test items. It also includes a general section on using films in teaching, a detailed description of each film, how to use it in class, and additional discussion questions.

We also suggest other films on each chapter topic and on each focus culture—these films are ethnographic films as well as a few especially relevant feature films—for those who wish to experiment and develop a course in a particular direction.

ORDERING OPTIONS

For the Third Edition, adopters have more flexible ordering options. They can order the *Seeing Anthropology* textbook alone using ISBN Order No. 0-205-38912-0 or they can order the package with the textbook and either the VHS tape with the ethnographic film clips or a CD-ROM with the ethnographic film clips as "mpg" files. (Please note that this is not a DVD.) To order the textbook with the VHS tape in a package, use ISBN Order No. 0-205-40486-3. To order the textbook with the CD-ROM in a package, use ISBN Order No. 0-205-40485-5. Adopters should contact their local Publisher's Representative with questions. Desk copies of *Seeing Anthropology* for adopters will include the VHS tape.

ACKNOWLEDGMENTS

I have learned so much about teaching and about film from so many people that I can't possibly name them all. I especially want to thank Robert Gardner, who invited me to join the Harvard Peabody Expedition to the Dani, and who introduced me to ethnographic film; and Timothy Asch, who was constantly innovating ways to use films in teaching, and whose untimely death was mourned by an extraordinarily wide range of friends. From the time that James Deetz and I were teaching fellows for William W. Howells at Harvard, to recently, when Cathryn Houghton, Curtis Renoe, Cynthia Miller, and Caroline Vinel assisted in my own introductory course at South Carolina, I have taught with dozens of people who have shaped my ideas. Among them, it was Kersten Bayt Priest who, more than anyone else, helped in reshaping this text. Whether or not they recognize their contributions, I thank them.

Those who read the manuscript at early stages, as well as the reviewers of the first edition (Donna M. Budani of the University of Delaware, William Leons of the University of Toledo, Dona C. Fletcher of Sinclair Community College, Andrei Simic of UCLA, and David Abrams of Sacramento City College), the second edition (Jill Dubisch, Northern Arizona University; Joseph Eisenlauer, Los Angeles Pierce College; Dona Fletcher, Sinclair Community College; Nicholas Freiden, Marshall University; Carol Hermer, University of Washington; Alice Horner, SUNY–New Paltz, Jon Schlenker, University of Maine at Augusta; and Susan Sutton, Indiana University–Purdue University Indianapolis), and the third edition (P. J. Capclotti, Penn State–Abington; Charles O. Ellenbaum, College of Dupage; Nicholas Freidan, Marshall University; James F. Hopgood, Northern Kentucky University; Michael Reinschmidt, California State University; Frances Rothstein, Towson University; and Harry Sanabria,

University of Pittsburgh) made many suggestions, some of which I accepted, some of which I resisted, but I am most grateful for their time and the thoughtfulness of their comments.

This book would not have been possible without the films and the cooperation of all who were responsible for making and distributing them. To mention just a few distributors with whom I spoke directly: Cynthia Close of Documentary Educational Resources, Daniel Bickley of the University of California Extension Media Center, and Elizabeth Enloe of the American Friends Service Committee provided invaluable advice and support. I also want to thank all of the filmmakers and anthropologists who made the films that are the centerpiece of this project. I received enthusiastic endorsement of the project from all of those I contacted directly, including J. Stephen Lansing and Andre Singer (*The Goddess and the Computer*); John Nathan (*Farm Song*); Ronald Simons and Gunther Pfaff (*Latah*); James L. Gibbs, Jr., and Marvin Silverman (*The Cows of Dolo Ken Paye*); Robert Gardner, Hilary Harris, and George Breidenbaugh (*The Nuer*); Tran van Thuy (*How to Behave*); Ellen Bruno and Ellen Kuras (*House of the Spirit*); Robert Gardner (*Dead Birds*); and Jerry Leach and Gary Kildea (*Trobriand Cricket*).

For still photographs, I thank Cynthia Close of Documentary Educational Resources, J. Stephen Lansing, Ronald Simons, Robert Gardner, Michael R. Dove, Christal Whelan, the University of South Carolina Publications Office, James L. Gibbs, Jr., Jonathan Gibson, Jerry W. Leach, and Margaret Lock.

Finally, as is customary, I take ultimate responsibility for this book. But the nice thing about a textbook is that it can always be improved in the next edition. I make this request and challenge to all who use the book, instructors as well as students: Please send me your thoughts. Praise is always welcome, but corrections and other suggestions will be even more useful.

Karl G. Heider
Department of Anthropology
University of South Carolina
Columbia, SC 29208
E-mail: heiderk@sc.edu

CHAPTER 1

The Study of Human Diversity

Trading ship. Borobudur, Java, 9th century C.E. *(Credit: Karl G. Heider)*

PRESS WATCH

HEADLINE ANTHROPOLOGY

Some of the subjects discussed in this chapter have made their way into current news stories. For example:

◆ A copper beech tree in Washington, D.C., long famed as a tree under which President Lincoln relaxed during the Civil War, was tested by radiocarbon dating and turned out to be at best 110–130 years old.

—The State (Columbia, South Carolina), *May 9, 2002.*

◆ Rene Levesque, Quebec archaeologist, who is searching for the bones of Samuel de Champlain, founder of French Canada, said "Finding Champlain would spur a move to go back to our language and culture."

—New York Times, *April 8, 2002.*

◆ As the (soccer) World Cup approached in 2002, co-host Japan worried about problems that might be caused by notoriously unruly English fans. In an attempt to head off trouble, the British Embassy distributed a pamphlet explaining some crucial cultural differences between Japan and England.

—New York Times, *June 2, 2002.*

INTRODUCTION

Anthropology is the study of different ways of life, both past and present. This field, as we know it today, is a relatively new discipline, emerging only in the late 19th and early 20th century as an aid to, and a reaction against, European colonialism. Above all, it is comparative and cross-cultural, combining elements from biology, linguistics, sociology, psychology, and history into a grand synthesizing endeavor. This book discusses in detail some of the major findings and approaches of just one branch, cultural anthropology. Other branches exist as well, which we will introduce before we begin our examination of the cultural side of anthropology.

THE FIELDS OF ANTHROPOLOGY

In the seventh century B.C., Archilocus wrote that "the fox knows many things, but the hedgehog knows one great thing." His sympathy seemed to lie with the hedgehogs. But for better or worse, anthropology represents the ultimate fox among the many disciplines of study possible. Look at what the various people in a good-sized anthropology department do—or look at the range of papers presented at the annual meetings of the American Anthropological Association—and you will quickly become convinced of two points: although each individual anthropologist may do research on specialized problems, all anthropologists wind up as generalists, and the courses required for a major in anthropology cover a greater span of subjects than those of any other department. This quality—the broad if somewhat superficial sweep of interests—is what makes anthropologists so adept at analyzing the connections among all aspects of a culture (the *holistic* approach). The eclectic nature of anthropology is especially evident when you consider some of the issues and problems studied by anthropologists in the four subfields that make up the discipline: biological anthropology, archaeology, linguistic anthropology, and cultural anthropology.

Biological Anthropology

Biological anthropology (previously known as physical anthropology) focuses on the human body, including its physiology (especially its skeleton), its diseases and other traumas, and its adaptations to and variations in different social and ecological contexts. Biological anthropologists study both living people and deceased ones, and some also study human evolution through human or prehuman fossil remains. Others, called **primatologists,** look at the biology and behavior of nonhuman primates like chimpanzees or macaques. One of the persistent questions that some primatologists attempt to answer is how closely primate communications systems approach human language. But others, working with chimpanzees, suggest that it is misleading to view these creatures merely as incomplete humans and try to measure how far they have climbed—or can be taught to climb—up our human ladder. If evolution results in diversity, we primates are each atop a different ladder. Therefore, the challenge to primatology is to explain the real differences, not the similarities, among primates:

> Evidence that human evolution was marked by the emergence of novel mental abilities is beginning to accumulate. . . . Humans developed a unique capacity to mentally represent a world of hidden causal forces, including mental states. (Povinelli and Bering, 2002:117)

This debate sounds intriguing, reminiscent of the one around human cultures in the late 19th and early 20th centuries: Were all human cultures evolving along a single line, with Victorian England at the forefront (see the illustration on page 16), or were cultures changing in many different directions? The rise of serious ethnographic descriptions of cultures made it clear that those "savages" were not merely incomplete Victorians. Perhaps a similar conceptual shift is under way in primatology (see also de Waal, 2002).

Biological Anthropology Case Study 1: Prehistoric Pueblo Women at Risk. Skeletons dug up from archaeological sites have long served as a staple of analysis for biological anthropologists. Traditionally, the main questions asked in these studies dealt with **descriptive morphology**—measuring the bones, noting anomalies—in an attempt to fit the ancient populations into racial categories. Today, these same skeletons are undergoing another anaysis with an eye toward putting them into more of a cultural context.

For example, Debra Martin (1998) has recently compared the skeletal remains from burials at two prehistoric Pueblo sites in the American Southwest. The La Plata site was a large, rich community with wide trade connections. The Black Mesa settlement was small, located in a poor, arid landscape, and kept isolated from other groups. On the surface, these two sites appear to offer a simple contrast between rich townspeople and poor rural farmers. Martin, however, discovered differences between the female skeletons that suggested something else. At La Plata, the skeletons of women show a much higher frequency than the male skeletons of broken bones, healed and unhealed, including serious skull fractures. Many of the most seriously damaged female skeletons were buried casually, without the usual grave goods. In contrast, the Black Mesa skeletons showed few signs of trauma, no differences with respect to gender, and no differences in elaboration or wealth of the burials. Obviously, at least some women buried at La Plata were at serious risk in ways that the women of Black Mesa were not. Putting these biological data into political-economic context, Martin suggests the following:

> Resource availability and ecological richness, however, did not ensure equality for La Plata women; women may have been subject to increased violence either as captured or enslaved laborers, or as recipients of physical exploitation caught in the struggle for control over labor, production, and resources. (Martin, 1998:184)

Biological Anthropology Case Study 2: The Effects of Tourism on Villagers' Health in Mexico.   Mexico, like other countries with warm beaches located close to the population centers of industrialized countries, has found that tourism brings in money. Unfortunately, this activity also has a downside. Biological anthropologists Margali Daltabuit of Mexico and Thomas L. Leatherman of the United States, together with their students, have been researching the effects of tourism in the Mayan communities of the east coast of Yucatán (Daltabuit and Leatherman, 1998). Traditionally, the Mayan villagers of the region have been subsistence farmers, growing maize and other crops for their own use. Because they had no money to develop the great hotels and other necessities for an international tourist industry, the capital for these developments came from the outside. The villagers are now in great demand as cheap labor. The men work in construction and the women toil as hotel maids. The money is hard to resist, and great numbers of villagers have left their farms to work in the tourist industry. Although much is changing rapidly, Daltabuit and Leatherman have paid particular attention to the effects of this trend on nutrition and health. Today, junk food and Coca-Cola are replacing the relatively balanced diet of the past. The biological anthropologists warn that new eating and employment patterns are likely to have adverse consequences for the people in the long run:

> The increased proportion of caloric intake that is met through sodas and snack foods cannot improve nutrition and may prove to be particularly detrimental. . . . It is unclear exactly what effects the tourist economy specifically has on women's health, but it is suggested that the disruptive effects to family relations and household economies may make women particularly vulnerable. (Daltabuit and Leatherman, 1998:335)

Promotion for Crush, a bottled soft drink, in Santiago Atitlan, Guatemala. *(Credit: © Paul Smith/Panos Pictures)*

Archaeology

Archaeology involves the study of peoples of the past through the analysis of their material remains—tools and other artifacts, house remains, bones, and the like. Typically, archaeologists' research centers on excavations of former living sites. Some archaeologists cross over into **paleontology** (the study of fossils) to search for early hominids; these scientists are called **paleoanthropologists.** Others study more recent cultures, reconstructing their lifeways from the traces that have been preserved in the ground. Prehistoric archaeologists are distinguished from historic archaeologists, who study more recent peoples through written records as well as through their artifacts.

The main raw data of archaeology include **material culture,** or **artifacts**—those things made by people. Tools, houses, and the like are excavated, described, and analyzed for what they tell us about the people of the past. Arrangements of artifacts, such as floor plans of buildings, scatterings of broken pots, and village patterns, all contribute information about past lifeways. The study of material culture is shared by archaeologists and those cultural anthropologists who examine art, architecture, and other aspects of life to see how cultural ideas are expressed in material form.

Earlier archaeologists tended to concentrate on the tools, buildings, and other remains that they dug up. They made precise descriptive categorizations and spoke in terms of assemblages of artifacts. In recent years, archaeologists have come to view artifacts differently. Rather than treating these items as ends in themselves, they are using the artifacts to reconstruct the lives of the people who made and used them. We usually reserve the term "cultural anthropology" for the study of living people, but certainly as archaeologists begin to examine the people of the past they, too, become cultural anthropologists.

Archaeological Case Study 1: The Kintampo in Ghana. Joanna Casey has been excavating at the Birimi Site in the northeast corner of Ghana since 1988 in an attempt to learn about the culture that existed there about 3,000 to 3,500 years ago (Casey, 1998). The prehistoric cultures of Ghana remain relatively unknown, though many sites of the prehistoric culture called **Kintampo** have already been found. (Curiously, no Kintampo sites have yet been identified outside Ghana.) The distinctive Kintampo artifacts include pottery and grinding stones, which suggest the possibility of farming, as well as stone projectile points, which suggest hunting. In addition, the sites hold many broken pieces of curious short rock cylinders, marked or decorated. Archaeologists call these items "terra-cotta cigars," but as yet no one knows their purpose.

As Casey's work crews carefully dig down to the level of the Kintampo occupation, they must separate out overlying materials from more recent Iron Age furnaces, which were made and used long after the Kintampo peoples had left. If they dig through the Kintampo levels, they come to a much earlier level marked by different, cruder tools. Many questions—some basic, some more subtle—remain to be answered about the Kintampo people: Where did they come from? With whom did they trade? How large was their settlement? What type of dwellings did they occupy? Were domestic animals important in their economy? Did they grow food crops and, if so, what kind? How sedentary were they? What was the division of labor between men and women?

To help answer these questions, Casey has also been studying the people who live around the site today to gain insights into the past. She has videotaped the ways in which they make, grow, and work things. This approach, called **ethnoarchaeology,** studies living people to obtain hints regarding how people of the past might have lived and how particular tools could have been manufactured and used. Although the analogies taken from ethnoarchaeological research cannot be used too literally, they remain a valuable tool for archaeologists.

Archaeological Case Study 2: Garbagology in Tucson. A final example focuses on the archaeology of contemporary culture. Often the richest part of an archaeological site is the midden, or trash heap. Broken tools, potsherds, animal bones, and other food remains are concentrated there. To better understand the process of discarding things—**garbagology**—in modern Tucson, Arizona, William Rathje and his students systematically examined garbage cans and trash bins in Tucson, finding an unexpectedly large amount of good food going to waste.

Dr. Casey consults with Adisa Tia, the senior wife of the Gambarana (chief of Gambaga) about grinding stones through translator Florence Loriba. She asks about grinding stones and other artifacts, including terra cotta cigars (just to the left of clipboard.) (*Credit: Ann O'Sullivan*)

Archaeology in the Public Eye. More than other anthropologists, archaeologists are featured in newspaper stories, because they sometimes discover things in dramatic ways. In contrast, the research of other anthropologists usually results in slow understandings that are rarely deemed front-page news. Probably the only anthropologist who is a worldwide household name is Indiana Jones, the fictional archaeologist of films like *Raiders of the Lost Ark*. His adventures are not exactly typical of archaeology, but if you asked any archaeologist under the age of, say, 40, he or she might sheepishly admit becoming interested in the field because of Indiana Jones.

Linguistic Anthropology

Linguistic anthropology analyzes languages and the ways in which people use them. In the 19th and early 20th centuries, anthropological linguists concentrated on **descriptive linguistics,** recording many of the world's languages, analyzing their grammars, and making up dictionaries. Franz Boas, the father of American anthropology, worked especially with the Kwa Kwaka' Wakw of British Columbia. He published thousands of pages of Kwa Kwaka' Wakw texts dealing with subjects as diverse as sacred myths and techniques for catching salmon. In 1785 the British scholar Sir William Jones recognized that Sanskrit, the ancient sacred language of Hindu India, was related to Greek and Latin. This realization opened the way for **comparative linguistics,** which attempts to discern the relationships between languages and to define the major language families like Indo-European, which includes languages employed from Ireland to India.

The job of descriptive linguistics is far from finished, however. Even as many tribal languages are disappearing, Christian missionary linguists continue to tackle the descriptive tasks and translate the Bible into other languages. Today's anthropological linguists have been asking new questions about how language is actually used in human interaction.

Linguistic Anthropology Case Study 1: Love Letters in Nepal.   When Laura Ahearn graduated from college, she joined the Peace Corps and taught English for two years in an isolated village in Nepal. She spent a third year as a Peace Corps volunteer trainer in Nepal, then entered graduate school to study anthropology. Next, Ahearn spent another two years in Nepal to carry out research for her Ph.D. dissertation in linguistic anthropology. By then, not surprisingly, she had an excellent command of the Nepali language used by the villagers.

A Nepalese couple who carried on their secret courtship and got married through love letters. *(Credit: Dr. Laura Ahearn)*

When she returned to Nepal, the children who had been her pupils during her first stay were young adults and close friends. Ahearn discovered almost by accident that many young couples, because they were not allowed to date or even be seen together in public, carried on long courtships through love letters that they exchanged secretly. Some of her friends, whose courtships ended in marriage, happily gave her bundles of these letters that they had saved. This find inspired a research project consisting of a detailed analysis of the linguistic aspects of these letters. Interestingly, the very fact of literacy (that is, of being able to write letters at all) was a skill that Ahearn herself had helped introduce into the village as a Peace Corps volunteer. Now this literacy is contributing to a change in the traditional process of arranged marriages, allowing the young people to work out their own arrangements.

Ahearn also analyzed the language itself as used in the letters. In one long exchange of letters that did culminate in marriage, the couple explored each other's interests, expressed their love, experienced misunderstandings and anger, voiced concerns about maintaining secrecy, and dealt with his desire to marry soon and her reluctance. As Ahearn guides us through the language of this correspondence, we gain an extraordinary understanding of the motivations and concerns of the couple (see Ahearn, 2001).

Linguistic Anthropology Case Study 2: Yiddish in South Philly.   Yiddish is a language spoken in the Jewish communities of Eastern Europe. It is basically a Germanic language, albeit one characterized by much borrowing over the centuries from Hebrew and Slavic languages. Yiddish was brought to the United States by Jewish immigrants and continues to be used in some Jewish neighborhoods. Rakhmiel Peltz studied how Yiddish was used and retained among the Jews of South Philadelphia. His work considered how English words were incorporated into Yiddish conversation and how Yiddish was in turn incorporated into English, how Yiddish proverbs were used, and what role Yiddish played in maintaining a sense of identity for first-generation Americans and their descendants. In particular, Peltz was concerned with evidence suggesting that Yiddish was being spoken less in later generations and, presumably, would soon disappear altogether from the community (1998).

Cultural Anthropology

Cultural anthropology, the focus of this book, studies peoples of the present. It looks at different ways of life, different cultures, different systems of meaning, and different peoples living today. On the one hand, as an anthropologist, you may travel thousands of miles to study a remote tribe in Africa. On the other hand, you may not require a passport or even a plane ticket to discover lifeways that are very different from your own. In most U.S. cities and towns, you can walk from one neighborhood to another and hear different languages or dialects, smell unusual foods cooking, and notice new clothing styles with unfamiliar materials and designs. We live in what is popularly and increasingly called a "multicultural" society. But what exactly is "cultural" about these differences that we see? What is "multi" or "diverse" about these ways, given that all of these people are members of the same species? Cultural anthropology seeks to answer these questions.

Cultural anthropology gathers information about cultures and develops theories and explanations to account for similarities and differences between cultural patterns. This discipline seeks to understand what it means to be human by examining similarities and variations between groups. Although terms such as "social anthropology," "ethnography," and "ethnology" are sometimes used to denote particular schools or approaches, here we use the term "cultural anthropology" to cover the entire field. The terms "cultural anthropology," "social anthropology," "ethnology," and "ethnography" are not always used consistently, however, and few people would fight to defend their boundaries these days.

Social anthropology usually refers to studies that focus on social organization, especially on systems that are strongly shaped by kinship relations. This approach is particularly associated with British scholars but has been adopted by some American universities as well.

Ethnography, the intensive study of a single culture, usually involves **fieldwork,** or firsthand immersion in the culture. Many ethnographers study distant nonindustrial societies and describe these groups in the **ethnographic present,** placing their subjects at a reconstructed imaginary moment when the culture was presumably functioning in isolation from outside contacts. In reality, few cultures were ever really isolated and unchanging. Other cultural anthropologists conduct their ethnographic fieldwork in their own cultures or in other cultures of the industrial world, such as peasant communities, farming communities, immigrant groups, occupational groups, and so on. These researchers are also more concerned with studying culture change and cultural interactions than in preserving, through ethnographic writing, a picture of a culture as it supposedly existed in some past time.

In contrast, the goal of **ethnology** is to discover the general rules or patterns that shape social behavior. Ethnology usually implies comparisons between cultures— that is, **cross-cultural studies** of one sort or another. This perspective provides the data necessary to make valid cross-cultural generalizations. The term "ethnology" is used today as the title of an anthropological journal that publishes mainly comparative articles, often demonstrating statistically significant associations among different cultural traits.

Cultural anthropology encompasses numerous specialized fields. The American Anthropological Association (AAA) as a whole has dozens of specialized sections, divisions, and subgroups, many of them including cultural anthropologists (Figure 1.1).

As we have seen, not only does each of the subfields have its own approaches, but much crossover also occurs between the fields. Archaeologists dig up prehistoric tools and then switch over to ethnoarchaeology, by asking living people how they use similar tools. Biological anthropologists use skeletons excavated by archaeologists to examine cultural behavior that affects the body. Linguistic anthropology is virtually a part of cultural anthropology in any case. In turn, cultural anthropologists look to archaeological findings to make sense of the development of contemporary cultures.

American Ethnological Society	Council on Anthropology and Education	Society for the Anthropology of Work
Anthropology and Environment Section	Council for Museum Anthropology	Society for Cultural Anthropology
Anthropology of Religion Section	Council on Nutritional Anthropology	Society for Humanistic Anthropology
Archeology Division	Culture and Agriculture	Society for Latin American Anthropology
Association for Africanist Anthropology	General Anthropology Division	
Association of Black Anthropologists	Middle East Section	Society for Lesbian and Gay Anthropologists
Association for Feminist Anthropology	National Association for the Practice of Anthropology	Society for Linguistic Anthropology
Association of Latina and Latino Anthropologists	National Association of Student Anthropologists	Society for Medical Anthropology
Association for Political and Legal Anthropology	Society for Anthropology in Community Colleges	Society for Psychological Anthropology
Association of Senior Anthropologists	Society for the Anthropology of Consciousness	Society for Urban, National, and Transnational Anthropology
Biological Anthropology Section	Society for the Anthropology of Europe	Society for Visual Anthropology
Central States Anthropological Society	Society for the Anthropology of North America	

FIGURE 1.1   Subgroups of the American Anthropological Association.
This list gives a good idea of some of the different ways in which anthropologists identified themselves at the end of the 20th century, creating groups of similar people (Senior Anthropologists) and similar interests (Feminist Anthropology). For more information on these groups, check out the AAA home page: http://www.aaanet.org.

Some college departments are characterized by an even balance between the four fields. In most departments, however, cultural anthropologists or archaeologists dominate, and some departments have no linguistic anthropologists at all. If you major in anthropology, you will learn something about all four fields. (Anthropologists may also teach courses in schools of public health, law, journalism, education, business, and medicine, as many disciplines have discovered that they need to know about culture.) Of course, each field has its own subspecialties. Likewise, the part of the world in which people do their research further subdivides the discipline, such that South Asianists or Africanists may participate in separate programs or institutes for regional studies.

Applied Anthropology

Applied anthropology is often considered a fifth subfield of anthropology. Applied or practicing anthropologists act as consultants, using the methods and insights of anthropology to tackle problems in the world outside academe. In contrast, academic anthropologists teach at colleges and universities and carry out research with the purpose of advancing the body of anthropological knowledge. This dichotomy can be somewhat misleading, however. An increasing number of anthropologists have found themselves doing pure research that has practical applications, so they are consulting as well as teaching.

This combination is exemplified by the Balinese work of Stephen Lansing, shown in the film clip from *The Goddess and the Computer* mentioned in this chapter. Lansing's research examines the complexities of the Balinese irrigation system. The key question addressed in the film is "How does the intricate network of canals manage to deliver water equitably and at the right time to hundreds of rice fields?" As we shall see, the "modern" Green Revolution was supposed to improve the rice yield but was failing because of its disregard for local wisdom and traditions. When Lansing took these insights to government officials, and when he provided the Balinese people with computerized ways to organize their water flow, he was applying anthropology.

We can cite many other examples of applied research. We have already seen how the study of nutrition in Yucatán raised important questions about the potential dangers to the local people stemming from the tourist boom. And in Chapter 14 we will encounter medical anthropologists who are providing their insights to fight HIV/AIDS and other public health problems.

Finally, it is worth noting that when U.S. anthropologists receive research grants from federal agencies, they must submit their research proposals to an Institutional Review Board (for academics, at their universities). This board asks about procedures to protect human subjects from physical or mental harm. It also requires the researcher to explain what, if any, benefits the research will have for the individual subjects and for people in general. This line of questioning does not rule out federal support for "pure" research, but rather prompts scholars to at least think about how their research may have real effects on people.

ANTHROPOLOGY AND OTHER DISCIPLINES

When we consider U.S. colleges and universities, we are used to thinking of neatly bounded disciplines in neatly bounded departments. You can major in English or in chemistry or in anthropology, but only rarely in an interdisciplinary program. Courses are given in physics, German, and sociology, but not in the sociology of physics. The fact that you are reading this book now almost certainly means that you are taking a course labeled "Cultural Anthropology." While a unique anthropological perspective certainly exists, as does a body of knowledge generated by anthropologists, anthropology includes knowledge gained through the work of other disciplines. To enforce honesty in labeling, we would have to call this course something like "Cultural Anthropology and a Lot of Sociology, Psychology, Biology, History, and Linguistics."

It is not easy to distinguish cultural anthropology from the other social sciences because so much cross-fertilization takes place, with a healthy exchange of theories and methods and knowledge across disciplinary lines. At one time, an-

These simple-looking fields are extraordinarily complex ecological systems. *(Credit: Karl G. Heider)*

thropologists confidently could claim that their discipline was *the* cross-cultural social science, but now other disciplines are making comparisons between cultures. Once only anthropologists carried out participant observation fieldwork research (see Chapter 3), but now some other social scientists have adopted this approach as well. The concept of culture (discussed in Chapter 2), which was originally developed by anthropologists, likewise is utilized by other disciplines. In fact, the new areas of cultural studies and multiculturalism are mainly the domain of scholars who have been trained in language, literature, and history, but *not* anthropology. Anthropology does not only export ideas. In fact, many anthropologists have benefited by borrowing from neighboring fields. For example, they obtain theories of class, power, and large-scale societies from sociology; a sense of development over time from history; the use of rigorous experiments from psychology; and the use of narration—even fiction and poetry—to express truths about people and peoples from literature. Many of these disciplinary crossovers will be pointed out in subsequent chapters. Nevertheless, it is still worth noting that departmentalization remains strong in American academia, and most faculty members in most U.S. departments of anthropology have a Ph.D. in anthropology.

To appreciate the eclectic nature of cultural anthropology, look carefully at the photographs of rice terraces on the Indonesian island of Bali. The pictures are pleasant, even beautiful, showing simple rural scenes. They do not appear very complicated at all. But what if you wanted to discover the true **context** of these pictures? Think of the many sorts of experts you would have to bring in to study the photos and explain what is going on:

A language expert to study Balinese language and understand what people are saying
A geologist to understand the rocks
A soil expert to analyze the soils
A rice expert to explain the rice planting cycle

A meteorologist to plot the rainfall
A geographer to describe the landscape
An economist to chart the costs and benefits
A political scientist to identify how power is allocated
An expert in Hinduism to determine who *really* runs things
A sociologist to find out how groups are organized
An engineer to explain the terraces and canals
A photographer to record it all
A writer to put it down on paper

Alternatively, you could rely on a single person who draws on all these fields: an anthropologist. This statement is not meant to claim that anthropologists are superhuman polymaths, but rather that they are generalists, trained to make connections.

KEY CONCEPTS IN ANTHROPOLOGY

Fieldwork is research, of course, and any research is designed to answer certain questions. It is based on some fundamental assumptions and employs certain tools. In this section, we will examine two assumptions of anthropological research: cultural relativity and holism. We will then consider some of the theoretical tools of anthropology.

Ethnocentrism and Cultural Relativity

One basic principle of anthropological research is the imperative of understanding a culture on its own terms. In the most literal sense, this idea demands that we know the language through which the people live and express themselves. In a broader sense, it means that we must learn about the key concepts, meanings, and patterns of thought that are fundamental to that culture.

The moral implication of that principle is called **cultural relativity,** the demand that a culture be appreciated and judged on its own terms, not ours. Cultural relativity acts as a powerful counter to **ethnocentrism,** which is the tendency to see, interpret, and judge other cultures based on the values of one's own culture. The 1984 film *A Passage to India,* for example, depicts India during the 1920s, with Hindus, Muslims, and British Christians trapped in cycles of ethnocentric misunderstanding.

Ethnocentrism results from the natural tendency of groups to establish solidarity by rejecting all that the group conceives itself *not* to be. In other words, people are habitually embedded in particular behaviors, traditions, norms, values, and beliefs that distinguish them as a group—or a *culture.* The group members will have a shared understanding of the world that leads to functional, comfortable behaviors that are commonly held and therefore interpreted as effective and "good." In contrast, other, unfamiliar behaviors and beliefs are understood as odd, strange, and uncomfortable and therefore interpreted as "bad." The natural outcome is an aversion to any way other than one's own. At its best, this phenomenon produces cohesion, identity, and a sense of belonging. At its most destructive, this cultural cohesion leads to an extreme ethnocentrism, which involves fear, prejudice, hate, and, sometimes, the destruction of others whose ideas and behavior do not match those of the group's culture.

Cultural relativism, however, implies a neutral stance or, at best, an attitude based on deep understanding and tolerance for a particular people. This idea is sometimes attacked by the device of taking it to the extreme, by saying things such as the following: "If anything that a culture values is acceptable for that culture, then we must understand the Nazi death camps and the Holocaust as just the outcome of German anti-Semitism and not be judgmental." More recently, a movement has emerged, especially among Western feminists, to force some African Muslim countries to end the practice of female genital mutilation. Some have defended this practice and attacked the would-be abolitionists on the grounds of cultural relativism: In those cultures, it is an important value to control women's sexuality, and so it is ethnocentric for Westerners to use their own value system to condemn others. (We will return to this vexing issue in Chapter 10, which deals with sex and gender.)

No widely accepted rule exists specifying where one should draw the line between legitimate cultural differences and behaviors that, however sanctified by cultural tradition (for example, persecution of Jews, control of women), are deemed to violate basic human morality.

Quite apart from moral judgment, the issues of the relativism-versus-ethnocentrism debate make a real difference in anthropological research; that is, they determine whether one describes a culture in its own terms or in terms of an outside system. Consider a simple example: How would one measure a Balinese house? One could state the dimensions in feet or in meters. In fact, Balinese houses traditionally were built to idiosyncratic specifications, using the particular body dimensions of the (male) owner. Unless one understood that cultural practice, one would come up with measurements in odd inches or centimeters instead of, say, a round number of the arm spans of a specific man. Even worse, unless one knew the Balinese system, one would miss the basic principle of harmony running through Balinese culture. In the case of the house, the harmony exists between the man and his constructed environment—his house. One could therefore obtain a precise measurement in meters, but still miss the cultural meaning of space.

Some realms of culture remain relatively immune to ethnocentrism. No one, on hearing people speaking Japanese, would say that they are speaking poor English. We easily accept the idea that people speak different languages, and even those who are promoting the view that English is the only acceptable language in the United States would agree that the use of Spanish is legitimate in Mexico. Other realms of culture are common targets of ethnocentric judgments: Balinese food ("disgusting eels!"), Japanese polite bowing ("hypocritical servility!"), and Dani meals ("boring sweet potatoes three times per day!") are all so different from North American cultural ideas that it is easy to be ethnocentric and reject these other patterns for not meeting our criteria. When I first looked at Indonesian movies, I was amused at how bad they were. Only when I moved away from my own (Western) ideas of plot, motivation, character, and symbols did I become able to understand these movies as Indonesian cultural products, concerned with order and disorder, not good versus evil.

This is the frontispiece of an 1879 book by J. G. Wood with the title *The Uncivilized Races of Men in All Countries of the World; Being a Comprehensive Account of Their Manners and Customs, and of Their Physical, Social, Mental, Moral and Religious Characteristics.* What does a close analysis of both title and picture reveal about the thinking of the time?

To avoid the ethnocentric predilection to categorize and judge reality from the standpoint of one's own culture, it is often necessary to practice using culture-neutral language to describe and analyze another culture. For example, in analyzing kinship terms (Chapter 9) we must distinguish between **culture-specific** concepts like "father," which reflect the way some particular culture (our own) construes the world of relatives, and **culture-neutral** terms like "age" or "gender," which should allow us to speak in a non-culture-bound way about the kinship terms of other cultures. The phrase *should allow* is important, though, for any language that we choose to use is necessarily rooted in some specific culture and cannot be completely neutral and scientific.

This dilemma is one of the challenges that we will face throughout this book, and we will at least be able to avoid the most egregiously culture-specific terms. In anthropology today, the term **emic** is often used for the culture-specific concepts, and the term **etic** is used for culture-neutral concepts. These terms were introduced by the linguist Kenneth L. Pike in 1954 and popularized in anthropology by Marvin Harris (1964). They are derived from **phonemics,** the study of the meaningful classes of sounds in a particular language, and **phonetics,** which defines spoken sounds in terms of their physical properties.

Some people use the terms *emic* and *etic* to connote different sorts of descriptions or explanations of behavior. A particular ritual might be explained emically, as the people themselves would, in terms of their beliefs in ghosts, or it might be explained etically, by the anthropologist, in terms of population control and stress reduction. In the following chapters, we will need to remain alert to the basic distinction between culture-specific and culture-neutral terms and explanations.

The great power that ethnocentrism holds over us comes from the inescapable facts that each of us has grown up immersed in some culture or other and that to express anything about another culture we must use a culture-bound language. The challenge, then, is to use this language (for anyone reading this page, it is English, of course) in as culture-neutral, or *etic,* a way as possible.

Those of us who speak English as our first, native language and who can travel around the world and find people everywhere who speak English, tend to forget just how culture-bound English (or any language) really is. The search for etic description is a first step toward understanding other cultures on their own terms.

Holism

Only connect.

—E. M. Forster, *Howard's End*

This epigraph to E. M. Forster's novel *Howard's End* encapsulates another important assumption in anthropology: that people exist in context, that things are interrelated in nontrivial ways. From this assumption follows the anthropological approach of **holism:** to understand any single aspect of culture, we must seek out its connections with other aspects of the culture. Although anthropologists have long recognized the importance of finding connections, other disciplines are only now discovering the importance of understanding interrelationships. Psychology, for example, has become much more concerned about the cultural context of behavior and thinking. This development is not really surprising. From our own experiences, we know that things are interconnected, that what we do here has some effect on what we do there.

Think about interconnectedness within a culture. Sometimes this relationship may spur political debate. For example, does a link exist between cigarette smoking and diseases like lung cancer and emphysema? Do childhood malnutrition, poverty, and minimal education result in high crime rates? Do watered lawns and golf courses in the central Arizona desert have long-range implications for drinking water? What are the effects of government subsidies of industry, art, and education?

For the most part, there is agreement that linkages exist, but disagreement persists regarding where they exist and what they mean. As we will see, holism—the recognition of interconnections—is an important concept in cultural anthropology.

A prime example of holism emerged from the research of Stephen Lansing, which is featured in the clip from *The Goddess and the Computer.* On the Indonesian island of Bali, the rice irrigation system serves as an integral part of the culture. It is not simply an economic arrangement of land and labor to produce rice. Instead, it is tied to the religious system: Hindu priests, with the many scattered water temples, assure the optimal distribution of water to the rice fields. The social organization of the Balinese villagers comes into play as well. The *subaks,* or irrigation societies, are local groups that manage the water and coordinate work on the canals. Intensive rice farming is made possible by an elaborate system of irrigation canals, which bring water to the different fields. In the early part of the rice growing cycle, the field must be flooded; as the rice matures, however, the field must be allowed to dry out. Thus the timing of water delivery through the irrigation canals is crucial. Water gates are opened or closed to direct the flow into one field and then into another. Although the irrigation canals are maintained by subaks, the overall control of the system remains the task of the religious practitioners, the Hindu priests, who work through the many local water temples and ultimately are controlled by the head priest of the temple of the goddess on the second highest volcano in Bali. In this example, the holistic approach has taken us far afield: from simple rice agriculture to social organization to religion.

When outsiders introduced the "Green Revolution," using better pesticides, fertilizers, and varieties of rice, they intended to increase the rice yield. These people, however, were unaware of how deeply rice growing was intertwined in other aspects of Balinese life. For example, the Hindu priests do not "just" lead rituals; they effectively run the rice system. Although the outside agricultural experts knew their agricultural science, they did not realize that they also needed to be familiar with the religious system. In short, they did not take a holistic view. By tinkering with one part of the system without knowing how all of the system components were interrelated, they inadvertently caused problems. Things *are* connected. (See Focus Culture: Finding the Connections in Contemporary Bali.)

Holism does not imply that everything is always harmoniously tied in with everything else. Cultures are not neat, total systems in the same way that a clock or a human body is. All human bodies and all clocks work in basically the same way. Different parts of these systems operate in predictable ways. The liver cleans the blood; if you damage the liver, you get blood poisoning. Cultures do not work like human bodies. There *are* connections, but those connections can work in many different ways.

Intensive irrigation agriculture, for example, requires heavy physical labor and usually occurs with kinship groups that are patrilineal (that is, reckoned through the male line) or bilateral (recruiting groups from both male and female lines). One can explain, logically, why that association works well. Because men generally perform most of the heavy work, and because brothers who have grown up together are more likely to cooperate well than are men who have married into a household, it makes sense to have a rule of patriliny and patrilocality. That is, after marriage, the wife moves in with the husband's family and so the brothers stay together. (Chapter 9, on social organization, covers this point in more detail.) Nevertheless, sometimes one does find irrigation agriculture in matrilineal societies, so the proposition that a simple and necessary connection exists between patrilineal social organization and irrigation agriculture does not hold. Although there certainly are connections, they are not hard and fast. That is, human livers have evolved one particular way to clean blood, but human cultures have worked out lots of ways to run irrigation systems.

DOING ANTHROPOLOGY

Find the Connections

Show the holism in your own life. Put some familiar object or event of your experience into holistic context. Think of Stephen Lansing, who traced Balinese rice production into religion and politics. As an example, consider your car, TV, VCR, CD player, or a piece of clothing and try to lay out the different spheres of action and thought in which the item you choose is interconnected with aesthetics, economics, government, social organization, gender, legal affairs, family, exchange, and psychology. Save your notes and try this exercise again after you have worked through the entire textbook.   ♦

Holism on an International Scale.   So far, we have described holism as an approach to one culture. As we will see in later chapters, we can also think of interconnections on a regional or even a worldwide scale. Think about interconnectedness of the world's cultures. If we look at the clothes we wear or the cars we drive, we see that we are linked to many different parts of the world. We depend on others to provide the raw materials, fabricate the cloth or the parts, and sew the clothes and bolt or weld together the parts of the car. This example clearly illustrates the interconnectedness of the world's economies. The fact that inexpensive clothes at discount stores often come from poorer countries not only points out our economic interdependence but also tells us something about relative wages.

FOCUS CULTURE

Finding the Connections in Contemporary Bali

OVERVIEW

Location: An island just south of the equator and east of Java
Geography: Active volcanoes along the north, fertile slopes stretching to the south
Population: 2,800,000
Language: Balinese, of Austronesian stock (related to most languages of Indonesia, Philippines, and Malaysia, as well as Madagascar and the Pacific Islands)
Religion: Mainly Hindu
Economy: Irrigated rice, fishing, and tourism
Sociopolitical Structure: Province of the nation state of Indonesia

Using a holistic approach, we have already seen in our discussion of the rice irrigation system that interconnections weave together the traditional aspects of Balinese life. We can also see interconnections in other ways when we examine a more recent phenomenon in Balinese culture—tourism. This development is a particularly interesting aspect of contemporary Bali because it strongly reflects the effects of globalization. Bali is one of the world's great tourist destinations, especially for Australians, Japanese, and Europeans, but also for Indonesian tourists from other islands.

Bali has everything: climate (mild tropical), scenery (active volcanoes and beaches), and a culture that is highly aesthetic in a visually elaborate way and immediately accessible and appealing to new arrivals. An intensity of ornamentation appears around the island, and everything seems to be decorated. Every household has a shrine with a carved god figure. The temples themselves are constructed of stone, carved on every surface with gods, demons, and floral designs. Each morning at dawn, people set out little offerings of flowers and incense at shrines, in doorways, and on sidewalks. Balinese painting is busy, with all available space being filled with figures. Balinese dance and theater use archaic languages but are so skillfully performed that even outsiders become enthralled. Perhaps a visitor cannot get below the surface easily in any culture, but in Bali the surface is so dense with visual elaboration that one has a feeling of deeper participation.

This elaborate art, architecture, and theater have attracted tourists, and Bali's economy is

largely dependent on its thriving tourist industry. To an unusual degree, Balinese have catered to foreign tourists, producing ever more accessible arts and crafts. Epitomizing this idea is an English-language sign in the heart of Bali proclaiming, "Antiques Made to Order." The most famous dance of Bali, the Monkey Dance, was developed in the 1930s for Western tourists. The south coast beaches provide foreigners with all manner of sex and drugs. Yet, in important ways, these enterprises are surface accommodations that hardly touch most Balinese, and the well-cultivated tourist market does keep Balinese artists of all genres employed. Many people, especially experienced Western tourists and expatriate residents, complain that Bali is not what it used to be. The answer, of course, is that it never was. Bali, like all cultures, changes constantly. The only difference is that Bali's changes are occurring more theatrically than those in most other cultures.

Tourism and Holism.   One million or more tourists come to Bali each year with money to spend. Not surprisingly, this money has effects throughout Bali. When we take a holistic approach, we do not simply estimate the economic contribution in dollars spent by tourists. Instead, we trace the ramifications of the tourist influx. First, hotels must be built and staffed. Rice fields, coconut groves, and pastures are turned into building sites, tennis courts, and even golf courses, yet there are ever more people demanding even better rice, coconuts, and beef. Someone—mainly Balinese—must staff these facilities. To fill this demand, many people leave their villages to learn management skills, language skills, and menial skills to care for the tourists. This trend leaves behind fewer rice farmers. But this transformation is just the beginning of the tourist effects, for all of these travelers come from inside Indonesia and from other countries to savor Balinese culture. The result is more performances and more carving, which in turn requires more dancers, musicians, carvers, and painters. Many Balinese who formerly dabbled in art as a sideline are now able to earn more money as full-time artists than they ever could as farmers.

With this holistic approach, we begin to see the complexity of interconnectedness. It would be easy to take this example even further. One million tourists need to be transported around the island, so think of what that need means in terms of extra vehicles, gas stations, drivers, and auto mechanics, not to mention exhaust pollution and the requirement of building and maintaining a road network. And one million tourists at the end of the day taking showers, dirtying sheets and towels, and flushing toilets have major ramifications for local water supplies. The holistic perspective suggests that tourist economics, art, and rice agriculture are interrelated.

Of course, not everything in Bali is perfectly meshed. Some Balinese stay isolated from these changes. In 1994, I saw some people in south Bali, just minutes away from the international airport, who spent their spare time collecting salt by evaporating ocean water on tidal flats. It was an extraordinarily long, tiring, labor-intensive process, and the salt that they finally produced brought them only pennies at the market. These people are fully Balinese, but are not really integrated into the economic web that we have followed from the tourist industry outward. (Interestingly, in my brief visit, I was unable to come up with an explanation for their apparent isolation.)

Bali has been called a "theatre state," and the audiences at a "big cremation ceremony" are not only Balinese but also foreign tourists, who are invited to observe. *(Credit: Karl G. Heider)*

Even Balinese politics can be understood as not just the exercise of power, but in terms of theater and religion. Clifford Geertz, an American anthropologist, wrote of 19th-century Bali as

> a theatre state in which the kings and princes were the impresarios, the priests the directors, and the peasants the supporting cast, stage crew and audience. The stupendous cremations, tooth filings, temple dedications, pilgrimages, and blood sacrifices, mobilizing hundreds and even thousands of people and great quantities of wealth, were not means to political ends: they were the ends themselves, they were what the state was for. (1980:13)

In short, Geertz suggests that we should understand that the function of Balinese kingship is to support the theater, rather than thinking of the theater as functioning to enhance the prestige of the kings. This idea of Bali as a theater state, of Balinese culture as performance, seems just as true today as it was in the 19th century. Visitors who stay longer than tourists—the many expatriate artists, hedonists, and anthropologists—gain ever-increasing rewards from this very theatricalism, for so much is expressed in a dramatic, public way.

Officially, Balinese are Hindu, but theirs is a local, Malay sort of Hinduism, both familiar and disconcerting to a visitor from India. In fact, wherever Hinduism spread in India, it absorbed local gods and customs. This **syncretism** happened in Bali as well. Balinese temple gates are massive stone structures, carved with Indian motifs but, surprisingly, split down the middle as if with a chain saw. A temple will have an anniversary ceremony in which men butcher cattle and serve *sate,* cattle meat paste baked on a stick. This practice would surely startle most Indian Hindus, who are vegetarian or who at least avoid beef. In addition, the dramatic plots of Balinese theater are based on Indian epics but throw in very un-Indian clowns from the Malay tradition to enliven the performance.

There is an intensity in Bali that is both religious and aesthetic. The people believe that power or sacredness is everywhere—in rocks, in trees, in houses—and they act accordingly. The flower and incense offerings that Balinese set out for the countless earth spirits each morning are testimony to how immediate and potentially threatening the supernatural world seems to the Balinese. More testimony to the immediacy of the supernatural comes in the form of the elaborate carvings on temples, the paintings jammed with people and things, and the care the Balinese take to ensure that buildings do not violate the natural order. (For example, houses must be oriented properly to natural features, and house poles must be erected root end downward or else the inhabitants will be out of harmony with nature and will become sick.) Above all, the Balinese people value order and harmony, as evidenced by their attempts to keep spirits in their places, dance with graceful controlled movement, and lay out house yards just so.

As Clifford Geertz described the "theatre state," in Bali even the ceremonies tend to be public. One rarely spends much time on a Balinese road without encountering some ceremonial act. It may consist of a procession of women carrying elaborate towers of fruit and flowers on their heads, accompanied by a male orchestra, escorting some candidates to a tooth-filing ceremony (to make the teeth less sharp and animal-like), or it may be a wedding procession or something else equally spectacular. Ritual seems to take place constantly. As Hildred Geertz has pointed out, this harmony of self, supernatural, and natural, however valued and sought, is somewhat illusionary, for

> the Balinese world is one in which the many elements are never harmoniously united, in which there is no single all-encompassing principle, no way of comprehending the whole. It is a universe of fluctuating, flowing, and shifting forces, which can sometimes be commanded by certain human beings, the masters of *sakti,* who momentarily and precariously can draw some of these forces together into a strong local node of power, which will inevitably later dissolve. (1994:95)

This passage points out the downside of the overwhelming concern for harmony. The Balinese feel that they are always on the brink of disharmony, and there can never be enough ritual to guarantee that the harmony will not dissolve. Only recently have a few scholars like Geoffrey Robinson (1995) and Margaret Weiner (1995) directly addressed the violent political history of "peaceful" Bali. (Trivia note: This

Margaret Weiner is the same person who recorded the sound and helped with interpreting on the film *The Goddess and the Computer*.) The many small kingdoms of Bali long waged war against each other. In the 1840s, the Dutch, who had secured control of Java, invaded Bali but managed to capture only the northern coast. The more numerous kingdoms of the South remained independent until the early 20th century. Then, seizing on various pretexts, the Dutch conquered the South. The single most memorable event of this conquest was the *puputan*, or Ending, at Klungkung in 1908. The Dutch army marched on the royal palace. Hundreds of men, women, and children, including the king, all dressed in white, came toward the Dutch guns and were slaughtered. (Wiener [1995] has made a powerful analysis of the meaning of the *puputan* for the Balinese and for the Dutch, then and now.) After gaining control of Bali, the Dutch reaped great profits from the opium trade and from heavy taxes, but Bali was hardly peaceful. Peasant resistance continued, with insurrections being put down by the Dutch forces (Robinson, 1995:64ff). The Japanese occupation of Bali lasted from 1942 until March 1946 (the victorious Allies had neither sufficient troops nor an interest in relieving the Japanese until then). This period was followed by four years of Balinese struggle for independence from the Dutch, the growing chaos of the Sukarno period, and the civil war of 1965–1966, when tens of thousands of Balinese were killed in hand-to-hand encounters (Robinson accepts a figure of 80,000, or 5% of the population killed [Robinson, 1995:273]). These aspects of Balinese history do not draw one million and more tourists to Bali each year.

The title of Wiener's book, *Visible and Invisible Realms*, acknowledges a complexly Balinese reference. On the surface, it evokes the Balinese cosmological ideas of a present human world and a parallel supernatural world. Weiner also means to say that one aspect of Balinese culture and history is spoken and written about and packaged for tourists, whereas another, less benign aspect remains largely invisible to visitors.

In the terrible years of 1997 and 1998, Bali, like other Indonesian provinces, suffered from a series of disasters that hit the region, including the El Niño drought, vast forest fires that blanketed much of Southeast Asia with smoke and soot, the collapse of the Indonesian currency, and the political chaos that forced President Suharto out of office. All this was topped by the terrorist bombing of a Balinese nightclub in 2002 that killed nearly 200 Balinese and foreigners. For Bali, all this bad news meant a precipitous drop in tourism, and at this point, it is too soon to predict how it will all turn out. ◆

SEEING ANTHROPOLOGY

The Goddess and the Computer

Filmmaker: Andre Singer   *Anthropologist: J. Stephen Lansing*

This film, with the combined words and visuals, lets the Balinese speak for themselves and gives us a richer picture of Bali than any words alone can provide. *The*

The Balinese Hindu temple at Batur plays a key role in regulating the irrigation system, as Stephen Lansing shows in the film *The Goddess and the Computer. (Credit: Documentary Educational Resources)*

Goddess and the Computer focuses on Stephen Lansing's cultural anthropological research on the intensive irrigation system of Bali. Lansing began fieldwork in the Balinese village of Sukawati when he was a college undergraduate, and he later returned in the mid-1970s to do further research for his Ph.D. dissertation. Although his topic was Balinese art, Lansing had already realized that "art" was hardly a realm unto itself. It pervaded the lives of ordinary Balinese (1995:4). Lansing was becoming aware of the basic holistic principle: that things are interconnected. During his next trips, he worked on an ethnographic film, *The Three Worlds of Bali,* each time revisiting Sukawati, which is perched dramatically on the cliffs overlooking the ocean. Over time Lansing became aware of the resistance the villagers were putting up to the "Green Revolution," a widely publicized development project that was supposed to make life—and rice growing—better for all. In 1983 he returned for a year to study the relationship between religion, ecology, and agriculture. It is this study that we see in *The Goddess and the Computer.*

The "Green Revolution" refers to a series of coordinated development projects in East and Southeast Asia after World War II that were designed to dramatically increase rice production so as to feed the burgeoning populations of the area and to provide an export crop. Experimental farms developed new, high-yielding varieties of rice, as well as adopting chemical fertilizers and pesticides necessary for their growth. The development agencies taught local experts, who in turn taught local farmers new cropping patterns that would allow three crops per year instead of the traditional two. Intensive agriculture became even more intensive, and some countries, such as Indonesia, did achieve a rice surplus.

The national and provincial bureaucracy liked the results, but the farmers soon saw problems. Over a period of a thousand years, the Balinese had worked out a system of growing rice that maintained an ecological balance in which humans, rice, water, hillsides, ducks, eels, and frogs were integrated into a smoothly functioning system. The development agencies saw their job as a simple agricultural problem—increase the rice yield—and ignored the centuries of local wisdom that had developed the old system. The film and Lansing's 1991 book summarize his attempt to understand what had happened.

The film leads off our selection of ethnographic films because it offers a splendid demonstration of holism. Bureaucrats and scholars in Bali had long considered Balinese temples to be "religion" and Balinese rice irrigation to be "economics," with the two being unrelated. Lansing walked the rice fields and listened to talk in the temples and made the connection, which he has described in film and in print. The film also provides an excellent introduction to anthropological fieldwork and an illustration of the close relationship that exists between theoretical and applied anthropology, showing the ways in which one cultural anthropologist used anthropological concepts to study a real-world problem and how he then attempted to solve it.

Resituating Holism. At the beginning of this chapter, you were introduced to holism and should have had a reaction on the order of "Yes, that certainly makes sense—aren't anthropologists smart to take this approach, crossing boundaries to discover interconnections!" By the time you have read this far and studied the film clip, you should be saying, "What's the great commotion all about? This holism is the most obvious approach in the world. Who would ever be so foolish to think that religion, art, politics, and economics really just existed in their own little boxes!" That is certainly what Stephen Lansing must have been feeling as he followed the irrigation canals from Sukawati, past the water temples to the great temple of the Dewi Danu.

The film clip introduces the Green Revolution in Bali, and talks about how ecology, religion, and agriculture are intertwined: for example, "the priests see no distinction between the practical and the religious aspects of water management." We see both Lansing and his collaborator, James N. Kremer, a specialist in ecological systems who helps to develop a computer program that explains the complexities of the system. We catch brief glimpses of the head priest of the main temple, the Gero Gde, a young man with long hair, wearing white. We see long shots of the ways in which the Balinese have carved rice terraces out of their hillsides. Along with Kremer, we get down into the "natural aquatic community" that is a rice field.

The complete film shows how a large crater lake, on the second highest elevation in Bali, serves as the reservoir that holds the water that drains down the slopes to the south and is ultimately channeled into the irrigation canal network. Behind the crater lake looms Mount Agung, the highest volcano in Bali, where an even more important temple lies. Our focus is on the temple of the crater lake, the temple of the Dewi (Goddess) Danu, which is concerned with irrigation. We see how the priests coordinate the timing of the irrigation system (as Kremer notes at the end of the clip, "Everything depends on carefully coordinated timing"). A new spring has been discovered, and the villagers in the neighborhood ask permission from the priests to tap into it, digging a tunnel with thousand-year-old technology to bring the water to their fields.

When Lansing and Kremer have completed their program, they bring it to the priests at the Dewi Danu temple. Their meeting is interrupted by government officials, who, for the first time, come to the temple to meet the priests. A classic turf war erupts. The functionaries from the lowlands suggest, not very subtly, that computers should be given to their offices in the provincial capital, rather than these ignorant priests—the bureaucrats still do not seem to understand how the irrigation system works!

Vocabulary.   Here are some Balinese words that you will hear. These translations will help you to understand the film:

> *Subak:* the irrigation cooperative and its district, the local group of farmers who are concerned with one section of the irrigation canals.
> *Agama tirta:* literally, "religion of holy water." What the Balinese call their own version of Hinduism.
> *Pura Dewi Danu Batur:* the temple of the *Dewi Danu,* the goddess of the crater lake.
> *Jero Gde:* the young man who is high priest of the temple.

Setup Questions for the Short Clip

Read these questions before you view the short clip, and think about them as you see it. They will help to orient your viewing and thinking about the clip.

1. In what ways is Lansing's research holistic? How did the holistic approach make a difference? On which disciplines does it draw?
2. What sort of ecological system is described? How have the people adapted to the environment?
3. Because the terraced fields produce rice, we call them *rice fields.* This term is much too simple, however, and because of its simplification, it is misleading and draws our attention away from the other organisms that thrive in the same space. What does the film mean by *the natural ecology?*
4. Why is the timing of the rice planting and harvesting cycles so important?
5. What do the Green Revolution experts fail to see?
6. What does it mean to say that these Balinese priests are not purely religious functionaries?
7. What different voices, or points of view, do we get?   ♦

HOLLYWOOD-STYLE ANTHROPOLOGY

Cultural Interaction in *A Passage to India*

A Passage to India, 1984, 163 minutes

Peggy Ashcroft as Mrs. Moore
Victor Bannerjee as Dr. Aziz
Alec Guinness as Professor Godbole
Judy Davis as Adela Quested
James Fox as Ronnie Heaslop (Mrs. Moore's son)

A Passage to India, E. M. Forster's 1924 novel, turned into film by David Lean, is one of the great statements about culture contact, exploring the understandings and misunderstandings among British Christians, Indian Muslims, and Hindus in a small city in northern India called "Chandrapore" under the British Raj in the 1920s. The film opens with a steamship officer warning, "East is East, Mrs. Moore. It's a question of culture." She is going to India to visit her son, Ronnie, a young magistrate in the colonial government, and she is bringing Adela, who may or may not be engaged to Ronnie. We soon meet the proper British, the improper British, various Muslims, and a Hindu professor, and the complications begin.

Setup Questions

1. Where is the film optimistic, where pessimistic, about understanding between people of different cultures?
2. Why does Mrs. Moore say that the "bridge party" is "the most unnatural affair"?
3. Why Adela's interlude at the ancient abandoned Hindu temple?
4. What is the importance of the photograph of Dr. Aziz's wife?
5. How are we to understand the relationship between Dr. Aziz and Adela Quested? ♦

CHAPTER SUMMARY

- Anthropology studies human behavior from many standpoints, with several major specialties.
- Biological anthropology examines the human body and its cultural adaptations.
- Archaeology studies distant (prehistoric) or more recent (historic) cultures, usually by excavating their remains from the ground.
- Linguistic anthropologists focus on the histories, structures, and uses of languages.
- Cultural anthropologists study the cultural behavior of living groups.
- Applied anthropologists are concerned with using anthropological knowledge to solve particular problems in the real world.
- Cultural relativity is a practical and moral position based on the imperative to understand a culture on its own terms before trying to judge or change it.
- Holism is the interconnectedness between different aspects of a culture.

KEY TERMS

anthropology	descriptive linguistics	Kintampo culture
applied anthropology	descriptive morphology	linguistic anthropology
archaeology	emic	material culture
artifact	ethnoarchaeology	paleoanthropology
biological anthropology	ethnocentrism	paleontology
comparative linguistics	ethnographic present	phonemics
context	ethnography	phonetics
cross-cultural studies	ethnology	primatologist
cultural anthropology	etic	social anthropology
cultural relativity	fieldwork	syncretism
culture-neutral terms	garbagology	
culture-specific terms	holism	

QUESTIONS TO THINK ABOUT

- Cultural relativity is one of the most important concepts in anthropology, yet at the same time one of the most problematic. Can one be open-minded and willing to understand cultural differences, yet at the same time consider that some practices, however traditional, are bad?
- Conversely, does ethnocentrism have its positive as well as its negative aspects?
- Look back at Biological Anthropology Case Study 1. Can you imagine any other explanation that would fit the facts of the two sites?
- See Archaeological Case Study 1: How might Joanna Casey possibly decide what those "terra-cotta cigars" were? Any ideas?
- In Linguistic Anthropology Case Study 1, Laura Ahearn followed some dramatic effects of literacy in Nepal. Do you think that the current shift from letter writing to e-mail might produce comparably significant effects on interpersonal relationships?

SUGGESTIONS FOR FURTHER READING

Auge, Marc
1998 (1994)   A Sense for the Other. The Timeliness and Relevance of Anthropology. Translated from the French. Stanford, CA: Stanford University Press. *The view from France.*

Boon, James A.
1977   The Anthropological Romance of Bali 1597–1972. Dynamic Prospectives in Marriage and Caste, Politics and Religion. Cambridge, U.K.: Cambridge University Press. *How anthropologists and others have interpreted Bali over the years.*

Borofsky, Robert (ed.)
1994   Assessing Cultural Anthropology. New York: McGraw-Hill. *An excellent and provocative collection of essays by leading anthropologists.*

Connor, Linda, Patsy Asch, and Timothy Asch

1986   Jero Tapakan: Balinese Healer. Cambridge, U.K.: Cambridge University Press. *Making a series of ethnographic films in Bali, by the anthropologist and the filmmakers.*

Geertz, Hildred

1994   Images of Power: Balinese Paintings Made for Gregory Bateson and Margaret Mead. Honolulu: University of Hawaii Press. *A fascinating insight into the Balinese representations of their natural and supernatural worlds.*

Peacock, James L.

1986   The Anthropological Lens: Harsh Light, Soft Focus. New York: Cambridge University Press. *An essay on the state of anthropology, from a senior American anthropologist.*

Look at current issues of anthropological journals like American Anthropologist, American Ethnologist, *and the* Journal of the Royal Anthropological Institute.

CHAPTER 2

Understanding Culture

Fishing and boating. Bayon, Angkor (Cambodia), 12th century C.E. *(Credit: Karl G. Heider)*

HEADLINE ANTHROPOLOGY

PRESS WATCH

Some of the subjects discussed in this chapter have made their way into current news stories. For example:

♦ Brown County joins 11 other counties in Wisconsin and 27 states in adopting English as the official language. One supporter said "English has been the most important unifier of our country for the last 200 years—it's a symbol of being American."

—New York Times, *July 19, 2002.*

♦ Among the many problems besetting a joint Israeli-Palestinian project to create a multicultural Sesame Street series was an Israeli story about an owl. Apparently for Arabs, owls are bad luck.

—New York Times, *July 30, 2002.*

♦ A former Wall Street speech writer describes how she learned about the "closed societies and rigid hierarchies" of financial services corporations: "I had to turn myself into something of an anthropologist."

—New York Times, *July 14, 2002.*

♦ "Jet Lag vs. Beauty Lag": in the *New York Times* Sunday Styles section, women explain how difficult it is to keep in tune with local standards of beauty as they fly from, say, London to Los Angeles. They mention especially manicures (and patching pedicures), whiteness of teeth, hips, hair, and breasts.

—New York Times, *April 14, 2002.*

♦ Cultural puzzles: in the US, there are strong regional preferences for car makes. Some are obviously related to weather or proximity to Europe or Asia. But why are Hondas so common in Boston, Cadillac Escalades in Brooklyn, Suburbans in Texas, Subarus in Portland, upstate New York, and Boulder? More puzzling, why are Subarus so popular among lesbians, Saabs among dog lovers, classic music lovers, and Internet users?

—New York Times, *April 5, 2002.*

Would you eat roast cat?
Would you want to stop other people from eating roast cat?
Would you eat roast cow? What if we called it "roast beef"?
Would you marry your first cousin?
Would you forbid—or encourage—a marriage between first cousins?

These questions are not frivolous. You probably know your own answer to each. Somewhere, however, there are people who feel just the opposite. They have learned, and share, quite different ideas about what constitutes appropriate food or about who can and should marry. These issues are matters of culture, and culture is the subject of this book.

The most central of all anthropological concepts is culture. Because the term "culture" has several meanings, it is important to examine and set aside some of these alternative usages before we define the anthropological use of it. When anthropologists use the term "culture," they are not referring to its exclusionary use for specialized public functions associated with "the arts," such as ballet, symphony, museums, and the like. We often refer to these types of activities as "cultural events." In this sense, "culture" emphasizes social class and is understood to involve polite and refined behavior, etiquette, and "a civilized manner." This usage, however, is much too narrow for our purposes. We also do not mean those "cultures" that chemists and biologists grow in their laboratories. Instead, this most central anthropological concept can be defined informally at its most basic level as learned, shared ideas and behaviors.

Let's consider Bali, the focus culture shown in the film clip from Chapter 1. Although the term *Bali* is used to designate a certain group of cultural characteristics, *Bali* has other meanings. Bali is also a natural geographical unit, an *island,* as well as a sociopolitical unit, a *province* of the Republic of Indonesia. In this island province live people of many different cultures, many of whom share "Balinese" ideas and practices that they have learned from other Balinese: that is, they speak Balinese, they eat in Balinese style, they live in Balinese ways. Culture is not geographically or politically bounded, however. For example, some cultural Balinese live on Lombok, the next island to the east; others live in Paris, Amsterdam, and Los Angeles.

The population of Bali is relatively homogeneous. In *The Goddess and the Computer,* the film from Chapter 1, we saw "typical" Balinese: artistic Hindus speaking Balinese and practicing intensive rice agriculture. Nevertheless, lots of people also living on Bali belong to other cultural groups: Javanese, Chinese, Europeans, Australians, and Americans. They may live on Bali and learn some of Balinese culture, but we would not call them "Balinese." In fact, on closer examination, even the Balinese show a great deal of variation. As Gregory Bateson and Margaret Mead warned 50 years ago,

> It is true that every village in Bali differs from every other in many conspicuous respects, and that there are even more striking differences between districts, so that no single concrete statement about Bali is true of all of Bali. . . . But through this diversity there runs a common ethos, whether one is observing the home of the highest caste, the Brahman, or of the simplest mountain peasant. (Bateson and Mead, 1942:xiv)

Bali is roughly the same size as Connecticut. Try to rephrase Bateson and Mead's statement to speak of the United States. We often refer to "American culture," but do all Americans share a common ethos? How could we formulate meaningful generalizations about the United States? Ordinary people in casual conversations do it—we call this practice "folk ethnography" or "common knowledge." Travelers cannot resist doing it ("The French are so different from us. Let me tell you what happened on our first day in Paris . . . "). Even some scholars try it. For example, the ambitious book, *Habits of the Heart,* by Robert N. Bellah and his collaborators (1985) suggests some fundamental organizing features of American culture, such as individualism. Nevertheless, all such attempts are necessarily broad generalizations and are forced to gloss over regional differences (New England versus the South versus California) and class differences, not to mention subcultures. The issues quickly become incredibly complex.

Cultural diversity has always been a characteristic of nation-states around the world. In fact, it is difficult to think of a sociopolitical unit such as a state, a province, or a nation that does not include people of more than one culture. These nation-states, however, have generally been held together by strong governments that promote the idea of a common ethos. That this common ethos may have been more political than cultural seems evident as we see the effects of the breakup of the Soviet bloc and the increasingly precarious status of nations like the United Kingdom. It has become almost a cliché to say that with the end of the Cold War, which was a struggle along ideological lines conducted at the national level, we have entered an era of smaller conflicts along ethnic lines. Sometimes the struggle takes place between an ethnic group and the larger state. In any case, various groups defined by their "culture" continue to do battle for independence, recognition, power, or territory. We can see these types of conflicts today in the former Yugoslavia, the former U.S.S.R., Mexico, Iraq, India, and Rwanda; undoubtedly, many more such struggles will occur in the future.

DEFINING CULTURE

In 1952, A. L. Kroeber and Clyde Kluckhohn published a famous study compiling and analyzing all the definitions of culture that they could find—some 300 pages of them, dating from the 18th century in German and then from 1871 in English, when the term was introduced by E. B. Tylor, who said, "Culture, or civilization . . . is that complex whole which includes knowledge, belief, art, law, morals, custom, and any other capabilities and habits acquired by man as a member of society" (1871).

Kroeber and Kluckhohn did not offer their own definition of culture. Instead, they said that, as of 1952, most social scientists could agree on the following:

> Culture consists of patterns, explicit and implicit, of and for behavior acquired and transmitted by symbols, constituting the distinctive achievement of human groups, including their embodiments in artifacts; the essential core of culture consists of traditional (i.e., historically derived and selected) ideas and especially their attached values; culture systems may, on the one hand, be considered as products of action, on the other as conditioning elements of further action. (Kroeber and Kluckhohn, 1952/1963:357)

This description still works a half-century later. For our purposes, we can use a stripped-down, basic definition that includes four primary properties of culture. **Culture** is

- learned
- shared
- ideas about and
- patterns of behavior.

Each of these characteristics is critical. Understood together, they form the core of the concept of culture. Nevertheless, we must immediately expand and qualify this definition.

Culture Is Learned

A crucial characteristic of culture is that it is not innate, or genetically passed on. Rather, it is learned. Although our genetic makeup is inherited through our biological mother and father, this genetic code does not determine our specific culture. For example, we inherit the shapes of our mouths and tongues from our parents. We inherit the ability to speak, but we do not inherit in the same genetic manner the language that we speak. Babies who are adopted at birth from one part of the world into new families far removed from their biological parents will not spontaneously vocalize speech used by the now-distant biological parents. Significantly, the children will vocalize the sounds to which they are exposed in daily contact within the new social context. In other words, language—an important part of culture—is learned. Although the ability to learn language is part of our biological capacity as a member of the species *Homo sapiens, which* language we speak is the result of learning. None of us has anything in our genetic instructions labeled *English* (or *Balinese* or *Yiddish* or *Malay*).

Enculturation is the process by which a child learns the ideas and behaviors that constitute his or her culture. From its earliest days, a child learns and absorbs these cultural patterns from many sources. These agents of **socialization** are everywhere in the child's environment. In the United States, they typically include parents, siblings, other babies, institutional settings like preschool and church, not to mention Barney and Mister Rogers and Sesame Street. The child is absorbing and imitating. Soon some formal teaching begins. Nevertheless, much of the process remains informal and even unconscious. By the time children are sent to school, they already have a command of much of their culture. They speak a language fluently long before being exposed to formal grammar lessons.

Would people be human if they were isolated at birth from any other human beings? Several famous stories explore this theme. For example, the plots of *Tarzan* and *The Jungle Book* revolve around an infant (Tarzan, Mowgli) who has been somehow abandoned by humans, then found and raised by very anthropomorphic animals. The adventures arise as the isolated child learns to survive in the animal kingdom. Clearly these stories are fantasy, but they are entertaining precisely because they play with questions of whether other living creatures have culture and what a human would be like without human contact.

Could an isolated human infant acquire human cultural ways of behaving apart from association with other humans? Or, taking the question one step further, do other animals have any sort of learned culture comparable to that of humans? Indeed, many animals do live in societies. These "social animals" include bees, beavers, bison, baboons, and bats. Bees, for example, have even been discovered to have complex communication systems. The direction and location of a particularly good spot to collect pollen is communicated by a "dance" that the scout bee performs while surrounded by fellow bees.

Other things besides information can be passed between individuals through movements, animal cries, and bird songs. For example, the famous case of the Japanese macaque monkeys shows that behavioral patterns can be learned. A troop of semiwild macaques on the coast of Kyushu was being observed by ethologists, who often tossed sweet potatoes to the monkeys to encourage the troop to stay in sight. One day one macaque took its sweet potato to the ocean and washed off the grit before eating it. Other members of the troop quickly took up this practice, and soon it was an established part of the group behavior. Thus this practice meets our formal definition of culture: learned, shared behavior. Nevertheless, although recent studies of chimpanzees have expanded our knowledge of their cultural capacities, they clearly remain minimal compared with humanlike *Homo sapiens* culture.

Anthropologists have pursued the question of culture and its acquisition further by studying nonhuman primates to see whether gorillas, baboons, or chimpanzees can learn to behave in human/cultural ways. In one approach, the anthropologists (primatologists) befriend the primates and use systematic stimulus–response methods to teach, providing a reward for learned behavior. The level at which these primates exhibit behavior that is actually symbolic, or meaningful, and therefore "cultural" continues to spur debate, however. This ongoing pursuit of primatologists remains one of the most interesting issues within anthropology.

We can say with certainty that, among all living creatures, the human infant is the most helpless for the longest period of time. It must rely on caregivers for an extraordinarily long childhood, comparatively speaking. One can observe the innate, genetically programmed behavior of newly hatched chicks that begin to hop and peck seeds within a few hours or the newborn foal that struggles upright on shaky limbs to quickly begin running. Human babies, in contrast, have much greater genetically inherited potentiality, but are notably "unfinished" at birth. That is, a human infant requires years of socialization through exposure to others of its own kind to become a completed *Homo sapiens*.

Culture Is Shared

Because culture is learned and can be learned only from other humans, it follows that humanness is achieved through contact with other humans. People will there-

fore come to share similar schemas, or basic ideas and ways of behaving. To paraphrase old anthropological wisdom (Kluckhohn, Murray, and Schneider, 1962:53),

> In some ways all people are the same.
> In some ways some people are the same.
> In some ways each person is unique.

Cultural anthropology focuses on the middle condition—that which is shared
by some people, but not all. Language is the most obviously shared pattern of behavior. It is difficult to imagine a language spoken by only one person, unless that
individual is the last surviving speaker of a dying tongue. Because people use language for communication, that kind of knowledge must necessarily be shared.
Think back to what we mean by Balinese culture: a shared language, a shared religion, shared concepts of health and sickness, shared music and dance, shared cui-
sine. All of these characteristics make up the culture that is common to the
Balinese. Even the worst tourist carvings, with designs invented last month for sale
today, are recognizably Balinese, for they partake of the same aesthetic for color
and form as do those objects that we would like to call "real" Balinese art in temples or museums.

Small-scale tribal societies of a few hundred or a few thousand people, like the
Dani discussed in Chapter 3, are especially noteworthy for the mutually shared features of their culture. In any one Dani area, all of the houses, gardens, funerals, and
games are virtually the same. When talking about the Dani, it is easy to begin sentences with "The Dani do . . . " or "The Dani believe . . . " But increasingly more variation occurs with larger groups, and it is difficult to make such generalizations with
huge complex nation-states. What do "Americans" believe? Malaysia (see the following Focus Culture) lies somewhere between the Dani and the United States in
terms of size and complexity, and the 12 million Malays share at least a language,
a religion, and some other cultural traits.

Generally, members of the same culture do not agree on everything and do not
share all knowledge. To explore the degree of common knowledge held by my Introductory Cultural Anthropology students, I have asked them with which novel
and movie they think everyone in the class is familiar. What is actually shared? (Try
this exercise yourself.) This question is a difficult one, and few students turn out
to be good ethnographers of their own culture.

Of course, at a less specific level, some things are shared, such as the English
language. Even in this case, however, people who ostensibly speak a common language will disagree about the exact meanings of particular key words. In my study
of emotions among Minangkabau of West Sumatra, Indonesia, I found that 80%
agreement on the precise meanings of emotion words was very high. Barbara Myerhoff was able to write about a common Yiddischkeit culture in her study of elderly Jews in the Senior Citizens Center in California (1979), but among these few
hundred people she found great differences. For example, some were deeply committed to Judaism as a religion, while others proclaimed themselves to be Jewish
atheists. At best, we can say that culture is more or less shared.

FOCUS CULTURE

Shared Malay Traditions and Local Variations

OVERVIEW

Location: Southeast Asia, on the long Malay peninsula, including southernmost Thailand and western Malaysia

Size: 127,584 square miles

Geography: Densely populated tropical coastal plains and inland mountains that are mostly covered by dense rain forest

Population: About 12,000,000

Language: Malay, an Austronesian language closely related to Indonesian

Religion: Islam

Economy: Rice agriculture, rubber, and palm oil; increasingly, manufacture of rubber and plastic goods, textiles, and processed food

Sociopolitical Organization: Malaysia is a constitutional monarchy with a prime minister and elected parliament. At the local level, bilateral or matrilineal descent groups with very important sibling relationships.

The Malay-speaking Muslims of the Malaysian part of the Malay peninsula provide a good example of a local cultural tradition—one that is a particular manifestation of a much wider Malay cultural pattern. Similar Malay people live on the neighboring Indonesian islands of Sumatra and Java. In a broader sense, we may speak of "the Malay world" as a great triangle that includes the Philippines, Malaysia, Brunei, and most of Indonesia, with some minorities in Thailand, Vietnam, and Hainan Island, China. Even on the Malay peninsula, national boundaries do not coincide with cultural boundaries. For example, four provinces of Thailand are inhabited by Malay-speaking Muslims. The Malaysian part of the peninsula includes significant numbers of Chinese and Indians (Tamil-speaking Hindus); in the interior, we find many small groups of what seems to be an earlier, pre-Malay population known collectively as the Orang Asli ("original people"), most of whom speak Mon-Khmer languages related to Cambodian Khmer and have animistic religions.

Most languages spoken in the Malay world are closely related members of the Austronesian (formerly called "Malay-Polynesian") stock. Austronesian speakers migrated into the "Southern Islands" (*austro,* southern; *nesos,* islands) from China several thousand years ago via the Philippines. Then, in one of the great sagas of maritime exploration, they spread halfway around the world, from Madagascar off the African coast in the west to Hawaii, New Zealand, and Easter Island, the far reaches of Polynesia, in the east. The Malays of the peninsula appear to be the descendants of Austronesians who had turned north again from the islands of Sumatra and Java. As they reentered the mainland, they would have encountered Mon-Khmer speakers whom they assimilated or crowded back into the deeper mountainous rain forests. This description gives a broad picture of this migratory saga, but we cannot know the details until much more archaeology is done in the region.

In some particulars, the peninsular Malays share a general Southeast Asian culture that has persisted for hundreds of years (Reid, 1988). These common traits include a diet based on rice, fish, coconut, and hot peppers; a habit of chewing a mild stimulant mix of betel leaf and other ingredients; bamboo and wooden houses raised above the ground on stilts; tools such as a small knife held in the palm and used for harvesting rice; piston bellows for working iron; belief in a sort of soul matter; and a relative degree of gender equality. At the local level, however, the groups lumped together as "peninsular Malays" show countless instances of cultural variation from state to state in Malaysia, and sometimes from district to district or from village to village. Even within a single village or household, not everyone shares exactly the same beliefs and attitudes or behaves in identical fashion. Nevertheless, we can talk about "peninsular Malays," describing commonalities and noting variations.

Peninsula Malays define themselves as Muslims who speak the Malay language and follow Malay traditions. This definition serves to distinguish them from the Chinese, South Indians, and many Orang Asli who also live in Malaysia. By the end of the first millennium of the Christian Era, much of Southeast Asia was at least nominally under the sway of local Hindu or Buddhist kingdoms. But in the 14th and 15th centuries, Muslim traders began bringing both textiles and Islam to the region; by the 17th century, Islam was firmly established in much of the Malay world. Today all peninsula Malays are Muslim. Indeed, this religion defines much of Malaysian culture, as the nation of Malaysia is becoming more and more an Islamic state. In addition, however, religious minorities (Hindu, Buddhist, and Christian) live in increasingly uneasy relationship with the Muslim majority. Malay Islam is part of the world of Islam, where the Koran and other writings guide behavior. Mosques are found everywhere, and the Five Pillars of Islam, if not always strictly observed, are considered fundamental. (The Five Pillars of Islam are daily prayer, the pilgrimage to Mecca, donations to charity, daytime fasting during the month of Ramadan, and the profession of faith.) Although all Muslims share these basic ideas, the total religious practice of Islam varies from culture to culture. Malay villagers tend to include much more than the "pure" forms of the "Great Tradition" of Islam in their Muslim practice. (We shall return

Children praying at an Islamic preschool at the National Mosque in Kuala Lumpur, Malaysia. *(Credit: © Steven L. Raymer/National Geographic Image Collection)*

to this issue of religious syncretism, the mixing of different traditions, in Chapter 12.) For example, most villagers use non-Muslim curers, called *bomoh* on the east coast. These *bomoh* (usually men) heal certain kinds of illness by communicating with spirits through trance seance rituals.　　　　　　　　　　　　　　　　　◆

Culture Is Ideas

Take that simple artifact of traffic control, the stop sign. This inert piece of metal contains a single word. It is thus related both to ideas and behavior. The whole bundle of related ideas about "traffic" is a **schema,** which includes several sorts of ideas. For example, a legal norm in the United States stipulates that drivers must bring their vehicles to a full stop at each stop sign. There is also a generally held notion that people should obey legal norms ("the law"). In addition, a commonly held perception indicates that it is not necessary to come to a full stop at a stop sign, especially if no other traffic is present and one cannot see any police officers. The result of these ideas—the *schema*—is a pattern of cultural behavior that includes erection of the stop sign itself, occasional police enforcement of some behavior, and ordinary motorists who either stop or roll past the stop sign. One could make a cultural study of how different sorts of people think and act when confronted with stop signs.

This norm ("a traffic law" in the United States) is one of the most explicit of all norms. *(Credit: Karl G. Heider)*

Culture as Symbol. In addition, a stop sign is loaded with symbols. The very word "stop" is a set of four particular sounds that have no inherent meanings, except to English speakers. For English speakers, they constitute a "word," which is a symbol with a particular meaning, a command to come to a halt. In turn, those four sounds are symbolized by certain graphic designs: "S" means, for English speakers, a certain sibilant sound. The stop sign's red color likewise conveys meanings of "danger" and, especially, of "stop." Finally, the hexagonal shape is a conventional symbol signifying "stop." We shall explore symbols and their meanings further in Chapter 4.

Let's consider another example of a less symbolic set of cultural ideas. A common North American schema for breakfast would be juice or fruit, cold or hot cereal, cooked eggs, toasted bread with butter and a sweet fruit spread, and a hot beverage, usually coffee. Notice some things about this cultural schema for breakfast. It is certainly learned; it is widely shared, though not by all North Americans, and many people outside North America order an "American breakfast"—for instance, at luxury hotels around the world—even though they would not consider themselves to be "Americans." Thus this schema describes both a set of ideas about what breakfast should include and a particular set of food items. It is explicit—that is, you can easily elicit a "breakfast schema" from anyone. Also, note that this schema is at a middling level of specificity. It mentions fruit or fruit juice but does not dictate the kind of fruit involved. In short, it leaves open some slots.

Malays and Balinese have a quite different schema for breakfast. Most importantly, they include rice, for without rice there can be no meal. They also include tea or hot water and perhaps some small fish or vegetables on the rice. Another major difference between American and Southeast Asian breakfast schemas is temperature.

For standard North American meals, most foods have a required temperature: fruit juice cannot be hot; coffee and tea must be steaming hot or ice cold, but cannot be lukewarm. On the other hand, temperature is not nearly so important for Southeast Asian meals.

For a more significant schema, or cluster of ideas, we can return to Malay ideas concerning health and sickness. In an important passage, Carol Laderman describes the goals of the *bomoh,* the spirit medium:

> A whole, healthy person normally has little to fear from hantu, but, should an imbalance of his component parts occur, whether due to depletion of semangat or accumulation of angin, the integrity of the person is breached, his "gates" no longer protect the "fortress within," but have opened to allow the incursions of disembodied spirits. The bomoh aims to return his patient to a state of balanced wholeness. (Laderman, 1991:40)

As an important theoretical aside, let us notice that Laderman uses four Malay words instead of one-word English translations. She translates two other Malay concepts within quotation marks. This usage is not intended to put off the non-Malay-speaking reader with impenetrable jargon. In fact, Laderman is a particularly lucid writer, and her works are a pleasure to read. But she has a thorny problem to solve. Some words represent ideas that are so fundamental and yet so deeply embedded in a particular cultural meaning system that simple one-to-one translations would hinder, rather than help, our understanding. She might have translated *hantu* as spirits, *semangat* as life force, *angin* as winds, and *bomoh* as shaman/spirit healer. Instead, Laderman spends pages, and even the entire book (1991) exploring these concepts.

Briefly, hantu are invisible supernatural beings or forces that can cause a wide variety of illnesses for people. The Malays have many names for different sorts of hantu. When a person suffers from an "unusual" illness (one not easily cured by more standard medicinal treatments), the individual can appeal to a practitioner called a bomoh, a man who has the special knowledge and power to intervene with the relevant hantu and effect a cure. These unusual illnesses involve a disturbance of a person's semangat, the vital force or soul matter that animates humans, animals, rice, and indeed everything in the world. Semangat is the essence of existence, but it can easily be disturbed, dislodged, or diminished. Once disrupted, it must be carefully nurtured back into order.

One literal translation of "angin" is wind, but the term has other implications as well. Winds are generally potentially dangerous to people and can cause sickness. One of our folk expressions and explanations for illness is "catch a cold"; Malays can say *masuk angin,* or "the wind enters the body." In addition, the east coast Malays have a concept of "inner winds," forces that exist in a person at birth and that determine the sort of person he or she will become, the talents the person will possess, and the success in life that the person will achieve. Laderman likens this concept to Western ideas of temperament and basic personality, and she compares these Malay conceptions to Western psychology and psychotherapies (1991:76–84).

Like semangat, the inner angin can become disturbed and demand the assistance of a bomoh to restore harmony. Ong describes a similar complex of beliefs on the west coast of Malaysia where, in the 1970s, incidents of "mass hysteria" afflicted Malay factory workers in American-owned electronic plants. To the puzzlement of the American management, bomoh were brought in to restore harmony (Ong, 1987:204).

In recent years, as Malaysia has become increasingly more strictly Islamic, the orthodox Muslim leadership has tried to abolish unorthodox practices like those of the bomoh. Abandoning this system has proved difficult, for the bomoh deals with problems that are deeply rooted in Malay beliefs, and, in any case, for the most part neither bomoh nor their clients feel that those beliefs and practices are inconsistent with Islam.

Culture Is Patterns of Behavior

When we say that culture is "ideas," we are pointing to cognitive, or mental, formulations—that is, those schemas of all sorts that people hold in their minds. Nevertheless, we must also affirm the close connection between ideas and **acts.** Thus we can next say that culture is patterns of behavior that are based on those ideas.

Take chairs. These items are common objects in many cultures. You are probably sitting on one as you read this book. The chair is a manufactured object, an artifact. Its making and its use follow from cultural schemas that we have in our minds about how one sits, where one sits, when one sits, and what constitutes an appropriate "sitting artifact." As I write this passage, I am looking at one of those "sitting artifacts" called a "chair," made nearly 200 years ago and once owned by my great-great-grandfather in Indiana. It is instantly recognizable today as a chair. It has four legs that hold a sitting surface about 18 inches above the floor, two arms, and a back. I still use it much as my ancestor did. Indeed, our cultural ideas for sitting have remained remarkably stable over the generations even as many other ideas and behaviors have changed beyond recognition. So, as Kroeber and Kluckhohn suggested, we consider this item and other chair-objects as part of culture. The advantage of considering chairs as cultural products of cultural ideas, however, is that the focus of attention is directed toward both those ideas about sitting and to the resulting chairs. Certainly some scholars study chairs as objects of intrinsic interest. In contrast, cultural anthropologists—and archaeologists—would tend to study chairs as a way of getting to broader cultural schemas, by asking myriad questions such as who sits on chairs (instead of sitting, squatting, or kneeling on the floor), what is the meaning of different chair-sitting postures (feet on the floor or tucked under the body; legs together versus ankles crossed versus legs crossed), when is it proper to stand or sit, what is the significance of the sudden appearance of chairs at a certain time or a certain level in an archaeological excavation, and so forth.

The task of accurate interpretation or representation of other cultures poses one of the greatest challenges for the anthropologist (a fuller discussion of this issue appears in Chapter 3 on fieldwork). We observe behaviors and attempt to interpret those behaviors based on what we know about a culture. Often, our initial interpretations change as we learn more about a culture. Much of this effort involves learning the language, which allows us access to the ideas that shape behavior. For example, during the first months that I spent with the Dani in New Guinea (see Chapter 3), I worked with half a dozen other members of the Harvard Peabody Expedition. We attended several funerals, where we saw and photographed the funerary behavior in careful detail. There was much display of goods, especially pigs and carrying nets, and objects were passed from one person to another. At first, I saw these events as displays of wealth, almost materialistic boasting. Only later, as I learned to speak better Dani, did I understand the real meaning of what was happening. As I began to work out the many Dani ideas involved in the funeral, gradually it became clear that the Dani were trying to impress and placate ghosts. All the wealth was directed more at the supernatural than toward other Dani. I had seen the actions, but to find the meanings, I had to ask the people themselves to learn their own, emic meaning of the funeral. And so I moved from acts to ideas.

Cultures Are Both Internally Consistent and Inconsistent

When we speak of the internal consistency of a culture, we refer to certain basic cultural patterns that run through and shape many different sorts of behaviors. Thus one theme that is frequently recognized deals with where, on an individualism–groupism continuum, a culture stands. Contemporary American culture lies far to the individualistic end of this continuum. This position reflects the shared value placed on the autonomy of the individual person. That is, in many different activities such as sports, marriage arrangements, and residence patterns, the interests of individuals take precedence over the interests of social groups. Peninsular Malay culture, on the other hand, is, on the whole, found more toward the groupism extreme, for much Malay behavior answers to group rather than individual goals.

As useful as it is to recognize such basic principles of a culture, we must also acknowledge that we are often struck by the presence of contradictory themes in the same culture. For example, the peninsular Malays are certainly in most respects group oriented, yet their concept of "inner winds" that shape a person's own personality is quite individualistic. Other people of the Malay world, for example, put more emphasis on the force of gender in determining a person's character.

Michael Kammen, a historian, wrote a book about the United States called *People of Paradox* (1972). In his book, he drew on anthropological ideas to examine such apparent contradictions as are embodied in Thomas Jefferson, who wrote the Declaration of Independence but nevertheless owned other human beings. Another famous example in the anthropological literature involves the Minangkabau of West Sumatra, Indonesia. They are matrilineal (that is, they emphasize descent through the female line), yet their religion, Islam, is strongly patriarchal. For a century, outsiders have tried to picture those practices as a debilitating contradiction. The Minangkabau historian Taufik Abdullah, however, has explained the apparent contradiction as part of the system: "In Minangkabau society institutional conflict is consciously recognized and even regarded as essential to the achievement of social integration" (1966:8).

Thus we must approach a culture as a systematically integrated whole, looking for interconnections while at the same time expecting to find real or apparent contradictions.

Culture, Society, and Ethnicity

It is one thing to define what we mean by "culture." It is much more difficult to specify the boundaries of a particular culture—that is, to say just who belongs to or shares in that culture. First, we must carefully distinguish between culture and society. A **society** is an organized group of individuals with specific boundaries, or criteria, of membership. We can speak of both societies and cultures in terms of levels of inclusiveness.

At the macro level, we call nations, states or provinces, counties, cities, and the like **social units,** or **societies,** because they consist of organized groups of people. Membership comes not only through the fact of one's body being within the geopolitical boundary, but also involves being registered and identified by that society as a member. This recognition is provided through identity papers such as birth certificates, visas, driver's licenses, voter cards, and so on. For example, the United States is a society, or social unit. It is made up of smaller social units such as Kansas, called "states"; they, in turn, are made up of even smaller units such as Douglas County or the city of Lawrence.

We define these social units by marking out their physical boundaries, by counting the people who are "members" within these boundaries, and by describing the organization of legislative, executive, and judicial bodies that exercise power within those social boundaries. Maps can show with precise lines the limits of social units such as cities, counties, provinces, and nations. A national or state government may take a census to identify its constituent members. Such governments may slot citizens into various categories that are arbitrary and often quite limited (for example, identity markers that allow individuals to categorize themselves in only one of five categories: white/black/Hispanic/Pacific Islander/ other).

We have already seen that the social unit called Malaysia encompasses people of various cultures. Not all Malaysian citizens are culturally Malay in the sense that they are Muslim, speak the Malay language, and follow Malay customs. Conversely, many people who are by those cultural criteria Malay live in other nations. We know that a majority of the people in the social unit called the United States speak English, call themselves Christian, and eat hamburgers. Many other people who are full members of that society are nevertheless of different cultures; they might speak only Navajo, be Jewish, or eat no meat. "Society" does not coincide with "culture," even though we sometimes erroneously use the two words interchangeably.

Clearly, it is much easier to demarcate arbitrary geopolitical boundaries of societies than to show the distribution of cultural ideas and behaviors. Therefore, these social units—these societies—should not be understood to reflect the precise borders or boundaries of cultural units. When someone says "American" or "Kansan," it is sometimes difficult to tell whether they mean the culture or the society or whether, more likely, they are confusing the two. These problems have prompted some to give up on the concept of culture. But if we use it with care, this idea can serve us well. It is important to be able to talk about the different cultures or subcultures within American society. Nevertheless, out of habit, we often fall back into the trap of misidentifying culture with society and speak of "American culture" or "Kansas culture." We can indeed lump people from different societies together when we say "Malay culture" or "Navajo culture." Nevertheless, we must be aware that societies are bounded, sociopolitically defined groups that are often territorial, whereas the patterns that constitute a culture form **"fuzzy categories,"** usually unbounded and poorly defined.

Ethnicity is a term whose recent popularity only confuses these issues. "Ethnicity," from the Greek, is close to "ethos" and, in meaning, to our term "culture." But today it is increasingly also used as a euphemism for "race," a term that has run into problems (see page 50). So, at the turn of the millennium, the very ambiguity of "ethnicity" makes it seem inoffensive or politically correct. But like all language, its meanings will change. Ethnicity, as cultural identity, is the subject of the film *Smoke Signals,* by and about the Coeur d'Alene Indians of Idaho.

Cultures and Subcultures: Operating on Different Levels

"Culture" is necessarily a generalization about shared ideas. The degree of sharedness always poses problems, however, because no cultural schemas are completely, 100%, shared. We therefore talk about culture at different levels or different degrees of sharing. At each level, we could try to describe what is known in common or we could focus on the variations between individuals. It is fair to say that anthropologists (like sociologists) tend to focus on the sharedness, whereas psychologists investigate individual differences.

As another example of these levels, we can speak of "the Malay World" in the broadest sense, narrow our focus down to Peninsular Malays, or further restrict it to one state, one district, or one village. A convenient term is **subculture,** a word referring to some clearly identifiable, shared cultural ideas and behaviors that are embedded within a larger, more general culture. This term is not especially precise, but it is useful when referring to a particular smaller set of ideas relative to a larger set. For example, we can identify gangs, or gays, or Greeks, or geographers as being subcultures within the broader culture of America. (Here, of course, *sub* refers to subdivisions and not to inferior forms.) Recently, these concepts have even crept into business sections of newspapers. Thus we may come across articles about culture clash when two banks or two airlines with different subcultures try to merge. An ethnographic examination of cultural dynamics in such a case would be interesting and important, but business executives seem to prefer reinventing their own ethnography in an effort to understand such situations.

In a fascinating recent study of very small subcultures, Kersten Bayt Priest followed two church congregations in the United States as they attempted but ultimately failed to unite into a single congregation (1998). Both churches drew members from the same part of the same city. They belonged to the same denomination, and their respective pastors had cordial relations. Theologically they seemed a good match. The process of unification began with much goodwill on both sides but, as Priest showed, it came to grief over music. It turned out that the churches had two subcultures, similar in many respects but distinguished primarily by differences in styles of singing, styles of body language while singing, and styles of choral direction. These two cultural schemas of worship music turned out to be so important to all concerned that the differences overrode all other cultural similarities.

At a more inclusive level, we can speak of **national culture,** including how it is created and how it is maintained. The 19th-century concept of America as a cultural "melting pot" has long been considered too facile to describe the reality of the perseverance of many subcultures. Yet one can still speak of an "American culture" that is widespread and easily identifiable, even if it is not shared by all American citizens. Movies, television, and national newspapers and magazines, as well as convenient long-distance travel, have strengthened this concept. This "American culture" includes a standard American English language and accent, shared knowledge of Super Bowls, World Series, celebrity murder trials, and presidential scandals, and even basic values like individualism that constitute the "American character" (see, for example, the Bellah et al. 1985 study).

In new nations like Indonesia, which have been recently and precariously cobbled together out of many diverse cultures and societies, with boundaries defined by fortuitous colonial empires frozen in the late 19th century, the issue of national culture is a governmental concern, too important to be left to chance. For example, in recent decades, the Indonesian government has worked to reduce the importance of regional languages and cultures while promoting a single Indonesian national culture. The Indonesian movie and television industries have played an important role in this effort by showing how people live in this national culture (Heider, 1991). Both Indonesian films and television series are produced in Jakarta for distribution throughout the country. Characters and scenery are identified as being from one recognizable region or another, but the actors all speak the national language, Indonesian, and dress in basic pan-Indonesian clothing (except for important ceremonies like weddings, when they wear distinctive ethnic dress). Their houses, their food, their work, and their play are all generically Indonesian. Not only does this practice deemphasize regional culture, but it also serves as a model and guide to show Balinese, Minangkabau, and Javanese how to be Indonesian. Thus these films (and now, increasingly, television dramas) are intended to be more than entertainment.

With the economic, ecological, and political turmoil of 1998, the flaws in the Indonesian national culture became apparent. One of the Five Principles of the Republic of Indonesia, proclaimed in 1945, was "belief in one God." This principle was intended to legitimize not only the majority religion, Islam, but also Christianity,

Buddhism, and Hinduism. The government officially emphasized toleration among religions. Under the stresses of the late 1990s, however, violence between Muslims and Christians increased. Rioting, burnings of mosques and churches, and even murders increased. It is too early to say whether the nation of Indonesia will survive as a multicultural society or whether it will fragment into smaller, more culturally homogeneous societies.

At an even more inclusive level beyond national cultures, one can recognize some aspects of emergent international culture, or global culture. This culture is shared by some people in all countries, its growth is facilitated by global communication technology, and, to the great distress of many, it has a distinctly American tone.

DOING ANTHROPOLOGY

Societies, Cultures, and Subcultures

Locate yourself culturally and socially. In which cultures do you share? Now think in terms of "society." Of which societies, or social units, are you a member? The list will be longer than you might think. It will be easy to work out your society membership: where you (could) vote, where your passport was issued, where you have memberships, and so forth. Your culture(s) will be more difficult. Try it.   ◆

Cultures Adapt and Change

To conclude our definition of "culture," we note that all cultures change continuously, although not all parts of cultures change at the same rates. Some features of culture may seem to remain stable for a long time. Older Americans, for example, often comment with displeasure on cultural change as if it were some nasty trick played on their generation. In fact, that reaction to change seems to be the fate of each generation. In Chapter 13, we will explore some of the many different forces behind culture change. We can predict one thing with certainty about cultures: they will be different in a generation. Even conservative people and conservative parts of conservative cultures inevitably change.

Modernization is a blanket term for the massive change that is affecting every culture in the world today, driven by new technology, including communication systems. Richard Lee (1993:23) describes being in the Kalahari Desert of southern Africa (see Chapter 10) in November 1963 and trying in vain to explain President Kennedy's assassination to the San. Less than 30 years later, he was again in the Kalahari at the time of the attempted coup against Mikhail Gorbachev in Russia; all of the San were glued to their radios, following those events with concern and knowledge.

Whether from internal dynamics, contact with other cultures, environmental alteration, or some combination of these factors, all cultures change all the time.

Note that cultures do not change out of some perverse desire to be different. Rather, they adapt to other cultures and to their physical environment. Of course, if a culture were totally maladaptive, it would fail to exist. Indeed, we have many examples of small-scale societies that simply vanished under the overwhelming force of larger societies.

Consider the Peninsular Malays. We know much about them from many excellent ethnographies, some of which are cited in the Focus Culture sketch in this chapter. These studies were all published between 1983 and 1996, however, and even the latest (Peletz, 1996) reports on the situation at the time of Peletz's latest fieldwork in 1987–1988. Even under normal circumstances, we can be sure that some things were changing for Malays in Malaysia although some aspects have remained largely stable. These people still speak Malay, although film, television, and radio must be having some effects on their language. The new technology of satellite dish receivers that bring in television channels from abroad must be exerting a significant influence. Basic beliefs in semangat and angin certainly persist, but what has been the fate of the bomohs, who have come under attack from orthodox Islam?

In reality, we have learned about these Malays as they were in the 1970s and 1980s, when the field research was being done. The term **ethnographic present** refers to this sort of time lag in our knowledge of a culture. It really has two meanings. Sometimes an ethnography intentionally attempts to recreate the culture as it was at some moment in the past, often under the assumption that before Europeans came into the area, before independence, or before some other watershed event, the culture was somehow in a pure and stable state. This denial of change is simply unjustified, as archaeologists and other historians have taught us. Cultural anthropologists have come to realize that they cannot limit themselves to what occurred in the brief moments of their fieldwork, but must consider the past to make sense of the present. For this reason, Peletz devotes the first half of his first book on the Malays of Negri Sembilan to 19th and early 20th century economic and social change. This first sense of ethnographic present, the imaginative reconstruction of an ideal past, is no longer commonly used. The second sense, the result of the time lag between fieldwork and publication, is unavoidable and in some ways more insidious. In recent years, Malaysia, like the rest of Southeast Asia, has been rocked by a series of political, economic, and environmental disasters that began with the 1987 collapse of the Thailand currency and the terrible drought caused by El Niño. Change must have accelerated in unimaginable ways. Although anthropologists are currently working in villages and cities and factories in Malaysia, it will be years before they have finished their fieldwork, analyzed their data, and written, rewritten, and published their findings. Thus today we are dependent on the picture of the ethnographic present of the previous decades as described in published books and articles.

Things could be worse, however. We are fortunate that the various ethnographers of the Peninsular Malays were attuned to historical processes of change. In most cases, these anthropologists even made return visits to their research sites to give us a sense of the dynamics of change.

THE CONCEPT OF RACE

There are no races, there are only clines.

—Livingstone, 1962

Race is a worldview.

—Goodman, 1995

The term **race** is often confused with culture. It has been used to refer to groups of people who share inherited physical characteristics. When scientists have tried to establish which traits are shared by which groups, however, they have found that no constant groupings of physical traits exist.

Humans vary greatly in our physical characteristics, along innumerable dimensions. Some of these variations are external and obvious, such as hair form, nose shape, and skin color. Some are internal, such as blood makeup and susceptibility to certain diseases. True, we are not as diverse as, say, dogs. Nevertheless, we are particularly attentive to even micro degrees of variation in ourselves (how often have you heard someone say, "She has her mother's eyes, but her paternal grandmother's mouth"?). We certainly do vary, albeit not in systematic ways. In other creatures, biological races are populations that we can reliably distinguish from each other by pointing out differences in inherited biological features or, more precisely, by genetic differences. In the human population, no genetic differences reliably define separate groups. Human variables do not sort out into neat groups; thus, from a biological standpoint, no "races" of humans exist (Brace, 1995).

Clinal Model of Variation

In a famous statement used earlier as an epigraph, Frank Livingstone said, "There are no races, there are only clines" (1962). He was referring to the continuous variation in human physical attributes **(clines).** Consider height. In any group of people, individuals vary in height, and the average heights of populations vary as well. There are tall people and there are short people, of course, but there is also every height in between. That continuum creates a cline: the continuous variation of a physical attribute. We can explain some clines in terms of adaptation, or evolutionary selection over many generations. Skin color, for example, is roughly correlated with levels of solar radiation. That is, the more sunlight, the darker the skin; the less sunlight, the lighter the skin. On the whole, then, darker skin is found closer to the equator. Even this adaptation takes millennia to develop, however. The principle works fairly well in the Old World—Eurasia and Africa—but not at all well in the Americas, where the migrants from Asia have had only 10,000 years or so to adapt. For example, the Inuit (Eskimos) of the Arctic have roughly the same skin color as equatorial South Americans.

Biological anthropologists demonstrate the irregular pattern of clines by juxtaposing maps of different physical variables such as skin color distribution, hemoglobin S (sickle cell) distribution, and tooth size (Brace, 1995) or form of navel, fingernail shape, hair coverage, skin color, stature, hair form, face size, hemoglobin S gene, and HLAB gene (Rice, 1997; see also Lieberman, 1997). Each of these attributes varies, but fairly independently. They do not covary. That is, knowing the value of one attribute does not allow a person to predict the value of another. Indeed, no groups of traits can be consistently found among any one population group.

Try this thought experiment about races and clines. Imagine a huge, square landmass located somewhere in the middle of an ocean. It is well populated, with people living in villages scattered throughout the entire area. Physically, these people vary in an interesting pattern. The people on the west coast are very tall; moving east, the stature declines until on the east coast the residents are very short. Along the north coast they are really fat; moving south, they get thinner until the south coast, which has skinny people. In the northwest corner people have small ears; moving diagonally toward the southeast corner, ear size increases until one reaches the big-eared people in the southeast corner. One day long ago, a ship from a distant land comes exploring and drops anchor off the northwest corner. The ship's crew walk into the nearest village and are struck by the appearance of the people: they are tall, very heavy, with small ears. Then the ship puts out to sea. Its next landing is on the southeast corner, where the sailors see short, skinny people with huge ears. The ship sails for home, where the captain reports finding a new land populated with two very distinct races: tall, fat, small-eared, and short, skinny, big-eared. At the time, this conclusion seemed perfectly reasonable. Only much later, when other ships return and the explorers land and walk from village to village, will they find every possible combination of these three traits. They will then be forced to revise their earlier description, concluding now that "there are no races, only clines."

This scenario gives us an idea of how Europe "discovered" race. According to C. Loring Brace (1995), early explorers who traveled on land, from Herodotus (5th century B.C.E.) to Marco Polo (14th century), were aware of human physical variation but were not tempted to think in terms of racial categories because they had experienced the variations, bit by bit, in all of these clines. Only with the advent of the great European ship voyages of the 15th century, which culminated in the European discovery of the New World, did the idea of "races" emerge. These ships later brought Europeans and West Africans together with the northeast Asians who had already reached the Americas. Ships allowed people to skip the intermediate populations. In terms of our imaginary tale, the sea-faring explorers saw only three extremes of the human continuum and, on the basis of their sample, erroneously concluded that human races existed.

"Race" as a Sociocultural Construct

"Race is a worldview," writes a leading biological anthropologist in an epigrah used earlier in this chapter and a "means of conceptualizing (and explaining) human variability" (Goodman, 1995:220). In other words, race is a **cultural construction** only loosely related to biological facts. But even as we discard the notion of **biological race,** we must recognize that many cultures, including the United States, have a long history of strongly held cultural schemas about races. This concept of **cultural race** has provided the basis for racist ideology worldwide. The fact that race has no biological validity is irrelevant to schemas about cultural race. Many people believe in race and act on those beliefs. On the one hand, biological race is a dead issue, scientifically speaking, although research on the clines of particular physical features remains important. On the other hand, as long as the cultural beliefs about race remain strong and crippling to the culture that harbors such beliefs, cultural race remains an important subject for anthropological research.

If cultural schemas of race simply consisted of false understandings of biology, they would be relatively benign. In reality, however, these cultural schemas include value-laden behavior and personality traits, holding that "race" is a bundle of physical and mental attributes of differential value. Not surprisingly, most people consider their own "race" more worthy than others, and those ideas are used to justify domination, discrimination, oppression, and even extermination of other "races." Such cultural schemas are not limited to the West. In 1956, after graduating from college, I spent a year traveling across Asia to Europe, from Yokohama to Vienna. I began with a clear awareness of the effects of racism in American society, but was repeatedly surprised to discover comparable cultural schemas, with comparable outcomes, in country after country. Cultural racism is not a trait of only one culture.

The closest that we can come to an official anthropological position on race is a statement from the Executive Board of the American Anthropological Association (May 17, 1998) that emphasized the lack of scientific basis for human races and spoke eloquently of the moral implications. According to this statement, "race"

> evolved as a worldview, a body of prejudgments that distorts our ideas about human differences and group behavior. Racial beliefs constitute myths about the diversity in the human species and about the abilities and behavior of people homogenized into racial categories. The myths fused behavior and physical features together in the public mind, impeding our comprehension of both biological variations and cultural behavior, implying that both are genetically determined. Racial myths bear no relationship to the reality of human capabilities or behavior. Scientists today find that reliance on such folk beliefs about human differences in research has led to countless errors. (*American Anthropologist,* 1998; 100(3):712–713)

The American Anthropological Association has taken an active role in combating racism in recent years. The special forum in *American Anthropologist* edited by Faye V. Harrison (1998a) is an important step. Harrison argues that

> exposure to correct information or valid anthropological analyses of the social phenomenon called race does not automatically lead to the democratization of the privilege, power, and wealth that sustain racialized—as well as classed—inequalities. (Harrison, 1998b:612)

THE INTERACTION OF BIOLOGY AND CULTURE

Determining the dynamics of the relationship between biology and culture is both one of the oldest intellectual problems and one of the hottest areas of current research. As far back as the fifth century B.C., Herodotus described a remarkable experiment intended to identify the oldest language. A king of Egypt, Psammetichus, had two babies removed from their families at birth and brought up in isolation to see which language they would speak. This experiment seems to have been based on the assumption that one language, the first human language, was innate and that all other languages were derived from it. As it happened, the first word that the babies were heard to speak sounded like the Phrygian word for bread, so it was declared that Phrygian was the oldest language. Even though the Egyptians knew nothing of modern genetics, they were making quite fine distinctions about what was inherited biologically in the absence of learning.

The fact is that we, as *Homo sapiens,* have an innate ability to learn language, but the language we learn is purely a matter of cultural learning. No evidence suggests that genetic markers for any specific language exist. Any normal human, whatever his or her culture, can learn any human language. (We explore this issue further in Chapter 4.)

Handedness offers another good example of the interaction of biology and culture in human behavior. We are born right- or left-handed, but culture gives meaning to the alternatives. *Handedness* is doing things more often and more skillfully with either the left hand or the right hand. It is one of the few basic and obvious ways in which *Homo sapiens* is asymmetrical. To look at us, we appear generally bilaterally symmetrical in both body and dress. But watch someone throw something, write a letter, or use a tool, and it immediately becomes obvious that the person has a predilection to use one hand rather than the other most of the time. In Chapter 4 we will discuss the symbolism of handedness, but we anticipate that discussion here by saying that most cultures attach negative meanings to being left-handed: it is unclean (in Asia), evil (in some European and North American cultures), gauche (in France), and sinister (in Italy). That is the cultural construction of meaning for handedness.

Another example involves food. The world contains a great number of substances that *Homo sapiens* can eat, but cultures include ideas that limit what is appropriate to eat. Such ideas constitute the cultural construction of food. Look at the following list:

Pork	Grubs	Fermented mare's milk
Broccoli	Liver	Blood pudding
Eyeballs	Tomatoes	Earth
Milk	Shrimp	Chicken eggs
Urine (human)	Dog	Fertilized chicken eggs
Flesh (human)	Beer	Snake
Testicles	Raw fish	Beef

Somewhere, each of these items is considered to be a food fit for humans, maybe even a delicacy. But no culture in the world would accept all of these items as food. Probably no individual eats all of them or even would be willing to try them all. The reason, of course, is culture: learned ideas and behaviors.

In this section, we have focused mostly on the diversity of human cultures. We have shown how cultures shape innate human abilities. Despite these variations, some cultural universals—features that all cultures share—do exist. If we started to list them, we would produce an impressive set of traits, both general and specific. All cultures know language, deal with the supernatural, use fire, and prohibit marriage between some relatives, just to name a few.

SEEING ANTHROPOLOGY

Latah: A Culture-Specific Elaboration of the Startle Reflex in Malaysia

Filmmaker: Gunter Pfaff   *Anthropologist: Ronald C. Simons*

This film focuses on one issue: the mix of biology and culture in **latah,** the startle syndrome of Malaya that has long fascinated anthropologists. The film follows the research of Ronald L. Simons, who was trained in both psychiatry and anthropology. This double training means that he was fully aware of both the biological and the cultural aspects of latah and therefore was not tempted to neglect one or the other.

The biological basis for the syndrome is evident in the fact that all people worldwide startle. That is, they have reflexive, autonomic reactions to sudden, unexpected stimuli. Any group, however, contains a wide range of intensity of these startle reactions, with some individuals, the **hyperstartlers,** showing quite extreme reactions. Although some cultures (like the United States) pay little attention to hyperstartling, other cultures (like the Peninsular Malays) have an elaborate syndrome, an overt cultural schema, with a special name, stereotyped response patterns, folk explanations, and judgmental, even moral, meanings assigned to the syndrome. This very explicit cultural schema contributes to the "cultural construction of startle behavior" in Malaysia. In contrast, Americans, who mostly ignore hyperstartle, have no cultural schemas at all for hyperstartling (except, perhaps, for the "jumpers" in Maine—see Simons, 1996:206–209).

Simons' research strategy was noteworthy. He was already a professor of psychiatry when he took leave from Michigan State University to study cultural and physical anthropology at the University of California in Berkeley. There he came across the literature on latah and recognized the startle reflex as a "hot tool"—that is, an ideal place to look at the intersection of biology and culture. As Simons wrote,

> The neurophysiology of startle, the personal experience of startle, and the interactive uses of startle (both actual and symbolic) comprise a system unusually amenable to straightforward analysis. Single startles, and the events that precede and follow them, make convenient analytic units. (Simons, 1996:7)

A latah woman explodes at her husband. *(Credit: Dr. Ronald C. Simons: Still from the film* Latah)

Incidents of startle are brief, frequent, visible, memorable, and often socially significant. To investigate latah, Simons went to the Malay village of Padang Kemunting on the west coast of the peninsula, where he lived for eight months and where the filming took place. He also worked with hyperstartlers in the Philippines, where a latahlike syndrome was culturally elaborated. In addition, Simons studied hyperstartlers in Michigan, where it is not culturally elaborated. Despite the absence of cultural elaboration of this syndrome in the United States, Simons did find accounts of hyperstartle in American literature and comic strips. In one of his most interesting analyses, he looks at how (in *Huckleberry Finn*) Tom Sawyer and Huck Finn deliberately turn Aunt Sally into a hyperstartler (Twain, 1884). Even comic strips show hyperstartle incidents (that obnoxious cat Garfield takes special pleasure in triggering hyperstartle in his housemates).

In his survey of the scientific literature, Simons found latahlike syndromes, each with its own name, from Maine (the "jumpers"), Siberia, Lapland, Burma, Thailand, Yemen, Japan, and the Philippines. Many of the features that we see in the Malay latah are present in other startle syndromes:

Matching, or imitative behavior
"Naughty talk," vulgar or obscene language
Violent, often aggressive body movements
Dropping or throwing objects

Which of these features can we trace to the biology of *Homo sapiens?* Certainly, the variable propensity to startle seems rooted in biology. But are hyperstartlers born or made? Perhaps some individuals who are naturally stronger startlers are worked on, under the proper conditions in midlife, and conditioned to become hyperstartlers. Part of the startle reflex is what Simons calls "attention capture"—a freezing, focusing, and then sudden release. This feature could account for some of the latah behavior. But what about the "naughty language"? Many "normal"-level startlers have experienced startle when, for example, they tripped over an unseen object and inadvertently and most inappropriately let out a strong oath. This scenario looks very much like the "naughty words" reactions that Simons traces through many of these startle syndromes.

Much remains to be discovered as we untangle the biological and cultural strands of this phenomenon. Implicit clues to the cultural side are suggested by what Simons has said about startle in interpersonal interaction:

> If one is startled while interacting with others, all the give-and-take of ordinary social intercourse, the fine mutually adjusting dance of speech and body, is broken, and the awkward and disconcerting lapse in seemly social presence must be acknowledged and remedied. Yet in spite of this, or to be more precise, because of it, people everywhere delight in startling one another. (Simons, 1996:3)

Why Latah? An Etic Explanation.   As outsiders, we can look for the function provided by this latah syndrome. It seems to allow people to get social attention and to have a central social role, albeit at considerable cost. Evidence indicates that most latah sufferers are relatively powerless in their particular contexts (for example, older poor widows with no relatives, living as unvalued dependents on the charity of nonrelatives). Latah offers a more visible, though temporary, social role of sorts for these people (see H. Geertz, 1968).

Why Latah? Emic Explanations from the People.   In the film, one woman explains latah as hereditary, biological—although she acknowledges that while her mother is latah, neither she nor her children are. A man suggests that anyone, if teased enough, would be latah. Others explain the preponderance of female latahs in terms of their ethnopsychological concept of semangat, or soul matter. In women, semangat is weaker, so women are therefore more susceptible to latah than are men. (We discussed the Malay concept of semangat on page 42.)

The video clip shows some latah behavior in the Malay village. Different villagers offer their explanations for this phenomenon, and we see that although most agree about what latah is, they do not agree on its cause. Most of the latah are older women, but we do see one man with this syndrome.

In the longer film, we see more extensive footage of latah performances, with a wide range of emotion. Most of these latah seem to express a mixture of pleasure and discomfort at the teasing and their own subsequent behavior. Simons and his filmmaker, Gunther Pfaff, include some 1936 footage of the Ainu, aboriginal pre-Japanese people of the northern Japanese island of Hokkaido. The Ainu syndrome, called *imu,* includes sudden hitting out, "naughty words," and imitation. A culture-specific feature of imu is that the stimulus usually involves snakes—an actual snake, a snakelike object, or even just the word "snake."

The complete film also shows two women, undergraduates at Michigan State University, in an experimental setting. A pistol is shot off unexpectedly behind each. One merely blinks, but the other goes into a major startle reaction. Simons says in the narration that this hyperstartler is occasionally startled intentionally by her family or friends. But, he continues, "I believe that if she were a Malay villager, she would be made into a latah."

Setup Questions

1. What is latah?
2. What insights do the personal histories give?
3. How does Simons' narration differ from the villagers' statements?
4. What is the folk theory of latah? Can you catch any logical inconsistencies?
5. Can anyone become latah?
6. Do latahs want to be latah? (Watch their faces carefully.)
7. What is semangat? How do villagers use the concept of semangat in their thinking about latah?
8. Is it strange that these Malay villagers go around poking each other in the ribs?
9. Why don't men generally become latah? ◆

HOLLYWOOD-STYLE ANTHROPOLOGY

Ethnicity in *Smoke Signals*

Smoke Signals 1998 89 minutes

Adam Beach as Victor Joseph
Evan Adams as Thomas Builds-the-Fire
Gary Farmer as Arnold Joseph
Irene Bedard as Suzy Song
Tantoo Cardinal as Arlene Joseph

On the Coeur d'Alene Indian Reservation in Idaho, on the 4th of July 1976, a house fire orphaned the baby Thomas. He grew up with his grandmother, and his closest friend was Victor, son of Arnold, who saved Thomas's life in the fire. The movie is set in 1998 (with flashbacks to 1976 and 1988). Arnold has disappeared, and dies in Arizona. Victor and Thomas make the trip to Arizona as a sort of quest. The film's voice is Indian throughout—funny, self-deprecating, proud, and terribly sad. (The screenplay is by Sherman Alexie from his own novel, *The Lone Ranger and Tonto Fist Fight in Heaven*.)

Setup Questions

1. How do the Indian self-images of Victor and Thomas differ?
2. What is the role of religion in the film?

3. What is fry bread and why is it important?
4. Explain the girls driving backward in the car.
5. What is the Spokane waterfall about?
6. "John Wayne's Teeth"?
7. What is Victor's moment of understanding?   ♦

CHAPTER SUMMARY

- We can define culture as
    1. learned (not innate)
    2. shared (fairly commonly held)
    3. ideas (mental models or schemas) and
    4. patterns of behavior.
- Schemas are organized sets of cultural ideas about something (for example, love, marriage, breakfast).
- We can talk about cultures on many different levels of generality, or inclusiveness. We often call the less inclusive levels "subcultures."
- Societies are organized groups of individuals. We can also talk about societies or social units at different levels of inclusiveness.
- Anthropologists often describe culture using an imaginary time frame of "ethnographic present," meaning either (1) a reconstruction of some pure, unchanged state before contact, or (2) the moment, years before publication, when the research was done.
- "Race" in the biological sense is not applicable to humans. There are so many different physical features that vary continuously (clines) and independently of each other that we cannot define discrete groups of humans.
- The biocultural model explains behavior like language, handedness, and latah as complex interactions between innate and learned behavior.

KEY TERMS

act	enculturation	race
biological race	ethnographic present	schema
clines	fuzzy categories	socialization
cultural construction	hyperstartler	social unit
cultural race	latah	society
culture	modernization	subculture
ethnicity	national culture	

QUESTIONS TO THINK ABOUT

- What are the implications of a society that is multicultural?
- What are the implications of a person who is multicultural?
- Does it make a difference if we define culture as just ideas (for example, schemas about something like sitting) or as ideas plus behavior and artifacts (for example, the schemas plus posture plus chairs)?

- If you were a teacher, how would you explain to your students the difference between the biological facts that say there are no human races and the cultural fact that people think races exist?
- The biocultural model accounts for some aspects of behavior, but for which aspects is it less relevant? Why?

SUGGESTIONS FOR FURTHER READING

Shore, Bradd

1996   Culture in Mind. Cognition, Culture, and the Problem of Meaning. New York: Oxford University Press. *An important recent discussion of the meaning of culture.*

Strauss, Claudia, and Naomi Quinn

1997   A Cognitive Theory of Cultural Meaning. Cambridge, U.K.: Cambridge University Press. *Developing the concept of schema and culture.*

Wiredu, Kwasi

1996   Cultural Universals and Particulars: An African Perspective. Bloomington: Indiana University Press. *A scholar from Ghana looks at culture.*

Zenner, Walter P.

1991   Minorities in the Middle: A Cross-Cultural Analysis. Albany: SUNY Press. *An anthropological survey of various relatively affluent immigrants in different countries.*

Look at current issues of the journal Cultural Anthropology.

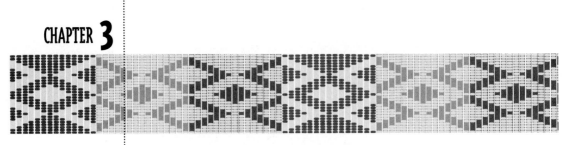

CHAPTER 3

Doing Anthropology:
Fieldwork and Theories

Cock fight.
Bayon, Angkor
(Cambodia),
12th century
C.E. *(Credit:*
Karl G. Heider)

HEADLINE ANTHROPOLOGY

PRESS WATCH

Some of the subjects discussed in this chapter have made their way into current news stories. For example:

♦ According to Gerald Zaltman, marketing professor at the Harvard Business School, focus groups are inadequate to learn what people really think, so he uses visual images to get at their real thoughts about products.

—New York Times, *February 23, 2002.*

♦ Consuming Rituals of the Suburban Tribe. Focus groups have their problems, so marketers are mimicking anthropologists and studying consumers in their native habitat: the home.

—New York Times, *January 13, 2002.*

♦ Anthropologist Paul Noguchi has analyzed lost-and-found collections in the US, England, and Japan for insights into local cultures.

—New York Times, *August 20, 2002.*

DOING FIELDWORK

There is no science in which the basic research is so exciting as in cultural anthropology. Cultural anthropologists study various cultures, their own as well as others, including subcultures in America such as company boardrooms, surgeons, gangs, body piercing, divorced men, and midwives. So many different research methodologies exist that it is impossible to find one approach that is used by all anthropologists. Nevertheless, there is a prototypical methodology, called **fieldwork,** which consists of research carried out while living in the midst of a group.

How do you learn about fieldwork? My own teachers were great fieldworkers, but they had been trained in the 1930s, an era when one simply did not discuss the actual process. They told us about everything except fieldwork. Today, it is difficult to understand or explain this reticence, but it must be acknowledged. A few early ethnographers did write about their experiences, but it was not until the post–World War II generations emerged that anthropologists began to develop ways to discuss their fieldwork. The great classic from that period was written by Laura Bohannon, who described her research among the Tiv of Nigeria. Perhaps because she was so ambivalent about the entire enterprise, Bohannon wrote it as a novel (*Return to Laughter*) under a pseudonym, Elenore Smith Bowen (1954). She also wrote a much-reprinted essay describing cultural misunderstandings in the field: "Shakespeare in the Bush." In this work, she tries to explain *Hamlet,* the play's ghost, and marriage to a deceased brother's widow to Tiv elders, who in turn patiently explain how necessary such marriages are, and who accuse her of totally missing the point. Most book-length ethnographies these days present at least some details about the actual research.

A few collections of essays from the field also date from this period. Significantly, they are written apart from the ethnographies, almost as if to distance the scientific research from the personal encounter (for example, Flinn and colleagues' 1988 work dealing with families in the field, and two collections edited by Philip P. De Vita about fieldwork mistakes [1990, 1992]). De Vita's titles give hints about the problem researchers face in this endeavor: *The Humbled Anthropologist* and *The Naked Anthropologist.* When a successfully overeducated adult walks into a field situation where he or she is less competent than a small child, the person is bound to make mistakes and feel humiliated—and few of us like to talk about our errors.

Faux Pas.   Doing fieldwork is inevitably to some extent a personally intrusive act and is successful only when the anthropologist has established good **rapport,** or relations, with the community. However sensitive the anthropologist is, and however careful he or she is not to destroy this rapport, many cultural booby traps wait to be sprung. Every fieldworker has stories of how he or she inadvertently violated some cultural expectation, and for every such incident of which the anthropologist is aware, there are probably others that the researcher never discovered. Michael Peletz describes his first months with the Malays in Negri Sembilan, before his fiancée joined him from America (1996). The villagers had strict Muslim ideas about proper separation between men and women. Consequently, when they perceived him as spending an inappropriate amount of time with a young single woman, many people distanced themselves from him. It took Peletz some time to restore good rapport. I raised eyebrows by wearing a red shirt in Japan (in 1956, red was still reserved for women) and by eating with my left hand in India (where it is considered impure).

Physical Dangers.   Often the fieldwork site poses dangers for anthropologists and their families, and a few have even lost their lives in the course of research. Perhaps this hazard is not surprising, considering the inaccessibility that anthropologists often seek out. In fact, most anthropologists can tell tales about their own foolish decisions and narrow escapes. Only slowly has an acknowledgment of danger come to be part of the training of fieldworkers. Nancy Howell has urged that basic health and safety instruction be incorporated into graduate training (1994), and another edited volume has discussed the issues faced by anthropologists who find themselves in the midst of civil conflict (Nordstrom and Robben, 1995).

In New Guinea, for example, my group observed several battles between Dani groups armed with spears and bows and arrows, but our main danger was self-induced. Neither side wanted to shoot at us (killing an outsider would apparently not have helped to placate the ghosts). For the first few battles, when we had little idea of what to expect, we stayed far back from the action. Later, as we grew more confident, we roamed into the range of arrows. Only dumb luck kept us from being hit. Perhaps the real surprise is that so many anthropologists have survived their research adventures.

Learning the Language

Being able to speak the language of the people seems so obvious and elementary a prerequisite for fieldwork that it hardly seems necessary to mention it. But for many anthropologists setting out to the field, this issue looms as a major hurdle. Of course, for anthropologists who do their fieldwork with people who speak their own native language, there are few problems on this score. In most cases, however, most fieldworkers are confronted with some sort of language barrier. If they can use a language that they have learned in school or college, they have a good head start. Unfortunately, schools and colleges in the United States generally teach only a handful of languages. A few teach some of the more exotic languages. Nevertheless, most anthropologists find themselves heading for a place where people speak a language that the anthropologist cannot possibly learn until he or she arrives.

Sometimes, anthropologists choose to use interpreters. It is usually possible to find someone who speaks English, Spanish, or another European language that was introduced during the colonial period. The main drawback of this approach is that an important link in understanding what is going on has been taken completely out of the anthropologist's hands.

Learning the language is certainly a most important step in understanding a culture, and time spent in language study is not wasted.

Sometimes, when I am at the annual meetings of the American Anthropological Association, surrounded by hordes of other anthropologists, I wonder how many hundreds of languages could be spoken in that room at that instant—and how many languages have been forgotten in that room. Anthropologists who spend a year or two learning and speaking an isolated tribal language when in their mid-twenties, and then do not have an opportunity to speak it again, will surely have forgotten it twenty or thirty years later. Nevertheless, language learning is part of the necessary investment for fieldwork.

Fieldwork Techniques

Participant Observation. **Participant observation** involves living with and taking part in the life of the people being studied and carefully observing and meticulously recording data. These activities are really the essence of fieldwork, and they differentiate anthropological fieldwork from the many other ways to study human beings. **Going native** is the somewhat old-fashioned term for an anthropologist

Participant observation: An American anthropologist and her daughter during fieldwork in rural India. *(Credit: © Doranne Jacobson)*

who has gone all the way, becoming more participant than observer. A few anthropologists have been able to completely merge with the culture for periods, but most could not do it even if they wanted to. Yet all practice this technique to some degree. They establish rapport by making friends, giving presents, and sharing meals. Speaking the language, however poorly, attending ceremonies, and taking part in daily life are all ways of building special relationships that allow the anthropologist to learn more about the culture. The anthropologist is accepted to some degree and perhaps given a special name, or even a kin relationship such as uncle or aunt, or daughter or son, to some key people in the group. Richard Lee (1993:61) tells of the moment when he was incorporated into the !Kung San naming system. He was given a !Kung name and suddenly had a sort of identity with everyone else who shared that particular name and was in a way husband to their wives, son to their fathers, father to their children.

Anthropologists probably do not get initiated into the tribe very often, but they are quietly tested in many ways to see whether they are really serious. In a famous anthropological anecdote, Clifford Geertz (1972) tells of attending a cockfight with his wife at the beginning of their fieldwork in Bali, at a time when they were being pointedly ignored and treated as nonpeople by the Balinese villagers. But cock-fighting was illegal, and when the police staged a raid, everyone—including the Geertzes—ran for it. The Geertzes found themselves pulled through a gateway, into a compound, and seated at a table, and tea miraculously appeared. When the police arrived to inquire, their host claimed them as old friends, completely innocent of the cockfight. From that moment, the villagers opened up to them, although there was much teasing about their undignified flight.

Napoleon Chagnon was fed false genealogies by the Yanomamo for his first months among them until they came to trust him and corrected their misinformation (Chagnon, 1992). Um'ue was my closest friend among the Dani, but it was not until my second visit that I learned his real name (or at least his more common name), Wali. He had gotten us to call him Um'ue so that if his sponsorship of our presence went wrong and the government came looking for someone named Um'ue, Wali would have deniability.

It is not easy trying to live in another culture, and all anthropologists have their favorite war stories. Nevertheless, the effects of participant observation are far-reaching. The fieldworker learns about events in context and finds out much more than had been anticipated in the original research proposal. Embedding oneself in a culture, using oneself as a research instrument, leads to the holistic perspective that is so characteristic of anthropology.

Participant observation is one of anthropology's major exports to other disciplines. In particular, sociologists who do qualitative research (rather than quantitative number crunching of data from large-scale surveys) use this approach. For example, Michael Burawoy spent a year as a factory worker in Hungary to study Hungarian factory culture. Burawoy and his sociology graduate students at the University of California in Berkeley reported on their participant observation studies in the San Francisco Bay area in a book with the provocative title *Ethnography Unbound*. Very explicitly, in the introduction, Burawoy wrote:

> We seek to unchain ethnography from its confinement as a quaint technique at
> the margins of social science. In our eyes participant observation is the paradig-
> matic way of studying the social world, and from this point of view anthropol-
> ogy becomes the paradigmatic social science. (Burawoy et al., 1991:3)

The political scientist James C. Scott carried out his early research on peasant revolts in Burma and Vietnam, based on materials from publications and archives (1976). Later, his interest in class conflict led him to think about "everyday forms of **resistance**," or the myriad ways in which subordinate classes can undermine and sabotage the goals of the superordinate classes. By very nature, these sorts of resistance are not publicized, and often are barely acknowledged by either side, yet they remain much more pervasive than open armed uprisings. To study this phenomenon, Scott took his family to live for two years in a Malay village, doing participant observation to learn about behavior that had escaped the notice of formal reports (1985). The point is that ethnographic research through participant observation, which has always been the anthropologist's dominant research tool, provides a unique opportunity to observe the dynamics of a culture from within.

Interviews.   Directed interviews are interviews that follow a protocol, or list of questions, and are replicated with each subject (in contrast to open-ended interviews, which are more exploratory). They are used to probe into specific subjects and to get comparable opinions on the same subject from several different people. For example, when Douglas Hollan and Jane Wellenkamp studied the emotions and life experiences of the Toraja in Indonesia, they worked with a checklist of important topics that they had devised in advance. They picked eleven representative people and carried out extensive interviews with each; Wellenkamp talked to the women, and Hollan talked to the men. The result (1994) was a rich account of the life experiences of Toraja men and women. By following the framework of their checklist, Hollan and Wellenkamp elicited comparable narratives on specific subjects from several different people.

Focus Groups.   Focus groups are interviews of small groups of people, four to eight at a time, where the leader's role is to orchestrate conversational agreement as well as disagreement. Focus groups are most familiar from politics and marketing campaigns, which have perhaps given them a bad name. Although many anthropologists have found that sitting in on informal group discussions is a good source of information, few have made systematic use of focus groups. There is a large literature on focus group methodology (see, for example, Bernard, 2000)

However, asking people questions about their thoughts and behaviors is not as straightforward as it might seem. Charles Briggs (1986), a linguistic anthropologist, has observed that different cultures have different ways of imparting information. If, for example, a standard (Western) question-and-answer situation is not a usual scenario, then forcing local people into it may not produce answers that are accurate or truthful in the sense that the questioner expects. A good analogy here is language itself—anthropologists know that it is to their advantage to know a people's language well enough to function in that language. By the same token, according to Briggs, the anthropologist must learn the people's own particular style of information communication. It is of course possible to "train" an informant—to teach both the anthropologist's language and style of question-and-answer. But to the extent that it is important to understand local people's ways of thinking and speaking, that goal is subverted by "training" informants.

A fine example is depicted in *I Love You: Hope for the Year 2000,* an ethnographic film made in Sumatra by Kathrin Oester and Heinzpeter Znoj. The anthropologist tries to question her closest friend about marriage arrangements in the village, but to no avail. Finally, she is invited to the friend's far-off rice field, where they are alone, and the friend explains things through little role-playing skits. It seems that role-playing has an appropriate degree of indirection, which straightforward questions and answers lack.

Questionnaires.   Questionnaires, which are used to survey large numbers of people, are more characteristic of other sorts of social science research but sometimes are useful to anthropologists. The results are not as rich as more open-ended interviews because people are usually restricted to short answers without the opportunity to follow up and expand on their thoughts, nor are they as likely to turn up surprises as are the less formal techniques. Nevertheless, the large number of precisely comparable responses allows statistical summarization and is the basis for more confident broad generalizations. What is lost in flexibility is gained in comparability.

Unobtrusive Data Collection.   **Unobtrusive data collection** involves the use of existing sources of data. In this type of research, the anthropologist does nothing to initiate or affect the data. The types of data cover a wide range, including archival work, use of historical documents, studying movies as texts, and the like (Webb, 1981).

Archaeology is the prototypical example of unobtrusive measures in anthropology. The behavior has happened, the people have gone, and the archaeologist comes along later to ponder what remains. Of course, the methods of excavation that the archaeologist chooses do influence the results, but it is too late to affect the data in the ground.

Anthropologists are beginning to look at feature films as cultural statements (Heider, 1994). Here, of course, one can be most unobtrusive. No matter how you look at a movie, you cannot affect the action. The drawback is that you cannot discuss anything with a film. Certainly, unobtrusive measures have their place in the anthropological toolkit, but they are just one of several useful approaches.

Recording Field Data.   In the early days of fieldwork, a typewriter and carbon paper were essential elements in the anthropological toolkit. When I first went to the Dani in New Guinea, my teacher Cora Du Bois wrote to remind me to make copies of all my field notes. Indeed, the lore of anthropology tells of the horrors of lost field notes. Today, anthropologists are more likely to take laptop computers to the field, with solar-powered battery chargers when necessary. Even more exotic equipment has been used to good purpose. When Napoleon Chagnon returned to the Yanomamo in 1990 and 1991, he used high-tech Global Positioning System instruments, which work with satellites and allowed him to precisely map the locations of Yanomamo gardens in the deep forest. George Morren has been using satellite photographs of New Guinea to study local horticulture.

Anthropologists have long taken both still and movie cameras to record events, and the results were used to illustrate books or to make ethnographic films. Traditionally, the problems of processing film in the field made conventional film difficult to use in actual research. Polaroid cameras, with their instant prints, have been useful for some sorts of research. Now that high-quality video cameras can be used in the field, many new possibilities have been opened up, but anthropologists have not caught up with the technology, and few have thought of ways to use these new tools. One possibility, which I tried in Sumatra, was to use clips from Indonesian feature films as eliciting devices, asking Minangkabau to evaluate the emotional behavior shown in the films. The great advantage was that people knew that the behavior was fictional and so were not embarrassed to discuss it with me, for they could not be accused of criticizing any actual person.

Fieldwork Settings

Any culture, any place in the world, can be the focus of anthropological research. We can categorize fieldwork situations into three types: the anthropologist goes to a tribe, the anthropologist goes to a modern nation, and the anthropologist stays at home.

The Anthropologist Studies a Tribal Culture. The traditional type of fieldwork involved the anthropologist studying a distant tribal culture. For the first decades of the 20th century, this approach was the most common type of fieldwork. Even to this day, many anthropologists continue to study tribal cultures. Several related reasons explained this attraction. First, there has long been a great curiosity about people with very different cultures from our own, and tribal cultures offered particularly extreme examples. Second, and less important perhaps, were the actual workings of cultures, a process that, of course, could have been studied in familiar as well as distant places. Third, anthropologists felt that those tribal cultures were being absorbed and assimilated by national cultures. Thus, if they were not recorded immediately, whole ways of life—including all associated knowledge, wisdom, and skills—would be lost forever. The national cultures were also changing, of course, but they seemed to be well documented. The mission of anthropology therefore became the preservation of the memory of tribal cultures before it was too late. This theme was repeated again and again in the writings of early-20th-century anthropologists.

In addition, it was in the national interests of the colonial powers of Europe, as well as Japan and the United States, to have information about the cultures of the tribal groups included in their empires. Knowledge is power or, as Bernard Cohn has put it, "the conquest of empire was the conquest of knowledge" (1996). Anthropologists provided that knowledge. Of course, not all anthropologists were agents of colonial governments, but their interests often coincided. The researchers needed government permission to carry out their work and often were supported and encouraged by the colonial administrations. Today, in the postcolonial world, the national governments that have succeeded the colonial administrations face many of the same problems of governing multicultural nations. As a result, they have generally continued to allow and encourage anthropological research.

Studying a tribal culture rather than a national culture or subculture has both advantages and disadvantages. Among the advantages is the fact that tribes tend to be relatively small, homogeneous, and isolated. It may be possible to know everyone in the tribe and to become familiar with the entire territory of the tribe in a year or so. More subtle considerations come into play as well. There are still so many tribes that often the anthropologist finds that he or she is the first person to write an ethnography of that group. Although anthropologists may be reluctant to admit it, they gain a certain satisfaction in being the first, or one of the first, to bring knowledge about a particular culture to the rest of the world.

Studying a tribal culture also has certain disadvantages. The less that is known about a tribe before fieldwork begins, the more difficult it is to plan focused research. Also, it is rarely possible to learn a tribal language before arriving in the field, so that one's first months are spent talking through interpreters, if they are available, and slowly working into the local language. Often it takes months, or even a year or more, to gain governmental permission to do the fieldwork. For graduate students with limited time and resources, this waiting period can prove a daunting obstacle. The more isolated the tribe, the more likely that living conditions will differ quite dramatically from those with which the anthropologist is accustomed, especially if accompanied by a family. In addition, real dangers may be associated with unhealthy conditions, inadequate medical care, and volatile political conditions in many areas of the world. It is quite possible to invest years in gaining knowledge of the anthropological literature on an area, some command of the language, permission to do research, and a research grant, only to find that a particular location has erupted in civil war.

FOCUS CULTURE

Fieldwork Among the Grand Valley Dani of Irian Jaya, Indonesia (West New Guinea)

OVERVIEW

Location: Central Highlands of the Indonesian Province of Irian Jaya (formerly Netherlands New Guinea), in the Grand Valley of the Balim River, 5,000 feet above sea level
Geography: High temperate valley surrounded by mountains
Population: About 50,000
Language: A Papuan language, like most of the New Guinea Highland languages, unrelated to any other major language stock
Religion: Belief in ghosts of dead people and spirits that live in the forests
Economy: Horticulture. The main food is sweet potatoes, which are grown by intensive digging-stick gardening. The Dani also raise pigs.
Sociopolitical Organization: Kinship-based. Patrilineal sibs and moieties are cross-cut by territorial confederations and alliances. The alliances are the largest social groups and have up to 5,000 people.

My first flight, in 1961, into the Grand Valley from the north coast of what was then the Netherlands New Guinea was something of an adventure. The plane was a one-engine Cessna that took off from the Sentani airfield where General MacArthur had his headquarters briefly during World War II. The flight left early in the morning in the hope of getting through the mountains before midday clouds closed off the passes. The flight lasted only an hour and traversed the swamps and Lake Plains

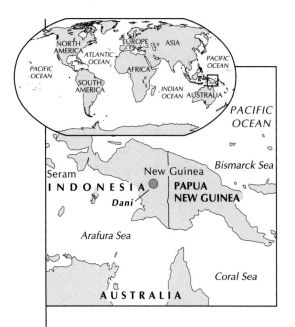

before entering the central mountain ranges of New Guinea. As we flew over the lowlands, we saw few signs of human occupation, and only an occasional isolated hamlet with its thatched-roof houses and sweet potato fields was visible in the mountains. Suddenly, the plane burst out of the narrow mountain gorges into the Grand Valley of the Balim River to reveal large and small collections of houses and everywhere the complex ditch systems of the sweet potato gardens. The Grand Valley is a great flat plain, some fifty miles long and as much as ten miles wide, with the Balim River winding slowly down the middle.

Before airplanes, the Grand Valley Dani were among the most isolated people in the world. Swamps, rain forest, steep mountains, and the apparent lack of any enticing economic resource like gold had combined to shield these Dani from outside traders or even explorers until the late 1930s. Only after World War II, and well into the 1950s, did the first Christian missionaries and Dutch colonial officials settle in the Grand Valley to begin their tasks of changing the Dani.

Even though metal was unknown to the Dani before 1938, these people were not completely cut off from the world. Throughout the Grand Valley, and indeed in virtually every village across the mountains of New Guinea, people used shells from the distant oceans for ornaments. One can picture a vast trading network, connecting village to neighboring village, tying together practically every person in New Guinea to every other and then to the world. This network was not effective enough to distribute metal tools, but it did deliver sea shells to every settlement in the mountains. It also spread the sweet potato, which had originated in South America, throughout the island. One even finds suggestive traces of a religious movement that spread for hundreds of miles across much of the highlands generations ago. Thus the isolation of the Dani was only relative.

In March 1961, the plane from the coast brought us for the first time to Wamena, the center for government and missionary activity in the Grand Valley. At that time, Wamena consisted of a handful of prefabricated metal buildings and an airstrip occupying land that had been abandoned by the Dani after a war. Today, Wamena has grown into a sprawling town with stores, banks, churches, hotels, a movie theater, and homes for several thousand people who have come from the outside to live and work in the temperate climate of the Grand Valley. The day we first arrived in 1961, we paid our respects to the Dutch and the Americans in Wamena, then moved across the Valley as soon as possible to set up our tent camp in a place that I called the Dugum Neighborhood, part of what is now called the Kurelu region. We wanted to live with Dani who were as unaffected by government or missions as possible. Even though the people of the Dugum Neighborhood were only an hour or so walk away from Westerners, some routes were blocked by ongoing wars; in other directions, nominal allies of uncertain friendliness resided. Thus, in the Dugum, with few trade goods to be seen and little outside influence yet to be felt, we had found something close to an "untouched" culture to study and film.

I was 26 years old, a graduate student in anthropology, planning to do research for my Ph.D. dissertation on material culture as a member of the Harvard Peabody Expedition. The expedition had been organized by Robert Gardner, an anthropologist and filmmaker at Harvard. Gardner had brought together a team that included Peter Matthiessen (author and naturalist), Michael Rockefeller (photographer and sound recorder), Eliot Elisofon (*Life* magazine photographer), Jan Broekhuyse (anthropologist and Dutch government official), Samuel Putnam (medical student and photographer), two policemen (whose protection we did not need but who were of great help in interpreting during the early days of the expedition), and a cook. Gardner's main goal was to make a film which he would call *Dead Birds* (described in *Seeing Anthropology*, pages 91–94). The expedition as a whole stayed for five months in 1961. Eventually, I spent a total of nearly three years in the region, gradually expanding my research on the Dani from stone axes to emotions.

In early April 1961, we were still getting settled into our camp in a grove of tall auracaria trees with its own spring of pure water. On our second day we were awakened by shouts traveling across the valley floor to announce a battle. Our neighbors were part of a group of 1,000 people on the southern front of the Kurelu Alliance, which was composed of about 5,000 people. Beyond the sweet potato gardens was a deserted strip of no-man's-land, and beyond it lay the gardens and compounds of the enemy alliance, the Widaia. Although the Kurelu and the Widaia were then members of different alliances, dozens of years earlier they had been allies, and they shared the same culture.

As men on both sides prepared for battle by putting on their best feather and shell ornaments and checking their weapons, we considered what we should do. Of course, we were eager to see and film as much as we could, but we did not know what to expect, and we could not predict how the Dani would receive our presence. An additional complication was the fact that the other outsiders in the Grand Valley—the missionaries and the government officials—were committed to ending Dani wars by persuasion and, if necessary, by force. They had succeeded in some parts of the Grand Valley, but battles were still taking place between the Kurelu and the Widaia. Both the government and the missionaries knew, of course, that we were living in an unpacified region and so implicitly condoned our presence—and our cameras—at battles. Also, a Dutch patrol officer who later wrote his doctoral dissertation on the Dani, together with two local policemen, were attached to our expedition to help us and, presumably, to keep us out of trouble. Nevertheless, we, as outsiders, would be taking a great interest in warfare and religious activities that other outsiders were trying to stop. This conflict of interests was inevitable, but only much later did we discover how strongly some of the missionaries resented what they saw as our threat to their moral authority.

We watched the first battle from a distance, only gradually learning through interpreters the Dani explanation of those events. Over the next weeks, we saw a total of eight battles. Months later, after the other expedition members had left and I had gradually improved my command of Dani, I got a better perspective on the warfare. From the beginning, of course, we could observe and photograph a great deal. There were the artifacts of war, including weapons, ornaments, watchtowers, and even the bamboo knives that served as surgical tools to remove arrows from bodies. There was the landscape of war, those fields on which the battles were fought, the abandoned no-man's-land, and the frontier with the watchtowers and other defensive arrangements like artificial ponds for ducks whose sudden noisy flight would warn of an enemy raiding party. We could also see and record strategies of ambush, attack, and retreat on the battlefields. In addition, we observed some ritual acts like the decontamination of the corpse of a man lost in a raid against the Widaia. The body had been returned by the Widaia, but its wounds were stuffed with magical objects that had to be neutralized before our friends could safely carry it home for cremation. Finally, we saw the emotional tone of the battles, which was a mix of excitement and wariness. The quiet raids were probably grim, but we could clearly see how the great battles were noisy and, despite the dangers, had a sportive element.

Later, when I was able to talk comfortably and privately with Dani leaders, I learned much more about the background, history, and motivations for Dani warfare. In part, it represented a ritual intended to loudly show the ghosts how much the living were doing for them, and to urge the ghosts to go away and leave the survivors alone. Later we realized how fortunate we had been to observe these battles of the Dani. After the Dutch and then the Indonesians imposed peace on the Grand Valley, no more great battles took place and much of what we saw was lost and could not be retrieved by later interviews.

Dramatic events like battles or funerals occurred only every couple of weeks. Most of the time, I just followed people around on their routine chores. Dani daily work revolved around the sweet potato gardens, pig herding, cooking, and, less frequently, building or rethatching houses. In my own life, I had never done any of these tasks but I set about to learn them.

To work out the gardening cycle, I made maps of large field areas and visited them every few weeks to get an idea of working patterns and to chart the progress of the sweet potatoes. It soon became clear that each family group had gardens in several different areas at different stages of growth. A woman would go out in the morning to clear the brush off a garden that was about to be replanted, then move to another to spend some time weeding, and finally drop by a third garden on her way home to dig up enough tubers to feed her family for the next day or so. Because there were no regular seasonal cycles in the Grand Valley, new sweet potato beds were being planted constantly and harvested every day throughout the year.

The labyrinth of deep ditches that separated the beds served to control moisture. In rainy periods, they drained water away from the sweet potatoes; during dry spells, they channeled natural streams through the system. These ditches represented a tremendous investment of labor. I often saw cooperative work teams of men clearing out old ditches and slopping the rich bottom mud onto garden beds preparatory to planting, but I never saw any new ditches being dug. In the Dugum area, at least, population size seemed to have reached an equilibrium with availability of prepared gardens. Someday, archaeologists will be able to tell us how old this intensive horticultural pattern of the Dani is.

Dani houses consisted of round domed structures with grass-thatched roofs. I spent much time at construction sites, for I was always able to find men with whom to talk. They made planks with their stone axes and adzes and then lashed walls and roof poles with split vines. Dani building always seemed a bit casual. Wall planks were never tightly fitted together, although this looseness had the advantage of letting smoke from the central hearth escape easily. People slept in the dark loft under the roof dome, and the smoldering embers in the fireplace provided enough warmth to keep people comfortable through the night and enough smoke to drive out mosquitoes. After a year in the expedition tents, I built my own house next to a Dani compound. It was light and airy, but I had to use a sleeping bag and mosquito net to sleep comfortably.

Dani men building a new compound in the hills above the Grand Valley floor. (Credit: Karl G. Heider, Film Study Center, Harvard University)

Stone tools were still being used by everyone in 1961. They were of particular interest, because by the second half of the 20th century few other peoples in the world had not somehow gained access to metal tools. The year before, I had done archaeology on a Classic Mayan site, Tikal, in Guatemala. There we were excavating ordinary house mounds, 1,000 years old, and found polished stone tools very much like those that the Dani were still using. The main difference was that I could talk with the Dani, explore their cultural schemas about tools, and watch them actually use the tools.

The Dani of the Dugum got their stones from a quarry far to the west of the Grand Valley. The blades were traded into the Grand Valley as finished tools, ground to a cutting edge. Much local variation was seen in the hafting of the blades (how the blades were attached to their handles). In the Grand Valley, they were hafted as either axes, set in a single wooden handle with the cutting edge parallel to the handle, or as adzes, with the blade perpendicular to the L-shaped handle and lashed in place with braided cord or split bamboo. There were a few other tools. Some men had small, finger-sized chisels that were used to make the hafting hole in an axe handle. In the Western Dani area, these small tools also had ritual importance; in the Grand Valley, however, they were only utilitarian. Small, unretouched stone flakes served for casual cutting or for preparing and decorating notched arrow points. The most versatile tool was a simple bamboo knife. Bamboo is a grass, whose silica content makes it an ideal cutting instrument. After use, it can be resharpened by pulling off a few strands to make a new edge.

Even after metal knives began to come into the Dugum in the 1960s, people preferred bamboo for butchering pigs because of the ease of use and resharpening. Similarly, most Dani were slow to take up metal axes and bush knives, for the stone tools were easy to get and easy to maintain, and the Dani were used to the motor skills necessary to wield the stone tools. Metal tools, which would not break easily, could be used with more force and greater body twist, but it took some time for the Dani to adjust to the new body movements. By now, all Dani are using metal, and stone tools are made only to sell to tourists.

Gradually, as I came to speak better Dani and the people became comfortable with me, I learned about the nonmaterial aspects of their culture—that is, the schemas that they held about social structure, political organization, and religion. The intensive gardening on the broad, flat floor of the Grand Valley supported dense populations. Within these populations, the families were organized into patrilineal descent groups. In a patrilineal system, a person is automatically a member of his or her father's group (in a matrilineal system, people belong to their mother's group). The patrilineal, extended family groups were bound together into higher-level social groups called sibs and moieties, larger organizations of patrilineally related families within the same village. Descent structure was important in establishing land use rights and reciprocal ties and obligations and in regulating marriages. The alliances were the largest social units of the Dani and were composed of several thousand people each, spread across many villages. In contrast to the sibs and moieties, which were largely social and economic in function, the alliances were political. There were about a dozen of these alliances in the Grand Valley, and until the 1960s, when the central government (first Dutch, then Indonesian) enforced peace, the alliances were in a state of constant war with each other.

Despite the warfare described earlier, these Grand Valley Dani seemed to be very low-key about most of life. There was little competition, and even the most important leaders (big men) were hardly distinguishable in their attire or belongings from ordinary people. They exercised leadership through influence and the force of their personalities but did not have the power to make people obey them. Although there was a wide range of intelligence, even the smartest people were not deeply intellectual. For example, they had no true number words to total large quantities of pigs, cowrie shells, or the like. Their interpersonal relations were very relaxed. Conflicts within the group were usually resolved by withdrawal. One party simply moved elsewhere. The most surprising fact about the Dani was that parents did not have sex with each other for five years after the birth of a child.

The Dani did not recognize any sort of supreme being but devoted their rituals to placating the ghosts of their own dead. These ghosts were somewhat threatening and caused illness and death, but the Dani did not live in terror of them. On the whole, their world was benign except for the ever-present danger of enemy attack.

After my first long visits to the Grand Valley, which lasted a total of nearly three years between 1961 and 1970, it was eighteen years before I returned. In 1988 and 1995, I made very brief trips to see my old friends. It was discouraging. So many people had died, and despite the economic prosperity enjoyed by Indonesia as a whole, the Dani had little part in this trend.

In the last few decades, as the Indonesian government has strengthened its control over the lives of the Dani, much has changed. The relatively informal leadership of the big men, based on consensus, has been replaced by the imposed power of the Indonesian army and police. The Grand Valley has no natural resources that the world wants except climate. Close to the equator, at an altitude of 5,000 feet, it is a temperate refuge in the tropics. Outsiders from elsewhere in Indonesia, as well as from other countries, have flocked to the Grand Valley to live or to sightsee, but the Dani themselves gain little economic benefit from all this influx, as even the most menial jobs are snapped up by outsiders. Indonesian schools have produced a generation of Indonesian-speaking Dani, and some move elsewhere in Indonesia seeking better opportunities. More and more Dani have become Christian, and unlike many other tribal peoples, the Dani are not being killed off, but rather assimilated.

The year 1997 was a terrible time for the Dani. The collapse of the Indonesian currency and the general political and economic turmoil meant that normal services on which the Dani had come to depend in the highlands were disrupted. In principle, they could have supported themselves as they had lived until the 1960s, but El Niño, which had brought floods to some parts of the world, caused a major drought in New Guinea. Many areas lost their sweet potato crops, and hunger and disease were everywhere. By 1999 the drought had eased, but the Dani are now so integrated into the world economy that they are still affected by the political and economic woes of Southeast Asia.   ♦

The Anthropologist Studies a Foreign Modern Culture. Small-scale societies such as tribes are not the only subjects of anthropological research. More and more, anthropologists are looking at the cultures of modern nation-states. Beginning in the 1930s, a few anthropologists began to study villages in Europe and elsewhere. By the 1960s, such village or peasant studies had blossomed. Today, many anthropologists work with regional or national cultures or subcultures rather than with tribes.

Many new problems arise when doing fieldwork in complex societies. Compared with a tribe of a few hundred people, nations have much larger populations, occupy more land, and are culturally extremely complex, often including groups that have quite different languages and cultures. In a year or two, living in a tribal culture, a single anthropologist can get to know most of the people and can see much of what is going on. This is impossible in a nation of millions of people. Some studies focus on a single village, considering it both as a self-sufficient society and as a representative of the entire national culture. For example, American anthropologists have been doing research in Japan for decades.

John Embree was one of the first anthropologists to study Japanese culture when he did fieldwork for a year in the small village of Suye Mura in the mid-1930s. His ethnography, published in 1939, was a general description of social organization, religion, economics, and the life cycle of the people. By taking the village as his subject, Embree was replicating the traditional anthropological fieldwork experience with the isolated tribe. Today, anthropologists studying Japan tend to avoid villages and to examine small parts of the national culture. Jennifer Robertson (1998) studied the Takarazuka Revue, a famous theater outside Osaka founded in 1913. It stages glitzy musical extravaganzas of Western shows and Western themes. Women play all parts, both male and female. Since its earliest days, Takarazuka has stimulated debate in Japan about sexuality and gender. Because of the way in which it challenges ideas about masculinity and femininity, Robertson found it an ideal place to study "sexual politics and popular culture in modern Japan" (her subtitle).

Although most fieldwork involves an anthropologist from one culture going to another culture, this boundary crossing was until recently almost always done by Westerners—Europeans or North Americans—who visited people of color in poorer, less powerful communities. Slowly, however, anthropologists from Asia, Africa, and Latin America have been doing fieldwork in Europe and North America. Americans have long been uneasily aware of the power of an outsider's insights. Alexis de Tocqueville, the French visitor of the 1830s, and the Swedish sociologist Gunnar Myrdal, who wrote about race relations in the 1940s, saw truths about racism in American culture that had somehow escaped some of the natives (de Tocqueville, 1835, 1840/1969; Myrdal, 1944).

An anthropologist from Nigeria, John Ogbu, did fieldwork in the late 1960s on a school system in Stockton, California. Elizabeth Colson, in her forward to Ogbu's book (1974), points out a particular advantage of being from another culture. As an obvious outsider, an African with a strange accent, Ogbu was able to elicit serious responses to questions that no American could have gotten away with, such as "Why do you have schools?"

If any American, white or black, had asked the same kinds of questions, informants would have been much less likely to respond with good will because they would have assumed that *Americans* ought to know how their fellow Americans live and the way the schools operate. Ogbu was seen as trying to understand something that was legitimately foreign to him, and the questions he asked were not those for which a routine reply was the accepted standard. (Colson, 1974:iii)

Ogbu wanted to discover why poor black and Hispanic children fail in school. He explored the ideology of American schooling and the different belief systems and expectations of the "subordinate minorities" and the "dominant whites." He came to the conclusion that school failure was to a great extent the result of unexamined assumptions about equal education, as well as realistic evaluations on the part of the children about their futures even with better education. (This status reflected the situation thirty years ago.)

The Anthropologist Stays at Home.   Many anthropologists do their research in their own culture, using their own native languages. Although they lose the cross-cultural outsider's perspective, they gain depth of insight because there are few problems of language learning and general adjustment.

Perhaps the greatest problem is that often older, more traditional anthropologists scorn such research. When Geoffrey Hunt was a student at London University, he ran into this attitude:

> On first learning that Camberwell in South London, and not India or Africa, was to be my fieldwork destination, my Professor informed me that Camberwell was neither exotic nor strange enough for fieldwork and that I was clearly playing at being an anthropologist. In spite of my efforts to emphasize the extent to which a syncretist West African religious group was culturally distant from my own white middle-class culture, he was not impressed and told me that to be taken seriously in anthropology I must remove myself completely from my own culture and conduct fieldwork in a far-off place. (Hunt, 1998:126)

Hunt persisted, and "so began a checkered anthropological career" (Hunt, 1998: 126).

Like Hunt, rarely, if ever, does the anthropologist study the very same group in which he or she grew up. And sometimes a small mistake in that type of self-study can create more problems than a large one. Recall what Elizabeth Colson said about John Ogbu studying a California school system: Because he was so obviously not an American, he could ask questions that an American could not get away with ("Why do you have schools?"). Similarly, Ogbu, as a Nigerian in California, would have been forgiven many mistakes that he might have made in interacting with the natives. A native anthropologist, however, has less leeway. Both Barbara Myerhoff and Rakhmiel Peltz fit the definition of anthropologists studying their own culture, even though Myerhoff was not actually fluent in Yiddish. Myerhoff describes how carefully the elderly Jewish ladies of the Venice, California, Senior Citizens Center monitored her behavior—indeed her life—and freely offered advice.

Certainly there are great advantages in studying a group of one's own culture, even broadly speaking. The anthropologist is already fluent in at least one of the languages and knows his or her way around the culture, based on personal experience with the basic schemas of that culture. A first term of fieldwork often lasts only a year or so. It does make a considerable difference if the ethnographer begins that year with little or no knowledge of the language and the rest of the culture or if the ethnographer can begin the research at full speed.

But what of the loss of perspective in studying one's own culture? Clyde Kluckohn liked to remind us that it would not be a fish that discovers water. He was alluding to the insights that an outsider with fresh experiences can gain from fieldwork. Ideally, an anthropologist should be something of an amphibian—comfortable in both air and water.

There are two ways to get some advantage of perspective and still study one's own culture. Barbara Myerhoff first immersed herself in fieldwork with a Mexican Indian tribe before returning home to study the elderly Jews in the Senior Citizens Center in Venice, California. In his Introduction to Myerhoff's 1979 book on the Yiddischkeit, Victor Turner, the great British anthropologist who wrote about ritual and pilgrimage, talked about the significance of Myerhoff's journey from her own culture to a distant one (in her case, the Huichol Indians of Mexico), where she made the exotic familiar, and then finally her return, as a changed person, to her own culture again:

> We find that the familiar has become exoticized; we see it with new eyes. The commonplace has become the marvelous. What we took for granted now has the power to stir our scientific imaginations. Most of us feel that our professional duty is done when we have "processed" our fieldwork in other cultures in book or article form. Yet our discipline's long-term program has always included the movement of return, the purified look at ourselves. (Turner, 1979:ix)

A second solution is to study an unfamiliar subculture within one's own society: the homeless, the drug scene, a gang, insurance executives, the scientific team on a research vessel or, as Geoffrey Hunt did, an immigrant religious group. This approach eliminates the need to spend a year or more in the study of a non-Indo-European language and even then having to base one's research on a less-than-fluent command of the language; it also avoids the problem of having to apply to a possibly reluctant government for research permission. Furthermore, this approach reduces much of the discomfort and danger of foreign area research.

After growing up in Kentucky (among other places), Ann E. Kingsolver went away to college and graduate school. She then returned to Kentucky to study the power and class relation of the local people. They were farmers who worked as wage laborers in a local Toyota factory but in turn hired Mexican migrants to work their tobacco crops. Kingsolver wrote that her

> aim in studying power, drawing on many approaches to do so, is to work on challenging those inequalities that are (thoughtfully or not) produced and reproduced in work settings. (Kingsolver, 1998:11)

Ann E. Kingsolver at her field site in east central
Kentucky. *(Credit: V. H. Kingsolver)*

Much fieldwork at home has been done with relatively disadvantaged people
such as the homeless, drug addicts, poor rural or urban residents, and recent immigrants. In 1972, Laura Nader wrote a famous paper "Up the Anthropologist," urging
her colleagues to "study up." She meant that we should look at the cultures of power:

> Departments of anthropology have generally believed that students should do
> their dissertation field work in a non-Western culture. At some points in time
> that was a useful policy to implement, if in training anthropologists one valued
> the importance of culture shock and the detachment which accompanies it. For
> many students today, the experience of working in a Washington law firm, in a
> company town, or in an international industrial complex would be more bizarre
> than anything a student anthropologist could find in a Mexican village, or in
> New Guinea for that matter. We anthropologists have studied the cultures of the
> world only to find that in the end ours is one of the most bizarre of all cultures
> and one, by virtue of its world influence for "bad" or "good," in urgent need of
> study. (Nader, 1972:301–302)

Quantitative Versus Qualitative Research: To Count or Not to Count

A story about Franz Boas, one of the great founders of modern American anthropology, beautifully captures the point of view of many anthropologists. Apparently,
Boas was giving a talk on Kwakiutl funerary ritual when someone in the audience
asked, "How many Kwakiutl funerals did you see, Professor Boas?" "Only one," he
answered, "that's all I needed to see."

What does this story mean? Should we assume that Boas was lazy, careless, or
arrogant? Did he think that all Kwakiutl funerals were identical? Or was he presenting

this particular funeral as a self-contained cultural statement? I suppose the last, that he was saying that the same language system, symbol system, and belief system were expressed in all Kwakiutl funerals and that although there might be some surface variations from funeral to funeral, one funeral should be sufficient to lead to the common underpinnings.

Like many early anthropologists, Boas was more interested in qualitative data than in quantitative data. **Qualitative research** depends primarily on subjective interpretations of an event or material. Participant observation is a qualitative method because the researcher does not remain an objective observer. **Quantitative research,** in contrast, relies on the statistical analyses of data. Statistical analysis requires gathering data that can be quantified (or counted) and then drawing conclusions on the basis of these data. These techniques may overlap. For example, researchers who are participant observers may use some quantitative techniques, such as systematically recording observed behaviors or doing interviews.

The question "What should be counted, when, and how?" points to a persistent dilemma in anthropological fieldwork. If you look at articles in the leading journals of psychology, sociology, and anthropology, you will be struck by how rarely anthropologists quantify their findings in comparison to their social science colleagues. You will also notice how often anthropologists make generalizations from one ethnographic study without providing the basis for these claims (the Balinese are Hindu, the Yanomamo are fierce, the Japanese are organized, and so on). Cultural anthropology offers no firm rules about counting or not counting, and there are some people who question whether it should even be included in the social sciences. (Physical anthropology is much more consistently "scientific" in approach.) In fact, a recent trend among ethnographers has been to highlight the subjectivity of anthropological research by focusing directly on the researcher's experiences.

In an ideal world, there would be a science of anthropology in which all findings were precise and all results could be replicated by anyone using the proper scientific methods. This idea is the illusion of positivism. (Positivism is a system of thought that deals only with measurable facts and phenomena that can be perceived by the senses, rejecting intuitive interpretation.) Indeed, some sorts of questions can be approached in this way. If we all measure a table and agree on the system of measurement (metric or not), we all should come up with the same answer. But most of our questions and observations concern extraordinarily complex phenomena that are in constant flux, and our results are necessarily affected by who we are and how, when, and where we approach the phenomena.

In the early 1980s the Australian anthropologist Derek Freeman attacked Margaret Mead's version of Samoan culture on the grounds that she had been biased by her gender, her sexuality, and her theoretical baggage. Mead had gone to Samoa to study a culture that treated puberty (coming of age) very differently than Americans did. She described the Samoan construct of puberty as being easy, free of the stress that Westerners felt. Most notably, she claimed that Samoan teenage girls had many guiltless sexual experiences before marriage. Freeman attacked Mead's emphasis on the cultural shaping of behavior and challenged her knowledge of

Samoan language and culture. In particular, he said that she had been misled by the Samoan girls on the issue of sexual freedom and that her theoretical biases had blinded her to the fact that puberty was actually a period of stress for Samoan girls.

Freeman's book (1983) caused a tremendous public stir, beginning with a front-page story in the *New York Times*. Freeman was certainly right on some counts, but he revealed himself as a naive positivist. Even as he attacked Mead for her biases, he refused to acknowledge that his own circumstances put a spin on *his* research. He was a tall New Zealand male who hung out with the Samoan chiefs far from Mead's site and more than fifty years after Mead had done her research. Mead, by contrast, was a short American female who hung out with the women and teenage girls. Mead certainly did come to Samoa with some theoretical assumptions to test. (Presumably, Freeman, considering himself a scientist, thought that he himself was free of assumptions.) A central question was whether young Samoan girls had extensive premarital sex.

This issue is a question of fact, but a fact that we can never discover directly. An anthropologist will not be able to observe this kind of activity, which is undoubtedly carried out in private. He or she must acquire knowledge through interviews and perhaps some observed behavior. There is always a question about the accuracy of interviews. Were the informants being honest? In other words, Margaret Mead's research is filtered through the instrument called Margaret Mead. Derek Freeman could not possibly have gotten the same information as Mead, as he conducted his research fifty years later. Cultures change, and so do people. Even if the sexual behavior had not changed, who is to say that the informants were not lying to Freeman? As a male who associated with the chiefs, he might have elicited different responses from his informants than a female would.

This is not to say that the truth is totally indeterminate or that the scientific method is a fraud. But for all of the advantages of the anthropological approaches to complex problems, it suffers from the drawback of the major mediating instrument, the human anthropologist. Anthropologists must always be careful to take note of the **Rashomon effect.** This idea refers to the fact that each individual's own circumstances, motivations, beliefs, and personality affect their versions of reality (Heider, 1988). *Rashomon* is a famous Japanese film directed by Akira Kurosawa. In the film, a person dies, and various people testify about what happened. Was it murder? If so, who did it? Was it suicide? Was a rape also involved? Each person gives a different account, shaped by his or her own self-interest. This fictional example is more extreme than most cases in which anthropologists disagree, but it provides a convenient label for the phenomenon of disagreement.

The moral is that we must, to some extent or another, be aware of our baggage and take it into account, remaining wary to the possibilities of distortion.

Ethics in Anthropology

Because of issues raised by anthropologists' involvement with U.S. policies in Vietnam and inspired by George Appell's 1978 case book on ethics, the national association to which a majority of anthropologists in the United States belong, the

American Anthropological Association (AAA), has adopted a code of ethics. This code was revised for the third time in 1997. (See Appendix B.)

Some of the points in the code are general principles for scholars of any discipline: Do not plagiarize, do not exploit others, do not use nonacademic criteria (gender, race, and so on) as a basis for hiring, and so forth. Other points are more specific to anthropology: Anthropologists have a primary duty toward their informants and should not exploit them. But in the end, the most vexing problems are unexpected and specific, and no code could anticipate them.

Just what constitutes exploitation? When an anthropologist descends on a community, stays for a year or two, and uses the resulting data to write a Ph.D. dissertation that leads to a job at a salary undreamt of back in the village, how does the anthropologist adequately compensate the people? Most anthropologists pay in goods or money for their room and board and perhaps for the time of some key informants. But what of the cultural knowledge that they acquired from the people, knowledge that anthropologists turn into tenured jobs and royalty-producing books. In truth, anthropology is a relatively low-paid job in academia, and university salaries are rarely glorious anyway. That perception, however, is relative to the home society. Compared with most of the people in most of the cultures that they study, anthropologists are fabulously wealthy.

In my own experience with the Dani, I walked into a different sort of **ethical dilemma.** One evening, we (the members of the Harvard Peabody Expedition) were eating dinner at our camp when we heard a commotion nearby. I ran toward the sound and arrived just in time to see a strange man, who was lying on the ground, give one last twitch and die. He had been killed by members of the Dani community—our informants and, more important, our friends. There was nothing I could have done to save him. But what if I had arrived a little earlier, when he was alive but badly wounded? Or even earlier, when he was about to be speared by our hosts? What should I have done then? Even now, the AAA code of ethics is not of much help. (Incidentally, when Robert Gardner arrived on the scene to film the sequence that he used in *Dead Birds,* the man was long dead.)

Most anthropologists can tell of similar ethical dilemmas. There are no neat solutions, but we now acknowledge an obligation to become aware that doing anthropology involves moral choices. (For example, until recently, no introductory text in cultural anthropology even mentioned ethics.)

As the Preamble to the third revision of the AAA ethics code (see Appendix B) states,

> In a field of such complex involvements and obligations, it is inevitable that misunderstandings, conflicts, and the need to make choices among apparently incompatible values will arise. Anthropologists are responsible for grappling with such difficulties and struggling to resolve them in ways compatible with the principles stated here.

The earlier, second revision ended this passage with the following sentence, since dropped from the code: "If such resolution is impossible, anthropological work should not be undertaken or continued." This sentence is remarkable in its demands, but it makes sense. Indeed, some anthropologists have done just that: given up research in midstream because of insoluble ethical problems. I know of one anthropologist who did so. This person was a senior scholar, already well known for work elsewhere, who was well into a new research project in a new area when it became clear that any publication would seriously hurt the people involved. (The stakes would be much higher, of course, for a graduate student who had studied a field language, gotten a research grant, and finally reached some remote place, only to find that ethically he or she could not continue.) However, I believe that a general rule is that the more a group's culture is respectfully presented to the world, the more secure that group is.

Ethics and the Yanomamo.   In the fall of 2000 a great uproar was caused by news of the imminent publication of a book attacking James Neel, a geneticist, and Napoleon Chagnon, an anthropologist, who had been doing long-term research among the Yanomamo (also called Yanomamö or Yanomami) of Venezuela and Brazil. The book was called *Darkness in El Dorado: How Scientists and Journalists Devastated the Amazon* (Tierney, 2000). Even before the book was actually published, its allegations were circulated by e-mail and then picked up in newspapers and magazines. The Yanomamo had been well known to anthropology for years through the writings of Chagnon and others (e.g., the many editions of Chagnon's case study [1992]). Both his methods and his conclusions had become the subject of considerable debate (see, for example, Chapter 11, pp. 336–337). But this new book went far beyond scholarly debate, accusing Neel, Chagnon, and others of a wide range of mistakes, sins, and crimes, including the spread of fatal measles epidemics among the vulnerable Yanomamo. For several months accusations and counteraccusations filled the air. The annual meeting of the AAA that fall was dominated by talk about the affair. The AAA and its committee on ethics moved quickly to determine the facts. A preliminary committee of inquiry was formed and reported on its recommendation that the executive board of the AAA establish a task force to conduct a detailed inquiry. The task force made its final report in the summer of 2002.

The AAA Task Force Report (for details, see the AAA home page at http://www. aaanet.org).   The task force concluded that Neel, who had since died, was not responsible for the measles epidemic, but that Chagnon, after being denied Venezuelan research permission, circumvented the authorities and "made numerous flights into the Yanomami area without any quarantine procedures or other protections for the indigenous peoples." This behavior, it concluded, was "unacceptable on both ethical and professional grounds and was a breach of the AAA's code of ethics." This report was immediately criticized (Gregor and Gross, 2002), and we were far from the end of things when this text was written. Surely, more articles and books were being written to clarify the missteps and correct the misstatements that surrounded this "El Dorado Affair" (see, for example, Fluehr-Lobban, 2003). But it had already emphasized the importance of teaching anthropologists about potential ethical dilemmas at an early stage. (See Appendix B, which contains the Code of Ethics of the AAA.)

WRITING AN ETHNOGRAPHY

So far we have considered a wide range of choices involved in actually doing anthropological research. A final set of choices must be made in creating the report of the research, be it a book-length ethnography or a shorter article (in a journal) or chapter (in an edited volume).

Reflexivity

One choice involves how much of the anthropologist to include in the account. **Reflexivity** refers to the ethnographic writing that describes how the presence of the author affected the behavior itself (the **Heisenberg effect**) and how the various characteristics of the author influenced the research (the Rashomon effect). When Julia Taylor analyzes the tango, the national dance of Argentina, we learn about it through Taylor's own experience, her apprenticeship to the tango (1998). This strategy is an extremely reflexive approach. In contrast, Jennifer Robertson in her ethnography of the Takarazuka Revue (mentioned earlier in this chapter) chose to be far less reflexive. She writes,

> I have no desire to dilute this investigation with an autobiographical account. Reflexivity for me lies in my sensitivity and attention to the competing historical forces and discourses shaping specific Japanese practices. I aim to complicate our image and understanding of Japan and not to problematize my own long and complex relationship to that country and culture. (Robertson, 1998:23)

ANTHROPOLOGICAL THEORIES: HOW WE ACCOUNT FOR CULTURAL BEHAVIOR

There can be no anthropological writing without some theoretical base, and many anthropologists identify themselves as much by their theories as by the world areas they study. But if you want to start a good fight in an anthropology department, talk about theory. There is nothing quite so contentious as questions of fundamental theory: Is anthropology a science or a humanistic discipline? Should it look like physics or like English literature? (We are assuming that these disciplines themselves are unified!) Should it be based on comparable replicable data that can be number-crunched or on the rich, lifelike qualitative descriptions that can be interpreted? At two U.S. universities, the department of anthropology ultimately fractured into two independent departments after a fierce battle over such issues. For other departments, harmony has come at the price of avoidance of serious theoretical debate. Despite the incredible proliferation of theories and variations on theories, the anthropological world is not really all that chaotic.

Theoretically eclectic ethnographic description is a realistic appraisal of much of cultural anthropology. It does not deny the role of theory, but recognizes that cultural anthropologists draw on assorted theories to account for their data. Anthropologists can be characterized as foxes, knowing many things. Theoretically, they are also magpies, opportunistically borrowing theoretical insights of many sorts. (As mentioned earlier in this chapter, they should also be amphibians, straddling air and water—quite a metaphorical menagerie!) To switch metaphors, we have a comprehensive theoretical toolkit containing theories of great variety, from which we can draw.

There can be no gathering of data or organizing of the information collected into an ethnography without some theoretical assumptions about the nature of humans. All cultural anthropologists would now agree on the importance of making these theoretical biases explicit.

Let me pass on some of the lore of anthropology. The time was spring 1960. The influential Harvard anthropologist Clyde Kluckhohn, in his last graduate seminar, was pushing us to examine the theoretical positions, both implicit and explicit, of various ethnographies. To emphasize the importance of being open about one's theories, Kluckhohn told the following story about himself:

In the mid-1930s, Kluckhohn spent a year at the University of Vienna, studying with Father Koppers and Father Schmidt, the leaders of the diffusionist Culture Circle School. They were Catholic priests, and one of the aims of the Culture Circle School was to discover the traces of Urmonotheismus, or original monotheism, existing in each culture. During that year, Kluckhohn visited Rome and had an audience with the pope, who seems to have been well briefed:

POPE: So, Mr. Kluckhohn, you are studying with Pater Schmidt. I suppose that you think his Catholic faith influences his anthropology.

KLUCKHOHN: Yes, Your Holiness.

POPE: Then, Mr. Kluckhohn, don't you agree that Pater Schmidt, whose beliefs are openly acknowledged, is being more honest than other anthropologists, whose beliefs are kept secret?

KLUCKHOHN: Yes, Your Holiness.

CURTAIN

I have always assumed that this story is true. It certainly should be, for it makes an important point: Theoretical assumptions must be explicit and open to examination. It would take more pages than this entire book contains to do justice to the many different theories that have guided anthropological research. To delve more deeply into theory, you could look at Marvin Harris's classic *The Rise of Anthropological Theory* (1968), Robert Borofsky's edited volume *Assessing Cultural Anthropology* (1994), or Robert Layton's *An Introduction to Theory in Anthropology* (1997). In this section, we will merely open up the anthropological toolkit, taking a quick look at some of the clusters or families of theories that are used in cultural anthropology and that we shall encounter in the following chapters.

Basic Assumptions

We have already discussed some of the basic assumptions on which this text is based, and on which most anthropologists today agree, whatever particular theories they may be using. Theories are normally made quite explicit, defended, and tested. In contrast, the following assumptions are now so fundamental to anthropology that they are rarely examined or even explicitly stated:

1. Culture is the sum of structured schemas of learned, shared ideas, and patterned behavior.
2. Some human behavior is a complex interaction of biology and culture.
3. Cultural behaviors are more or less interrelated (holism).
4. Cultures adapt to and interact with their natural and cultural environments.
5. All cultures change all the time.

Basic Assumptions and the Dani.   Even though the preceding five basic assumptions are stated in today's language, they were present in some form in the anthropology of 1960, when I was preparing to study the Dani. In one way or another, they were relevant to my Dani research. In fact, I started out not with any great theoretical orientation but with the intention to apply assumption 3 (holism) to Dani artifacts. I had been thinking about artifacts—tools, pottery, and the like—from the point of view of archaeology and had been both inspired by and disappointed with ethnographic attempts to describe the artifacts of various living groups. These descriptions tended to be little more than exhaustive lists of things. It seemed important to take the assumption of holism seriously and to show, as far as possible, how the objects of Dani life were interconnected. For instance, using assumption 1, if Dani personality could be described in terms of some cultural norms about Dani psychology (we did not use the term "schema" yet), surely that personality would be manifested in some material ways. To take one possibility, perhaps men with different personalities would wear different sizes and shapes of penis gourds. Perhaps living arrangements and settlement patterns would reflect Dani kinship and social organization. This approach turned out to be only partly successful for two reasons. First, not everything was actually connected with everything else in any significant sense (penis gourd size and shape did not reflect personality). Second, the holistic model is a vast multidimensional web of relationships, but a book has to be written in one-dimensional linear sentences that are interspersed with two-dimensional diagrams. (That is, using words in sentences, the writer must consider one connection at a time, even when multiple simultaneous interactions are taking place.)

Assumption 4, that people adapt to their environment, led me to spend a lot of time exploring how the Dani related to their flora and fauna, how they worked their sweet potato fields, and what they gathered and hunted in the high forests surrounding the Grand Valley. Assumption 5, that cultures are in constant change, was always in the back of my mind. For the first months, however, I was occupied with making sense of what was going on in front of me. Only slowly did I begin to recognize evidence of change.

Assumption 2, that a biological basis exists for some cultural behavior, seemed so alien to the anthropological atmosphere of the time that I never thought seriously about it. Only in later years, after I had finished my study of Dani artifacts and begun to look at sexuality and emotion, was I ready to think about any sort of bio-cultural model.

Theory Families

The intellectual toolkit on which anthropologists draw includes not only the basic assumptions mentioned previously, but also myriad theories. These theories can be roughly grouped into one of three families, each of which asks a different sort of question about cultures and cultural traits:

1. Where did it come from and how did it evolve? (historical and evolutionary theories)
2. How does it work, and what are its effects? (functional and interactional theories)
3. What does it mean? (symbolic and interpretist theories)

    In describing each family, I shall indicate how I drew on it to account for some Dani behavior. Nevertheless, it should be emphasized that this structure is merely one possible way to summarize the vast array of basic assumptions and theoretical approaches that cultural anthropologists apply in their attempts to describe and explain cultural beliefs and practices around the world. Many other structures are also possible.

    Historical and **evolutionary theories** address the questions of cultural origins. **Historical particularism** asks how a particular cultural pattern developed, whereas evolutionary theories focus on broad stages in the development of human cultures. Both approaches trace the development of cultures over time, showing how the current culture came to be by following its emergence from earlier forms. Much 19th-century anthropology was concerned with these sorts of questions: What was the origin of the family? The origin of language? The origin of sailing vessels? The emphasis could be on internal dynamics **(evolution)** or external influences **(diffusion)**. In the mid-19th century, much of the inspiration for these approaches came from the interaction between ethnography, Darwinian thinking about physical evolution, and the discoveries of European archaeologists who were demonstrating that prehistoric tools developed in complexity from the middle Palaeolithic through the Neolithic Age to Metal Ages. We shall discuss change more extensively in Chapter 13.

History and the Dani. As I worked within the holistic model, looking for coherence among the various aspects of Dani culture, numerous discordances emerged. Clearly the Dani, with their vast sweet potato gardens that provide 90% of their diet, are settled horticulturalists (see Chapter 6). Yet many of their traits seemed more like those of nomadic foragers. These seeming anomalies included such things as a particular feast in the boys' initiation ceremony where everything eaten consisted of hunted and gathered foods; songs that were characteristic of foragers rather than horticulturalists (Lomax, 1968); and the Dani's practice of referring to their semipermanent settlements by the name of a nearby spring or hill, rather than giving the settlement itself a name. No one of these characteristics would have been important taken in isolation, but the entire collection taken as a whole does show a pattern. Certainly the Dani's distant ancestors had been foragers before they adopted their intensive gardening life. Thus it seems likely that these "anomalies" can be explained as archaic survivals from the earlier stage, testifying to an ongoing transition to horticulture.

Functional theories address the question of what the trait or institution does. What effect does it have on the rest of the culture? Why do people say that they behave in such a way? (This explanation gets at their folk ideas, the **explicit function.**) What effects can the anthropologist discover of which the people themselves may not be aware (the **implicit function**)? In extreme cases, the functionalism of early anthropology assumed perfectly harmonious, never-changing cultures with traits meshing and spinning like the mechanisms of old clocks. In fact, this idea is a caricature of functionalism, for cultures are not nicely tooled clockworks. Instead, one of the more revealing questions that can be asked of any trait focuses on its function. Classic functional approaches, which had been linked closely to general theories of societal needs that had to be fulfilled, turned out to be too rigid and have fallen into disuse. Nevertheless, most anthropologists use some version of functional approach, even if they do not employ that label. Among the most important is **cultural materialism,** which places priority on infrastructural features (for example, technology) as causal, shaping social and ideological features.

Marvin Harris, the most influential proponent of cultural materialism, has used this approach to explain the sacred cattle of Hindu India. It had traditionally been assumed that the Hindu prohibition on slaughtering and eating cattle stemmed from religious beliefs about cattle and their close association with gods. According to this view, cattle shared sacredness and were to be revered and protected despite the high material costs, which include supporting useless herds and not utilizing an obvious source of protein. Harris turned this idea around. Instead of saying that the religious beliefs caused great material waste, he analyzed the role of cattle in India to show that slaughtering cows for food would be wasteful. The cattle provide nourishment (as milk and yogurt), traction (pulling plows and vehicles), and cooking fuel (dried dung), and they are relatively inexpensive to maintain. This scenario provides a good example of the cultural materialist position, by stating that the material, technological conditions are primary and the religious beliefs function to support a successful cattle complex (Harris, 1979b:242–257).

Similar to cultural materialism, **cultural ecology** emphasizes adaptation between cultures and the environment. Stephen Lansing's research on Balinese rice agriculture (discussed in Chapter 1) shows the complex interplay between Balinese landscape and Balinese agriculture.

Function and the Dani. One could ask, Why do the Dani fight wars? Alternatively, one could ask a broader question, What are the functions of Dani warfare? One of the most important problems of Dani ethnography was to account for Dani warfare. The basic question, "Why did the Dani fight war?", was not answered simply in terms of a single factor like shortage of land, desire for revenge, or loot, however. The cultural materialist approach, which had been used to explain warfare in other New Guinea highland groups as primarily the result of population pressure on limited natural resources (see, for example, Rappaport, 1968), seemed to be too narrow to encompass all that we knew about Dani warfare. Certainly in the Dani case, population pressure was at best a very minor contributing factor. Instead, it was possible to identify a couple of dozen preconditions that shaped Dani warfare and outcomes, or results of that warfare (see Chapter 11).

Interactionist theories stress patterns of behavior that emerge from interaction between two or more people. An important inspiration for this family of theories was Mauss's work on "the gift" (1925; see Layton, 1997). In Chapter 7, we will discuss how "gifts" are actually exchanges in which the delay in reciprocating builds social ties. In anthropological linguistics, conversation analysts have similarly demonstrated how talk between people is not an alternating set of canned speeches but rather an "emergent form" negotiated between interactors.

Interaction and the Dani.   The film *Dead Birds* includes a ten-minute sequence of a boy's funeral that is not part of the short clip. The scene occurs in the courtyard where the cremation will take place. Several hundred people are gathering, for this event is a "fresh blood" ceremony—one for a person killed by the enemy. The potential danger from ghosts, especially the ghost of the victim, must be countered by an especially large display and exchange of pigs, carrying nets, and cowrie shell belts to placate the ghosts. We see people gather, with the men working out the redistribution of the shell goods, preparing the corpse, lighting the pyre, and performing a ritual act to release the spirit and encourage it to leave the dwelling area and go off into the woods. We—the Americans of the expedition—were stunned by the death and the ceremony, and our reaction is reflected in the filming and editing of the event. The film sequence emphasizes the mournful sadness in both visuals and the soundtrack. In other words, for the emotional tone of the funeral, we concentrated on intensifying the internal emotions—sadness—of the individual participants.

When Robert Gardner shot and edited the scene, I (as anthropological consultant) agreed that it was accurate. Since then, our understandings of emotion behavior have developed considerably. In retrospect, I would now reinterpret what happened in an interactionist framework. During the funeral, which lasted an entire day, various sorts of interactions—greetings, presentation of goods, gossiping, negotiating the redistribution of goods—took place. For each event, a different mix of appropriate emotion was displayed to others. An interactionist approach to the filming of the funeral would have devoted more attention to the changing nuanced interactions and subtle emotional changes that occurred among the many participants.

We got much of the funeral right, such as things like economic exchange (funerary "gifts"), symbolism, and religious beliefs about ghosts—all those areas of culture in which we had been trained as graduate students in the late 1950s. Today, with interactionist theories being more prominent in the anthropological toolkit and emotion behavior being a prominent anthropological concern, we would have gotten the rest right as well.

Symbolic and **interpretive theories** deal with meanings in peoples' minds—that is, their interpretations and understandings of themselves and their culture rather than origins, development, or functions. What is the meaning of totem poles or totemism (discussed in Chapter 4 and Chapter 12, respectively)? Myths, for example, may present historical events, and the telling of myths may serve certain functions. Myths themselves, however, use metaphor to convey meanings and explanations of life, death, love, and the relations of people to nature or to the supernatural (see Chapter 4).

Interpretive theories are especially associated with Clifford Geertz. In his famous piece on the Balinese cockfight (1972), he does not trace its origins and only briefly mentions its functions (for example, the way betting on the cocks redistributes wealth). Instead, he analyzes the cockfight's symbolic meanings ("cocks" have much the same male sexual connotations for Balinese as for Americans), and he interprets the risk taking for bettors in relation to Balinese men's personalities.

Symbolism and the Dani.   Often, in the early 1960s, Europeans or North Americans reported that when encountering unfamiliar Dani in the Grand Valley they would hear whispers of "belal," or "snake." Why were the Dani calling us snakes? To put it in a better way, what meaning did "belal" have that would cause the Dani to apply that word to us? At first, I did not see this issue as a problem. My own culture uses "snake" as a derogatory epithet, and I assumed that the Dani were doing the same. Only gradually did I realize that the answer must lie in the Dani symbolism, which was not necessarily the same as mine.

Today I would suggest that it is rooted in the Dani mortality myth, which tells of a race between a bird and a snake. The contest was won by the bird, and as a result people and birds became associated in various ways. The most important link was that both people and birds had to die and could not shed their skins and continue to live, as do snakes (the Dani rarely see snakes). The significance of this opposition is based on a general Dani belief that snakes do not die, but merely shed their skins and continue living. As birds and snakes are thought to be opposed symbols, it follows that birds and people are associated with death. (The image of "dead birds" is so important in Dani symbolism that Robert Gardner choose it as the title for his film on the Dani.) Now, we have a formula: *People = Birds ≠ Snakes.* Snakes, then, were immortal, as opposed to birds and people, who could die.

When Europeans came into the Grand Valley, they brought all manner of miraculous artifacts, such as airplanes, radios, and guns. Most remarkably, Europeans were not seen to die, for those who became seriously ill were flown out to hospitals on the coast. The Dani apparently made sense of these outsiders by completing the equation in the following way: *Dani people:European people::birds:snakes.* Thus the meaning of calling us snakes was to acknowledge that we were a different sort of being that did not appear to die.

DOING ANTHROPOLOGY

Recognizing the Theory

Examine the articles in any current issue of a journal like the *American Anthropologist, American Ethnology,* or *Current Anthropology.* Usually the article will begin with a statement of the theoretical position to be taken. You should be able to recognize in a general way where it draws from the theoretical toolkit described in the preceding pages (and probably it will be eclectic, utilizing more than one theory family). Also, because theoretical innovation is so highly prized in cultural anthropology, you will likely see how the author(s) carve out a unique theoretical niche for the article. ♦

SEEING ANTHROPOLOGY

Fieldwork Among the Grand Valley Dani: *Dead Birds*

Filmmaker: Robert Gardner
Assistant Camera: Karl G. Heider

Sound Recording: Michael Rockefeller,
Anthropological Advice: Peter Matthiessen,
Jan Broekhuyse, and Karl G. Heider

This film about the Grand Valley Dani was shot by Robert Gardner in 1961 when traditional intertribal warfare was still being waged in that part of the New Guinea highlands, and stone tools were still more numerous than metal ones. (We have discussed this film in many places; see R. Gardner, 1971, 1972; Heider, 1972a, 1976b, 1997; and Loizos, 1993.)

Gardner had been trained in anthropology and had experience in filmmaking as well as film editing. In 1960 the head of the Bureau of Native Affairs of Netherlands New Guinea came to the United States to drum up interest among American anthropologists to do fieldwork in New Guinea. Gardner saw an opportunity to put together a team that would combine anthropology with filmmaking in a dramatic cultural setting. At the time, only a handful of ethnographic films had been made. One model was Robert Flaherty's films. His first one, *Nanook of the North* (1922), followed an Inuit (Eskimo) man, Nanook, as he triumphantly coped with the harsh Arctic environment. Flaherty's later films also concentrated on one or two individuals, showing their culture through their adventures. In the late 1950s, John Marshall's first Kalahari film, *The Hunters,* which Gardner had just helped to edit, was built around four Ju/'hoansi (!Kung) men on a giraffe hunt.

When we arrived in New Guinea and settled into the Dugum Neighborhood, Gardner immediately looked for an individual to follow. He found two candidates: Weyak, a man, and Pua, a young boy. Gardner spent most of his time getting to know them, their families, and their daily lives. Jan Broekhuyse, the Dutch government official who had been assigned to the expedition, often accompanied Gardner to help translate and to introduce him to the culture. The rest of us followed our own interests during the day, but each evening gathered around the dinner table to swap information and insights. When an event like a battle or a ceremony occurred, we would all attend, taking care to stay out of camera range. At one point Gardner considered shooting footage of each of us among the Dani, to make up a sort of preamble or postscript to the film, but eventually decided against it. Today it would be normal, almost obligatory, to be reflexive and reveal oneself on film. In the early 1960s, however, it was unheard of to do so.

Gardner used an Arriflex 16-mm camera with a 400-foot canister. Using an experimental battery belt that he devised, he could shoot up to twelve minutes in a single take. Today, when even cheap video cameras can shoot for an hour, a mere twelve-minute shot seems like nothing. In my own backup filming, however, I used standard 100-foot rolls of film that could shoot for only three minutes. Of course, at that time no field equipment was capable of recording sound that was synchronized with the visuals (again, today's video cameras give us the luxury of synchronized sound). Michael Rockefeller was responsible for the sound recording. He often accompanied Gardner or went out on special assignment to capture particular sounds that would be matched to the visuals in the editing process.

The Dani did not know about cameras, and it was many years before any of them saw *Dead Birds*. We had heard reports of cultures where people believed that cameras "steal the soul," so to avoid misunderstandings we simply did not explain photographs to them. Later in the expedition, when proof sheets of our still photographs began arriving, we kept them out of sight from the Dani. In retrospect, this precaution was probably unnecessary. When I returned to the Grand Valley in 1988, I brought copies of our books as presents. As soon as I handed them out, people forgot me completely and pored over the photographs. Older people explained the battle photos to those too young to remember, and images of long-dead people were examined with special interest, but no one was upset by seeing images of the dead.

In this short clip, we see men at battle and women collecting brine from a salt well. In the complete film, Gardner covers a much wider range of Dani life. As it turned out, the battles and rituals that occurred during the five months that Gardner was in the Grand Valley provided a good story line, something for Weyak and Pua to live through. Not every battle or ceremony was included, but the major events in the film did occur as shown. Occasionally Gardner used a setup shot, asking Pua to stand still and look into the distance, for example. All of the significant events were filmed as they occurred naturally, however, and in no case were they staged. Today, if you visit the Grand Valley as a tourist, young Dani men will perform a battle for you to photograph. Because they were born long after pacification, I suspect that they learn about battles the same way that you do—by watching Robert Gardner's *Dead Birds*.

Elsewhere in New Guinea, youth who have left their homes to attend schools have been deeply embarrassed and ashamed when pictures of their relatives from a previous generation were shown in classes. I do not know if any Dani have experienced this reaction, but certainly those still living in their villages were pleased and proud to see our photographs from the 1960s when I visited them years later.

The short clip begins with a battle, with Dani men on both sides firing arrows and throwing spears. Wounded men are brought back from the front lines for treat-

Robert Gardner shooting footage for *Dead Birds* at a Dani battle in 1961. *(Credit: Karl G. Heider, Film Study Center, Harvard University)*

ment. While the men are at battle, a party of women go to the brine pool to soak banana bark in the salty water. One man got an arrow in his buttocks, and Tuesikhe was hit just below his collarbone. Another man works the broken arrow tip out of the wound. Then steps are taken to restore Tuesikhe's soul matter (his *edai-egen,* or "seeds of singing").

The complete film follows a Dani man (Weyak) and boy (Pua) through their daily routines punctuated by battles and other rituals. The film is inspired by the Dani mortality myth about a race between a bird and a snake "to determine if men would be like birds, which die, or like snakes, which shed their skins and have eternal life. The bird won, and from that time all men, like birds, must die." The title of the film comes from the Dani term for battle trophies ("dead birds" or "dead men"). The main events are shown as they happened in 1961. As a local group was performing a *wam kanekhe* ritual, renewing its sacred relics, most of the people of the neighborhood were in attendance. Although the front was unguarded, a gang of boys ventured down to the Aikhe River and ran into a Widaia ambush; one of them was killed. A few weeks after his funeral, an enemy man was killed in turn, and the ghost threat was momentarily diminished.

Setup Questions for the Film Clip

1. You have just arrived in the Grand Valley to do fieldwork with the Dani. A battle takes place. You know no Dani language yet, but you can observe behavior. From what you see in this film clip, what can you say about:

   Tools
   Weapons
   Ornaments
   Attire
   Food
   Surgery
   Emotional tone of battle
   Battle tactics
   Individualism in battle

   The narration gives you some hints about Dani concepts of the "soul matter," or edai-egen.

2. Look carefully at the battle scenes. You can follow individual men in action. How would you describe their strategy?

3. Using both the short clip and the textbook, think of the various ways in which Dani war is different from what you know of modern war (for example, World War II). ♦

HOLLYWOOD-STYLE ANTHROPOLOGY

Different Versions in *Rashomon*

Rashomon   1951   83 minutes   Japanese, with English subtitles

Toshiro Mifune as Tajomaru, the Bandit
Machiko Kyo as The Woman
Masayuki Moro as The Man

Rashomon is one of Akira Kurosawa's greatest films (it won an Academy Award for best foreign film), and it stands as a very loose metaphor for the "Rashomon effect," where different anthropologists present different versions of the same culture. The film takes place during the feudal period in Japan and is set under the Rashomon, a great ruined gate in Kyoto. It is raining, and three men seeking shelter discuss a recent case in which a man was killed and his wife perhaps raped by a famous bandit, Tajomaru. Through flashbacks we get different accounts of what happened: from a passing firewood collector; from a priest; from the bandit; from the woman; from the dead man (speaking through a spirit medium in trance); and again from the firewood man.

Setup Questions

1. How is each version of the incident shaped by the narrator's interests?
2. What is the role of the unnamed third man at the Rashomon gate? ♦

CHAPTER SUMMARY

- Fieldwork is the most distinctive form of anthropological research. The researcher becomes involved with a community, often lives with the members of the community, and to some extent shares their lives (as a participant observer) without completely "going native."
- Fieldwork means gaining rapport with people, and in some cases learning a new language.
- Other research tools used by cultural anthropologists include interviewing, giving out questionnaires, observing, and making unobtrusive collections of data.
- As technology has evolved, tape recorders and video cameras have joined pencil and paper as recording devices.
- Cultural anthropologists use these research methods in their own culture as well as in quite different cultures around the world. They may talk with everyone in a small-scale society or may examine a limited subculture in a large nation. They may emphasize quantitative data, counting and measuring, or they may gather richly qualitative data like individual life experiences.
- Increasingly, anthropologists are becoming sensitive to ethical dilemmas arising from their fieldwork, necessitating sometimes painful decisions so as not to damage the people that they study.
- Theories that anthropologists use to account for different cultural behaviors and institutions can be very roughly grouped in three great families: historical (where did it come from?); functional (what does it do?); and symbolic (what does it mean?). Most anthropologists are eclectic, drawing on different theories to handle different problems.

KEY TERMS

cultural ecology	going native	quantitative research
cultural materialism	Heisenberg effect	questionnaires
diffusion	historical particularism	rapport
ethical dilemma	historical theories	Rashomon effect
evolution	implicit function	reflexivity
evolutionary theories	interactionist theories	resistance
explicit function	interpretive theories	symbolic theories
fieldwork	participant observation	unobtrusive data
functional theories	qualitative research	collection

QUESTIONS TO THINK ABOUT

- What are the advantages and disadvantages in studying cultural behavior (1) in your own subculture, (2) in a subculture slightly different from yours, or (3) in a very different culture? If you were to do fieldwork for a year or two, which would you choose and why?

- If you were to do fieldwork, which of these choices would you make and why?
  Working alone or with a research team?
  Participant observation, interviewing, using questionnaires, or all of the above?
  What equipment would you bring along: pencils, tape recorder, video camera?
- Can you imagine doing fieldwork on the Internet? What could you study? Would it be fieldwork?
- If you use a functional approach, what would the difference be between functions that the people claim for something and functions of which they are unaware but that you can figure out?
- Similarly, what would be the differences in meanings of symbols that people tell you about and meanings of which they are unaware but that you work out?

SUGGESTIONS FOR FURTHER READING

Gardner, Robert, and Karl G. Heider
1969 Gardens of War: Life and Death in the New Guinea Stone Age. New York: Random House. *The Dani through still photographs taken by the Harvard Peabody Expedition.*

Geertz, Clifford
1995 After the Facts: Two Countries, Four Decades, One Anthropologist. Cambridge, MA: Harvard University Press. *A leading American anthropologist describes his life in anthropology.*
1988 Works and Lives. The Anthropologist as Author. Stanford, CA: Stanford University Press. *A lively account of the lives and works of some giants of anthropology.*

Matthiessen, Peter
1962 Under the Mountain Wall: A Chronicle of Two Seasons in the Stone Age. New York: Viking. *A novelist and natural historian on the Harvard Peabody Expedition describes the Dani and their environment.*

Narayan, Kirin
1994 Love, Stars, and All That. New York: Pocket Books. *An anthropologist uses fiction to describe a cultural situation.*

Look at the series of books History of Anthropology, *edited by George W. Stocking, Jr., for the University of Wisconsin Press.*

CHAPTER 4

Meanings: Language, Symbols, and Art

A discussion. Prambanan, Java, 9th century C.E. (Credit: Karl G. Heider)

HEADLINE ANTHROPOLOGY

PRESS WATCH

Some of the subjects in this chapter have made their way into current news stories. For example:

◆ New Yorkers complain that negotiating their crowded sidewalks has been complicated by newcomers who do not understand the local rules of walking (and by natives distracted by their cell phone conversations).

—New York Times, *July 16, 2002* (and Letters, *July 20, 2002*).

◆ A boy carries the bridal slippers which the bride will change into at the altar—they signify purity and cleanliness in Seventh Day Adventist weddings.

—In a photo montage in the Sunday Styles section, New York Times, *June 30, 2002.*

◆ In Pennsylvania, the Swartzentruber Amish violate state law by using grey reflective tape and lanterns instead of bright orange reflective triangles on their horse-drawn buggies. Other Amish groups are willing to use the orange triangles. The law may be changed.

—New York Times, *June 7, 2002.*

◆ In 2001, the Taliban in Afghanistan destroyed not only the two giant figures of the Buddha at Bamiyan, but also "systematically ransacked" the art objects in the National Museum as part of their campaign against idolatry.

—New York Times, *April 15, 2002.*

President George W. Bush is criticized (perhaps jokingly) for his frequent use of the word "fabulous," which is not a properly Texas expression.

—New York Times, *March 18, 2002.*

LANGUAGE

Meaning is so central to being human that we need to address this issue immediately. It is useful to distinguish between **signs** and **symbols.** Signs indicate, symbols mean. All creatures must attend to signs. A rabbit knows, or must learn, that the smell of a wolf indicates danger. Lightning indicates that rain is coming. The sign has a direct, immediate connection to what it indicates. *Homo sapiens* also make use of such indicating signs. Unlike the rabbit, however, we attach arbitrary meanings to things, creating an arbitrary relationship that we call symbolic. Thus we see lightning and know that rain may come, but we also may load some symbolic meanings into lightning. We may think that Zeus is angry and throwing thunderbolts, or we may hear thunder and think "rain" as well as "elves moving furniture in the sky" or "giants bowling." Alternatively, when someone tells us about Zeus, the furniture, or the bowling match, we may think, "That person is superstitious."

In addition to the significance (the indicating property of signs), we humans add layer on layer of symbolic meanings. Thus our cultural schemas consist of bundles of ideas with complex meanings. These meanings are not only arbitrary, but also culturally variable. Thunder and lightning indicate rain everywhere (unless it is deep summer, when they may just indicate "heat lightning"). But Zeus, the furniture movers, and the bowlers—all symbolic meanings—are culture-specific and in no way intrinsic. You—or your grandparents—may well have quite different symbolic meanings attached to these natural events. *Darmok,* an episode of the "Star Trek: The Next Generation" television series, plays with the idea of a language so loaded with culture-specific symbolism that it cannot be translated into English.

Perhaps it is going too far to suggest that *Homo sapiens* are the only creatures who understand the meanings of symbols. Experimental primatologists have succeeded in teaching chimpanzees to use very simple symbols. Someday, real symbol use may be found in other creatures. Certainly, we have no vested interest in keeping the title of "symbolizer" limited to ourselves. Nevertheless, it seems unlikely today (at the beginning of the 21st century) that other animals will ever command the complex layering of symbols, much less approach the symbolic repertoire, of any normal adult human being.

In this chapter, we discuss the meanings of symbols in language and in other nonlinguistic realms such as art. Let us begin with language. Language pervades all aspects of human thought and interaction. Culture is stored in language and transmitted by language. Here is an old question: Can we do or think anything at all without language? Perhaps you can come up with some examples. For instance, we could suggest the lightning-fast plays in Ping-Pong or basketball, reactions experienced while driving a car in fast heavy traffic, or attempts to explain the taste of exotic food or smell of a new perfume. Even these events can be discussed and analyzed in language, however, and it is possible to learn a whole vocabulary to describe tastes or aromas.

We store cultural knowledge in words, in our memories, or, in some cultures, in written form. We pass cultural knowledge on to others through spoken or written words. In Chapter 5 we will discuss a kind of learning called *embodied* or *situated.* In this sort of learning, for example, a dance teacher passes on her knowledge not so much with words as by touching, by shaping and guiding her pupils' movements with her own hands. Some cultures rely more on words, calling out instruction or even having students read manuals on "how to dance." Nevertheless, even the most nonliterate cultures use language extensively in teaching.

To use language is the very essence of being human. Language is our ultimate, defining tool. Most of us learned our first language so early in life that we have no memory of what it is like to be without language. But consider the well-known story about how Anne Mansfield Sullivan taught language to Helen Keller. Keller describes this event in her autobiography (1902). She was born in 1880, and at the age of 19 months an illness left her deaf and blind. What little language she had acquired soon deteriorated. Keller was six years old, and reduced to signing her wants with her hands, when Annie Sullivan came to be her tutor. Keller described in unforgettable terms the moment at the pump, when she suddenly realized that spelling out "w-a-t-e-r" in her hand meant water. This revelation has also been dramatized as a play and movie, *The Miracle Worker.* Keller describes the events leading up to her epiphany:

> . . . Miss Sullivan slowly spelled into my hand the words "d-o-l-l." I was at once interested in this finger play and tried to imitate it. When I finally succeeded in making the letters correctly I was flushed with childish pleasure and pride. Running downstairs to my mother I held up my hand and made the letters for doll. I did not know I was spelling a word or even that words existed; I was simply making my fingers go in monkey-like imitation. (Keller, 1902/1958:17)

Although her autobiography was published when Keller was only 20, it is significant that her recollection of herself at six was "monkey-like," not really human. But then one day Keller and Sullivan walked to the well-house in the garden:

> Some one was drawing water and my teacher placed my hand under the spout. As the cool stream gushed over one hand she spelled into the other the word water, first slowly, then rapidly. I stood still, my whole attention fixed upon the motions of her fingers. Suddenly I felt a misty consciousness as of something forgotten—a thrill of returning thought; and somehow the mystery of language was revealed to me. I knew then that "w-a-t-e-r" meant the wonderful cool something that was flowing over my hand. That living word awakened my soul, gave it light, hope, joy, set it free! (Keller, 1902/1958:18)

What do we learn from this story? Perhaps, more than anything, we see this six-year-old suddenly gaining (or recovering) the most human of all tools—language—in all its complexity. Never again, despite being unable to see or hear, could she consider herself "monkey-like." So what does it mean to say that other organisms communicate but only humans have language?

In fact, it used to seem very straightforward: We *Homo sapiens* had language, and all other species lacked language. But careful studies of animal behavior (**ethology,** not to be confused with *ethnology*) have shown that other creatures do indeed have fairly complex communication systems. Bees can communicate information about a distant source of nectar. Bird songs are territorial messages. Experimental research has shown that chimpanzees and dolphins can be taught words. Anyone who has lived long with dogs or horses has the sense that they talk with us. (Cats raise all sorts of other questions. Do they want to talk with us?)

In one sense, most human behavior could be considered communication. Architecture and attire are statements about people's identity. We talk of using the legal system "to send a message to criminals" or war "to send a message to the enemy." Rituals function to allow humans to communicate with the supernatural.

Here we narrow in on that part of human culture that is primarily concerned with communication. For convenience, we call this area *language* and mean both verbal and nonverbal systems of communication.

The linguist Charles F. Hockett helped to pin down just what we mean by *language* in this strict sense. In the 1960s, he described sixteen **design features** of human language. Some are found in the communication systems of other creatures, but only in human languages are all present. (See Table 4.1.)

TABLE 4.1   Hockett's Sixteen Design Features of Human Language

Design Feature	Definition
1. Vocal–Auditory Channel	Messages originate from the vocal apparatus and are received by the auditory apparatus. This stipulation immediately focuses us on spoken and heard language and cuts out much communication, including written messages.
2. Broadcast Transmission and Directional Reception	Speech goes out in all directions, and the receiver can identify the direction of the source of the sounds.
3. Rapid Fading	The speech messages do not last.
4. Interchangeability	Any speaker can utter any message. This feature addresses the extraordinary flexibility of human language.
5. Complete Feedback	The speakers can monitor their own speech, although we often are not fully aware of what we are communicating.
6. Specialization	Speech is solely for communication. (Houses, clothing, and rituals have many other functions in addition to communication.)
7. Semanticity	Words have meanings.
8. Arbitrariness	The sounds of the words do not have any necessary relationship to what they mean. This feature is observed even when we try to write down noises. For example, in German, roosters say "kikeriki," and in Indonesian, guns go "dorr."
9. Discreteness	Messages are composed of separate and separatable units. Changing one sound (a phoneme) changes one word into another word; changing a word makes the sentence different.
10. Displacement	Messages may describe things and events distant in time and space.
11. Openness	New, unique utterances are easily made.
12. Duality	Significant sounds (phonemes) combine into meaningful units (morphemes).
13. Cultural Transmission	Specific languages are learned.
14. Prevarication	Speakers can make false statements.
15. Reflexiveness	Speakers can talk about talking.
16. Learnability	Speakers of one language can learn another language.

Source: Hockett, 1960.

What seems to be most important about human language, as distinct from the communication systems of other animals, is that our languages are learned (features 13 and 16), with a huge number of words (7) that can be arranged in an infinite number of statements (11) to speak about distant (10) and counterfactual, or false, (14) subjects or even about speaking itself (15).

One or another of these features can be found in the communication systems of one or another nonhuman species. Perhaps only reflexiveness (feature 15), the self-conscious discussion of language itself, is lacking in nonhuman systems.

It is safe to say that no other species has a communication system approaching human language, as measured by Hockett's criteria. In recent decades, however, another sort of question has been hotly debated: Even if there are no nonhuman natural languages, is it possible to teach nonhumans to use a real language? After some apparent success with chimpanzees, skepticism won out, and the general consensus was that the answer was no. Even though trained chimpanzees could make a variety of hand gestures and could associate certain hand gestures with certain objects (food) or states (hunger), none seemed able to achieve the infinite creativity of human language. It was also argued that apes lacked the sort of brain capacity that allows humans to learn languages.

Primitive Languages and Primitive Peoples

Primitive is not a very useful word in any case, and it has such negative connotations that anthropologists shy away from it. Nevertheless, we must use it to address one of those logical but false ideas about human languages—namely, that "primitive peoples" (those with small-scale social organizations and simple technologies) have "primitive languages." One might think that if we can list sixteen design features for human language and find no other creatures that use more than a few of those sixteen, then it stands to reason that some human languages will be less developed than others. This is not the case.

Travel accounts, even by people who should have known better, have long reported primitive languages. The great 19th-century English explorer and translator Richard Burton came across some Arapaho on a trip across North America and claimed that their language "has never, I am told, been thoroughly learned by a stranger. It is said to contain but a few hundred words and these being almost all explosive growls, or gutteral grunts, are with difficulty acquired by the civilized ear" (1861/1963:158). Furthermore, because Arapaho had so few words, it depended on hand gestures to supplement the words and on light to see the hand gestures, so they "can hardly converse with one another in the dark: to make a stranger understand them they must always repair to the camp fire for a 'pow-wow' " (1861/1963:136). This idea of primitive languages was not just a 19th-century conceit. In the 1930s the Austrian traveler and ethnographer Hugo Adolf Bernatzik reported that the Phi Tong Luang, mountain folk of Thailand, had a similarly rudimentary language (1938).

When I was struggling to learn Dani, the German mountain climber and explorer Heinrich Harrer visited New Guinea and reported that the Dani language was "simple and word-poor." At that time, I was trying to master Dani verbs. The Dutch linguist Piet van der Stap O. F. M. had estimated that with prefixes, infixes, and postfixes, each Dani verb had 1,680 different possible forms! So much for simplicity. Harrer wasn't completely wrong, for he had learned a bit of a stripped-down, simplified "police talk," which the Dani used in communication with outsiders. (I always assumed that they considered us not quite up to learning real speech.)

At any rate, although languages vary tremendously in the grammatical features that they elaborate and the realms in which they have a large vocabulary, there is no justification for talking about "primitive languages."

Elements of Language: Channels of Communication

Language is only part of the human communication system. Usually, by *language,* we mean only the phonology (sounds), lexicon (words), and syntax (grammar) of a language. Hockett's sixteen design features of language address only these aspects. Until recently, if you took a language class in Spanish or German, those aspects are all you would have been taught. Gradually, however, "language" teachers are realizing that there is much more to any language than sounds, words, and grammar. The most important channel of communication is language, as described above—phonology, lexicon, and syntax. Paralanguage, however, is also critical in the communication process. It includes intonation, pacing, pauses, and accenting—a myriad of special effects that speakers use and hearers take in, for the most part unconsciously. In fact, you cannot speak without employing paralanguage; even a monotone communicates something. And think of all the different ways in which an apparently simple "yes" or "no" can be uttered. Finally, there is nonverbal communication, a variety of uses of "body language" and space.

Languages are amazingly elegant cultural constructions. The few sounds in a language can combine to make many thousands of words that can be arranged in a huge number of utterances (sentences). The number of such possible combinations is virtually infinite. Consider the sentence that you are now reading. It is unique—that is, it has never been written or said before—and yet you have no trouble in understanding its meaning.

Phonology.   We can begin outlining the elements of language by delving into **phonology,** the study of the sounds of language. Most languages make use of only about 30 sounds, which are called phonemes. A **phoneme** is a basic sound that makes a difference in the meaning of a word. For example, "bat" is composed of three phonemes, which we symbolize in writing as "b," "a," and "t." If you change the "b" phoneme to, say, a "p" phoneme, you have a different word, "pat."

If we pay close attention, we realize that any particular phoneme may have several slightly different sound forms, depending on its context. Turn "bat" around, into "tab," and the "b" phoneme sounds a bit different. Say the two words, holding your hand close to your mouth, and you can feel the difference in the amount of air being pushed out between your lips. These slight variations of the same phoneme are called **allophones.**

The branch of linguistic analysis that identifies the clusters of allophones constituting different phonemes is called **phonemic analysis.** It is the way in which we identify the clusters of sounds that are meaningful for that language. Native speakers recognize the allophones as one phoneme and ignore the slight variations, even as they unconsciously make the appropriate sound shifts. It is also important to be able to describe in precise ways the exact sound of each allophone. Because native speakers do not pay attention to these variations, linguists cannot ask them for their own categories. Instead, they must rely on scientific, or **culture-neutral** criteria. Thus we could say that the "b" phoneme is a bilabial (made with the lips), with one allophone (as in "bat") and a stop (a slight explosion of air between the lips), and that another allophone (as in "tab") is not a stop.

We could also analyze the physics of the sounds. Such a culture-neutral description of sounds is called **phonetic analysis.** From the two words "phonetic" and "phonemic" comes two broader concepts of cultural analysis, **emic** (using native categories) and **etic** (using culture-neutral criteria).

Morphology and Semantics.   At the next level, **morphology** is the study of how phonemes, or sounds, combine to form units that have meanings. A **morpheme** is one or more phonemes that have meaning. Morphemes can stand alone, like the word "wrap," or they can be bound, like the "un-" of "unwrap" and the "-ed" of "unwrapped." Some, like the morpheme for the plural of nouns, have variations called **allomorphs.** (Try the plurals of "bat," "horse," and "ox.")

A somewhat different approach to language at the level of words is **semantics,** the study of meanings. It usually focuses on words and particular **semantic fields,** or sets of related words. A semantic analysis could involve working out the meanings of and relationships between kinship terms, emotion words, or names of gods.

Syntax and Discourse Analysis.   **Syntax,** or grammar, refers to the regular patterning, or rules, that speakers use to form words into strings of words, or utterances (or sentences). "Rules" sounds quite formal; indeed, we find them laid out in "grammars" when we study new languages in school. Still, we learn the patterns of our first language at an early age easily, when we are quite unaware of these "rules."

Although formal grammar usually refers to the basic rules, it also has the implications of proper or appropriate language utterances. "Proper grammar" has almost a moral connotation. **Discourse analysis,** or **conversation analysis,** studies the ways in which people actually speak, looking for the rules or patterns in our normal informal talk—for example, where we use incomplete sentences, pauses, interruptions, and interjections like "uh" and "you know."

Paralanguage.   **Paralanguage** refers to vocalizations other than words that are used in ordinary utterances. They include the ways in which words are said, including the intonation, stress, and tempo, as well as other vocalizations like "ah," "um," and "mmm"—all those additions that conversation analysts find so significant in normal conversation between people. In fact, the category of paralanguage is often included as part of the phonology, semantics, and syntax of language.

Nonverbal Communication.   When people talk face to face, not only do they use the vocal channels of language and paralanguage, but they also employ their bodies in a variety of ways to add **nonverbal communication** to their utterances. Hand movements, facial expressions, and use of personal space are just the most obvious of these nonverbal channels.

Emblems and Other Gestures. A classic study of gestures was done in the 1930s by David Efron, a student of Franz Boas. German anthropologists during the Nazi period devoted much time to trying to develop surefire ways of identifying Jews. One of their "findings" was that gesticulating while talking is an innate trait of the Hebrew race. Efron's research (1941/1972) refuted this conclusion. He studied gestures in New York City among first- and second-generation Southern Italians and Eastern European Jews. He found, not surprisingly, that the second generation, born in New York and speaking English, had lost many of the gestures of their parents. Thus gestures were evidently learned, and not biological.

Of most interest to us now was Efron's analysis of the differences between the two sorts of gesturing. The Italians used what Efron called **emblems,** discrete gestures with specific meanings that could be used without speech. The Jews used **illustrators,** hand and arm motions that accompanied speech but had no direct translatability and were meaningless apart from speech. Emblems are mainly hand

A Dani man pulls at his eyebrow (*left*) to indicate that a person is a member of his sib. The same man flicks his penis gourd (*right*) with the fingernail of his forefinger to express wonder or amazement at something. There are dialect variations: In the Grand Valley, men use one hand; Western Dani use two hands simultaneously. A Dani man who wears pants and a wristwatch may flick the crystal of his watch. *(Credit: Karl G. Heider, Film Study Center, Harvard University)*

gestures with meanings, like the thumbs-up "okay" or the two-finger "V for Victory." Illustrators beat time to speech and have little meaning other than adding emphasis. It is said that Fiorello LaGuardia, mayor of New York City in the 1920s, was fluent in English, Yiddish, and Italian. He often appeared in the newsreels of the time, and supposedly one could easily tell which language he was speaking even without the sound because he used the appropriate hand gestures for each of his languages (Birdwhistell, 1970:102).

More recently, David McNeill has suggested adding a category of emblems that he calls **Butterworths,** or "gestures that occur specifically as part of an effort to recall a word and/or find an appropriate sentence structure" (1992:77).

The same gesture may have different meanings in different cultures. The American thumbs-up emblem is an obscenity in Southeastern Europe (as some American hitchhikers have found out). The thumb-and-forefinger circle that Americans use to mean *A-OK* means *money* in Japan and is an obscene emblem for women in the eastern Mediterranean.

Emblems, like other aspects of communication, change over time. When Saint Nicholas rose up the chimney "laying his finger aside of his nose," 19th-century Americans knew that he was indicating secret complicity. Danny Kaye in the film *The Inspector General* (1952) sings "Give Them the Finger" using the same gesture, but by now Americans miss the gesture and understand the words differently.

Emblems may be class-specific. When Winston Churchill, the aristocratic British Prime Minister, started using the "V for Victory" emblem that he made famous in World War II, he performed it with the back of his hand to the receiver. For lower-class English, this gesture was a powerful obscenity. Churchill was soon advised to clean up his act.

The earliest studies of emblems were often little more than inventories, or dictionaries, of the hand gestures of a language. Recently, interest has grown in learning how these emblems become incorporated in speech. Brenda Farnell (1995) showed how Assiniboines of Fort Belknap, in northern Montana, use the hand signs of Plains Indian Sign Talk in their speech. (Farnell's solution to the problem of representing the complex visual and oral data was to use a sophisticated notation system in her book and to accompany it by visuals on a CD-ROM.)

Much work has now been done on emblems, and the results are often used in newspaper features stories and travel guides for serious tourists and business people. For example, the volume on Thailand in the *Culture Shock!* series spends six pages explaining the nuances of meaning attached to the *wai* in Thailand and instructing foreigners on its use and misuse (R. Cooper, 1996:12–17). Thais make the wai by pressing their palms together and lifting the hands to the head as they bow the head. This emblem is a sign of respect toward people as well as sacred objects. The higher the hands are raised and the lower the head is bowed, the greater the expression of respect and deference. According to Cooper, "it is the most significant of the many social actions that reinforce Thai social structure" (1996:13).

Proxemics: Space as Communication. The anthropologist Edward T. Hall developed the concept of **proxemics,** the cultural use of space, when he was advising Harvard Business School students on cross-cultural communication. Hall had observed that North Americans, when speaking to each other, kept a greater distance apart than did either Arabs or Latin Americans. Although some individual variation occurs, one can make rough generalizations. In casual, man-to-man conversation, most Arabs stand close to each other, almost touching, and often speaking so that each feels and smells the breath of the other. To keep a greater distance would be a sign of unfriendliness, even disdain. Most North American men would be very uncomfortable at such close quarters. It would imply an intimacy inappropriate for a casual conversation. As a consequence, they generally keep a greater distance. Exactly how far depends on many situational factors: the setting, the relationship between the two men, and the topic of conversation. Thus, if an Arab man is talking to a North American man, each tries to adjust into his own comfort zone, but in doing so creates a distance that is uncomfortable for the other.

Hall tells the story of a Venezuelan chasing a New Yorker around the room at a cocktail party. No sooner had the New Yorker stepped back to his comfortable distance than the Venezuelan moved into his, and so they went (Hall, 1959).

Hall identified several different features in the proxemics bundle:

- The distance between people
- The degree of eye contact
- The shoulder axis angle (open to closed) of the two people
- The degree of touching (or nontouching)
- Vocal volume

Not only is each of these factors a cultural variable, but on the whole, they are out of awareness. The New Yorker and the Venezuelan know about language differences and realize that they both have to speak English or both have to speak Spanish. But they may not be aware of the importance and the cultural differences in these other, nonverbal features. Hall called them the *silent language.*

Research with foreign students in Colorado (Watson, 1970) and observations at ethnic churches and bars in Chicago (Carrucci et al., 1989) suggest that some cultures can be characterized as high contact (southern Europe, Latin America), others as low contact (northern Europe, East Asia), and some as mixed (India, with much touching but little eye contact).

Eye contact is especially interesting. Not only does it vary greatly from culture to culture, but it has moral connotations; that is, each culture has a "normal" range of eye contact that is appropriate for a particular context. If someone looks too intently or too little, it is likely to be seen not as an ordinary error but as indicating some moral deficiency.

Obviously, then, the chances for miscommunication are great. As an example, in South Carolina, everyone is aware of some differences between Low Country (Charleston, and regions nearby) and Up Country (Greenville, Spartanburg, and so on). What seems to an outsider to be a generalized Southern accent is two quite distinguishable accents. In proxemic terms, Up Country is high eye contact, and Low Country is low eye contact. For someone from the Up Country, the Charleston level of eye contact is evasive, shifty-eyed, lazy, and untrustworthy. Charlestonian children, on the other hand, are told "Don't bore a hole in him with your eyes," and the intense eye contact of the Up Country is felt to be aggressive, even threatening. Low Country schoolchildren show respect by averting their gaze from the teacher, but an Up Country teacher demands that the children "look me in the eye while I am talking to you!"

We are acutely aware that people speak different "languages," but by that we usually think only of vocabulary and grammar, for we expect those features to vary from culture to culture (and from language to language). Most people rarely think of nonverbal features as part of language and thus are surprised when they vary. If one party was speaking French or Hindi, they would immediately grasp the problem. Eye contact, like that practiced in South Carolina, is out of awareness as a cultural variable, so people are not even conscious of what signals they are sending.

These findings about the importance of space in interaction are directly relevant to anyone who wants to communicate with people of another culture, especially to the extent that the other culture has different proxemic norms. If an English-speaking American tries to do business with Thais in Thailand, both sides know that someone has to yield and speak the other's language. If some sort of adjustment is not made to the proxemic channels as well, however, one or both will misread the messages. Perhaps an extraordinarily sensitive person will make changes without really thinking about it, but for most of us it will take a conscious effort. There are really three steps involved. First, one must take note of one's own basic proxemic behavior by becoming aware of one's own preferred speaking distance, or level of eye contact. Second, one must recognize the proxemic pattern of the other people. Again, think in terms of Hall's list of proxemic features. Third, one must decide how far one is willing to go to make the other party comfortable. For Americans traveling abroad, this three-step process of accommodation is complicated by the fact that many people in other countries have learned English vocabulary, grammar, and pronunciation, but retain their own paralinguistic and nonverbal patterns. Of course, it is not necessary to travel to a different country to meet up with people of different cultures.

Try this exercise: Analyze your own proxemic patterns. When you are talking to friends, how far away from them do you generally stand? What about strangers? How much eye contact do you usually make? Do you face the person directly, stand at right angles, or stand shoulder to shoulder? Do you touch people as you speak with them? How loudly do you speak?

With this self-awareness, become conscious of other people's cultural patterns. Think about how you can adjust to ease their concerns and, of course, to facilitate your communication with them.

This experiment illustrates that space is not just there, where interaction happens. Space can be manipulated for its different meanings, as words themselves are. Alessandro Durante, a linguistic anthropologist studying Samoan speech, came to realize the significance of space in the *fono,* the Samoan council of chiefs. A fono takes place in a large round structure whose thatched roof is supported by posts around the outer circumference. The participants sit in a circle around the edge. Some are entitled to lean against a post, others are not. Durante describes his early encounters with this proxemic pattern as

> a dimension of human interaction in which the locations of the actors, the proximity of their bodies, their most minimal physical reactions meant more than I could understand. (Durante, 1994:54)

The key word here is "meant"—this space has meanings. The Sunday after-church meal with the pastor's family and other church dignitaries was another Samoan setting where space had meaning. Durante describes an experiment that he once conducted at such a meal. One Sunday, instead of sitting with the high-status people, he moved across the room to sit with the unimportant guests. This change immediately redefined him and he was not shown the usual respect, but rather treated as a low-status Samoan and received only leftovers (1994:58ff).

In this photograph from northern Ghana of the Nayiri, the paramount chief of the Mamprusis, and some subchiefs, what clues tell you which is the Nayiri? See the answer at the bottom of the page. *(Credit: Dr. Joanna Casey)*

Answer: The most important man sits at a higher elevation that the others.

Kinesics and Choreometrics. Various ways of holding and moving people's bodies in interaction have been studied not just for their aesthetic aspect but as communication. Ray Birdwhistell introduced the term **kinesics** for this study of body communication. For example, Birdwhistell described how tertiary sexual attributes express and communicate gender identity (1964/1970). Primary sexual attributes are those that are directly involved in reproduction, such as ovaries and testicles; secondary sexual attributes are physical features that are more loosely associated with gender, such as breast development, body and facial hair, and musculature. Birdwhistell used the term *tertiary sexual attributes* for the learned behaviors that communicate masculinity and femininity. Some examples are intrafemoral angle (males sit with knees apart, females with knees together); pelvic angle (women stand with their lower hips forward, upper hips back, while men do the opposite); arm position (men walk with their elbows away from their sides, women with their elbows close to their bodies); wrist angle (men keep their wrists straight, women bend their wrists and let their fingers droop loosely). As you read this description and check it out with your own experience, you must remember that Birdwhistell's observations were especially valid for American culture in Kentucky in the 1950s. Much has changed in the last fifty years, especially, perhaps, in the intrafemoral angle feature. This change is particularly noticeable in college settings, for as women increasingly have worn pants, they have been less likely to sit with their knees together. At the time when Birdwhistell wrote, male and female were strongly differentiated in middle America, and these kinesic markers were an important part of how people, especially college-age people, communicated information about their identity. They are still part of gender communication in some contexts in many parts of America today.

One research direction that emerged from Birdwhistell's work was Alan Lomax's study of dance and work movement, called **choreometrics** (1968). Lomax studied film clips of dance from dozens of cultures around the world, developing a coding system that helped to detail several widespread movement patterns. For example, Lomax described two main torso movements. In one, the trunk is held rigid and moves as a single unit. In the other, the trunk moves as two units, with the hips and the shoulders moving separately. European dances such as the waltz, the square dance, or clogging and American Indian dances all use the one-unit trunk style. Sub-Saharan African dances and Polynesian dances such as the Hawaiian hula use the two-unit trunk style. In the United States, these two styles came together most dramatically in the 1950s, when Elvis Presley introduced his hip-swiveling African American movements into mainstream pop culture. Today, most young Americans at least try the two-unit trunk style of dance, while older Americans of European background tend to stick with one-unit trunk movements. Trunk movements are just one of many movement features that Lomax described. He combined these features into dance styles that extend across specific language and culture barriers.

Alan Lomax stressed that movement is communication and that it is one way in which cultures communicate their sense of self and their pride in their own traditions.

Elvis Presley introduced a two-unit trunk body movement into mainstream American entertainment. *(Credit: Photofest)*

DOING ANTHROPOLOGY

Full-Channel Shakespeare

As a good illustration of how important each of the different communication channels is in making up the entire bundle of acts that we call communication, let us look at a passage from William Shakespeare's *Hamlet*. Hamlet, Prince of Denmark, has been shocked by his father's death and his mother's hasty remarriage to his father's brother. He sets a trap for the royal couple, inviting a troupe of players to act out a drama that parallels the events as he has imagined them. The royal party assembles for the play. It includes Ophelia, whom Hamlet has been courting. Here is an exchange:

QUEEN: Come hither, my dear Hamlet, sit by me.
HAMLET: No, good mother. Here's metal more attractive.
POLONIUS: [to the King] O, ho! do you mark that?
HAMLET: Lady, shall I lie in your lap?
     [Sits down at Ophelia's feet.]
OPHELIA: No, my lord.
HAMLET: I mean, my head upon your lap?
OPHELIA: Ay, my lord.
HAMLET: Do you think I meant country matters?
OPHELIA: I think nothing, my lord.

HAMLET: That's a fair thought to lie between maids' legs.

OPHELIA: What is, my lord?

HAMLET: Nothing.

OPHELIA: You are merry, my lord.

HAMLET: Who, I?

OPHELIA: Ay, my lord.

HAMLET: O God, your only jig-maker! What should a man do but be merry? For look you how cheerfully my mother looks, and my father died within 's two hours.

(Act III, Scene 2, lines 115–135)

This passage is all that we have from Shakespeare—only words, sentences, and two incidental stage directions. The staging of Hamlet brings this scene to life by adding pronunciation (accents), paralanguage, and all the nonverbal features like use of space, body movements, and facial expressions that make up nonverbal communication. This particular scene has been played in many ways. One important decision concerns the state of Hamlet's mind. Is he mad? Sad? Indifferent? Angry? Does the Queen feel guilty? How does Ophelia react? Is Hamlet making subtle innuendoes or bawdy jokes? Depending on what choices of paralinguistic and nonverbal acts are used, the scene has different possibilities and the play quite different meanings. Speech is impossible without these features. We are so taken by Shakespeare's words that we forget how much of their meaning he left up to the actors.

Try to act out this short scene by yourself or in small groups. See how many different meanings you can give to this short exchange. ♦

Language, Culture, and Biology

The biocultural model is particularly useful in approaching the nature of language. On the one hand, language is obviously learned. Even now, you may be struggling with a second language. For those of us with an immigrant parent or two, it seems somehow unfair that we did not inherit proficiency in German, Vietnamese, or whatever. In fact, there are no genes for particular languages, so we have as much trouble learning our grandparents' tongues as anyone else does. On the other hand, one of the most wonderful aspects of human maturation is the speed and ease with which babies become fluent speakers of their first languages. The best accounting for these facts is a model that embraces both innate capability and learned specifics.

Universal Grammar: The Biological Basis of Language. One dramatic event in the recent development of the social sciences was the so-called Cognitive Revolution, which began in the 1950s. Until then, American psychology had been dominated by behaviorism, whose main theoretical position was learning theory. Research was directed toward exploring the mechanics of learning, and psychologists were not interested in the possibility that human behavior included an innate component. Anthropological linguists were still working out the differences between human languages, so they also tended to ignore the commonalities of languages.

Noam Chomsky, more than anyone else, triggered the Cognitive Revolution. He pointed out the shortcomings of behaviorism and proposed a new concept: a basic, innate, species-wide **Universal Grammar** that would account for the ease with which young humans become fluent productive speakers of one language or another.

This Universal Grammar consists of very basic universal principles of grammar that are part of our genetic makeup as *Homo sapiens.* These principles have a limited number of potential manifestations, and what we call *learning a language* involves selecting the manifestations that are appropriate to one particular language. Thus, in the Universal Grammar, there is the ability to deal with subjects, verbs, and objects and to learn the order that any particular language uses (and so babies learning English learn the subject–verb–object pattern). According to psychologist Steven Pinker,

> Universal Grammar is like an archetypal body plan found across vast numbers of animals in a phylum. For example, among all amphibians, reptiles, birds, and mammals, there is a common body architecture, with a segmented backbone, four jointed limbs, a tail, a skull, and so on. The various parts can be grotesquely distorted or stunted across animals: a bat's wing is a hand, a horse trots on its middle toes, whales' forelimbs have become flippers and their hindlimbs have shrunk to invisible nubs, and the tiny hammer, anvil, and stirrup of the mammalian middle ear are jaw parts of reptiles. But from newts to elephants, a common typology of the body plan—the shin bone connected to the thigh bone, the thigh bone connected to the hip bone—can be discerned. Many of these differences are caused by minor variations in the relative timing and rate of growth of the parts during embryonic development. Differences among languages are similar. There seems to be a common plan of syntactic, morphological, and phonological rules and principles, with a small set of varying parameters, like a checklist of options. (Pinker, 1994)

The development of the idea of Universal Grammar is an example of what Thomas Kuhn called a revolution in scientific thinking. Behaviorism was the normal science of its time, setting the problems and the research agendas to solve those problems but ignoring certain anomalies. Chomsky and others turned their attention to the anomalies. To solve them, they came up with a whole new set of problems and a revolutionary research agenda: they no longer asked "What are the mechanisms of learning?" but "What are the inborn abilities that allow learning?" Steven Pinker (1994) has written an excellent account of this Cognitive Revolution, and Barkow, Cosmides, and Tooby (1992) provide a more anthropologically oriented discussion of the same issues.

Anthropologists have watched the research on Universal Grammar from a distance with either fascination or disdain. In the greater scientific division of labor, the task of anthropology is still to work out the details and the implications of cultural variation, but we are increasingly becoming aware of how much this variation rests on a common biological base.

Linguistic Determinism Versus Linguistic Relativity.   A great question that has been asked in one form or another for centuries concerns the relationship between language and cognition (which includes thinking, perception, and memory). This question pertains to linguistic determinism: Does the particular language that a particular people speaks shape, in whole or in part, the way they think? Or, more broadly, does language shape culture?

In anthropology, Franz Boas introduced this question at the beginning of the 20th century. By midcentury, it was called the **Sapir–Whorf hypothesis** after two particularly influential linguists, Edward Sapir (a student of Boas) and Benjamin Whorf (a brilliant amateur linguist who worked with Sapir). John Lucy (1992a) has carefully traced the development of this idea, particularly as it was explored by Boas, Sapir, and Whorf. All three were careful not to claim evidence for causal connections between language and culture. Perhaps Whorf made the most definitive statement on the Sapir-Whorf hypothesis: "There are connections but not correlations or diagnostic correspondences between cultural norms and linguistic patterns." Furthermore,

> there are cases where the "fashions of speaking" are closely integrated with the whole general culture, whether or not this be universally true, and there are connections within this integration, between the kinds of linguistic analyses employed and various behavioral reactions and also the shape taken by various cultural developments. (cited in Lucy, 1992a:66)

The debate over the Sapir–Whorf hypothesis only quickened and deepened in the 1990s. Although much reference is still made to earlier works, especially Whorf's papers from the 1930s (collected in Whorf, 1956), this question is now a concern of the fast-breaking cognitive sciences, where linguistics, psychology, computer sciences, and anthropology study "thinking" (see especially Lucy, 1992a, 1992b; Lee 1996; Gumpertz and Levinson, 1996a).

The debate centers on two very closely related concepts. The first concept is **linguistic determinism,** which implies that language shapes thought. In the words of Gumpertz and Levinson, linguistic determinism "should be understood to imply that there is *at least some* causal influence from language categories to non-verbal cognition; it was not intended to denote an exclusive causal vector in one direction . . . " (1996b:22). The second, or corollary, concept is **linguistic relativism,** the idea that significant differences between languages cause or are at least related to significant differences in cognition.

For anyone who has struggled to learn a new language, linguistic relativism seems obvious: Languages are different, and they involve different ways of thinking. The problem lies in nailing down these differences. Although much anecdotal evidence exists both for and against linguistic relativism, little systematic comparative work has been done on linguistic variation in relation to cognitive variation. The main issues can be summarized as follows:

1. Assuming that a common human deep structure for language actually exists, are the differences between languages significant? And what, exactly, are they?

2. Is all human cognition (thinking, perception, memory) similar, or do significant cognitive differences exist between cultures?
3. If the differences outlined in (1) and (2) are real, can the linguistic differences be linked to the cognitive differences?
4. If the answer to (3) is "yes," can we identify cause and effect? Which way does the causal arrow point? Does language shape cognition? Or vice versa?
5. Given the answer to (4), how strong is the influence? For example, if we accept linguistic determinism, does language determine, merely limit, or just influence cognition?
6. How do we handle variations within a language, different ways to express something such that a speaker is not caught in a single confining frame? (Paul Kay argues that because these options do exist in languages, they undermine the basis of linguistic determinism [1996].)

For example, Dani, Chinese, and Indonesian (quite unrelated languages with quite different cultures) do not force a choice between singular and plural noun forms, as does English. Yet each language has ways to make the distinction between one and more than one. To suggest that Dani, Chinese, and Indonesian force people to not perceive, speak of, or remember the differences between "one" and "more than one" is not logical, however. But to what extent does the easily available non-specifying noun form influence thought? The answer to this question is not at all clear and, as John Lucy has insisted (1992b), can be decided only by carefully designed comparative research. Clearly, the matter of linguistic relativism remains an important area for research.

Sociolinguistics: Language in Social Context

In recent years, a tremendous growth has occurred in **sociolinguistics,** the study of language in its social context. This field focuses on not just how women, or gays, or Cambodian peasants use their particular ways of speaking to indicate who they are (identity), but also on how talk and social context mutually influence each other (see especially Goodwin and Durante, 1992).

Gender and Language

Gender hierarchies display themselves in all domains of social behavior, not the least of which is talk. Gender ideologies are socialized, sustained, and transformed through talk, particularly through verbal practices that recur innumerable times in the lives of members of social groups. (Ochs, 1992:336)

So writes Elinor Ochs, who has studied in painstaking detail the ways in which Samoan women create, maintain, and negotiate their status as women and as mothers through their talk. For example, Samoan mothers, unlike American mothers, do not use baby talk with their children. Where American mothers establish their low status through their talk to children (by altering their speech to accommodate the child's level of comprehension), Samoan mothers hold off engaging their children in talk until the child is able to actually understand. As Ochs says,

> When I examine transcripts of children's interactions with others, I see a set of cultural meanings about the position of mother, hence about women, being conveyed to children hundreds of times in the course of their early lives through linguistic forms and the pragmatic practices these forms help to constitute. (Ochs, 1992:354)

Whereas Ochs focuses on how women use speech to define their own status as mothers, another "ethnographer of communication," Jennifer Coates, has analyzed tapes of conversations among groups of women friends (1996). She was interested in the different ways that women have of "doing femininity":

> It seems to me that the talk we do with our women friends is particularly important in terms of our sense of ourselves as women, because in our talk we collaborate in constructing a shared view of what constitutes womanhood. (Coates, 1996:261–262)

Another take on gendered language and the ways in which it is used can be found in the studies of lesbian speech (for example, Cummings, 1994; Lewin, 1993) and of gay men's English (Leap, 1996a, 1996b). Leap describes in detail how gay men use Gay English when meeting other men of unknown sexual orientation to identify themselves as gay and to determine whether the other person is gay or straight. Leap's analysis of the lexical content of conversations showed that Gay English is not distinguished by a distinct vocabulary or grammar but rather by more subtle clues like references to certain people (Bette Davis), places (San Francisco), and even drinks (vodka tonic) that have special meanings within gay communities. Similarly, in her study of lesbian speech in Columbia, South Carolina, Elizabeth Busbee found "that women in lesbian speech communities identify their speech and their conversational space as lesbian *not* by numerous linguistic phenomena but by virtue of the topics they choose to discuss and perspectives from which they present these topics for discussion" (1998:50).

Busbee emphasizes the limited, regional nature of lesbian speech communities—code words reported from elsewhere in the United States were unknown to the Columbia community. Also, undoubtedly, videotape records would show paralinguistic and nonverbal cues. As Leap shows, however, Gay English is an intentionally obscured code, intended to be recognized only by other gays.

Language, Status, and Power. In many languages, a speaker's choice of words indicates his or her status relative to the listener. The most common place to locate this feature is in the pronouns, and particularly in the second-person plural pronouns. The system of pronouns often gives insight into the system of relationships in a culture. Certainly, anyone who wants to function in that culture must take pains to master the pronouns together with the personal names and titles that are part of the naming system. Standard American English is remarkable for having only one second-person form, *you* (although regional dialects may add *you-all, youse, y'uns,* or *yez* for more than one person). German, French, and Spanish still have two second-person forms that distinguish between formal and intimate, or superior and inferior relationships. (In the 19th century, German had four options, which calibrated social status even more finely.) At the extreme, Khmer (Cambodian) has some twenty-eight second-person forms to precisely calibrate relative status. In many languages, the proliferation of these second-person forms correlates with a cultural concern with hierarchy as expressed in levels of status and degrees of respect and so supports the simpler version of the Sapir–Whorf hypothesis.

The forced choice among different pronoun forms expresses basic facts about the relationship. In European languages, for example, if both parties to a conversation choose to use the same pronoun, they are agreeing to have relatively equal status and, furthermore, to have a relationship that is either relatively formal or relatively informal and intimate. If the two parties use different pronoun forms, this discrepancy indicates inequality or power differential: the speaker using the informal form is of higher status than the one using the formal word.

Forced choice between words with hierarchical implications is not limited to pronouns. In Japanese, for example, if you stay at an inn and ask the maid whether the bath is ready, you use the basic word *furo* for bath. In her reply, the maid will attach an honorific *o,* saying *ofuro.* She is not honoring the bath itself, but rather marking the status difference between guest and servant.

The many studies of gendered talk, especially "woman's language," have been based on the assumption that because men, on the whole, have higher status and more power than women, and because it can be shown that men and women use language differently, then these differences should reveal how power is asserted in talk. Indeed, men's talk does differ from women's talk in many ways: men interrupt more than women do, men are more direct and confrontational, and so forth. Deborah Tannen, a linguist who has published both technical and best-selling books on gendered speech, cautions against jumping to conclusions, however. She emphasizes that

> all linguistic strategies are potentially ambiguous. The power-solidarity dynamic is one fundamental source of ambiguity. What appears as attempts to dominate a conversation (an exercise of power) may actually be intended to establish rapport (an exercise of solidarity). (Tannen, 1994:23–24)

Further complicating the issue is the fact that, quite apart from any power variables, ethnic or cultural variables come into play. For example, speakers differ in how long they can pause without being interrupted—that is, when they signal, by the length of their pause, that another speaker may begin. Tannen summarizes various peoples' research on this issue, pointing out that Jewish New Yorkers are generally seen to interrupt Californians, but Americans are seen to interrupt Scandinavians, and Swedes and Norwegians are seen to interrupt Finns, and finally, within Finland regional variations occur (Tannen, 1994:68)!

Language and Identity. Language is the single most important cultural feature of identity. The language that you speak and the way in which you speak it identify you and your group more definitively than any other cultural trait. Neither food, nor clothing, nor music, nor religion is as important.

In pre–World War I England, George Bernard Shaw wrote the play *Pygmalion* (which became the musical *My Fair Lady* in 1956) to demonstrate how the English were locked into a particular class and region by the English they spoke. Henry Higgins, a linguist, bet that he could pass Eliza Doolittle, a flower girl, off in the highest social circles if he could teach her how to speak the appropriate upper-class English. She learned, they fooled the linguistic police, and Higgins won the bet.

When the U.S. government wanted to strip North American Indians of their culture, the most effective weapon was to prohibit the speaking of native languages in schools. After the 1965 civil war in Indonesia, the new Suharto government clamped down on Indonesians of Chinese ancestry by banning the use of Chinese languages and the display of Chinese writing. And as we shall see with the Focus Culture for this chapter, a major step in the cultural resurgence of the Kwa Kwaka' Wakw is to teach children their language again.

SYMBOLS, ART, AND IDENTITY

Certain aspects of culture are highly symbolic. Language consists entirely of a vast set of symbolic meanings. Sometimes there is a logical connection between the symbol and what it represents. For example, the leaf of the maple tree stands for Canada, the cedar for Lebanon, and the banyan tree for Indonesia. Each type of tree is an important feature in each country's landscape. But in language this logical relationship between the symbol and what it symbolizes is missing. The letter "T" stands for some particular sounds (called *unvoiced alveolar stops*), and the combination TREE means certain woody stemmed plants, but in both cases, the relationship between symbol and thing symbolized is quite arbitrary.

Religion, because it deals so much with mysteries, is particularly rich in symbols. Nevertheless, all areas of culture use some symbols, and there is a tremendous variety of these things that stand for other things. Next we examine some of the more clearly symbolic ideas developed in different cultures, focusing on the ways in which they are crafted together into systems, or symbolic structures.

Gauche Sinister Left Hands.   Of all symbols, the most pervasive and ever-present is that based on the human hands. Symbolically, right is right or correct, and left is in some way sinister (*left* in Latin), gauche (*left* in French), or polluted. One can speculate that handedness and gender were the first and most immediate binary oppositions. A biocultural model is particularly applicable here, for apparently, in all populations, the great majority of people are born right-handed. That is, they are naturally inclined to use their right hands, and it is their right hands that are more dexterous (from the Latin for *right*), or adroit (from the French for *right*). But if biology makes most people do most things best with their right hands, it is cultures that construct the meanings about right and left. Logically (I speak as a left-hander), there is no reason why the symbolism could not be reversed. Why not have the right hand, which does most of the work, be thought of as lower status and the left hand be considered noble? After all, many cultures sort people out that way. In fact, no culture values the left hand over the right. In virtually all cultures, the right hand is used in rituals, in greetings, and in eating; in metaphor, it is considered to be better than the left. In much of Asia, the left hand is not just symbolically impure, but people use it, with a bowl of water, to wipe themselves after defecation: It is physically polluted.

Many cultures have handed artifacts that can be used comfortably by right-handed people only. Recently, novelty stores in the United States have been catering to left-handed people and their relatives who are looking for left-handed scissors and the like. The Dani are one of the few cultures that have no handed artifacts; the artifacts that they do have can be used equally well with either hand. In fact, even the Dani language does not have words for *left* and *right;* instead one talks of *main hand* and *other hand,* depending on the person's handedness.

Handedness is a source of great interest to left-handers. As one of them, I was very aware that the choices for president of the United States in 1992 were among three left-handers. If you are sitting in a classroom now, you probably have no choice but to be sitting at a right-handed desk, even if a disproportionate number of your fellow anthropology students are left-handed. (I think that anthropology draws many left-handers, but I cannot explain why.)

This very arbitrariness of symbols creates problems. A symbol may have any meaning, for no intrinsic property exists to keep one single meaning firmly attached. Thus symbols change meanings and have multiple meanings depending on place and time. In the 1960s the "V for Victory" hand gesture was used by President Nixon (meaning "victory") in the United States. In contrast, the same gesture meant "peace" for those opposed to the American–Vietnamese War.

Swastikas.   Some symbols are vested with powerful cultural and emotional meaning and may have different meanings for different people in different cultures. The graphic image seen in the photos on the next page is found in many parts of the world (Wilson, 1986). It is called **swastika** in Sanskrit and is a common Buddhist and Hindu symbol. Among the Navajo, it is used as a design motif in rugs and jewelry. Malcolm Quinn (1994) traced the "aryanization" of the swastika in Europe from the late 19th century up to the point when it was adopted by the German National Socialist (Nazi) Party in 1919 and took on a variety of new meanings: strength and unity for Germans, inhuman barbarism for others, especially Jews.

Symbolic Structure in Narrative Art

All cultures have *myths, legends,* and *folktales,* which are forms of narrative art having particular meaning for the culture. These narratives generally use symbols to tell about or explain unusual or supernatural peoples and events, and they function as entertainment, ritual, or both, often incorporating symbols.

One of the first anthropologists to develop a systematic approach to the study of symbols was Claude Lévi-Strauss. In a series of immensely influential books, he

The swastika (*left*), appropriated by the German Nazi Party in the 20th century, was one of the world's most widespread symbols. Here it is woven into a Navajo rug from the 20th century. *(Credit: Karl G. Heider)* The swastika symbolizing the American Nazis (*right*). *(Credit: © Dennis Budd Gray/Stock, Boston, LLC)*

presented his structural analysis of myth. For Lévi-Strauss, myths are symbolically encoded solutions to the basic questions of the human intellect, especially "What are we?" Myths, said Lévi-Strauss, present binary oppositions such as culture versus nature. Then they mediate or reconcile the opposites. Often, only after he collected and analyzed many versions of similar myths from closely related cultures could he identify the complete structure.

Analysis of a Folktale: *Goldilocks and the Three Bears.* Eugene Hammel (1972) made an ingenious analysis of *Goldilocks and the Three Bears* in the Lévi-Straussian style. Hammel chose this folktale because it is familiar and because so many versions have been published. He was able to use eighty-four dated examples, published over 140 years in England and the United States.

The earliest versions of the story tell of three bears who are visited by a fox called Scapefoot. Through the 19th century, a general sharpening of the story occurs, making the different elements steadily more oppositional. In particular, the nature–culture opposition is developed. The intruder, who in early versions is just another animal (fox), becomes in later versions a human girl with silver and then golden hair. The bears, at first three undifferentiated creatures, become a differentiated family of father, mother, and baby bear. The action takes place between the girl intruder (who as a human represents culture but who acts wild and naturelike) and the bears (who are animals, of course, but who have a family and the household artifacts of culture). The plot has the human acting "naturally" as she encounters the "natural" beasts acting "humanly." In every case, after a period of confusion, Goldilocks leaves, presumably returning to her culture, and the bears remain happily in their (natural) forest.

A second structural regularity is the use of threes: three bears, three things that Goldilocks encounters (the porridge, the chairs, and the beds), and her three attempts to use each. This structure allows for opposition (too hot, too cold; too hard, too soft), which is then resolved (just right!). In his analysis, Hammel goes much further, but this discussion is enough to show clearly that this simple children's story is more than a unique product of someone's imagination. It incorporates and refines some basic symbolic oppositions and structural principles that are widespread. As the story becomes refined over the years, it gets better in the sense that the oppositions and principles become clearer.

Symbolizing History: The Swamp Fox, the Wizard Owl, and the Gamecock.　An even more elegant example of the emergence of symbolic structure comes from South Carolina (Heider, 1980). By the late 19th century, a generally accepted story of the Revolutionary War recalled the exploits of three militia generals, each with an animal sobriquet, as they led the colonial troops against the British forces. They were Francis Marion, of the Low Country, called "the Swamp Fox"; Andrew Pickens, of the Up Country, "the Wizard Owl"; and Thomas Sumter, "the Gamecock" of the Midlands.

At first glance, this story is an extraordinary Lévi-Straussian triad: the burrowing animal in the Low Country, the bird in the Up County, and in the middle, mediating, a flightless bird, the gamecock. But a careful look at the historical record shows that it took 165 years to polish the story. During the war, there were actually several generals; they had to be whittled down to the three and made into two extremes and a mediating middle. The "Gamecock" nickname for Sumter was used scornfully by the British and did not acquire positive connotations until the 1840s. Likewise, Marion was not called "the Swamp Fox" in a positive sense until the 1840s. Pickens was not even included in the set with the other two until the early 20th century, and it was not until 1940 that all three, complete with sobriquets, were in place. The symbolic structure is now elegant, but it took generations of people working it over to produce the elegance.

As another example, intense and often bitter public debate has erupted for years over the flying of a Confederate flag above the South Carolina state capital building. The flag was first raised there in the early 1960s to commemorate the bravery of the Confederate soldiers in the Civil War (according to some) or to symbolize resistance to federal attempts to desegregate the public schools (according to others). Today, whether it means racism, Southern heritage, or antigovernment sentiment or is just used for its shock value, the Confederate flag is a powerful multivocalic symbol that exacerbates divisions among the peoples of South Carolina. Attempts to redefine the flag have failed. Today, it remains necessary to some, a public abomination to others. The moral: You can use a symbol, but you cannot control its meanings.

Symbols are evident everywhere in culture. They are often quite visible within the cultural landscape, providing guideposts for behavior. In many cases, symbols are culturally constructed; in other cases, symbols have been created with the intent that they transcend cultural boundaries. Many of the symbols guiding travelers, for example, are meant to have some universal meaning, such as bathroom signs or road signs.

As we have seen, symbols can also be very specific to a culture. Consequently, understanding the symbols and the meanings attached to them is a very important part of understanding a culture. One particularly symbol-rich aspect of culture is **art.** Art, like language, is an expressive aspect of culture. Studying it can reveal much about the values, ideas, and beliefs of a culture as well as those of an individual artist. Many genres of art exist: visual art, which includes sculpture, painting, drawing, and the like; filmmaking; performance art; narrative art, including written and oral storytelling; and craft arts, such as weaving, pottery making, and glass blowing.

In craft art, we often see the use of symbols as designs. Although these designs may not always carry meanings, they often do. In fact, the use of designs or symbols is what turns an artifact into art.

Art can be defined as the nonutilitarian elaboration of a thing or an act. For example, the Dani have minimal art. They rarely do more than is necessary to manufacture any of their artifacts. Other New Guinea cultures, especially those residing along the coasts, have made elaborately carved shields, carried by warriors to protect them from arrows and spears. In addition, these shields were carved with designs representing protective magical powers or mythical creatures; these carvings make the shields become art.

Art and Identity

Among the displays in the British Museum in London are two collections acquired in the 19th century that particularly involve cultural identity. The first is a set of marble sculptures taken from the Parthenon in Athens by Lord Elgin through an arrangement with the Turkish occupiers of Greece. The second is a set of cast bronze plates ripped off the palace of Benin in what is now Nigeria, West Africa, by British soldiers. Pressure to repatriate these objects of art has been growing, and they will likely be returned to their original owners in the 21st century. These and other treasures stolen, smuggled, or otherwise spirited away from their sites of origin are increasingly the focus of controversy. Art has meanings at various levels, and one of the most powerful meanings is to symbolize cultural identity. Art styles are as distinctive as languages, and objects made in these distinctive styles have particular potency as symbols of identity.

An exhibit of Kwa Kwaka' Wakw potlatch masks and other objects at the American Museum of Natural History in New York demonstrated the contentious nature of artistic identity markers (see the analysis of the exhibit by Joseph Masco [1996]). The museum had invited several Kwa Kwaka' Wakw to participate in mounting the exhibit. One of these people was Gloria Cranmer Webster, great-granddaughter of George Hunt, Boas's collaborator (we meet her in the film clip *Box of Treasures*).

The exhibit began with an unresolved conflict over what to call these people, Kwakiutl or Kwa Kwaka' Wakw. The museum wanted to present the materials in terms of Boas's anthropological understanding as of the late 19th century; the people themselves wanted to tell the story about how they had changed, adapted, and survived. The museum focused on "Kwakiutl" and "potlatch" because those terms were so well known. For the Kwa Kwaka' Wakw themselves, however, the potlatch was merely one part of their ceremonial exchange life over the decades. The museum wanted to celebrate its own caretaking of Boas's collections, whereas the Kwa Kwaka' Wakw wanted to tell of their cultural resistance and resilience even during the period when potlatching was suppressed. Obviously, the art objects and old photographs do not speak for themselves. Masco shows how this tension between "ethnographic authority" (Boas on the "Kwakiutl") and cultural identity (as experienced by the Kwa Kwaka' Wakw) was eventually solved by presenting both positions in different parts of the exhibit.

Art in Context Versus Art on a Pedestal

Generally, art museums hold collections of Western art from different times and places, displaying their best pieces in their galleries for their visitors to see. They are little concerned with cultural contextualization—that is, putting their objects into context—because such museums have been created to display the sorts of Western art that were created to hang on walls of museums. These items typically consist of paintings, suitably framed, spaced on the walls. Understanding the meanings of these works of art does not pose a great cultural challenge. Visitors today have some general idea of the cultural context of 17th-century Netherlands, 19th-century France, or 20th-century America.

When the same approach is applied to objects from radically different cultures, such as tribal cultures that are largely unknown to museum visitors, it is a different matter. These objects, whose meaning depends so heavily on their cultural context, are stripped of that cultural information and become decultured forms. Two extreme examples make this point.

On Fifth Avenue, in New York City, the Michael C. Rockefeller Wing of the Metropolitan Museum of Art has one room populated with magnificent "*bis* poles," which Rockefeller collected on the Asmat Coast of what is now Irian Jaya, Indonesia, straight south of the Dani (*bis* is pronounced like "bish.") These bis poles are strangely evocative of the Northwest Coast totem poles. They contain one thin male figure after another, each standing on the shoulders of the lower figure, often with prominent erections, in a style as unmistakably Asmat as the totem poles are immediately recognizable as Northwest Coast. One of my own personal epiphanies was wandering through the galleries of the Tropical Museum in Amsterdam and suddenly coming upon an array of bis poles that had been collected and sent to Holland in the 1920s. They were stunning. In New York, these great carvings are mounted as pure dramatic form and as such are successful. People coming on them for the first time gasp, as I had gasped that day in Amsterdam. The museum, however, gives no clue as to the ritual significance and the cultural context of these objects. Furthermore, the casual visitor is not challenged with the fact that these stunning creations are made by people who, according to Fifth Avenue standards, are nearly naked, filthy, ill-mannered, former headhunters. A chance has been lost to make that art meaningful in its own terms and, not incidentally, to open the visitors' eyes to the idea that a very different sort of people can produce great art.

Now consider a positive model for cultural contextualization. A few years ago, the same Tropical Museum in Amsterdam presented a wonderfully worked-out exhibit of a working-class slum in Calcutta. A few small houses were constructed in such a way that one could wander around the streets, peer into rooms, and see realistic settings with artifacts and art in place. The walls, plastered with real cow dung, even smelled genuine. On a video monitor, one could watch a long shot of people, animals, shops, and traffic on the streets of Calcutta, probably taken with a concealed camera in a pedicab that was unobtrusively wheeling through the streets of the city. Although this exhibit contained less dramatic art than the rooms that displayed Asmat bis poles, what was present had been carefully placed in its cultural setting.

FOCUS CULTURE

Art and Ceremony of the Kwa Kwaka' Wakw of the Northwest Coast

OVERVIEW

Location: The Northwest Coast of North America: on Vancouver Island, the straits islands, and their adjacent mainland, British Columbia, Canada

Geography: Settlements along the rugged coastlines

Population: About 4,000

Languages: Kwakwala, of the Wakashan Stock, and now English

Religion: Officially mainly Anglican, but much of the traditional religion has been retained

Economy: Until the 20th century, technically foragers, fishing, and hunting and gathering in the incredibly rich maritime zone. Today there is much commercial fishing

Sociopolitical Organization: Traditionally heirarchical chiefdoms

For one of the most striking art styles in the world, we go to the Northwest Coast of North America, which extends from Washington through British Columbia to the Alaskan panhandle. This region is a land of temperate rain forest, wet, dank, green, with the great cedars and Douglas firs coming down to the ocean. Fjords, bays, inlets, river mouths, and islands indent the coastline. This land has long been recog-

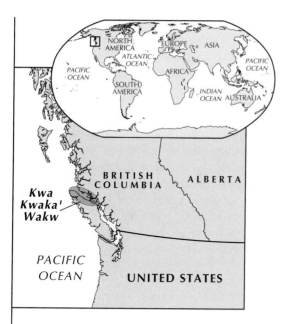

nized as a "culture area," for although the people living here spoke several different languages, they shared many culture traits.

The natural environment of the Northwest Coast has two outstanding features that the people successfully exploited: salmon and the red cedar. The salmon swarmed up the rivers in countless numbers. They, along with the other creatures of the sea and the forest, provided plenty of food. The red cedar was easy to split and fine to carve even with stone and bone tools. From it, the people made grand houses and carved out one of the world's great art traditions.

Naming and Identity. We will focus on only one of the Northwest Coast cultures: people organized in some two dozen different independent units, or tribes, all speaking a language called Kwa Kwala. These Kwa Kwala speakers call themselves Kwa Kwaka' Wakw (pronounced more or less **Kwa Kwa**ka **Wa**ku) and wish others to call them by that name despite the fact that they were made famous by Franz Boas as "Kwakiutl." (That term is the name for one of their local groups, but Boas used it to describe all these people.)

The Kwa Kwaka' Wakw groups live in the southern part of the Northwest Coast, on the northern end of Vancouver Island, on the mainland across the Queen Charlotte Strait, and on various smaller islands in the strait itself.

The name is merely one part of the broader linguistic aspect of cultural identity. The Kwa Kwaka' Wakw are trying to restore their cultural identity by reviving the Kwa Kwala language itself before it is lost. Most Kwa Kwaka' Wakw had been discouraged or forbidden to use their own language, so now only some elders are really comfortable speaking it. Today, however, a move is afoot to restore it as a living tongue by teaching school children to speak Kwa Kwala. This choice is controversial, for even as the children are being urged to strengthen their identity as Kwa Kwaka' Wakw, they are being bombarded by other messages advertising the benefits of joining contemporary Canadian national culture. Several scenes described in the complete film for this chapter, *Box of Treasures,* present this dilemma. Of course, the same problem affects many people around the world today.

The Great Anomaly. In Chapter 6, where we look at various subsistence styles, we will make the generalization that hunters and gatherers, or foragers, because they must range far in search of their food, live in small groups with temporary dwellings, own only the few objects that they can carry with them, and are relatively egalitarian. That is a good generalization. The Kwa Kwaka' Wakw are exceptions on each count, however. Their food swims up the rivers to them. Thus, in each of the respects that we mentioned, they resemble farmers more closely than foragers. They build large multifamily houses of broad cedar planks painted with symbolic designs of real and supernatural creatures. Settlements often consist of several such houses located on a narrow strip of shore with forest behind and sea in front. Old photographs of Kwa Kwaka' Wakw villages show canoes, some holding as many as fifty people, drawn up on the shore. Totem poles rise high above the roofs. Although the word "totem" comes from an Algonquian language of eastern North America, the most generally known use refers to the "totem poles" of the Northwest Coast. These poles consist of carved and painted cedar, made to honor a particular person and depicting a series of creatures, animals, humans, or mythological beings one above the other. Each figure represents what Boas called a "crest," a symbol of a totem of an individual or of a person's kin group (the *numaym*), of a person's guardian spirit, or in some cases of particularly significant events. Thus the pole summarizes the person's status as shown by the crests and events to which the person is entitled, and it serves as a public proclamation of the importance of that person.

The Kwa Kwaka' Wakw are strongly hierarchical. The tribes themselves are ranked, as are the subdivisions of tribes (the numaym). Individuals, too, are ranked according to their offices and titles.

In addition, the Kwa Kwaka' Wakw were wealthy. They had easy access to plentiful food, most of which could be accumulated in a few months of the year, leaving

A contemporary Kwa Kwaka' Wakw dance at the U'mista Cultural Center (still from the film *Box of Treasures*). *(Credit: Documentary Educational Resources)*

the winter months essentially free for ceremonial activity and, above all, for potlatches. Potlatches are great competitive feasts where one chief invites his rivals from other villages to watch him build his status by giving away or destroying great amounts of valuables. The guests must, in turn, reciprocate or lose out in the status rivalry.

Kwa Kwaka' Wakw art is stylized and obviously carries much deep symbolic meaning. If the artists had made completely naturalistic representations of real animals and birds, an outsider could immediately appreciate (and have at least the illusion of understanding) the artists' minds. Obviously, however, so much more is going on in the art. The artists are not representing reality so much as referring to an elaborate system of symbolic meanings.

Of course, Kwa Kwaka' Wakw culture has been changing constantly. The visits of European ships to the Northwest Coast from the 18th century on certainly speeded the change, as the visitors introduced metal tools. Although the red cedar could be worked with stone and shell blades, iron and steel made fine carving possible. George Hunt, in an 1899 letter to Boas, reports a surprising discovery:

> . . . in the old times I found that there was no masks made of wood, for they had
> no knives to carve with, so all the masks was made out of Red cedar Bark . . .
> (quoted in Jacknis, 1991:192)

The ending of war in the mid-19th century removed one way for Kwa Kwaka' Wakw men to achieve renown. Nevertheless, the most dramatic change related to the drop in population from perhaps 19,000 before European contact to around 1,000 at the beginning of the 20th century. At the same time, the number of titles or ranks stayed the same and wealth increased. With more wealth available, greatly increased competition for titles ensued in more elaborate potlatches.

Although we may quibble about whether the Dani really have art, absolutely no question exists about the Kwa Kwaka' Wakw. If we look at their houses, for instance, we can readily see the nonutilitarian embellishments. The traditional house was made of cedar planks, and its front face was painted with an elaborate design representing some of the crests or titles associated with the house. Inside, two or more large tree trunks, or "roof poles," held up the central ridgepole. These roof poles were often carved and painted with images of crests much like the freestanding "totem poles" outside the houses. Clearly, the painting and the carving go beyond the merely utilitarian and are "art."

The aesthetics of Northwest Coast art was explored in a remarkable book-long conversation between Bill Holm, a scholar studying that art, and Bill Reid, a Haida carver. The two men spent three days with the DeMenil collection at Rice University examining each piece. Their discussions about provenance, form, and aesthetics form the body of the resulting book (Holm and Reid, 1975). A few excerpts from some of Bill Reid's comments give an idea of how a native artist thinks about an art style:

> These objects weren't merely used at ceremonial affairs. They were treated
> as art objects, passed from hand to hand, admired, fondled, examined closely.
> Everyone was a critic and connoisseur. Everyone probably felt some direct

relationship with the objects in his immediate family, and maybe even with those in the whole community. These were communities of connoisseurs. (Holm and Reid, 1975:97)

Bill Reid's family was Haida, a group living just north of the Kwa Kwaka' Wakw. Although Reid continued the Haida carving tradition, he had lived away from the coast long enough to have some sense of seeing the art as an outsider. He said,

One of the great joys I've gotten out of the Northwest Coast is the feeling I have that these people looked at the world in a very different way than we do. They weren't bound by the silly feeling that it's impossible for two figures to occupy the same space at the same time. So we have this human figure, plus a bear's head or whatever, coexisting in space and time. (Holm and Reid, 1975:46)

Edmund Carpenter, in his Introduction to the Holm and Reid volume, called this idea "visual punning." He says, "Such visual puns did more than express complexity; they depicted transformation. Before one's eyes, Bear became Wolf, then Bear again. The image didn't change, of course. What changed was the observer's organization of its parts. But the effect was one of transformation" (Carpenter, 1975:9).

Bill Reid continues:

I think what appeals to those of us interested in Northwest Coast art is the enormous number of levels of aesthetic appreciation involved. A piece can become part of a costume and, as such, disappear into an overall effect. Or it can be held in the hand, a thing of beauty in itself. And beyond this, there are many other levels of meaning and expression in every individual part. This can be said of great art of all periods, but it's such an obvious, pleasurable thing with Northwest Coast materials. (Holm and Reid, 1975:71) ♦

SEEING ANTHROPOLOGY

Art and Identity of the Kwa Kwaka' Wakw: *Box of Treasures*

Produced by the U'Mista Cultural Society
Filmmaker: Dennis Wheeler   *Narrator: Gloria Cranmer Webster*

This film focuses on Kwa Kwaka' Wakw identity as expressed in their art and ceremonies. It does not home in so much on what different forms symbolize, but rather on the importance of the art itself to their identity. The Canadian government had long felt that the potlatch ceremonies were harming the Kwa Kwaka' Wakw. In 1885, it made the potlatch illegal. According to Douglas Cole (1991:140), several reasons underlay this move. Potlatches and other winter ceremonies took place every night for two months in the dead of winter, and the exertion and visiting from village to village promoted disease. Women resorted to prostitution to pay for the potlatch gifts. It was difficult to keep schools going when the children and their families were involved in the intense ritual life. Perhaps most important, the fact that the people were amassing wealth only to squander it on gift giving was so alien to mainstream Canadian culture that it seem immoral and antithetical to modernization.

Despite the ban, the Kwa Kwaka' Wakw managed to continue potlatching until 1921. In that year, an especially large potlatch organized by Daniel Cranmer (Gloria Cranmer Webster's grandfather) was broken up, the participants were jailed, and the potlatch objects—many of them great artistic treasures—were confiscated and sent to Ottawa.

Ultimately, in 1951, the ban on potlatching was quietly dropped. After much negotiation, the Canadian government agreed to return the confiscated objects if the Kwa Kwaka' Wakw would prepare a proper place to preserve them. This film is the story of the return of tribal treasures to the cultural center known as U'Mista, in Alert Bay, on Vancouver Island. For particularly good accounts of U'Mista and the films, see Webster (1991) and Morris (1994:123–136).

The short video clip gives us the voices of many different Kwa Kwaka' Wakw, including an old woman, a mask carver, some politicians, a fisherman, and especially Gloria Cranmer Webster. They talk of loss, of what was taken away after Chief Dan Cranmer's potlatch in 1921. We see a deserted village with its abandoned totem poles. The film then cuts to the town of Alert Bay, where many Kwa Kwaka' Wakw now live and "where we have begun the task of reclaiming all that was almost lost." They insist that they are not gone, but are still very much alive and well.

The complete film shows the opening ceremonies for the U'Mista Cultural Center, with speeches (mainly in English). Much talk focuses on reclaiming the culture—not only the art treasures, but also the dances and the language. A linguist discusses his work in analyzing and recording the language, and we see children learning to speak Kwa Kwala. People acknowledge that it is difficult to compete against television and other modern attractions, but they do it for the children: "It is important for them to know who they really are."

Setup Questions

1. What are the meanings of the potlatch for the Kwa Kwaka' Wakw people? For the Canadian government?
2. The crate from the Ottawa Museum of Man sent to U'Mista is marked "Works of Art." Is that label accurate?
3. How have the Kwa Kwaka' Wakw tried to make their U'Mista Center a proper non-museum setting for their treasures?
4. "The Center was to be far more than a museum." What does that statement mean?
5. What does "U'Mista" mean in Kwa Kwala?
6. Can you get an idea of what Bill Reid was saying about aesthetics of Kwa Kwaka' Wakw art from the film clip and the photographs in the text? ♦

HOLLYWOOD-STYLE ANTHROPOLOGY

The Cultural Translation of *Darmok*

Darmok   "Star Trek: The Next Generation," Episode 102   1991, Stardate
45047.2   45 minutes

Patrick Stewart as Captain Jean-Luc Picard
Paul Winfield as Captain Dathon

You don't have to be a Trekkie to know that "Star Trek" often deals with problems of culture. In this episode, the Starship *Enterprise* encounters a Tamarian starship, and for once the Universal Translator, which renders any possible language of the universe into 20th-century American English, fails: "We can't even say hello to these people." Utterances come out part English, part Tamarian. Captain Picard and the Tamarian captain, Dathon, are beamed down to a planet deserted except for some force entity that is trying to kill both of them. It is essential that they work out a way to communicate.

Setup Questions

1. Why is the Universal Translator ineffective?
2. What does "Darmok" mean?
3. What does "shaka" mean?
4. Why does Captain Picard tell the Gilgamesh story?
5. Explain "Juliet on the balcony."
6. At the end, Picard is reading "Homeric hymns" in Greek—why? Which Homeric work? Why that one?   ◆

CHAPTER SUMMARY

- Although other creatures have systems of communication, none has—or can learn—anything comparable in its various design features to the human languages that each normal *Homo sapiens* learns with ease in the very first years of life.
- Human communication systems use a complex combination of meaning-carrying acts: "language" consists of the sound system (phonology), the vocabulary (lexicon), and the grammar (syntax). In addition, these communication systems encompass paralanguage (tone, pauses, and the like) and various channels of nonverbal communication such as hand gestures, proxemics (the use of space in face-to-face interaction), kinesics (expressive uses of the body), and the styles of body movement in work and dance (studied with choreometrics).
- Language is a prime example of the mixture of innate and learned, for we *Homo sapiens* are born with immense innate but general language structure that allows us to quickly learn any of the human languages to which we are first exposed.

- Sociolinguistic research shows how language is used in context to express gender and other facets of a speaker's identity.
- Symbols, like a swastika or a flag, also have meaning and can express identity.
- Art is the nonfunctional elaboration of things and acts and speech. It also expresses cultural and personal identity.

KEY TERMS

allomorph	illustrators	primitive
allophone	kinesics	proxemics
art	linguistic determinism	Sapir–Whorf hypothesis
Butterworths	linguistic relativism	semantic fields
choreometrics	morpheme	semantics
conversation analysis	morphology	signs
culture-neutral	nonverbal	sociolinguistics
design features	communication	swastika
discourse analysis	paralanguage	symbols
emblems	phoneme	syntax
emic	phonemic analysis	Universal Grammar
ethology	phonetic analysis	wai
etic	phonology	

QUESTIONS TO THINK ABOUT

- Are we, perhaps, too eager to claim too great a gulf between human speech and the communication systems of other animals? Why?
- Do you share in a subculture that has words and gestures not known to the larger culture?
- When you speak (or try to speak) a second language, do you change your style, personality, or perceptions? Do you think a person fluent in two languages would experience such changes?
- Do you think that you speak differently when you speak with someone of your own gender, compared with when you speak with someone of the opposite gender? How about someone of a very different age?
- How does the art that you like express your identity? (Take this one step beyond "because it's the real me.")

SUGGESTIONS FOR FURTHER READING

Ardener, Shirley (ed.)
1992   Women and Space: Ground Rules and Social Maps. Oxford: Berg. *Relationship of public architectural space in expressing gender.*

Errington, J. Joseph

1998   Shifting Languages: Interaction and Identity in Javanese Indonesian. Cambridge, U.K.: Cambridge University Press. *Tensely negotiated, high-stakes relationship between a local and a national language.*

Errington, Shelly

1998   The Death of Authentic Primitive Art and Other Tales of Progress. Berkeley: University of California Press.

Jonaitis, Aldona

1991   Chiefly Feasts: The Enduring Kwakiutl Potlatch. Seattle: University of Washington Press. *Richly illustrated collection of important essays.*

Kuipers, Joel C.

1998   Language, Identity, and Marginality in Indonesia: The Changing Nature of Ritual Speech on the Island of Sumba. *Language as a ritual device.*

Morris, Rosalind C.

1994   New Worlds from Fragments: Film, Ethnography, and the Representation of Northwest Coast Cultures. Boulder, CO: Westview Press. *An analysis of how ethnographic films, including* Box of Treasures, *have depicted the peoples of the Northwest Coast.*

CHAPTER 5

Psychology and Culture

A servant expresses surprise. Prambanan, Java, 9th century C.E. *(Credit: Karl G. Heider)*

HEADLINE ANTHROPOLOGY

PRESS WATCH

Some of the subjects discussed in this chapter have made their way into current news stories. For example:

◆ Yao Ming Yao, the new 7'5" center for the Houston Rockets, said that he did not dunk the ball in games in China because it would be considered disrespectful.
—New York Times, *August 4, 2002.*

◆ Emmanuel Anati, Italian archaeologist, says that prehistoric rock art "is a mirror of the workings of the human mind over the past 50,000 years."
—New York Times, *April 21, 2002.*

◆ Traditionally, Brazilians have considered Argentines as "arrogant and excessively formal," while Argentines have thought of Brazilians as "darker, happy-go-lucky inferiors wallowing in tropical indolence." Today, with both their political and economic systems in chaos, Argentine attitudes have changed, and they look to Brazil for leadership, both political and personal: "We need to learn from them how to be more cordial and less pedantic," said one Argentine.
—New York Times, *August 5, 2002.*

◆ A major problem is treating depression in Japan is the strong stigma attached to any sort of mental illness (as well as to psychiatrists who treat mental illness). Japanese feel that depression is a character fault, and that they should tough it out through "a cultural impulse known as 'gaman,' or the will to endure."
—New York Times, *August 10, 2002.*

In this chapter we look at psychological, or mental, processes as they are shaped in different cultural contexts. First, we look at overall psychological themes in culture, ways of thinking about the individual self, and psychological processes such as learning, cognition, and emotion. Then we proceed to examine sexuality across cultures.

We will find the biocultural models to be very important, even though we emphasize cultural construction. Also, even though we examine a single aspect of human behavior, we must be aware of the holistic aspect of what humans do and realize that psychologies do not float around unconnected, but instead are integral parts of all human behavior.

Psychology is a great umbrella term for many sorts of human behaviors and mental processes that show important cross-cultural variation:

Personality: a person's unique characteristics and behaviors
Cognition: ways of thinking, knowing, problem solving, and remembering

Perception: the organization and interpretation of sensory information
Emotion: a feeling state involving physiological, cognitive, and expressive
  components
Learning: the development of skills, capabilities, and behaviors
Mental illness: maladaptive or dysfunctional patterns of thinking and behaving

Psychologists, of course, have learned a tremendous amount about these processes, by looking both at commonalities and at individual differences.

Remember the paradigm (p. 37):

> In some ways all people are the same.
> In some ways some people are the same.
> In some ways each person is unique.

Although the tradition of psychological research has concentrated on the first and third conditions, anthropology, using the concept of culture, has focused on the second condition. At the moment, **psychological anthropology** is the most commonly used term for all of those different sorts of research into cultural variations in psychological processes. The basic question driving research in psychological anthropology can be formulated as follows: How does culture affect personality (or cognition, or perception, or emotions, or mental illness)? The answer to this research question comes from the description of some psychological processes in one culture or, comparatively, in several cultures. But the more profound theoretical question, which is still debated, goes back to the biocultural model (recall Chapter 2): What is the mix of biology and culture in any one of these processes?

There is often a certain tension between psychologists, who have been trained in a tradition that has had little use for the concept of culture, and anthropologists, whose most fundamental tradition is theories of culture. For a long time, communication between psychology and anthropology seemed like a one-way street, with anthropologists using some insights and discoveries of psychology while psychologists ignored anthropology. This situation has now changed, and many psychologists are paying attention to cultural variables in their research. If you are taking an Introductory psychology course today, your textbook probably has a cross-cultural section. If you could find an introductory psychology text from a couple of decades ago, however, it would probably not mention culture.

Compare the definitions of personality supplied by Victor Barnouw (1985), an anthropologist, and Lester Lefton (1994), a psychologist. Victor Barnouw defines *personality* as

> a more or less enduring organization of forces within the individual associated with a complex of fairly consistent attitudes, values, and modes of perception which account, in part, for the individual's consistency of behavior. (Barnouw, 1985:8)

Barnouw does not explicitly mention the environment or culture in his definition. Lefton, on the other hand, reflects the recent appreciation for the culture among psychologists by including a reference to the environment in his definition, which refers to *personality* as

> a set of relatively enduring behavioral characteristics and internal predisposi-
> tions that describe how a person reacts to the environment. (Lefton, 1994:426)

Yet even anthropologists would say the following about the study of psychology in a culture: Of all important aspects of culture, *subsistence* is the most obvious, *ritual* is the most photogenic, and *psychology* is the most elusive. Not incidentally, of the thousands of ethnographic films, a majority show rituals of some sort, some show subsistence activities, and practically none even hints at psychological issues. (As you will see, our film for this chapter is quite different from our other films.)

Yet an awareness of psychological differences between cultures or nations must be as old as thought. One of the oldest ideas around is the notion that the natural environment is not just part of the mix, but the crucial shaper of culture. This concept is called **environmental determinism.** Often, it has been pushed far beyond explaining basic economic patterns. In the fifth century B.C., Hippocrates tried to explain the differences between the personalities of Greeks and Persians (whom he called Asiatics) as the result of climate:

> And with regard to the pusillanimity and cowardice of the inhabitants, the prin-
> cipal reason why the Asiatics are more unwarlike and of more gentle disposition
> than the Europeans is, the nature of the seasons which do not undergo any
> great changes either to heat or cold or the like. . . . It is changes of all kinds
> which arouse the understanding of mankind, and do not allow them to get in to
> a torpid condition.

Another example of pushing environmental determinism far beyond economics came more than two millennia later. Thomas Jefferson, naturalist, archaeologist, and architect, spun out an elaborate account of environmental effect on personality. In a letter of September 2, 1785, he wrote:

> My idea of the characters of the several states:

In the North they are:	In the South they are:
cool	fiery
sober	voluptuary
laborious	indolent
persevering	unsteady
independent	independent
jealous of their own liberties, and just to those of others	zealous for their own liberties, but trampling on those of others
interested (tight fisted)	generous
chicaning	candid
superstitious and hypocritical in their religion	without attachment or pretensions to any religion but that of the heart

These characteristics grow weaker and weaker by gradation from North to South and South to North, insomuch that an observing traveler, without the aid of the quadrant, may always know his latitude by the character of the people among whom he finds himself.

Jefferson was speaking a bit tongue-in-cheek. In any case, such mechanical determinism is not convincing today. Both mechanical determinism and environmental determinism are marvelous, if wrong, statements of **folk ethnography,** or folk psychology. The notion that climate or other aspects of one's environment affect one's personality has failed to hold up under scrutiny. It bears some resemblance to astrology, which assumes that the positions of the planets at the time of one's birth determine one's personality. Both ideas are firmly believed by many (and most American newspapers carry a daily astrological column), but neither has scientific support.

CULTURE, PERSONALITY, AND THE SELF

Childhood

Many theories of human personality have emphasized the importance of early experience in shaping an individual's personality. In turn, these theories have stimulated ethnographic research on children. For example, John and Beatrice Whiting and their colleagues have long been carrying out cross-cultural studies with large samples of ethnographies backed up with on-site ethnographic research, in an effort to identify which childrearing practices can be reliably associated with other cultural traits.

John Whiting (1990) discusses one such logical chain that begins with the cross-cultural finding of two basic patterns of mother–infant contact. In some cultures, mothers and infants remain in close contact during the day and sleep together at night; in others, the infant spends most of its time in a crib or cradle, not actually touching the mother, and not sleeping with the mother. In the close-contact cultures, children are not separated from their mothers until they are several years old; in the crib and cradle cultures, they are separated from their mothers at birth.

Whiting suggests that the different caretaking arrangements have a major effect on the psychological development of a male. This influence does not necessarily come in the sexual area, as Freud might have suggested, but rather it occurs in terms of dependency and aggressiveness. In the first situation, the baby boy identifies closely with the mother for the years when he is in constant contact with her. When he is finally "weaned from her back," he faces a gender identity conflict that must be resolved. In many cultures, the resolution takes the form of a dramatic puberty rite often involving circumcision. For cradle or crib babies (all boys), who have been separated from constant contact with the mother since birth, the psychodynamics are quite different. Such cultures tend to lack the intense male initiation rites but do have beliefs in high gods or guardian spirits who substitute for the distant or missing parents. Thus, Whiting suggests, the contact/noncontact patterns in infancy are significantly correlated with the presence or absence of intense male initiation rites and beliefs in high gods or guardian spirits. This association seems to make sense in psychological terms. Whiting does not claim absolute determinism or invariable chains of cause and effect, but only general trends and statistically significant associations. His hypotheses have stimulated much fieldwork directed at the specific details of these early childhood dynamics.

Other anthropologists have turned to experiences in later life, rather than those confined to infancy, to identify significant cultural shaping of psychological patterns. Robert Paul, for example, has said,

> I believe everybody has sado-masochistic impulses and fantasies; but whether these end up being tapped directly by men as a source of motivation for participation in a life of war and raiding, or transformed by the defense of "reaction formation" into an institution of piety and non-violence like Tibetan monasticism depends on the subsequent cultural shaping and experience of middle childhood, adolescence, and beyond. (Paul, 1994:92–93)

Increasingly, anthropologists are studying childhood not so much for its developmental psychological implications, but rather to determine the political and economic effects of conflict on children (see, for example, Scheper-Hughes and Sargent, 1998). Alternatively, they may examine how children learn and use a language (Schieffelin and Ochs, 1986).

Margaret Mead and the Cultural Construction of Puberty and Gender

The 1920s and 1930s saw the first great surge of anthropological interest in psychological issues. Bronislaw Malinowski's seminal book *Argonauts of the Western Pacific* (1922) had staked out certain areas of interest for anthropology: fieldwork, ritual, economics, exchange, and social organization. Two years after this book was published, a young American woman from Columbia University in New York City named Margaret Mead began research in an area that Malinowski had neglected: sex and gender. These studies would later inspire many others to follow her lead. Out of Mead's work came a rather technical monograph that few would read (*Social Organization of Manu'a,* 1930) and a book that is still in print seventy years later, *Coming of Age in Samoa* (1928). This book popularized anthropology and made Mead famous. In this book, she investigated the cultural construction of puberty (coming of age) among Samoan youths.

At the time Mead began her research in Samoa, anthropologists were interested in exploring cultural diversity, and they had found much evidence of these differences—in language, religion, social structure, clothing, food, and so forth. It was generally assumed that sex and gender were so completely biological that cultural variation would be insignificant. Mead, however, found that this assumption was not the case. The prevailing view was that puberty was a time of turmoil and that the stress was purely biological and should be a universal characteristic of adolescence. This situation did not prove to be the case in Samoa, where Mead

Samoans boarding a bus. *(Credit: © Tony Perrottet/Omni-Photo Communications)*

found the transition from childhood to adulthood to be a fairly smooth one, with little of the upheaval that U.S. adolescents experience. It was clear to Mead that despite human biology, many aspects of behavior at puberty are culturally constructed (see Table 5.1).

Later, when Mead went to the Sepik River basin in New Guinea to study sex roles, she once again found diversity, not uniformity. Each of the three cultures that she studied had very different ideas of what it meant to be female and male. She found that the Arapesh women were similar to women in the United States—

TABLE 5.1   Mead's Paradigm on Puberty, Reformulated in Terms of Our Biocultural Model

Biological Givens	*Cultural Construction of Puberty*
In their early teens, *Homo sapiens* undergo massive physical and chemical changes. This transformation is called *becoming adult.*	In the United States in the 1920s, adolescence was a time of great emotional stress in the area of sexuality, which was very constrained. In Samoa in the 1920s, sexuality was freely expressed, and adolescence was a time of little stress.

generally gentle, nurturant, and nonviolent. What was surprising was that men exhibited the same traits. Violence and aggressiveness were considered unacceptable
behavior. The Mundugumor resembled the Arapesh in that there were no definable
differences in the behavior of the men and women. However, the dominant traits
among both men and women were completely the opposite of those of the Arapesh,
resembling the typical stereotype of a macho male: aggressiveness and violence.
Adults in general tended to be abusive or indifferent to their children, selfish, and
very sexual. In the third culture, the Tchambuli, Mead found sex-role differences,
but they were the reverse of ours. The women were in control, sexually dominant
and responsible for running the household and providing food for the family. They
tended to dress practically and showed a businesslike, common-sense approach to
life. The men, by contrast, contributed very little to the economic well-being of the
community. They were artistic, moody, and vain, spending most of the day painting, adorning themselves, and gossiping.

On the basis of her work with the three New Guinea groups, Mead concluded
that gender is culturally constructed (see Table 5.2):

> The material suggests that we may say that many, if not all, of the personality
> traits which we have called masculine or feminine are as lightly linked to sex as
> are the clothing, the manners, and the form of head-dress that a society at a
> given period assigns to either sex. (Mead, 1935:190)

By the time of Mead's death in 1978, she was a household name, the best-
known social scientist in the world. This status largely reflected her willingness to
bring her anthropological insights to bear on matters of public policy. After her
death, both her early research and her life were subjected to a critical scrutiny that
is usually reserved for politicians and movie stars.

Mead's brilliant insights were both her strength and her weakness. She never
became fluent in any of her field languages, but she could sense what was going on.
Her periods in the field were so brief that she gained little temporal perspective.
For instance, when Mead was with the Tchambuli (doing the three-culture study of
gender), the men were busily carving figures for the cult houses, and the women
were selling produce at markets. From these facts, Mead built a picture of passive
males and aggressive females into the Tchambuli construction of gender. When

TABLE 5.2   Mead's Paradigm on Gender, Reformulated in Terms of Our Biocultural Model

Biological Givens	*Cultural Construction of Gender*
Homo sapiens are male or female.	United States: Men are aggressive, women are nurturers.
	Tchambuli: Women are aggressive entrepreneurs, men are withdrawn artists.
	Arapesh: Both men and women are gentle nurturers.
	Mundugumor: Both men and women are aggressive.

Deborah Gewertz (1983) restudied the same people (now called *Chambri*), she learned that Mead's visit had coincided with an unusual historical event. The Chambri had been driven from their homes by enemy neighbors, had lived in exile as refugees, and then, just before Mead arrived, had been able to reclaim their old territory. Mead found them in the midst of reconstruction, the men rebuilding the cult houses while the women temporarily filled in for them at the markets.

Certainly, in her concern to develop the idea of cultural conditioning, Mead was attacking the notion that individual cultures are transmitted genetically—"that the minutiae of cultural behaviour are carried in the individual germ-plasm" (Mead, 1935:191). Her strong opposition to this form of biological determinism led her to a hostility toward any consideration that some cultural capabilities are found in the biological heritage of all *Homo sapiens*. But as the most effective proponent of anthropology for decades, she was instrumental in making the field what it is today.

Mead's Samoan work has been the target of numerous attacks and counterattacks that began shortly after her death in 1978 and show no signs of letting up (see Shankman, 1996; Freeman, 1999; Orans, 1996). Certainly ethnographic field methods as well as theories have developed and changed immeasurably since the 1920s when Mead did her pioneering research in Samoa. Nevertheless, many of the basic lessons that she taught, and even the biocultural model that, perhaps despite herself, underlies her research are still alive and well today.

From "National Culture" to Cultural Themes

Many attempts have been made to develop a way of describing the general psychological makeup of a people. We have previously seen how Herodotus in the 5th century B.C. and Thomas Jefferson 22 centuries later tried to achieve this goal. The attempt itself seems eminently reasonable. Our folk beliefs certainly have no doubt that "the English" are not the same as "the French" or that "Minnesotans" can be distinguished from "Texans." After all, they live in different places, speak differently, eat differently, drink differently, and play differently. So surely they *are* different in some basic psychological sense. As long as we were dealing with relatively homogeneous, relatively isolated tribes, about which most of us knew relatively little, that concept apparently worked well.

The phrase, **national character,** has been discarded. In part, it was rejected because it suggests a common cultural pattern for a nation, which is by definition a social entity, not necessarily a cultural one. The general idea of a **national culture** persists, however, and has resurfaced in many different forms.

Ruth Benedict and *Patterns of Culture*.   During those same years between the world wars when Margaret Mead and others were exploring psychology through fieldwork, Ruth Benedict, Mead's mentor at Columbia University, was developing a theoretical model of cultural patterning based on psychological traits. Her book *Patterns of Culture* (1934) was another landmark in anthropology.

The idea of cultures as interrelated wholes was not new, and many different attempts had been made to discover basic principles of patterning. Economically oriented scholars, for example, emphasized subsistence strategies, and this focus produced the categories of foragers, horticulturalists, agriculturalists, and pastoralists. Another approach, which emphasized political organization, produced the set of bands, tribes, chiefdoms, and kingdoms. Benedict gave primacy to psychological or personality features. She looked at three cultures (none of which she herself had studied) from a psychological standpoint and described their dominant personality configurations:

> The Zuni, a Pueblo culture in New Mexico, where people were aesthetic and mild, she labeled *Apollonian* (drawing on Nietzsche's use of Greek prototypes).
> The Kwakiutl, now called Kwa Kwaka' Wakw, of British Columbia, where people were aggressive and competitive, she called *Dionysian* (again, after Nietzsche).
> The Dobu, an island participating in the Kula Ring off the eastern tip of New Guinea, where people lived in fear of witchcraft, she called *paranoid.*

The assumption that each culture produced a dominant personality configuration seemed to hold. In a sense, this model was Benedict's attempt to elevate folk ethnography—those stereotypes that people hold about other people—to a science. Very soon, however, other anthropologists, who knew those particular cultures much better than Benedict did, joined the discussion, saying that things were not so simple and uniform.

At first, the criticisms of Benedict dealt with the idea that, in her desire to formulate a single consistent pattern of culture, she had overlooked other, discordant elements. Helen Codere, taking her cue from Franz Boas, from whom Benedict had gotten most of her information about the Kwa Kwaka' Wakw, noted that in addition to the themes of "vigor, zest, violence, jealousy of prerogatives, acquisitiveness, competitiveness, the will to superiority and self-glorification, and great sensitivity to shame" that Benedict had described, the Kwa Kwaka' Wakw were amiable, sociable, and cooperative (1966:7). Codere, in a famous article on "The Amiable Side of Kwakiutl Life" (1956), pointed out that the play potlatch, which was marked by "funmaking" and even satire, took place in the midst of the winter rituals. (See also Barnouw, 1985:66–71).

More recently, Stanley Walens has made a different sort of reinterpretation of the Kwa Kwaka' Wakw worldview on the basis of a careful examination of the literature, especially Boas's work. Walens suggests that Benedict is wrong when she interprets certain speeches or behavior by tribal chiefs as evidence for megalomania. The chief is not displaying individual psychological behavior, Walens proposes, but rather acting out a social role following the demands of rhetorical style and the hierarchical social organization. Likewise, when the chief displays great anger at being insulted at a feast, it is because the insult affects his entire social group (the *numaym*). To be sure, anger is involved, but it is a socially scripted performance on behalf of the group, not individually felt anger. Similarly, Walens reinterprets intense ritual dancing, suggesting that the Kwa Kwaka' Wakw seek not the transcendental feelings of ecstasy but the transcendental feelings of superhuman self-control and purity that characterize feelings of sacredness. The transcendantal feelings the Kwakiutl seek are not in the least Dionysian, but are Apollonian. The Kwakiutl seek not excess but order. (Walens, 1981:41)

Another attempt to discern a national character occurred in World War II, when many American anthropologists used their skills in military intelligence. This situation involved urgent applied anthropology. The U.S. military recognized that in fighting Japanese troops they were encountering a very different culture that they did not understand. They also recognized that they needed answers to some cultural puzzles. (The same is probably true of all American wars—even the Civil War between North and South—but the 1940s marked the first time that cultural anthropology was openly enlisted in the war effort.)

One of the most immediate problems was posed by Japanese soldiers who had been taken prisoner in the South Pacific by American troops. Instead of giving only the standard information of name, rank, and serial number, they willingly told their captors all that they knew about the disposition, morale, and plans of the Japanese forces. This turnabout astonished the Americans, who desperately wanted to know what was going on and, especially, whether they could trust this information. Ruth Benedict was able to explain the behavior in terms of Japanese ideas of obligation and loyalty. As strongly as those soldiers were bound to Emperor and country, once they were captured they might as well have been dead. They had lost their standing as social beings and no longer had a place in the web of social obligation. They therefore talked, and yes, their information could be trusted.

Benedict summed up the results of her study of the Japanese prisoners of war in *The Chrysanthemum and the Sword,* published the year after the war ended (1946). She used the holistic model of her earlier studies to characterize the Japanese personality, but now, to accommodate the complexities of Japan, she described two dominant patterns. One was the aesthetic ("the chrysanthemum"), manifested in Japanese art, haiku poetry, and Zen practices such as flower arranging and the tea ceremony. The other was the military ("the sword"), exemplified by the samurai warrior and later the kamikaze pilot.

National character studies are no longer particularly important in anthropology for various reasons. Perhaps most important, the problems of grand generalizing soon became apparent. Each of these nations included so much cultural variation that any statements were vulnerable to contradiction and difficult to verify. Nevertheless, it is difficult to avoid the feeling that there is something like "national character" that can offer a partial answer to questions such as "Why did Japanese prisoners of war betray their comrades?" or, in the cases that follow, "Why did they kill?"

Why Did They Kill? The Cambodian Case.   Cambodians (or Khmer) were known as gentle, friendly, artistic people and, like other mainland Southeast Asians, were Theravada Buddhists who valued all forms of life. So the events of 1975–1979, which occurred when the Khmer Rouge (Red Khmer) ruled the country, took the world by surprise. The Khmer Rouge emptied the cities and systematically murdered and starved to death priests, intellectuals, former government officials, and the country's entire middle class. In the end, perhaps 2 million people out of a total population of only 8 million were murdered. (An American film, *The Killing Fields,* dramatized these events.) Why did they kill? These acts were often called genocide, although perhaps fratricide would be a more accurate description. To say that the Khmer Rouge killed for ideological reasons does not seem adequate, for others who had been trained in the same communist theology in Paris did not act so ruthlessly.

Alexander Laban Hinton has looked at psychological features that contributed to the killings (1996, 1998). At least part of the explanation lies in very general psychological principles. Another part lies in Khmer culture—specifically, in Khmer cultural models or schemas that are so deeply embedded that they have retained their power to influence behavior through many different political regimes.

Although many foreign observers in the past commented on Khmer gentleness, Hinton suggests that Khmer culture included both a "gentle ethic" and a "violent ethic." The gentle ethic dominated interaction between familiar people within the face-to-face community. This ethic may be common in small communities generally, but in the Cambodian instance it was strongly reinforced by the principles of Theravada Buddhism. Harmony and knowing one's place in the hierarchy were strong values. Likewise, the violent ethic had long been part of Cambodian culture. Hinton suggests that it had roots in Hinduism, which, like Buddhism, came to Cambodia in the first millennium A.D. and manifested itself over the centuries in wars against other social groups as well as ruthless destruction of domestic enemies. During the reign of the Khmer Rouge, this violent ethic was turned against the regime's perceived enemies, who were identified as others even though they were fellow Cambodians.

Around the world, similar ideas are held by many peoples. The process of **Othering,** where people turn some category of humans into "The Other," dehumanizes those individuals. Psychologically, this perception of outsiders makes it easier to treat them badly, even to enslave or kill them. In Cambodia, the Khmer Rouge attacked its political opponents by deliberately manipulating these schemas so that Khmer were prepared to kill even family members who had been identified as enemies of the people.

In addition to taking advantage of this widespread process of Othering, the Khmer Rouge were able to play on very specific aspects of Khmer culture (Hinton, 1998). Khmer society has long been hierarchical, with social rankings carefully delineated. Even the language reinforces that stratification, for it has dozens of different pronouns that precisely calibrate the difference in status between people. These rankings are relatively flexible, however, and a person can rise or fall in the hierarchy. The opinions of other people are crucial in this process. Indeed, the Khmer speak of *mukh,* which Hinton loosely translates as "a sociocentric self-image that is based on the evaluations of others and shifts along an axis of honor and shame" (1998:101).

Certainly, none of these cultural features alone would turn the Khmer into killers of their own people. The Khmer Rouge, however, skillfully played on their

Cambodian cultural values. They commanded their recruits to execute opponents of the regime in group settings, where both their respect for hierarchy and fear of public shame came strongly into play. In this way, they strengthened the violent ethic and, by suppressing Buddhism and the village organizations, undermined the gentle ethic. Executions took place in public, and, in horrible obedience to their own values, the Khmer became murderers.

In his analysis, Hinton goes beyond simply explaining the killings as obedience to fanatical Maoism. By drawing on the concept of cultural themes consisting of shared psychological traits, he has advanced our understanding of such extreme behavior. Consider the many attempts to account for Nazism and the Holocaust (see Ingham, 1996:216–220). Recently, Daniel Goldhagen has tried to explain the Holocaust as a result of pervasive and extreme German antisemitism (1996). Although Goldhagen is a political scientist, he used the anthropological concept of cultural model, or schema, to understand the Holocaust. His work is an important example of how other disciplines have been able to use anthropological insights. As Goldhagen says,

> The study of Germans and their antisemitism before and during the Nazi period must be approached as an anthropologist would a previously unencountered preliterate people and their beliefs, leaving behind especially the preconception that Germans were in every ideational realm just like our ideal notions of ourselves. (Goldhagen, 1996:45)

Goldhagen concludes that Germans had long held a cultural schema of antisemitism—in fact, not just antisemitism, but "eliminational antisemitism" that justified the killing of Jews. He rejects the possibility that only a few fanatical Nazis were involved or that masses of Germans were coerced to kill against their consciences. Carrying out the Holocaust demanded that many tens of thousands of ordinary Germans be willing to kill Jews. The Nazis, in turn, were able to take advantage of that cultural schema.

The definitive history of the Spanish Inquisition by Henry Kamen, another historian who is asking these anthropological questions about general cultural themes, closes with these words of despair:

> Even when all explanations have been offered, the questions remain. How could a society as apparently tolerant as Castile, in which the three great faiths of the West had coexisted for centuries and into which the mediaeval Inquisition had never penetrated, change its ideology in the fifteenth century, against the instincts of many great men in both Church and state? How could a clergy and population that had never lusted for blood except in war (Queen Isabella thought even bullfighting was too gory) gaze placidly upon the burning alive of scores of their fellow Spaniards for an offense—prevarication in religion—that had never hitherto been a crime? How could the Spanish people—who were the first Europeans to broaden their vision by travelling the oceans and opening up the New World—accept without serious opposition the mental restrictions proposed by the Inquisition? The preceding pages have tried to offer the elements

of an answer, but it is in the nature of the inquisitorial phenomenon that no answer can match the complexity of the questions. (Kamen, 1997:320)

The Importance of Cultural Themes.   In the years since Ruth Benedict first popularized the concept of "patterns of culture," anthropologists have tended to turn toward a search for the major psychological themes of a culture, those basic principles by which everyone plays out his or her life, whether in accordance with the themes of the culture or in conflict with them. The focus has shifted to those themes that are recognized by the people themselves as important, rather than categories imposed from the outside like Benedict's Apollonian/Dionysian/ paranoid characterizations. In short, this trend features a turn from etic to emic concepts.

Thus anthropologists have examined culture by focusing on a key concept or a pair of opposites. Jane Bachnik and others (1994), for example, have analyzed the Japanese cultural theme of inside and outside (*uchi* and *soto*) as it is manifested in speech, in fiction, and in thinking about the world. They say that the Japanese think about themselves in these terms. The private, inside behavior is kept quite separate from the outside, public behavior. This is not to say that uchi and soto are so Japanese that only the Japanese can understand the concepts. Rather, uchi/soto, or inside/outside, is an especially salient opposition in the Japanese construction of the world and the self.

In other cases, anthropologists are drawn to comparisons of two different cultures that seem to exhibit opposing cultural themes.

Peaceful Versus Fierce.   The Yanomamo, as described by Napoleon Chagnon and as shown in many of Timothy Asch's films, are certainly volatile and aggressive. In the early editions of his case study, Chagnon used the subtitle *The Fierce People.* (He dropped it in the fourth edition because the word *fierce* implies an animallike quality to many Spanish and Portuguese speakers, and he does not want to further compromise the Yanomamo in the eyes of the national governments.)

Fights, often of a serious nature, are frequent within Yanomamo villages, and villages are in constant danger of attack. Men fight, and women encourage them. The introduction of shotguns, which are supposedly used only for hunting, has escalated the violence. But Yanomamo people do not embody pure aggression. Some who have known the Yanomamo from other areas have questioned Chagnon's emphasis on male violence, and some of Asch's films do show a gentle side to these people. Chagnon is careful to explain that not all Yanomamo are aggressive all the time, contrasting some leaders who are habitually violent with others who maintain their positions through more subtle means.

The Dani, on the other hand, seemed to me in many ways the opposite of the Yanomamo. Despite their constant warfare, in which people are killed, the general tone of their life is calm and relaxed. Fights within the group are rare, and confrontation is avoided. Even war is not carried out in a spirit of anger. It is more like deer hunting in the United States, in which the hunter tries to kill but without aggressive emotion. When I wrote the case study on the Dani, I chose the subtitle

Peaceful Warriors to contrast with Chagnon's *The Fierce People* and to emphasize this apparent contradiction in Dani life.

Individualism Versus Groupism. Anthropologists have gone beyond Benedict in exploring themes of Japanese culture, as have many writers. Americans, in particular, find Japan fascinating, perhaps because its cultural emphasis on **groupism** is so foreign to the American obsession with **individualism.** Indeed, Western interest in Japan has produced art and literature that explores Japanese character and culture more or less explicitly. For example, there is Pierre Loti's *Madame Chrysanthème,* a romantic novel (1888). John Luther Long's short story *Madam Butterfly* (1898) was turned into a stage play and then in 1904 made into an opera by Puccini; it also had echoes in the 1990 play *M. Butterfly.* James Michener's 1954 novel *Sayonara* became a popular film starring Marlon Brando (1957). Gilbert and Sullivan's comic opera *The Mikado* (1885) and James Clavell's novel *Shogun* (1975) were also based on Japanese culture. Robert Whiting, although not an anthropologist, used the cultural themes of group membership (in contrast to American individualism) to analyze Japanese baseball in his entertaining book *The Chrysanthemum and the Bat* (1977). Michael Crichton, a novelist who had majored in anthropology as an undergraduate at Harvard, based his best-selling novel (and later film) *Rising Sun* (1992) on cultural themes of individualism and groupism in the corporate cultures of the United States and Japan. (The novel is good ethnography, but its politics have been criticized as Japan-bashing.)

Each society is made up of individuals or selfs, but whether each self should strive for autonomy or try to be a team player in the social group is a matter of cultural construction. The dominant American conception of the self is as an independent, autonomous individual who is not dependent on another. Children are taught independence, and too much dependence is a matter for concern. In Japan, the same idea of the autonomous individual is not valued, and individuals are taught to be dependent members of the group. The Japanese psychiatrist Takeo Doi (1971) has written about the concept of *amae*—a sort of dependence of child on parent, of guest on host, of employee on boss. Amae is highly valued in Japan but not approved of in the United States.

The difference between baseball in the United States and baseball in Japan reflects the basic cultural themes of the two cultures (Whiting, 1977). Although the formal rules of baseball are the same in the two countries, the manner of play—indeed, the whole organization of the game—is shaped by the culture. Japanese players are expected to be totally dedicated to the group—the team—and to subordinate their personal interests to those of their team. The sacrifice bunt, a strategy in which a batter intentionally risks being put out (and having a lowered batting average) to advance a base-running teammate, is rare in the United States but common in Japan. Free agency, in which a star player can change teams for a higher salary, is routine in the American game but considered scandalous in Japan.

Little cross-cultural experiments occur whenever a Japanese major league team hires an American player. The frictions that often arise in such cases have little to do

Hiromi Makihara of the Yomiuri Giants receives the MVP award during the Japanese World Series. *(Credit: Ronald C. Modra)*

with skill or performance and much to do with different cultural expectations. The 1992 movie *Mr. Baseball* plays on these themes as it follows an American professional baseball player's cultural mishaps as he tries to survive in Japanese baseball.

The power of groupism in many cultures has been particularly striking to anthropologists from the United States, for late-20th-century American culture is strikingly individualistic. Robert Bellah, a sociologist whose Ph.D. dissertation was on Japanese religion, organized a team research project that looked at the "habits of the heart," the customs of white, middle-class Americans in the late 1970s and early 1980s. The researchers concluded,

> Individualism lies at the very core of American culture. . . . We believe in the dignity, indeed the sacredness of the individual. Anything that would violate our right to think for ourselves, judge for ourselves, make our own decisions, live our lives as we see fit, is not only morally wrong, it is sacrilegious. (Bellah et al., 1985:142)

Francis L. K. Hsu, who grew up in China, studied anthropology under Malinowski, and was a professor at Northwestern University and President of the American Anthropological Association, has written about the American theme of rugged individualism:

> Most individuals in all societies around the world may be self-sufficient. That is to say, the individual is able to take care of his own physical and mental needs. But American rugged individualism means that one is not only self-

sufficient as a matter of fact but he must strive toward it as a militant ideal. (Hsu, 1983:4)

Both Hsu and the Bellah team recognized that the formulation of groupism versus individualism, as valuable as it is, cannot be taken as an absolute either/or dichotomy. The most individualistic person may have some committment to some group, while in the most group-oriented cultures, some people are encouraged to act individualistically. Despite the exceptions and countercurrents, this idea remains a powerful dimension of contrast. In Chapter 8, we shall see how it plays out in marriage, differentiating arranged marriages from love marriages.

The Vietnamese film for this chapter, *How to Behave,* serves as a running commentary on the same ideas, praising the themes of groupism ("kindness") and using leprosy as a metaphor for those who are cut off from society. This film, made by Vietnamese for Vietnamese audiences, provides an inside, emic exploration of these basic psychological principles of Vietnamese culture. Though no anthropologist was involved in the filming, it offers a remarkably anthropological-like examination of cultural themes and national character.

FOCUS CULTURE

Cultural Themes in Vietnam

OVERVIEW

Location: On the mainland of Southeast Asia, Vietnam extends south from China a long, narrow S-curve, bordered by Cambodia and Laos to the west and the South China Sea to the east.

Geography: Tropical with monsoons. Thinly populated forested mountains in the west; densely populated delta regions in the north and south, which are the chief agricultural areas; and coastal lowlands, where rice is raised and fishing is an important industry.

Population: 74,000,000 live in Vietnam. Many live in Cambodia and overseas, including about 500,000 in the United States.

Language: Part of the Austro-Asiatic language family, related to Cambodian with tones and vocabulary resulting from Thai influence. It is the only national language on the Asian mainland except Malay that is written in a Roman script.

Religion: Mainly Mahayana Buddhism mixed with Confucianism; many Roman Catholics, and many smaller religions

Economy: Mostly intensive agricultural (70 percent of workers are farmers), with some fishing

Sociopolitical Organization: Socialist government tightly controlled by the Communist Party

On a map Vietnam appears to be part of Southeast Asia, forming the easternmost coastal part of that land mass. Over the last two millennia, however, it has usually been more tightly linked to China than to its neighbors to the west.

The two great river valleys—the Red River to the north around Hanoi and the Mekong in the south around Ho Chih Minh City (formerly Saigon)—had quite different histories. The center of classic Vietnamese culture was in the North. The South was sparsely settled, mainly by Cham, an ethnic group speaking an Austronesian language closely related to Malay and Minangkabau. Only in the 19th century, when the French undertook extensive drainage projects to convert swamps to rice fields, did large numbers of Vietnamese move into the South.

While village agriculture continues even today, the French developed large rubber plantations when they arrived in the 1800s. Many Vietnamese who lived and worked on these plantations were influenced by the French, and many of the cities that grew up during this time had a strong French flavor.

The history of Vietnam has been one of war, rebellion, and colonization for 2,000 years. During most of that time, Vietnam was under the control of the Chinese or the French. The country has known more war in the past half-century than most nations have experienced during their entire existence. The First Vietnam War was fought for independence from the French from 1945 to 1954. The Second Vietnam War pitted the North, which received some assistance from the Soviet Union, against the South, which was actively aided by the United States and its allies, from 1965 to 1975. The Third Vietnam War involved the invasion of Cambodia by Vietnamese from 1975 to 1985. And this litany of warfare does not include the country's sporadic border conflicts with China. Today, however, Vietnam is at peace and rapidly increasing its economic ties with the United States.

Although little anthropological research on Vietnam has been published, we do have village studies from both the South (Hickey, 1964) and the North (Luong, 1992). Robert McNamara, the U.S. Secretary of Defense under Presidents Kennedy and Johnson, also wrote a recent book on Vietnam. In his book, he claims that one reason for the American failure in the Second Vietnam War was ignorance of Vietnamese culture among U.S. government officials (1995:322). McNamara was concerned with winning the American–Vietnamese war, but his belated insight could well be extended to the overall American–Vietnamese relations after World War II.

Today, with the help of such young scholars as Hy V. Luong and Neil L. Jamieson, the gaps in our knowledge of this culture are slowly being closed.

Traditionally, Vietnam was an agricultural society built on strong family ties, with extended families living together and worshipping their ancestors. The family, with its obligations of filial piety and wifely obedience, was the essential building block of Vietnamese society. As Jamieson said about the annual Tet, or New Year's celebration, "Celebrating Tet with one's family was an essential part of what it meant to be Vietnamese, to be a complete human being" (1993:28).

The traditional village was Neo-Confucian and Mahayana Buddhist (not the Theravada Buddhism of the rest of mainland Southeast Asia). These religions stressed the importance of a balance between a more male *yang* principle and a more female *yin* principle. Jamieson sees recent Vietnam as oscillating between the yang subsystem of Chinese-oriented Confucianism, with its rigid hierarchical principles based on court life, and the yin subsystem of village-based Buddhism, a more egalitarian, village-based pattern (1993:15). That is, neither subsystem was "the" real, authentic Vietnam, but both were variations played on the same basic values. According to Jamieson, several fundamental themes of Vietnamese culture persisted throughout all the surface changes:

Ly encompassed the idea that there was a basic order to the universe.
Hieu means filial piety, the moral debt (*on*) that children owe to parents.

Urban street scene in Vietnam. *(Credit: © Andrew Holbrooke/The Image Works)*

De, another of the essential Confucian relationships, consisted of the proper behavior between brothers. Younger brothers were to be submissive to their nurturing older brothers (and similarly women were to be subservient to men—their fathers, brothers, and husbands).

Nghia is the correct behavior to fulfill the Confucian obligations.

Nhan and *tinh* were more Buddhist virtues, somewhat opposed to the obligatory Confucian obligations-cum-responsibilities already mentioned. They implied compassion. According to Jamieson, they "provided an emotional balance to the rationality of righteousness embodied in *nghia*" (1993:20).

Clearly, we have come a long way from Ruth Benedict's attempts in the 1930s to characterize a culture by a single classical Greek allusion (Dionysian, Apollonian). Rather than forcing a culture into one of our patterns, Jamieson has chosen to examine the Vietnamese's concepts about their own culture and to translate and explain those concepts to us in terms of a dynamic oscillation between two ideal, but never realized patterns. In the film clip for this chapter, we shall see how the Vietnamese themselves draw on these concepts. ♦

Privacy and the Self

Traditionally, anthropologists have tended to examine and compare the personality traits that are found in individuals in particular cultures. In the 1990s anthropologists seem to be more concerned about examining subjective views of the self, and particularly the cultural construction of the self. Less concerned about determining the bundle of features that make up the personality, current research on the self emphasizes the various dimensions that define the ways in which individuals think about themselves and others. This emphasis on the emic, or native, ways of thinking about personhood distinguishes our contemporary emphasis on the self from the earlier focus on personality. The phrases **indigenous psychologies** (Heelas and Lock, 1981) and **ethnopsychologies** (White and Kirkpatrick, 1985) have been used to refer to this perspective.

Anthropologists who studied personality often used standard procedures such as the Rorschach ink blot test or Thematic Apperception Tests to elicit reactions from informants. These tests had been widely used on European and American subjects, so there was a base of data and theory to which the reactions from people of other cultures could be compared. But with the shift from cross-cultural comparisons of personality features to a concern with culture-specific understandings of person and self, the use of standardized testing has diminished.

One area of current research focuses on the cultural construction of privacy. In any society, whether the emphasis is on individualism or groupism, the self is constantly interacting with other individuals. In this interaction, the boundary of the self becomes an issue. This boundary defines privacy: what is reserved to the self and what is available to others. We can speak of a cultural construction of privacy—that is, the norms that restrict access to a person are cultural norms. Different cultures set the boundary at different places. Clothing and architecture are among the more obvious ways in which the cultural boundaries of privacy are signaled and maintained. Americans, accustomed to clothing that covers and bedroom doors that close, would find Yanomamo life disconcertingly public, for the Yanomamo have little clothing and no walls, not to mention doors, and so seem to have no privacy at all. Indonesians who visit the United States are surprised at the public nature of sexuality when they see heterosexual couples holding hands on the street or embracing on the grass. Americans who visit Indonesian villages, by contrast, are struck by how much public defecation and urination they see. On the whole, Americans and Indonesians have opposite notions of privacy in relation to sex and elimination. But, as Ernestine Friedl has pointed out (1994), the act of sexual intercourse is almost universally a private matter.

The philosopher Ferdinand David Schoeman (1992:14ff) suggested distinguishing between two sorts of privacy norms. One sort limits access to standard behaviors (elimination, sex, eating, salaries, and the like) and to body parts (genitalia, breasts, faces, ankles, and the like). The other sort limits access to behavior that is private, personal, and expressive. (Contemporary U.S. political debates focus on this second sort, in the name of freedom or autonomy.) Anthropologists frequently comment on the first sort of privacy in passing, especially as they inadvertently stumble on unexpected boundaries of privacy.

Robert Murphy wrote a classic paper on the veils worn by Tuareg men (1964). The Tuareg are Muslim pastoralists and long-range traders of the Sahara Desert. Day and night, at home and abroad, the men—but not the women—conceal their faces except for their eyes with a carefully adjusted veil. Murphy explained the veil in relation to a feature of Tuareg social organization. To an unusual degree, Tuareg marry within their own group (a practice called *endogamy*). Therefore, a Tuareg man interacts equally with his own blood kin and his in-laws. They are the same people. If he marries a cousin, his father's brother is also his wife's father. The Tuareg has a problem: Does he deal with the man as an intimate uncle or a distant father-in-law? The particular Tuareg solution is to wear a veil, keeping a formal distance from everyone.

LEARNING STYLES

In the previous section, we referred to the cultural construction of various psychological behaviors. This construction necessarily depends on learning, as do all aspects of culture. However, just as diversity has been a common theme in our study of culture, so we will encounter cultural differences in styles of learning.

The Cycle of Learning

John W. M. Whiting used a model of learning in which children learn from adults in culture-perpetuating circles as the children grow into adults, who teach children, and so on. It is not a closed system, so Whiting's model takes into account how various factors influence and change what is learned. An alternative model emphasizes how much is learned from other children, not adults. Iona and Peter Opie, who made an exhaustive study of children's games in Great Britain (1969), emphasized how much of the culture is passed from child to child in a sort of secret underground pool of knowledge, to be quite forgotten by the individual children as they grow into adulthood. They distinguish between nursery rhymes, which are known, controlled, approved, and told by adults, and the "school rhyme," which escapes the notice of adults altogether. In fact, anthropologists such as Marjorie H. Goodwin have slipped into this secret world to study the speech and play of children (1990).

I was struck among the Dani by the complete lack of explicit teaching. There were no schools, but I was prepared for that absence. But even when a child helped his or her parents or sat at an adult's elbow watching a task, the adult never explained it or instructed the child. I was disappointed. I had tried to eavesdrop, my pencil and notebook handy, to get a quick idea of what was going on. But no one explained anything. The child just watched. I come from a culture that explains, instructs, teaches, and advises, in words spoken and printed. Whatever it is, there is a class to teach it, an expert to explain it, a book to describe it. But not among the Dani.

Teaching and Learning Styles

Jean Lave has described two quite different styles of teaching and learning (1990, 1991). One is the formal, school-based verbal lectures and testing of abstracted knowledge reflecting a **culture of acquisition** based on the theory that a student acquires culture as a body of knowledge. You are engaged in this type of learning at this moment, and you will soon be asked to write out answers to some questions as a test of your successful acquisition of that body of knowledge that we call cultural anthropology. Lave's other sort of teaching and learning style is based on a theory of **situated practice** that assumes that

> processes of learning and understanding are socially and culturally constituted, and that what is to be learned is integrally implicated in the forms in which it is appropriated. (Lave, 1990:310)

The Dani, for example, have learned their own culture in this way—in an informal manner, practicing the activity in context, learning from those who know "by doing it with them as legitimate peripheral participants" (Lave, 1990:311). No lectures, no final exams.

Lave studied how tailors' apprentices in West Africa learned their trade (1990). She used the term **situated learning** to describe the process, as the apprentices are situated in the context of doing the activity. They sit with the master tailors, watching them work. There are no formal classes. Gradually, however, the apprentices take on the simpler tasks such as ironing the finished suits. This duty gives them an intuitive grasp of the end product. From there they work backward, doing finishing tasks, then sewing pieces of cloth together, and finally cutting the cloth.

Minimal verbal instruction is provided; rather, the apprentices learn by observing what is going on around them in the tailor shops.

You are now learning about anthropology in a most unembodied, nonsituated manner. You hear lectures; you read what is written on the chalkboard and on these pages. The ethnographic films are a way to get you situated in another culture. Ideally, each anthropology class would let you spend some time with the Balinese, the Dani, the !Kung, and the Japanese and even take part in their work. That type of education would be situated learning.

COGNITION

Cognition generally refers to how people think, which, undoubtedly, has an effect on their learning styles. Anthropologists are concerned with how different cultures organize knowledge and what meanings they give to it. We may begin with sets of labels and wind up with symbolic meanings. To take a very simple example: All cultures can see stars in the night sky, but different cultures see different groupings, or constellations of stars, and attribute different meanings to stars and groups.

Cognitive Style and Intelligence

Shirley Brice Heath (1983) studied two neighboring but separate communities in the U.S. Southeast, looking at how children were taught. She described two quite different cognitive styles, or ways of thinking about the world. In the white community, the children were constantly being quizzed with questions demanding answers of knowledge, questions whose answers the adult questioner knew. In the black community, children were posed questions that had no particular right answers, questions that evoked creative responses. The implications of this difference became painfully apparent when the different children faced intelligence or aptitude tests that were structured in the mode of the first of these two cognitive styles. The white kids were home free; the black kids floundered in an alien cognitive style.

Intelligence is difficult enough to talk about in our own culture. It is much more problematic cross-culturally. When I was with the Dani, I felt intuitively that some people were highly intelligent, some were really slow, and most were scattered in the middle, but I had no idea how to demonstrate this distribution. We are accustomed to thinking in terms of intelligence quotient (IQ), a single dimensional measure of intelligence in which 100 is the average and people's scores fall in a normal curve on either side of 100. Because of the problems posed by culture-specific knowledge questions and by the culture-specific cognitive styles of the set of the questions, however, there is no reason to assume that these tests have pan-cultural validity.

Howard Gardner has proposed a theory of multiple intelligences (1983, 1993), which makes a compelling argument that intelligence is not a single, unitary skill. Rather, **multiple intelligences** exist. Gardner suggests that at least seven can be identified: musical, bodily-kinesthetic, logical-mathematical, linguistic, spatial, interpersonal, and intrapersonal (1993:17–26). Most of us would probably measure high on some and low on others. It seems likely that we could say that most cultures emphasize some sorts of intelligences but neglect others.

On the whole, anthropologists watch the vehement but inconclusive debate over intelligence and intelligence testing in the United States and remain agnostics, simply not trying to work it out across cultural boundaries. Alan Hanson, an anthropologist who has studied testing in the United States, wrote of "our addiction to testing" and described how it "influences both society and our selves as socially defined persons" (1993:1). (Hanson may or may not be on your final exam.)

You have probably already taken some intelligence-based tests, most likely several versions of the SAT, and you may well soon be taking GREs and the like. On the assumption that the scores on these tests are accurate predictors of future success in college or graduate school, admissions officers use them as gatekeeping devices. In Hanson's "institutional analysis," he examined the actual effects of such testing. One function is to define the person. (On the day I wrote this page, I heard a friend refer in amazement to a high school senior: "Joe has a 1500 SAT and he didn't apply to a single college!" Joe was being defined by his SAT.) Another function is control of individuals. We are given

> tests to determine if we have done our homework, if we can drive competently, if we have taken drugs, if we have lied, if we were at the scene of a crime, if we have contracted a sexually transmitted disease, and so on ad infinitum. (Hanson, 1993:4)

In fact, such tests are not unknown in other cultures. The film for Chapter 11 (on norms and conflict resolution), *The Cows of Dolo Ken Paye,* shows the Kpelle of Liberia using a hot knife ordeal, a sort of magical augury, to discover who had committed a crime. In any case, we in the United States have certainly far outreached other cultures in our enthusiasm for testing.

DOING ANTHROPOLOGY

A New Intelligence Test

You may have taken an IQ test, and you may even know your score. But now try to judge yourself on Gardner's multiple intelligences, as they are explained in the following list by Kersten Bayt Priest. To imitate the standard IQ tests, you might give yourself 100 if you rate as average on a type of intelligence, and so on. Do not get carried away, however. At the end, you will be tempted to sum or average the total. Think: What would that aggregate number actually tell you?

1. Musical intelligence: The ability to access the sensed world most effectively by translating events, thoughts, and feelings into rhythm and sounds; producing music by composing, singing, and/or playing on an instrument.

2. Bodily-kinesthetic intelligence: The ability to imagine and perform movement with the body through dance, sports, and/or other acts that require the smooth integration of the body's part in an activity (for example, sewing, painting, hunting, fishing, woodwork, pottery making).

3. Logical-mathematical intelligence: The ability to internally visualize and manipulate symbolic qualities, quantities, and distances, thereby using the mind as a tool to interpret realities and solve puzzles/problems in the material world. Note that this ability is not limited to paper-and-pencil applications of these skills, for individuals can be very good at everyday quantitative estimations of such basic things as comparative grocery prices.

4. Linguistic intelligence: The ability to accurately hear and decode spoken sounds and words; the ability to carefully read, comprehend language, and write effectively (that is, the oral version of this "intelligence" is demonstrated in public speaking, storytelling, and elaborate joking).

5. Spatial intelligence: The ability to look at physical objects, mentally visualize them in their three-dimensional component parts, and understand how they function (for example, the auto mechanic who can take an engine completely apart and put it all back together again so that it works).

6. Interpersonal intelligence: The ability to interact with other people, understand them, and intuit correctly what is required to communicate effectively (for example, a friend who seems to "really understand" you, some politicians . . .).

7. Intrapersonal intelligence: The ability to think introspectively about oneself, extrapolate about others, and identify uniquely insightful ideas about human realities (for example, poets, philosophers, counselors).

Next, perform a cross-cultural thought experiment. Take one or more of our focus cultures and try to work out in which of these "multiple intelligences" might they be strongest or weakest. (Be wary of overgeneralizations, for just as you and your closest friends undoubtedly vary on these dimensions, so would a group of Dani or Balinese or Kwa Kwaka' Wakw.)   ♦

Organization of Knowledge

Much anthropological research has been concerned with categorization: How do people divide the world into units? From a linguistic standpoint, the emphasis has been on the words that are used to label the categories. From a psychological standpoint, the emphasis has been on the cognitive processes, the structure of the categories, the cognitive processes of categorization, and the ways in which the categories affect behavior.

All cultures make categories. The Argentine essayist Jorge Luis Borges wrote a wonderful story, "Funes the Memorius," in which he imagined a person who was incapable of thinking in categories:

> Locke, in the seventeenth century, postulated (and rejected) an impossible language in which each individual thing, each stone, each bird and each branch,

would have its own name; Funes once projected an analogous language, but discarded it because it seemed too general to him, too ambiguous. In fact, Funes remembered not only every leaf of every tree of every wood, but also every one of the times he had perceived or imagined it. . . . I suspect, however, that he was not very capable of thought. To think is to forget differences, generalize, make abstractions. (Borges, 1964:65, 66)

Of course, no culture could exist without the elementary cognitive process of category making. How, then, is the world divided up? An extreme relativist position would suggest that categories are completely arbitrary impositions of particular cultures, bearing no relation to the natural occurrences. That is indeed true of the sounds that make up the labels of categories. No logic claims that *tree* (in English) is more appropriate than *pohon* (in Indonesian) or *o* (in Dani) for those tall, woody plants. Likewise, *bird* (in English), *burung* (in Indonesian), and *tue* (in Dani) are equally arbitrary sounds for those feathered creatures.

The categories themselves are remarkably similar, however, and are close to the biological givens of the natural world. Where they are not exactly the same, they do not vary by much. For example, the English bird category and the Dani tue category both include all feathered creatures that each culture knows. The Dani category also includes furry flying mammals: bats and flying foxes. Strictly speaking, this classification is a biological error, but it does make a lot of sense. (In fact, many English speakers put bats in the bird category.)

"Weeks" and "months" are culturally constructed cycles of time. This calendar from multicultural Indonesia plots several different cycles: Javanese, Chinese, Christian, and Muslim. Can you figure them out?

What we do not find is disjunctive categories, which would include radically different members. No culture has a basic category system that lumps birds and elephants in one box and horses and snakes in another. (Of course, there are secondary cultural categories, such as the forbidden foods in the Book of Leviticus in the Bible, which include pork, shrimp, and some birds.)

Color Categories.   Although phonetic naming of colors is random and the number of categories varies from culture to culture and even among members of the same culture (I use one word, *red,* where my neighbor the painter recognizes *crimson, vermilion, garnet,* and others), there is remarkable universal agreement about the best examples of colors (Berlin and Kay, 1969). As it happens, we have one of the clearest etic, or culture-neutral, systems to describe colors: the objective physical measures of wavelength. The Munsell Company publishes a set of color chips that literally covers the spectrum and that can be conveniently carried into the field and used to question people about their color terms.

It turns out that strong cross-cultural agreement exists regarding which chip is the best red, which is the best blue, and so forth. These hues are the focal colors. Cultures do differ, however, on how many chips they include in the red category, and some cultures do not even have terms for some colors.

Classification of Living Things.   The realm of living things—the fauna and flora—also demonstrates this combination of cultural variation on universal categories. The research of Brent Berlin (1992) and many others has shown that cultures divide the natural world into categories very much like the "scientific" Linnaean system. Furthermore, just as the Linnaean system has different levels of inclusiveness (phylum, family, genus, species, variety), so different cultures have similar levels.

Kinship Classifications.   Kinship terms represent a third sort of category that all cultures use. Here, the biological facts are that a male and a female together produce a child. From those two biological facts (sexual intercourse and birth), any person can trace relationships to many other people. No culture has separate terms for each particular relationship. But exactly which relationships are grouped together in categories labeled with kinship terms is a cultural variable. In English, *uncle* lumps together men to whom one is related by blood or by marriage on the father's side and the mother's side. In Dani, *opase* includes some English *uncles* and the English *father.* However, kinship terms are not completely random. No culture lumps, say, grandmothers and nephews under a single kinship term.

We shall return to kinship in Chapter 9. Nevertheless, kinship terms, together with color categories and systems of living things, demonstrate the same principle: On a base of physical givens, cultures segment the natural world into categories that vary widely but not completely randomly.

EMOTIONS

In emotions, we see culture-specific constructions of behavior on a biological base, providing a good illustration of the usefulness of the biocultural model. Until recently, psychologists had treated emotions as universals, unaffected by culture. Anthropologists had either ignored emotions altogether or assumed that they were as culture-specific as words in a language.

Now, however, it appears that the psychologists were right to some degree. A few basic emotions are fairly similar across all cultures, with the same meanings and the same facial expressions. The English versions of these emotions are happiness, sadness, surprise, anger, fear, disgust, and perhaps contempt.

The psychologist Paul Ekman and his colleagues (1983) found that when someone makes the appropriate facial expression—that is, moves the right set of facial muscles for an emotion—whether the person is feeling that emotion or not, certain autonomic nervous system reactions such as skin temperature or heart rate will be triggered in a pattern that is specific to that emotion. Furthermore, even someone who has not been previously feeling that emotion will start feeling it. This finding suggests that these few basic emotions are hard-wired in human beings; in other words, connections between the facial muscles, the autonomic nervous system, and the brain are part of our human biological heritage. This component is the *bio-*part of the biocultural model.

What of the *-cultural* part? In addition to the biological basis, Ekman also identified a culturally constructed component of emotions. First, Ekman resolved the old standoff between psychologists and anthropologists by introducing the concept of **display rules,** culture-specific rules for behavior when one is feeling a particular emotion. If one is feeling a certain degree of anger, for example, the cultural display rule might be to show more anger, to show less anger, to show no emotion at all, or to **mask** the anger with the expression for another emotion.

Cultural Display Rules

In both Bali and Japan, for instance, the rule is usually to mask anger with a smile. The Yanomamo exaggerate their anger expressions. The Dani mask anger with the disgust nose wrinkle. In the United States, norms vary. In much of the South, anger is masked with happiness; in parts of the North, it is displayed realistically or even is dramatically exaggerated. We also have rules for specific contexts: If you draw four aces in a poker game, you should mask your joy with a "poker face." If you lose a beauty contest, you should mask your dejection with a happy smile.

Such rules complicate intercultural communication. Because the expressions for the basic emotions are easily read by outsiders, and because most cultures use culture-specific display rules only for a few kinds of situations, we go along thinking that we are understanding what is happening—until we are hit by a display rule, and then we are thrown for a loop. There is a saying that "the Javanese have a smile for every emotion." My guess is that it is a Dutch saying from the colonial period, expressing Dutch frustration at not being able to read Indonesian expressions. I also

Cultural display rules #1. In the Miss South Carolina contest of 1999, both winner and losers mask their inner feelings with the appropriate display rules. *(Credit: Photograph by Erik Campos/The State)*

suspect that these expressions are slightly different smiles and that Indonesians themselves have no trouble reading the nuances. Think of all the different smiles that we know in English: grins, smirks, doleful smiles, sarcastic smiles, and many more.

In some cultures, individuals learn to mute certain emotions. Muting is slightly different from masking. Circumstances may lead people to mute certain recurring and extremely painful emotions. For example, Nancy Scheper-Hughes has written of how the desperate poverty and high infant mortality of northeastern Brazil have muted the supposedly basic human emotion of mother love (1992). The apparently unemotional indifference of mothers to the deaths of their babies is thus put into cultural context.

Anthropologists must also be aware of the emotional norms in a culture so that they can avoid inappropriate emotional displays. Jean Briggs (1970) was one of the first anthropologists to write an ethnography based on emotion. She experienced firsthand the consequences of inappropriate emotion behavior when she lost her temper while living in northern Canada with the Utku, who value emotional control:

> Indeed, the maintenance of equanimity under trying circumstances is the essential sign of maturity, of adulthood. The handling of emotion is thus a problem that is of great importance also to the Utku themselves. (Briggs, 1970:4)

Cultural display rules #2. In the penultimate moment of the 1999 women's soccer World Cup play, the American keeper has just blocked the Chinese player's shot, assuring the U.S. team of the championship. Each player follows the appropriate display rule of her culture. *(Credit: AP/Wide World)*

During Briggs' research, sports fishermen set up elaborate camps and commandeered the Utku's two canoes. The Utku politely acquiesced, but Briggs could see how the loss of their boats inconvenienced them. Finally, she writes, "I exploded" (1970:284) and told the sportsmen to back off. Actually, her reaction sounds like a fairly moderate case of venting North American middle-class indignation, and her intention was to protect the Utku. Her vehemence went far beyond the bounds of what was allowable, however, and must have shocked and even frightened them. As a consequence, Briggs was ostracized for several months. Although she still lived in the camp, she was ignored as much as possible until finally an exchange of letters with an Utku living in the nearest town eased relations.

In her ethnography, *Never in Anger,* Briggs stresses the importance of understanding the ways in which particular cultures manage emotion. She also recognizes the impossibility of using simple one-to-one translations of emotion terms from one language to another, suggesting the development of rich schemas or scenarios of emotions, based on extensive ethnographic descriptions of emotion events. It is significant that, although Briggs uses our word "anger" in her title, her nuanced analysis shows that no single Utku word precisely matches it. In an appendix, she discusses at length seven Utku words under the general heading of "ill temper and jealousy" (1970:328–337).

Translating Emotions into Words

Probably, most languages have labels for unique or unusual emotions that are not of much interest to other cultures. *Amae,* the particular Japanese concept of dependence, is an example. Michelle Z. Rosaldo (1980) wrote an entire book to explain the idea of *liget,* which is held by the Ilongot of the northern Philippines; it is something like anger but has some joy and some sadness mixed in. The Indonesian words that a dictionary translates into English as *love* are actually close to *sad nurturance.* And in medieval Europe, there was a well-known concept, *accidie,* a kind of laziness that we no longer discuss (Harre and Finlay-Jones, 1986:221).

Grief: Emotion and Culture

The death of Diana, Princess of Wales, in 1997 unleashed an intensity of emotion in Great Britain that took everyone, especially the British, by surprise. At the same time, an undercurrent of condemnation targeted the royal family for appearing so unmoved. This event offers a striking example of cultural display rules and culture change.

The untimely, unexpected, and violent death of someone who plays a meaningful part in people's lives and imaginations triggers a mix of emotions. Anger, guilt, and sadness are particularly common. Sadness is a basic, pan-cultural emotion; indeed, the "sad" face is recognized universally. The actual behavior—that is, the performance of sadness—is culturally variable, however. Everyone may feel sad at the death of someone near and dear, but what they will actually express on their faces is to a great extent a cultural matter. Cultural display rules designate the appropriate public emotion reaction.

In fact, cultural rules even apply to the emotional meaning attributed to a particular event. In some cultures where the death of a child is believed to be caused by a witch, people may react with more fear than sadness—fear that the witch may strike again. When my mother was a young girl in a Presbyterian Church in St. Augustine, Florida, about 1910, one of her little friends died. For the rest of her life, my mother remembered how her Sunday School teachers told their charges that they should feel happy and rejoice, for their friend was now in the hands of Jesus. This interpretation was the cultural meaning of that event at that time in that culture. (My mother also remembered that the Sunday School teachers were unable to follow their own cultural rules and broke down in tears.)

In 1963, when President John Kennedy was assassinated, his widow Jacqueline was widely praised for her dignified control, for not breaking down in public tears. No one doubted her inner grief, and all admired her demeanor. In 1983, when Princess Grace died in an automobile accident, her husband Prince Rainier wept publicly at her funeral. The American press took Rainier to task for losing control, for not behaving as a man should. The irony, of course, was that Rainier followed the display rules of his own, Euro-Mediterranean culture but was judged by Anglo-Saxon, or northern European, display rules, which mandated a more Jacqueline Kennedy–like restraint of emotion. A decade earlier, Senator Edmund Muskie of Maine saw his presidential ambitions fatally damaged when he appeared to weep in angry frustration while defending his wife at a press conference.

By the 1990s, the display rules for northern Euro-Americans had shifted. Today, the president of the United States can, in some circumstances, freely express emotion and even weep in public. Cultures change. As noted in earlier chapters, all cultures change all the time. But not all aspects of culture change at the same rate. And not all people change with their cultures. In fact, many people consider the state of the world when they were ten years old to be the normal state, with everything since representing decay. Nevertheless, cultures do change.

The British royal family faces another dilemma. An exceptionally isolated family, hemmed in by tradition, they expressed emotion appropriately according to the cultural display rules of a past generation, or even a past century. Meanwhile, the emotion culture of Britons generally has been changing. The intense scrutiny of the media during the extraordinary events since Diana's death merely brought this cultural gap into public view.

Furthermore, cultural differences often take on moral import: different is bad, especially when these differences concern matters as central to human identity as emotion. The British have felt a certain ambivalence toward the "foreignness" of their royals since the Germanness of Kings George and Prince Albert, as well as the Greekness of Prince Phillip, became an issue—perhaps even since the Normanness of William the Conqueror.

Thus the Windsors are not just different, but their differences are morally suspect. It is not too much to suggest that the future of the British monarchy rests on this matter of cultural display rules of emotion. One thing can be predicted with certainty: the display rules governing emotion behavior today will themselves change. Future generations of British people—and Windsors—will think that *their* emotion patterns are right, proper, and eternal and will find those emotional display rules of 1997 puzzling and incomprehensible.

SEEING ANTHROPOLOGY

Cultural Themes in Vietnam: *How to Behave (Chuyen Tute)*

Directed by Trần Văn Thủy

How to Behave (Chuyen Tute) was made by a Vietnamese film group in documentary form. As one of the filmmakers is dying of cancer, he tells his comrades to go out and make a film that tells the truth about Vietnam. After his funeral, the survivors take their cameras around the country asking people questions such as "What is happiness?" and "What is leprosy?" These are simple, even banal questions, but the film gradually builds a picture of some of the basic themes of Vietnamese culture.

How to Behave (Chuyen Tute) is a very different sort of film, and one that is much more difficult to watch, than a standard didactic ethnographic film made about another culture by Americans for Americans. It takes some shifting of mental gears to appreciate the film.

The short film clip shows a series of instant interviews as the camera asks a variety of people "What is kindness?" and then moves on to talk about leprosy and how that disease brings out kindness in some, particularly nuns.

The complete film begins with the scenes of the dying filmmaker being visited by his colleagues, as he challenges them to make a different sort of film. After his funeral, as they are shooting a scene at a brickyard, the brickmaker angrily chases them away, also demanding that they tell the truth in their films. They acknowledge that the propaganda films they have been making are dull and unreal, so they begin to search for the realities of Vietnamese life and culture (in our terms, **cultural themes**). They begin with "the people," then go on through "kindness," "leprosy," and "greatness." Finally, they return to their friend's funeral, concluding that kindness is indeed essential.

Think of the clip as a report of anthropological fieldwork, designed to probe some central cultural themes of the Vietnamese. As you watch the interviews, think back to the basic Vietnamese concepts that Jamieson identified and to the individualism–groupism continuum. Culture is supposed to be shared. How much agreement can you find? What might account for the differences in the responses? Identify the respondents as far as you can by age, gender, and social status. Does that information give you any leads?

Setup Questions

1. How much disagreement is there among the various Vietnamese speakers on the meaning of *tu te* ("kindness")? How do these differences relate to the idea of culture as shared ideas? What sorts of people have what sorts of ideas (for example, the old Confucian scholar versus the young truck driver)?
2. Compare the Vietnamese concept of *tu te* (translated in the film as "kindness") with the English/American concept of kindness.
3. In the repeated questions and answers about concepts (the people, kindness) can you begin to recognize the Vietnamese words being used?
4. Do you think that this film is a spontaneous documentary or a carefully scripted production? What cues do you use? Does it matter?
5. Can you discern the old Confucian rules of respect?   ◆

HOLLYWOOD-STYLE ANTHROPOLOGY

Individualism and Groupism in *Mr. Baseball*

Mr. Baseball   1992   109 minutes

Tom Selleck as Jack Elliot
Ken Takakura as Coach Uchiyama
Aya Takanashi as Hiroko Uchiyama

Jack Elliot, a fading star first baseman with the New York Yankees, is sent to the Chunichi Dragons in Nagoya to play baseball Japanese style. From the beginning, he makes cultural missteps, unintentional as well as intentional. His greatest problem is the very different style of baseball, as played under Japanese cultural rules—well described by Robert Whiting in *The Chrysanthemum and the Bat.* The film nicely illustrates the individualism-versus-groupism continuum. You don't really have to know much about baseball, but it helps.

Setup Questions

1. Try to list all the cultural differences that are revealed by Jack's faux pas.
2. Identify individualism and groupism in the film.
3. How is the Japanese bow used as a narrative device?
4. What do the Americans miss out on when they dismiss the Japanese "politeness" as hypocritical?
5. What does "hai" mean?
6. What does harmony mean for Japanese behavior?
7. How is the visit to the temple a key turning point?
8. What is the role of apologies?
9. Explain the function of getting drunk.
10. What does Jack teach the Japanese team?
11. What is the meaning of Jack's last at-bat?
12. How does Jack finally approach Hiroko?   ◆

CHAPTER SUMMARY

- Early learning is often studied for clues to personality.
- In the 1920s and 1930s, Margaret Mead went to Samoa and New Guinea to study the events around puberty—coming of age—in various cultures. Her work examined influences that shape personality, particularly gender differences.
- Cultural themes are broadly shared psychological features that are recognized, generalized, and caricatured in folk ethnography. They have been systematically studied by psychological anthropologists in many cultures.
- Events like the Spanish Inquisition, the Holocaust, and the Khmer Rouge killing of millions of their fellow Cambodians have attracted special attention from scholars looking for the cultural bases of such behavior.
- Cultures can be located on a continuum from extreme individualism to extreme groupism, which turns out to be a very fundamental principle that seems to account for much culturally variable behavior.
- Learning styles can be characterized on a continuum from formal to situated. Formal learning takes place apart from the actual events, often through lecturing with a chalkboard; situated learning occurs in the real context, practicing as apprentices do.
- What we mean by "intelligence" is better measured as "multiple intelligences" rather than on a single "IQ" dimension.

- Classification, or organization of knowledge, in areas like time, colors, living things, or kin, is strongly shaped by culture even though it is based on biological or physical facts.
- Emotions are cultural constructs rooted in basic *Homo sapiens* physiology. Cultural display rules such as masking rules are important in interpersonal interaction.

KEY TERMS

cognition	groupism	national culture
cultural themes	indigenous psychologies	othering
culture of acquisition	individualism	perception
display rules	intelligence	personality
emotion	learning	psychological
environmental	masking	anthropology
determinism	mental illness	situated learning
ethnopsychologies	multiple intelligences	situated practice
folk ethnography	national character	

QUESTIONS TO THINK ABOUT

- Anyone who has a sibling is aware of how much variation in personality can occur within a single family. How true can generalizations about the psychology of entire groups of people be?
- Does Thomas Jefferson's description of Northern versus Southern character fit at all with your own experiences?
- Think of some folk ethnographic characterizations of different cultures or nations. How true are they? How could you study and verify them?
- What examples of masking are you familiar with?

SUGGESTIONS FOR FURTHER READING

Briggs, Jean L.
1998   Inuit Morality Play: The Emotional Education of a Three-Year-Old. New Haven, CT: Yale University Press. *Six months in the life of an Inuit girl, by the great pioneer in the anthropological study of emotion.*

Hardin, C. L., and Luisa Maffi (eds.)
1997   Color Categories in Thought and Language. Cambridge, U.K.: Cambridge University Press. *A balanced collection of essays about a key issue in the linguistic relativity debate.*

Hendry, James B.
1964   The Small World of Kanh Hau. Chicago: Aldine. *Another early ethnography.*

Hickey, Gerald Cannon
1964 Village in Vietnam. New Haven, CT: Yale University Press. *An early village ethnography.*

Jessor, Richard, Anne Colby, and Richard A. Shweder (eds.)
1996 Ethnography and Human Development: Context and Meaning in Social Inquiry. *An important collection of essays bringing the revived interest in learning up to date.*

Try a novel by a Vietnamese, such as Bao Ninh's The Sorrow of War, *1995, Riverhead Books, New York, or one of the Penguin Books volumes.*

Look at current issues of the journal of the Society for Psychological Anthropology, Ethos.

CHAPTER 6

Patterns of Production

Food preparation. Bayon, Angkor (Cambodia), 12th century C.E. *(Credit: Karl G. Heider)*

HEADLINE ANTHROPOLOGY

Some of the subjects discussed in this chapter have made their way into current news stories. For example:

◆ Lee Secrest, who lives in an isolated part of Montana, uses a traditional Native American technique of tanning hides with brains. His brain-tanned hides are used in museums and in movies (e.g., *Dances With Wolves*).

—New York Times, *May 26, 2002.*

◆ "Never underestimate the importance of local knowledge" in a full page ad for HBSC, a bank, with photos of an American football ("USA football"), a soccer ball ("UK football"), and an Australian Rules football ("Australia football").

—New York Times, *March 12, 2002.*

If you take a course in economics, you will deal with the classic concerns of production, distribution, and consumption as measured in monetary terms in nation-states. Cultural anthropology studies basically the same phenomena, but instead of looking at modern nations, which compute gross national products in dollar values, the anthropological focus has usually been on much smaller societies, which often lack any sort of money or at least deem that money is not important. So the traditional perspectives and approaches of economic anthropology are understandably somewhat different from those of economists, for much of what we are looking at takes place on such a smaller scale and is so much less formal that it often escapes the notice of "real" economists.

Small-scale informal transactions are not limited to tribal societies. As an experiment, go into an average American home and inventory the furnishings. Check everything that was bought new for cash from a store. Those transactions registered on the economic screen. Everything else—inherited portraits, borrowed chairs, wedding gift silver, tables from garage sales, homemade bookcases—to some extent or another slipped beneath the economic radar. Yet they represent transactions that are significant in social terms, even if neither money nor sales taxes were paid.

A major theme of economic analyses is those *transactions* or *exchanges* where goods and services are transferred for some consideration from one person or group to another. We shall explore this broad question of exchange in Chapter 7. In this chapter, we will look at **production,** the creation and reproduction of goods like food, tools, and other artifacts together with the knowledge involved in making and using them.

CULTURAL ADAPTATION AND PRODUCTION

Production always takes place in the context of a real setting, so when we look at how cultures produce food and other goods, we must immediately consider the interaction between culture and the natural environment. All cultures exist and interact within an environment whose elements include the natural setting plus neighboring social groups. This interaction results in some degree of accommodation among all elements, a process that we call **cultural adaptation.** Cultural adaptation is not a static state. For any culture in any environment alternative adaptations always exist, and adaptation is always in progress.

Human beings are intelligent, observant, innovative, and opportunistic. Recall Howard Gardner's concept of multiple intelligences (Chapter 5). Any group probably includes some people who excel at continuing the patterns of previous generations. Others are opportunistic and are constantly trying out new things, seeking to build artifacts a little differently, or striving to open up a new food source. Food production strategies—whether foraging, farming, pastoralism, or some combination of these strategies—represent the most crucial of all adaptations and offer the greatest opportunities for innovation. This innovation, in turn, leads to two sorts of change: (1) cultural change, when new ideas take hold, and (2) environmental change, when people alter the environment. Most Americans live in communities that demonstrate both sorts of alterations. In the last few generations, we have changed our culture, replacing fans and wood-burning stoves with central air and heating systems. Likewise, we have adapted the environment to our convenience by leveling hills, filling in gullies, and paving over streams.

If we think of our focus cultures so far, we see that the Malays, the Dani, the Balinese, the Kwa Kwaka' Wakw, and the Vietnamese represent different permutations of cultural adaptation. The Balinese have done the most to alter their landscape, turning steep slopes into irrigated rice terraces. Nevertheless, each culture has undergone massive changes in response to the demands of living and growing certain crops under specific environmental conditions. For groups such as the Yanomamo and the Dani, which lack written histories, the changes are lost in the mists of time. However, for the Balinese and the Vietnamese, we have written records of the process of cultural adaptation. And, of course, today we can actually see the changes taking place as these cultures get new tools, new crops, and new commercial opportunities.

Whether the adaptation is major or minor, it is important to be aware of the specifics of the adaptation when attempting to make changes in a culture. As we have seen in Bali, ecological systems are involved in adaptations. If the precise interactions that are part of the systems are disrupted, a successful adaptation can go awry. We can see this interaction in the Dani practice of keeping pigs in their house compounds.

Case Study: Dirty Dani Pigsties.   In the 1960s, some Indonesian officials became concerned that the Dani practice of keeping pigs (which produce pig droppings) in their house compounds was a health hazard to the people. Especially concerned were the many officials who were Muslim, a religion that considers pigs to be abominations. They proposed to force the Dani to move their pigsties a good distance away from the human dwellings. Fortunately, this plan was never carried out, for it overlooked several ways in which pigs were part of an ecological system.

First, Dani pigs are scavengers. They live on foods that humans reject or garbage that humans discard. Pigs forage around the houses for their food. If they were kept far away from the kitchens and eating areas, the human cost of collecting and delivering garbage to the pigs would be much higher.

Second, pig manure is nasty, smelly, and germ-ridden, but it is also great fertilizer. The Dani plant many kinds of food, as well as their tobacco, in the pig-enriched soil around their houses. It is likely that these crops would not thrive in the absence of pigs.

Third, one of the Dani's favorite crimes, and a source of disruption of the civil peace, is pig stealing. Pigs housed next to the sleeping houses are difficult to steal. But if the sties were even a short distance away, the rate of pig theft would likely shoot up, with all sorts of unintended consequences.

The point here is not to claim that the Dani pig system is perfect or to deny that pig droppings may be a health problem. Dani pigs are part of a system, however, and before tinkering with one element in the system, it is well to explore that system as a whole.

These interacting ecological systems do not come completely labeled, and the actors themselves might not be fully aware of how the systems work. We often recognize such a system only when a well-meaning development plan disrupts the traditional system and unanticipated consequences bring chaos. In the last few decades, many governments and nongovernmental organizations have started development projects without first understanding all ramifications of the conditions that they want to change.

Michael R. Dove, an anthropologist who has spent many years observing development projects in Indonesia and Pakistan, has warned against rejecting the ecological system embodied in traditional cultures:

> In Indonesia, as in many other developing countries, development is widely interpreted as meaning and necessitating change. That which is old and unchanged is reflexively categorized as undeveloped. This especially applies to culture. Traditional cultures and lifestyles are regarded as clear signs of underdevelopment and as formidable obstacles to necessary socioeconomic advancement. Accordingly, one ubiquitous element in development planning is the deprecation and attempted alteration or elimination of traditional culture. . . .
>
> In contrast, I maintain that traditional culture is intimately bound up with and directly supports the basic social, economic, and ecological processes of society. I further maintain that traditional culture is dynamic, is always undergoing change, and as a result is not inimical to the processes of development per se. (Dove, 1988a:1)

Here, Dove argues that we pay attention to the **local knowledge** contained in traditional cultures. James C. Scott has considered at length the ways in which grand reformist schemes ranging from planned cities (India, Brazil) to collectivization of agriculture (USSR, Cambodia under the Khmer Rouge) have come to grief because they did not take into account local wisdom. Scott has proposed a new term, *metis,* for this "wide array of practical skills and acquired intelligence in responding to a constantly changing natural and human environment." (1998:313).

Production of food and goods, then, does not "just happen." Instead, production is carried out through the interaction of a particular culture with a particular technology in a particular natural setting.

Technology

Technology is the means of manufacture and production. It includes tools and other artifacts as well as knowledge involved in the production of all manner of goods, including food. It is important to emphasize both aspects of technology—the cultural ideas (schemas) and the actual tools and other material objects. The crucial role played by technology in cultural adaptation is especially apparent in cases of adaptation to extreme environments, such as the Inuit in the Arctic. Even in temperate climates, however, technology is crucial. For example, the intensive sweet potato gardens of the Dani depend on remarkable knowledge to accompany their deceptively simple toolkit made up of stone axes, stone adzes, wooden digging sticks, and fire-making equipment. (In 1961, a government agricultural specialist from the experimental station on the coast visited the region and was stunned by the sophistication of the Dani gardens.)

The important role of technology is illustrated by Jeanne E. Arnold's study of boat making in prehistoric North America (1995). Along the West Coast of North America, from California to Canada, no agriculture took place, though the many cultures living on the Pacific Coast made some use of inshore maritime resources. Two areas, the Channel Islands near Santa Barbara and the Northwest Coast (especially of British Columbia), boasted a fortuitous combination of environmental opportunities: shelter provided by offshore islands, a rich sea life fed by nutrient-carrying currents, and plentiful boat-building wood. Both the Chumash in the South and the Nootka in the North (neighbors of the Kwa Kwaka' Wakw) developed boats in which they could not only exploit the offshore sea life (whales and the like) but also engage in long-distance trading. In both cases, the cultures that took advantage of these opportunities were able to accumulate wealth, status, and power in an increasingly hierarchical society. Arnold is careful not to claim too much for the technology, but she does show how important these boats were in the total cultural-environmental mix of both Chumash and Nootka.

One of the most dramatic illustrations of the interconnectedness of tools and knowledge is traditional Polynesian voyaging. By the time European explorers finally made it into the Pacific Ocean (between Magellan in 1520 and Cook in the 1760s and 1770s), Austronesian-speaking people setting sail from Asia had long since discovered and settled virtually every possible island in the South Pacific. Some scholars thought that these trips were merely accidental voyages of boatmen who lost control of their vessels and wound up on new islands. But the best understanding today is that the people whom we call *Polynesians* (a Greek neologism) were not only superb boat builders but also expert navigators. In addition to finding every island that was to be found, they had the artifacts and the knowledge to make regular planned voyages between island groups (Finney, 1994).

What Does the Environment Determine?

Julian Steward, one of the founders of modern cultural ecology, did fieldwork with hunting and gathering groups that lived in Utah, such as the Shoshoneans who lived in the extreme arid conditions of the Great Basin, where environmental effects were quite immediate. In his formulation of the problems, Steward emphasized the interaction between technology, environment, and what he called "levels of socio-cultural integration"—namely, the size and complexity of the social group. He pointed out that technologies have different outcomes in different environments:

> They may be used differently and entail different social arrangements in each environment. The environment is not only permissive or prohibitive with re-spect to these technologies, but special local features may require social adap-tations which have far-reaching consequences. (Steward, 1955:38)

Some cultural features are less tied to environment and technology, as seen in the contrast between Australian Aborigines and the Ju/'hoansi (San) of the Kala-hari in Southern Africa (our focus culture in Chapter 10). In many respects, the cul-tures of the two peoples are similar. Both groups live in deserts (although they are green deserts, alive with arid-adapted plants and animals). Both are foragers, hunt-ing with bows and arrows and using digging sticks for getting out roots and the like. Both live in small, mobile bands. But they differ in respect to kinship and art. The Ju/'hoansi have little concern about tracing relatives beyond the immediate family, and their art is minimal. The Australian Aboriginals, by contrast, have some of the most complex, far-reaching systems of kinship reckoning known anywhere. (See, for example, Tonkinson, 1991, Chapter 3, for a good description of an Aboriginal section system.) And they have elaborated to an extraordinary extent a cosmolog-ical mythology about what they call the Dreamtime, a supernatural world, and pro-duce vivid graphic arts and rituals that depict the events of the Dreamtime.

The Inuit (Eskimos) and the Kwa Kwaka' Wakw adapted foraging strategies to two quite different environmental challenges. In the far North, where only stunted plant life grew and farming was impossible, the only source of food was in the waters—that is, the oceans and rivers. No trees were available from which to build houses or boats or to burn for firewood, however. Winters are bitter cold and sum-mers are short. Surely it is one of *Homo sapiens'* greatest achievements to have in-vented ways to survive in this part of the world. The Inuit made houses of snow, clothes of skins, rope and thread of sinews, and dog sled runners of frozen fish iced together end to end. One old story dates from the 1940s, when the American and Canadian military forces were establishing radar bases in the far North. They hired some local labor and were amazed to discover that Inuit quickly mastered this state-of-the-art technology and became master radar technicians. How curious, they thought, that illiterate hunters who had no machinery themselves could learn West-ern technology so quickly. Obviously, whatever skills the Inuit lacked in some directions, they had been developing a technological intelligence for many generations under circumstances where the stakes were literally life or death. At least some of these skills had been developed over a period of 10,000 years, since the last great Ice Age. With this cultural adaptation, the greatest achievement was survival.

In contrast, the Kwa Kwaka' Wakw and the other Northwest Coast cultures lived in a land incredibly rich in food and materials. The Haida carver, Bill Reid, in an elegiac appreciation of Northwest Coast cultures, lists the resources of the sea and says "Even today, only a stupid man could starve on this coast, and today is not as it was" (1971:38). Survival is assured. What, then, did the Kwa Kwaka' Wakw do with their environmental possibilities? They did not just eat, they feasted; they did not just fish, they stockpiled; they did not just build shelters, they carved and painted. They distributed their vast wealth unequally and developed hierarchies of power and social status, expressing the social ranks in carved and painted crests.

Another example of the ways in which a culture adapts to the environment can be seen in a comparison between northern and southern Vietnam. Jamieson makes a strong case for environmental influence in this region as he considers "ecology as history" (1993:3–6). The two concentrations of Vietnamese population are in the North and the South. In the North, the Red River comes shooting down out of the mountains of southern China and its lower reaches, around Hanoi, to form a fertile but dangerous environment. Floods, droughts, disease, and pests make life in the North uncertain. In contrast, the Mekong River, in the South, has wandered through the lowlands of Cambodia and Vietnam for a couple of hundred miles, losing its power. In addition, this region has an unusual safety feature in the great Tonle Sap lake of Cambodia. Usually the lake drains into the river. When the river rises, however, the flow reverses itself and the access water actually backs up into the lake, mitigating flood possibilities. Without ignoring historical differences, Jamieson suggests that

> these ecological differences between the Red River and the Mekong delta have been of immense significance in generating differences in cultural emphases and social organization between the two core regions of Vietnam. (Jamieson, 1993:5)

Specifically, he argues that

> life has been easier and more secure in the southern third of Vietnam, and the harsh discipline found in the north has been always considerably moderated there. Southern villages have always been more open, less corporate, more tolerant of individual initiative and heterodoxy. (Jamieson, 1993:5)

Although the environment allowed this system to develop, we cannot say that the environment determined it. We have no reliable way to predict in what directions a culture will elaborate. Having a ready excess of food is an obvious factor. Here we can compare the Kwa Kwaka' Wakw and the Dani. The Dani have an easy and reliable supply of food (sweet potatoes and pigs), but do not resemble the Kwa Kwaka' Wakw otherwise. First, they are farmers. Second, they have little excess floating wealth to play around with. Some have suggested that social and artistic elaborations are possible only when a society has plenty of spare time.

Again, good counterevidence exists. It is likely that both the Ju/'hoansi and the Australian Aboriginals—two foraging cultures—had comparable spare time, but the Aboriginals developed elaborate graphic art traditions and the Ju/'hoansi did not. I often wondered, sitting around with Dani men, why they seemed to spend so much time chatting and smoking instead of developing a great art. There is no easy answer to this question. The bottom line is that environment and culture are part of one interactive system in which the environment may limit possibilities (Inuit cannot have irrigated rice fields) and pose challenges, but does not determine the cultural outcome.

THE DIVISION OF LABOR

Production of anything—food or any other goods—depends on the labor of human effort. Nevertheless, a huge degree of variation appears in the ways that labor is allocated and utilized in different societies.

Specialization: Mechanical and Organic Solidarity

One of our most useful concepts was developed by the French sociologist Emile Durkheim, who wrote a series of influential books in the 1890s, including *The Division of Labor in Society* (Durkheim, 1893/1964). Faced with a growing emphasis on individualism in European societies, Durkheim expressed the following concern: "Why does the individual, while becoming more autonomous, depend more on society?" (Durkheim, 1893/1964:37).

His answer, in brief, recognized that as individuals became more **specialized,** doing more varied sorts of jobs—that is, as the **division of labor** in a society increased—those individuals became more, not less, dependent on their fellows. In such a case, the question then arises, "What holds a society together when there is no necessity for interdependence?"

To explore this apparent paradox, Durkheim examined the cross-cultural data on production and work that were available then. He examined the degree of specialization in different societies and the implications. At one end of a continuum of specialization are societies such as the Dani, in which there is some specialization according to gender and age but rarely more than that. This minimal division of labor is the least in any human society and is largely based on physical and mental capabilities.

According to Durkheim, the degree of specialization is not enough to hold these types of societies together. Instead, they maintain cohesiveness through **mechanical solidarity,** which is based on strongly held and shared values, beliefs, and customs. In these societies, everyone performs the same tasks, and the total effort is the sum of the parts. Everyone has the same basic worldview and everyone engages in the same activities. Their society is held together by what the people have in common. There is very little specialization, and the family acts as a self-sufficient economic unit.

The Dani are a good example of this type of society. Basically, all adult Dani men command the same knowledge and produce the same things. There are no full-time specialists or even part-time specialists. There are what we can call *spare-time specialists,* people who are especially good at carving arrow points, hunting in the forest, or running a curing ceremony. But, in theory at least, a single man and woman and their children could carry on Dani culture in isolation. This idea sounds like a twist on the old joke "How many Xs does it take to screw in a lightbulb?" Here it would be, "How many Dani does it take to run the economy?" (The answer would tell us something about the purely economic side of cultures but would ignore the fact that in social life, economics is deeply intertwined with other activities. No Dani couple would actually be happy living alone.)

In groups such as the Dani, in which, in theory, there is no economic necessity for people to stay together, their common beliefs bind them together. Before the Christian missionaries came to the Grand Valley, there were no atheists among the Dani. Their ghosts and spirits were facts that everyone understood and more or less acted on. These beliefs were a strong part of their culture. Increasing contact with the modern world has disrupted this commonly held system of beliefs, and the cultural solidarity has weakened noticeably.

At the other end of the specialization continuum are societies such as those of Japan and the United States, with their vast array of different occupations. In the United States, farmers produce only one sort of food, and cultural anthropologists do not understand the laboratory work of the physical anthropologists down the hall. Few if any Americans command the range of knowledge and skills that would allow them to exist alone. Even the "survivalists" in the United States are dependent on sporting goods stores, manufacturers of survival equipment, and the like.

In these societies, which are characterized by what Durkheim called **organic solidarity,** each member has specialized knowledge and skills, and each contributes differently to the whole. For example, compare building a house among the Dani with building a house in the United States. Any normal adult Dani male can build a house by himself, possibly gaining some assistance from his wife, who would gather the thatching grass for him. In the United States, most houses are built by a team of specialists: architects don't know roofing, electricians don't do paneling, and painters don't install the plumbing. To describe this phenomenon, Durkheim used the analogy of an organism like the human body, with its specialized limbs and organs. As this interdependence grows, the necessity of having strongly shared cultural beliefs diminishes.

Division of Labor by Age and Gender

Although a clear economic division of labor does not exist in all societies, there does exist division of labor based on other factors, such as age and gender. With the long maturation time needed before humans reach their full strength, children take up normal adult tasks only gradually. By middle childhood, around five or six years of age, Dani children are already beginning to help out a little with jobs such as caring for infants or herding pigs. By their midteens, Dani are expected to do fully adult shares of the work.

Different cultures have different expectations for how long childhood lasts and how carefree it should be. Middle-class Americans tend to postpone fully responsible adulthood and extend the formal learning period into the late teens or early twenties. In 19th-century England, however, children were often working full time at age ten, doing quite difficult and dangerous jobs such as mining coal.

Just as division of labor by age is found in all cultures, division of labor by gender is also a cultural universal. No culture assigns males and females the same jobs. There are fairly general cross-cultural regularities in how work is allocated: Men do heavy labor (hauling logs, rocks, and so on), labor that involves short spurts of intense energy (breaking sod, chopping wood), and work that is far from home (deep-sea fishing, long-range hunting, trading trips). Women do long-lasting work (such as bearing babies, cultivating gardens, and weaving) and home work (such as cooking).

There are obvious biological bases for this division of labor. On the whole, men are stronger, especially in their upper bodies, than women are. And, of course, only women become pregnant, give birth, and breast-feed. So it would seem logical that cultures would assign weaker women to less physical tasks and would exempt new mothers from certain tasks. But in any group, some women are stronger than some men, and not all women are bearing children all the time. One might imagine a com-

Male potters in India. *(Credit: Karl G. Heider)*

pletely gender-neutral rational culture that takes into account these physical differences but uses gender as a secondary criterion and does not separate all women from all men. However, there are no such cultures. In the contemporary United States, attempts are being made to override the habits of gender separation in many areas, though these attempts are met with considerable resistance, legal as well as informal.

FOOD PRODUCTION STRATEGIES

One of the most fundamental adaptations of any culture is the way in which people get their food. There are only three main **food production strategies: foraging,** in which people hunt, fish, and gather food that they played little or no part in raising; **farming,** in which people plant and harvest vegetable food; and **animal husbandry,** in which people raise animals for food. It has been customary to label groups by their dominant subsistence strategies as "hunters and gatherers," "agriculturalists," or "pastoralists." These labels have two major drawbacks. First, most groups use **mixed production strategies** if at all possible. For example, as we shall see in Chapter 10, the Ju/'hoansi of the Kalahari Desert got most of their food from foraging, but would plant seeds of gourds and other edible plants when there was enough rainfall. The Dani ate mainly sweet potatoes from their gardens, but also raised pigs and sometimes hunted. The Nuer (Chapter 9), so famous for their cattle herds, raised grain on the side.

The second problem with these subsistence strategy labels is that each includes such a wide range of cultures. "Hunters and gatherers" include the Kwa Kwaka' Wakw of the lush temperate rain forests of the Northwest Coast, the Inuit of the Arctic, and the Ju/'hoansi of the Kalahari Desert. "Farming" includes the intensive rice growers of Bali and Vietnam, the cassava gardeners of the Amazon Basin, and the wheat farmers of Kansas. "Pastoralism" lumps llama adaptation to high altitude in Peru together with camel herders in Arabia. The solution to these labeling problems is to first describe some prototypical subsistence strategies and then be alert to the various mixes of strategies used by different cultures. Mixed strategies are the rule, although a few exceptions occur. The Inuit have been able to utilize only the foraging strategy, because they could not grow plants in the arctic and their only domestic animals, dogs, were too valuable as traction beasts, pulling sleds, to be used for food. Another exception involves the cultures of the Northwest Coast, where the richness of the ocean life and the coastal regions made hunting, fishing, and gathering an extraordinarily productive strategy and both farming and animal husbandry virtually nonexistent.

Foraging

Foraging (traditionally called **hunting and gathering**), the original human food-producing strategy, has continued as the dominant strategy of many groups even through the 20th century. The several peoples of the Kalahari Desert in southern

Africa were still extensively engaged in foraging after World War II. Because they have been studied by so many anthropologists, they have become the main image of foraging in the minds of the public as well as in the anthropological literature. Although we will refer to them throughout this text as an example of one foraging strategy, we need to be aware of other sorts of foraging. The following list mentions groups that have practiced the foraging strategy exclusively in the last century or so:

Inuit, living in the arctic north of Canada and Alaska fish, hunt, and gather.
Kwa Kwaka' Wakw, Nootka, and other groups on the temperate rain forest of
    the Northwest Coast of North America, fish, hunt, and gather.
Australian Aboriginals, in the central deserts of Australia, hunt and gather.
Ju/'hoansi and others of the Kalahari Desert of southern Africa hunt and
    gather.

Other cultures have increasingly mixed foraging with other food-producing strategies. For example, people like the Yanomamo of the Brazilian-Venezuelan rain forest use both foraging and farming strategies about equally. Large groups like the Grand Valley Dani show considerable within-group variation in their balance of strategies: Those who live in the central valley do almost no foraging, but grow sweet potatoes and pigs for food, whereas Dani who live on the periphery of the Grand Valley, on the higher forested mountain slopes, cultivate some vegetables and pigs, but also spend time hunting back in the high forests. (I lived with people on the valley floor and labeled them as "horticulturalists," so it never crossed my mind to pay attention to how much food the slope dwellers were getting from their forests.) In his study of an Appalachian community (1973), George L. Hicks found many people who augmented their garden-grown food with hunting, and also gathered the wild galax to sell for cash to florists who used the leaves to make up flower arrangements.

With this range of foraging strategies, it is difficult to find any common features. Even if we take those cultures most single-mindedly committed to foraging, such as the Inuit, the Kwa Kwaka' Wakw, and perhaps the Australian Aborigines and the Ju/'hoansi, we find a wide range of land use, kinship patterns, property rights, division of labor, and tools. What is impressively common to all, though, is the profound adaptation to a particular unusual natural environment. We can use our focus culture for Chapter 10, the Ju/'hoansi (San, or !Kung) of the Kalahari Desert, as one example of these many foraging adaptations. The film clip for that chapter is taken from a film by John Marshall called *N!ai*. In Chapter 10, we will use it to discuss gender roles and sexuality, but you may want to skip ahead and view it now for its glimpses of Ju/'hoansi foraging strategies.

We must be careful not to equate modern foragers, such as the Ju/'hoansi of southern Africa, exactly with our early ancestors, for several reasons:

1. People like the Ju/'hoansi have long been trading with farmers and ironworkers and have gotten goods and ideas from them that were not available to foragers 50,000 years ago.

Foraging, a major subsistence activity of Ju/'hoansi women in the Kalahari Desert. *(Credit: John Marshall, photo courtesy of Documentary Education Resources)*

2. People like the Ju/'hoansi have been changing—as all cultures do—for as long as any other culture. It is misleading to think of them as some 50,000-year-old culture preserved as if in amber, unchanged.
3. Perhaps most important, the foragers whom we know today are magnificently adapted to their extreme environmental niches: desert, arctic, and deep rain forest. But surely before the advent of farming, the concentration of foragers would have been in the lush fertile valleys that teemed with food—just those places where farming took hold and squeezed out the foragers.

Yet with all these reservations, we can look at Ju/'hoansi foraging for some clues to what people were like before farming.

Ju/'hoansi Culture.   Names are a major problem when discussing these foragers of the Kalahari Desert. Although they clearly share a general cultural pattern, few agree on what overall label to use for them. Until the 1950s, these people were simply called Bushmen. That term had derogatory connotations and was later dropped in favor of terms that the people themselves use, like *San, !Kung,* or *!Kung San.* Richard Lee (1993) has proposed *Ju/'hoansi,* and some anthropologists have taken up that term (for example, Kelly, 1995). Susan Kent, in her edited volume (1996), uses the term *Baswara,* but one of the book's chapters, by Mathias Guenther

(1996), uses *Bushmen,* as does the index for the volume. To complicate things even more, Richard Lee, in 1998, referred to *African Bushmen* (1998:ix). In this book, we shall stay with Ju/'hoansi.

Until recently, the Ju/'hoansi were primarily foragers, living on roots, nuts, and other plant foods and a wide variety of animals. Anthropologists long assumed that foragers like these people must be living on the constant edge of starvation, trying to wrest a living from the hostile desert with rudimentary tools. As we have seen, however, technology is more than artifacts. It encompasses knowledge, and the knowledge that the Ju/'hoansi have of their environment is extraordinary. Lee wrote:

> The Ju/'hoansi are such superb trackers and make such accurate deductions from the faintest marks in the sand that at first their skill seems uncanny. For example, both men and women are able to identify an individual person merely by the sight of his or her footprint in the sand. There is nothing mysterious about this. Their tracking is a skill, cultivated over a life time, that builds on literally tens of thousands of observations. The Ju hunter can deduce many kinds of information about the animal he is tracking: its species and sex, its age, how fast it is traveling, whether it is alone or with other animals, its physical condition (healthy or ill), whether and on what it is feeding, and the time of day the animal passed. (Lee, 1993:52–53).

Knowledge of plants is equally profound. The Ju/'hoansi know more than 100 different species of edible wild plants (Lee, 1993:45). One of their most important artifacts is the *kaross,* a great leather cape-cum-carrying bag that women use to transport food back to camp.

Men are hunters, and their skills at bringing down large herbivores such as kudus, wildebeests, and even giraffes are most celebrated. It turns out, however, that in many areas, the most important food is the protein-rich mongongo nut, gathered by women and children. Richard Lee made a detailed study of the Ju/'hoansi diet and found that the people were remarkably well nourished.

Perhaps even more surprising, they did not have to work especially hard to get the food. Lee found that, on the average, they spent 2.4 days, or 20 hours per person per week, finding food.

The Ju/'hoansi live in small camps in the desert or close to Bantu cattle farms, where they may work. The camps are formed around siblings and their spouses. From Lee's study of work production it is clear how interdependent women and men are (1979:276). Men do most of the hunting, and women do most of the gathering. Although men spend more time at foraging than women (21.6 hours per week versus 12.6 hours per week), they bring in less food than women do. Women build the shelters, and men spend more time making and maintaining tools. Lee calculated that the men in his study spent 44.5 hours per week on food production, tools, and housework, whereas women spent 30.1 hours per week (1979:278).

For part of the year the Ju/'hoansi, whom Lee examined, lived in small camps of rarely more than a couple of dozen people. At the beginning of Lee's study in

Hunting, a major subsistence activity of Ju/'hoansi men in the Kalahari Desert. *(Credit: John Marshall, photo courtesy of Documentary Education Resources)*

1964, these camps were based near water holes or rich nut tree groves; within a few years, however, some people had moved to a European settlement and split their time between foraging and wage labor. The traditional camps had fluctuating membership but were formed around a core of siblings and their spouses. These core people "owned" or controlled the water hole and food resources in the neighborhood, albeit via a relatively informal understanding. That is, people from other groups could use the water or gather the food with permission.

Lee found a seasonal rhythm of dispersal and concentration of Ju/'hoansi settlements. In winter, camps could grow to 100 or 200 people. This season was a time of intense socialization, initiation ceremonies, curing ceremonies, and trading, all of which the Ju/'hoansi valued. The downside of the large winter-time groups was the increase in conflict:

> The largest grouping the !Kung could muster thus had an inherent contradiction. People sought the stimulation of a more intense social life, but there was always the danger of serious conflict. The !Kung annual round was structured to allow both kinds of social life—the intensity of the public life, with its inherent dangers, and the domestic tranquility of smaller groupings in the private life. (Lee, 1979:367)

In thinking about technology and adaptation, it is easy to overlook the knowledge it takes to adapt and survive, especially in severe environments. Obviously, surviving in the Kalahari Desert takes great knowledge of the environment, an aspect of

Ju/'hoansi technology that has recently been studied. Europeans who came in contact with the Ju/'hoansi have long been impressed by a particular skill important in hunting and gathering in the Kalahari—namely, "dead reckoning." This skill is the ability to know where one is, and after hours of walking to know how to go straight home without having to retrace one's route. There was—and still is—a commonly held belief in South Africa that the Ju/'hoansi, being primitive and closer to animals, had an inborn, instinctive ability to orient themselves. Thomas Widlok has investigated these skills, treating them as cognitive skills, as a way of organizing knowledge (1997). Widlock worked with Hai//om people in Namibia, who are closely related to the Ju/'hoansi. He devised an experiment utilizing a global positioning system (GPS), a handheld device that can use satellite transmissions to show a person's precise location. He took Hai//om, both men and women, old and young, deep into the bush and then asked them to point the directions to various places. He, of course, could verify the exact direction with his GPS. Their overall accuracy was extraordinary, with an average error of 16.40 degrees. (Try this same exercise in your classroom. You most likely will not come close to this level of accuracy.) Widlock suspects that some of his informants' error was caused when people pointed at the path they would take avoiding major obstacles, rather than indicating the absolute direction of the target.

From a cognitive standpoint, the intriguing question is, How does this system work? We know how the GPS works—an individual holds an instrument that locks into satellite transmissions and transforms that information into a maplike representation of locality. The Ju/'hoansi skill is mental, however—not high tech. Widlock rejects the idea that the Kalahari Desert people employ some sort of mental map, comparable to what most of us use if we have several errands around a region and after the last can return to our starting point without retracing our steps. Widlock suggests that a Hai//om

> has throughout his or her everyday life continually accumulated information about plant use, the topographical transitions between countries, the travels and travel accounts of fellow Hai//om, the exchanges between social groups and other relevant information. Hai//om orientation skills may *seem* puzzling because Hai//om individuals are closer to reconstructing and influencing the basis on which their cognitive system is built. They therefore seem more independent of any cultural artifacts, but their skills in the last instance depend as much on a network of social relations and on communicated knowledge as those of the anthropologist who uses a GPS. (Widlock, 1997:328)

In short, dead reckoning is not an instinctive skill at all. It is a socially constructed body of knowledge exchanged and shared among the group, appropriate to their subsistence adaptation.

Animal Husbandry and Pastoralism

A second food production strategy is animal husbandry **(pastoralism),** raising animals for food and other products. It ranges in importance, with some groups like the Dani raising pigs for ceremonial exchanges and occasional feasts, whereas other cultures do no farming but spend all their time with their herds.

The Nuer of the upper Nile region of East Africa are prototypical pastoralists. They (1) depend greatly on their animals for subsistence, (2) focus much of their symbolic, ritual, and social life around their animals, (3) move their settlements according to the rhythm of the seasons, and (4) live in fairly marginal land that is not suited for intensive horticulture or agriculture. They are not "pure" pastoralists, however, for they also maintain yearly farms where they grow grains and other crops. This pattern depends on certain types of animals—in particular, a few larger ungulates that live in herds and are domesticatable:

Cattle, in the Near East, East Africa, and Central Asia
Yaks, in Central Asia
Sheep (and goats), as with the Navajo of the U.S. Southwest, and generally
  mixed in with Asian cattle pastoralism
Llamas, alpacas, and vicuñas, the cameloids of the Andes
Camels, from North Africa to India and Central Asia
Reindeer, in arctic Eurasia

Pastoralism in Siberia, Russia. In thin forest just south of the tree line, a Nenets herder lassoes a stray reindeer that has wandered into another herd during a snowstorm. *(Credit: © Maria Stenzel/ National Geographic Image Collection)*

The regular movement of pastoralists varies from relatively fixed settlements to quite wide-ranging nomadism. A notable pattern is **transhumance,** where people move their flocks or herds back and forth between seasonal camp areas. The Bakhtiari of western Iran had a particularly dramatic version of transhumance. Twice each year, they packed up their black tents and moved their millions of head of livestock—sheep, goats, and camels—across rivers and over the snow-covered Zagros Mountains in search of grass. One of the earliest and most dramatic of all ethnographic films followed one Bakhtiari trek. The film was called, not surprisingly, *Grass* (1926) and was made by Merian C. Cooper and Edward Schoedsack (who later went on to make feature films like *King Kong* [1933]). *Grass* is silent, in black and white, with intertitles that are sometimes corny, but it still has a breathtaking authenticity. Watching the people swimming their herds across flooding rivers, or taking off their shoes and walking barefooted as they chop paths up the mountain face through the snow, one is struck by the extraordinary rigors that this sort of human adaptation demands—twice each year! Whereas the film *The Nuer* (Chapter 9) emphasizes the poetry and beauty of pastoralists' relations with their cattle, *Grass* shows the grim reality and costs of having to move so much so far.

Not all transhumance has quite such demands. One fall, driving through the Austrian Alps, I came across a herd of cattle decorated with flowers and cowrie shells. They were being brought down for the winter from their high-altitude summer pastures, and the ornaments celebrated a season without mishap.

Not many decades ago, this pastoralist adaptation seemed to protect the people who practiced this type of food production, for their lands were too dry, too cold, too high, or too remote to be threatened by others. By the end of the 20th century, however, they had become beleaguered. Technology, politics, population growth, and even ecological sensitivity threatened the pastoralist way of life. Hydroelectric dams in Norway took Saami (Lapp) lands; in Tanzania, state-run wheat farms spread into Barabaig grazing lands; also in Tanzania, the Maasai lost first the Serengeti Plain and then the Ngoro basin to wildlife preserves; and the Nuer were caught between sides in long-term wars in the Sudan and Ethiopia (Fratkin, 1997). Eliot Fratkin, who has studied the Ariaal of Kenya, nevertheless remains somewhat optimistic:

> I believe that pastoralism still has a future, as it remains one of the few mechanisms by which humans can wrest food and livelihood from the world's arid lands. For pastoralism to survive, however, there must be changes in both pastoral practices as well as the policies of national governments and international development agencies aimed at pastoral peoples. (Fratkin, 1998:39)

Central Asia has seen a dramatically different development. Since decentralization, decollectivization, and the increase of privatization and market economies in Mongolia, China, and Tibet, pastoralism has actually increased. To some extent, the precommunist social organization, which centered on small kin-based herding groups, has reemerged (Fratkin, 1997).

Farming

The third major food production strategy is farming, the planting and harvesting of vegetable foods. After scrounging for food for nearly 100,000 years, some groups of *Homo sapiens* became farmers. That flat statement implies a tremendous transformation, the details of which archaeologists are still working on. V. Gordon Childe, the late British archaeologist, named it the *Neolithic Revolution,* although of course it must have happened relatively gradually.

We can engage in some speculation here. Certainly, those foragers must have known a lot about their environment just to survive. Don't forget, we know things that *Homo sapiens* 10,000 years ago didn't, but there is no reason to suppose that we today are any wiser, more clever, or more observant. The wisest, cleverest, and most observant women and men of those days must have realized that seeds that were spit out of a person's mouth, dropped, or left in particular places turned into plants and that seeds from the best fruits produced the best fruits.

Before long, some groups had committed themselves to farming, with tremendous consequences: They settled down to protect their crops instead of ranging far after game and ripening plants. They began to accumulate things instead of making only what they could carry. Women who didn't have to carry children on long treks had more children, closer together, and the population increased. And so forth and so forth.

Even our prototypical foragers, the Ju/'hoansi, began planting some seeds and harvesting some food in periods of particularly good rainfall. They were opportunistic, always ready to fall back on foraging in the more common dry periods. So we could think of them as *occasional horticulturalists.* Some farmers seem almost nomadic, like the Orang Asli of Malaysia, *slash-and-burn horticulturalists* who carve out fields from the forest, plant them for a couple of seasons, and then clear other fields. Some have considerable investment in the land itself and are *intensive horticulturalists,* like the Dani, who have been working the same ditched fields for ages. There are *irrigation agriculturalists* (or *intensive agriculturalists*), like the Balinese with their immense reshaping of the hillsides into irrigated terraces, as we saw in *The Goddess and the Computer.* And in many industrialized societies today, we can speak of *agribusiness,* in which huge fields are tilled, planted, and harvested by machines.

All manner of plants have been domesticated and improved far beyond their wild varieties to serve as staples: corn, beans, squash, and potatoes in the New World; rice in Southeast Asia; other grains in the Near East; plantains in Africa. Then these plants were spread by early voyagers, many even before 1492, when the great Columbian exchange began.

In sorting out all these kinds of farmers, the main variables are the following:

1. Tools, which range from simple digging sticks to plows and tractors
2. Land tenure, which ranges from constantly shifting fields to centuries-long occupation
3. Alteration of the land, which ranges from virtually none to ditching, terracing, and irrigation canals

4. Soil enrichment, which ranges from minor (ashes from trash fires) through local fertilizers (pig droppings) to high-tech imported insecticides and fertilizers
5. Crops, which range from mixed cropping to huge single-crop fields (monoculture)
6. Purpose, which ranges from minor dietary supplements to subsistence (to feed the household) to cash cropping

If we look at our focus cultures in terms of their use of techology in farming, the occasional Ju/'hoansi are at the minimal end, the Vietnamese and Balinese are at the high-technology end, and the Dani in the center.

Slash-and-Burn, or Swidden, Farming. **Slash-and-burn horticulture,** also known as **swidden farming** or **shifting horticulture,** is the typical farming pattern used in tropical hilly forestland around the world. It is a nonintensive, shifting form of farming. Small fields are opened by felling or just killing trees, burning off the underbrush, and then planting seeds, roots, or cuttings for one or two growing cycles. As new underbrush begins to reclaim the land, that field is abandoned and new fields are opened. It has been characterized as ecologically sound, for the forest is barely disturbed and quickly allowed to return. Although the tropical soils are often not particularly fertile, they are enhanced by the ash of the fires. In any case, before the soil has a chance to be exhausted, it is renewed by its return to forest. When there is great population pressure, however, fields are kept open too long, the system gets out of control, and the soil becomes permanently depleted. Thus slash-and-burn horticulture is a sustainable system when there is plenty of forest and low population size, but as populations increase and forests are clear-cut for lumber, this strategy becomes counterproductive in the long run.

Slash and burn is rarely anyone's sole strategy. Because the people are living and farming in the forests instead of clearing the land, they usually do a great deal of foraging to supplement their food supply.

Horticulture. Farming practiced on relatively permanent fields but with hand tools like digging sticks instead of plows or draft animals is called **horticulture** (or **gardening**). It is midway between the very diffuse slash-and-burn strategy and the intensive plow or tractor **agriculture.**

FOCUS CULTURE

Horticulture of the Grand Valley Dani

The Grand Valley Dani of Irian Jaya, Indonesia, whom we have met already, produce most of their food by horticulture. In fact, the Grand Valley Dani grow their sweet potatoes not only on the flat valley floor, but also on higher ground at the edges of the valley and on the high forested slopes bounding it. The first two locations nicely fit our definition of horticulture, but on the higher steeper slopes the Dani use slash-and-burn techniques. Here we can expand the general description of Dani culture from Chapter 3 by concentrating on their horticulture.

Once, what is now the Grand Valley of the Balim River was probably a great lake. At some point, the waters broke through the natural barrier at the south end of the lake, draining it and leaving only the river winding its way along the broad, flat floor of the old lake bed. The ground must have been waterlogged and swampy. Eventually the Dani arrived, probably practicing their slash-and-burn farming on the higher slopes. We do not know what happened next, for the Dani are not particularly interested in history and archaeology has yet to work out the story. Somehow, in a great adaptive move, some Dani began to drain the swamps, using their digging sticks to construct networks of drainage ditches to lower the water table and raise the garden beds. It looks as if the population had become fairly stable by the 1960s, for no new areas were being drained by then.

The ditch systems are carefully maintained and serve many purposes. During wet spells, they drain water off the sweet potato beds; during dry periods, they channel the water available from natural streams into the gardens. When people weed their gardens, they throw the trash into the ditches, where it decays and enriches the ditch mud that is smeared on the beds at the next planting. The ditches also protect the growing sweet potatoes from marauding pigs (on the midslope gardens, which lack such ditches, it takes much labor to build fences). Finally, the digging sticks themselves, after being shaped with stone adzes and baked over fires, are left in the ditch mud to soak up water for greater heft.

Dani men use fire-hardened digging sticks to prepare gardens for planting.
(Credit: Karl G. Heider, Film Study Center, Harvard University)

Dani women tend the gardens, weeding and turning the sweet potato vines to the sun. *(Credit: Karl G. Heider, Film Study Center, Harvard University)*

The Dani system includes a definite gender-based division of labor. Men clear brush and trees off fallow gardens, turn the soil with their heavy digging sticks, clear out the ditches, and smear the fertile mud on the fields. Then women take over, planting the sweet potato cuttings, weeding, and finally harvesting and cooking.

The Grand Valley lacks predictable seasons. Wet alternates with dry, but not on a yearly cycle. Sweet potato gardens are planted throughout the year, and every day women harvest enough tubers and leaves for their household needs.

Pigs are an important part of this ecological system. After a particular garden area has been worked out by the women, they herd their family's pigs onto the garden to root around, eating the last small tubers and fertilizing the ground with their droppings.

Land rights are fairly informal. There was no strict ownership of land, no formal titles. Men—and sometimes women—continue to farm gardens that they had farmed before. A newcomer would confer with the important men of the neighborhood and with those who had used the land last, then would be allowed to take over old garden areas. No shortage of land was apparent, and in the area that I studied I came across no disputes over land. In recent years, this informality, which worked well a generation ago, has become a great disadvantage to the Dani. Outsiders have come into the Grand Valley and found ways to buy up Dani land. They have followed the laws of the Republic of Indonesia, which assume a level of ownership quite foreign to the Dani system. Such "legal" alienation of native land is an old story, and one that is quite familiar in North America.

The Dani garden cycle alternates growing with a fallow period. A particular garden area would be used for a time—which varied greatly in length from one to ten or more years—and then allowed to rest. Weeds, grass, and small trees would gradually take over. When it was needed again, the land would be reopened for planting. I never discovered a strict pattern to this rotation system, nor any explicit Dani theory about fallowing. Nevertheless, the areas around each settlement included gardens at every stage of the cycle. The wide strips of unoccupied land between warring groups constituted another sort of fallowing, lasting a decade or two while fighting on that front continued.

Sweet potatoes make up about 90% of the Dani diet. The tubers are roasted or steamed, and the leaves of the vines serve as the major edible greens. The Dani also grow many other foods: tubers like yams and taro were sometimes planted with the sweet potatoes, and in small house garden plots one could find bananas and two sorts of pandanus (nuts and fruits), as well as sugarcane, cucumbers, and even tobacco.   ♦

Intensive Agriculture.   **Intensive agriculture** refers to those farming patterns that combine extremes of the six variables listed on pages 187 and 188: plows and tractors, permanent occupation of fields, often irrigation systems, fertilizer and insecticides, usually single-crop fields, and cash cropping, rather than merely subsistence farming. Often a relatively few people engaged in intensive agriculture can feed a large population, releasing many to work in factories and service industries. We have already examined the irrigation rice farming of the Balinese in Chapter 1, which nicely exemplifies a much more intensive pattern than either slash-and-burn or horticulture.

Intensive agriculture is generally associated with draft animals, which are domesticated mammals large enough to pull plows. As Jared Diamond has pointed out (1997:157ff), very few of the large mammals of the world were capable of being domesticated for traction. These few were found in Eurasia and North Africa but were absent from sub-Saharan Africa, the Pacific, and the Americas. By 2500 B.C., all of the large mammals capable of pulling plows (or wheeled vehicles) had been domesticated. Since then, none of the remaining candidates has been successfully domesticated. This factor seems to have been the major constraint on the spread of intensive agriculture, for it was not until Europeans brought their cattle and horses to the New World that intensive agriculture became possible there. The few areas of dense population in pre-Columbian America had been fed by slash-and-burn techniques (for example, the Lowland Mayans) or digging stick horticulture (for example, the Pueblo cultures in the southwestern United States or the Mound Builders east of the Mississippi).

To summarize the farming strategies introduced so far: each of these variations —slash-and-burn, horticulture, and intensive agriculture—has been practiced for

Intensive agriculture in the United States. A team of combines harvests wheat, dumping the grains into the truck. *(Credit: © Cotton Coulson/Woodfin Camp & Associates)*

centuries throughout the tropical and temperate world, often by the same people exploiting neighboring ecological niches and usually, to some extent, in combination with animal husbandry and even foraging strategies. Despite the artificiality of these categories, it is useful to be able to recognize ideal types, or prototypical expressions, of each strategy. Table 6.1 details characteristics of each farming technique.

Food Production Strategies in Industrial Societies

For centuries, even millennia, the range of food-producing strategies could be summed up by the traditional types described previously. Now, with industrialization and globalization, significant new forms have taken shape. Following is a very small sample of strategies that anthropologists have studied.

Commercial Fishing. The Gulf of Mexico, with its shallow warm waters, teems with sea life. In prehistoric times, it was a prime place for foraging. In fact, the coast is marked by numerous huge deposits of shells discarded by ancient peoples. Today, anthropologists have studied a very different sort of maritime exploitation: small-scale commercial fishing, especially shrimping. Paul Durrenberger, in Alabama (1992), and Robert Lee Maril, in Texas (1995), paint similar pictures of men (and a few women) who go out in small boats alone or with a deckhand hoping to net

TABLE 6.1   Traditional Farming Strategies

Slash and Burn (Swidden, Shifting)	Horticulture (Gardening)	Intensive Agriculture
Usually tropical	Tropical and temperate	Tropical and temperate
Adzes, axes, digging sticks	Axes, adzes, digging sticks	Animal-drawn plows, tractors
Land not altered	Some field preparation	Land leveled, often irrigation, terraced
Temporary shifting fields	Semipermanent fields	Permanent fields
Minimal fertilizer use	Rare fertilizer use	Common fertilizer use
No ownership	Informal ownership	Formal ownership
Movable settlements	Semipermanent settlements	Permanent settlements
Gender, age division of labor	Gender, age, some occupational division of labor	Extensive occupational division of labor

enough shrimp to at least break even. They are fiercely independent, competing against each other at sea, yet dependent on each other for society on shore. In all cases, the overwhelming facts of their lives involve government fisheries regulation and competition from imported shrimp. Recently, Vietnamese refugees have settled on the Gulf Coast and entered the shrimping business. Although they have quickly learned the technology of shrimping, their ignorance of the unwritten norms by which the Americans mitigate conflict has resulted in serious culture clashes.

Subsistence Strategies within Industrialized Settings.   On the whole, Americans buy their food in stores drawing from the global economy. At most, they may try to grow a few tomato plants each summer. Nevertheless, anthropologists have been able to find some people who produce and forage for much of their own food even as they live in the shadows of supermarkets.

Jo Ann Koltyk has studied the Hmong community in a small central Wisconsin city (1998). The Hmong were highland people of southern China who centuries ago began moving south into Southeast Asia to escape the dominance of the Chinese. They were recruited by U.S. forces to fight against the North Vietnamese but then were abandoned when the U.S. military withdrew from Vietnam in 1975. Many escaped to Thailand, and eventually some settled as refugees in the United States. The Hmong had used both foraging and slash-and-burn farming techniques in Southeast Asia, and they seemed singularly unsuited for urban American life. Koltyk describes how they have adapted to small-city Wisconsin opportunities. Virtually all Hmong families grow much of their vegetable needs in small gardens and preserve the food. Freezers are especially important appliances, for they allow people to buy whole pigs or cows, butcher and share the meat, and freeze it. Also, the Hmong do a great deal of hunting and gathering. Men and boys hunt deer, squirrels, and birds; families fish; and the people generally are skilled gatherers, foraging for all sorts of edible plants that their neighbors of European ancestry completely ignore. Koltyk tells of a day she spent with some Hmong women gathering watercress. On their return home with a huge harvest, they made up small bundles to give out to friends and relations. Koltyk emphasizes how important these subsistence activities are: Not only do the people become relatively independent of the formal grocery store economy, but also they use their excess foods in exchanges to strengthen the community. By the same token, they reaffirm their own identity as Hmong.

The Milagro Beanfield War shows a Hispanic community in New Mexico trying to maintain their small family farms, a scale of subsistence agriculture being threatened in this instance by resort developers.

DOING ANTHROPOLOGY

Food Production Strategies in a Supermarket Culture

As the result of extreme division of labor, most Americans no longer produce any of the food that they eat. They have other sources of income and use money to buy food that others have produced. Nevertheless, hunting, fishing, gardening, and even gathering are still practiced in America, not just for sport or entertainment but as a food strategy.

Use your ingenuity to explore these alternatives to supermarket shopping. Talk with people who hunt, fish, garden, or even gather. Search the Internet or contact government agencies for statistics on hunting and fishing licenses issued and on game killed or caught. Check stores or newspaper columns that are aimed at these people. ♦

SEEING ANTHROPOLOGY

A Horticultural Strategy: *Dani Sweet Potatoes*

Filmmaker: Karl G. Heider

I shot the footage for this film after I had been following Dani sweet potato production for nearly two years and had developed a good idea of the major steps in the process. There was no story line and no concern to show any individual Dani as people; rather the goal was to show the process of producing sweet potatoes step by step as I had come to understand it. I had been hanging around, living in the neighborhood, following people to the gardens—and everywhere else—for so long that they pretty much ignored me behind the camera. In the clip, we see only a part of the farming sequence, but in the complete film we follow things through the cooking and distribution at a minor ceremony. I omitted the farming in the lower-slope gardens as well as the slash-and-burn process on the steeper slopes above the settlements.

The film clip begins with the clearing of a garden area. A pig herd passes by three young men who are cleaning out an old ditch system. On another garden area, the clearing is progressing, and dried trash is burned off. Then we join a cooperative work group that is clearing out the ditches and smearing the ditch mud on the garden beds. Even without sound, one gets some sense of the fun that the men have, working together in the muddy ditch. Then we see the women's part in the process—planting, weeding, and harvesting.

The complete film begins with men and boys clearing an area to reopen gardens that had lain fallow for some time. The action in the short clip is followed by more harvesting, and a woman brings the tubers back to the compound. Next we see the making of a steam bundle for cooking large amounts of sweet potatoes (and often other vegetables and pork). Men and women heat the rocks in a fire, then build up the steam bundle with layers of hot rocks, grass, and sweet potatoes, before finally closing it up in a grass envelope. After an hour, the steam bundle is opened and the sweet potatoes and other vegetables (there was no pork this time) are distributed to everyone attending the event. (It was a sort of memorial feast for a distant relative who had died far away.)

Setup Questions

1. What evidence of division of labor can you recognize in the clip?
2. What can you sense about the atmosphere of the mudding crew?
3. Why would so many men get together to spread the mud?
4. Why would the Dani harvest sweet potatoes every day? What are the implications of that strategy?
5. Compare this view of the Dani with what you saw in the *Dead Birds* clip.   ♦

HOLLYWOOD-STYLE ANTHROPOLOGY

Family Farms in *The Milagro Beanfield War*

The Milagro Beanfield War   1988   118 minutes

>   Chick Vegnera as Joe Mondragon
>   Sonia Braga as Ruby Archuleta
>   Ruben Blades as Sheriff Bernabe Montoya
>   Carlos Riquelme as Amarante Cordova
>   John Heard as Charlie Bloom
>   Daniel Stern as Herbie Platt

In the high dry country of northern New Mexico the Hispanic farmers with their tiny bits of land are disheartened. They are no match for the well-funded and politically powerful resort developers. But the last holdout, Joe Mondragon, decides one desperate day to take water from the irrigation ditch and plant beans in his field. Thus begins the Milagro Beanfield War. Then there is the subplot around Herbie Platt, a sociology graduate student (he might as well be an anthropologist) from NYU who descends on Milagro to do research for his dissertation.

Setup Questions

1. How could these small family farms possibly survive? How have they kept going for 300 years?
2. Given that pigs are poorly adapted for dry climates, how does this one survive? And why?
3. Describe Herbie Platt's research methodology. What does he do well? Where are his weaknesses?
4. What is the sign of Herbie's understanding?
5. Who is the old man who dances and plays the accordion and talks with Amarante?
6. Who is the *zopilote* and what is the meaning of the name? ♦

CHAPTER SUMMARY

- This chapter deals with production, the first of the traditional concerns of economics (along with distribution and consumption), which is the creation and the reproduction of goods.
- Production, especially of food, is closely dependent on the natural environment. The interplay of human effort and the environment represents cultural adaptation.
- Cultural adaptation is achieved through the means of technology, which includes both tools and knowledge. When examining technology of very different cultures, it is often easy to understand the tools but to overlook the knowledge that has developed over generations.
- Although the environment does not fully determine the production of food and the like, in combination with the technology it may limit the production possibilities.
- Specialization, or the division of labor, is present in every society at least along the lines of age and gender.
- Societies with mechanical solidarity have minimal division of labor—everyone does much the same thing. Societies with organic solidarity, in contrast, have a great range of specialists.
- There are three major strategies for food production: foraging for food from land, water, and air; farming vegetable food; and raising animals (animal husbandry, or pastoralism). Most societies concentrate on one strategy or another but nevertheless use an opportunistic mixture of several techniques.
- Prototypical foragers like the Ju/'hoansi live in small groups with meager material objects and move about their marginal territories using their profound knowledge of the environmental possibilities to find food.

- Prototypical pastoralists like the Nuer focus their attention on their animals, investing much symbolism in them, often not even eating much meat but making extensive use of animal products such as milk, blood, wool, hides, and even dung.
- Farmers may be seminomadic, slash-and-burn gardeners who clear plots in the forest, use them for a time, and then move on. Horticulturalists are more settled farmers, using simple tools like digging sticks to work their land. Intensive agriculturalists employ plows or tractors with fertilizers and insecticides to farm large permanent fields.

KEY TERMS

agriculture	horticulture	production
animal husbandry	hunting and gathering	shifting horticulture
cultural adaptation	intensive agriculture	slash-and-burn
division of labor	local knowledge	horticulture
farming	mechanical solidarity	specialization
food production strategies	mixed production strategies	swidden farming technology
foraging	organic solidarity	transhumance
gardening	pastoralism	

QUESTIONS TO THINK ABOUT

- Imagine the genius that it took to develop the knowledge component of technology: to discover that California acorns or Amazonian cassava, both poisonous when eaten raw, could be soaked, leached, and processed into a staple food.
- Imagine yourself as Robinson Crusoe, the Swiss Family Robinson, Tarzan's parents, or any of the other fictional castaways who had not studied cultural anthropology. How could you possibly survive?
- Why is gender such a common and strong basis for division of labor? Why do at least some cultures not use strength, interest, or some other directly relevant criteria?
- Why do so many cultures have such a mixture of food-producing strategies?
- The more efficient the food production of a group, the more time the members have for other things. What might influence the ways in which people actually use the rest of their time, whether in art, in ritual, or simply sitting around?

SUGGESTIONS FOR FURTHER READING

Dobres, Marcia-Anne, and Christopher R. Hoffman (eds.)
1999   The Social Dynamics of Technology: Practice, Politics, and World View. Washington, DC: Smithsonian Institution Press. *A holistic approach to production of artifacts.*

Ginat, Joseph, and Anatoly M. Khazanov (eds.)
1998   Changing Nomads in a Changing World. Portland, OR: Sussex Academic Press. *Pastoralism in Africa and Asia today.*

Gowdy, John M. (ed.)
1998   Limited Wants, Unlimited Means: A Reader on Hunter-Gatherer Economics and the Environment. Washington, DC: Island Press. *Classic and current papers.*

Netting, Robert M.
1993   Small Holders, Householders: Farm Families and the Ecology of Intensive, Sustainable Agriculture. Stanford, CA: Stanford University Press. *A broad consideration of intensive agriculture as practiced by household farms. The author is an anthropologist who has done fieldwork in West Africa and Switzerland.*

Sciama, Lidia D., and Joanne B. Eicher (eds.)
1998   Beads and Beadmakers: Gender, Material Culture, and Meaning. Oxford, U.K.: Berg. *Another example of the current approach to material culture.*

Wilk, Richard R.
1996   Economics and Culture: Foundations of Economic Anthropology. Boulder, CO: Westview.

CHAPTER 7

Distribution and Consumption

Bringing food. Barobudur, Java, 9th century C.E. *(Credit: Karl G. Heider)*

HEADLINE ANTHROPOLOGY

PRESS WATCH

Some of the subjects discussed in this chapter have made their way into current news stories. For example:

♦ In the US there are some 2500 "swap meets" (in the West) or "flea markets" (in the East) at which goods are sold informally in a sort of "parallel economy," below the radar of official economic statistics.

—New York Times, *April 28, 2002.*

♦ By fermenting mare's milk, herders in Kyrgyzstan make kumiss, with an alcohol content of 10%, and skim off the whey, which is three times as strong.

—New York Times, *July 19, 2002.*

♦ A popular gourmet restaurant in Guangdong Province, near Hong Kong, had made its reputation by serving "extreme food," rare wild animals like flying foxes, snake, lynx, wildcat, and also rat.

—New York Times, *June 25, 2002.*

♦ New York City has some 4000 street fairs scheduled each year where individuals and groups can sell goods.

—New York Times, *April 28, 2002.*

♦ In Chiapas, Mexico, the Roman Catholic church, on orders from the Vatican, has stopped ordaining lay deacons, who, with their wives, have been carrying out many of the normal duties of priests (short of consecrating communion and hearing confessions). The Vatican is particularly unhappy with the amount of both pre-Columbian elements and liberation theology that the deacons have introduced.

—New York Times, *May 26, 2002.*

If individuals were truly self-sufficient, if everyone produced everything he or she needed, there would be no distribution, no economics, and also no societies. **Exchange,** the distribution of goods and services, forms the strands of social networks that bind the members of a group to each other and, reaching beyond, ally one group with another. Mutual interest may be the motivation for these associations within and between groups, but it is exchanges, both substantial and symbolic, that forge the real ties.

DISTRIBUTION: MECHANISMS OF EXCHANGE

In Chapter 6, we looked at production. Here, as we turn to other main interests of economics, **distribution** and **consumption,** we face a different sort of problem. As anthropologists first encountered other cultures, they found different manners of producing food, tools, or other goods, but these techniques were easily understood. They differed in details only, not in principle, from what the anthropologists had encountered at home. In contrast, distribution, or exchange, in small-scale tribal societies dealt with a whole new set of principles and posed different problems. Most importantly, there were rarely stores or markets selling products for money on an impersonal basis. Instead, many of the transactions took place as deeply embedded components of social relationships.

Anthropologists generally follow Karl Polanyi (1957), who recognized three major patterns, or **forms of integration,** by which societies manage distribution: reciprocity, redistribution, and market exchange. These patterns blur into each other and so are not absolutely clear-cut. Also, in many societies, more than one pattern may coexist at different levels. Table 7.1 gives a general idea of what distinguishes each pattern and where each occurs.

We will approach distribution as anthropologists did, beginning with reciprocity (the mechanisms that dominate exchange in small-scale societies), then moving to redistribution (or pooling, which is characteristic of societies with strong central leadership), and finally considering the market exchange of large-scale societies with money.

Generalized Reciprocity

Reciprocity refers to a wide range of exchanges involving goods and services between relatively equal individuals or groups. Various permutations of this form of integration characterized traditional tribal societies before they were incorporated into the money economies of larger states. Following Marshall Sahlins' classic statement (1965), we recognize three major forms of reciprocity: generalized reciprocity, balanced reciprocity, and the special case of negative reciprocity. We are really talking about a continuum along an axis of social distance,

TABLE 7.1   Exchange and Society Size

	Reciprocity	Redistribution	Markets
Small-scale societies (bands, tribes)	Yes	No	No
Midsized societies with some central power	Yes	Yes	No
Large-scale societies with strong centralized power	Yes	Yes	Yes

with generalized reciprocity appearing at one end and negative reciprocity found at the other end.

Generalized reciprocity is the form most extensively studied by anthropologists, because it is the key to mechanisms of exchange in nonmarket economies. Also known as delayed reciprocity, it occurs between closely related or allied people or groups and involves an indirect exchange that takes time to complete: A gives to B, but B does not immediately reciprocate. This delayed exchange is made possible by close social ties (preexisting or newly created) and often creates or maintains complex relations between people. ("If friends make gifts, gifts make friends" [Sahlins, 1965:139].)

Another way of formulating generalized reciprocity as a form of integration is through the concept of **gift.** One of Durkheim's students, Marcel Mauss, analyzed this sort of exchange in his important book *The Gift: Forms and Functions of Exchange in Archaic Societies* (1925/1954). Mauss saw exchange, which was largely gift exchange in these "archaic societies," as deeply embedded, what he termed a "total social phenomenon." Taking a holistic perspective, he recognized that gift giving served many different functions: legal, political, domestic, religious, economic, aesthetic, and structural. But he insisted that

> we are dealing then with something more than a set of themes, more than institutional elements, more than institutions, more even than systems of institutions divisible into legal, economic, religious, and other parts. We are concerned with "wholes," with systems in their entirety. . . . It is only by considering them as wholes that we have been able to see their essence, their operation and their living aspect." (Mauss, 1925/1954:77)

Of course, gift giving is important in more than tribal societies. As a homey example, let's take an American middle-class ten-year-old's birthday party. The birthday child invites a dozen friends, each of whom brings a gift having a value of a few dollars. The children get food (ice cream, cake, soft drinks), perhaps a minor present to take home, and entertainment (home games, an expedition to a skating rink, or the like). During the next year, the birthday child can be expected to be invited to twelve birthday parties, and should bring an exactly comparable present (sometimes, depending on the current fads, it is the same thing—a Barbie doll or Pokémon trading cards, for example). At the end of the annual cycle, everyone should be about equal. There should not be any great variations in cost of the present, impressiveness of the entertainment, or the like. So what is the point? Obviously, one function of this shuffling about of interchangeable goods and services is to strengthen ties by keeping everyone constantly in someone's debt. There is no specialization; each child buys presents at one of the same few toy stores. But the social network is being constantly strengthened. A birthday party, in Mauss's words, allows us to "catch the fleeting moment when the society and its members take emotional stock of themselves and their situation as regards others" (Mauss, 1925/1954:77, 78).

What is interesting here is that the cultural idea of *gift* in English is something given freely, without thought of return. From an anthropological viewpoint, we

An American birthday party with presents. *(Credit: © Pickerell/The Image Works)*

could hypothesize that there is almost never such a thing as a gift in that sense. There is virtually always the expectation of return. But that very cultural ideology of the "free" gift, while technically incorrect, is part of what binds the social network.

Mauss's formulation includes three obligations: to give gifts; to repay those gifts; and, most interestingly, to accept gifts. In these sorts of interactions, it is not acceptable to reject the social ties that a gift brings with it. There is the implication that all gifts are of this sort, implying social obligations with the expectation of return.

Is it possible to have truly free gifts? Christians are exhorted to tithe, to give one-tenth of their goods to their church. One of the five essential principles of Islam is the obligation to give generously to charity. You are probably paying tuition to a college or university now; as soon as you graduate you will be asked to "give" to variously named alumni funds. Such gifts do not fit into Mauss's concept.

Mauss's book on gift giving and receiving is one of the few theoretical works from the 1920s that remains a standard reference. It was important because it described the workings of a kind of exchange that had escaped the notice of traditional economics. Mauss was open to two kinds of misunderstandings:

1. Although he showed the prevalence of "gifts" that are in fact delayed reciprocity, this finding does not exclude the possibility of "pure gifts," or gifts without reciprocity.
2. Because Mauss drew on ethnographic writings to show how important gifts were in tribal societies, people sometimes fell into a simplistic trap: we have

markets, they have gifts. As a very broad generalization that statement is not bad, but things are much more complex in real life.

Ceremonial Gift Exchange Among the Trobrianders

The Kula Ring. The most famous gifts in all ethnographic literature are the simple shell bracelets and coral necklaces of the Kula Ring of the Massim District, off the eastern tip of New Guinea, which were memorably described by Bronislaw Malinowski in 1922. The Massim area includes several island and atoll groups that lie in an approximate circle (see Figure 7.1). Malinowski, doing fieldwork on the Trobriand Islands, saw how his chiefly friends had ritual counterpart partners located in neighboring villages both to the east and to the west. At regular intervals and with great ceremony, a chief would sail with his entourage to the east or west to pick up a gift from his kula partner. If he went to the west from the Trobriands, the gift would be a shell bracelet; if he went to the east, the gift would be a red coral necklace. Later, there would be return visits with more gifts. As Malinowski worked out the regional implications of the **kula exchange** system, he found that the bracelets circulated all around the circle in a clockwise fashion, while the necklaces went in a counterclockwise fashion. Malinowski described in detail how these gifts were embedded in regional social and religious systems.

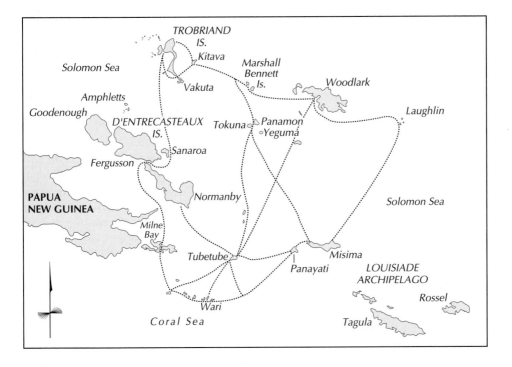

FIGURE 7.1   The Kula Ring.

Mauss (in *The Gift*) used Malinowski's account of the Kula Ring as his prime example of a total social phenomenon. He emphasized how much other ordinary trade was carried out under the protection of the chiefly gift giving. While the leaders were engaged in the kula ritual in the village, their followers were conducting lively barter on the beach. Different islands produced different things—fine pottery, canoe wood, great yams, greenstone, or whatever—and thus the ceremonial kula exchange allowed the exchange of these other, more usable goods.

Why the Kula Ring? What does it mean? What are its functions? It is certainly one of Mauss's total social phenomena, for the kula involved much of Trobriand culture: ritual (in the gift-exchange ceremonies), technology (in crafting and sailing the great seagoing canoes), politics (in the jockeying for influence), and economics (in the trading for ordinary crafts and produce that accompany the kula voyaging). Annette Weiner, who studied the Trobriands half a century after Malinowski, emphasized (1988) how men (and a few women) are motivated to participate in the extraordinary complex manipulations to establish, maintain, and profit from their kula paths (the ties they have with their various kula partners on other islands). At one level, the kula exchange represents a great context for status, with winners and losers. Weiner emphasized how the kula event is a chance for the principals to gain some international renown, a fame that they could never achieve as players at the local village or island level:

> Through the shells, a villager transcends the history of his or her own ancestral lineage and becomes a part of kula history. What is of consequence is that this kula history legitimizes a person's right to win while others lose. (Weiner, 1988:156)

Once it seemed as if the Kula Ring was an example of *visiting trade institutions* (exchange between antagonistic trading partners), in which the dangers of the Massim area would be overcome by the ritual of the kula, creating close kinshiplike ties between the trading partners. Ordinary trade could then be safely conducted under the umbrella of the kula. Weiner, however, pointed out (1988:146) that in the past, as today, straightforward trading voyages were safely made between islands without any kula protection. So, although trade does take advantage of the kula, it does not depend on the kula.

Funerary Gift Exchange Among Women. The Kula Ring is just one example of Trobriand exchange. Sixty years after Malinowski's study, Annette Weiner went to the Trobriands to study tourist art. On her first day in the village, however, she was taken to a funeral ceremony where women were giving away goods. To her surprise, Malinowski had not dealt with this particular ceremony. In following it up, Weiner learned about the important role played by women in Trobriand ritual exchanges. So, as it turned out, first Malinowski and then Weiner were drawn to exchange as a key to the organization of Trobriand society.

In her first book, Weiner drew attention to the fact that many anthropologists working in other cultures had missed the importance of this sort of women's exchange. In particular, she focused on women's exchange of cloth (her definition of cloth included a broad range of artifacts, mostly made by women by processes of weaving, plaiting, knitting, netting, and sewing) and cited (1976:93) among others my own ethnography of the Dani. Weiner's analysis was right on the mark. I had included a photograph captioned "at a funeral, women redistribute the nets that had been brought as funeral gifts," but then I dismissed this event as "strictly a woman's affair, and the men ignore it" (Heider, 1970:156, 157). Had I paid attention to the nets, I would have learned much about the Dani women's roles in their society.

This funeral exchange does several important things. First, it reaffirms the integrity and status of the matrilineage passing out the gifts. Second, it dramatizes the links between the dead person's mother's and father's matrilineages. Third, the exchange places the women at the very center of Trobriand social and ritual life at least for the duration of that ceremony. Finally, the ceremony is frankly competitive, but unlike the men's competition that Malinowski described, it occurs between women:

> Women's mortuary ceremonies constitute a game (*mwasawa*) of sorts in which women strive to be first. To be first, a woman must be affluent enough to give away more than five thousand bundles of banana leaves and twenty or thirty skirts in one day. . . . Women constantly deal in bundles and skirts just as men traffic in yams and male valuables. In all competitive activities that men undertake (e.g., *kula,* cricket, warfare, *kayasa*), villagers say that men play games. In the women's mortuary ceremony, women have the opportunity to play similar games. (Weiner, 1976:91, 92)

Food Sharing as Insurance.   One function of gifts for Trobrianders, then, is to forge ties between potentially hostile villages or islands. But similar practices have other functions. For many of these cultures, enough environmental variability and uncertainty occur—the rain doesn't fall, the game is scarce—that no person or household unit can be assured of having enough food all the time. Sharing one's surpluses with others, in the expectation that food given out will eventually be returned, is a way of safeguarding against the inevitable bad times. This has been called a *social refrigerator.* We can see a double outcome of sharing. Food is distributed, and the social network is strengthened. There are many ways to institutionalize sharing.

The Feasts of the Horticultural Kantu'.   The Kantu' of West Kalimantan are generally sober, but on occasions of ceremonial feasting (once a week or so), they get thoroughly drunk on potent rice wine. The drinking is necessary for communication with their gods or spirits. The host provides the liquor for the guests, who come from other households or even other longhouses. The host's role is to force the guests to drink as much as possible, vomit, and then drink more.

How do we make sense of such a cultural pattern? The Kantu' themselves say that by so pleasing the spirits, they will have good rice harvests. Furthermore, by pleasing their human guests, they will share in the good fortune of those guests. But the costs are high. The host must use great quantities of his precious rice to

A drinking feast of the Kantu' of Kalimantan (Indonesian Borneo). *(Credit: Dr. Michael R. Dove)*

make the liquor. The guests become severely intoxicated, become nauseated, vomit, are often delirious, and have long hangovers.

According to the authority on the Kantu', Michael Dove (1988b), these drunken ceremonies play an important part in the Kantu' ecological system. Kantu' grow rice in small plots that are widely dispersed through the rain forest. The ethos of the Kantu' is one of competitive independence. Yet so many uncertain variables plague the agricultural process that every household, no matter how skilled, has seasons of success and seasons of failure. So, although ecology and psychology create an atomistic society, the same ecology creates a need for social integration, for some means to shift rice from "the temporarily lucky to the temporarily unlucky" (Dove, 1988b:165). These ceremonies accomplish this goal by maintaining long-term ceremonial relationships between households. The ceremonies not only create the relationships, but also inform each side about the strength and wealth of the other. Then they facilitate the movement of rice, other goods, and labor to help out in times of need. Of course, drunken feasts are not the only possible route to survival in an uncertain world. In fact, Dove points out that in recent times, the Kantu' have begun to plant rubber trees to provide a fallback resource for times of need; as a result, the ceremonial feasting has diminished.

The Everyday Sharing of Food among the Ju/'hoansi.   The environment of the Ju/'hoansi (the !Kung San) in the Kalahari Desert of southern Africa could hardly be more different from the rain forest of the Kantu', but it is similar in one important respect: uncertainty of resources, particularly game in this case. No matter how skilled a hunter is, he inevitably will have periods of failure. The Ju/'hoansi have their own pattern of sharing, very different from the Kantu' but with the same results: It strengthens their social ties with other groups, it distributes meat from the temporarily lucky to the temporarily unlucky, and it promotes an egalitarian ethos.

Much Ju/'hoansi hunting is done with poisoned arrows, and hunters frequently use other people's arrows. They say, "The owner of the arrow is the owner of the meat." That is, the person who decides how the meat shall be distributed is not the hunter himself, but the man or woman who provided him with the arrow. As Richard Lee explains,

> The reason for this . . . arrow sharing is not hard to find. A meat distribution brings prestige to the hunter, but it also can be a heavy burden, bringing with it the risk of accusations of stinginess or improper behavior if the distribution is not to everybody's liking. A practice that tends to diffuse the responsibility for meat distribution and spread the glory (and the hostility) around is therefore a blessing in such tense situations. (Lee, 1993:55, 56)

Another Ju/'hoansi custom that promotes sharing and egalitarianism is what Lee calls "insulting the meat" (1993:54). Instead of celebrating a successful hunter and praising the meat that he has brought in for distribution, everyone, including the hunter himself, downplays and even disparages the event. Thus,

> Even though some men are much better hunters than others, their behavior is molded by the group to minimize the tendency toward self-praise and to channel their energies into socially beneficial activities. As a result, the existence of differences in hunting prowess does not lead to a system of Big Men in which a few talented individuals tower over the others in terms of prestige. (Lee, 1993:55)

Marriage as Exchange.   The most common institutionalized sorts of generalized reciprocity are the exchanges that are triggered by marriage. Although we now tend to think of marriage as the union of two individuals, in most societies marriages are more nearly unions of two groups that the fact of the marriage obligates to exchange goods and services of spouses over time. In Chapter 8 we shall explore how the extensive exchanges that take place serve to integrate, or bind together, the two groups.

Analysis of wedding exchanges among the Kwa Kwaka' Wakw clearly shows the gift exchange dynamics (Suttles, 1991:71ff). The generalized reciprocity begins when the groom's party arrives in their canoes at the bride's village with lavish gifts for the bride's family. They all feast together. Afterward, the bride's father hands his daughter to her new husband, along with gifts of skins, fish oil, carved dishes, and new names for the groom and his children by a previous marriage (if he has any): one set of names for the summer (the secular season) and a second set for the winter, when important rituals are performed. The groom's party then goes home and the bride's party distributes those first gifts to four other clans, presumably as delayed reciprocity for earlier gifts. During the winter, the bride's people pay a return visit, bringing reciprocal gifts to the husband. The most valuable of these gifts are ownership of certain powerful winter dances. Later, when a child is born, the mother's clan brings more gifts. This series of gift exchange, triggered by the wedding, is straightforward generalized reciprocity.

Among the Trobrianders, marriage exchanges are very complex because they involve an effort among women to "keep while giving" (Weiner, 1989:40). This attempt is manifested in various ways. The Trobrianders have matrilineages and matri-clans, but patrilocal residence. Although a women remains a key member of her matri-clan, with her children being the next-generation members of that clan, she lives in her husband's hamlet (usually not far from her own). Thus brothers and sisters—both members of their mother's clan—are separated as adults. Of course, this sort of problem (scattering of clan members' residences) exists for virtually every society, because brother–sister incest prohibitions force brothers and sisters apart.

The Trobrianders did their best to counter this spread of clans in two ways. First, their beliefs about the origin of children emphasize the importance of the mother's clan and deny a role to the father. They say that when a person dies, his or her spirit goes to an island in the west and later returns to be reborn as a new member of the same clan. Conception, then, is the work of the mother and the spirit, both of whom are members of the same clan. When Malinowski reported this belief, stating that the Trobrianders did not understand the physical role of the father in conception, he triggered a long debate about local knowledge and the Oedipus complex that continues today. Perhaps we can say that, at some level, the Trobrianders do emphasize only the role of the matrilineage and ignore the role of the father in conception itself (although they believe that it is important for the father and mother to have sexual intercourse between conception and birth to help form the child). Sometimes this belief is even used in legal arguments. Weiner tells of a woman who became pregnant while her husband was away. He complained of adultery but she claimed that she had not had sex with anyone—the conception involved only her and the baby's new spirit. Perhaps also there is another understanding of the biological, "scientific" process of conception that does not limit itself to the culturally paramount ideas about matrilineage continuity. (It does sound as if the aggrieved husband was not completely buying the traditional belief about conception and new spirits.)

The second means of "keeping while giving" for Trobrianders is a very complex exchange system that binds together matrilineages related through marriage. Although their children must "marry out," they are kept close. For the Dani, long-term wedding gifts keep two lineages involved with each other long after the wedding itself. The Trobriand exchanges are even more elaborate. They begin with the birth of a child, when the mother's husband (the baby's father) begins a lifelong series of gifts and supportive acts toward the child. By the time the child is grown and dies, it will have accumulated a huge debt. That is, its (mother's) matrilineage will owe much to the matrilineage of the father. Weiner encountered this concept on her first day in the Trobriand village. A person had died, and the women of the matrilineage had prepared a vast quantity of "cloth"—skirts and woven banana leaf bundles. They had made them, borrowed them, bought them, and in the name of themselves and their matrilineage passed them out in repayment of the debts incurred by the life of the dead person.

Balanced and Negative Reciprocity

Balanced reciprocity is found further along our gift-giving spectrum (see Table 7.2). This type of exchange takes place between more distant people (distant in geographical or social terms), the reciprocity is more immediate (without a long delay), the goods involved are of relatively balanced or equal value, and the long-term social consequences are less important. **Barter,** the overt negotiation of exchange, is more likely to occur. The Kula Ring of the Trobriand Islands, for example, was a two-tiered economic institution: In village ceremonies the high-status men presented gifts that would eventually be reciprocated (generalized reciprocity), while their followers brought goods to be unceremoniously bartered on the beach (balanced reciprocity). Another example of balanced reciprocity can be found in the barter economy that involves many people in the United States today. A dentist and an auto mechanic may exchange services, thereby avoiding cash and income tax liability.

Negative Reciprocity.   Continuing along our continuum, as the social distance increases, the nature of the exchange shifts from a concern for social ties toward

TABLE 7.2   Three Types of Reciprocity: the Reciprocity Continuum

Most anthropological attention is paid to generalized reciprocity, "gift giving," in tribal cultures, but the entire spectrum can be identified in most cultures. The extreme cases are not, strictly speaking, "reciprocity," for in neither "true gifts" nor in plunder do we see any expectation of return; rather, they are the logical extension of these principles. The visiting trade institution reproduces generalized reciprocity at the far right.

	Generalized Reciprocity		*Balanced Reciprocity*		*Negative Reciprocity*
	"Pure" gift	**Gift**	**Barter**	**Bargaining**	**Theft, plunder**
Time lag of reciprocity	Never	Delayed	Short term	Immediate	Never
Social distance	Intimate (kin)	Close (kin, neighbor)	Medium (friend)	Medium (friend)	Extreme (enemy, Other)

an antagonistic stance of maximizing personal gain. Bargaining becomes sharper and eventually we wind up at the far right of the spectrum with outright trickery, theft, and plunder, which are, indeed, types of **negative reciprocity.** The parties are no longer kin, allies, or friends but rather enemies or the Other. It is therefore safe to consider them deserving of abuse (if one can get away with it). The Vikings practiced negative reciprocity for centuries, swooping down out of Scandinavia to plunder the English coastal settlements of goods and slaves.

A Solution: Visiting Trade Institutions.   If these principles were absolute laws, long-distance trade would be impossible. But trade is desirable, and one widespread solution is to create a nominal kinshiplike relationship between distant and otherwise unrelated people. These individuals are often called "trading partners." For example, the distant partners of kula exchange, which we discussed under the aegis of "generalized reciprocity," could often be part of visiting trade institutions.

Redistribution

Redistribution involves the distribution of some of a rich person's wealth, or the gathering together, or *pooling,* of resources in a common pool, followed by a reallocation of these resources. In these cases, no expectation of reciprocity exists. Individuals may relinquish some of their resources, perhaps in the expectation that they will later benefit in some way. Redistribution usually requires some centralized power to assure the incoming contributions and to determine the outgoing expenditures.

Taxation is a prime example of that redistribution. When the rich contribute proportionally more than the poor, it is called *progressive taxation* and has some economic equalizing, or **leveling effect.** When the poor contribute more in proportion to their wealth, it is *regressive taxation* and increases the economic stratification.

The Kwa Kwaka' Waka potlatch distribution and the Chiapas Mayan cargo system both involve the distribution of rich individuals' wealth to others, which has a leveling effect. We first met the Kwa Kwaka' Wakw of the Northwest Coast in Chapter 4. Thanks to Franz Boas's writings, the Kwa Kwaka' Wakw (Boas called them the "Kwakiutl") are famous in the anthropological literature. Their **potlatch** ceremony is a standard example of "ritual distribution and exchange" (Goldman, 1975:122ff). Basically, the host of a ritual event would hand out to his guests from other clans or even tribes massive amount of objects—furs, skins, carvings, food, and even "coppers," which are painted and inscribed shields of beaten copper. In return, the giver received the guests' recognition of his claims to high status. Although there was no expectation of delayed reciprocity, a rival chief, so as not to be eclipsed in everyone's eyes, might be moved to counter with his own, grander potlatch. Occasionally, the rivalry between chiefs became so intense that they would try to outdo each other by destroying coppers or other valuables rather than simply redistributing them.

It is difficult to reconstruct the psychology of those old potlatches. To some extent, they must have served as economic leveling institutions through which the most wealthy chiefs gave away goods to gain status. In the Focus Culture, Frank Cancian analyzes this aspect of another redistribution system, the Mayan cargo ritual.

Marcel Mauss, who had discussed gifts and generalized reciprocity in the kula exchange, also pointed out that the potlatch was, like the Kula Ring, a **"total social phenomenon."** That is, he forced people to look in a holistic sense at the various ways in which this redistribution institution, the potlatch, was involved in Northwest Coast cultures: in religious, mythological, shamanistic, economic, social organizational, and legal senses (1925/1954:36, 37).

FOCUS CULTURE

The Redistributive Cargo System of the Zinacantan Mayans of Chiapas, Mexico

OVERVIEW

Location: The Mexican state of Chiapas

Geography: Settlements are concentrated in the rugged mountains of Chiapas; many people also have farms in the adjacent lowlands.

Population: Of the total of 5 million Maya living in Mexico and Central America, more than 100,000 live in the Chiapas Highlands. Some 22,000 live in Zinacantan.

Language: Tzeltal, Tzotzil, and other Mayan languages, in addition to Spanish

Religion: Mainly Roman Catholicism with much traditional Mayan elements; recently some evangelical Protestantism

Economy: Mainly small-scale maize farmers

Sociopolitical Organization: Within the Mexican state of Chiapas, municipios (townships) contain small hamlet settlement clusters

The great Mayan civilization of the first millennium A.D. flourished in the lowland jungles of what is now southern Mexico, Guatemala, and Honduras. Its achievements in temple architecture, astronomy, and mathematics (they and the Hindus were the only cultures to invent the concept of zero) were long known to Europeans. Indeed, in the early 1500s, Spanish invaders met and conquered their descendants. For the most part, the kingdoms had collapsed hundreds of years earlier, for reasons still hotly debated, and much of Middle America was dominated by the Aztec empire by the time of the Spaniards' arrival.

Today, however, Mayans still occupy much of their old territory. They no longer form powerful independent kingdoms, but rather are citizens of modern nations. They speak one or another of the Mayan languages and sometimes Spanish. Their religious practices are ostensibly Roman Catholic, sprinkled with much evidence of older Mayan beliefs. We will focus on the Tzotzil-speaking Mayans of Chiapas, the southernmost state of Mexico, and particularly on the municipio of Zinacantan (like

an American township or county), high in the mountains, surrounded by pine forests. Since the 1950s, Zinacantan has been studied as intensively as any region in the world through a project organized by Evon Z. Vogt of Harvard University (see Vogt, 1994). Also, in the 1990s, the Zapatista Rebellion in Chiapas made front-page news.

Maize (corn) is the Mayans' main crop. From it, the Mayans make the baked tortillas that are the essential part of any meal. Maize is grown in small garden plots. The Mayans practice slash-and-burn horticulture using metal hoes and machetes to clear the bush from the fields at the beginning of the growing season. The brush is dried and burned, the maize planted, and the crop eventually harvested. Beans and squash are the other main food crops. This triad of maize, beans, and squash has been the basis of New World horticulturalists' diet since long before European contact. Other foods, like hot chile peppers, are also grown or bought in markets.

In their home territory, at 7,000 feet altitude in the mountains, there is not enough land to support the entire Mayan population. Consequently, most families rent plots in the lowlands. Reaching this land involves a strenuous hike of several hours and 5,000 feet of difference in altitude.

Chickens and pigs are kept around the houses, and some Mayans have horses to carry burdens. Sheep are kept not for food, but for wool.

From this wool and from store-bought cotton thread, the women weave the traditional clothing. Highland Mayan women, especially, wear skirts, blouses, and shawls with colorful designs that are distinctive markers of local identity. When Carol Hendrickson studied the meanings and making of the dress of a Mayan group in Guatemala, some 250 miles east and south of Zinacantan, she described it as "a powerful and densely meaningful expression of social identity and a vital element of life in the highlands" (1995:6). Generally, the dress of Zinacantan men is not as spectacular as that of the women, but on festive days they do wear broad-brimmed hats decorated by rainbows of ribbon streamers. Vogt suggests that this headgear is the modern version of Classic Mayan feathered headdresses shown in paintings and bas reliefs (1970:57).

Religious activity is an obsession in Zinacantan. According to Vogt,

> The Zinacanteco way of life emphasizes ceremony. Hardly a day passes in Zinacantan Center without some ritual being performed as the annual ceremonial calendar unfolds; hardly a week passes, even in the smaller hamlets, without at least one ceremony being performed by a shaman to cure illness, dedicate a new house, or offer candles in a maize field. (Vogt, 1970:78)

Among our focus cultures encountered so far, this ritual intensity is matched only by the Balinese. Like the Balinese, these Mayans have an extremely syncretic mix of religions—in this case, Mayan and Roman Catholic. At first glance, they seem quite simply to be Catholic. The main center of Zinacantan boasts the churches of San Lorenzo and San Sebastian, both built in Spanish colonial style. Scattered around the landscape are shrines with great wooden crosses. Indeed, the yearly ritual cycle is full with Catholic saints' days and the main celebrations of the Christian year—Christmas, Easter, Epiphany. Yet many of the meanings assigned to these Catholic symbols and events come not from Rome but from old Mayan traditions. Even the settlement pattern has a traditional look. Hamlets, where the farmers actually live, are scattered across the municipio, and government and ritual life focus on a classic Mayan ceremonial center, albeit one with churches and the city hall instead of temples.

Although Zinacantans grow much of their own basic food—maize, beans, and squash—their dominant method of exchange is market exchange. They shop in markets in the region and beyond for most tools, household goods, and clothing, as well as for the large amounts of rum liquor and other things necessary for ceremonials.

Mayans in Chiapas, Mexico, carrying their assigned cargoes during a ceremony. *(Credit: © D. Donne Bryant)*

The **cargo system,** a redistributive mechanism, is also an essential element in the Mayan economy.

One of the most important Mayan institutions is the system of religious offices, which are arranged in four hierarchical levels. Each office is held by a man for one year and carries with it increasingly elaborate duties, at increasing expense to the office holder. The word "cargo" is Spanish, referring to the idea that an office holder "carries" the burden of office for a year before passing it on to the next carrier. The image of a carrier evokes the Classic Mayan concept, illustrated in their art, of gods bearing a great stone block with the symbol, or glyph, for a particular year held on their backs by a rope that goes over the forehead of the carrier (Vogt, 1970:19).

The cargo system results in great redistribution of wealth, for the cargo offices require the men holding them to spend time and money on ceremonies and to provide food to the community even as they take away the cargo bearers' own ability to accumulate wealth. This redistribution, like the potlatch, is very much a "total social phenomenon," to use Mauss's term. Frank Cancian, who described the cargo system in Zinacantan as it existed in the 1960s, showed how deeply entwined it was in people's economic life, religious life, social prestige and hierarchy, and politics, even though the Mayans themselves strictly differentiate it from the civil administrative offices. Hierarchy plays an important role in Mayan life generally, and its status is reflected in the cargo titles and their behaviors. There are 55 positions in the four levels. Within each of the levels, the positions are ranked. The higher the level, the fewer the cargos:

> Level 4: 3 cargos
> Level 3: 4 cargos
> Level 2: 14 cargos
> Level 1: 34 cargos

The higher the level, or the higher the rank within the level, the more duties the carrier has. The rankings determine who sits where in ceremonies, who is served rum liquor before whom, what the cargo holder's duties are, how much money the incumbents must spend during their year of service, and, at the end, how much prestige each has garnered for his efforts. "Ritual is the principal product of the hierarchy, and the performance of ritual is the principal duty of the cargoholders" (Cancian, 1965:51).

Depending on the particular office, the cargo holder is involved in many rituals over the course of the year. He is a leader, a participant, and a sponsor. Many rituals involve long parades where men carry sacred images of Catholic saints around to different important spots in the area. The cost of the office is mainly in the liquor and food that the cargo holder must provide for all participants and helpers in the particular ceremonies for which he is responsible as the holder of that title for that year. Cancian figured that virtually every man in Zinacantan could afford a first-level cargo. If their ambitions led them to higher levels, however, by the time they reached the fourth level, the costs would be considerable. One must also add in the time required to meet the office's demands in addition to the actual outlay of money. The usual maize farmer must spend weeks away from home tending his field in the low country. Many cargo holders move to the ceremonial center for the year to devote themselves to their ritual duties, thus neglecting their fields. At the end of the year, virtually every cargo holder has overextended himself and is in debt to his close kinsmen.

A man's identity as a Zinacantan is marked by his ability to speak Tzotzil, his distinctive clothing, and his participation in the cargo system to the extent that he can. Most men hold only a first-level cargo, and only the richest men can afford to move through all four levels. In discussing the functions of the cargo system and its importance to Zinacantan, Cancian emphasized its integrative aspect, for it truly binds the men of the muncipio together. The trade-off of money for prestige reduces the difference between the very rich and the rest of the population, and it particularly reduces possible jealousy toward the rich, for their wealth will be channeled back into community ritual. Because so much money goes into ceremonies within the community, less is available for consumption and investment in the wider realm of Chiapas and Mexico. In 1976, Cancian predicted:

> As long as the traditional norms are held by all Zinacantecos, and the alternatives to being an Indian are unattractive, the cargo system would seem to be a very satisfactory way of converting economic surplus into social position. However, if and when the norms weaken and the non-Indian environment becomes more attractive, the expenses of cargo may only add to individual motivation to reject the traditional system. (Cancian, 1976:136)

And what role do the women of Zinacantan play in this system? They are virtually invisible, for they hold no cargo positions and only sometimes are glimpsed assisting their husbands.

The Mayan cargo system can be analyzed in terms of all three families of theories (refer back to Chapter 3). Although Cancian pays attention to both the historical and the symbolic aspects of the institution, as an economic anthropologist he is most interested in the functional questions: What effects does the cargo system have on Mayan life? What are the consequences of cargo? Cancian discusses two, quite different functions: (1) by recognizing and rewarding wealth, the system legitimizes stratification, but (2) by inducing the richer men to redistribute wealth, spending so much money on food and drink for others, the cargo system serves as a leveling mechanism. Cancian summed up his analysis of the cargo system of the 1960s in the following way:

> Service in the cargo system legitimizes wealth differences that do exist and thus prevents disruptive envy. There is, in effect, sufficient leveling (the result of differential economic contribution to cargo service) to satisfy normative prescriptions, but not enough to produce an economically homogeneous community. (Cancian, 1965:140) ♦

Market Exchange

In the institution of **market exchange,** goods and services are exchanged for money, with the price being set by the "market forces" of supply and demand (Plattner, 1984; Narotzky, 1997). Unlike the forms of reciprocity, market exchange functions in an impersonal way, unaffected by ties of kinship or other alliances. In fact, the ideal function of supply and demand is often overridden by other forces, particularly the monopolistic powers of producers or distributors or the governmental powers of the state. These issues quickly merge into political or moral issues. "Price fixing" is a negative term for monopolistic violation of the supply and demand function, and "black market" is a negative term for the functioning of supply and demand in the face of state monopolies.

Anthropological studies of market systems have described many situations that seem to fit the definition of market exchange well but on closer examination appear to function through extensive personal networks. The classic study of Haitian market women by Sidney Mintz (1961) showed how buyers and sellers in the market were linked by long-term personal relationships and were actually not acting on moment-to-moment supply and demand principles. Many people were more concerned with their long-term social ties than with getting the greatest monetary value from their purchases.

James M. Acheson described a similar situation in the marketing of lobsters. Recognizing the broad social implications, he titled his paper "The Social Organization

A Haitian market. *(Credit: Teun Voeten/Panos Pictures)*

of the Maine Lobster Market" (1984). Acheson describes how little the lobstermen understand and are able to manipulate the actual mechanics of the system, saying,

> From the point of view of the fisherman, anyone connected with the marketing of lobsters is at least slightly tainted, if not an outright crook. Yet ironically, the fisherman's response traditionally has been to form very close ties with one particular dealer—a man who he often suspects is part of a conspiracy to defraud him at every opportunity. (Acheson, 1984:105–106)

Garage Sales: Blending Markets and Gifts.   Even as we deal with various sorts of reciprocity, redistribution, and market exchange, it is important to remember that these categories are not absolute and exclusive. Any individual, or any culture, is likely to use more than one in its economic life.

An ethnographic study of U.S. garage sales, for example, showed how the principles of markets and gifts can be blended. Gretchen M. Herrmann did her fieldwork in upstate New York, attending more than 1,000 garage sales and interviewing more than 200 participants (1997). Garage sales (and their close cousins like yard sales) have been commonplace in the United States since the late 1960s and are now an important means of circulating all manner of household goods, clothing, books, and other items that are still usable. Herrmann describes the cultural schema for a garage sale:

- It is held in or near the residence of the seller (not on sidewalks, in empty lots, or from stalls at a swap meet).
- The goods are personal possessions, used by the seller.
- The goods are in decent condition, and the prices are well below retail prices.
- Buyers are expected to act almost like guests—not arriving before the stated time, and not bargaining too aggressively—and are to buy for their own personal use, rather than for resale.

In short, the bundle of cultural ideas that makes up the garage sale schema melds market with gift. Of course, goods are sold for money, but the impersonal and profit-maximizing features of the market are severely mitigated by giftlike features. Buyers are not really personal guests of the sellers, but some of that relationship is suggested. The goods are not exactly given away, but the prices are unreasonably low. In fact, Herrmann describes many instances where the sellers virtually give away extra objects because they feel that the buyers will provide "a good home."

DOING ANTHROPOLOGY

Your Own Transactions

Think of all the transactions in which you have been involved recently. You could categorize them as reciprocity, redistribution, or market exchange, but you would soon think of instances that did not fit nicely into any of these categories. Go beyond the labels, and use the following attributes to describe your transactions:

1. What was the nature of the reciprocity (immediate, delayed)?

2. What social ties were involved (nonexistent, casual, lifelong)?

3. Was the transaction voluntary or obligatory?

4. What is being exchanged (goods, services, currency)? ♦

CONSUMPTION—FOOD

The third general concern of economics is consumption, or how things are used. We can look at how houses, or tools, or clothing is used. But here let us concentrate on food, for of all sorts of consumption, eating and drinking reveal the most about a culture—about its social relations and patterns of meaning. Food is newly produced, distributed, and consumed daily by virtually every human being. Its consumption is important and overt, and it is a part of daily decision making to a far greater degree than, say, housing or attire.

Foods That Are Not Eaten. If you make a list of all the possible foods available to *Homo sapiens,* it is almost endless. Each item is probably eaten somewhere by someone, but no one person would willingly eat everything. There are many reasons for this reluctance:

- *Personal idiosyncratic preference:* Even people who generally share the same culture commonly vary in what they like to eat. If you grew up in a large family or regularly eat in a school cafeteria, you are well aware of this variability.
- *Health reasons:* Following the advice of a physician or for self-imposed reasons, many people abstain from certain foods in the hope that they can improve their overall health.
- *Moral reasons:* In otherwise omnivorous societies, some people may practice some degree of vegetarianism out of a dislike of killing animals.
- *Religious reasons:* An explicit proscription on eating (or drinking) certain things may be part of formal religious doctrine. Alcohol, caffinated drinks, beef, and pork are the best known such prohibitions.

Case Study: Explaining the Cow and Pig Taboos

Explaining religious prohibitions has long been a challenge. Maimonides, the 12th-century Jewish philosopher, used the approach of **medical materialism.** He argued that since pork could cause sickness, the prohibition was based on sound medical principles. Marvin Harris (1979a) had explained the Hindu ban on killing zebu cattle and eating their meat in similar functional terms, an approach that he called cultural materialism: the products of the zebu cattle—namely, their dung, their milk, and their traction power pulling plows and wagons—had become so essential in the Indian economy that it made sense to prohibit wasting them as food.

While this argument makes sense in the case of the Hindu cattle, the matter of the pig is more complex. True, pork can carry the trichina worm that causes trichinosis in humans if the meat is not thoroughly cooked, but many other cultures safely eat well-cooked pork. True, in arid lands pigs are expensive luxuries, for they require water holes for heat regulation, as well as specially grown food when there is little garden trash and garbage, but many cultures tolerate luxuries. Yet, the most serious problem with a materialistic explanation of the pork ban is its context. Take a look at Leviticus 11 and Deuteronomy 14, where not just pork but dozens of creatures are banned. It is possible to make a convincing materialistic argument for pork, but difficult to use that logic for the entire array of banned foods.

Mary Douglas developed an alternative explanation, one of symbolic natural history (1966). Douglas suggests that these prohibitions are based on a culture-specific natural history that speaks in terms of categories of creatures. There are acceptable, clean categories whose members can be eaten. But creatures that fall outside those categories are unclean and may not be eaten. Thus, for land animals, the clean category is defined as those animals that have cloven hoofs and chew their cuds. But animals that have only one of the crucial attributes, like the camel that only chews its cud, or the pig that has only cloven hoofs, are unclean and not to be eaten. Similarly, the clean category of water creatures is defined as those with fins and scales. By implication, shrimps and shellfish do not qualify and are forbidden. Many other prohibitions laid down in Leviticus (18, 19, 20) and Deuteronomy (22) show a similar concern with purity, defined in terms of certain categories of things and behaviors, and forbid the mixing of these categories, such as meat with blood in it, planting a field with two kinds of seeds, or wearing clothing woven from two kinds of yarn (Leviticus 19).

Fasting.   In addition to certain prohibitions for certain foods, many cultures ban eating (and, often, sex) at certain times. Most famous is the Muslim fasting during the ninth month, Ramadan, when eating, drinking, and sexual activity are forbidden from dawn to dusk. Christians may fast, or at least abstain from a favorite food, during Lent, the 40 days before Easter. And until recently Roman Catholics in the United States ate fish instead of meat on Fridays.

Eating Together: Social and Ritual.   **Commensuality,** sociable eating together at ritual occasions, is one of the most widespread human practices. (Think of all the different social and religious meanings of group eating in your own experience.) In Chapter 12 (p. 349ff) we shall discuss rituals as rites of intensification, which function to create or strengthen social bonds. There seems to be no more effective way to bring together friends, relations, or strangers than to serve a communal meal.

But it is not just eating itself that does the job. Often specially meaningful foods are prescribed. In the United States such special foods may symbolize the in-group members in contrast to particular others: the Thanksgiving turkey is not-English;

Feasting in Greece. Joyous reunion on Easter Sunday brings together three generations of the Loukas Sklavounos family in the village of Vasilika. *(Credit: © James P. Blair/National Geographic Image Collection)*

the Easter ham is not-Jewish. At the culminating feast of the Dani boys' initiation an array of archaic foods are served (Chapter. 12, p. 372). Although I found no Dani who said as much, it seems obvious that these particular foods are from an earlier, foraging stage of Dani culture.

Case Study: Consuming Sugar

A classic anthropological analysis of consumption was Sidney W. Mintz's study of sugar (1985), which incorporated each of the three approaches mentioned previously. In 1948, Mintz began fieldwork in the Caribbean, in a sugar-producing region of Puerto Rico. From his firsthand view of sugarcane farming, his interest expanded to the entire economic life of sugar, in historic perspective. Mintz sums up the story of sugar:

> In 1000 A.D., few Europeans knew of the existence of sucrose, or cane sugar. But soon afterward they learned about it; by 1650, in England the nobility and the wealthy had become inveterate sugar eaters, and sugar figured in their medicine, literary imagery, and displays of rank. By no later than 1800, sugar had

become a necessity—albeit a costly and rare one—in the diet of every English person; by 1900 it was supplying nearly one-fifth of the calories in the English diet. (Mintz, 1985:5, 6)

The production of sugar from sugarcane began in Asia, and Arabs introduced it to Europe. European consumption took off in the 17th century, when Europeans developed plantations in the Caribbean worked by enslaved Africans. At first, sugar was used as a spice, as a medicine, for decoration (wedding cakes are still ornamented with sugar-base constructions), for preservation, and, of course, as a sweetener (especially in the early days with three newly introduced but bitter drinks—tea, coffee, and chocolate). When it was still scarce and expensive, sugar in these forms was used by the rich. Its use and its sharing symbolized high social status and power. By the 19th century, sugar had taken on quite a different cultural role. Its cost had plummeted, and sugar became the source of cheap calories—energy for the working classes, a role it continues to play around the world today. The "Coca-Cola-ization" of the world is the triumph not so much of American culture, but of cheap sugar for the world's poorer consumers.

Nutritional Anthropology.   In recent decades these various interests in food have merged into an important new subfield called nutritional anthropology. It adds a strong biological aspect to the functional, ecological, social, and symbolic points of view. And there is a strong applied component, as it investigates chronic undernourishment and even starvation in a world that produces food surpluses. In Chapter 1 (p. 4) we discussed a study of the effect that tourism in Yucatán has on the nutrition of local people who have left their farms to earn cash working in the luxury beach hotels of the area.

Foodways.   The term **foodways** is used for studies that approach a culture with a broad perspective via the people's food. It is a food-based ethnography of a culture, starting with the food and following it in a holistic manner, tracing how the food relates to the various other realms of the culture: social ties, magic and religion, medicine, sexuality, architecture and other artifacts, identity—these are just some of the aspects of culture that are tied to food. Not surprisingly, much had been written about Chinese foodways, exhaustively cataloging Chinese foods (Simoons, 1990) and emphasizing the development of Chinese foodways from prehistoric times to the present (Chang, 1977). Eugene Anderson emphasizes the cultural context of food:

> Chinese use food to mark ethnicity, culture change, calendric and family events, and social transactions. No business deal is complete without a dinner. No family visit is complete without sharing a meal. No major religious event is correctly done without offering up special foods proper to the ritual context. (1988:244–245)

And Anderson points out the surprising statistic that in Hong Kong "expenditures on food as a percentage of total actually rise as people get richer" (1988:245).

This fact indicates the importance, in southern China, at least, of the consumption of food in social interaction. And the Japanese film *Tampopo* explores the meanings of food in Japan.

DOING ANTHROPOLOGY

Global Consumption

The global economy did not begin in recent decades—the centuries-long history of tea, coffee, and chocolate sweetened by sugar is a neat example of the story of global trade. To what degree are you today consuming products from around the world? Make a list of the origins—to the extent that you know them—of your food and clothing. How many countries have contributed to your lifestyle?   ♦

SEEING ANTHROPOLOGY

Appeals to Santiago

Photographer and Director: Arnold Baskin   *Ethnographers: Duane Metzger and*
Written by Carter Wilson   *Robert Ravicz*

Appeals to Santiago describes the cargo system of the Mayans in Chiapas, Mexico. It was shot in Tenejapa, in the Tzeltal Maya region, some 16 miles from Zinacantan, the center of Tzotzil Maya, where Frank Cancian studied a comparable cargo system. The film uses a native voice, or point of view, rather than that of an analytical anthropologist. It is not didactic or etic, but emic. The opening words are "My name is Alonso The . . . ," and it presents the cargo system through his perspective as Alonso The comes into the town of Tenejapa: "I've come to work in the Fiesta of Santiago." Ostensibly, there is no analysis, just the voice of Alonso The presenting the Mayan understanding of these ceremonies.

The short clip begins with a prayer in Mayan that is then translated into English. The cargo bearers describe how they prepare the saints' images, dressing them in their sacred vestments and jewelry. We then follow the procession that carries the images around the town, stopping at important places to eat and drink in the saints' honor.

The complete film begins with Alonso The walking into Tenejapa from his home two hours away and explaining the roles of the cargo officers, the mayordomos, and the captains. We see the cargo officials of the previous year handing over bundles containing the ornaments of the saint figures to Alonso The and the others who are taking on the duties for the coming year. Although this event is a Christian ceremony, centered on the Roman Catholic church in Tenejapa, the entire focus is on the laymen who serve their year's duty as cargo bearers. There is no sign of the Catholic priest.

Setup Questions

1. Listen carefully to the prayers in Mayan. Can you hear the poetic cadence of Mayan Catholicism?

2. Look carefully at what people are wearing. The Chiapas Mayans are famous for their colorful woven cloths and ribbon-decorated hats. Each local area has its own designs. Identify the Tenejapa costumes and look for visitors from other Mayan areas.

3. How does the emic Mayan understanding of the cargo system differ from Cancian's etic analysis?

4. What seems to be the role of alcohol in these rituals?

5. How do you read the emotional tone of these events?

6. Where are the women?   ◆

HOLLYWOOD-STYLE ANTHROPOLOGY

The Mystique of Food in *Tampopo*

Tampopo   1987   114 minutes   Japanese with English subtitles

    Nobuko Miyamoto as Tampopo
    Tsuomu Yamazaki as Goro

This movie is a hymn to food—preparing it, eating it, studying it, savoring it, even having sex with it. The main story concerns a widow, Tampopo, with a noodle (ramen) shop. One day Goro, a truck driver, and his assistant Gun, stop by for a meal. When they admit that the noodles are unimpressive, Tampopo begs Goro to become her teacher. He takes over and drills her relentlessly, as her support group grows to five men. Slowly, by fair means and foul, her noodle shop becomes famous. Meanwhile, interspersed through the film are numerous shorter episodes that have nothing to do with the main plot but add delicious perspectives on food.

Setup Questions

1. Try to note all the different words used to characterize noodles good and noodles bad.
2. How does the music comment on the events?
3. Most critics recognize this film as a parody on American westerns. Why?
4. Answer Tampopo's question: Why are you doing all this for me?
5. How is social class used in the film?
6. Explain the gangster's story about the wild boar.
7. Explain the final scenes.
8. And how about the scenes under the final credits?   ◆

CHAPTER SUMMARY

- Human social groups are never completely self-sufficient, but always seem to exchange some products with other groups. The social ties resulting from these exchanges may be more significant than the value of the goods themselves.
- There are three forms of distribution or exchange that move goods and integrate different social groups together (however loosely): reciprocity, redistribution, and market exchange.
- Reciprocity is the exchange of goods between relatively equal parties. When the reciprocity is completed immediately, the exchange is called balanced reciprocity and usually involves barter; when the exchange is delayed or left incomplete, we are dealing with "gifts." The giving of gifts (and the expectation of reciprocal giving) creates special bonds, often involves rituals, and establishes kinlike ties and other cultural features composing a "total social phenomenon" in holistic terms.
- The special case of negative reciprocity is the attempt to get something for nothing through theft or trickery; it is really an antireciprocity.
- The most famous example of the total social phenomenon of gift giving is the Kula Ring exchange involving the Trobriand Islanders and their neighbors of Papua New Guinea.
- Redistribution, or pooling, occurs when goods are gathered together and then redistributed, usually for the benefit of the leaders who are powerful enough to command compliance. Taxation is a good example of redistribution, as are the potlatch competitive feasting ceremonies of the Northwest Coast and the Mayan cargo system.
- In market exchange, products are valued in money terms and exchanged for money.

KEY TERMS

balanced reciprocity	foodways	medical materialism
barter	forms of integration	negative reciprocity
cargo system	generalized reciprocity	potlatch
commensuality	gift	reciprocity
consumption	kula exchange	redistribution
distribution	leveling effect	taxation
exchange	market exchange	total social phenomenon

QUESTIONS TO THINK ABOUT

- Can there be "pure gifts"? Can you give examples? Can you formulate principles that would govern the existence of "pure gifts"?
- Thinking about the ambiguous nature of garage sales, can you analyze similarly ambiguous institutions in your own culture (like bake sales, for example)?

- Power, in the hands of individuals, is a major variation from culture to culture—some have much, some little. How does this idea relate to the three forms of distribution?
- Thinking about the Mayan cargo system, can you predict how it is evolving today, and why?
- Why shouldn't social groups strive for self-sufficiency and bypass distribution altogether?

SUGGESTIONS FOR FURTHER READING

Cancian, Frank
1992   The Decline of Community in Zinacantan. Stanford, CA: Stanford University Press. *Cancian's third book on Zinacantan, following the culture's changes, especially in the cargo system.*

Collier, George A., and Elizabeth Lowery Quaratiello
1994   Basta! Land and the Zapatista Rebellion in Chiapas. Oakland, CA: Institute for Food and Development Policy. *An economic anthropological background to the recent uprising.*

Counihan, Carole, and Penny Van Esterik (eds.)
1997   Food and Culture: A Reader. New York: Routledge. *An excellent collection of papers.*

Goodman, Alan H., Darna L. Dufour, and Gretel H. Pelto (eds.)
2000   Nutritional Anthropology: Biocultural Perspectives on Food and Nutrition. Mountain View, CA: Mayfield. *A more biologically oriented collection.*

Harris, Marvin
1985   Good To Eat. Riddles of Food and Culture. New York: Simon and Schuster. *A collection of Harris's cultural materialist essays on cows, pigs, and other food.*

Mintz, Sidney W.
1996   Tasting Food, Tasting Freedom. Boston: Beacon Press. *One of the great figures of economic anthropology begins this collection of essays saying, "My father was a cook."*

Vogt, Evon Z.
1994   Fieldwork Among the Maya: Reflections on the Harvard Chiapas Project. Albuquerque: University of New Mexico Press. *An account by the director of the most ambitious anthropological project ever.*

Wiesner, Polly, and Wulf Schiefenhoevel (eds.)
1995   Food and the Status Quest: An Interdisciplinary Perspective. Providence: Berghahn. *Integrates production, distribution, and consumption of that basic commodity.*

Wilson, Carter
1965   Crazy February: Life and Death in the Mayan Highlands of Mexico. Berkeley: University of California Press. *A novelist who worked with the anthropologists tells it his way.*

Wong, Bernard
1998   Ethnicity and Entrepreneurship: The New Chinese Immigrants in the San Francisco Bay Area. Boston: Allyn and Bacon. *Chinese business abroad.*

CHAPTER 8

Marriage and Family

Woman with
swaddled baby.
Prambanan,
Java, 9th
century C.E.
*(Source: Karl
G. Heider)*

HEADLINE ANTHROPOLOGY

PRESS WATCH

Some of the subjects discussed in this chapter have made their way into current news stories. For example:

◆ Owen Aldren, 82, of Bluffdale, Utah, has 8 wives (aged 64 to 93), was excommunicated from the Church of Jesus Christ of Latter-Day Saints (Mormon) in 1942 for polygamy, but is now patriarch of the Apostolic United Brethren Church.

—New York Times, *23 February 2002.*

◆ At the end of June 2002, the Canadian Province of Quebec legally considers gay and lesbian couples' rights equal to heterosexual couples in terms of children, inheritance, and insurance, even though short of marriage (which is under federal law).

—New York Times, *June 25, 2002.*

◆ With the brutal civil war in Sierra Leone over, the more than 4,500 children forced to fight are being returned to their families.

—New York Times, *May 9, 2002.*

◆ In Japan, where married women still have relatively few rights, a movement for women to be buried apart from their husbands had gained popularity as a gesture of independence.

—New York Times, *May 9, 2002.*

◆ First cousin marriage is legal in 18 states of the US.

—National Survey of State Laws, 1999, *in* USA Today, *April 4, 2002.*

◆ Recent research on the incidence of genetic disorders among children of first cousins suggests that there is only a small increase for some diseases (from 5% in the general population to 7–8% among such children). Some genetic counselors maintain that this is still a reason for first cousins not to marry.

—USA Today, *April 4, 2002.*

DEFINITIONS AND FUNCTIONS OF MARRIAGE

Marriage is the socially recognized union of a male and a female, marked by some sort of public wedding ceremony, that establishes a *family,* a social unit whose functions are to regulate sexual activity, to produce and raise children with a particular social identity and cultural skills, and to constitute a basic economic unit. That definition serves us fairly well, but there are exceptions, somewhere in the world, for each of these points. For example, same-sex unions exist in various forms (although many people in the United States resist calling them marriages). In addition, not all cultures make a big public ceremony out of weddings. Often, nuclear biological families (mother-father-child) are subsumed into domestic household units. We could cite many other exceptions to the definition of marriage. Linda Stone, in her recent survey of kinship and marriage, notes the widespread occurrence of such exceptions and concludes that

> perhaps the only generalization one can make about marriage is that everywhere it entails intimate, if not emotionally charged, relationships between spouses, and everywhere it creates in-laws. (Stone, 1997:183)

In short, marriage brings together two individuals as well as two groups of people. What are the functions of marriage? According to Stone, its primary function is to create new social ties, or families (spouses and in-laws) that provide a setting for important sexual, economic, and educational activities.

Sexual Regulation.   Generally speaking, a marriage confers exclusive sexual access to a woman on her husband. To a much lesser degree, wives have exclusive claim on their husband's sexuality. This issue is greatly complicated by the coexistence of quite conflicting norms, especially for men. According to an ideal principle,

Chinese family memorial service in Honolulu, Hawaii. The ceremony is called Ch'ing Ming ("Bright and Clear") or Bai San, and is conducted each April to pay homage to deceased ancestors. Paper money is burned, food and drink are offered, and firecrackers frighten away evil spirits. *(Credit: Carl Hefner)*

men have sex only with their wives but in fact are expected to be sexually active outside marriage. The same is rarely true of women. Such behavior is tolerated for men as long as extramarital affairs are not made public.

Economic Cooperation.   Given the pan-cultural division of labor by gender, it is difficult for a single adult to function without a partner of the opposite gender. This need is especially evident in subsistence cultures, in which the family is a fairly self-sufficient unit. In traditional Japanese villages such as Suye Mura, intense cooperation within and between families made single-person households unlikely. Robert J. Smith, who studied another small Japanese village in the 1950s and again in the 1970s (1978), reported only a couple of single-person households. But in Theodore Bestor's Tokyo neighborhood in the 1980s, single-person households accounted for nearly 15% of the population (and actually 38% of the households) (1989:272). Of course, in Tokyo, the village pattern of economic cooperation is replaced by cash transactions for goods and services.

Education of Children.   The family or the household is required to educate the children or provide for their education so that they can function as productive members of society. The ideal American pattern, in which the child and her or his parents live in a separate nuclear family household, makes the child dependent on a very few people for early education. Then the child is entrusted to a wide range of strangers in separate educational institutions called *schools,* which provide mass education for groups of unrelated children. Although this pattern is generally found in complex modern societies, it is far more common worldwide for the child to be educated by the household or village. Children grow up in sprawling, multifamily households and are raised by the neighbors. Early childhood education is often provided by older siblings or nearby children. Parents, village elders, designated relatives, and sometimes teachers also educate the children as they grow older.

Human sexuality must be controlled lest it get too disruptive to the social group; human infants have a long maturation period during which they must be cared for; most social behavior is not innate, so infants have much to learn; and human beings need to be located in some supportive social network. But for all the cultural variation, it is noteworthy how commonly cultures have a ceremony to ratify a union between two people who have more or less exclusive claims on each other's sexuality and who share in the raising of children. Let us look at some of the main variations in marriage and in families.

The search for the one precise and accurate definition of marriage goes on, however. This quest is built on the assumption that because all cultures have something like marriage, we should be able to define the universal essence of it. We shall proceed to talk about some fairly mechanical cultural variations in marriages— arranged versus love, different marriage exchanges, forms of postmarital residence, and so on. First, let us explore another approach to marriage, looking at the **cultural schemas of marriage.** What is the set of ideas that people have in their minds about marriage, what does marriage mean to people, how do they express these ideas, and how do such schemas influence behavior?

Naomi Quinn has been exploring American schemas for marriage by interviewing people at length about their own marriages. As people talk about their marriages, they make extensive use of metaphors. Quinn has found that even in a small and fairly heterogeneous sample, certain metaphors constantly recur. These standard shared metaphors indicate the cultural ideas about marriage that are held by Americans. For example, her interview subjects often used language to suggest that they think of marriage as a thing that has been constructed, "a manufactured product." Quinn offers several quotes from her interviews:

> "When the marriage was strong, it was very strong because it was made as we went along—it was sort of a do-it-yourself project."

> "And I suppose what that means is that we have both looked into the other person and found their best parts and used those parts to make the relationship gel."

> "They had a basic solid foundation in their marriages that could be shaped into something good." (Quinn, 1987:175)

Quinn has identified some eight related sets of metaphors that seem to characterize the "American marriage." Presumably, future research that works out the metaphors and schemas of marriage in other cultures will give us a much different understanding of the rich range of marriage schemas across cultures than the one that simply notes such features as "arranged marriage, with bridewealth and patrilocal residence." For example, another cognitive anthropologist, Dorothy C. Holland, has studied the **schemas of romance** held by American undergraduates (1990). This line of investigation could eventually take us into far richer cross-cultural descriptions of courtship (or premarital maneuvering) than merely saying that marriages are either arranged by families or by people "in love."

FORMS OF MARRIAGE

Marriage is a major event, not only for the two individuals who are most directly involved, but for the society itself, as it marks a new alignment of ties and obligations between groups. So it is not surprising that marriage reflects and expresses basic cultural principles in several ways.

Arranged Marriages Versus Love Marriages

The major cultural variable of groupism and individualism shows up clearly in the degree of freedom the individual has in choosing a mate. Is marriage seen as primarily a group concern or primarily an individual concern? In many societies, marriages are part of political and economic processes, ways to gain advantage by creating alliances between groups. So groups use their young people as particularly valuable chips in alliance-forming exchanges, leading to **arranged marriages.**

Lying behind this issue is the question of how a culture sees individuals, how it defines the self. As we discussed in Chapter 5 on cultural psychologies, some cultures, such as the United States, define the self more as an autonomous, independent individual, while other cultures put more emphasis on the self as an integral part of a social network. On the one hand, it follows that autonomous individuals emphasize their own feelings of love and romance, looking for like-minded individuals to fall in love with. On the other hand, it also follows that where individuals are, first of all, parts of the group, the group should use the marriage of individuals in its overall strategy.

While some cultures may insist on arranged marriages in all cases, many have both arranged and independent marriages. In our focus cultures, we have examples of arranged marriages among the Nuer, Ju/'hoansi, and Japanese, and to a lesser extent among the Dani and Balinese. Among the Minangkabau of West Sumatra, Indonesia, people who are wealthier, and thus have more at stake for the clan segment, have arranged marriages. Poorer people are left more on their own by their relatives. In any case, should higher-status people's first marriages end through divorce or death, they are allowed to manage their own subsequent marriages.

Things are changing, however, and the arranged marriage looks more and more endangered for many reasons. Recall, for example, Laura Ahearn's study in a Nepalese village (Chapter 1). With schools came literacy, and with literacy came the opportunity for young men and women to bypass marriages arranged by their parents and to work out their own romantic relationships through the secret exchange of love letters (Ahearn, 2001). The dramatic increase in migration from continent to continent has also loosened the traditional family control of marriage arrangements as more young people, finding themselves far from home, choose their own spouses, marry, and only then inform their families.

DOING ANTHROPOLOGY

Schemas of Love and Marriage

Take a novel, film, or play that you know or are studying and work out its schemas for love or for marriage. (*Moonstruck* explores schemas of love and marriage in a New York Italian neighborhood.) Not every work of fiction you read or see is concerned with these experiences, but you should have no trouble finding a good rich source of statements about such schemas. In most cases, the work will probably present at least two schemas in opposition to or in tension with each other. ("She loved me for the dangers I had passed, and I loved her that she did pity me.") For each schema, list the principles involved. Look for metaphors or other images about love or marriage ("my love is like a red red rose . . . "). Be sure to note the culture, and the time period, and other specifics (gender? age?) that each schema is supposed to represent.   ◆

It has long been taken for granted, even by anthropologists, that romantic love was a Western development, and a recent one at that. Perhaps it is better to say that the ideal marriage in most cultures, most of the time, is arranged by others, while the ideal marriage in the West today is contracted between two individuals who are in love. As William R. Jankowiak and Edward F. Fischer found in a broad cross-cultural survey, romantic love is in fact found "in almost every culture" (1992:153). Jankowiak's historical survey of Chinese literature showed that the idea of romantic love is an old one in China, not the result of either Western influence or communist ideology (1995). And in Jankowiak's study of a Chinese city, he encountered much discussion of romantic love leading to a **love marriage** (1993).

Some of the surprise at Jankowiak's various findings comes from the fact that a single culture can support quite different schemas for marriage. Older people, especially men, hold to an arranged marriage pattern, while young people may well act on a romantic love model. It is possible to fall into the trap of listening to the official version and to ignore what is actually going on. Bali is a case in point. Although formal religious wedding ceremonies take place, the most common form of marriage is either elopement (according to Fred Eiseman) or "wife capture" (according to Stephen Lansing). Elopement is a strategy for carrying out a love marriage in the face of pressure to have an elaborate arranged marriage. The couple publicly spend the night together, and then the girl's parents, equally publicly, express great outrage (but of course do not have to pay for the expensive wedding ritual) (Eiseman, 1990:97).

Minangkabau wedding party in West Sumatra, Indonesia, makes a formal visit to the groom's house before returning to the bride's house, where the couple will take up matrilocal residence. *(Credit: Karl G. Heider)*

Wife capture can be more or less an elopement, or it may sometimes involve actually forceful abduction (Lansing, 1995:39).

In small-scale societies in which different kin groups are well known to each other and are already engaged in long-term jockeying for alliances and for advantages, the children and their potential marriage partners are part of this maneuvering when they are quite young. Among the Ju/'hoansi, children are promised in marriage at an early age, so the advantages of in-law connections between groups can begin years before any actual wedding. John Embree, writing about a Japanese village in the 1930s, said, "Marriage is primarily a social and economic arrangement between two families" (1939:203). The same is true in many societies of the world.

Monogamy Versus Polygamy

Monogamy is the situation of having only one spouse at a time. **Polygamy,** the pattern of multiple spouses, characterizes another type of family that is more common than one might think. When one man has more than one wife **(polygyny)** or in a situation so rare as to be "an ethnographic curiosity" (Murdock, 1949: 25), when one woman has more than one husband **(polyandry),** the multiple spouse configuration may or may not constitute a single household. These terms are used for marriages and also for the sorts of families that they create (see Figure 8.1).

How frequently does polygyny occur? Most cultures in the world allow polygyny (about 75%) but most married people in the world are in monogamous marriages (even in cultures that allow polygyny, most people are monogamous) (Altman and Ginat, 1996:40; Killbride, 1994:41). In Murdock's sample of 238 societies, only 43 were strictly monogamous in that they did not allow plural marriages. In many societies, a man may have a long-term relationship with another woman who is not recognized as a legitimate wife. This practice is called concubinage, not polygyny. Practically speaking, even in societies that permit or even value polygyny, most men are monogamous or even bachelors. Murdock considers societies where polygynous marriages represent less than 20% of total marriages as being

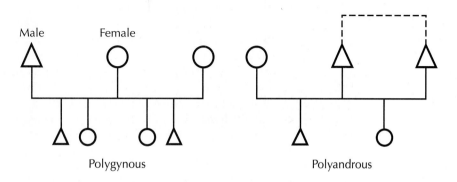

FIGURE 8.1   Two Types of Polygamy

Analyze this picture of a Japanese family; then read the footnote on the next page. *(Credit: Christal K. Whelan)*

essentially monogamous. Polygynous families are especially common in tribal horticultural societies, in which women do significant subsistence work and a man's wealth depends on the number of wives he has in his household work force.

However, if one man has more than one wife, then some men must have no wives. For the Dani, this problem was offset by warfare, which killed off perhaps 25% of the young males, and by a staggered age of marriage. (Women usually married at an age several years younger than men, so there were considerably more women in the marriage pool than men.) The result was that there was no significant number of eligible bachelors among the Dani. In polygynous Near Eastern Muslim societies, on the other hand, many men must remain permanent bachelors or, at best, wait to marry the widow of a rich man. Chagnon describes how Yanomamo polygyny unbalances lineages, allowing groups with polygynous families to quickly build their strength (1992:150). However, the tendency of larger groups to split apart in conflict serves as a counterbalance.

Polygyny puts a strain on familial relations. Nearly half of Dani men had polygynous families in the 1960s. Most of these men had only two or three wives. More often than not, co-wives did not get along together and lived in different house-holds, often some distance apart. With more wives to care for his pigs, a man could participate in exchanges at funerals and other ceremonies and build up his influence, but it was at the expense of running multiple households.

The Ju/'hoansi have polygyny, and although Ju/'hoansi men greatly desire it, Ju/'hoansi women do not. In one sample, Richard Lee found only 5% of 131 married men living in polygynous households, and most of them were powerful healers. It is "sexual jealousy, pure and simple" (Lee, 1993:85) that keeps the rate of polygyny down, for Ju/'hoansi women clearly have considerable voice in deciding whether they will join polygynous families.

Polygyny has a long history in the Judeo-Christian tradition, beginning with the Patriarch Abraham and continuing into the early modern era in Europe. It was definitively rejected by the Roman Catholic Church in the 16th century, however (Altman and Ginat, 1996:42).

Members of the Church of Jesus Christ of Latter-Day Saints (commonly known as Mormons) adopted polygyny early in their move west from New York state. By the time they settled in Utah (from 1847), it was a major and distinctive tenet of their religion. Much of the general opposition to Mormons focused on their practice of polygyny. Federal pressure against polygyny intensified, and in 1890, four years after Utah became a state, the Mormon Church itself officially renounced polygyny. Since then the church has excommunicated those who persist in polygynous marriages. Nevertheless, some in fundamentalist splinter groups have continued the practice. Somewhere between 20,000 and 50,000 Mormons live in polygynous families today (Altman and Ginat, 1996:x). Irwin Altman, a psychologist, and Joseph Ginat, an anthropologist, did extensive fieldwork among those living in "plural families and fundamentalist communities" and have written an ethnography of this illegal but widely practiced pattern. They conclude,

> Fundamentalist groups are growing, people are not leaving in great numbers, and those with whom we spoke are committed to their lifestyle. Why is this the case? A major reason is that they believe in their religion. Mormon fundamentalists hold fast to 19th-century notions regarding plural marriage, a patriarchal family and religious structure, an afterlife with husbands as "kings" and wives as "queens" governing in their own heavenly universe and surrounded by their children, and other doctrinal teachings. (Altman and Ginat, 1996:439)

Polyandry, in which one woman has several husbands, is rare indeed and best known from the Himalayas. There, brothers who are often away from home on long trekking trips may marry a common wife (fraternal polyandry). But on the whole, maintaining a single polyandrous household, even with brothers, would be difficult. How, then, can we explain a pattern of behavior that is so rare and so apparently

When Christal Whelan was making a film about Christians on the Goto Islands of Japan, she wanted to take a photograph of the family with which she was staying. The mother, father, and daughter began to pose for her, but the mother said that a picture of just three people was bad luck, so she got a doll to make four in the photo.

difficult to manage? Melvyn C. Goldstein (1987) has studied polyandry among Tibetans living in Nepal. Interestingly, polyandry is just one of their options, which also include monogamy and polygyny, and divorce is easy for those who find marriage unpleasant. Surprisingly, there seems to be no sexual jealousy when brothers share one wife. All the husbands equally share the responsibility for raising the children of their wife. The reason that these Tibetans give for polyandry is economic. The family land and livestock do not need to be divided into unviable small parcels. Goldstein also points out that polyandry slows down population growth. In the area that he studied, 31% of the women of childbearing age were unmarried, and although some of them did have children, a fair number of women were not bearing children at all. But polyandry remains an extremely rare and geographically limited solution to land and population problems.

MARRIAGE AS EXCHANGE

One way of looking at marriage is as a transaction between two kin groups—families, clans, or whatever—involving goods and services moving back and forth, tying the two groups together. These exchanges include **dowry,** by which a woman brings some significant wealth to her new family; **bride wealth,** by which the husband's group pays or compensates the wife's group with some goods; and **bride service,** by which the new husband works for his father-in-law for a period, often of years, before he and his wife are free to go their own way.

Bride Wealth and Dowry. While dowry and bride wealth, at first glance, seem to be mirror images of each other, they are in fact quite different (see Goody and Tambiah, 1973). In the case of bride wealth, pigs, cattle, or some other commodity is removed from the husband's kin group to the bride's kin group even as the bride herself moves out of her natal home into her new home (Figure 8.2). To put it in depersonalized terms, her services—economic, sexual, and reproductive—are exchanged for the bride wealth. That wealth often keeps moving, as her kin group uses it for the marriage of one of their sons to a daughter of yet another kin group. The dowry goods, by contrast, come with the bride as her contribution to her new household, and remain her own property; they are not folded into the joint property.

Steven J. C. Gaulin and James S. Boster (1990) noted that while dowry is fairly rare, it occurs mainly among socially stratified societies that do not permit polygyny. This "female competition" model suggests that dowries are ways for a woman to attract the most valued, most wealthy husband in competition with other women.

Although the dowry usually gives the new bride some economic leverage of her own, things do not always work out that way. John Van Willigen and V. C. Channa (1991) have described how the custom of dowry in India has led to the murder of hundreds of women. In Hinduism, dowry giving is expected, even a religious obligation. But often, the groom's family is not satisfied with the dowry, and after the wedding, with the bride in their hands, they harass her, demanding more contributions from her family. Eventually, if more is not forthcoming, they may burn

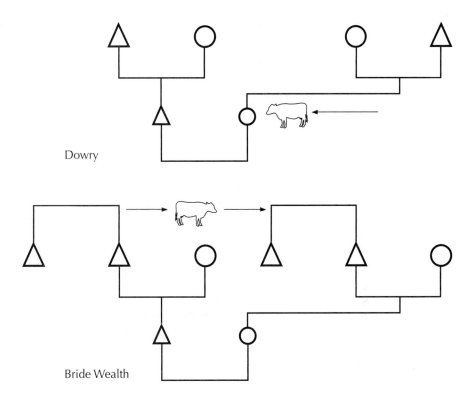

FIGURE 8.2 Wedding Exchanges: Dowry and Bride Wealth

her to death with kitchen stove kerosene. Since 1961, the government of India has passed a series of laws intended to abolish dowries. They have been unsuccessful, and to the extent that the dowry should strengthen the bride's position, these attempts to end dowries may have actually weakened women's power and increased dowry death.

In an article on dowry death, Van Willigen and Channa go far beyond merely describing the pattern. They actually offer suggestions for easing the problem. (This piece, significantly, was published in *Human Organization,* the journal of the Society for Applied Anthropology.) They advocate increasing the economic value of women by changing inheritance laws, which now strongly favor males and make it easy to disinherit women after the dowry has been paid. But there are always unintended consequences. Splitting the holdings of one generation among all the children of the next generation could destabilize families by, for example, splitting a barely adequate farm into economically unviable pieces. Van Willigen and Channa therefore also recommend strengthening families by making it easier to have a civil wedding (which would avoid the huge expenses of a religious wedding) and by instituting universal governmental registration of marriages to allow some control over dowries and establish the interest of the government in marriage.

Bride Service Societies. The holistic embeddedness of marriage exchanges in the total cultural mix is also evident in a study that Jane Fishburne Collier (1988) made of wedding exchanges, power, and conflict resolution among classless societies (bands and tribes). For example, Collier contrasts *bride service societies,* which are generally hunter and gatherer bands, like the Ju/'hoansi or horticultural or hunting groups, like the Yanomamo, with *equal bride wealth societies,* which are commonly small tribal societies without chiefs or such formal leadership, like the Dani.

The most telling difference between the two types is that bride service is worked off by the groom himself (Figure 8.3), while the bride wealth is exchanged between the couple's elders. The groom who performs bride service is not indebted to anyone, is not under the control of the elders, and in conflict situations is expected to work things out himself, often in physical confrontation with his opponent. But in societies in which the older generation provides the valuables for the younger generation's wedding, the younger generation is to a greater extent dependent on the elders, and conflict tends to be resolved by conferences of elders.

Dani weddings involve a relatively balanced exchange between the kin of the bride and the kin of the groom, as shown in Figures 8.4 and 8.5. Generally, pigs move from his side to her side, while sacred stones and shell goods go the other way. The exchange continues for a generation. At the wedding, some of the pigs given by the groom's kin to the bride's kin are immediately passed on to her mother's kin, so as a new round of exchanges begins, an old round is concluded. Not only are the kin groups linked by long-term exchange, but as Collier has described for just this sort of society, the older generation also provides and receives goods on behalf of the younger.

If one were to map the exchanges in a typical middle-class American wedding, one would find a similar balancing out (Figure 8.6). The personal histories are especially important in such reckonings. Many wedding presents are gifts from elders to the young couple that are returns for other wedding presents given a year or a generation before. (When the Smith girl marries the Jones boy, the elder Browns give an expensive present matching one given by the elder Smiths to the younger

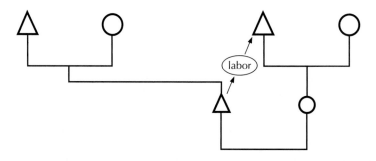

FIGURE 8.3   Bride Service

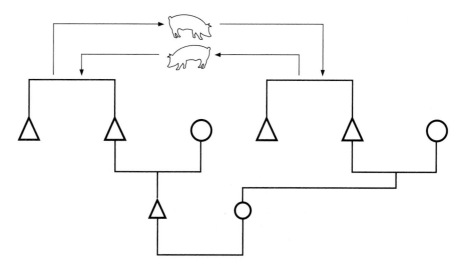

FIGURE 8.4   Balanced Wedding Exchange (Dani)

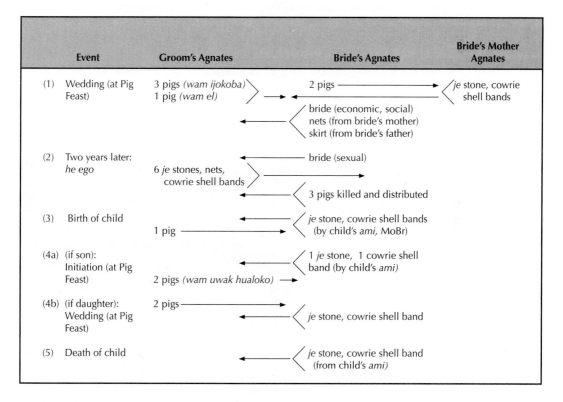

Event	Groom's Agnates	Bride's Agnates	Bride's Mother Agnates
(1) Wedding (at Pig Feast)	3 pigs *(wam ijokoba)* 1 pig *(wam el)* →	2 pigs → ← bride (economic, social) nets (from bride's mother) skirt (from bride's father)	*je* stone, cowrie shell bands
(2) Two years later: *he ego*	6 *je* stones, nets, cowrie shell bands →	← bride (sexual) ← 3 pigs killed and distributed	
(3) Birth of child	1 pig →	← *je* stone, cowrie shell bands (by child's *ami*, MoBr)	
(4a) (if son): Initiation (at Pig Feast)	2 pigs *(wam uwak hualoko)* →	← 1 *je* stone, 1 cowrie shell band (by child's *ami*)	
(4b) (if daughter): Wedding (at Pig Feast)	2 pigs →	← *je* stone, cowrie shell band	
(5) Death of child		← *je* stone, cowrie shell band (from child's *ami*)	

FIGURE 8.5
Dani wedding exchanges over the years between the groom's agnates (members of his patri-sib), the bride's agnates (from her patri-sib), and even an exchange left over from the previous generation involving the bride's mother's agnates. *(Source: Heider, 1972b. Reprinted by permission of Oceania Publications.)*

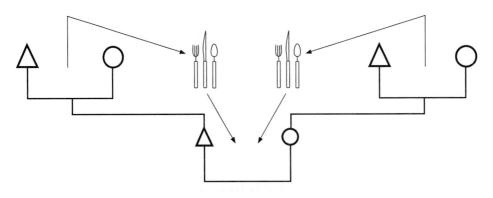

FIGURE 8.6 Balanced Wedding Exchange (United States)

Brown girl when she was wed. This exchange seems complex, but the Joneses, Smiths, and Browns know the details as well as the Dani remember whose pig was given to whom.) In this respect, Ju/'hoansi marriages are similar. They involve a continual exchange of goods between the respective parents for a decade or more before the wedding and often for years afterward (Lee, 1993:80).

The events of a Dani wedding ceremony are spread out over a couple of years. The first step is a group event, when the young brides (the three on the left) are given married women's skirts, a set of new carrying nets, and a digging stick, and are escorted to their husbands' compounds. *(Credit: Karl G. Heider)*

MARRIAGE RULES

Marrying Out (Exogamy) and Marrying In (Endogamy)

No culture allows people to marry whomever they choose. There are always rules specifying whom you should marry and rules specifying whom you should not marry.

Exogamy rules prohibit people of the same social group from marrying. Clans, sibs, and similar groups, which are especially common in tribal societies, are usually exogamous. Dani sibs are exogamous, but the more inclusive moieties are also exogamous. Because half the entire Dani population is in one's own moiety and so is categorically prohibited, a person's marriage choices are considerably constricted. In China, people of the same clan name are not supposed to marry. And there are echoes of a similar family name exogamy in the old American feeling that even people whose family names begin with the same letter of the alphabet should not marry:

> Change the name and not the letter,
> Change for worse and not for better.

Rules of **endogamy** stipulate that marriage must take place within a group. In Hindu India, the occupational caste groups, for example, are endogamous: Marriage is supposed to take place only within a caste, and people of different castes are traditionally not allowed to marry. In the United States and other complex industrial societies, such explicit endogamy does not exist, but we can speak of a more generalized preference for **homogamy,** which is marriage within the same religious group, social class, or socially defined racial category. A major goal of the Japanese marriage go-between is to bring together people of similar sorts and thereby to promote homogamy.

Incest Prohibitions

Every culture has some specific **incest** prohibitions, designating some kin relationships for which marriage or sex is forbidden. Incest prohibitions and rules of exogamy are similar in that both work to prohibit certain kinds of relationships. Incest rules cover both marriage and sex and specify certain kin relationships, however, while exogamy rules concern marriage only and speak to group membership.

The most commonly prohibited relationships are those between direct lineal kin (for example, parents and children) and between siblings. Even in this case, there have been some exceptions. The royal families of certain kingdoms (Hawaii, Egypt, and Inca) were considered so sacred and separate from the ordinary people that brothers and sisters (or, more commonly, half-brothers and half-sisters) could marry only each other, for anyone else would be too polluting.

The most puzzling exception is the pattern of culturally approved and commonly occurring brother–sister marriages that was recorded from the Graeco–Roman population living in Egypt during the period of Roman rule (the first three centuries

A.D.). Explaining this pattern in the face of an otherwise general condemnation of brother–sister marriage complicates an already difficult anthropological puzzle. To the question "Why incest?" we now add "Why brother–sister marriage among these Egyptian Greeks?" Brent D. Shaw suggests (1992) that these Greek settlers were such a small community and so violently contemptuous of the surrounding Egyptians that they turned inward for marriage partners and felt justified in allowing brothers and sisters to marry. Seymour Parker (1996) suggests that additional economic and social factors were involved. In the first century A.D., Roman pressure to obtain Egyptian grain grew. Good agricultural land reserved for Greeks was scarce, however. At the same time, legal reforms allowed daughters to inherit equally with sons (with more heirs, the land would be split in more parts). This combination of factors made it especially advantageous to keep the family estate intact by marrying brothers and sisters. Unfortunately, the historical record gives no details on this brother–sister marriage pattern. How did people feel about the biological and social effects of this long-term practice? It remains a puzzle.

Of course, violations of the incest rules have made for fascinating drama from the ancient Greeks (Oedipus and his mother) through the Germanic epics (Siegfried's parents were brother and sister) to lurid headlines in yesterday's newspapers.

Although cultures generally agree on prohibiting sex and marriage between core lineal and consanguinal relatives, there is great disagreement on which, if any, other relatives should be prohibited. In the United States, incest laws are fairly esoteric. Even most lawyers do not know exactly what is prohibited. Most Americans believe in a folk model that marriage between first cousins is prohibited, even though nearly half the states in fact do allow first cousin marriages (Heider, 1969b). The prohibition against a man's marrying his deceased wife's sister was regularly debated in the British parliament for fifty years before it was finally repealed in 1904. People feel very strongly about such things.

Explanations of Incest Prohibitions. Why do all cultures have some incest prohibitions? This question has long been a topic of debate in anthropology. Although we do not have the definitive answer, at least four sorts of contributing factors exist.

One factor is the *biological inbreeding disadvantage*. Supposedly, people early on realized that children of close relatives often had physical defects, and so incest prohibitions amount to primitive eugenic codes. This factor presumes a level of scientific insight that we do indeed find in realms other than genetics among tribal peoples. But it does not account for variations, such as why cousin marriage prohibition exists in some cultures but cousin marriage is preferred in other cultures. Certainly, Americans, if asked to explain the incest prohibitions, usually offer the inbreeding explanation. But folk wisdom is not necessarily accurate, and serious questions have been raised about the scientific basis for this explanation (see, for example, Leavitt, 1990).

A second biologically based explanation says that close family members have an *instinctual repulsion* toward incest and the social taboo merely reflects this natural response. However, if it were instinctual, there would be no need for the taboo, and incest would never occur. In fact, there are plenty of instances of violations in different types of societies.

As a third factor, we can point to the advantages of the *social alliances* between families or clans that result when marriages within families are prohibited. One can imagine that over the millennia, the groups that had forbidden their sons and daughters to marry each other, and that sent them off to other groups, would have long-term advantages over groups that did not follow this course; they would have a ready-made basis for political, economic, and military alliances. The special case of dynastic marriages among European royal houses certainly demonstrates this principle. As the Austrian Hapsburgs were piecing together their empire, there was a saying about Felix Austria ("happy Austria"), which weds instead of wages war, their brides bringing as their dowries strategic territory to strengthen the Hapsburg holdings.

A fourth factor, and more subtle social theory, holds that incest laws prevent *social role conflicts* that might be caused by marriage between core relatives. Thus the relation of parent to child, or brother to sister, might conflict with the relation of husband to wife, so societies make sure that no one is both parent and spouse to another person.

Other explanations are based on psychological principles. One argument proposes that people who are raised together will be very attracted to each other and, for some of the reasons stated above, must be strongly prohibited from marrying and from having sexual relations. Sigmund Freud was one of the major proponents of this theory. The opposing theory, associated especially with Edward Westermarck, posits that living in the same house for a prolonged period of time dulls the sexual appetite and breeds a *habit of avoidance.* This situation is another case in which the taboo merely formalizes an existing inclination. Studies of marriages between unrelated people who have grown up together on an Israeli kibbutz (Spiro, 1958) seem to support this second view. It was found that even though marriages between people raised together on the same kibbutz were not discouraged, they rarely occurred. This disinclination was attributed to sexual indifference.

Further evidence of this lack of interest among intimates was discovered by Arthur Wolf in his work with the Chinese in northern Taiwan. When Wolf began his fieldwork in 1957, he came across a unique marriage pattern, recognized its importance, and has been working on it ever since (1995). The most common form of marriage is the familiar arranged marriage between adults, in which the bride joins the groom's household. Wolf calls this the "major marriage pattern." Another pattern, which Wolf calls the "minor marriage," is common in Taiwan and South China. In these cases, an infant girl is brought into her future husband's household, and the two are raised together. Some steps of the marriage ceremony are performed immediately, incorporating the infant into her new family, and she is thereafter called *sim-pua,* "little daughter-in-law." The marriage is finalized years later when a wedding ceremony is performed.

Despite exhaustive efforts, Wolf was unable to establish a relationship between wealth, class, or beauty and the type of marriage employed by a couple. In fact, over the last century, most girls were married in the minor marriage fashion.

Only if they were from small families with few or no older siblings did girls tend not to be sent off into minor marriages. Wolf found that these minor marriages, between people who had grown up together, were significantly less successful than major marriages, as measured by the higher rates of adultery, high divorce rates, and lower fertility. He concluded that childhood association is statistically more likely to reduce the sexual attraction that makes for lasting marriages and many children.

Wolf's line of argument is that inbreeding is disadvantageous because it leads to fewer offspring. Outbreeding, which seems to lead to happier marriages and more children, is adaptively advantageous. Consequently, there has been selection for people who have an aversion to inbreeding. This aversion becomes the moral repugnance that underlies the incest prohibitions that are expressed in terms of kinship. In the end, Wolf does not claim to have finally solved the incest riddle, but he does think that this idea is the right direction to take and that, at the least, "association during the early years of life inhibits sexual attraction" (1995:515).

Cousin Marriages

Even though cultures do try to prohibit some marriages on the grounds of close relationship, cultures on the whole seem to encourage homogamy, marriage between generally similar people. Homogamy has not been an issue for isolated and relatively homogeneous societies such as the Dani or the Yanomamo, but in heterogeneous societies such as the United States, one often hears pleas for young people to marry within their own kind, despite the obvious advantage to the society as a whole in breaking down communalism of all sorts.

Among the best-known sorts of preferred marriages, we find two sorts of **cousin marriage.** In societies with unilineal exogamous descent groups, **cross-cousin marriage,** marriage between children of a brother and a sister, are the closest relatives who are allowed to marry. A cross-cousin marriage reactivates and strengthens the ties between two groups that have already been forged in the parental generation. For example, if we start with a brother and a sister, if she then marries into another clan, and then his son marries her daughter (or his daughter marries her son), the two clans are bound together more firmly than ever.

Parallel cousin marriage, marriage between children of same-gender siblings, is less usual than cross-cousin marriage. Certainly, in societies with unilineal descent groups, marriage between children of brothers or children of sisters would likely violate the rule of exogamy. The Balinese, however, are an example of a society that actually prefers marriage between children of brothers (patriparallel cousin marriage) even though both are of the same descent group. Stephen Lansing (1995:38) suggests that this type of alliance is preferred because it strengthens the descent group by keeping goods at home, and it allows the bride to remain in the descent group where she grew up. This idea makes sense, but it is no more logical than the opposite argument that it is in the group's interest to create marriage alliances with other groups and increase its strength in that way.

In any case, preferred parallel cousin marriage is rare, found mainly among Arab societies, in which it is customarily explained along the same lines that Lansing used for Bali.

Social Repairs: Preserving Lines of Descent

The patrilineal descent group (clan, sib, or lineage) is obviously a successful mechanism for organizing people into social groups. However, this mechanism is successful only if marriages produce male children in each generation to provide for continuity. The obvious question arises, "If a man has no sons, what is he to do?" Several ingenious solutions have been devised to address this problem.

The Levirate.   One solution is the **levirate,** in which the brother of the dead man marries the widow, assuming the responsibility of taking care of her and her children. This type of marriage is best known from the Bible, where it is described thus:

> When brothers live together and one of them dies without leaving a son, his widow shall not marry outside the family. Her husband's brother shall have intercourse with her; he shall take her in marriage and do his duty by her as her husband's brother. The first son she bears shall perpetuate the dead brother's name so that it may not be blotted out from Israel. (Deuteronomy, 25:5–6)

Thus, if a man dies without male heirs, it is the duty of his brother (the widow's brother-in-law, or *levir* in Latin) to have children by her who will be counted to the dead man's line. The most famous story about the levirate concerned a man named Onan. When his brother Er died, Onan presumably wanted to inherit the family wealth. But if he were to have a son by Tamar, Er's widow, that son would have inherited before Onan:

> And Judah said unto Onan, Go in unto thy brother's wife, and marry her, and raise up seed to thy brother.

> And Onan knew that the seed should not be his; and it came to pass, when he went in unto his brother's wife, that he spilled it on the ground, lest he should give seed to his brother.

> And the thing which he did displeased the Lord; wherefore he slew him also. (Genesis, 38:8–10)

In the end, Tamar tricked Er's father, Judah, into having intercourse with her and fathering twins, thereby fulfilling the spirit of the levirate at least, by having children with the help of the deceased husband's kin.

The Nuer Solutions: Female Husband and Ghost Marriage.   One Nuer solution to the problem of sonlessness is the institution of **female husband.** For the Nuer of East Africa, as we will see in Chapter 9 on social organization, continuity of the male line is essential to maintain religious rituals and preserve the right to inherit cattle. If a man has only daughters, the Nuer allow one of his daughters to take on the social role of a man, marry a woman in the standard wedding ceremony, and then serve as social father to the wife's children. These children are then counted to her lineage. (The biology of this procreation—namely, just who is the physical father—is less important to the Nuer than the social fact that she, as a member of the lineage, is the social father.) In theory at least, this female husband could also marry a man and bear children by him, but they would be counted in his lineage. Thus female husbands allow symbol and society to triumph over biology (see also O'Brien, 1977).

Another Nuer solution to the lineage continuity problem is **ghost marriage.** If a man dies without sons, one of his kinsmen marries a woman, usually the widow, to have sons in his name. They are in the dead man's lineage and are considered to be his sons. Evans-Pritchard described the ghost marriage:

> The woman is *ciejooka,* the wife of a ghost, and her children are *gaatjooka,* children of a ghost. The family that develops out of a ghost-marriage may be called a ghost-family in acknowledgment of the ghostly status of the pater of the children. It consists of a ghost, his wife, his children born in the union of marriage, and the kinsman who begat these children and acts as father to them. (Evans-Pritchard, 1951:110)

Social Repairs: Saving the Alliance

Another potential threat to the social order is the death of a spouse. In a society where marriage is primarily an individual matter, the death of one partner leaves a widow or widower, but has relatively few social reverberations. Where marriage has deeply involved two social groups, where wedding exchanges have begun and are meant to continue, or where a presumption of long-term alliances between groups exist, however, then the death of a spouse has broader social implications. In such a situation, the levirate or sororate is often an optional way to repair the damage.

We have already considered the obligatory levirate in the Bible, where a widow continues her deceased husband's lineage by having sons in his name, fathered by his brother. A second function of the levirate is to provide a new and equivalent substitute for the dead man. The sororate, the mirror image of the levirate, has the same function. So, when an obligation or a preference specifies that the widow be remarried to her deceased husband's brother (levirate) or an obligation or preference specifies that the widower be remarried to his deceased wife's sister **(sororate),** the alliance between the two groups can continue as before. (This type of marriage is not to be confused with **sororal polygyny,** where a man is simultaneously married to sisters.) Murdock reported the **preferential sororate** from 100 of a sample of 159 societies (1949:29).

However common it might have been around the world, for at least half a century the sororate was bitterly opposed in Great Britain. The Marriage Act of 1835 made sororate marriages "null and void." Bills to permit it—"marriage with a deceased wife's sister"—were introduced to Parliament 28 times between 1850 and 1900 and finally adopted in 1906 (for the colonies) and 1907 (for the United Kingdom), although even then clergymen who objected were specifically exempted from having to perform such a wedding (Anonymous, 1911).

FOCUS CULTURE

Marriage and Family in Japan

OVERVIEW

Location: Japan is a nation in East Asia

Geography: An archipelago of four main islands and many smaller ones

Population: About 150 million, mostly Japanese, with some aborigines (Ainu) and long-term Korean residents

Language: Japanese is not closely related to any other language. It is written with Chinese ideographic characters and two alphabetical scripts.

Religion: Shinto, an ancient religion focusing on the emperor and ancestors, coexists with Mahayana Buddhism. Many Japanese practice both religions.

Economy: Farming, fishing, and industry. Fish and rice are staples.

Sociopolitical Organization: The emperor is the symbolic head of the country, but it is governed by a parliamentary democracy.

Of all the large nation-states, Japan is perhaps the most culturally homogeneous, but it is still difficult to generalize about 150 million people. Japanese culture is essentially a mixture of very ancient patterns, with a strong Chinese element added in the 8th century A.D., and much American influence dating from the period of post–World War II U.S. military occupation. Of our focus cultures, Japan is the only one about which Americans know much, but that knowledge is limited. Japan sends us cars, television sets, cameras, and VCR players, and we know something of Japanese corporate culture. But the traffic in television programs, movies, fashions, and even baseball players is almost exclusively from America to Japan.

It is easy to see Japan in terms of cultural contradictions. It is very much more traditional, yet it is also innovative and modern in many ways. Ancient forms of theater are revered, but there is a thriving movie and pop music culture. There is strong emphasis on the group, yet

fierce individualistic competition for entrance into the best universities. The family is important, yet, as we shall see in *Farm Song,* people resist its power.

Japan is too big, too diverse, too contradictory, and too rapidly changing for us to generalize about it. Nevertheless, anthropologists persist in trying. Marilyn Ivy, in her postmodern anthropology of Japan, expresses this unease in her opening paragraph:

> The subject of late twentieth century Japan confounds the simplicities of world order, whether new or old. . . . "Japan" appears ubiquitous, nomadic, transnational. Yet at the same time Japan seems to reinscribe the distinction ever more sharply between the "West" and itself. . . . Japanese themselves commonly insist that theirs is a small island country (shimaguni), a homogeneous place. (Ivy, 1995:1)

If we consider the individualism–groupism spectrum (see Chapter 5), it is clear that while the United States generally tilts toward the individualism end of the spectrum, Japan tends to be found more toward the groupism end. This generalization is exemplified nicely in the comparison between American and Japanese styles of playing baseball (described in Chapter 5). Arranged marriages are another index of where a culture stands on this continuum. Although arranged marriages have almost vanished from the American scene, they persist more generally in Japan.

Often, there are special people who act as go-betweens, or marriage brokers, to facilitate arranged marriages. In traditional Japan, the go-between, or *nakodo,* was a trusted friend of both parties who not only brought the two groups together and vouched for their suitability, but also gave a speech at the wedding itself. Kalman D. Applbaum (1995) describes how, in urban Japan today, professional nakodo services are playing the same function. The problem is to find two people and two families who are compatible in education, social standing, astrological readings, and religion, as well as personal attractiveness. Too much disparity between families or individuals would cause problems. Positive attributes, especially higher education, as well as negative attributes, such as physical deformities or neighborhood reputations, are carefully considered. Applbaum points out that these new professional nakodo constitute an adaptation to urban life while retaining the feel of neighborhood traditions and providing the assurance of social stability that seems to the Japanese to be so lacking in Western-style love marriages.

Of course, we are dealing with a generalization here, and, as in perhaps any culture, there are inherent tensions in the demands of both the groupism mode and the individualism mode. In the film *Farm Song,* we see evidence that not all Japanese go along with the demands of groupism.

Although Japan has been generally patriarchal, with emphasis on the continuity of lineages traced through men (patrilineal), there is also a strong focus on the house, rather than any descent groups like clans. Japan social organization is best understood as a **house society.** In traditional Japan, the *ie,* or *house,* was both the structure and the people living in it as a household with considerable continuity over time. It included an extended family, with the patriarch, his wife and unmarried children, his eldest son and family, and perhaps other relatives and non-kin. We see such an arrangement in the film *Farm Song,* in which we encounter an extended four-generation family. (We shall return to house societies on page 278.)

Although the continuity of the *ie* is critical, it is also important in this patrilineal society to preserve the lines of descent. In Japan, the levirate is not used for this purpose. Instead, a Japanese family may adopt an adult male who takes the family name and then marries a daughter of the family and sires children who will bear the family name. In this case, the wedding is performed with the man in the role of the bride and the daughter of the house in the role of the groom (Embree, 1939:213). This arrangement is perfectly logical if one thinks of the person in the role of the bride not primarily in terms of gender but as "the one marrying into the family" and one considers the groom as the family member. As in the case of the Nuer female husband, the biological fact of gender is redefined in the interests of social continuity. ♦

FAMILY AND HOUSEHOLD FORMS

The family is different from a descent group in that the father and the mother are joined by marriage, a tie that is not one of descent or kinship as measured by blood (and, in fact, is easily broken apart). The biological family, composed of parents and offspring defined by sexual intercourse and birth, is the essential core on which all cultural constructions of kinship organization build. The family in cultural terms takes various forms and is often submerged in a larger domestic group or household.

From a purely biological standpoint, the **nuclear family** is the basis of all social organization. It consists of a mother, a father, and their children, often living in an independent household, apart from relatives (Figure 8.7).

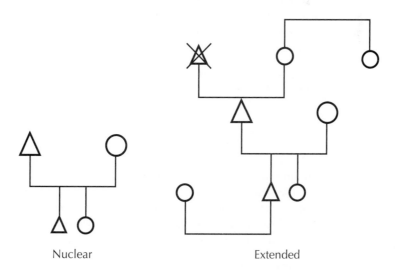

Nuclear   Extended

FIGURE 8.7   Families

In contemporary American political discourse, "the family" and "family values" are powerful vote-getting slogans. But who is to say that the nuclear family is worth fighting for? It is far from the most common family form, cross-culturally. Even in the United States, more often than not, nuclear families split up, recombine, or are submerged in other social groupings such as the **extended family.** An extended family has more than two generations and may include siblings and their spouses. Grandparents and grandchildren, as well as cousins, may be living together.

As David Schneider has pointed out, there is tremendous cultural variation in American kinship organization. Although the nuclear family may be the middle-class white Anglo-Saxon ideal, it does not reflect the range of forms within the United States or in other industrial nations. Schneider attributes some confusion in the ethnographic literature about the primacy of the nuclear family cross-culturally to the fact that many ethnographers have assumed that family and household were synonymous. In fact, the **household,** which is defined as a basic economic interacting unit, is often made up of both kin and friends who happen to live in the same house and does not constitute a single family unit. Schneider believes that this faulty analysis

> may be a consequence of the fact that most ethnographers are middle class and the middle class tends to treat the family and the household as one and the same thing. The lower class does not. Co-residence is not nearly the great symbol of unity for the lower class family that it is for the middle class. (Schneider, 1980:122)

Among the 350 Dani whom I knew best and the many hundreds of others I knew slightly, there was only one nuclear family household. The father was a real loner. People liked him, but he was not particularly sociable. When other men went to battle, he worked his sweet potato gardens.

Napoleon Chagnon, counting Yanomamo nuclear families, whether they constituted an independent household or lived within a larger, more miscellaneous household, calculated that

> by the time a Yanomamo reaches the ripe old age of about 10 years, only about one out of three live in a family containing his yet-married mother and father, and by the age of 20 years, only about one in ten comes from such a family! (Chagnon, 1992:155)

Is any variation from the nuclear family household a sign of sociocultural pathology? Ethnographers avoid answering this question directly. Rather, they study how alternative patterns function. For example, Carol B. Stack, in her study of an African American community in the Midwest (1974), emphasized strategies of survival. Stack's ethnographic study of the community showed how relatives and nonrelatives were involved in complex, flexible patterns of cooperation, exchange, and support. Stack concluded,

> Distinctly negative features attributed to poor families, that they are fatherless, matrifocal, unstable, and disorganized, are not general characteristics of black

families living substantially below economic subsistence in urban America. The black urban family, embedded in cooperative domestic exchange, proves to be an organized tenacious, active, lifelong network. (Stack, 1974:125)

POSTMARITAL RESIDENCE PATTERNS

The location of the residence of a newly married couple has important consequences for their economic, political, and social activities. The major sorts of **postmarital residence** patterns are **matrilocal** (living with the wife's kin group; see Figure 8.8), **patrilocal** (living with the husband's kin group; see Figure 8.9), **neolocal** (establishing an independent residence; see Figure 8.10), and **avunculocal** (living with an uncle; see Figure 8.11).

Patrilocal residence seems the most obvious choice. It makes it easy for groups of related men to form work groups, fighting groups, and ritual groups, and then of course they bring their wives in from outside. In fact, patrilocal residence and patrilineal descent groups are the overwhelmingly popular choices, accounting for something like 80% of all societies.

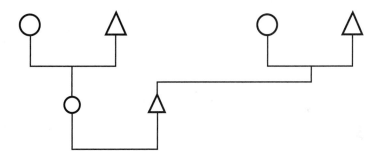

FIGURE 8.8 Matrilocal Postmarital Residence

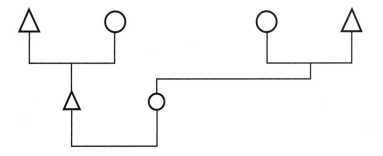

FIGURE 8.9 Patrilocal Postmarital Residence

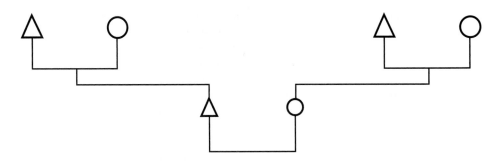

FIGURE 8.10   Neolocal Postmarital Residence

If patrilocality is so effective, what are the reasons for matrilocality? Certainly, male kin activities are disrupted when brothers and male cousins are dispersed, each living with his wife's family. William Divale proposed a solution to this puzzle by looking for the conditions that actually favor matrilineality, with its weakened male kin groups. Cross-cultural research shows that male kin groups, associated with patrilineal residence, are likely to fight among themselves as well as carry on external war. However, matrilineal societies, lacking these male kin groups, may carry on external war but are unlikely to have internal conflicts (Ember and Ember, 1971). Divale, looking at pre-state societies (bands, tribes, and chiefdoms), pointed to migration as being key (1984). In normal settled condi-

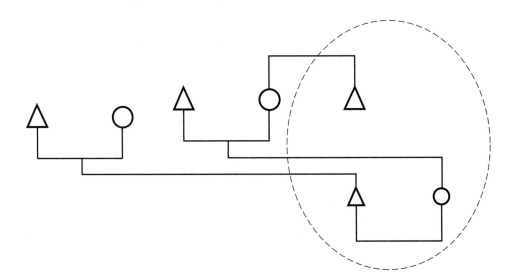

FIGURE 8.11   Avunculocal

tions, societies are patrilocal and patrilineal, with these feuding and warring groups of male kin. Then, when migration brings one society into close and antagonistic competition with another, internal fighting threatens survival. A society that shifts to matrilocal residence will dissipate the power of its male kin groups and can concentrate its fighting force on external war. This brief summary of part of Divale's argument reveals the implications of different forms of postmarital residence.

CHANGING FAMILY FORMS IN WESTERN CULTURES

By now we seem to have found and labeled all possible transformations of the human family. In reality, the basic principle of culture change is still at work. Looking at the second half of the 20th century from both historical and cross-cultural perspectives, we see several major trends of change, despite considerable variation within and between countries, and despite the inherent problems of using national states to represent cultural entities (following, especially, Goode, 1993):

- Divorce rates have increased.
- Single-parent family rates have increased.
- Cohabitation rates have increased (cohabiting being a less stable arrangement than marriage).

Something is happening here, and a few anthropologists are looking beyond the aggregate statistical picture to examine the human implications.

There are probably no societies that do not have some standard way of ending marriage, although the actual form and permissible reasons for divorce vary greatly. With the extraordinary rise in the frequency of divorce in the industrialized West have come major changes in the structure of personal networks. Bob Simpson, a British anthropologist who has worked for years in the world of social policy research, pointed out (1994) that the number of divorces in England and Wales had risen from 700 in 1911 to 160,000 in 1985. This trend means not just the dissolution of many nuclear families, but the constitution of countless of what Simpson calls **unclear families.** Divorced people and their children do not just survive in the fragments of nuclear families. The old family ties, especially those between parents and children, may be maintained or they may be broken off. Relations can be immensely complicated as single parents bring their children into new households, marry, and create new families with multiple parent, child, and sibling ties, any of which may or may not be actively recognized. As Simpson emphasized, rather than simply pass this trend off as the result of social failure, these families must be seen and studied as the creative, flexible, even transient social forms in which an increasingly large number of Westerners actually live.

Simpson described one such "unclear family" (1994:934–936). A man with a child by a woman out of wedlock and a second child by a wife whom he later divorced is married to a woman with a child by a husband whom she later divorced.

The man and the woman have two children together. (You can try to diagram this situation, using the kinship symbols from Chapter 9.) In our previous descriptions of families, it was always clear where affinal and consanguinal ties lay, who was what kin to whom, who would live where, who would share the common resources, and so forth. Consanguinal ties may be permanent, although parents do sever them by "deserting" their children. Affinal ties are much more fragile and are easily severed. In a family such as this one, much is unclear. Who is kin to whom? Who pays for what? Who has claims on whose salary? Who is on whose insurance policy? For grandparents, who have lived through jarring family changes, which are "their" grandchildren? The man has children whose mothers are his wife, his ex-wife, and his former lover. What are their relationships? (With minimal fieldwork, you could probably turn up even more complex situations.) The point is that our neat rules are useless in such situations. The people must work out patterns of behavior as they go, on the spur of the moment, with little cultural guidance. "Unclear families" indeed!

Thus we can see that one of the major changes in American culture today concerns marriage. Marriage, which was once the prerequisite for respectable heterosexual couples who wished to live together and have children, is no longer so. Children of unmarried parents are no longer condemned as illegitimate or labeled *bastards.*

On the other hand, while opposite-gender couples are increasingly rejecting marriage, same-gender couples are demanding it. In the 19th century genteel American women who were not blood kin but who had long-term living arrangements were said to have *Boston marriages.* This label was a respectful acknowledgment of an emotional and economic interdependence, had no legal status, and ignored any sexual implications. Today, many gays and lesbians are seeking the legal advantages of heterosexual marriages, such as health benefits, retirement plans, inheritance, and rights to adopt children. Many also want formal religious marriage ceremonies that are comparable to those for heterosexual couples. Legislatures, insurance companies, employers, and churches are tied in knots trying to arrive at solutions that will satisfy everyone. They must consider both the same-gender couples and the parts of their constituencies or congregations that strongly condemn any public approval of homosexuality. In fact, the lesbian and gay communities in the United States are divided on this issue (see Sherman, 1993). Some believe that legalizing same-sex marriages would be an important step toward official recognition of their situations; others believe that heterosexual marriage has not proven to be a great success and are reluctant to bring it on themselves. Meanwhile, even some mainline Protestant churches allow ceremonies of commitment for same-gender couples, as long as they are not called *weddings.*

On the whole, parentage has been a fairly unproblematic concept. With marriage ostensibly controlling sex, the presumed father of a child was the husband of the mother. Special circumstances such as adoption, adultery, and the levirate made it useful for anthropologists and lawyers to distinguish between the biological father (*genitor*) and the social father (*pater*). But technological advances at the end of the 20th century have greatly complicated matters.

SEEING ANTHROPOLOGY

An Extended Family in Rural Japan: *Farm Song*

Consultant and interviewer: John Nathan

In *Farm Song,* we have a version of Japanese culture that is isolated, traditional, and vanishing. We see an extended family living on a farm in an isolated valley far to the north of Tokyo. The film does not involve an anthropologist, but it gives an excellent picture of a fairly typical, old-fashioned Japanese family. There is Opi, the old grandfather, a widower; Masao, his son, and Masao's second wife Toshi; Masao's son Masashi and his wife Hisae, and one of their sons. Opi is always around, but we mainly see him praying at one shrine or another. We encounter the teenage boy only at the end of the film in a remarkable double interview, in which he first gives the proper responses in the presence of his family, and then, alone with the film crew, he voices his doubts about the future and hints that he will leave home as soon as possible.

But the main characters are the two women, Toshi and her daughter-in-law Hisae, who is still known as "the new wife." In various interviews together and alone, the two women reveal much about the ambiguous position of a woman who marries into a strongly patrilineal, patriarchal household.

The objects that we see in the film range from the archaic mask of the rice cauldron god to the television set, which stays on, unwatched, through the meals. The

Women working in the rice fields in rural Japan. *(Credit: Karl G. Heider)*

rice seedlings are transplanted by tractor, but people have to fill in the gaps by hand.

The short clip begins as Masashi describes his arranged marriage. Then his father, Masao, talks about his marriage to Toshi. Next, Toshi gives her somewhat grimmer story of the marriage. Finally, Opi, the old grandfather, talks about his marriage.

We follow the New Year's house cleaning, and the women make the special holiday rice dumplings. On New Year's Day, the family has a feast. Sake is drunk and things get a bit rowdy.

In another interview, Toshi and her daughter-in-law Hisae discuss relations between the women of the house, including the old grandmother, Opi's wife, who is deceased.

The complete film sets the family in context in rural Japan, in the far north. We follow the technology of rice production. Men use some machinery, while the women do hand labor. After the interviews and New Year's events (seen in the short clip), the film includes an interview with Masahi's teenage son, who subtly raises doubts that he will spend his life on the farm as his father has assumed. More individual interviews with the women reveal their unhappiness with life in the family.

Setup Questions

1. Think about what this film reveals about gender roles in that family. How would you describe them? Do women have power?
2. How are marriages brought about?
3. How is emotion handled? What display rules are used to cover felt emotions?
4. Do you think that Toshi and Hisae have the same understanding of their relationship?
5. How much evidence do we see of changes in this rural Japanese family?
6. Describe the *ie,* the household. Who is in it, and what do they contribute?
7. What is the function of the New Year's events?   ♦

HOLLYWOOD-STYLE ANTHROPOLOGY

The Family in *Moonstruck*

Moonstruck   1987   103 minutes

   Cher as Loretta Castorini
   Nicolas Cage as Ronny Cammareri

The last words of the film are a toast: *A la familia!* To the family! The toasts are in Italian and in English, for although this is an American film, it is very Italian in details like language and music, but especially in its constant exploration of love, marriage, and family. Loretta Castorini, a young widow living in the huge family house with Cosmo and Rose, her parents, agrees to marry Johnny Cammareri, but as he leaves for Sicily to see his dying mother, he begs Loretta to invite his estranged brother Ronny to the wedding. Cosmo's aged father and Rose's brother and his wife fill out the family picture. It all takes place in three days and two nights, under the influence of a full moon.

Setup Questions

1. Cut to the final scene: how is this different from a more typical American love story?
2. What is the meaning of the final camera movements?
3. How is space used? Especially contrast the kitchen with the dining room.
4. Why *La Bohème,* an opera about some French artists in Paris who are called Bohemians?
5. Who uses "ti amo" when?
6. What are the Italian touches in the film? Could this film be set in a Kansas farm town?
7. How are all the little extraneous vignettes used to support and comment on the main plot?
8. How are love, marriage, and family each pictured in contradictory terms?
9. There are only two non-Italian-American characters of any significance—what are they doing in a film like this? ◆

CHAPTER SUMMARY

- Something like marriage is found in all societies. A reasonably comprehensive definition of marriage includes (1) social acknowledgment of (2) a union of a male and a female functioning to (3) regulate sexual activity, (4) produce and raise children with social and cultural identity, and (5) constitute an economic unit. Although exceptions to each of these points exist somewhere in the world, this definition is a good start.

- A major area of variation in marriages is how they are originated. In strongly group-oriented societies, marriage tends to be arranged by family or similar social groups; in strongly individualistic societies, marriages tend to be love-based arrangements contracted by the two principals.

- Polygamous marriages involve more than one spouse. If one man can have more than one wife at a time, it is called polygyny; if a woman can have more than one husband at a time, it is called polyandry.

- Every society forbids some potential unions and encourages others. Incest prohibitions forbid certain close relatives to marry (or have sexual relationships). Rules of exogamy force people to marry outside their group (clan or other group). Homogamy is the principle of marrying similar people. Endogamy is the rule that one must marry within a particular social group (such as a caste).

- Marriage always, to some extent, brings together two groups in some sort of exchange. Bride wealth is given to the bride's group as she herself moves into the husband's group; dowry is made up of the goods that the bride owns and brings to the union; bride service is performed by the husband for his father-in-law for a period after the wedding.

- Various forms of social repairs are brought into play if something goes wrong in a marriage, such as the early death of a spouse. One of the most common repairs is the levirate, used especially in societies where maintenance of the male line is threatened by the death of the husband. In levirate, a relative of the deceased marries or at least impregnates the widow, to produce a son in the name of the deceased man.
- The nuclear biological family (man, woman, child) is often less important as a basic economic, residence, social unit because it is submerged in multigenerational families or households that include non-kin.

KEY TERMS

arranged marriage	female husband	nuclear family
avunculocal	ghost marriage	parallel cousin marriage
bride service	homogamy	patrilocal
bride wealth	households	polyandry
cousin marriage	house society	polygamy
cross-cousin marriage	incest	polygyny
cultural schemas of	levirate	postmarital residence
marriage	love marriage	preferential sororate
dowry	marriage	schemas of romance
endogamy	matrilocal	sororal polygyny
exogamy	monogamy	sororate
extended family	neolocal	unclear families

QUESTIONS TO THINK ABOUT

- Officially, the dominant schema for U.S. marriages is the love marriage. But to what extent are people actually constrained by families, friends, or social norms in their choice of spouse?
- Why is there such a strong feeling against recognizing same-gender unions as families?
- If first cousin marriage is permitted so widely in the United States, why does it inspire general disapproval?
- Why has there been such strong feeling against (Mormon) polygyny in the United States?

SUGGESTIONS FOR FURTHER READING

Bestor, Theodore C.
1989 Neighborhood Tokyo. Stanford, CA: Stanford University Press. *An ethnography of urban Japanese families.*

Ember, Melvin, and Carol R. Ember
1983   Marriage, Family, and Kinship: Comparative Studies of Social Organization. New Haven, CT: HRAF Press. *Utilizes the large sample base of the Human Relations Area File.*

Harrell, Stevan
1997   Human Families. Boulder, CO: Westview. *An ambitious attempt to consider the world's families in terms of six major categories, or clusters.*

Imamura, Anne E.
1996   Reimaging Japanese Women. Berkeley: University of California Press. *An important updating of the pictures of Japanese women in the film* Farm Song.

Ingoldsby, Bron B., and Suzanna Smith (eds.)
1995   Families in Multicultural Perspectives. New York: Guilford Press. *A reader.*

Weisner, Thomas S. (ed.)
1997   African Families and the Crisis of Social Change. Westport, CT: Bergin and Garvey.

Yamada, Haru
1997   Different Games, Different Rules: Why Americans and Japanese Misunderstand Each Other. Oxford, U.K.: University of Oxford Press. *A sensitive exploration of some of the more implicit cultural norms of the two cultures.*

CHAPTER 9

Social Organization and Kinship

A noble
couple.
Prambanan,
Java, 9th
century C.E.
*(Credit: Karl
G. Heider)*

HEADLINE ANTHROPOLOGY

PRESS WATCH

Some of the subjects discussed in this chapter have made their way into current news stories. For example:

◆ In North Carolina, the spouse and family of a murder victim can claim compensation from the state. The Crime Victims Compensation Commission has ruled that those cohabiting with, but not legally married to, victims were also entitled to compensation.

—New York Times, *September 1, 1999.*

◆ Inspired by a Louisiana law requiring elementary school students to address their teachers as "sir" or "ma'am," South Carolina leaders are discussing the possibility of instituting a similar law there.

—The State *(Columbia, South Carolina), August 30, 1999.*

◆ A Columbia University study shows that teenagers with poor relations with their fathers are especially likely to abuse tobacco, alcohol, and drugs—more so than teenagers who have had no contact with their fathers.

—New York Times, *August 31, 1999.*

◆ Sonia Gandhi, the Italian-born daughter-in-law of one Prime Minister of India and widow of another, as well as leader of the Congress Party, is running for parliament and, presumably, for the post of Prime Minister, but has formidable opposition.

—New York Times, *August 20, 1999.*

◆ As Hillary Clinton was on a tour of North Africa, the King of Morocco welcomed her visit, saying "We will not only treat her as a head of state, but as a member of my family" and invited her to visit the royal family's mausoleum.

—The State *(Columbia, South Carolina), April 1, 1999.*

Societies are organized groups of people. Recall the discussion in Chapter 2, which distinguished between "society" and "culture." The concept of a society centers on patterned relationships, or ties (the **social organization,** or **social structure**) between people. The concept of a culture, however, centers on cognition, shared ideas or knowledge (the cultural schemas). Although we (even anthropologists) sometimes use "culture" and "society" interchangeably, they do have importantly different meanings.

For example, we can call the people who pierce their body parts a culture or, more accurately, a subculture, because they share some schemas about bodies and ornaments. Yet these people are not automatically a society (or social unit). But what if there were (there probably is, somewhere) a Piercing Club open only to Pierced People? That group would be both a social unit and part of a subculture. Of course, some Pierced People (culturally speaking) might not be members (socially), and perhaps some who share the cultural schemas but have not yet gotten around to actually being pierced might be accepted as members.

Think about the term "members." It also means body parts. Members of a club, or social unit, or society, are joined in an organized whole, as are the parts of a living body. Nevertheless, we do not speak of "members of a culture" but of people who "share" a culture. You can be thrown out of a social unit ("dismembered"?) but you cannot be removed from a culture or subculture (unless, perhaps, with our piercing example, you "change your mind").

In Chapter 2, we saw that cultures are fuzzy categories with no clear boundaries. In contrast, societies and social units generally have precise boundaries. A person either is or is not a member of a social unit. Cultures and societies are similar, however, in that each concept can be used at various levels of inclusiveness. We can use the term "society" for the largest groups, and "social units" for smaller groups (this relationship is comparable to the one between "culture" and "subculture").

Within any society, there are many different social groups, large and small, that are organized according to different sorts of principles and that perform different functions. Some groups constitute embedded series, or units within units with different degrees of inclusiveness. For example, a *nation* (the United States) is made up of fifty *states,* each of which is made up of many *municipalities* (cities and counties). In addition to such embedded series, other groups may cross-cut each other so that a person may be associated with some people in one group but with other people in a second group (such as a college fraternity or sorority made up of people from many different states).

In summary, groups can be defined according to a number of different criteria:

1. *Recruitment:* How do people become members of a group? By being born into a kinship group (such as a clan), by residence (such as a local group like a neighborhood association), by age (such as Generation X), by choice (such as a club), or by a combination of several criteria?
2. *Organization:* Does the group have explicit formal membership, leadership, and functions (such as the United States or a Rotary Club)? Or is it more of a broad category or class of people such as farmers, Irish Americans, or senior citizens?
3. *Boundedness:* Is the group limited to a certain place, or does it extend across territorial boundaries?
4. *Corporateness:* Does the group own or control real or intellectual property such as land or ritual knowledge?
5. *Function:* What does the group do? Does it wage war, regulate marriage, run an irrigation system, or perform religious ceremonies?

We can look at social organization in terms of the recruitment criteria and focus especially on the relative importance or nonimportance of kinship in constituting these groups. We have already seen how different groups function to arrange marriages. In subsequent chapters, we will encounter groups conducting religious ceremonies, resolving conflict, and fulfilling other needs.

The most basic type of group is a kinship group. Anthropologists have long been impressed with the importance of **kinship,** which can be defined as the various cultural constructions or elaborations of *marriage,* creating **affinal** relatives (in-laws), and *birth,* creating **consanguinal** (blood) relatives. To summarize: *Kinship = Affinity + Consanguinity.* This idea is a simple formulation, to be sure, but many of the best minds in anthropology have spent the last century and more working out the ingenious variations that human cultures have played on those themes. Kinship groups are universal, but the patterns and rules that govern kinship ties vary dramatically from culture to culture.

The realm of kinship is a prime example of interaction between biology and culture, our "biocultural model." Recall our British example of an "unclear family" from Chapter 8, where we saw a complex tangle of consanguinal and affinal ties. Sex and birth are part of our biology. Nevertheless, those relationships are elaborated in myriad ways in different cultures, leading to the "cultural construction of kinship."

On the whole, *domestic household groups,* at the small end of the social unit scale, are kin-based, built around a *nuclear family* (wife, husband, and child), an *extended family* (three or more generations), or *related families* (two siblings and their families). By the time we move up in size to social units that we can call *settlements* (village, hamlet, or compound cluster), we are no longer dealing with only kin, and we find many unrelated people who for one historical reason or another are linked in that social unit. At the large end of the social unit scale today are *nations* (for example, Malaysia, Canada, Indonesia), in which kinship ties are of minimal significance.

When trying to understand the social structure of a society, you can use three general rules of thumb:

- The smaller the society (the maximal social unit), the more prominent a role kinship will play in organizing the subunits (the constituent social groups).
- The larger the maximal social unit, the more different sorts of subunits there will be.
- The larger the maximal social unit, the more the subunits will be organized on principles other than kinship.

CLASS AS CATEGORY

In addition to the various groups that we have already discussed, organized by kinship, age, or voluntary principles, social organization can be analyzed in terms of social class, which is a category rather than an actual set of groups.

Traditionally, people who studied large-scale societies (most sociologists) have paid more attention to non-kinship-based categories such as social class and occupation. Anthropologists, who have traditionally studied smaller-scale societies, have tended to look much more intensely at kinship ties and kinship-based groups. The theories of kinship that have emerged from anthropology over the past century have been concerned with such factors as principles of descent and inheritance in the broadest sense and of affiliation and exchange of goods and services between in-laws. Theories that have emerged from sociologists have tended to be more concerned with power relationships between classes. Now, however, as more anthropologists study modern industrial societies, they must consider both kinship and class in their analysis of social structure.

As an example of an anthropological approach to class, Kathryn Marie Dudley has been studying people who have lost their jobs or their farms, yet cling to a middle-class identity. In her fieldwork, Dudley was able to identify the ways in which these downwardly mobile people regard being "middle class" as a cultural attitude rather than as some sort of economic measure. In particular, being middle class is seen by them in individualistic moral terms:

> Membership in the middle class is thus not just a matter of achieving a certain standard of material success and, once having done so, resting back on one's laurels; it requires the unremitting performance of a distinctive moral character—one which, in every community, is as much culturally-defined as it is economically-based. (Dudley, 1999:4)

Studying Class, Power, and Inequality

Much anthropology that is emerging at the turn of the century uses the traditional anthropological methods and concepts to explore human situations at home. It is perhaps controversial to emphasize the continuity of anthropological tradition, for much is being challenged. I would argue, however, that the road to the best of modern anthropology still leads through the past, through Boas and Malinowski, through Mauss and Margaret Mead. Questions of function still arise, but no longer with the idea of a society as a hermetically sealed machine spinning along smoothly. Rather, we see factions within a society contesting major aspects of their machinery. The concept of culture is difficult to avoid, but instead of emphasizing the shared nature of cultural schemas, the focus is on conflicting schemas (think of the wide disparity in cultural schemas that can be held by twenty people in a single college classroom). And what of the study of exotic tribes? The distinguished French anthropologist Marc Auge writes of studying groups close to home. He uses the term "the proximal other" (1994/1998) to emphasize that one does not have to cross an ocean to find great cultural differences. *Pygmalion,* set in early 20th-century London, is a brilliant depiction of class in this sense.

Another strong trend in anthropology today is what has been called "relevance." Often the focus is on such pressing social issues as abortion, race, gender, and class. Very often, a more or less explicit part of the agenda is the conviction that this anthropological investigation can make things better. That is, awareness of injustice can lead to justice. As Michaela di Leonardo has pointed out, such studies have a long history in anthropology (1998:28).

One recent example is a collection of essays on workplace ethnography edited by Ann E. Kingsolver (1998). These studies look at how, in U.S. workplaces, people use notions of power and class to maintain or to challenge various sorts of inequality. Kingsolver describes her own research in eastern Kentucky, where farmers were able to work two jobs, tobacco growing and factory labor (1998:1–20). As the factory opportunities for overtime began to cut into the time they could count on to tend their own tobacco fields, the farmers began to hire migrant workers from Mexico. This example is no simple picture of labor and management, of employer and employee. The farmers worked for multinational factories (Toyota and textiles) and multinational tobacco companies, but grew the tobacco as self-employed farmers and then became employers of the Mexicans.

One of the studies in the Kingsolver volume described "Seeing Power in a College Cafeteria." Daniel Cogan was a college undergraduate who had eaten in the cafeteria and then worked in it. He began to notice how the student workers were distanced from the nonstudent workers and how the nonstudent workers were made invisible to the students who ate there. The university was constituted as a place of study and not as a workplace. The cafeteria operation had been contracted out to a large, off-campus food service corporation, so the nonstudent workers had no official relationship to the university. They were kept out of sight of the student customers, being confined to the kitchen. In contrast, the student workers were out front, interacting with the customers. Students were considered students who worked and were given all sorts of benefits, such as book-aid bonuses that were denied the nonstudent workers. As Cogan put it,

> The privileges bestowed upon student workers in the workplace of the cafeteria reinforce their position as trainees of the university and nonstudents as reproductive laborers at the university. (Cogan, 1998:174)

As part of his study, Cogan made a videotape called *A College Cafeteria.* He enlisted the workers as much as possible to make it a truly collaborative product. The sound track had only their voices, not his narration. His intent was to use the videotape to raise awareness on the campus of the way in which inequality was being managed under everyone's eyes. As it turned out, the making of the video—rather than the tape itself—had that effect.

Despite current efforts in anthropology to examine non-kin aspects of social organization, the early overemphasis on kinship sometimes led to a distortion in the view of the importance of kinship in organizing social behavior and threatened the precept of holism. The fact is that kinship is just one element among many that structure social behavior. (That point, incidentally, becomes apparent when we look for a film "about kinship." Few exist. Instead, many of the films that we see, especially *The Nuer,* show kinship as a factor in the action.) Kinship systems do provide rules of behavior, as well as a rationale for organizing people into groups that interact regularly and have a common identity. Finding general rules, in turn, allows us to summarize lots of different human solutions to the problem of organization. The rules exist, of course, but we cannot expect them always to be followed precisely. In the field, in an actual village, we see how actual people play out their lives more or less in accordance with the rules.

DESCENT GROUPS

The most important of the kinship groups are **descent groups,** which contain the people who are united by a direct line of descent from a common ancestor. These groups can be **unilineal,** in which descent is traced through only one parent (the most widespread form of descent group), or **non-unilineal,** in which descent is traced through either or both parents. In the United States, for example, the most common descent pattern is non-unilineal. However, that is far from the norm.

In unilineal descent, membership in the descent group is automatically determined at birth by one of two rules of descent. In patrilineal societies, the person is a member of his or her father's group (a **patrilineal descent** group) or in matrilineal societies, descent is reckoned through the mother (a **matrilineal descent** group). Unilineal descent groups vary in size, in function, and in how explicitly people can trace their genealogical relationships.

Descent groups usually have several attributes. They are generally

- exogamous.
- **corporate.** (Some property is usually owned jointly, in the name of the group as a whole. It may be land, livestock, or sacred objects or even sacred knowledge.)
- **totemic.** (Descent groups often are associated in some ritual or symbolic sense with particular animals, birds, or other aspects of nature, an idea we will explore further in Chapter 12.)

All manner of other social and religious activities may also be organized by these descent groups. The groups themselves may be egalitarian, or they may be ranked in a hierarchy. We differentiate unilineal descent groups mainly on the basis of size.

Lineages, Clans, and Sibs

The **lineage** is the smallest unilineal descent group, in which everyone knows the other members of the groups and how they are related. In societies in which these lineages make up parts, or segments, of larger units, we speak of **segmentary lineage systems** (we find these in Nuer social organization, as discussed later in this chapter).

Clans and sibs are larger unilineal descent groups in which people believe that they can trace their descent back to some founding ancestor and therefore have a sense of collective identity. However, the line of descent is only assumed and cannot be reconstructed. Clans and sibs are generally exogamous, marriage being forbidden between members of the same group. A distinction is often made between groups that are territorially bounded and own property in the name of the group and are called **clans,** and groups that are more widely dispersed and have no corporate holdings and are called **sibs.** Clans or sibs may be made up of clearly recognized lineage segments, as with the Nuer, or may be more internally undifferentiated, as with the Dani, who do not emphasize lineages.

Phratries and Moieties

Unilineal descent groups like clans or sibs are commonly found in medium-size tribal societies. Some such societies have also developed further combinations. A **phratry** is a loose association of several clans or sibs. And a few societies are divided into halves, called **moieties,** with a person belonging to one of two moieties, according to the descent rule (matrilineal or patrilineal). Moiety systems are usually found in societies made up of clans or sibs and collect each of the clans or sibs into one of two larger social units.

While moieties are relatively rare, the Dani have them. The Dani system works this way: Each Dani is born into the father's patri-sib, which in turn is included in one or the other patri-moiety. All 50,000 Dani in the Grand Valley belong to one of the two moieties and one of the several dozen sibs. Members of the same sib are spread out across the entire Grand Valley. Here is where the unilineal descent groups (sibs and moieties) are qualified by local territorial units, the most important of which is what I call the Confederation. Confederations are named, usually after their most important sibs, often one sib from each moiety. For some events, such as warfare, or some rituals held every few years to commemorate the dead, the entire Confederation takes part. But it is the local members of a sib who are the closest allies. They mutually own and safeguard some sacred objects, and together they perform rituals around these objects.

The main function of the Dani moiety is to regulate marriages. In most clan societies, one must marry outside one's own clan (the rule of exogamy). But in societies with moieties, like the Dani, people are not only prohibited from marrying anyone in their own sib, but also cannot marry into any other sib belonging to their moiety. This rule of moiety exogamy severely restricts a person's choice of marriage partners by eliminating many potential partners. I knew of no violations of the rule among the Dani, but the relatively large population of the Grand Valley means that a person has access to a fair number of acceptable mates anyway. One can imagine that in small-scale societies, an exogamous moiety system would pose real hardships for young people wanting to get married.

For example, matrilineal clans are the most important unit of social organization for the Hopi, who are Pueblo Indians of northeastern Arizona (Eggan, 1950). The members of a single clan consider themselves to be descended from the same female ancestor. Each clan is named after the clan totem. These totems are usually creatures like Bear, Crow, or Badger, but may include objects like Carrying Strap, Tobacco, or Sun's Forehead. The clans are corporate, owning common land, houses, and even some ritual knowledge. They are also exogamous. Furthermore, Hopi clans are linked with other clans into phratries that seem to celebrate not common descent, but historical partnerships. These phratries, too, are exogamous. Although they have no economic, ritual, or political duties, a major function of the phratries is to safeguard the survival of sacred knowledge, for if one clan has no more daughters and so dies out, its ceremonial duties can be taken on by a partner clan of the same phratry.

The clans themselves are composed of smaller units (lineages) that are the main channel for inheritance of goods and knowledge. A boy learns ritual

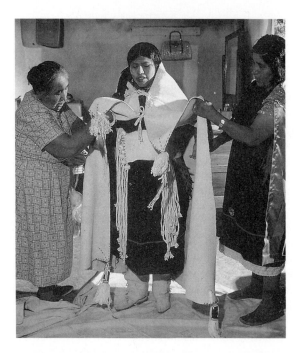

Hopi ceremonies are organized by their matrilineal clans. *(Credit: © Terry Eiler/National Geographic Image Collection)*

knowledge from his mother's brother, a member of his immediate matrilineage. At the core of the household is a particular lineage segment composed of a few related women plus their children (their husbands belong to different clans). In addition to these unilineal descent groups, the Hopi have many ritual societies concerned with war, fertility, or other activities, whose memberships cross-cut the descent groups.

Patrilineal Descent

There are far more patrilineal societies than matrilineal societies. In patrilineal societies, a person is born into his or her father's group. Property is inherited through the male line, and often family names or titles are passed down through males. As we saw in Japan (in Chapter 8), strong patrilineal emphases in naming and inheritance can exist without strongly developed patrilineal descent groups. Likewise, European societies have long used patrilineal principles for family names and for inheritance but lacked formal descent groups. As we shall see in Chapter 10, all societies—whether patrilineal or matrilineal—are **patriarchal.** That is, they vest most of the real power in men.

FOCUS CULTURE

Patrilineal Descent of the Nuer of the Upper Nile

OVERVIEW

Location: The upper Nile region, straddling the Sudan–Ethiopia border

Geography: Open grassland

Population: 1,000,000

Language: Nuer is considered one of the Eastern Sudanic family

Religion: Animism (belief in spirits in nature), traditional belief in a high god. Now many are Christian.

Economy: Primarily cattle herding but some horticulture

Sociopolitical Organiztion: Patrilineal, segmentary lineages and clans

We have already met the cattle-herding Nuer of the upper Nile (Sudan and Ethiopia) as a prototypical example of pastoralism. The Nuer have also long been famous exemplars of a patrilineal descent system. For the Nuer of the 1930s (Evans-Pritchard's Nuer), the most important principle of this system is that men—not women—form the significant links in the social organization. The Nuer are organized into exogamous patrilineal clans and lineages. Evans-Pritchard describes some functions of clans and lineages beyond exogamy:

> Clans and lineages have names, possess various ritual symbols, and observe certain reciprocal ceremonial relations. They have spear-names that are shouted out at ceremonies, honorific titles by which people are sometimes addressed, totemic and other mystical affiliations, and ceremonial status towards one another. (Evans-Pritchard, 1940:193)

Lineages play a key role in marriage arrangements of these Nuer. When a young man marries, he is unlikely to have enough cattle of his own to put together all of the bride wealth. He must therefore look to the older men in his lineage—his father and father's brothers—to loan him the cattle. This act puts him in substantial debt to these lineage elders. In this way, the demands of marriage exchange strengthen the bonds of lineage.

The Nuer have what is called a *segmentary lineage system,* for as a single lineage gets so large as to be unwieldy, a sublineage (sons and grandsons of a younger brother) break off, and this segment begins to function as a lineage in its own right. In the ideal Nuer system, a man has two sons, each of whom has two sons, and the lineage includes five families in three generations. By the fourth generation, however, the lineage may break into two segments. Each of the segments acknowledges the old ties and remains members of the same clan, but the two segments have become relatively independent social groups, or lineages, in their own right. In Figure 9.1, we see how Evans-Pritchard and a Nuer have visualized Nuer lineages.

Even the Nuer, with prototypical unilineal descent culture, qualify their kinship ties with allegiances to other groups. For example, in the film *The Nuer,* we catch a

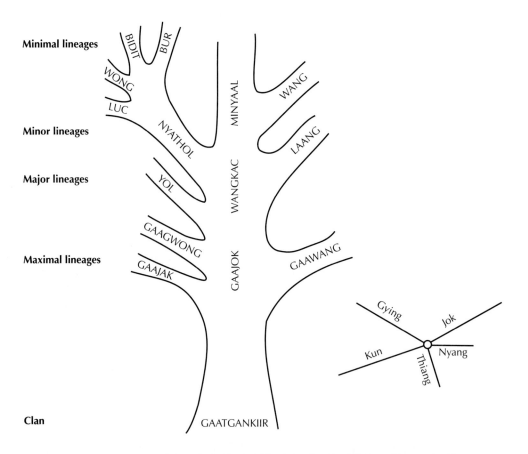

Minimal lineages

Minor lineages

Major lineages

Maximal lineages

Clan

FIGURE 9.1 Two versions of Nuer Segmentary lineages. On the left is a diagram by Evans-Pritchard showing the entire clan with its various lineages branching out. On the right is the way the Nuer would draw local clan relations in the dirt, indicating how people living in one local community are related. (*Source: Evans-Pritchard (1940:197, 202). Adapted by permission of Oxford University Press.*)

brief glimpse of men sitting around a great pottery vat drinking homemade beer together. This group is an **age set,** which is composed of members from various lineages and clans who are linked by age, not by kinship. Members of an age set are all born about the same time and share a group identity. They grow up together, are initiated into adulthood together, fight as a unit in war, and generally socialize together. Age sets cross-cut descent groups, so a man's allegiance to his descent group might well conflict at times with his loyalties to his age-set mates.

What of Nuer women? Because of rules of exogamy and the postmarital residence rule of patrilocality (the rule that the newly married couple lives with his relatives, not hers), the women of a clan seem to vanish from the picture after marriage. They move out of the village where they were born and no longer stay connected to it. Because the wives of the males in the village must all come from other lineages and clans, according to the rules, and they are not members of the local lineage, their activities tend to be overlooked.

In fact, for the Nuer, both marriage ties and age sets create social bonds and arenas of social interaction and loyalties that cut across the unilineal descent groups. The Nuer define themselves in social terms not as members of a particular lineage, but as belonging to a particular local community. This local community, called *cieng,* includes men who are members of a single lineage but also other, non-related men as well as the married-in women.

In effect, what lineages actually do is to regulate marriage through the rule of exogamy, perform some ceremonies, and have some legal responsibility in murder cases.

Here, as a counterpoint to Evans-Pritchard's Nuer, we will look at the Nuer of Sharon E. Hutchinson, who spent two years with Nuer groups in the 1980s and 1990s, half a century after Evans-Pritchard. We also have the film version, *The Nuer,* which offers yet a different take on this group.

When Hutchinson first visited the Nuer, she was surprised to find that it looked much as Evans-Pritchard had seen it in the 1930s—swamps, marshes, and lakes in the wet season when the people move to high camps; parched land in the dry season; and always, Nuer settlements with sights and sounds and smells of cattle. Even today, the Nuer spend much of their time at pastoralism, caring for their cattle and exchanging them in marriage ceremonies. In the 1930s, reported Evans-Pritchard, they talked mainly about cattle. Hutchinson, however, found that cattle talk had been superseded by concerns with national politics, development programs (or the lack thereof), and often very basic philosophical debates triggered by the changing importance of money, the intrusions of northern Arabs, and Christianity.

One dilemma with which the Nuer have been coping is the shift from three earlier basic factors of social cohesion—namely, blood (kinship), cattle, and commensuality (eating together)—to the new factors coming in from the outside—money, guns, and paperwork (from the government bureaucracy) (Hutchinson, 1996:56–102). When Evans-Pritchard first came to the Nuer, money was unimportant. Wealth was contained in cattle, but it was not a moneylike wealth. For those people (mainly males) who owned cattle, these cattle were an extension of themselves, of their own power. Later, national civil wars in the 1960s and again in the 1980s wreaked havoc

Nuer with their cattle in camp. *(Credit: © Betty Press/Woodfin Camp & Associates)*

on the herds and drew young men to cash-earning jobs in the military or the capital in the north, Khartoum. With more money available and a greater need for replacement cattle, people simply bought cattle instead of receiving them from their clan elders through the traditional ritual kinship exchange channels. Even then, however, people paid attention to the source of the money. Bride wealth cattle could not be bought with just any money, but only that money gotten from the sale of cattle previously in the bride wealth system or money from respectable sorts of labor.

The introduction of this "cattle of money," which came without traditional kinship obligations, transformed the entire social world. The Nuer were slow to accept this kind of cattle as appropriate bride wealth, but when a young man could buy cattle to be used in his wedding payments (bride wealth) and could even replace a few of the required cattle with cash, he was more independent and individualistic than if he were still dependent on his kin ties for help with the bride wealth. Use of money to build up a bride wealth payment that is not entangled in kinship obligations created an independence that now reverberates through all links of Nuer society and that is just one aspect of continuing social change. As Hutchinson put it,

> Although cattle could not be converted into money and vice versa, the cattle of money and the money of work could not be used to reinforce transgenerational bonds of dependence among kinsmen in the same way as the cattle of girls because, as Nuer put it, money has no blood. (Hutchinson, 1996:99)

Of course, money has no blood, but cattle, which are in some ways like people, have blood. The exchange of cattle therefore remains the basis for the traditional ties, or entanglements, that held Nuer clans together. ♦

Matrilineal Descent and the Minangkabau

We need to distinguish matrilineal descent, the rule of descent through women (or the principle that a person takes his or her social location from the mother, not the father), from **matriarchy,** a theoretical society where women, not men, yield the power (see the discussion of this system in Chapter 10). In theory, a matrilineal system is just the mirror image of a patrilineal system. In practice, however, because of the dominance of males in every society, this matrilineal system turns out to be not all that different from a patrilineal system. As an example of a matrilineal society, we will look at the Minangkabau.

Although an overwhelmingly large majority of unilineal descent group systems are patrilineal, a significant minority are matrilineal. These groups include widely separated cultures such as the Navajo and the Hopi in North America; many sub-Saharan groups; some cultures in India, especially in the southern state of Kerala; and the largest of all, the Minangkabau of West Sumatra, Indonesia (see Krier, 1995; Blackwood, 1995).

The Minangkabau heartland is a series of high valley bowls surrounded by volcanoes, lying just south of the equator. The old Hindu kingdom of Minangkabau had been rich in gold, which it exported to early modern Europe. (Marco Polo may have visited Minangkabau on one of his trips to China.) By the end of the 18th century, the gold was running out, and spices, tea, and coffee production became more important. During the first decades of the 19th century, a militant reformist Muslim movement swept out the Hindu rulers. By the middle of the century, the Minangkabau were firmly Muslim and firmly under the Dutch colonial empire but retained their matrilineal system. For a hundred years now, social commentators and social scientists from the West have been puzzled by the apparent contradiction of the strongly patriarchal Islam coexisting with the matrilineal descent system. Minangkabau scholars have insisted that there was no real conflict, and in fact matrilineal Muslim societies have long existed in Africa as well.

It is not clear just how the Minangkabau social organization worked during the days of the Hindu kingdom. But by the mid-19th century, the Minangkabau were living in small, independent territorial units called *nagari.* Each nagari contained a few thousand people living in a few villages near their rice fields. Each nagari was proud of its independence and emphasized the uniqueness of its culture, even while the residents recognized their overall Minangkabau identity.

Even today, each Minangkabau is a member of a *suku,* a matri-clan. These clans are nonterritorial, extending across the entire Minangkabau landscape. The local clan segment, or lineage, is the significant descent group. At its core is a group of women—mothers, daughters, and sisters—plus their brothers, sons, and husbands. The men are nominally at least secondary clan members. The lineage owns, in the name of the women, real property in three categories. First, the great house, the *rumah gadang,* with its graceful upsweeping multiple roofs, is one of the most beautiful house forms of Southeast Asia. It has apartments for each of the adult women and a room for the men to store their things. Second, rice fields also are owned by the women of the clan. Third, the clan has a collection of ceremonial heirlooms, mainly fine antique textiles. (The Minangkabau have long specialized in weaving, and their repertoire of different kinds of weaving in cotton, silk, and gold is one of the world's richest.)

Clans are exogamous, so men marry women of other clans and sometimes other nagari. A husband sleeps in his wife's apartment but during the day returns to his own clan house to work the rice fields of his mother, sisters, and aunts. Children are raised primarily by their own clan members, which means their biological mothers and mothers' brothers.

The Minangkabau are famous in Indonesia for both their matrilineality and their pattern of out-migration. For generations, Minangkabau men, and now increasingly families, have been encouraged to leave the heartland for a few years to

A great house of the matrilineal Minangkabau of West Sumatra, Indonesia. The house, the rice fields, and the heirlooms are owned by the women of a matrilineage. The roof line is one of many Southeast Asian elaborations of roofs, but here people say it represents the horns of the water buffalo. *(Credit: Karl G. Heider)*

have adventures, to see the world, and to earn money to send back to the home villages. It has often been suggested that this out-migration, or *merantau,* serves as a safety valve for the strongly patriarchal Muslim men to alleviate, for a while, the constraints of the matrilineal order.

In fact, although the Minangkabau are matrilineal in their clan organization, they are not matriarchal in its assignment of power. Although the women own the important property, their sons and brothers exercise control over it as the actual managers. To be sure, Minangkabau women are influential and independent, but the main power to make economic, political, and social decisions is in the hands of the men. The Minangkabau are also Muslim, and Islam emphasizes the role of men. Islamic law on inheritance and other aspects of descent strongly mitigate the matrilineality of Minangkabau custom. Finally, there are many loopholes. When the Minangkabau migrate from the heartland to the coast, or to other parts of Indonesia, they are removed from the power of custom and can own their own land and houses.

Challenges to Unilineal Descent Systems

In his influential work on the history of science, Thomas Kuhn (1970) has described how revolutions in science occur when conventional understandings ("normal science") of one moment are found wanting, unexplainable anomalies pile up, and then, in a relatively sudden fashion, a new understanding emerges to replace the old.

We can see something like this at work in kinship studies. For much of the 20th century, the study of kinship was inspired by British social anthropology. In the **genealogical method,** ethnographers were urged, as their first task in the field, to collect genealogies to locate each person in a descent line. Those data were then used to recognize important social groups, which turned out to be, not surprisingly, descent groups. By happy coincidence, many of the most important scholars studied societies in which unilineal descent was indeed important. We have discussed Evans-Pritchard's work with the Nuer, a prototypical example of unilineal descent organization, with its clans and segmentary lineages. But we have also seen how there were other principles at work in Nuer social organization, such as locality, age sets, and exogamous marriages.

The importance of unilineal descent was so fundamental to the normal science that even when anthropologists reported on other sorts of cultures, they tried to force them into unilineal modes. Malinowski described the Trobriand Islanders as matrilineal (with lots of exceptions). Raymond Firth, in his work on the Polynesian Tikopia, defined the *paito* (literally "house") as a unilineal descent group by focusing only on the men's descent and ignoring the women's marriage ties. For whatever the paito is, it is made up of men born into it and their wives who have married into it. Thus, Firth said,

> Every individual family of father, mother, and children is part of a larger group known as the paito and composed of similar families, tracing their relationship ultimately to a common male ancestor through male forebears in each case.
> (Firth, 1936:345, quoted in Bouquet, 1993:66)

However, "in each case" means "in the case of each male." Women are members of the paito, but through marriage, not through unilineal descent. And only men with patrilineal links to the main lineage can become chiefs or elders. In fact, we are getting very close to "house societies," discussed in a later subsection.

African Models in the New Guinea Highlands. In 1962, J. A. Barnes wrote an influential paper called "African Models in the New Guinea Highlands." Barnes was a British social anthropologist who had done his early fieldwork in Africa, where the unilineal descent model fit fairly well. He then moved to the Australian National University, where he became familiar with the ethnographic data that were coming out of New Guinea. Although these highland cultures certainly used patrilineal principles in organizing their social groups, there was no hard and fast patrilineal rule. People had much choice as to which group they could join, groups included members and even leaders who were not patrilineally related, and there was little interest in remembering patrilineal genealogies. In short, said Barnes, "it seems prudent to think twice before cataloguing the New Guinea Highlands as characterized by patrilineal descent" (1962:6). And, Barnes mused, what if social anthropology had been developed on the basis of New Guinea Highland ethnographies instead of African ethnographies? He said, "It would be interesting to work out how, say, the Nuer might have been described if the only analytical models available had been those developed to describe, say, Chimbu and Mbowamb" (1962:9).

The Case of Ethnocentrism. A fascinating and quite different sort of challenge to unilineal descent system orthodoxy came from the experience of Mary Bouquet (1993). Bouquet was trained in anthropology at Cambridge University, and in the mid-1980s she taught anthropology at a university in Portugal, asking her students to read the classic British social anthropology books in English. The Portugese students were puzzled, not because of language problems, but because of basic cultural assumptions. The British emphasis on genealogies and pedigrees, which, as we have seen, leads to recognition of unilineal descent organization, was not self-evident to them. It turns out to be a culture-bound, British way of approaching social organization. The Portugese pattern emphasizes a person's ties with both father's and mother's sides instead of concentrating on the father's side only.

As Bouquet thought about her students' reactions, she came to see how the unstated assumptions of British culture had shaped the British social anthropology that was being exported abroad. Most tellingly, Bouquet quotes Evans-Pritchard himself as he acknowledges that even the Nuer think of a person not as part of the sort of segmentary lineage system that he has presented, but as part of an interacting network. For them, their own social system is seen "primarily as actual relations between groups of kinsmen within local communities rather than as a tree of descent" (Evans-Pritchard, 1940:203, quoted in Bouquet, 1993:75).

An Alternative Model: House Societies. What do we learn from all this? Actually, it is not that the genealogical method is wrong or that unilineal descent does not exist. Rather, we can see that unilineal descent principles may not be the only, or even the principal, way in which different societies are organized. As the paradigm shifts, it does not discard the idea of unilineal descent, but it puts it into context.

Recognizing the very mixed nature of important social groups in many societies, anthropologists have recently talked about *houses,* getting away from kinship implications altogether.

Claude Lévi-Strauss, in a short but seminal piece (1982/1979:163–187) shows how the social units in some societies have long given analysts trouble. If we look back at Franz Boas's analysis of Kwa Kwaka' Wakw social organization (1897), we begin to appreciate the problem. Boas noted the variations in Northwest Coast societies, and he had no trouble recognizing the southern tribes as patrilineal and the northern tribes as matrilineal. By that time, in the late 19th century, enough ethnographic information had been gathered to show that most tribal societies were organized according to the principles of descent through the male line (patrilineal) or through the female line (matrilineal). These two categories worked broadly, if not quite universally. In fact, we still use them—albeit cautiously—today. The Nuer of Evans-Pritchard's time were clearly patrilineal. Even today the Minangkabau are certainly matrilineal. Of course, there are always a few footnotes to add. For instance, a Minangkabau man is by birth a member of his mother's matrilineal clan, but at certain moments (like marriage) he receives support from his father's matrilineal clan. In addition, some titles are passed down through men. Nevertheless, this patrilineal linkage does not invalidate the general proposition that the Minangkabau are matrilineal.

Thus, if the two ends of the Northwest Coast could be handled with the concepts of the time, the Kwa Kwaka' Wakw, in the center, seemed anomalous. Boas drew on the historical, evolutionary thinking of the 19th century to try to resolve the puzzle by suggesting that Kwa Kwaka' Wakw clans were originally patrilineal and then picked up some matrilineal traits under the influence of the northern tribes. He concluded that the Kwa Kwaka' Wakw represent "a peculiar transitional stage" (1897:322).

Boas's dilemma is a good example of how even brilliant scholars can be constrained by their conceptual tools. His categories of matrilineal and patrilineal worked for most cultures but not for a few exceptions. In the end, Boas gave up in frustration and used the Kwa Kwaka' Wakw term for these peculiar groups, *numyan.* Later, Lévi-Strauss traced the course of Boas's thinking, showing how similar principles could be found elsewhere in the world. Indeed these cultures were all anomalous, or "peculiar" if one were stuck in a matrilineal/patrilineal paradigm. Lévi-Strauss resolved the problem by introducing a new term, **house society** (*societé á maison*). House societies are those in which groups center on a single large house and are composed of many sorts of people related in many ways. They are found especially in Southeast Asia (Carsten and Hugh-Jones, 1995), Japan (see p. 250), and Europe. Lévi-Strauss discussed at length medieval European royal houses. More recently, Frances Pine has pointed out the importance of the house in the social organization of peasant and pastoralist societies in marginal regions of Europe (Basques, Portugal, Transylvania, and southwestern Poland). These societies are characterized by

> social identification with a named house group, the perpetuation of groups through marriage, fostering, or adoption, and a high degree of ritual elaboration revolving around the house and its members. (Pine, 1996:443)

In the anthropological literature on Bali, generations of anthropologists have expressed their frustration at trying to come to grips with the Balinese ancestor group called *dadia*. It is important in some areas but not elsewhere. While it resembles conventional categories such as clan, it is not a good fit with any. James Boon concluded that it was like a lineage, a caste, a cult, a faction, and a political party—in other words, a complex mixture (1977:145).

An important theoretical question triggered by Lévi-Strauss's proclamation of house societies is the following: "Given that many cultures have important groups that do not match our neat unilineal descent group thinking, does it help to consider them house societies, and to elevate the house to the status of a cross-cultural category?" We cannot live without cross-cultural categories, yet we get into trouble when we take them too literally.

Non-unilineal Descent

There are ways to constitute descent groups other than through a strictly unilineal rule (be it patrilineal or matrilineal). Some societies form **cognatic descent groups**

House societies are centered on those who live in a great house rather than on unilineal descent group organization. *(Credit: Dr. Frances Pine)*

by allowing individuals to choose whether to become affiliated with their father's descent group or their mother's descent group. This choice is often tied to residence. A person has relatives in several areas and so is entitled to join any of these groups but chooses one, gaining rights to land and other benefits through that group. Cognatic descent groups, then, are corporate groups that own some valuables in common.

Linda Stone draws a useful distinction between cognatic societies and bilateral societies (1997:178). **Cognatic societies** are organized into cognatic descent groups, and every person has chosen membership in one out of several groups that he or she is eligible to join. **Bilateral societies,** which are common in Europe and Southeast Asia, also recognize descent through both father and mother but do not have actual organized descent groups. People can inherit through both father and mother and, as we shall see in the next section, kinship terms for cousins, uncles, and aunts do not distinguish the father's side from the mother's side. In bilateral societies, however, one can often recognize a *unilateral bias* in one realm or another. For example, most Americans follow a patrilineal principle in family names, but there is an unrecognized matrilineal bias in postmarital residence as well as where you eat Thanksgiving dinner (check this idea out).

KINSHIP TERMINOLOGY SYSTEMS

Among the first really good sets of ethnographic data were **kinship terms,** the words that people use to talk about their relatives. There were lots of reasons for this development. Kinship terms are easy to discover. People talk about kinship freely. People use kinship terms openly. Even in cultures in which personal names may be really personal, private, or even secret, people are forthcoming about their kinship term system. In the 19th century, one could send kinship term questionnaires out to European colonial administrators and missionaries and get back reliable results. In other words, kinship terms posed a middle-level problem that could be solved by the good ethnography and cross-cultural comparisons of the time and that led straight into the core of human social organization.

Diagramming the Kin Universe

There are many ways to show kinship ties on paper. Sometimes "family trees" are drawn literally like trees, starting with a single ancestor (the important founder, or apical ancestor) and branching up. Sometimes the diagrams hang down like a branching chandelier (see, for example, Figure 8.2). Sometimes the focus is on a single person, the "I," or the speaker, placed in the center with parents and grandparents radiating out in widening concentric circles.

Try collecting someone's genealogy. You will quickly find that unless that person has a very standard simple family, in which no one married more than once and there are no stepsisters, half-cousins, or the like, your diagram will quickly get complicated and overloaded. For convenience here, we can just map married couples and the set of children associated with the first marriage (see Figure 9.2). Using this simple diagram, you should be able to map all the relatives.

Every culture has a finite and fairly small set of words that label categories of relations. This vocabulary is called their *kinship terminology*. It includes **terms of reference,** which are used when speaking about another person ("He is my father.") and **terms of address,** which are used when speaking to another person ("Hey, Mom!"). Terms may refer to relatives by marriage (affines) or to biological relatives (consanguines), or they may cover both (such as *uncle,* who may be a father's brother or an aunt's husband).

There may be multiple terms, each denoting the same person but with different connotations (*pop, pa, dad, daddy, papa, father*). Complicating things, kinship terms are often extended metaphorically to non-kin (Uncle Sam, Mother Teresa, Brother Cadfael, Father Christmas).

Another problem arises when members of a society refer to someone by using a kin term when no biological or marriage relationship exists. It may just be an expression of friendship or collective identity. One example is the use of the term *brother* among African Americans in the United States. It is more an expression of solidarity and shared identity than a definition of a biological relationship.

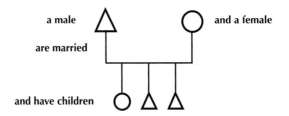

From here, with a large enough piece of paper, you can map any relationships. For example, here is a more complicated family. The first wife of the man (A) died; he and his second wife divorced. What are the English kinship terms for A and B? B and C? C and D?

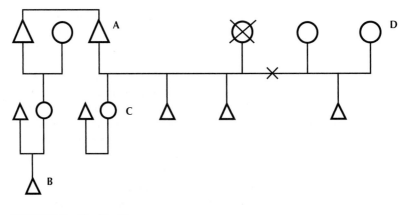

FIGURE 9.2   Kinship Diagrams

Culture-Neutral Kinship Analysis

The need for a set of culture-neutral (etic) terms to describe kinship relations in different systems is obvious, because the words from any one system are specific to that culture. A. L. Kroeber, on the basis of an exhaustive study of North American systems, came up with a means to perform a culture-neutral analysis of a kinship system (1909/1952). He concluded that, for all the apparent variation, only eight principles or dimensions were involved in establishing kin relationships when speaking to an informant. They were the following:

1. *Generation,* which distinguishes people of one's own generation from that of one's parents and that of one's children,
2. *Age within generation,* which distinguishes, for example, one's older brother or sister from one's younger brother or sister
3. *Lineal versus collateral,* which distinguishes direct-line ancestors and descendants from those who are farther removed, such as the English term *aunt* or *cousin*
4. *Gender of the other,* which distinguishes between male and female relatives, such as uncle/aunt and brother/sister
5. *Gender of the speaker,* in systems in which men and women use different terms for the same relative
6. *Gender of the person who links the speaker with the relative,* in systems in which, for example, a father's brother would be distinguished from a mother's brother
7. *Consanguinal versus affinal,* which would distinguish an aunt by marriage from an aunt who is a parent's sister
8. *The other's condition of life,* which would indicate whether the relative is alive or dead, single or married

Doing a Componential Analysis.   To see how Kroeber's system works, write down the English kinship terms, define them in relation to the speaker (or the user of the term), and distinguish every term from the others using Kroeber's dimensions. (*Hint:* You need to use only four dimensions, and you do not always need that many.)

This exercise is called a **componential analysis** of a kinship system, which involves determining the basic underlying principles, formulated in an etic language, and then using them to define the terms of a particular culture. If you have done the analysis successfully, you will have come to the following results:

> *Father* is male (Kroeber's criterion 4), one generation older (Kroeber's criterion 1), and lineal (Kroeber's criterion 3).
> *Mother* is female, one generation older, and lineal.
> *Grandfather* is like father but two generations older.
> *Aunt* is like mother but collateral (criterion 3).
> *Grandson* is like grandfather but two generations younger than the speaker.
> *Cousin* is same generation but collateral.
> *Brother* is male, same generation, lineal, and consanguinal.
> *Brother-in-law* is like brother but affinal instead of consanguinal.

We could code these various terms as follows:

Father: G + 1, LIN, MALE, CONS
Mother: G + 1, LIN, FEMALE, CONS
Grandfather: G + 2, LIN, MALE, CONS
Aunt: FEMALE, G + 1, COLL
Grandson: MALE, G − 2, LIN, CONS
Cousin: G 0, COLL, CONS
Brother: MALE, G 0, LIN, CONS
Brother-in-law: MALE, G 0, AFF

Four of Kroeber's eight criteria are not used in the English system. Some are rare, but criterion 2, which distinguishes older siblings from younger siblings, is found in many cultures.

Kroeber's eight North American dimensions do not exhaust all of the possibilities. Elsewhere in the world, some other criteria are used. For example, the system in Truk (a Micronesian culture in the Caroline Islands) uses Kroeber's criterion 4, gender of the other, but also uses a criterion to distinguish relatives of the same gender as the speaker from relatives of the opposite gender as the speaker (Goodenough, 1956). The Dani system uses a dimension that distinguishes between relatives in the same moiety as the speaker and relatives in the opposite moiety.

As a further experiment, collect kin terms from another culture and make a componential analysis of that system, trying to work out the principles on which it is based. How many dimensions do you need to define each kin term in a way that differentiates it from each other term in the system?

Using an Emic Approach

In the early days of kinship analysis, before people really understood the importance of etic definitions, some serious misunderstandings arose because of the use of emic (culture-specific) definitions of kinship relationships.

One such error went like this: In many cultures, people lump fathers and father's brothers together. This grouping was supposed to be evidence of an earlier time when people did not know the difference between their own biological father and other, similar men, a time of so-called primitive promiscuity, when all of the men were having sexual relations with all of the women. It is easy to be scornful of such logic now, but that was actually a fairly ingenious attempt to explain differences between kin term systems.

Now we would phrase it quite differently. For example, the Dani term *opase* can be defined as "male, one generation older, same moiety." It can be glossed as "father," "father's brothers," and "father's father's sons." We understand it as a term that labels a group of males who are similar in certain culturally significant senses.

The etic definition shows us which dimensions are important in the Dani system. Where the English system is concerned with differences between ancestors and closely related nonancestors (fathers versus uncles, mothers versus aunts), the Dani system is concerned with distinguishing people of the same moiety from people of the opposite moiety. In fact, there are other important behavioral differences having to do with moiety membership, so this approach is not a trivial labeling exercise.

Whether these distinctions are made is likely to indicate cultural concerns but cannot be used as a measure of cultural ignorance. For example, English, unlike German or French, does not distinguish between male and female cousins. Historical reasons having to do with the development of each language explain this difference, but we cannot go much further. Certainly, it would be hard to argue that French and Germans are more interested in cousins than are the English or to suggest that the English do not recognize the difference between male and female cousins. It is merely that such differences are not encoded in the vocabulary.

NON-KIN GROUPINGS

Kinship is not the only means of grouping people in a society. As we saw with the Nuer, age is another dimension along which members of that society and others are organized. Many of the more complex societies are characterized more by involvement in voluntary organizations, such as churches, corporations, clubs, and the like, than by groupings that are determined at birth.

Organization by Age

Many societies group people, especially boys, by age cohorts that cut across descent groups. We have seen this pattern among the Nuer. The cohort, called an *age set,* is formalized with an initiation ceremony in the early teens. Because neighboring Nuer tribes do the same thing, a man traveling away from home can claim ties with the age set that is equivalent to his own. So the Nuer age set members provide social and political support to each other and are allies in conflicts.

Other cultures of East Africa, such as the Masai of Kenya, have elaborated age sets into major units of the society. Boys as well as girls of adjacent years are called into age sets in childhood and proceed though a series of age grades together. Like Nuer age sets, these groups provide social and political support. The age sets also form fighting units, however, and the whole age-set complex of the Masai has a military tone that is lacking in the Nuer system.

Western societies include some structures that are generally equivalent to age sets. In Austria, people are labeled by their birth year, rather like a good wine (for example, Jahrgang 1977). In the United States, high school and college classes are identified by the year of their graduation, and they celebrate their collective identity with class reunions every five or ten years.

Voluntary Associations

Large-scale industrial societies such as the United States are characterized by social groupings that are based not on inherent attributes such as ancestry or date of birth but on the individual's choice. This structure allows for a vast number of social groupings, in contrast to descent groupings, which are more limited. If you were to list the different groups to which a Dani, or a Ju/'hoansi belongs, you could come up with perhaps a dozen, at most, for each, many of which would be determined by a descent rule.

However, the distinction between automatic and voluntary group membership is not as clear as it seems at first glance. On the one hand, ethnographers who describe kin-based societies inevitably come across cases in which people manipulate or even break the rules, even as they are ostensibly agreeing with them. On the other hand, in the United States, many of our "voluntary" social groups are those of our parents. Churches, schools, and clubs all have a degree of family continuity. Even though they are technically voluntary, we somehow wind up in our paternal or maternal groups.

One of the most ambitious fieldwork studies of such **voluntary associations** in the United States was conducted by two psychologists, Roger G. Barker and Herbert F. Wright. They and their research team exhaustively cataloged all of the "behavior settings" in which the residents of a small Midwestern town interacted:

> The Presbyterian worship services, the high school basketball games, and the post office, for example, persist year after year with their unique configurations of behavior, despite constant changes in the persons involved. These persisting, extra-individual behavior phenomena we have called the standing behavior patterns. (Barker and Wright, 1955:7)

Boy Scouts are one type of volunteer social group, where descent is fairly unimportant. *(Credit: © Catherine Karnow/Woodfin Camp & Associates)*

Of the 585 behavior settings identified, many revealed ongoing voluntary associations in the town, from formal (Boy Scouts) to informal (high school kids at the drug store soda fountain). An analysis of kinship groups in the town would have given only an incomplete picture of social activities there. In fact, most activities were organized through voluntary associations.

DOING ANTHROPOLOGY

A Second Look at Your Social Groups

Recall the "Doing Anthropology" exercise in Chapter 2, where you listed the various social groups to which you belong. Redo this exercise. Using the criteria for groups given in this chapter, characterize your groups, both voluntary and descent based. ♦

SEEING ANTHROPOLOGY

Social Organization and *The Nuer*

> *Filmmakers: Hillary Harris, George Breidenbaugh, and Robert Gardner*

The Nuer, shot in 1968 in Ethiopia, is surely one of the most beautiful of our films. Hillary Harris, who shot most of it, was already famous for his New York dance films, and his sensitivity to Nuer movement shows clearly. Robert Gardner, who had made the Dani film *Dead Birds* (Chapter 3) seven years earlier, visited Harris in the field for a couple of weeks with a synchronous sound camera and shot the interview sequences.

The short clip begins as a Nuer man describes the importance of cattle in Nuer life. We see scenes of domestic activity: milking, cooking, and fetching water from a river. A group of men try to work out a problem: one man's wife has not borne him a son, so he wants to divorce her and have the bride wealth cattle returned. More domestic scenes follow, and then the men of an age set gather to drink beer together.

The complete film opens with poetic sights and sounds of Nuer moving about a village as day begins. We hear about the boys' initiations (*gar*), when deep cuts are made across the foreheads, leaving scars that last a lifetime. We hear much about the importance of cattle—how a boy receives an ox and a special name when he is initiated, how cattle are given as bride wealth at marriage.

Next, we see a ceremony to cure a woman who has been possessed by the spirit of her husband's brother, a man who died without fathering sons. Through a spirit medium, the dead brother asks for a "ghost marriage" (recall Chapter 8)—a woman will be married to his ghost and then she will have children that continue his lineage. They agree.

The dry season ends, and the young people move the herds to wet-season camps. Two boys are initiated with the *gar* ceremony.

Setup Questions

1. Think about the problem of filming kinship. Although one cannot see kinship, what evidences of kinship are possible to film? What evidences do you see in this film?
2. How does the film use emic, or native, statements to augment the etic narration?
3. What various uses do the Nuer make of cattle and cattle products?
4. How are the cattle poetic metaphors for the Nuer?
5. Did you catch the attempt to make visual generalizations, to show a range of behavior beyond the specific examples of a single photograph?
6. What does the divorce case suggest about cattle and social organization? ◆

HOLLYWOOD-STYLE ANTHROPOLOGY

The Sociolinguistics of *Pygmalion*

Pygmalion   1938   black and white   96 minutes

Leslie Howard as Professor Henry Higgins
Wendy Hiller as Eliza Doolittle

Pygmalion is a profoundly cynical statement about social organization and language by George Bernard Shaw. The play opened in 1913, this movie of the play in 1938, and the musical version, *My Fair Lady*, in 1956 (movie version, 1964). The plot: In early 20th-century London, Professor Henry Higgins, who seems to have invented phonetics, the science of speech, makes a bet that he can teach Eliza Doolittle, a Cockney flower girl, to speak such good English that she can pass as a duchess. He wins. It is a cutting exploration of the relationship between language and class in the England of a century ago, with several subplots that mock the English class system.

Viewing advice: the last 20 minutes or so become tedious, and the ending subverts Shaw's own ending. And Professor Higgins' relentless misogyny is a bit hard to take. You may prefer the musical version (it won an Academy Award for best picture, whereas the 1938 version was only nominated for best picture). I suggest both.

Setup Questions

1. Why would a shop girl in a flower shop have to speak better English than a duchess? (And why does Nepomuck, at the ball, declare Eliza a fraud?)
2. Explain Eliza's parrot (in the play there is only an empty bird cage).
3. What is Mrs. Pierce's role in this class system?
4. What does Alfred Doolittle mean by "the undeserving poor" and "middle-class morality"?
5. Does Professor Higgins have to be so totally insensitive toward Eliza? (He does get along with other women.)
6. Who do you think Eliza winds up with? (In his postscript to the play, Shaw explained the outcome, saying that it is perfectly obvious.)
7. It turns out that class lines are not impenetrable: did you notice the movement up and down? ◆

CHAPTER SUMMARY

- Social organization refers to the ways in which a society is subdivided into constituent subgroups or smaller social units.
- In organizing themselves, all societies use principles based on the biological facts of procreation: affinity, the (marriage) links between a man and a woman, and consanguinity, the "blood" link of descent connecting parents and children.
- Unilineal descent groups are formed by the rule that a person is by birth a member of the father's group (patrilineal descent) or of the mother's group (matrilineal descent). These groups are usually exogamous, corporate, and totemic.
- Small unilineal descent groups, where everyone knows everyone and the links are common knowledge, are called lineages; larger groups, in which the exact relations may no longer remembered, are called clans and sibs. Groups of clans linked together are called phratries. There are also some rare unilineal systems that divide the entire society into two superarching groups called moieties.
- An example of patrilineal organization is the Nuer of the upper Nile, and an example of matrilineal organization is the Minangkabau of West Sumatra, Indonesia.
- Societies where kinship is not such an important criterion for organization, but groups of kin and non-kin form a household (often in a single great house), are called "house societies."
- Some societies use a principle of non-unilineal descent, forming cognatic descent groups where people use either patrilineal or matrilineal links to claim membership in a particular group.
- Most kinship terms are like "uncle," lumping several different sorts of people together in a single category. This choice is not an arbitrary one, as the sets of kinship terms in a culture give clues about the structure of the interpersonal relationships. The terminology tends to lump together people who are alike in culturally salient ways and split apart those who are different in culturally important ways.
- Componential analysis reveals the principles used to form kinship term categories (for example, gender plus relative age plus direct lineality).
- Common non-kinship criteria for forming social units are age (age sets) and voluntary associations (such as clubs).

KEY TERMS

address, terms of
affines (affinal)
age grades/sets
bilateral societies
clans
cognatic descent groups
cognatic societies
componential analysis

consanguines
 (cosanguinal)
corporate
descent groups
genealogical method
house society
kinship
kinship terms

lineage
matriarchy
matrilineal descent
moiety
non-unilineal descent
patriarchal
patrilineal descent
phratry

reference, terms of	social organization	unilineal descent
segmentary lineage	social structure	voluntary associations
system	societies	
sibs	totemic	

QUESTIONS TO THINK ABOUT

- Why are patrilineal systems so much more common than matrilineal systems?
- American English and Inuit use the same sort of kinship terms. Why? (What could they have in common? What sorts of theories could you use to answer this question?)
- In large-scale societies, kinship principles seem less important than in small-scale tribal societies. What does this fact suggest about the advantages and disadvantages of kinship organizations?
- Can you identify changes in (ideas about) social organization between older and younger generations today?
- English-language kinship terms are fairly uniformly agreed on, except for terms for grandfather and grandmother. Collect some examples. Can you suggest reasons for this variation?

SUGGESTIONS FOR FURTHER READING

Deng, Francis Mading
1972   The Dinka of the Sudan. New York: Holt, Rinehart and Winston. (1984 reprint by Waveland Press, Prospect Heights, Illinois.) *Evans-Pritchard wrote disparagingly of the Dinka, neighbors of the Nuer, but this ethnography by a Dinka anthropologist paints a rather different picture of the situation.*

Kelly, Raymond C.
1985   The Nuer Conquest: The Structure and Development of an Expansionist System. Ann Arbor: University of Michigan Press. *Yet another take on the Nuer.*

Scheffler, Harold W.
1978   Australian Kin Classification. Cambridge, U.K.: Cambridge University Press. *One of the last of the classic kinship studies.*

Strathern, Marilyn
1992   After Nature: English Kinship in the Late Twentieth Century. Cambridge, U.K.: Cambridge University Press.
1992   Reproducing the Future: Essays on Anthropology, Kinship, and the New Reproductive Technologies. Manchester, U.K.: Manchester University Press.

CHAPTER 10

The Cultural Construction of Gender and Sexuality

An orgy. Borobudur, Java, 9th century C.E. *(Credit: Karl G. Heider)*

HEADLINE ANTHROPOLOGY

Some of the subjects discussed in this chapter have made their way into current news stories. For example:

◆ 250 women in Athens, Georgia, attended the 4th annual Southern Girls Convention, "dedicated to the notion that is O.K. to be a feminist in the South."

—New York Times, *July 22, 2002.*

◆ *Cosmopolitan* sponsored an international conference of magazine editors to explore how to translate *Cosmo*'s "tangy fusion of sex and empowerment" to the nearly 50 countries it now publishes in.

—New York Times, *May 26, 2002.*

◆ Recent studies in the US show that women feel pain more than men, and receive even less medication for pain than do men.

—New York Times Special Section on Women's Health, *Sunday, June 23, 2002.*

◆ A painting of a baby nursing at its mother's breast was removed from a public exhibition at the Stewart International Airport in Orange County, New York, because of 15 complaints that it made some passengers uncomfortable.

—New York Times, *28 February 2002.*

◆ In the US South, a new pattern of "secondary virginity" is emerging—abstaining from sex for weeks or months before marriage. It seems to be a compromise between generally accepted premarital sex and various southern religious campaigns promoting premarital abstinence.

—New York Times, *August 4, 2002.*

DIFFERENTIATING SEXUALITY AND GENDER

The terms *sex, sexuality,* and *gender* have been used in so many different ways that we must be very explicit about what we mean by them. Using the biocultural model helps to sort things out. We begin with the physical facts of *Homo sapiens.*

As a biological term, **gender** refers to the fact that humans are overwhelmingly either male or female. Culturally, however, gender is constructed in a bewildering variety of ways. Not only is there tremendous variation in what it means to be "male" or "female," but, as we shall see, there may be more than two cultural genders. The organization of cultural activity by gender is pervasive. Not only do all cultures use gender in this way, going far beyond the obvious biological facts of conception, childbearing, and breast-feeding, but gender differences show up in most aspects of life. Practically every subject that we touch on in cultural anthropology shows the workings of the cultural construction of gender, and gender is an issue in nearly every chapter of this book.

Sexuality is closely linked to gender. Again, in the terms of our biocultural model, we begin with the biological fact that *Homo sapiens* reproduces through sexual intercourse between male and female, an act that seems to be basically plea-surable for the participants.

Then there are the culture-specific elaborations on that act of **sex:** sexual be-havior and the meaning of sex as well as all the culture-specific elaborations of eroticisms and other sexual pleasures. Although sexuality has spurred a tremen-dous amount of interest through the ages, anthropologists have neglected this en-tire subject. This omission may be in part because of a cultural disinclination to examine sexuality publicly. It is too fraught with our own ideas of privacy and of impropriety. Somehow it has been deemed less appropriate for real scholarship than kinship or ritual is. Also, ironically, sexuality is too important. On the surface, perhaps, it is pleasure and procreation. In fact, sex is so embedded in issues of power, gender, social structure, and the person that we must go far beyond just the ideas of pleasure and procreation to understand it.

HOW MANY GENDERS? HOW MANY SEXUALITIES?
THE PUZZLE OF HOMOSEXUALITY

Homosexuality is, for most 21st-century Americans, a particular puzzle. Is it bio-logical? Is it learned at an early age? Is it an adult choice? Just how our biocultural model fits (what is innate, and what is learned?) is the subject of much scientific research and increasingly acrimonious political debate. Sometimes the line be-tween science and politics is quite unclear. Another part of the debate takes place on moral grounds, where the biological facts are considered irrelevant to whether homosexual behavior is condemned or accepted.

Anthropology contributes to this debate in two ways: by examining the cul-tural assumptions of the Western model of gender and sexuality and by exploring the ideas of other cultures. *Tootsie,* which was made as cinematic entertainment, is a flippant exploration of these same cultural associations.

As Gilbert Herdt put it, Western thinkers, including anthropologists, have been prisoners of a "principle of **sexual dimorphism.**" This model emphasizes two gen-ders, male and female, whose purpose is reproduction (Herdt, 1994:21ff). While the principle does account for much social life of all societies, it relegates other cul-turally constructed genders as well as nonreproductive sexuality to marginal or de-viant status at best. Of course, the West recognizes the existence of alternative genders and pleasurable sexuality beyond reproduction, but people and govern-ments have had an uneasy time with both. The ethnographic data will take us to a more complete view of how *Homo sapiens* constructs both gender and sexuality.

Alternative genders from other cultures have often been described in the an-thropological literature. Commonly, such people were thought of as transvestites or cross-dressers—that is, members of one gender who simply switched genders symbolically. As long as the dimorphism model was used, there was little inclina-tion to credit the possibility of a third (or fourth) gender in other cultures.

Among North American Indian tribes, there have been many variations on gender behavior that go far beyond a simple male–female dichotomy. In the

Male-to-female cross-dressing transformation. According to Carl Hefner, "This former player in a Javanese folk theater (*ludruk*) now owns a beauty salon in Surabaya, Indonesia. While acting in the persona of a female on stage, such players challenge conceptualizations of male and female gender. Audiences are engaged in the transvestite's symbolic dialogue when they accept the convincing female persona, yet at the same time possessing the knowledge that the person portraying the female is biologically male." *(Credit: Carl Hefner)*

anthropological literature, the term **berdache** has often been used for individuals (usually males) who took on female roles. In *The Zuni Man-Woman* (1991), Will Roscoe summed up the current understanding of these patterns in North American Indian culture, saying that the most important attributes of this gender were their economic activities (males did woman's tasks, females were active in "warfare, hunting and leadership") and their special supernatural powers. Their attire and even their sexual activity were generally less important. They were usually full, respected members of their groups and often outstanding figures (Roscoe, 1994:332ff).

More recently, a consensus has emerged among Native Americans and anthropologists who are concerned with the issue that the term "berdache," which was perhaps originally a derogatory word from Arabic, is inappropriate. A new term, **two-spirit,** has been proposed (Jacobs, 1994). Again, we are guided by the principle that we should adopt a term or a name preferred by the people themselves and should drop a derogatory or inaccurate word no matter how established in the anthropological literature it might have become.

In any case, a variety of patterns that complicate gender identities seem to be widespread in Native North America. For example, the Northern Athapascans, of northern Canada, do not seem to have the sorts of variations that had been labeled "berdache." They believe in reincarnation, however, and when the spirit of one person is reincarnated in the body of a person of the opposite gender there can be, at least temporarily, doubt about real gender identity (Goulet, 1996). We can formulate a general principle for Native North America: Although male and female are the basic genders, the various cultures in different ways provide socially acceptable alternative gender roles for some individuals.

Serena Nanda has written about the **hijras** of India. She titled her book *The Hijras of India* (1990). Even though Hindu culture has a strongly dualistic concept of male and female, there is room for alternative genders:

> In Hinduism, the complementary opposition of male and female, man and woman, represents the most important sex and gender roles in society but by no means the only ones. The interchange of male and female qualities, transformations of sex and gender and alternative sex and gender roles, both among deities and humans, are meaningful and positive themes in Hindu mythology, ritual and art. (Nanda, 1994:375)

Men become hijra by having an operation that removes their maleness—their genitals. They have two main social roles simultaneously and (apparently) in contradiction: as sacred ritual specialists and as prostitutes for men.

There are many other culturally constructed "extra" genders: *mahu* in Tahiti, Hawaii, and elsewhere in Polynesia (Besnier, 1994); a pattern of women "becoming" men in the Balkans, which may or may not represent a real third gender (Gremaux, 1994); the *kwolu-aatmwol* of the New Guinea Sambia culture, who are biologically hermaphroditic and a culturally constructed third gender (Herdt, 1994); and alternative genders such as *banci* and *waria* in Indonesia (Oetomo, 1991).

But what of sexuality between males or between females where there is no particular third gender? It is this issue, of course, that has attracted so much attention in the United States in the 1990s. Only recently have anthropologists come to write about such patterns. For example, various people writing about New Guinea cultures had referred rather obliquely to homosexuality, but it was not until the 1980s that Gilbert Herdt began describing a New Guinea Highland group that he called *Sambia,* whose pattern of cultural construction of male homosexuality and heterosexuality was quite unusual (see, particularly, Herdt, 1987).

The Sambia believe that girls are born complete and have only to grow up to be able to have children. Boys, on the other hand, are born without semen. Before they can procreate, all boys, at about ten years of age, are removed to a special male village. There, they ingest semen daily, performing fellatio on a few young men whose duty it is to service them. After several years of this practice, in their later teens, the boys are discharged from the male village, are married to young women, and from that moment lead exclusively heterosexual lives.

The ability of Sambia males to make such a sudden and complete transformation from homosexuality to heterosexuality came as a great surprise to Western thought, and the implications are still being worked out.

THE ROLE OF GENDER IN SOCIETY

Once again, folk wisdom plays a large role in our thinking about gender. We swing from thoroughgoing biological determinism ("the biological differences between men and women shape vast behavioral differences") to complete relativism ("it is only culture that makes male and female different"). The issue is complicated by strongly held political views at either extreme.

Much basic biological research on male/female differences is going on now, and as the preliminary research reported in the popular press is either supported or modified, our understanding of the biocultural model deepens. Watch the news magazines and the *New York Times* Tuesday science section for constant reports of new findings. For example, gender differences have been found (for both humans and rats) in cravings: Males desire protein and fat-rich red meat, and females desire chocolate. Also, males and females use different parts of their brains to solve the same sorts of problems.

The Impact of the Feminist Perspective

In Chapter 5, we discussed Margaret Mead's book on her study of gender in three New Guinea cultures, *Sex and Temperament in Three Primitive Societies* (1935). Her thesis was that, although gender division of labor and other differences between gender were the cross-cultural rule, it was all arbitrary. There were no occupations, artifacts, or personality traits that are inherently male or female. The three cultures that she described did, indeed, shuffle things around.

Despite Mead's flair for recognizing and dramatizing important problems, anthropological interest in gender did not become widespread until the feminist movement began to gather momentum again in the 1960s. Many anthropologists, especially young women, were inspired to ask new sorts of questions. The first task was to find out about women. Initially, the questions focused on the roles of women in different societies. Even though there had long been many influential women anthropologists, their anthropology had concentrated on men. Cultures were described from the male perspective, and female perspectives were played down.

Perhaps the single most important American publication to open this new era in anthropology was *Women, Culture, and Society* (1974), edited by Michelle Zimbalist Rosaldo and Louise Lamphere. In their Introduction, the editors noted that, with very few exceptions,

> anthropologists in writing about human culture have followed our own culture's ideological bias in treating women as relatively invisible and describing what are largely the activities and interests of men. In order to correct that bias, to

alter our conceptions of the female, and to understand their source, what we need are new perspectives. Today, it seems reasonable to argue that the social world is the creation of both male and female actors, and that any full understanding of human society and any viable program for social change will have to incorporate the goals, thoughts, and activities of the "second sex." (Rosaldo and Lamphere, 1974:2)

Revisiting the Trobriand Islands.   It is difficult to explain today why anthropologists so long slighted the women's side of cultures. Recall Annette Weiner's restudy of Trobriand Island culture discussed on page 205. Bronislaw Malinowski's work had made the Trobriands famous from the time of his first book on it (1922). In 1971 and 1972, Annette Weiner, then a graduate student, spent a year in that "sacred place." Her dissertation research plan was to study woodcarvings made for the tourist trade. The day after she moved into a village, however, she was summoned to a women's mortuary ceremony. The high point was a massive exchange of goods among women that lasted five hours. That evening, back in her house, she referred to Malinowski's publications and found nothing about the events that she had just witnessed.

> My original research project was not concerned with the study of women, but from that first day I knew that women were engaged in something of importance that apparently had escaped Malinowski's observations. The women's mortuary ceremony was a Pandora's box; it opened up the whole question of relationships between men and women. The exchanges, each differing in objects, style, color, quality, and quantity, gave as much information about the living as they did about the dead. (Weiner, 1976:7,8)

Weiner concluded,

> To devote only one chapter of an ethnography to women or to produce a book about the kinship system of a particular society from only male informants' points of view is to reduce the study of society and culture to an impoverished view of human interaction. (Weiner, 1976:228)

If we can resist the wisdom of hindsight, it is perhaps not so shocking that Malinowski, for all his brilliance, focused his research on the men, and the high-status men at that. Surely, it must have seemed to him that there was where the key events took place. Recall Evans-Pritchard's similar experience with the Nuer in the 1930s (discussed in Chapter 9). Weiner shook anthropology out of that perspective. She went to the Trobriands to study tourist art and came back a feminist. More importantly, she made all anthropologists feminists, in the sense that today, it is increasingly difficult to ignore gender issues, and any ethnography that describes only men is suspect. This transformation has been a matter not merely of adding chapters on women to chapters on men, but of looking at how men and women are regarded in different cultures and how cultures dramatize the differences.

Woman the Gatherer. Another major reinterpretation of the role of women that was stimulated directly by feminist perspectives concerned foraging strategies, particularly among the foragers of the Kalahari Desert. Although the focus through the 1960s had been on "man the hunter," by the 1970s it had expanded to include "woman the gatherer." Careful fieldwork showed that the women, in fact, provided more food than the men did. We shall return to this issue in the Focus Culture in this chapter.

The Meanings of Macho. Societies are not just women plus men, but women and men interacting. Interestingly, the emergence of feminist anthropology has not just added women to our picture of cultural behavior. It has thrown new light on men. Where Malinowski and Evans-Pritchard had simply made assumptions about men, anthropologists now began to pay attention to men, to problematize men and masculinity in ways not considered before. Matthew C. Gutmann studied "the meanings of macho" in Mexico City (1996, 1997) and contributed the photograph on page 299. Gutmann has stressed the importance of going beyond seeing gender as a matter of similarity or difference, equality or inequality, and looking at the interaction of men and women—the "ambiguous relationship" between genders.

Gutmann has said that he could not have studied machismo in Mexico if he had spoken with only men (1997). In his book, he wrote,

> In April 1989, while walking through downtown Mexico City, I passed a musical-instruments shop and something inside caught my attention. I took a photograph of a man holding a baby. When I later showed the photo to anthropologists and other friends in the United States, many had a curious reaction. "That can't be," one said in surprise. "We know they're all machos in Mexico." The implication was that although machos may sire many children, they do not attend to them later because that is women's work and machos by definition shun these kinds of duties. . . . I always carried this photo with me in Mexico, and . . . I recorded . . . responses . . . from people living in Santo Domingo as well as from anthropologists and residents of other areas of Mexico City and other parts of the country. . . . Responses to the photograph were not just different but fell into two completely opposed categories: the photo depicted either the most natural, common situation in the world, hardly worth commenting on, or an anomaly, an aberration that it would be irresponsible of me to interpret as representative of any significant number of men in Mexico. . . . The responses to the photograph . . . reveal something about the viewers' own life experiences with fathering as well as myriad preconceptions about the fathering experiences of others. (Gutmann, 1996:54–57)

Gender in Politics and Economics

Politics is the study of power relations in a society: who has it, how they get it, how they exercise it, how they lose it. One of the most striking regularities is that human societies are **patriarchal:** Men hold the major positions of power, and women do not have access to power over men. There are matrilineal societies, of course, in

Macho in Mexico? See page 298. *(Credit: Dr. Matthew C. Gutmann)*

which descent is reckoned through the female line and one is a member of one's mother's descent group. There are societies such as the Iroquois, where women had much influence (Wallace, 1969), or the Minangkabau of West Sumatra, who express "matrifocality both as an ideology and as a lived reality" (Sanday, 1990:141). There are instances of exceptional or accidental women who became rulers (Cleopatra, Queen Elizabeth I of England, Indira Gandhi, Margaret Thatcher). But we know of no societies in which women normally rule—that is, **matriarchial** societies.

Joan Bamberger (1974) raised the fascinating question, "If there are no documented cases of matriarchy, then why are myths of ancient matriarchal societies so common around the world?" Bamberger concluded that the myths do not so much celebrate women as tell how women, through their foolishness and irresponsibility, have forfeited their right to rule. The myths thus validate patriarchy.

We have already discussed, in Chapter 6 (on economics), how strongly pancultural is the division of labor along gender lines. Even in societies such as Minangkabau or the United States, where women may own more wealth than men, men are the real managers of that wealth.

Gender in Social Organization.   In Chapter 9 (on kinship) we discussed how gender is used as a primary organizing criterion, using either matrilineal or patrilineal principles to organize groups. It is so common for societies to vest economic, political, and ritual power in men and to give men power over women (especially within the family) that the question arises: "Does any society have real gender equality?"

The answer depends on definitions. What do you mean by *equality* and *power?* Certainly there are societies such as the Yanomamo, in which men freely dominate women, beat them, and hold them in low regard. And there are societies such as the Dani, in which men and women like and respect each other, physical abuse is rare, and women are strong and independent. But even among the Dani, men are unquestionably in charge.

Maria Lepowsky has written (1990, 1993) about Vanatinai, an island in Melanesia near the Trobriands, with a nearly gender-equal culture. Not surprisingly, Vanatinai is matrilineal, so things are not skewed toward males from the beginning. And warfare, with its celebrated male heroes, has long since been stopped. As Lepowsky writes,

> On Vanatinai there are no ideologies of male superiority and female inferiority.
> There is considerable overlap between the roles and activities of women and
> men, and the actions of both sexes are considered equally valuable. Men have no
> formal authority or powers of coercion over women except for the physical vio-
> lence that both sexes abhor and that is rare in the extreme. It is not a place where
> women and men live in perfect harmony and where the privileges and burdens of
> both sexes are exactly equal, but it comes close. The rules of social life stress re-
> spect for the will and personal autonomy of each adult. (Lepowsky, 1993:viii)

It should be noted that Vanatinai is not really egalitarian, for there is considerable competition for status. But women and men have equal access to inequality.

The Impact of Cognitive Differences.   An increasing body of evidence shows gender differences in thinking, which are presumably the result of evolutionary selection over 2 million years of human foraging existence. Helen Fisher, an anthropologist who has written much about sexuality and gender, suggests that as the special talents developed by women become more appreciated, they will have radical effects on societies. Fisher points to several strengths of women:

> Women, on average, take a broader perspective than men do—on any issue.
> Women think contextually, holistically. They also display more mental flexibility,
> apply more intuitive and imaginative judgments, and have a greater tendency to
> plan long term. (Fisher, 1999:4)

And so Fisher sees a future in which these strengths of women will be given full play to change our world:

> I am optimistic about the future—not only for women but for men. Women's
> propensity to think contextually and their intense curiosity about people will
> add variety and texture to what we watch on television. Their faculty for lan-

guage and appetite for diversity and complexity will enrich what we read in newspapers, magazines, and books—and influence our feelings and beliefs. With their people skills, women will continue to invigorate the service professions, adding comfort and novelty to our work and leisure hours.

Women already bring compassion and patience to hands-on healing. They offer imagination in the classroom. They are broadening our perspective of justice. Their facility for networking and reaching consensus will become more and more important as companies dismantle hierarchical management structures and emphasize egalitarian team playing. With their long-term and contextual view, their need to nurture, and their prominent role in civil society, women will also make major contributions toward solving our worldwide social and environmental ills. (Fisher, 1999:xx)

MANIFESTATIONS OF SEXUALITY

Sexuality as Biological Procreation

The biological essence of sexuality is sexual intercourse for the purpose of creating a child. It would be hard to imagine a culture in which sexuality began and ended with the procreative act. Even the Roman Catholic Church, which considers sexuality as being primarily for procreation and proclaims any act that is designed to thwart procreation to be "intrinsically evil," states that within marriage for the sake of procreation, "sexuality is a source of joy and pleasure" (Catholic Church, 1995:2370 and 2362, respectively).

Sexuality in Art

A major theme in much art, both visual and verbal, is sexuality. Such art is not necessarily about the act of sex itself, but rather hints at or recounts the desires, pleasures, and disappointments of sex, the quests for or escapes from it, and the imaginings about it. Sexuality is particularly evident in literature, theater, and dance but less obvious in architecture or music. Although the religious arts of the Judaeo–Christian tradition are virtually devoid of overt sexuality (the Song of Solomon is a famous exception), Hindu art and literature are strongly sexual. There are even Hindu temples in India and Nepal that are covered with depictions of many varieties of sexual intercourse, reflecting the importance of sexuality in Hindu theology.

One of the interesting implications of the culturally patterned depictions of sexuality is that there are limits on what can legitimately be depicted. When these limits are breached, we call the depiction *pornography*. In cultures such as those of Europe and North America during the last century or two, in which the limits have been relatively restrictive, there have been tremendous production and consumption of pornography along with intense social interest in defining and combating pornography. In theory, there should be limits to the depiction of sexuality in every culture, but the identification and repression of pornography do not seem to be important everywhere.

Sexuality in Attire

Clothing may function in a utilitarian way to protect the body from the elements, but it is also a means of nonverbal communication, conveying a wide range of messages about gender, age, status, and often sexuality (Barnes and Eicher, 1993). Even in societies in which very little clothing is worn, there are often specific bodily adornments that carry a sexual message. For example, among the Mehinaku, who live in the Amazon rain forest some 1,200 miles from the Yanomamo, women wear a string belt called the *inija:*

> The inija is a twine G-string. The "tail" leads from the body of the garment, which rests on the pubis, through the labia and the buttocks, emerging in the rear, for all the world like an actual tail. For the men, the inija is a titillating symbol of female sexuality, irresistibly focusing attention on the vagina. In part, it is so attractive because it is worn during rituals and in the late afternoon, when women wish to make themselves especially attractive. A man who might be indifferent to an unpainted and beltless woman suddenly finds she is of sexual interest when she paints up, and especially when she wears an inija. (Gregor, 1985:47)

In 17th-century Netherlands, even the making of clothing was related to sexuality:

> Seventeenth-century Dutch emblems of spinning, embroidering, and lacemaking presented erotic visual plays, based on popular Dutch metaphors for copulation derived from the motion of the textile professions' tools. (Stone-Ferrier, 1989: 221–222)

For the Dutch of this period, the wearing of elegant clothing, especially that ornamented with lace or embroidery, sent a message of available sexuality: "Rich dress served only to attract men, which endangered a lady's chastity" (Stone-Ferrier, 1989:224). There is nothing intrinsically sexual about either lace or embroidery, but 17th-century Dutch culture read both as symbols of sexuality.

In a similarly symbolic way, the Kodi of Sumba, an Indonesian island just east of Bali, wear beautiful dyed and woven *ikat* cloth in ceremonies. The designs on a bride's attire symbolize the goods exchanged at the wedding, but these textiles also have an erotic appeal that enhances the bride's sexual attractiveness (Hoskins, 1989:158).

Sometimes, it is too easy to read sexuality into attire. From childhood on, Dani males wear a penis gourd, a dried hollow gourd covering the penis and held upright by a string around the body (Heider, 1997:60–62). Elsewhere in New Guinea and in Africa, South America, and 15th- and 16th-century Europe, men wore similar phallic exaggerations as statements about sexuality (and definitely more than just gender markers). But not the Grand Valley Dani. "Perhaps the most remarkable aspect of the Dani penis gourd is that it is not, in any explicit way, a focus of Dani sexuality or eroticism" (Heider, 1970:247).

The 17th-century English poet Robert Herrick sang of the sexuality of clothes:

> A sweet disorder in the dress
> Kindles in clothes a wantonness . . .

Dani men at a ceremonial pig feast wearing penis gourds
for modesty, not display. *(Credit: Karl G. Heider)*

In the contemporary West, we are made very aware of how clothing, especially
women's but also men's, can signal sexuality. Clothing plays out themes on culturally eroticized body parts, revealing, suggesting, and concealing.

DOING ANTHROPOLOGY

Expressive Clothing

Clothing is an important channel of communication, especially as it expresses gender
and sexuality. Most people around you today own enough different articles of clothing so that they can make quite nuanced choices of expression about gender and sexuality at any one moment in any given context. Explore this idea with observations of
your own choices in different situations, observations of those around you, films or
television shows, or magazines (ads are especially good for this exercise).   ♦

King Henry VIII of England wearing a codpiece.
(Credit: © The Granger Collection)

Gender-Specific Alterations of the Body

At the intersection of gender and sexuality, where cultural symbol meets the human body, we find a great variety of things that are done to permanently transform the human body. These acts go beyond temporary alterations of clothing and un-clothing, of painting the skin, and of hair length and arrangement.

Explicitly or implicitly, most of these transformations either enhance or di-minish sexuality. It is often difficult to discover a single reason, especially for the more widespread practices. People justify them in a variety of ways simultaneously, mixing symbolic readings, gender identity, and sexuality.

Genital Alterations

Male Circumcision.　The removal of the foreskin covering the penis, **circumcision,** is perhaps the most common of all genital alterations. It is explained in the Old Testament as a symbol of God's covenant with Abraham (Genesis 17:9–14) and is still done by Jews on the eighth day after birth, in a ceremony called, in Yiddish, *bris.* Celebrating the same event, Muslims carry out circumcision in a ceremony called *sunnat,* which usually takes place around the tenth year of a boy's life. In the first century A.D., Paul (Galatians 6:11–16) declared that circumcision was irrelevant to Christians. But in the late 19th century, many Western countries reintroduced circumcision, mainly for supposed physical and mental health reasons (to reduce dangerous male sexuality), although at the end of the 20th century only the United States and Australia still maintain the custom for those reasons. Many other cultures practice circumcision as part of the boy's initiation ceremony. This procedure may be either the full removal of the foreskin or, as among the Wana of Sulawesi, Indonesia (Atkinson, 1989), merely a small cut in the foreskin.

The most extreme surgery is subincision, practiced by some Australian Aboriginal cultures, in which the boy's initiation into manhood involves slitting the penis open along the entire lower length.

In East and Southeast Asia and, most famously, in Borneo, small gold beads are implanted under the skin of the penis or short pins are inserted transversely through the penis. Donald E. Brown surveyed the reasons that people give for this family of practices (1988). The most interesting explanation is the widespread report that men wear these inserts to increase women's pleasure in sexual intercourse. This idea is extraordinary, if true, for it would be a unique instance of men undergoing alteration—radical, painful alteration—on their own bodies for the sake of women's pleasure. Brown himself did not fully endorse this view. Certainly the inconvenience, pain, and risk of infection would seem to be drawbacks for the men involved. But, as he and others have pointed out, this case may be an example of men's fantasies about women's sexuality.

Female Genital Mutilation: Clitoridectomy and Infibulation.   Various sorts of **female genital mutilation** are practiced widely on girls, especially in Africa but also elsewhere in the world. The most drastic forms of female genital mutilation involve the excision of all or parts of the clitoris **(clitoridectomy),** the labia minora, and the labia majora, and **infibulation,** in which, after much or all of the labia majora is excised, the vulva is pinned shut with thorns or sewn with thread and grows scar tissue, in effect closing the vulva except for a small opening to allow urine and menstrual blood to pass. Sexual intercourse and childbirth necessitate breaking open the scar tissue, which is subsequently reinfibulated, or closed. Clitoridectomy was widely practiced by mid-19th-century English and American physicians (apparently all males) as a recommended cure for masturbation and other mental problems (Sheehan, 1997).

Female genital mutilation is carried out by women on their own kin, and although the reasons for it differ in detail, the common rationale has to do with reducing women's sexuality to an absolute minimum on the grounds that it is polluting or otherwise dangerous to men. Female genital mutilation is particularly common in non-Arab sub-Saharan Muslim cultures but is also practiced by Christians and others (Lightfoot-Klein, 1989; Dorkenoo, 1994).

Recently, female genital mutilation, euphemistically called *female circumcision,* has been the subject of intense international debate, especially among feminists. The American writer Alice Walker has written a novel (1992), made a film called

Warrior Marks, and published a journal of the making of the film (Walker and Parman, 1993) in an attempt to focus worldwide public attention on female genital mutilation. Walker and other opponents say that the practices are not essential to any religion and do serious physical and psychological harm to the women and that the inhumane cruelty of these practices puts them beyond the protection of cultural relativity.

Countering this campaign to end female genital mutilation are people such as Ellen Gruenbaum, who has carried out research in the Sudan. She urges that before outsiders jump into the debate, they consider the cultural context of the practices:

> In my research in Sudan, for example, rural women find that marriageability is necessary for economic survival throughout the life span. Where there is little or no opportunity for girls' education, women's employment or women's independent economic activity, there is little alternative to the pattern of marriage, child-bearing and dependence on one's successful children for old age security. Such conditions limit the ability of families to challenge the idea that infibulation defines virginity and morality, hence marriageability, and parents are concerned to ensure that their daughters be physically modified to ensure their marital and economic security. The tight reinfibulation, where it is practiced, is said to be highly desirable sexually, which many view as important for maintaining the husband's continued loyalty and preventing divorce or polygyny, which might undermine a woman's financial security. (Gruenbaum, 1995:14. Reproduced by permission of the American Anthropological Association.)

Similarly, Janice Boddy, who also did fieldwork in the Sudan, warns, "Those who work to eradicate female circumcision must, I assert, cultivate an awareness of the custom's local significances and of how much they are asking people to relinquish as well as gain" (1997:322).

Exaggerations of Women's Bodies

Chinese Footbinding. Over a period of centuries, lasting well into the 20th century, upper-class Chinese women's feet were transformed into small, useless, but—for Chinese men—extremely erotic stubs. The process of **footbinding** began at age six or eight. By the mid-teens, the bones of the foot had grown permanently distorted into the desired position. The feet caused the women constant pain, and normal walking was out of the question.

Corseting. During the second half of the 19th century, in a similar practice designed to reshape a woman's body, English and American women of the middle and upper classes were subjected to extreme corseting. Their waists were constricted to a diameter of some twelve inches or so by an undergarment that was laced tight and shaped by stays of steel or whalebone. Corseting began before puberty, and sometimes the girl's lower ribs were surgically removed to allow the waist to be molded. The internal organs were displaced, and general health, not to mention the

A Chinese woman's feet deformed by binding. *(Credit: © Culver Pictures)*

progress of pregnancy, was greatly hindered. It has been estimated (Davies, 1982) that corseting so disrupted the anatomy that it was responsible for a significant drop in the birthrate of middle- and upper-class America and England. The goal was to create an hourglass figure, which was the cultural ideal of the time.

Breast Implants.   In the late 20th century, some 4 million American women had sacks of jelly surgically implanted in their breasts to better match a particular cultural image of female sexuality. Since the late 1980s, there have been many claims of medical complications resulting from leaky implants.

Taken as a whole, these alterations testify to the extraordinary lengths to which cultures have gone to proclaim and exaggerate gender and sexuality. Making distorted feet, waists, or breasts a focus of eroticism is culture at work. Many of these instances speak to gender power—namely, to men's control over women. Cultures that practice clitoridectomy and infibulation are very specific about their intent to control women through their sexuality. Footbinding and corseting, which significantly are limited to upper-class women, not only satisfy cultural ideals of beauty but also physically limit the activity and indeed the health of the elite women who submit to them. The feminist reading of these practices as symbolizing and actualizing male power over women is surely accurate. This concept was pointed out long ago by the economist Thorstein Veblen, in his famous book *The Theory of the Leisure Class,* in which he cited both corseting and footbinding as prime examples of **"conspicuous consumption"** or, more particularly, "conspicuous waste" by which wealthy men could proclaim their high status (1899:115). Thinking along these lines, though, makes the Borneo penis pin more remarkable, for it is apparently the only one that puts males at discomfort, even risk, for the pleasure of females.

SEXUAL ETHOS

It is possible to go beyond the ethnographic particulars of sexuality and make broader generalizations, characterizing the ethos of sexuality of a culture as a whole. The dangers of this approach are similar to those of the national character approach (in Chapter 5): overgeneralizing and ignoring variations.

Sexually Permissive Cultures: Polynesia

The first European sailors—all men—who visited the islands of Polynesia had no doubt that they were no longer in England or France. By the late 18th century, after the first tentative contacts had been made and ships were making return voyages to islands, the chroniclers told of encountering a sexuality that was very different from what they were used to. This was the time when Jean Jacques Rousseau was writing of "the noble savage," uncorrupted by civilization, and the sailors saw his ideas realized in Tahiti, the Marquesas, and elsewhere in Polynesia. K. R. Howe quoted the French captain Bougainville as he described the encounter:

> For Bougainville, Tahiti was La Nouvelle Cythere: "The very air the people breathe, their songs, their dances . . . all conspire to call to mind the sweets of love, and all engage to give themselves up to them." Such descriptions by Bougainville, and similar ones by Cook and Banks, took the reading public of Europe by storm, fascinating those who were predisposed to see such people as Noble Savages, and horrifying those with a narrower moral outlook. (Howe, 1984:84)

Between the sailors, who praised Polynesian sexuality, and the later Christian missionaries, who abhorred it, there was fair agreement about its openness.

Anthropologists such as Bengt Danielsson (1956), Robert C. Suggs on the Marquesas (1966), and Donald S. Marshall in the Cook Islands (1971) contributed to this view. But there seemed to be parts of Polynesia where sexuality was not so open. Samoa, especially under Christian missionary influence and colonial government control, was one of the more restrained. As Bradd Shore has shown in his writings (1981, 1982),

> The Samoan attitude towards sexuality is complex and suggests neither the thorough prudishness of missionary morality nor the casualness and erotic abandon reported for traditional Marqueses or Tahitian society. (Shore, 1981:196)

Shore describes the different gender ideals of sexuality: Males are expected to be sexually active before and outside marriage, while unmarried females' virginity enhances their brother's honor. But Shore also points out a sort of situational double standard: Sex is freer at night away from the village, more controlled during the day and in public places.

Sexually Restrictive Cultures: Inis Beag

In contrast to Eastern Polynesia, a pattern of restricted, obsessive sexuality is exemplified by John Messenger's description of a traditional Gaelic-speaking island community of western Ireland, which he studied intensively for nineteen months between 1958 and 1966 and which he called Inis Beag (Messenger, 1969, 1971).

In some respects, Inis Beag resembled a small Polynesian island: a few hundred islanders farming and fishing with little involvement from a central government. In terms of sexuality, however, the cultures are very different. The people of Inis Beag are devout Roman Catholics but strongly anticlerical, and they secretly have many pre-Christian beliefs and practices.

Marriage is late, on the average, at age thirty-six for men and twenty-five for women. People are profoundly ignorant and misinformed about sex. Messenger calls them "one of the most sexually naive of the world's societies" (1971:14,15). The slightest degree of nudity is shunned, and even bared feet are considered embarrassing. Although men go fishing at sea in canoes, none knows how to swim, for that would involve unacceptable nudity.

The "sexual puritanism" is taught to the children early and is reinforced by the conservative priests and monitored by private gossip and public ridicule. Certainly, Inis Beag is an extreme case, and not even typical of Ireland as a whole. In the early 1930s, Conrad M. Arensberg and Solon T. Kimball (1940) studied a rural community in County Clare, not far from Inis Beag, where the people were not quite so puritanical or ignorant of sexual matters.

Sexually Indifferent Cultures: The Dani

Polynesia and Ireland provide two extreme examples of sexual ethos, and the Grand Valley Dani represent a third extreme, one of relative indifference to sexuality in word or deed. They practice **postpartum sexual abstinence,** a period of about five years after the birth of a child when the parents do not have sexual intercourse with each other. Also, the Dani have virtually no premarital or extramarital intercourse, nor do they have homosexual sex or other outlets. As well as I could discover, these are the ethnographic facts. Another anthropologist, Klaus Koch, working among the Eastern Dani, or Jale, reported a similar abstinence period (1974:90).

In fact, this extraordinarily long postpartum sexual abstinence is consistent with other aspects of Dani culture that suggest a generally low intensity of intellectual elaboration, low intensity of ritual, and low intensity of emotional involvement.

In terms of our biocultural model, the Dani do, of course, have sex, but the cultural construction of sex, the intensity with which they act or think about sex, is extraordinarily low. For contemporary Westerners, who have imbued the Freudian hydraulic model of sexuality, which posits a high amount of innate, biologically determined fluidlike libido that can be expressed in sex, dammed, or rechanneled into other activities, the Dani case seems unbelievable. But if one understands the cultural construction of sex to be the construction of the very level of sexuality itself, then it makes sense.

FOCUS CULTURE

Gender and Sexuality of the Ju/'hoansi (!Kung San)

OVERVIEW

Location: Kalahari Desert at the border of Botswana, Angola, Namibia, Zambia, and South Africa

Geography: Desert

Population: Richard Lee (1993:10) estimates 82,000 in the five countries.

Language: One of the San family. It is a "click" language, having four different clicks. One of the clicks is like the English "tsk tsk"

Religion: Centers on placating potentially dangerous ghosts of their own dead

Economy: Until recently, the San were classic hunters and gatherers, or foragers, eating a wide variety of plant and animal foods.

Sociopolitical Organization: Small mobile bands, organized bilaterally around siblings

Nisa, a Ju/'hoansi (!Kung San) woman, talking to Marjorie Shostak:

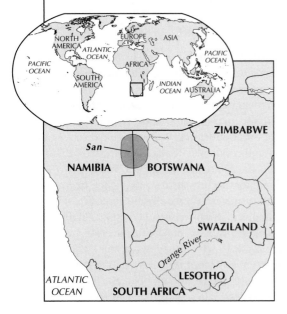

Marjorie, those people who tell you that when people live in the bush they don't have lovers, or that people only learned about it recently from the blacks, they are deceiving you. They are giving you lies and are trying to fool you with their cleverness. But I, I am like your mother and don't offer you deceit; only the truth is what I give you. I am an old woman and when I see what other people tell you, I can see through them. Because affairs—one married person making love to another not her husband—is something that even people from long ago knew. Even my father's father's father's father knew. There have also always been fights where poison arrows are shot and people are killed because of that. Having affairs is one of the things God gave us. (Shostak, 1981:271)

Shostak turned thirty hours of interviews with the woman she called Nisa into an autobiography in Nisa's voice, supplemented with background information in Shostak's anthropological voice. This remarkable collaborative effort gave a woman's perspective to a culture that had been mainly known for its hunting skills in the extreme conditions of the Kalahari Desert. We have already considered the Ju/'hoansi (also called San, !Kung, and Bushmen) for their foraging strategies in Chapter 6 (production). Here we look at Ju/'hoansi gender and sexuality, taking our cues from Shostak's story of Nisa and John Marshall's film *N!ai,* about the life of another Ju/'hoansi woman.

According to Shostak, sex is almost as important a topic of Ju/'hoansi conversation as food. Marriages are intense but often short-lived, and people frequently take lovers. Ju/'hoansi men and women have great self-esteem. Even though the culture includes ideals of beauty that not everyone can meet, physical beauty seems to be relatively unimportant and Shostak says that "most women think of themselves as attractive" (1981:270) and feel that they can attract lovers if they wish.

Sexual play begins at an early age. Children do little work—both hunting and gathering are easier if children are left in camp. There boys and girls play as equals, easily experimenting with sex. Traditionally, marriages were arranged for girls by age 10 or 12, and for boys ten years later. The great difference in maturity between spouses intensified the strains on the marriage, but the girl's family realized significant benefits from her marriage. The custom of bride service among the Ju/'hoansi brought the husband to the wife's camp where he worked with and for his father-in-law for several years.

Status of Women. Both Shostak (1981:13) and Richard Lee (1979:447ff) agree that Ju/'hoansi women and men had relatively equal status. They each worked about the same amount of time, but women produced more of the food. Women did most of the child care, albeit with the help of the whole camp. Because of the bride service pattern, married men were often outsiders in their wife's family, giving women special influence. Men may have had somewhat more political influence, but women did play strong roles. There was relatively little violence against women and rape was rare (Lee, 1979:463). Shostak sums it up by saying, "Women may in fact be nearly equal to men, but the culture seems to define them as less powerful. In other words, their influence may be greater than the !Kung—of either sex—like to admit" (1981:13).

Man the Hunter, Woman the Gatherer. In the first wave of post–World War II studies of these Kalahari foragers, attention was focused on "man the hunter." That was the title of the seminal book edited by Richard B. Lee and Irven DeVore in 1968, and it had been the subject of John Marshall's first, and now classic, film, *The Hunters* (1957). In the 1970s, however, the rise of feminist anthropology changed our thinking about cultures around the world—not just in the Trobriand Islands, but also in the Kalahari Desert. Careful ethnography turned attention to include "woman the gatherer" (the title of a 1981 book edited by Frances Dahlberg).

The 1960s research of Richard Lee gives us some measures of the relative contribution of food by Ju/'hoansi men and women (1979:450). Men did the hunting, and women did four-fifths of the gathering of roots, fruits, and nuts. If one figures contribution by weight and calories, men brought in about 44% and women about 56% of the food. (Shostak estimates women's contributions at 60%–80% [1981:12].) In terms of work effort and productivity, men worked more but women produced more, as hunting is always an uncertain enterprise. By a third measure, however, the Ju/'hoansi certainly put more value on the meat produced by men's hunting than they did on the real staple of their diet, the mongongo nuts produced by gathering. (Those anthropologists who first concentrated on men's hunting were responding to the Ju/'hoansi's own sense of priorities—killing a large game animal is more exciting than scooping up mongongo nuts.) ♦

SEEING ANTHROPOLOGY

Sexuality and Change in the Life of a Ju/'hoansi (!Kung) Woman: *N!ai: The Story of a !Kung Woman*

Filmmaker: John Marshall

N!ai: The Story of a !Kung Woman is about one woman called N!ai, and how she has survived change. It is a powerful statement about both gender and sexuality. The filmmaker is John Marshall, who uses footage that he shot of N!ai and her people beginning in 1951 and continuing for twenty-seven years. As N!ai tells her story, the film moves back and forth in time.

The earlier scenes, shot in the 1950s, show a time when "our hearts were free." The people then still lived primarily from foraging and were relatively independent and unconcerned with either their Bantu neighbors or national politics. These scenes give us a sense of prototypical foragers living in a timeless world. Later in the film, Marshall takes us forward to the late 1970s, when the South African government was recruiting Ju/'hoansi to fight against the SWAPO guerrilla forces in Namibia.

The film evokes Marjorie Shostak's book about another !Kung San woman, *Nisa* (1981). Both film and book address the question "What is it like to be a woman in Ju/'hoansi culture?" Both N!ai in the film and Nisa in the book tell us quite frankly about their own sexuality.

There is a fascinating sequence in *N!ai* in which Marshall films a commercial film crew shooting a feature film near N!ai's settlement. That film turned out to be *The Gods Must Be Crazy,* which became a great international hit and was the top-grossing foreign film in the U.S. market. Many anthropologists who know the Ju/'hoansi have criticized it for its simplistic view of Ju/'hoansi life.

The film suggests that after people were forced into settlements and were incorporated, however disadvantageously, into the South African economy, the old gender equality gave way to more gender inequality. Considerable discussion of this issue has appeared in the anthropological literature. There does seem to be variation

N!ai, a !Kung woman. *(Credit: John Marshall, photo courtesy of Documentary Educational Resources)*

among different foragers groups, and many who became more sedentary manage to retain a fair degree of gender equality. Thus sedentary life cannot be the only causal factor influencing the degree of gender equality (see Kent, 1995).

The short clip is a flashback using earlier footage that Marshall shot of N!ai. It tells of her arranged marriage at age 8 to Gunda, thirteen years older. Problems occurred between them. We see a difficult childbirth. N!ai watches as two men try to cure mother and child.

The complete film opens in 1978 on a reservation that the South African government established for 800 Ju/'hoansi on the Namibia–Botswana border. N!ai receives food for herself and her children and begins to tell her story. We cut back to life as they lived it in 1952. N!ai describes gathering food with her mother and tells of a giraffe hunt involving her father, which produced enough meat for fifty people for ten days.

After the segment shown in the short clip, we continue with curing ceremonies. Gunda becomes a healer, going into a trance. The couple's marriage is troubled, and N!ai takes various lovers. N!ai works for tourists and photographers but she doesn't share her money with others. *The Gods Must Be Crazy* is being shot on location. N!ai's daughter is accused of prostitution by jealous people. The South

African army recruits the Ju/'hoansi to fight against guerrillas. The film ends on a pessimistic note.

Setup Questions

1. What is N!ai's view of the past (her ethnographic present)? Do you think that she is exaggerating or romanticizing?
2. What does N!ai tell us about her marriage?
3. What does N!ai tell us about sexuality?
4. Can you pick up any differences between what Nisa told Shostak and what N!ai says to the camera?
5. What do we learn about a !Kung schema of femininity? Do we see hints of their schema of masculinity?   ◆

HOLLYWOOD-STYLE ANTHROPOLOGY

Gender Confusion in *Tootsie*

Tootsie   1982   116 minutes

    Dustin Hoffman as Michael Dorsey
    Dustin Hoffman as Miss Dorothy Michaels
    Jessica Lange as Julie Nichols

Michael, a good actor, scrapes by somehow in New York. Finally, desperate for a role, he auditions for "Southwest General," a television daytime soap, disguised as a woman, Dorothy. He is cast as Miss Emily Kimberly and immediately becomes a major star. But this is a comedy (most of the time) about gender line crossing. We know that Dorothy is Michael, his roommate knows, his agent knows, but everyone else assumes that Dorothy is a woman and behaves accordingly.

Setup Questions

1. Explain how each of the principals reacts differently when they know about Michael's subterfuge.
2. How does Michael alter his nonverbal behavior when he is Dorothy?
3. What is the meaning of the title of the movie?
4. Why does Michael finally say, "I was better as a woman"?
5. What does the final freeze frame promise?   ◆

CHAPTER SUMMARY

- Both sexuality and gender are examples of the biocultural model, showing greatly varying culture constructions based on a common *Homo sapiens* biology.

- Gender refers to maleness and femaleness and the elaborations thereof; sexuality refers to sexual intercourse and elaborations thereof.
- Homosexuality and lesbianism are also cultural constructions in many cultures, apparently based on the biological fact that the male–female distinction in *Homo sapiens* is to some degree a bimodal continuum rather than an absolute dichotomy.
- The anthropological awareness and study of the cultural constructions of gender were greatly stimulated by the rise of feminist anthropology in the last decades of the 20th century.
- Particularly significant "discoveries" include the previously neglected role of women in the Trobriand Island Kula exchange and the importance of women as gatherers in foraging societies. ("Discoveries" is enclosed in quotation marks because the people themselves knew about it all along.)
- The cultural construction of sexuality includes culture-specific ideas and practices involving beauty, love, eroticism, and the like.
- Cultures usually adorn or decorate the body to enhance gender ideals. Some cultures carry out drastic body alterations. Examples are Chinese footbinding, Western corseting, male circumcision and female genital mutilation, and breast implants.
- The degree to which sexual activity (especially intercourse) is allowable outside marriage varies greatly from sexually permissive cultures to sexually restrictive cultures to sexually indifferent cultures.

KEY TERMS

berdache	footbinding	postpartum sexual
circumcision	gender	abstinence
clitoridectomy	hijra	sex(uality)
conspicuous	infibulation	sexual dimorphism
consumption	matriarchal	two-spirit
female genital mutilation	patriarchal	

QUESTIONS TO THINK ABOUT

- Much current homophobia is fueled by religious fundamentalism (Christian and Muslim). What insights does cultural anthropology offer?
- How could so many anthropologists have neglected the roles of women in cultures for so long?
- Is it conceivable that there could be a culture with total gender equality? Why?
- To what extent does the practice of female genital mutilation challenge cultural relativity? Should the West support the moves to end it in Africa? Should the West outlaw it among immigrants? Does it change matters to call the practice "female circumcision"?
- Why has the Dani pattern of sexuality seemed so strange, even to some anthropologists?

SUGGESTIONS FOR FURTHER READING

Atkinson, Jane Monnig, and Shelly Errington (eds.)

1990   Power and Difference: Gender in Southeast Asia. Stanford, CA: Stanford University Press. *An important collection of papers that explores the case for Southeast Asia as an area of relative gender equality.*

Marks, Stuart A.

1991   Southern Hunting in Black and White: Nature, History, and Ritual in a Carolina Community. Princeton, NJ: Princeton University Press. *An ethnographer who had previously studied hunters in Zambia writes an ethnography of the quintessential mark of maleness in a North Carolina county.*

Ong, Aihwa, and Michael G. Peletz (eds.)

1994   Bewitching Women, Pious Men: Gender and Body Politics in Southeast Asia. Berkeley: University of California Press. *The continuing analysis of this very important world area case study of gender relations.*

Ruby, Jay (ed.)

1993   The Cinema of John Marshall. Chur, Switzerland: Harwood Academic Publishers. *Comprehensive coverage of John Marshall and his films, including* N!ai.

Sinha, Mrinalini

1995   Colonial Masculinity: The "Manly Englishman" and the "Effeminate Bengali" in the Late Nineteenth Century. Manchester, U.K.: Manchester University Press. *The cultural construction of gender in colonial India.*

CHAPTER 11

Power and Politics

Armies aboard ship. Bayon, Angkor (Cambodia), 12th century C.E. *(Credit: Karl G. Heider)*

HEADLINE ANTHROPOLOGY

PRESS WATCH

Some of the subjects discussed in this chapter have made their way into current news stories. For example:

♦ In Major League Baseball, a Cardinals coach accused a Cubs base coach of breaking an unwritten rule of baseball by stealing signs, somehow communicating to Sammy Sosa what his next pitch would be.

—New York Times, *May 12, 2002.*

♦ Plane spotting, like train spotting, is a peculiarly British hobby, but 8 Britons were sentenced to three years in jail as spies for plane spotting by a judge in Kalamata, Greece.

—New York Times, *April 28, 2002.*

♦ In Finland, where traffic fines are adjusted to the offender's income, Anssi Vonjoki was fined US$103,000 for going 46.5 in a 30 mph zone.

—The State *(Columbia, South Carolina), April 15, 2002.*

POWER

In this chapter, we look at political life in its broadest sense as the story of power. This concept encompasses the ways in which leaders of groups channel and exercise power; the ways in which power of all sorts serves to command conformity to cultural norms; the methods by which power is brought into play to reestablish harmony when people violate norms; the ways in which conflict between societies, in the absence of social control, escalates into war; and finally strategies for achieving peace between societies.

In the previous chapters, we considered several different principles involved in organizing people into groups: kinship through birth, kinship through marriage, locality (place of residence), language or other cultural practices, exchange, and the like. These principles, used alone or in combination, define a limited number of social groups to which an individual belongs. We have discussed what different sorts of groups do—that is, what their function is. Now we turn to another aspect of social groups—namely, power and **political organization.** All social groups have some sort of leadership and thus some sort of hierarchy or ranking. By **power,** we mean the ability of some people to get other people to do things. There are four basic questions to ask about power in human societies:

• How is it acquired?
• What kinds of people get it and what kinds do not?

- How strong is it?
- What is it used for?

A useful distinction can often be made between actual power, which implies the use of physical force or the threat of physical force, and **influence,** which is the ability to talk people into doing things without the use of force.

All human societies have leaders, but their power varies greatly along this influence–power continuum. Even the most egalitarian groups include, at a minimum, some differential use of influence, the weak form of power. The focus on power leads us from leadership (the use of power in groups), social control of behavior, and conflict resolution to questions of war and finally of peace.

Big Men and Chiefs

Leaders at the powerful end of the continuum have always been easy to recognize. At the weak end, however, the influence of leaders is often concealed by subtlety and deviousness. This case was particularly true in Melanesia and New Guinea, where Marshall Sahlins saw the difference between **big men** and **chiefs** (1963). Groups like the Dani, and most other highland New Guinea peoples, have big man leaders (whatever their actual physical size, they are often called literally "big men," making size a metaphor for influence). Elsewhere in the Pacific, like the Trobriand Islands, the most important leaders have not just influence but real power and so can be called chiefs.

The difference between big men and chiefs is not merely a matter of power. Big men, because they depend on persuasion, are more likely to be charismatic personalities. They tend to achieve their positions through their own efforts, and their hold on those positions is more likely to be more tenuous. Table 11.1 summarizes these differences, although it is important to remember that these characteristics are continuous attributes, not absolute dichotomies.

These categories are hardly rigid, and if you look at the Focus Cultures, you will see how much of a range really exists. For example, in the 1960s I watched the Dani big men gain power and become chieflike as first the Dutch and then the Indonesians established their control over the area. Both governments wanted Dani chiefs to act as their go-betweens, relaying their orders to the people. For example, traditional Dani work groups consisted of friends and neighbors who exchanged work to help each other prepare garden areas or to build houses. The outside governments,

TABLE 11.1   Big Men Versus Chiefs

Big Man	Chief
Uses influence	Wields power
Individually achieved	Inherited
Temporarily held	Lifetime tenure

however, required uncompensated Dani labor to build roads for the convenience of their own vehicles (the Dani, of course, used footpaths and lacked both vehicles and roads). They made these demands known through the big men, held the big men responsible for turning out road crews, and rewarded the big men who achieved this goal while punishing the big men who did not. By giving these big men an unprecedented amount of real power, the government officials in effect turned big men into chiefs. Although these chiefs could now, with the backing of the Indonesian forces, order their people to do things like building roads, they themselves were located far down in the Indonesian governmental hierarchy. Even minor problems were taken out of their hands and handled by the national police. In effect, the big men with broad influence had become chiefs with quite narrow powers.

The Political Organization of Societies

One way of categorizing societies is in terms of political power, by answering the following questions: How much political power is available? How is it allocated to leaders? Generally, the answers are correlated with the size of the society. That is, the larger the society, the more powerful the leaders. Furthermore, the answers are roughly correlated with subsistence type but only very generally with principles of social organization like descent groups or patrilineality versus matrilineality.

Band Organization. Social units of a few dozen people with informal leadership, which are often mobile or even nomadic foragers, are called **bands.** Bands often roam over vast expanses of land that is too marginal to support even pastoralists. Famous examples of band organization include the Inuit (Eskimos) of the North American Arctic, the "pygmies" of the Congo rain forest, the aboriginal peoples of Australia, and, of course, the various Ju/'hoansi peoples of the Kalahari Desert, whom we saw in *N!ai,* the film from Chapter 10.

Tribal Organization. The term **tribe** has been used for midsize societies ranging from a few hundred to a few thousand people, with somewhat more power available to leaders. Three societies that we have already seen on film fit in the tribal category, although in their variations they demonstrate the breadth of the category: the Dani (Chapter 3), with their big man leaders, horticulture, and long-term settlements; the Kwa Kwaka' Wakw (Chapter 4), with more powerful chieflike leaders, permanent villages, and, anomalously, a subsistence strategy based on fishing, hunting, and gathering; and the Nuer (Chapter 9), who have powerful leaders (chiefs) but practice seminomadic pastoralism with some horticulture on the side. (In Chapter 13, we will meet another tribal society with chiefs, the Trobriand Islanders.)

Chiefdoms. **Chiefdoms** are groups of several hundred to many thousand people with powerful leaders and, usually, some degree of bureaucracy, or hierarchically ordered layers of leadership. The Kpelle of Liberia, whom we meet in this chapter, are a typical West African chiefdom. In English, the most important Kpelle is called

The oni, or chief, or ife in Nigeria. *(Credit: © W. Robert Moore/National Geographic Image Collection)*

the "paramount chief," and then in descending levels are the positions of "chiefs" and "elders."

Nation-States. **Nations** and *states* are terms used for social units with thousands to millions of people in large bureaucratic societies with much power concentrated in explicitly organized institutions and individuals at various levels. We have seen the Balinese (Chapter 1), who live in a province of Indonesia; Vietnamese (Chapter 5); the Malaysian villagers (Chapter 2); and the Mayans in Mexico (Chapter 7). All of these cultures are embedded in nation-states.

We must use these terms with great care. They are of little precise analytical use because so much variation occurs within types and so many intermediate examples exist. Also, the terms have been compromised by casual use over the centuries. Nevertheless, it is difficult to avoid these terms. They do give a general idea about the concentration of political power, and they point to the very important issue of leadership and power. For example, we can question whether the Dani, Kwa Kwaka' Wakw, and Nuer are "tribes," not because the answer to that question is so useful in itself, but because it focuses attention on the nature of leadership and political organization of each.

Power Differentials

Power differentials—the unequal allocation of power—are found in all societies. Put another way, there are no truly egalitarian societies. Recall our discussion in Chapter 10, where we stated that a few societies seem to approach but do not achieve gender equality. At the other end of the spectrum, however, examples of nearly absolute power of one person over another are common.

Slavery.   Slavery, *serfdom,* and *indentured servitude* are just a few of the English terms that have been used to describe conditions of extreme servitude. In his recent book, *The Slave Trade,* Hugh Thomas sketches the history and distribution of slavery:

> Most settled societies at one time or another have employed forced labor; and most peoples, even the proud French, the effective Germans, the noble English, the dauntless Spaniards and, perhaps above all, the poetical Russians, have experienced years of servitude. (Thomas, 1997:25)

The states of antiquity all had economies based on slave labor: Greece, Rome, Sumer, Egypt, China, and the Aztecs and Incas of the New World. Slave labor was one solution to the common problem of too much land, too few workers. These conditions still hold in many parts of the world. Although slavery in the strict sense of the word is practically nonexistent today, large numbers of foreign workers with minimal rights continue to be found in the homes of the Gulf States, in the vegetable fields of California, on the Ivory Coast, and in the mines of South Africa and Peru, just to name a few examples.

This extreme exercise of power over individuals, once so common, was gone by the time that anthropological fieldwork began. We therefore have no firsthand ethnographic accounts of it. At best there are rich studies from documents. Charles Joyner (who has Ph.D.'s in both history and folklife) used testimonies of former slaves recorded during the 1930s in the Waccamaw Neck region of South Carolina to reconstruct an ethnography of slave life (1986). Nevertheless, if slavery itself has vanished, then the other sorts of near-servitude—such as foreign "guest workers" in Europe and the Near East or migrant laborers in the United States—persist, although anthropologists have shown little interest in studying them.

Colonialism.   In 1961, when I began to study the Grand Valley Dani (see Chapter 3), I lived with the other members of the Harvard Peabody Expedition. When they left, I stayed on by myself in a tent and then in a house that I had built beside a Dani compound. Every few weeks, I would walk across the broad valley floor to Wamena, the small settlement established by the Netherlands New Guinea government. I would pick up mail and supplies, chat with Dutch and American missionaries and government officials, and compare notes on the Dani with Father Piet van der Stap, a linguist. I considered these trips a welcome break from my intense and lonely ethnographic immersion among the Dani.

Only years later did I realize what an opportunity I had lost to study the last days of the Dutch colonial empire in Southeast Asia. For more than three centuries, the Dutch had been expanding their imperial power in the region, with increasingly greater effects on local cultures. The Dutch reached the Dani in 1956. By the time we arrived in 1961, they had already made changes in Dani life. In the early 1960s, however, virtually no anthropologists were studying colonialism in places like New Guinea. We were resolutely ignoring that cultural interaction in favor of describing an "ethnographic present," the shape of the culture at the imagined pristine moment before Europeans came on the scene. Since the 1960s, anthropology has paid increasingly more attention to what is often called "the colonial encounter."

In **colonialism,** one society, a nation-state (in recent times, usually European), establishes (usually through military conquest) overwhelming power (administrative, economic, political, cultural—although never total control) over another state. From the earliest historical times, we have records of colonizing by empires in China, the Fertile Crescent, Peru, Mexico, and, most recently, Europe.

The "best example," or prototype, and certainly the one most analyzed, is the British raj in India during the 90 years from the Sepoy Mutiny of 1856 to India's independence in 1947. In the last two decades, some scholars have been examining colonialism with the idea that the many players among both colonizers and colonized have influenced each other—that the culture of colonialism was an emergent form, worked out among all concerned. For example, they are beginning to consider ways in which Great Britain today has been shaped as strongly by India as India today has been shaped by Great Britain, if in different ways. More attention is beginning to be paid to the role of those "natives" in the colonial encounter. In India, a movement called Subaltern Studies, which has its own journal, has since the mid-1980s written about the role of the *subalterns* in shaping their culture (Indians serving in the British Indian civil service were labeled dismissively as "subalterns") (Guha, 1997). The tremendous vitality of this scholarship gives us a whole new slant to the cultural history of colonial studies (see also F. Cooper and Stoller, 1997; Clancy-Smith and Gouda, 1998; and Kaplan and Pease, 1993).

Resistance.   **Resistance,** in one form or another, is found where power differentials are great. We have already discussed James C. Scott's fieldwork in a Malay village in Chapter 2. Scott's general subject was the class structure, but during his two years in the village he became increasingly more aware of the subtle ways in which poor people were able to carry out resistance against rich people. Open revolt was not a realistic path, and even open confrontation was rare. However, constant small acts, such as sabotaging farm machinery (which put poor laborers out of work), killing livestock, and stealing rice, were carried out in secret against the more powerful. Scott suggests that this "class resistance"

> includes *any* act(s) by member(s) of a subordinate class that is or are *intended* either to mitigate or deny claims (for example, rents, taxes, prestige) made on that class by superordinate classes (for example, landlords, large farmers, the state) or to advance its own claims (for example, work, land, charity, respect) vis-à-vis those superordinate classes. (Scott, 1985:290)

Kpelle women hoe land cleared from the forest. *(Credit: © Sean Sprague/Panos Pictures)*

The film for this chapter, *The Cows of Dolo Ken Paye,* begins with just such an "everyday form of peasant resistance" (Scott's term): the farmers of the Kpelle village are constantly tyrannized by the cattle of the rich chiefs and elders. Their crops can be protected only by costly fences. Even then, cattle manage to break through and damage crops. Finally, a farmer secretly wounds a marauding calf. In this case, the resistance seems to fail, for the farmer is caught and punished. (In Scott's Malay village, perpetrators were rarely caught.)

SOCIAL CONTROL

Culture, we have seen, refers to learned, shared ideas about behavior. Now we can take a further step and examine the mechanisms that ensure that people will share ideas or at least that, on the whole, their behavior will reflect those ideas. There are many ways to conceptualize cultures, depending on what sets of questions one wants to pursue. Sometimes we can think of a culture almost in the abstract, as a collection of principles that a group of people act on. Or we can get more particular and speak of the schemas that people share. To arrive at a shared culture is not an easy task. Let's imagine culture as an ungainly collection of principles that are available to a lot of unruly individual human beings who have their own motivations and impulses to go their own ways and not follow perfectly the principles of their cultures. Thinking of culture in this light raises such questions as "Why do people in a culture conform as much as they do?" and "What happens when people don't follow the rules?" Answers to these questions provide us with a framework for understanding social control in a society. These questions are addressed by *High Noon,* which presents a picture of a tenuous system of social control in a small social unit.

This point brings us to the anthropology of law, the cross-cultural study of law.

Studying the Laws of Others

Some of the earliest systematic studies of other cultures looked at law and legal institutions. This interest grew out of the immediate practical problems faced by European colonial powers that had acquired, through military conquest, large chunks of the world. If they were to reap any economic benefit through extracting resources or selling products, they needed peaceful conditions and a set of common rules to govern economic exchange between the local societies and the Europeans. To some extent, the Europeans imposed their own legal system, but there was also accommodation between the indigenous legal system and that of the Europeans, especially if the colony was large and powerful.

In the 18th century, as the British were extending their rule in India, a debate about the essence of Indian law ensued (Cohn, 1996:60–75). Some British, overwhelmed by the foreignness of India and not finding the sorts of legal codes that they knew at home, gave up. They had concluded that India was despotic, arbitrary, and thus lawless. The other camp, which prevailed, realized that by learning Sanskrit, Persian, and Arabic, they could have access to Hindu and Muslim law. They could then codify it, annotate it, translate it into English, and make this knowledge into a tool of justice controlled by the British. As Cohn has argued, "The conquest of India was a conquest of knowledge" (1996:16). It is not difficult to recognize one of the precursors of anthropology in this 18th-century legal project.

People quickly realized that simply looking for a local version of Western law was insufficient. The formal legal codes, elaborate constitutions and courts, and prisons supported by powers of coercion that characterize our legal system were minimal or even absent in many societies. Instead, custom, or customary law, governed social behavior. The Yale sociologist William Graham Sumner called these customs *folkways.* In the Netherlands East Indies, the Malay term *adat* was used for this less-than-law area, while the Arabic term *hukum* was reserved for formal law. What often developed was a dual set of rules of conduct consisting of the local customary law and the formal European law, a situation called **legal pluralism.**

Legal pluralism, the term used to refer to the colonial imposition of a (usually) European legal system over an indigenous system, now seems much more complex. As Santos has written,

> Legal pluralism is the key concept in a postmodern view of law. Not the legal
> pluralism of traditional legal anthropology in which the different legal orders
> are conceived as separate entities coexisting in the same political space, but
> rather the conception of different legal spaces superimposed, interpenetrated,

and mixed in our minds as much as in our actions. . . . Our legal life is constituted by an intersection of different legal orders, that is, by interlegality. (Santos, 1987:279–280).

In other words, these legal orders resemble the rest of culture in their heterogeneity. This variation sometimes creates special difficulties. For example, the Navajo live under a mix of Navajo and U.S. law. But a Navajo who kills a supposed witch (appropriate, even necessary behavior in Navajo terms) is liable for homicide under U.S. law (which does not recognize witches or their threat to the community).

Law as a Reflection of Basic Cultural Postulates. As the great European empires began to be dismantled, a more profound theoretical concern emerged. The study of local social rules moved away from trying to fit them into the Western mode, focusing instead on understanding how the study of a culture's laws leads to an understanding of other fundamental principles of that culture. The American anthropologist E. A. Hoebel perhaps best exemplified this approach in two important works. The first was a collaborative effort with the legal scholar Karl Llewellyn, *The Cheyenne Way: Conflict and Case Law in Primitive Jurisprudence* (1941). In the second, Hoebel's classic *The Law of Primitive Man* (1954), he elaborated the thesis that laws have meaning because they are based on the basic postulates of a culture and that to understand the laws, one must understand these basic **cultural postulates.**

Hoebel reworked the ethnographic literature from a number of cultures to show how law flows from basic postulates. For example, for the Inuit (Eskimo), two of the nine basic postulates that Hoebel derived were the following:

Postulate I. Spirit beings, and all animals by virtue of possessing souls, have emotional intelligence similar to that of man.

Corollary 1. Certain acts are pleasing to them; others arouse their ire.

Postulate II. Man in important aspects of life is subordinate to the wills of animal souls and spirit beings.

Corollary 1. When displeased or angered by human acts they withhold desired things or set loose evil forces. (Hoebel, 1954:69)

Hoebel continued:

Out of Postulates I and II with their attendant corollaries one can feel emerging a legal principle that willful and persistent violation of tabus shall be sanctioned by extrusion from the community. . . . The violation of a tabu is a sin supernaturally sanctioned; willful and repeated sinning becomes a crime legally punished. Penalty: exile—in the Arctic. (Hoebel, 1954:74)

It is always easier to make generalizations about a culture that one knows only from a finite number of books and articles written by others. Having firsthand knowledge complicates things. This problem becomes apparent if one tries to apply Hoebel's approach to a contemporary American polarizing issue such as abortion or gun control. Certainly, one cannot frame a set of postulates about either issue that is held in common by "Americans." They are political issues precisely because two contradictory sets of postulates are held by large numbers of Americans. Even though the federal and state laws about abortion and gun control are fairly clear at any one moment, there is constant pressure to change them because no commonly accepted basic postulates about the matter exist. Articulating the opposing sets of postulates held by different groups of Americans can help to clarify just where the disagreement lies.

Even the basic cultural postulates change. If one were to take Hoebel's set of postulates back to an Inuit community today, one would surely find some people who recognize them and subscribe to them fully. Undoubtedly, one would also find many Inuit who question and even reject them.

There is an interesting parallel here with how psychological anthropologists developed a concern with basic themes, or patterns of culture. Look back at Chapter 5, on cultural psychologies. In each case, the anthropologists were attempting to formulate the very basic parameters of cultures themselves. In important ways, both Ruth Benedict with her patterns of culture and E. A. Hoebel with his basic cultural postulates were working toward the same sort of essence of a culture. The concept of schema also resembles cultural postulates as a way of laying out in systematic form the basic beliefs of a group.

Not only does legal anthropology lead to consideration of the basic postulates of a culture, but it also has a most dramatic and rich source of behavioral data, the *trouble case,* arising when someone violates a norm of law. When the humdrum routine of normal life is disrupted by a dispute of some sort and that dispute is resolved in some way, much is revealed about a culture. Trouble cases bring cultural postulates to the surface. Lawyers like to say that hard cases make for bad law, but we can add that difficult cases make for great anthropology. This point is well demonstrated in James Gibbs's film on the Kpelle of Liberia, *The Cows of Dolo Ken Paye.* In the film, an aggrieved poor man fatally slashes the marauding cow of a rich man, and the resulting proceedings lead the anthropologist to some of the major tensions of the village. We discuss this event in more detail later in this chapter.

Defining Law. In earlier times, it was common to divide cultures between those that have law and those that do not. Today, the tendency is to look for comparable features or attributes across all cultures, for certainly the challenge of social control is pan-cultural. The older solution to the definition problem is to reserve **law** as a term specific to cultures like our own and to use a broader, more culture-neutral term for the whole range of human behavior. Thus one can begin from the paradigm that describes the American legal system as formally conceived and uses the labels *laws, crimes, courts, adjudication,* and *punishment.* Each of these terms has a clear meaning in the American context but is really a subset of a broader culture-neutral concept. A second solution is to use more culture-neutral terms to reformulate the paradigm of social control with the following general terms: *norms* (including *laws*), *transgressions* (including *crimes*), and *resolutions* (including *courts* and *punishments*). This approach avoids a precise definition of "law," but locates it at one extreme of several attribute dimensions in the consideration of norms, transgressions, and resolutions.

Cultural Norms

Laws, or written codes, are the most formal part of the entire range of cultural **norms,** or cultural rules for behavior. Norms are the essence of culture. As we have seen, they are rules, ideas, or postulates for behavior of all sorts, and they cover homicide, property rights, foodways, kinship terms, grammar, pronunciation—everything that people do. Figure 11.1 illustrates the wide realm of norms as a set of variables, usually ranging from the more formal (where we find law) to the less formal.

When viewed this way, as a continuum, it is hard to find a sharp dividing line between law and custom. Also many cultural norms change, lack consensus, or vary depending on the situation, so the laws may reflect only the prevailing view at the time the law was made and concern only a particular set of circumstances. One must be careful not to assume that laws and rules are always an accurate reflection of the range of acceptable behavior and ideas.

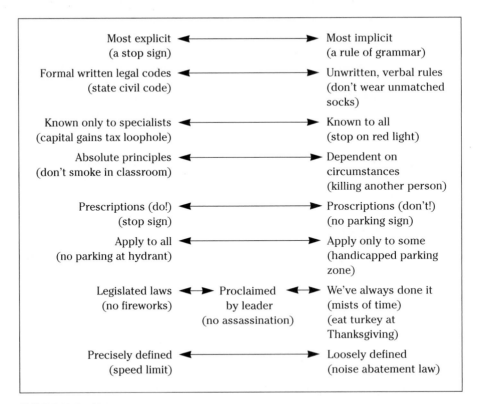

FIGURE 11.1 Norms.
The variations are shown in terms of different attribute dimensions.

One must also realize that laws and norms vary tremendously across cultures. For example, all societies define some homicide as *murder,* homicide that is illegitimate. But there is tremendous cultural variation. Even within a society, people may disagree. For example, consider the bitter debate about abortion and capital punishment in the United States today. The debates hinge on two fundamental questions: "When does a fetus become a human and thereby have the right to live?" and "When does a human being forfeit the right to live?"

The Ten Commandments, the basis for the Judaeo–Christian tradition, include the flat admonition, "Thou shall not kill." However, virtually all Jewish and Christian thinking has come up with qualifications specifying when killing of a human being is accepted, approved, or even required. For example, the new Catechism of the Catholic Church states, "The fifth commandment forbids *direct and intentional killing* as gravely sinful. The murderer and those who cooperate voluntarily in murder commit a sin that cries out for vengeance" (Catholic Church, 1995:2268). But then (in 2308) the Catechism lays out the conditions for a just war.

Although every culture draws some lines about what body parts can be exposed when and where, norms vary from culture to culture, over time, and situationally. The norms are sometimes written into formal law but often are more informal customs. Dani penis gourds reveal men's scrotums, but should a man's gourd be knocked off, revealing his penis, he is terribly embarrassed. On March 30, 1994, Muslim fundamentalists in Algeria shot and killed two young women who went out in public without covering their heads (*New York Times,* March 31, 1994, p. A3). Slacks or shorts, which are quite acceptable for most American college undergraduate women in classrooms today, would have been unacceptable in the same classrooms in the 1950s. And what is routinely modest beach attire would be quite unacceptable in a church or classroom.

DOING ANTHROPOLOGY

Backpacks on Campus

An example of a very implicit norm, a norm never actually put into words, is one found until recently on college campuses in the United States. Women carried their books in one arm or two and, if two, pressed them against their bodies. But men carried books in only one arm, and that arm was extended straight down at the side. No sign, no college regulation, ever put this norm into words. No campus police ever were on the lookout for violations. Yet the norm was obeyed virtually without exception. Today, it is difficult to observe this behavior because of a technological revolution on campuses: the backpack, suspended by one or both straps down the back, has made older ways of carrying books obsolete.

Here is a fieldwork exercise: Is there any normative pattern for backpacks on campuses? Under what circumstances is only the left strap used? Only the right strap? Both straps? (I have not yet figured out a pattern, but on principle one can predict that one should emerge if backpacks last long enough.) ♦

The book-carrying norm on American college campuses in the early 1990s allowed women to carry their books raised against their bodies, but men carried their books with arms extended, against their legs. This norm was never written or spoken, but was almost universally obeyed. *(Credit: University of South Carolina Publications Office)*

Transgressions

Unacceptable deviations from cultural norms are known as **transgressions.** These acts of **deviance** vary according to how serious they are thought to be. Some are viewed with horror; others are merely irritating or strange. Minor transgressions, such as rolling through a stop sign, taking a pen from the office, or trespassing on a neighbor's property, are committed all the time by normal people, who rarely experience consequences.

Criminal law has developed a huge vocabulary for labeling various sorts of transgressions. *Torts,* wrongs against individuals that are remedied by actions pursued by the individual, are distinguished from *crimes,* which are violations for which the government pursues remedies. Crimes include *treason,* an act against the state itself; *felonies* (serious, usually punished by death or imprisonment); and *misdemeanors* (less serious).

Violating supernatural or religious norms is a sin. The biblical books of Leviticus and Deuteronomy specify numerous such sins, covering all aspects of life. The Hindu prohibition on killing or eating Zebu cattle is widely observed today. The Catholic Church defines sin as "an offense against God" (Catholic Church, 1995:1849) and subdivides sins in various ways, one of which is the distinction between *mortal sin,* "whose object is grave matter and which is also committed with full knowledge and deliberate consent" (1995:1857), and *venial sin,* which involves a less serious matter or is committed with less full knowledge or less deliberate consent. In the 13th century, Saint Thomas Aquinas gave blasphemy, perjury, homicide, and adultery as examples of mortal sin, and "thoughtless chatter or immoderate laughter" as examples of venial sins (Catholic Church, 1995:1856).

Zebu cattle in a street in India.
(Credit: © Doranne Jacobson)

Violating linguistic norms may be *mispronunciation, grammatical error, speaking with an accent, lisping,* or *stuttering.* Violating more general cultural norms may be a *mistake,* an *error,* a *faux pas,* a *goof,* or a *boo-boo.* You could easily extend this list of transgression words. It is obvious from this large vocabulary that we are interested in the precise definition of transgressions. Most other cultures are not as concerned with labeling their transgressions.

Transgressions vary cross-culturally. They may be precisely defined or vaguely defined, and the boundaries of acceptability may be clear or vague. The offense may be against another person, against a group, or against a supernatural being.

Conflict Resolution

If we look at institutionalized systems of **conflict resolution,** we find that an essential variable is power. Do third parties (be they judges or mediators) have the legitimate social power to force a settlement and then make it stick (adjudication), or do they derive their power from their own personal influence (mediation)? Do the mediators have any power at all?

A second variable is the degree of formal procedure involved. The 1995 trial of O. J. Simpson in Los Angeles made the general public aware of the complexities of U.S. courtroom procedure. Other conflict resolution systems involve considerably less procedure.

A third variable is the intended outcome of the conflict resolution proceedings. Is the system intent on finding fault and punishing the guilty, often by imprisonment or death? Or is the goal to reestablish, to some extent, the situation that existed before the transgression? Or is the purpose of the proceedings to demand the payment of some sort of restitution?

Mediation. **Mediation** refers to systems that are less formal, involve less coercive institutionalized power, and are aimed more at reconciliation of the opposed parties. In mediation, the third party generally must rely on his or her own personal power to enforce judgments and resolve disputes. When that fails, there are no institutions to prevent the escalation of violence. However, as we will see, among the Yanomamo, the conflicts are often carefully controlled exercises that serve to settle an issue while avoiding death or serious injury.

The Dani are temperamentally more like the Ju/'hoansi than the Yanomamo, and they do have more means of conflict resolution. For example, if someone steals a pig, kills and eats it, and is discovered, then some of the big men of the area will get together and confer about it and then tell the culprit to give the pig's owner two pigs in compensation. The important men do not have the power to force the person to make the repayment, but there is strong feeling in the area that he should. This form of conflict resolution is effective if all concerned are from the same vicinity and if only minor theft is involved. If the parties are from different political groups, or if one person kills another, then there is often no way to resolve things peacefully. Once, in a case that I knew well (Heider, 1997:92), the killer and his friends moved to another neighborhood a few kilometers away to ease matters. Dani often resort to withdrawal in the face of conflict. It does not necessarily resolve things, but it does avoid further exacerbation.

Another form of mediation is a sort of group therapy session known to many Pacific Island cultures. Although there is considerable variation in the forms that it takes, the term *disentangling* refers to the whole family of practices.

Tangles—interpersonal conflict, disagreements, moral dilemmas—are at the heart of social life. People talk about their troubles, and in seeking solutions through talk, they create valued images of self and community. *Disentangling* refers to cultural activities in which people attempt to straighten out their tangled relations (Watson-Gegeo and White, 1990:3).

The *ho'oponopono* is the Hawaiian form of disentangling. Although there was considerable variation in the Hawaiian ho'oponopono, the main outlines are clear (following Boggs and Chun, 1990). Ho'oponopono is used to set things right in a family through a series of frank, open discussion sessions that explore the family problems with the intention of resolving them, thereby untangling the family members. There are some procedural rules about the choice of leader (a high-status, respected person who may or may not be a family member), confidentiality of the discussion (which makes it difficult to study directly), willingness of all family members to participate, and the various religious elements such as prayers and Bible readings. Above all, there are rules of speech that regulate the way in which people bring out resentments, listen to others, apologize, and ask forgiveness.

Adjudication. Adjudication is another method of conflict resolution that is a bit more formal than mediation. Both techniques involve a third party, but in adjudication the third party has the power to impose a judgment on the disputing parties. In mediation, the disputants are negotiating with the help of a third party, but the mediator does not have the authority to hand down a decision. However, the line between mediation and adjudication is not always clear.

The Zapotecs, who live in the Mexican state of Oaxaca, are said by themselves and others to be particularly peaceful. But conflicts do arise and are handled through a court system, which Laura Nader studied. The local courts, which deal with relatively easy cases, are primarily concerned with restoring harmony. The *presidente,* or judge, encourages the parties to talk, airing their grievances. Eventually, he makes his decision of fine or compensation for damages not in the spirit of punishment but "to make the balance" between the two parties involved. As Laura Nader put it, the presidente is "mediator, adjudicator, group therapist" (1969:85).

An example of Zapotec justice is "The Case of the Damaged Chiles" (Nader, 1969:74–75). A merchant laid out some chile peppers on the edge of a road, and a truck ran over some, damaging them. The presidente heard the accusations of carelessness on both sides and finally told the driver to pay three pesos for the damaged chiles and admonished the merchant to be more careful in the future. This Zapotec case illustrates just how difficult it is to draw a clear distinction between mediation and adjudication, for it is only a notch more formal than the Hawaiian ho'oponopono. As we will see in the film about the Kpelle justice system, both mediation and adjudication are often employed in the same culture. They are just different levels of conflict resolution. As the complexity of the culture increases, so does the complexity of the various resolution strategies.

FOCUS CULTURE

Adjudication in a Kpelle Village

OVERVIEW

Location: Liberia and Guinea, west coast of Africa

Geography: Liberia has a narrow coastal plain rising to a forested plateau. The climate is generally hot and humid, but most of Liberia has a dry season and a rainy season.

Population: 530,000
Language: Kpelle is a tonal language, related to Mande, in the Niger-Congo family
Religion: A supreme God and various spirits
Economy: Slash-and-burn horticulture; dry rice farming, vegetables, and some cattle
Sociopolitical Organization: Chiefdom within a nation-state; members of widespread West African secret societies, Poro (for men) and Sande (for women)

Much of this description of the Kpelle is based on the research of James L. Gibbs, Jr. The Kpelle live in Liberia and neighboring Guinea, where Gibbs did his field work. The village featured in the film was in central Liberia. As might be expected of such a large population, there is considerable cultural variation, and the language has several distinct dialects.

The Kpelle grow dry rice (unlike in Bali, complex irrigation systems are not necessary), cassava, and vegetables and fruits, using slash-and-burn horticulture. It takes a tremendous amount of hand labor to clear the fields of undergrowth, which springs up between plantings.

Traditional Kpelle houses were round, with cone-shaped roofs thatched with palm leaves. More recently, as corrugated metal sheets became available for roofing, the house shapes changed from round to rectangular to accommodate the new material.

The Kpelle sociopolitical organization is a chiefdom characterized by patrilineages and local territorial units. The territorial units are, from smallest to most inclusive, the family household; then town quarters, headed by elders; then towns, headed by chiefs; then districts with their chiefs; and finally the chiefdom itself, which is headed by a paramount chief, who was also a Liberian government employee.

The town quarters are especially important groupings in Kpelle life. They are territorial, and people think of themselves as being related to other members of their quarter. However, this concept is perhaps more a matter of using kinship as a metaphor for unity than a literal way to determine relationships (Gibbs, 1965:207). Secret societies—the Poro for men and the Sande for women—are also important; they across both kinship and local groupings. Social control is exercised by the Poro, which enforces general cultural norms; by the formal courts; and by moots (as discussed later).

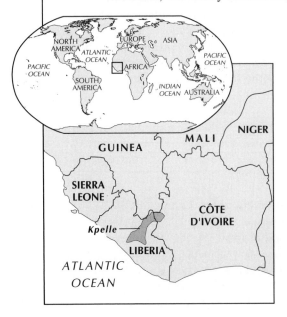

Sometimes it is said that the United States is the world's most litigious society. Certainly in terms of proliferation of courts at many levels, of the ability to appeal decisions to ever-higher courts, and of full-time specialists like lawyers and judges, this statement seems likely to be true. West African societies like the Kpelle are also highly litigious, however. Gibbs collected reports on involvement in legal cases from each household in the village of Fokwele (where our film for this chapter takes place). Villagers reported 999 disputes. Even though the Kpelle system does not rely on lawyers, and various district and paramount chiefs take their turn as judges in the formal courts, theirs is a society very familiar with legal proceedings.

Gibbs identified two main ways to handle disputes, through courts or through moots. Courts handle the more serious cases, amounting to slightly less than half of the total. The most serious cases like murder are taken out of the Kpelle system and dealt with in a federal Liberian court. Cases are brought before chiefs, who hear the plaintiff, defendant, and witnesses, and then announce the verdict. This form of resolution consists of adjudication. Court proceedings are formal, with such touches as official uniformed "messengers" who assist the judges.

There are also more casual, informal ways to resolve trouble cases: **moots,** or **house palavers.** They work through mediation, somewhat like the Hawaiian ho'oponopono discussed earlier. Moots are held in a home and are attended by the complainants and an ad hoc group of their friends and relations who join in hearing the complaints and helping the principals reach a resolution. The emphasis is on restoring harmony. After the matter is resolved, perhaps with a formal apology, everyone has a drink.

Gibbs found that the main conflicts coming to both courts and moots had to do with marital discord—sex, violence, bride wealth problems, friction between co-wives, and the like. He was particularly interested in how the culturally patterned psychology of the Kpelle interacted with the conflict resolution process. For example, Gibbs identified an important bundle of Kpelle values marked by indirection, nonconfrontation, and particularly indirect expression of anger. Although this pattern may have reduced some open physical conflict, it was in itself a cause of many trouble cases. Examples of this link appeared when people did not fulfill obligations (like repaying debts) or when cases were brought to court for reasons other than the apparent ones. Gibbs gives one example in "The Case of the Indebted Fisheater" (1969:191–192). One man sued another for a trifling debt of two cans of fish. The Fisheater could well have paid for the fish, but he was more interested in inconveniencing the shopkeeper, and the case provided an indirect channel for his aggression. We shall see how the Kpelle play out these various themes in the film, *The Cows of Dolo Ken Paye*.   ◆

Conflict Resolution in Modern Industrial Societies.   Legal anthropologists have become increasingly more interested in studying the conflict resolution systems in modern industrial societies, including the United States. In eastern Massachusetts, where there is a full-blown formal court system, S. E. Merry has looked at the ways in which people bring their personal family and neighborhood problems to the court for resolution. From the point of view of the court officials, these disputes over dogs, property, and domestic violence are "garbage cases" that do not belong in proper courtrooms. Yet people persist in bringing them, rather than taking them to mediation programs. Merry explains this use of the legal system as

> part of an effort by working-class Americans to escape from the control of local political authorities and from dependence on violence to a less violent, more autonomous, more legally regulated social life. (Merry, 1990:176)

Ironically, though, this search for autonomy leaves people dependent on a complex and unfriendly legal system.

Anthropologists have long listened to what people say in courts. More recently, in a convergence of linguistic anthropology and legal anthropology, they have been making fine-scale analyses of talk in legal cases. This has been called "the ethnography of legal discourse" (Conley and O'Barr, 1990), and the analysis focuses on how people actually manage language in courtroom situations.

For example, Charles Goodwin (1994) made a microanalysis of testimony in the first Rodney King trial in Los Angeles. In 1992, Rodney King, an African American man, was stopped by white Los Angeles police for a minor traffic violation and severely beaten. The beating was recorded on videotape by an amateur photographer, and it seemed to present overwhelming evidence of extreme unprovoked police brutality. But even videotaped behavior does not speak for itself. The policemen were indicted, tried, and acquitted. Goodwin showed how the police officers' defense attorney and their expert witnesses used talk and selected slow-motion fragments of the incriminating videotape to construct an image of professionally restrained law officers subduing an out-of-control, threatening citizen. (In a second trial, the prosecution was more effective, and several police officers were convicted.)

PATTERNS AND CAUSES OF WAR

When conflict resolution fails, conflict results, and no matter how effective the mechanism, it never works all the time. In cases where the conflict occurs between two maximal social units, conflict often becomes **war.** Among the Dani, for example, the conflict resolution mechanism works fairly well in resolving trouble cases within confederations. When grievances cut across confederation boundaries or involve people of different, supposedly friendly alliances, however, it is much more difficult to resolve them. Grievances pile up, resentments fester, and eventually one side or the other ends the peace with a sudden attack, killing many people, rearranging frontiers, creating new no-man's-lands, and setting off a long-term state of war between the newly constituted alliances that can last for years.

The course of a war is punctuated by battles and raids that continue long after the original disputes are forgotten. Eventually, these alliances in their turn explode, a new alignment is made, and the new cycle of war begins.

The most famous study of conflict in the ethnographic literature is Chagnon's work on the Yanomamo. Napoleon Chagnon described Yanomamo warfare as a longstanding pattern of conflict attributable to particularities of social organization, ecological pressures, and the "fierce" personality type. But Brian Ferguson disputed this interpretation, arguing that the "extreme conflict mode" of the

The two sides in this Dani war face each other along a low ridge. The men carry spears or bows and arrows. The lines stay static for a while as a few young men at the very front test the enemy. *(Credit: Karl G. Heider, Film Study Center, Harvard University)*

Yanomamo is "clearly attributable to the exogenous factors of Western contact" (1992:225, 1995). More recently, Leslie Sponsel has summarized data that call into question the characterization of the Yanomamo as extremely aggressive (1998). In the Papuan New Guinea Highlands, Strathern found that the introduction of guns led to the revival and intensification of warfare (1992). By the late 1980s, both crude homemade zip guns and modern manufactured weapons were being used in tribal warfare.

Groups in the North American Plains such as Comanche and Dakota, armed with guns and mounted on horses, were famous warrior cultures by the 19th century. However, before the 17th century, they had neither horses nor guns. Frank Secoy described (1953) what happened as English and French pressed in from the north and Spanish from the south. In the north, the individual English and French traders competed with each other for Indian business and freely exchanged guns for furs. In the south, horses were introduced by the Spanish and turned Apache groups into highly mobile raiders and hunters. The Dakota, who had been sedentary horticulturalists in the Minnesota forests, were pushed west, onto the Plains, propelled by a domino effect of better-armed enemies moving in from the east. By the late 18th century, the Dakota had also acquired guns and horses and swept westward, dominating large areas of the Plains, hunting buffalo, and raiding farming tribes along the major rivers.

This description is certainly not meant to suggest that the Plains had been peaceful before European intrusion. There is archaeological evidence from the 14th century, long before European influence, for hard times and intense warfare. The archaeological excavations at the village called Crow Creek in South Dakota revealed extensive fortification ditches and palisades. Skeletal remains of perhaps 500 people were found in one of the fortification ditches. Forensic anthropological examination of the bones showed that the people had been malnourished in life, met violent deaths, and were mutilated after death. A reasonable interpretation is that this group, although having a marginal economy, invested a lot of energy in defensive construction. It appears, however, that these attempts at defense were futile, and the people were killed anyway. If this story is correct, and if it is not a unique occurrence, the Crow Creek massacre is eloquent testimony to pre-European levels of violence (Bramforth, 1994).

Nevertheless, some evidence indicates that societies which have not had access to weapons but have experienced the protection of the state no longer engage in the types of wars that were commonplace in precontact days. For example, we saw in *Dead Birds* (Chapter 3) the traditional Dani pattern of war, which was a significant feature of the culture in 1961 and showed no evidence of European influence (Shankman, 1991). However, the Dani have not gained access to guns, and warfare between the alliances seems to have ended.

Causes of War

One of the most puzzling questions about war remains. Why, if all societies have fought war, is there such a great range in the frequency of war from society to society? The Dani had a system that kept them more or less constantly at war. Other groups rarely engaged in war.

One explanation looks at psychological patterning. Cultures that encourage aggressive personalities are often at war. Certainly, Chagnon's picture of the Yanomamo as a culture that values male aggression supports this theory. But the Dani, who at home are quite mild and unaggressive, are strong counterexamples.

In a fascinating comparative study that was designed to address this problem, Clayton and Carole Robarchek did fieldwork with one of the most warlike cultures known, the Waorani of Ecuador, and one of the most peaceful, the Semai Senoi of Malaysia (1992). In some respects, the two groups are similar: Both live in deep rain forest, practice slash-and-burn horticulture (growing sweet manioc, plantains, and bananas), fish and hunt game with blowpipes and poison darts, and lack alcohol and hallucinogenic drugs; both live in small bands, reckon kinship bilaterally, and lack unilineal descent groups such as clans. The Robarcheks quickly rejected environmental differences as a crucial factor, for the warlike Waorani actually have richer natural resources than do the Semai Senoi.

So they looked to other factors such as worldview. The Semai live in a terrifying, threatening world, and they use much magic ritual and taboo to cope with their environment. The Waorani world, on the other hand, which is seen as benign, has little need for taboos and magic. The Semai cling desperately to their little kin groups, while the Waorani are individualistic and independent. Generally, internal fighting is associated with male interest groups such as clans that promote group solidarity against each other. But the Waorani are an exception to this trend.

Social control systems also differ greatly. The Semai avoid conflict and immediately act to defuse potential conflict. For the Waorani, in their individualism, "no institutionalized mechanisms exist for the resolution of disputes and the restoration of amity" (Robarchek and Robarchek, 1992:204). In summary, the Robarcheks fall back on differences in "internal psychocultural dynamic" to explain war and peace.

Certainly, the determinants of war are always complex and must be seen in context, in holistic perspective. It is never useful to look for a single cause of war, be it tribal war in the Amazon or World War II.

The Nature of War

When we look at the nature of war from a cross-cultural perspective, four common characteristics emerge from the data:

- All societies have war (with variable frequency).
- War is an almost exclusively male undertaking.
- War involves homicide.
- Wars have rules.

War Is Universal (but with Greatly Variable Frequency). Much of the current research seems to indicate that war is universal in the sense that all societies have had some experience with war, but this claim needs to be strongly qualified. There is, in fact, a wide range of warring, from societies that are most frequently at war to societies that are most frequently at peace. Despite the existence of many cultures at the peaceful end of the spectrum, which include cultures that do not wage war now and may not have when initially studied, no autonomous society (excluding societies that have been absorbed into a larger empire or nation) has been found that is *completely* ignorant of war and has never participated in war. There may have been other societies that have never known war, but at most they represent a tiny fraction of the total number of *Homo sapiens'* social endeavors, and it is true that the vast majority of societies engage in or have engaged in warfare.

One of the most interesting questions concerns the tremendous variation in the frequency with which different societies have engaged in war and the frequency with which any particular frontier has been the scene of war. Much is still to be learned about how these variations are related to the specific nature of specific societies or to critical pairings of societies.

War Is a Male-Dominated Endeavor. Men fight wars; women do not. This idea is one of the strongest generalizations emerging from the ethnographic literature. The exceptions to it are few. There were the famous "Amazons" of the kingdom of

Dahomey, in West Africa, where in the 19th century, women formed units in the army and engaged in warfare (Polanyi, 1966:36). These women were called "the King's wives" or "our mothers," but contradicting the implications of these titles, there is a strong possibility that they were not actually considered to be women:

> The Amazons are not supposed to marry, and, by their own statement, they
> have changed their sex. "We are men," say they, "not women." (F. E. Forbes,
> cited in Herskovits, 1938:85)

There are other, less reliable reports of women warriors. The original Amazons were a legendary monarchy of women, ruled by a queen and composed exclusively of women, that waged war against other states in Asia Minor and the Aegean.

By the second half of the 20th century a few nations—China, Israel, the United States—began to train women for combat. And there are a few earlier instances of women assuming a male role and entering combat (Molly Pitcher of the American Revolution, for example). This concept is reminiscent of the "female husbands" in the Nuer society (see Chapter 8). The principle of exclusively male warfare seems to be part of the general pattern of the gender division of labor (for example, women do not hunt big game animals or build houses).

War Produces Homicide. Killing can be seen not simply as a defining attribute of war, but as a logical and necessary consequence of war that is justifiable and acceptable. In other words, sanctions against homicide that exist *within* societies are not applicable in conflicts *between* societies. Once again, wars are seen as institutional conflicts, not individual conflicts.

War is conflict between parties that are not subject to a single, bipartisan conflict-resolving institution, so it follows that war produces homicide. When the parties to a conflict are members of the same society, that society provides means of resolving the conflict in some manner short of homicide. But in intersocietal conflict the hostile acts easily escalate to the ultimate hostility: homicide.

Wars Have Rules. Every society has a set of rules and patterns that govern war. Some rules are strategic; others are defensive. But what is unexpected is the regular occurrence of rules that restrict the violence of war, such as constraints on the killing of innocent citizens and the use of chemical weapons, and norms that limit the extent of death and destruction.

The best evidence for cultural restrictions on war comes from the European tradition (Bailey, 1972; Karston, 1978). In medieval times, there were already explicit rules, royal ordinances, and other laws that specified the manner of declaring war, the acceptable fighting tactics, details of ransom, privileges of ambassadors, treatment of prisoners of war, division of booty, and the like. In the 19th century, as weapons became more sophisticated and war damage more extensive, European nations tried to formulate comprehensive rules of war. A series of Geneva Conventions (1864, 1906, 1929, 1949) specified the treatment of wounded, of prisoners, and of civilians. A parallel series of Hague Conventions (1868, 1899, 1925, 1954) attempted to regulate weapons and other practices of war (Bailey, 1972).

THE NATURE OF PEACE

The End of War

One of the great challenges for the anthropology of the 21st century is to think about the condition of **peace** as thoroughly as, during the last decades of the 20th century, we have thought about the condition of war. One direction will be to explore conflict resolution (see, for example, Fry and Bjorkqvist, 1997); another will be in a more psychological direction (see, for example, Sponsel, 1998). Yet another research program will be to better define those components that go into making societies more peaceful or more warlike and those components that make societies more violent or more nonviolent, for they are not necessarily the same.

The cross-cultural perspective yields an understanding of the pan-societal nature of war. Now we will apply our understanding of culture to try to discover how wars end, leading to a period of peace between wars.

A model of war that is based on holistic description seems at first glance to offer a way to end war. If we can specify preconditions, causes, or motivations for war, then perhaps we can find functional equivalents that will satisfy the needs that gave rise to war.

Much depends on how one explains war. For example, for William James, the psychologist, writing in 1910, the major function of war was to unite and discipline a nation, an end of which he approved. But he was a pacifist and abhorred war as immoral, so he urged a "moral equivalent of war." (Actually, he proposed a "conscription of the whole youthful population to form for a certain number of years a part of the army enlisted against nature," the last being a phrase that startles our ecological sensibilities in the late 20th century. But he meant that all youth should be conscripted into manual labor jobs, which would give them moral and physical toughness.)

This idea that if one could specify the reasons for war, then one could end it, was held most forcefully by Margaret Mead. She argued (1940/1964) that "war is only an invention" to fulfill certain needs and, like other inventions, can be made obsolete and replaced by other social inventions that would fulfill those needs at less human cost.

It has been suggested that sports can replace war. This idea assumes that war functions to fulfill some aggressive instinct that can better be fulfilled by athletic competition. The modern Olympic Games are often proclaimed for their promotion of international peace. Murdock described how the Truk (in Micronesia) were convinced to "wage baseball" instead of war (1948/1965). I have heard missionaries and government officials propose soccer as a substitute for Dani warfare. In reality, it would be hard to show that the Olympic Games actually promote peace. Indeed, the Games were canceled three times (1916, 1940, 1944) because of war. At best, the Olympic Games are a result, not a cause, of peace. And baseball in Truk or soccer among the Dani became possible only after war had been ended.

We can return to the basic definition of war that implies that war is a societal imperative. War occurs between autonomous bounded societies, and war is the result of the boundedness of these autonomous societies. If we examine the instances when societies have given up war, we find that they do not occur when societal or psychological needs are fulfilled through alternative activities but rather when the societies have lost their autonomy.

Therefore it seems misleading to talk in grand terms of a functional equivalent or substitute activity as a means of ending war. We have seen that war occurs in and is a result of an intersocietal no-man's-land and that when this zone is abolished, war is no longer possible. In other words, war ends with a structural alteration in societal autonomy such that societies merge into an overarching authority. Stalemates, such as the recent Cold War, are at best fragile peaces.

Margaret Mead thought that a general absence of war on a global scale could be accomplished only by the development of a complex boundary-crossing sort of international development, perhaps the United Nations (1968). In more recent years, multinational corporations have been filling just this role.

In the past, warfare ended and societies were absorbed into others by two processes: forceful incorporation with pacification and voluntary union. Forceful incorporation with pacification is still incomplete in a few remote areas of the New Guinea Highlands and the Amazon Basin. Effective voluntary union may possibly still develop in Europe and Central America. But it seems unlikely that these historical processes can go much further. Nation-states seem to have reached their maximal possible sizes in the early post–World War II period. In fact, during the last decades, nations have split apart, getting smaller rather than larger: Malaysia, Pakistan, the Soviet Union, Czechoslovakia, and Yugoslavia are striking examples of this trend, and Canada and Indonesia could well follow soon. Loose confederations of United Nations–like organizations, which leave the constituent nations relatively intact, do not completely rule out the possibility of warfare between the nations.

Taking another tack, one can talk of peace in two senses. One is the momentary interlude between wars, which is the peace that is most often talked about. A more fundamental sort of peace implies the absence of the capability for war. In the pursuit of this condition, much attention is focused on armaments. If armaments are decreased, the argument goes, then war will be less likely. In fact, the precise level of technology seems to be relatively unimportant. Wars continue with or without poison gas. Societies with nuclear capability continue to fight in conventional (nonnuclear) war. Successive disarmament treaties could abolish successive types of weaponry, reversing the evolution of weapons back to the Palaeolithic level, but as long as the crucial condition for war, the intersocietal no-man's-land, still exists, the potential for war will be present.

It would be difficult to show that, as a general principle, war is eliminated by a change in armaments. On the other hand, it is clear from history that the possibility of war between two societies is ended when the societies relinquish part of their autonomy to a larger sociopolitical entity that exercises greater power—and weaponry—than its constituent parts.

But there is a final cautionary irony. Before central governments emerge, we see that war, with the attributes discussed previously, occurs between societies.

When the central governments are strong in their conflict-resolving power, serious mass conflict does not occur. There is a zone of transition, however, between the internal peace of a strong society or nation and the state of intersocietal (or international) warfare, in which serious mass conflict does occur. These conflicts lack the legitimacy of wars and are thus likely to be more ruthless and bloody than wars. During the 1990s the fighting in the former Yugoslavia and that in Rwanda exemplified this principle to a horrifying degree. From this standpoint, then, while the uniting of societies does away with war, the hazard of a weak union is that conflict more terrible than war may break out.

Peace as a Social Condition

Anthropologists, who have so long studied war and aggression, are now beginning to study peace (Howell and Willis, 1989; Sponsel and Gregor, 1994) and nonviolence (Montagu, 1978; Silverberg and Gray, 1992). There is even a quarterly news journal, *Human Peace,* published by the Commission on the Study of Peace, a unit of the International Union of Anthropological and Ethnological Sciences.

A basic problem is distinguishing between the peace that is merely an interlude between wars and the peace that is a permanent state or social condition. We have seen how many cultures intensified warfare as Europeans pressed in on them. But others gave up warfare as they came under the sway of colonial or national governments and missionaries. Both the Waorani in the Amazon and the Grand Valley Dani in New Guinea ended their wars abruptly, leading anthropologists to wonder just how deeply rooted those patterns had been (Robarchek and Robarchek, 1992:205; Heider, 1997). The Kawelka of the Papua New Guinea Highlands, who had given up war in the 1960s, resumed it in the 1980s when guns became widely available. On another scale, in 1914, European nations had known a period of relative peace for a century after the Napoleonic wars. But then they fought two world wars in a period of thirty years.

SEEING ANTHROPOLOGY

The Cows of Dolo Ken Paye: Resolving Conflict Among the Kpelle

Filmmaker: Marvin Silverman   *Anthropologist: James L. Gibbs, Jr.*

The Cows of Dolo Ken Paye was shot in the Kpelle village of Fokwele by Marvin Silverman, in collaboration with the anthropologist James L. Gibbs, Jr. The film shows how conflict is resolved in a chiefdom in which the leaders—elders and chiefs—have real power to adjudicate problems and make their decisions stick.

Silverman and Gibbs first intended to make a film about a day in the life of the village. Then, in the midst of filming, a crime took place, and the camera was fortuitously present as the search for the villain unfolded. Because Gibbs had done research in the village years earlier, the film is able to bring historical depth to the story, even using black-and-white still photographs from his earlier work.

Also, note in the early part of the film how people hull rice in wooden mortars, winnow it in woven rice *fanner* baskets, and cook it in clay pots. All this domestic technology, along with the rice-growing technology itself, was brought by West Africans to the South Carolina Low Country in the 18th century (see L. Ferguson, 1992). As we see in the film, it also takes quite a bit of effort to protect the maturing rice from marauding cattle (not to mention rice birds and other pests).

The Kpelle territorial units come into play in the film as the trouble case is worked out. We also see the effects of social stratification, for it is the richer people who own the trouble-causing cattle. Gibbs calls it "an incipient class system" (1965:214) based on material wealth. It is the richer men, with the most wives and children, who are the strongest candidates for political offices.

The short clip begins on a peaceful Sunday morning as the people of Fokwele are going to church. Suddenly, two young men bring in a calf that has been slashed by a bush knife. The calf belongs to the town chief, so the case is moved up to the clan chief and then up to the next level, the paramount chief, who sends for an ordeal operator. Meanwhile, we learn about ordeals. Formerly poison was used, but now hot oil and hot knives have taken their place. Using them, the ordeal operator discovers the guilty party—the innocent are not burned, the guilty are. In fact, most cases are tried through the testimony of witnesses and cross-examination. One man hopes that the person who attacked the calf will just confess.

Clan Chief Samuel Paye, Town Chief Carboy, and other Fokwele townspeople watch the first screening of *The Cows of Dolo Ken Paye* in Fokwele in 1972. *(Credit: James Lowell Gibbs, Jr.)*

The complete film opens by introducing the bush town of Fokwele, a Kpelle settlement in Liberia. The people grow mainly rice by the slash-and-burn technique. There is constant tension between the poor farmers who have to fence their fields against cattle and the rich cattle owners. We flash back to a trouble case that occurred during one of Gibbs' earlier periods of fieldwork (illustrated by his old black-and-white still photographs). Dolo Ken Paye was then paramount chief, and some men attacked one of his bulls that had been ruining their gardens. They were tried and fined for the attack. After this background material, we see the short clip, introducing the current trouble case involving a calf from the herd of the late Dolo Ken Paye.

After the short clip ends, the ordeal operator arrives and prepares to work. He builds up an atmosphere of tension as he heats the knife that he will use. He calls one man to represent the community. The man flinches under the hot knife, showing that the culprit was a local person. Then the ordeal operator reveals that, in fact, the guilty man had come to him the previous night and tried to bribe him. The name is revealed, the guilty man confesses publicly, and he is held until the judges decide what restitution he will have to pay.

Setup Questions

1. What do we learn about the structure of the Kpelle chiefdom?
2. How do you think this mix of secular and supernatural works in the Kpelle legal system?
3. What can you tell about Kpelle ideas of self-dignity?
4. Can you spot Gibbs, the American anthropologist, in his Hitchcock-like cameo appearance?
5. Why might the informal palaver be passed over in favor of the hot-knife ordeal? ♦

HOLLYWOOD-STYLE ANTHROPOLOGY

Social Control in *High Noon*

High Noon   1952   black and white   85 minutes

Gary Cooper as Marshall Will Kane
Grace Kelly as Amy Fowler

Hadleyville, a small isolated cow town somewhere in central California perhaps, long ago. Frank Miller, murderous thug, is coming back to revenge himself on the town and especially on Marshall Will Kane, who sent him up. Kane is getting married and plans to leave town with his bride, but when he learns that Miller is on his way, decides that he must stay to protect the town. It is Miller and three of his gang against Kane, alone, since none of the townspeople will help. Kane wins out, throws his badge on the ground in disgust, and rides away.

High Noon is a classic western, about a hero facing his duty. But it is also about social control in a society too small, too weak, to have any effective way to control crime. Although Hadleyville is nominally part of the Territory, which in turn is part of the United States, in fact it gets no support from those higher levels of social control and is on its own.

Setup Questions

1. Compare Hadleyville to a tribe or band in terms of social control, law, and power. What are the similarities; what are the differences?
2. What role does Helen Ramirez play in the social order of Hadleyville?
3. In many westerns, the good guys wear white, and the bad guys wear black. How is color used in *High Noon?*
4. What is the judge's "lesson in civics"? ◆

CHAPTER SUMMARY

- Social organization refers to the ways in which groups are subdivided, whereas political organization is the allocation of power to individuals and groups within a social unit. Social organization is usually an accepted situation, but the allocation of power is usually contested.
- Societies vary tremendously in the amount of power that is vested in leaders. In middle-level societies, leaders with minimal power, who must use their personal influence to effect any action, are called big men. Leaders with real power are called chiefs.
- Bands are small social units with little formal power. Tribes are larger units with big men or even chiefs. Chiefdoms are led by chiefs with considerable power. Nation-states have layered bureaucracies, with much power residing in each layer.
- Societies with minimal power differentials among people are called egalitarian. Maximal power over individuals is called slavery, and colonialism is maximal power over other societies. Those subject to maximal power often develop subtle means of resistance.
- Every society has norms—that is, ideas or schemas of how to act. The most formal, explicit, enforced norms are called laws. Even societies without these formal laws have norms that are enforced by informal means.
- All laws, norms, or the like are subject to transgressions of some sort. Those transgressions, in turn, bring about some degree—however ineffectual—of social reaction to correct the situation.
- Conflict within a society triggers some sorts of conflict resolution activity. Mediation is relatively informal, without resorting to power but rather relying on a negotiating middle person. If it involves something like a judge and courts with real power, it is called adjudication.
- War is violent conflict between two maximal societies. It is carried out by men, involves homicide, and is fought according to some rules. Although all societies seem at least to have known war at some time, there is tremendous variability in the frequency with which societies have gone to war.

- Peace as a permanent state is more than the absence of war. Understanding it is one of the great challenges facing anthropology.

KEY TERMS

adjudication	influence	postulates, cultural
bands	law	power
big men	legal pluralism	power differentials
chiefdoms	mediation	resistance
chiefs	moots	slavery
colonialism	nations	transgressions
conflict resolution	norms	tribe
deviance	peace	war
house palavers	political organization	

QUESTIONS TO THINK ABOUT

- In the Doing Anthropology exercise in Chapter 9, you listed the social units in which you are involved. Now describe the leadership of each: Do they have big (wo)men, chiefs, or another type of leader?
- Resistance is best recognized in the extreme conditions of slavery or colonialism, but it can be a tactic used by subordinates in any situation of power differential. Discuss some examples of resistance in your own experience.
- Where would you look for basic postulates of American law? How are they used?
- Could you come to school wearing socks of obviously different colors? Why or why not?

SUGGESTIONS FOR FURTHER READING

Bellman, Beryl L.
1984   The Language of Secrecy: Symbols and Metaphors in Poro Ritual. New Brunswick, NJ: Rutgers University Press. *An important study of Kpelle before civil war made research difficult.*

Bellman, Beryl L., and Bennetta Jules-Rosette
1977   A Paradigm for Looking: Cross-Cultural Research with Visual Media. Norwood, NJ: Ablex. *An unusual investigation of how people approach visual media.*

Bledsoe, Caroline H.
1980   Women and Marriage in Kpelle Society. Stanford, CA: Stanford University Press. *A rigorous study of Kpelle women's life and work.*

Gay, John
1967   The New Mathematics and an Old Culture: A Study of Learning Among the Kpelle of Liberia. New York: Holt, Rinehart and Winston. *A cognitive study of Kpelle thought and learning.*

Rosen, Lawrence
1989   The Anthropology of Justice: Law as Culture in Islamic Society. Cambridge, U.K.: Cambridge University Press. *An ethnographic study of the actual process of law in a Moroccan court.*

Werbner, Richard (ed.)
1998   Memory and the Postcolony: African Anthropology and the Critique of Power. London: Zed Books. *An important collection contributing to the anthropology of colonialism.*

Wolfe, Alvin W., and Honggang Yang (eds.)
1996   Anthropological Contributions to Conflict Resolution. Athens: University of Georgia Press. *Chapters on how conflict is ended and peace achieved.*

CHAPTER 12

Facing the Supernatural:
Magic and Religion

A Buddha and
flying spirit.
Borobudur,
Java, 9th
century C.E.
*(Credit: Karl
G. Heider)*

HEADLINE ANTHROPOLOGY

Some of the subjects discussed in this chapter have made their way into current news stories. For example:

◆ A consortium of universities in the US and Europe is building an observatory to house the world's largest telescope on what they call Mt. Graham in Arizona, and what the resident Apaches consider their own sacred site.

—The Chronicle of Higher Education, *June 28, 2002.*

◆ Some 250,000 members of the Native American Church, which use peyote cactus in their religious rituals, get their peyote from Miranda City, Texas. Peyote contains mescaline, a powerful hallucinogenic substance, but state and federal law allows its use by Native Americans.

—New York Times, *May 7, 2002.*

◆ In Singapore, four seven-year-old Muslim girls wearing headdresses for religious reasons have been banned from their schools under a law intended to prevent religious polarization.

—New York Times, *March 2, 2002.*

◆ The mayor of the Florida town of Inglis has banned Satan from the town by mayoral proclamation.

—New York Times, *March 14, 2002.*

All cultures have ideas about the **supernatural** and have ways to interact with the supernatural. All cultures talk about supernatural beings: gods, spirits, ghosts, and the like. All cultures are concerned with supernatural power and have patterned **rituals** to help people get through climactic moments, especially at significant moments of the life cycle such as birth, coming of age, marriage, and death.

Once again, we are faced with the prospect of using a few English words such as *God, religion, ghosts,* and *spells* to talk about a bewildering array of ideas and behaviors. Even the word *belief* runs into problems in the cross-cultural perspective. We can ask Americans whether they are Christians or Muslims, whether they believe in God or spiritualism or channeling. The culture offers options. But to say that the Dani believe in ghosts or that the Balinese believe in water spirits is rather like saying that they believe in trees. Ghosts and trees are simply there, part of the world around them.

Even the word *supernatural* comes from medieval Christian theology and has now become dependent on our current scientific understanding of what is "natural." Having said that, we nevertheless use the term to categorize ideas about entities and forces that are not recognized in our scientific "nature." It is by this very culture-specific criterion that we recognize ideas about the supernatural in all cultures.

LOOKING FOR THE ROOTS OF RELIGION

Much of early anthropology was devoted to describing and explaining the many cultural manifestations of religion. If religion is a universal cultural phenomenon, there should be some unifying theory to account for it.

One of the great works of 19th-century European scholarship (although it was published in the early 20th century) was *The Golden Bough,* by James Frazer. It constitutes an extended search through the religions of the world to solve the puzzle of what was said to have taken place in the sacred grove of Nemi, in Italy. Frazer began his work with this memorable description:

> In this sacred grove there grew a certain tree round which at any time of the day, and probably far into the night, a grim figure might be seen to prowl. In his hand he carried a drawn sword, and he kept peering warily about him as if at every instant he expected to be set upon by an enemy. He was a priest and a murderer; and the man for whom he looked was sooner or later to murder him and hold the priesthood in his stead. Such was the rule of the sanctuary. A candidate for the priesthood could only succeed to office by slaying the priest, and having slain him, he retained his office till he was himself slain by a stronger or craftier. (Frazer, 1922:2)

Frazer's goal was not just to understand this account from classical European antiquity in its own terms, but to place it in pan-cultural context, to

> prove that these motives have operated widely, perhaps universally, in human society, producing in varied circumstances a variety of institutions specifically different but generically alike. (Frazer, 1922:3)

It is significant that when Bronislaw Malinowski published his first great study, *Argonauts of the Western Pacific* (1922), he asked Frazer to write the preface. Each, in quite different ways, was looking for general principles that would apply to all human cultures.

Theories of religious activity have tended to emphasize either social or individual themes. Emile Durkheim, the French sociologist, in *The Elementary Forms of Religious Life* (1912), emphasized the collective representations (what we now call *culture*) that people hold about religion and proposed that religious ritual was an acting out of the society itself, a dramatization of the moral community of the group.

Others have interpreted rituals such as initiation ceremonies as ways to alleviate individual anxieties at critical life moments. Certainly, religion in general, and religious rituals in particular, have multiple functions on both the societal and the individual level, as we shall see.

Magic, Science, and Religion

It is useful to distinguish among these three related concepts, even as we acknowledge that they are hopelessly culture-bound terms. Bronislaw Malinowski, in a famous essay proposed the following:

Science is instrumental, which is to say it is the practice of doing things, and it is based on a rational understanding of physical principles. All cultures have these practices based on an empirical knowledge of the world.

Magic is also instrumental but invokes supernatural powers through words or other acts that are thought to automatically coerce the supernatural. Magic, like religion, is based on faith rather than on scientific proof.

Religion, like magic, is based on belief and invokes supernatural powers. Rather than using coercive spells, however, it works through prayers that beseech the supernatural.

These three concepts represent ideal types, and their analytical value lies in pointing to some crucial variables: The difference between natural and supernatural is not recognized by all cultures; the difference between beseeching prayer and coercing spell is not always clear. To illustrate the ambiguous nature of these boundaries, think of the arguments that would be generated in trying to label the following as either magic, or science, or religion:

Astrology (looking up one's horoscope in the daily paper, or having it "read" by a specialist)

Use of a lucky number in making decisions

Turning on a television set (for a person completely ignorant of electronics)

Malinowski's distinction between magic, science, and religion has always rested on the assumption that magic is not rational, or scientific, but uses words in some metaphorical way to make things happen. To make this judgment, in turn, demands that the ethnographer has an understanding of what is going on that is as full or fuller than the people themselves have.

In trying to rethink this problem, Michael F. Brown tells of a song sung by women raising chickens among the Aguaruna of the Amazonian rain forest of northeastern Peru (1997). The song looks like magic: it demands that a particular spirit make the chickens grow. When singing it, the women feed their chickens with the leaves of an aquatic plant called duckweed, which is known for its rapid growth. At first glance, this case seems to be a fine example of contagious magic: the rapid growth of the duckweed is transferred to the chickens. Brown points out, however, that duckweed leaves are particularly nutritious for fowl (hence its English name). So now, as we understand the ethnobotany of the case, this "magic" begins to look more "scientific." In short, Brown suggests that the strict separation of magic from science may often be a mistake. It may result from our own ignorance. Further, he suggests that

we could reserve "magic" as a provisional label for moments of ethnographic breakdown, when our understanding is challenged by that of our interlocutors, a situation demanding deeper exploration of local ideas about how things come to pass in the world. (Brown, 1997:130, 131)

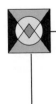

DOING ANTHROPOLOGY

Magic, Science, and Religion

Find examples of each pattern (magic, science, and religion) in your own culture. You may well be able to discover them in the experience of a single person. Do you have any problems distinguishing among the three concepts?   ♦

An Aguaruna woman. *(Credit: Dr. Michael F. Brown)*

The Anxiety Theory of Religion

Bronislaw Malinowski (1925/1948), in his research on the Trobriand Islanders, discovered that these people relied on three sources of information to guide them in their daily activities: religion, magic, and science. He made a useful distinction between the concepts of magic and religion. In religious acts, people beseech or pray to a supernatural power, asking for help, whereas magic uses words or other acts that are thought to automatically coerce the supernatural. In fact, there is not an absolute line dividing these realms. Magic and religion (prayer) are probably used in different circumstances by most people.

Malinowski went further, making one of those seminal observations that lead to real insight. When the Trobrianders fished inside the lagoon, they relied on science, or technology (knowledge and tools), alone. That is, they used their knowledge of the seas, along with their boats and fishing tools. When they sailed beyond the reefs into the open ocean, however, they supplemented their science with various magical spells to protect them from uncertainties. Malinowski's point was that all cultures rely heavily, but not exclusively, on science to accomplish their goals. The Trobrianders are, in fact, expert canoe builders and skilled sailors, reading sky and water to navigate on their voyages. As long as they stay within the lagoon, they are in no danger, for their technology is quite adequate to cope with any eventualities. But the open sea is considerably more unpredictable and dangerous, and once they sail outside the lagoon even the best sailors in the best canoes can be overwhelmed. That is where magic comes in. Presumably, the magic "works" not by actually calming the storms but by reducing the anxiety of the voyagers.

This concept leads to the **anxiety theory of magic:** People will use their scientific technology as far as it will extend and then will resort to magic or religion to reduce anxiety. The theory addresses individual psychology. There are side effects, however, because ineffective ritual, or even doubts that ritual has been properly performed, may actually increase anxiety. Nevertheless, this principle can be observed in many contexts.

George Gmelch, a professor of anthropology who once played professional baseball, described baseball magic in these same terms (1971). Gmelch pointed out that players use magic where their skills leave significant uncertainty. Playing the outfield is a relatively sure thing, and errors are rare. But when the same players come up to bat, even the very best fail most of the time, and much magic is used at the plate. Likewise, pitchers, who often give up several runs in each nine innings, use magic. The magic behavior takes many forms. It may involve wearing special clothing or amulets or performing a sequence of acts that have to be performed before each game. This pattern of magic can be observed in many spheres of ordinary life.

The reliance on religion to cope with anxiety is evident in a saying that is attributed to an American chaplain in the Philippines during World War II: "There are no atheists in foxholes." The meaning is obvious. When men go into combat, they turn to God. War produces an extreme situation of anxiety; indeed, otherwise skeptical soldiers frequently use both religious prayers and magical charms (often a mixture of the two) to relieve anxiety. In Chapter 11, on war, we discussed four general principles of war. A fifth principle of war, which we can add now, is that war involves supernatural beliefs and ritual practices. These beliefs and practices are evident in preparation for battle, in battle, and afterward, especially for any who have actually killed an enemy (Ferguson, 1988:vi).

Sympathetic Magic

The anxiety theory of magic is a functional theory, for it answers a basic question: What does this institution do for people? But at an earlier stage of anthropology, before functionalist questions became popular, anthropologists emphasized the collection and categorization of the cultural customs of the world. Out of this tradition came a recognition of three sorts of magic, which could be formulated in terms of principles, or "laws":

> **The law of contagion.** Objects that had once been in contact remain in some sense always in contact, and a change in one will continue to affect the other. This law appears in a widespread belief that a person is vulnerable to sorcery though discarded hair or nail clippings or even feces.

The law of similarity. A fundamental and real connection exists between similar things or acts, such that doing something to one object will have a similar effect on its likeness.

The law of opposites. The reverse of the law of similarity, this law states that opposite objects or acts have a connection, and that what affects one can affect the other.

These principles are called **sympathetic magic** because, unlike a more general act such as casting a spell on someone or something, they are supposed to work because of a very particular affinity between two things. Nineteenth-century anthropologists recognized the significance of these widespread principles. In 1871, Edward Tylor wrote:

> The principal key to the understanding of Occult Science is to consider it as based on the Association of Ideas, a faculty which lies at the very foundation of human reason, but in no small degree of human unreason also. Man, as yet in a low intellectual condition, having come to associate in thought those things which he found by experience to be connected in fact, proceeded erroneously to invert this action, and to conclude that association in thought must involve similar connections in reality. (Tylor, 1871:115, 116)

For Tylor, then, such ways of thinking characterized lower forms of culture and were evidence of "a low intellectual condition." The racist, evolutionary framework in which Tylor presented his ideas later served in a way to discredit them. Only recently have contemporary psychologists such as Paul Rozin and Carol Nemeroff (1990) reopened this question by looking for basic psychological processes and using American college students as subjects. Thus some 19th-century insights, when reformulated, have made powerful contributions to our modern understandings of sympathetic magic.

Rozin and Nemeroff explain the law of contagion in terms of transfer of essence—that is, an essence that can be moved from one person to another directly, or via an object, through touch, smell, or ingestion. In experiments they conducted at the University of Pennsylvania, subjects were asked about their feelings toward using a hairbrush after it had been used by someone they liked and by someone they disliked. There was some positive effect with the hairbrush used by people they liked, but a much stronger negative effect for hairbrushes used by people they disliked. This idea is called "forward contagion"—you are affected by an object that has been affected by someone else. "Backward contagion" occurs when your hairbrush is used by someone else and you are retrospectively, as it were, affected when the other person affects your hairbrush. A strong minority of people felt both positive and negative effects from this backward contagion. Rozin and Nemeroff posed the Hitler's sweater puzzle to probe the strength of negative forward contagion: Would you be willing to wear a sweater that had been worn by Hitler? What if it were dry cleaned? What if it were unraveled and the yarn rewoven into a new sweater?

According to the law of similarity, things that seem alike have an identity. Rozin and Nemeroff found strong evidence for this law. Their subjects were reluctant to hold a joke shop plastic replica of vomit between their lips, or to eat chocolate fudge molded into the shape of dog feces. Interestingly enough, the idea of contagion seems to increase with the age of subjects, whereas the law of similarity decreases in strength with age, suggesting that contagion is a more sophisticated principle than similarity.

In summary, Rozin and Nemeroff suggest the following:

> The laws of sympathetic magic may well be universal beliefs or laws of thought. The overtness of belief, and the domains in which the laws operate, vary both across cultures and across individuals within culture. We believe that the laws are factors in decision making in U.S. culture. (Rozin and Nemeroff, 1990:229)

SACRED POWER

Sacred power comes in many forms. Some forms are personal spiritual forces that reside in a supernatural being that has special abilities and characteristics. Most of these beings are seldom, if ever, visible to humans. We have many words in English for them: *God, gods, spirits, ghosts, imps, sprites*—a thesaurus lists dozens by specific and generic names. Few native speakers could distinguish among them, much less successfully apply these English words to ideas of other cultures. Evans-Pritchard (1956) translated the Nuer word *kwoth* as *God,* then immediately glossed it as *Spirit.* Then he spent a chapter explaining what the Nuer really mean by kwoth: the Spirit of the Sky, close to humans but different from them, present and distant—in short, a complex theological concept that is only crudely hinted at by using *God* as the translation.

One form of this belief in supernatural beings is **animism,** which is generally associated with tribal cultures. This belief system imbues all of nature, animate and inanimate, with vital spiritual powers. In the Dani world, for example, there are some places such as pools in the forest that are inhabited by vaguely defined spirits. The flat stones that are owned by descent groups and kept in the rear of a men's house have a particular supernatural power. In 19th-century evolutionary thought, animism was considered to be a developmental stage preceding **polytheism** (belief in many gods, having human or animal-like forms and strong personalities) and **monotheism** (belief in one god).

Other types of spiritual forces are more impersonal, existing in the universe but having no personality or locus. This type of force can be concentrated in an individual or an object but is not inherent in the object; it merely resides there. A belief in this type of pervasive force is called **animatism,** and the best example is mana, which will be discussed later.

Soul Matter

Soul matter is a large and reasonably cohesive set of ideas about the vital essence or spiritual power that all or most cultures have in varying degrees. Shelly Errington has written about an Indonesian version of soul matter called *sumange* and says, "The idea that a cosmic energy suffuses and animates the world is an extremely common one in island Southeast Asia" (1989:35).

Many religions that are practiced around the world today believe in some type of human soul. For example, the Malay villagers in the film *Latah* (Chapter 2) call this spiritual force *semangat* and say that the reason more women become latah is that they have weaker semangat than do men.

The Dani speak of *edai egen,* the "seeds of singing," which develop slowly in an infant. By the time the child is about two years old, the edai egen is fully grown and can be seen throbbing below the sternum. (This stage coincides with the age at which a child can walk confidently and talk coherently.) If a person is seriously ill, his or her edai egen is in danger. When Tuesi, the warrior in *Dead Birds,* took the arrow in his chest, his edai egen was affected. It became smaller and retreated toward his backbone. He was warmed by the fire, and curing magic was performed to restore his edai egen.

The Ju/'hoansi call it *n/ um:*

> N/ um is a substance that lies in the pit of the stomach of men and women who are n/ um k"ausi medicine owners and becomes active during a healing dance. The Ju/'hoansi believe that the movements of the dancers heat the n/ um up, and when it boils it rises up the spinal cord and explodes in the brain. The n/ um k"au then feels enormous power and energy coursing through his or her body. The legs are trembling, the chest is heaving, the throat is dry. And strange visions flood the healer's senses. . . .
>
> The n/ um of the healing dance is just one of many forms of n/ um. The word has a wide range of meanings for the Ju/'hoansi. N/ um can mean medicine, energy, power, special skill, or anything out of the ordinary. Menstrual blood, African sorcery, herbal remedies, a vapor trail of a jet plane, tape recorders, and traveling in a truck at high speeds are just a few of the contexts in which the word n/ um is used. (Lee, 1993:115)

In Christianity, this life force is called *the soul.* For example, the new Catechism of the Catholic Church says,

> The Church teaches that every spiritual soul is created immediately by God—it is not "produced" by the parents—and also that it is immortal: it does not perish when it separates from the body at death, and it will be reunited with the body at the final Resurrection. (Catholic Church, 1995:366)

In Hinduism and Buddhism, the soul, after death, comes back reembodied (reincarnated), and its position in the social order depends on the merits accrued in the previous life. So it might come back as a higher-status human or as a lower animal.

Mana and Taboo

Whereas soul matter is a personal power that is associated with an object, **mana** refers to an impersonal supernatural force and is an example of animatism. Mana exists in the universe and can reside in people, animals, plants, and objects. There are many different manifestations of mana. In Melanesia, luck, misfortune, and exceptional personal prowess are all attributable to mana, which can be acquired by anyone through chance or certain actions.

In the more stratified societies of Polynesia (where the term originated), *mana* refers to the derived power of a particularly important or noble person. This power or essence is sometimes considered to be actively dangerous to lower-status people. In old Fiji, some chiefs were so full of mana that they were carried about on litters because if their feet touched the ground, that piece of earth would be forever dangerous to ordinary people.

In Hawaii, ritual cannibalism might be practiced to gain mana:

> In *lua* (hand to hand) combat, a warrior might eat some part of his brave but defeated enemy, so that he might incorporate in himself some of the man's courage. Legend tells that Kamehameha's mother craved and ate the eye of a shark during her pregnancy, thereby taking in and giving to her infant the daring and fierceness of the shark. (Pukui et al., 1972:151)

Taboo is the word that Polynesians use for the dangerousness of mana. We now use taboo widely for whatever is forbidden, but its original meaning was that something was forbidden because it had so much mana or similar supernatural power. In old Hawaii, certain surfing beaches were taboo, reserved only for the high chiefs who had much mana. (Surfing was not invented by 20th-century California teenagers.) The highest royalty had so much dangerous mana that their only safe choice in marriage would be their own sibling, a person with equal mana. (Shakespeare referred to a similar idea when he wrote, "There's such divinity doth hedge a king" in *Hamlet*, IV.5:123.)

The Dani speak of *wusa,* a kind of sacred force that is around anything to do with ritual. The Dani are a relatively egalitarian society, so not surprisingly, there are no high-status people with wusa. But anyone who handles a corpse, for example, must have the wusa removed. The little enclosures where cremated bone fragments are dumped are also said to be wusa, meaning both that they are filled with sacred power and that they are dangerous or forbidden to approach. In this way, wusa is like mana and is strongly taboo.

Recent attempts to amend the U.S. Constitution to prevent the burning of the American flag have used this idea. Although opponents base their concerns on the principles of freedom of expression, those who favor an amendment want to prevent the desecration of the flag. That is, they want to officially establish the sacredness of the flag and make taboo its misuse. A Hawaiian king would understand this feeling well.

To make a broad analogy, mana is like electricity: It is useful if handled properly but dangerous—even fatal—if misused.

Totems

In the summer of 1952, between high school and college, I was a shovel hand on a University of Kansas archaeological dig in South Dakota. We lived on a Dakota reservation, and many of the other diggers were Dakota teenagers. One evening, Bill Voice, a Dakota Indian who owned the land on which we were camped, told the story of how his grandfather had gone on a vision quest to get a totem. He climbed to the crest of a low hill and fasted and meditated. Eventually, a blue racer snake passed by, slithering over his foot. Bill Voice's grandfather followed the snake into a village, where in front of each tepee sat a person with an ailment of some sort. Next to the person was growing a plant that would cure that ailment. He observed it all carefully, and when he returned to his own camp, he used that knowledge to become a famous healer. To indicate his special relationship with the snake, he painted an image of the blue racer on his war shield.

This story involves complex symbolism. The image of the blue racer on the shield represents the man and his new power. The snake also represents his vision, which is also full of symbolism. The snake, then, becomes Voice's grandfather's totem, which represents his special relationship with nature and holds special meaning for him. The whole package of ideas involved in his vision and what it means, we call *totemism,* an Algonquin word meaning *relative* that has become the general term for a vast variety of such mystical relationships between humans and nature. It is one of the most widespread of all religious beliefs.

In the prototypical example of totemism, a descent group such as a clan or sib takes its name from its totem, which is a symbol that represents the common identity of the group members and their special relationship to the totem. This relationship is often explained by a myth about a common ancestry. These myths often tell a story about the founding of the clan. The people who refer to themselves as their totem—bears, wallabies, or whatever—use visual symbols of their totem in their art and are not allowed to kill or eat their totemic creature. This human–nature identification is quite widespread, turning up in many different parts of the world.

The Dani, for example, tell of a time when people and birds lived together. One day there was a disagreement of some sort, and the birds went off to live by themselves. Each sib remained identified with a particular species of bird, however, and even today the people of that sib say that they are related to that kind of bird, which they would never eat or kill. This restriction is not a very significant food prohibition, as birds are, at most, a minor part of any Dani's diet. So, in fact, this totemic relationship is somewhat esoteric and not particularly important or even obvious in everyday Dani life.

Although the word "totem" comes from an Algonquian language of eastern North America, the most generally known use refers to the "totem poles" of the Northwest Coast. These totem poles are made from carved and painted cedar, created to honor a particular person, and depict a series of creatures, animals, humans, or mythological beings one above the other. Each figure represents what Boas called a "crest"—a symbol of a totem of an individual or of a person's kin group (the numaym), of a person's guardian spirit, or in some cases of particularly significant events. The pole summarizes the person's status by showing the crests and events to which the person is entitled, and it serves as a public proclamation of the importance of that person.

Kwakiutl totem pole. *(Credit: Department Library Services, American Museum of Natural History)*

The various groups of Australian Aborigines had the world's most complex totemic systems known. Individuals had totems, various different groups were identified with totems, and even categories such as gender had totems. Any one person could have several different totems, and these totems could be any sort of plant or animal or even other natural phenomena such as clouds or mud. People and their totems were considered to share the same flesh and in some ways the same destiny. The totems served as a constant connection between people and the Dreamtime, an important Aboriginal concept of the time of creation, when the landscape of the world, down to its every stone and stream, was created. Even today, the Dreamtime exists in some form. The Mardu, one group of Western Desert Aborigines, speak of a conception totem, a spirit child from the Dreamtime who becomes a human being (Tonkinson, 1991:80).

We mentioned that among the Aborigines, some totems were related to gender. A. P. Elkin, the great Australian anthropologist, distinguished between social totemism, which is matrilineal and concerned with relationships such as marriage, and cult totemism, which is patrilineal and concerned with religion and relations with the Dreamtime (1938/1964:148). As W. E. H. Stanner pointed out, the fact that Aboriginal religious concepts were so involved with nature is not particularly surprising, for, after all, they were hunters and gatherers. Traditionally, these foraging groups had intimate relationships with nature in terms of the spirits that inhabited all of the natural world. However, it was the identification of humans with a natural counterpart, which was then ritually celebrated, that differed from other animistic beliefs. Thus, when the Aborigines celebrated their totems, they were honoring themselves. The real significance of totemism for them was the way it bound people together into "sacred corporations in perpetuity" (Stanner, 1965:237).

Explanations for Totemism.   There have been many attempts to account for totemism. In the early days, it was explained as the result of "primitive thinking." Peoples with primitive technologies were thought to have primitive minds, so they simply didn't know any better and actually thought that they *were* beavers, hawks, or whatever. We now see this explanation as the result of primitive anthropology, as taking a symbolic metaphorical system literally.

A second line of explanation was that people used these totemism metaphors as a sort of magical means to gain for themselves characteristics of the totem, such as the power of a bear or the swiftness of the eagle. In yet a third line of thinking, Claude Lévi-Strauss developed a symbolic structural approach in which he teased out the sort of thinking that related the different totems of a culture to each other. He insisted on considering all totems of a culture as a system and suggested that this system represented a symbolic way of stating the relationships of humans to each other. He said that groups of humans are related to each other in the social world as totems are related to each other in the natural world.

Just as the natural world is constituted by kinds of things—bears, wolves, and other species—so the human world is divided into groups such as clans, lineages, or territorial groups. The people of the bear clan are to the people of the wolf clan as bears are to wolves. Bears and wolves are clearly not the same, but in some senses they are complementary. Those complementary oppositions may be dramatized in myth. They are used as a metaphoric, symbolic model for the way in which one clan (bear clan) is different from but the complement to another clan (wolf clan). Lévi-Strauss concludes, "Totemism is thus reduced to a particular fashion of formulating a general problem . . . how to make opposition, instead of being an obstacle to integration, serve rather to produce it" (1962/1963:89).

This emphasis on the intellectualizing basis of totemism leads to Lévi-Strauss's famous line, that in totemism, "natural species are chosen not because they are 'good to eat' but because they are 'good to think' " (1962/1963:89).

It may well be that we have lumped many quite different phenomena under the single label of *totemism,* thus making it difficult to explain the various totemisms by a single theory. At best, it is a great family of generally similar ideas linking individuals or groups of people with some particular natural entity. There seem to be no particular sorts of cultures that have totemism. As common as totemism is, among our focus cultures only the Dani seem to have ideas that could be called totemism. Cultures may conceptualize a relationship with a personal supernatural entity in other ways. For example, some Americans have a very vague idea of a guardian spirit. Balinese believe that a child is born with four "sibling spirits" who can both threaten and aid the child as he or she grows (Lansing, 1995:35).

Totemism in the United States.   Ralph Linton described totemism in the 34th, or "Rainbow," Division of the U.S. Army during World War I (1924). The 34th Division was made up of men from many different states and so got the nickname "The Rainbow Division." Linton described how a full-blown totemism emerged around the nickname as the men moved closer to combat in France. Finally, on the front, people reported seeing guardian rainbows before battle (even when, as Linton pointed out, meteorological conditions made that impossible). Linton presented his account as an argument against the "primitive mentality" explanation of totemism. It was not just "those savages" who had totemistic beliefs, it was also American men in uniform. According to Malinowski's anxiety theory of magic, discussed earlier in this chapter, the rainbow belief may have developed as one way to reduce anxiety among these American men who found themselves in dangerous and uncertain circumstances.

Another, less mystical manifestation of totemism in American life today is the so-called **mascots** of schools, their sports teams, and professional sports teams. This pattern began in the late 19th century with some sports teams and some colleges. By the end of the 20th century, it had spread to include not just colleges, but high schools, middle schools, and even grade schools and kindergartens.

Mascots are still primarily a U.S. phenomenon, and no other country takes this practice to such an extreme. If you are in college, it is a safe bet that you cannot help knowing your totem and that you own some representation of it (you may even be wearing it in word or picture). You are aware of the symbolic status of the totem but still are willing to say that you are a Brave, a Lion, or whatever. At the least, you likely have no hesitation in referring to the athletic teams of your school as Braves or Lions. If an anthropologist from Mars tried to find out whether you really knew the difference between humans and lions, you would be amused or annoyed.

Most colleges have elaborate stories (myths) about how their totems came about. The most popular totems at the college level have traditionally been various sorts of Native Americans (Braves, Warriors, Chiefs, and so on), followed by various great cats (Lions, Tigers, Wildcats, and so on). These at least have fairly obvious reference to strength and ferocity, which the athletic teams supposedly display. (In recent years, a few colleges have given up their Indian totems when Native American groups objected to being portrayed as bloodthirsty, tomahawk-wielding savages.)

Among the rare or unique college totems are relatively mild ones such as ducks, birds, and even horse chestnuts (Ohio State Buckeyes). Colleges and high schools often use kinds of humans, which are far from tribal totems. There is some tendency for colleges to use more occupational or historical figures (Cornhuskers, Boilermakers, Sooners, 49ers), whereas high schools tend to use mythical figures (Demons, Dragons). As totem marketing and performances have evolved, schools need images for bumper stickers, and they want some figure to dress up and perform with the cheerleaders. This trend has given rise to the Unmentionable Totems. For example, the University of Alabama totem is officially "The Crimson Tide" and that of Cornell University is "The Big Red," but visually neither is satisfactory. So each has an animal totem that is never spoken but is portrayed on T-shirts, on decals, and at games. (Alabama has an elephant; Cornell has a bear.)

The University of South Carolina gamecock ("Cocky") and the Duke University Blue Devil meet at a football game. *(Credit: University of South Carolina Publications Office)*

Following Lévi-Strauss's theory, one might look for evidence of symbolic relations between the totems of opposing teams, but this evidence is hard to find. Headline writers sometimes play on the totems ("Braves Scalp Dodgers"; "Bears Maul Steelers"). The University of South Carolina Gamecocks lend themselves to ingeniously obscene bumper stickers, especially when playing the archrival Clemson Tigers or the University of Southern California Trojans. But having spent the 20th century getting these totems in place, American schools and colleges can take a lesson from Professor Lévi-Strauss and devote the 21st century to forging logically systemic symbolic structures out of them.

Human Mediators of Sacred Powers

Given the vast and all-encompassing nature of sacred power in many cultures, it is not surprising that human beings are often designated as mediators of this power. In English, we use names such as *magician, sorcerer, witch, spirit medium, medicine man,* and *shaman.* Such people can be women but are more likely men. Usually ordinary human beings, they facilitate communication between humans and the supernatural world. In some cases, they use supernatural power to harm others. This skill is either acquired through study and apprenticeship or considered an inherited trait.

Shamans: Using the Power for Good. In the Balinese film *The Goddess and the Computer,* we met the Agung Gede, who as a child was discovered to have special powers and became the major priest in the central Hindu temple on Bali. There are also a large number of Balinese called *balian,* who are spirit mediums and healers. Timothy Asch, Patsy Asch, and Linda Connor made four films about a balian called Jero Tapakan. In one film in the series (*A Balinese Trance Séance*), a bereaved family comes to Jero to ask her to communicate with their son, who has died, to find out what happened to him. Jero goes into a trance and, speaking in different voices, tells the family of the errors that they made in his funeral and how to correct them (Connor et al., 1986).

While the Dani believe that some people are better at communicating with and controlling supernatural power than others, they are not completely sure about who these people are. If one curing ceremony does not work, they have no hesitation about asking someone else who claims to be a healer to give it a try.

The word **shaman** comes from the Tungus people of Siberia and was used in many early ethnographies. It refers to a particular kind of healer who goes into an ecstatic trance state, communicates with spirit helpers, and can even have out-of-body experiences. Over the last century, generally similar practices were identified in many cultures throughout the world and were labeled with this Tungus word.

As a methodological note, one can easily imagine the problems that this free and easy use of the Tungus word has created. Calling so many sorts of healers by the same term creates the supposition that they are the same and related to each other. In fact, what might properly be the end result of cross-cultural analysis has become the opening assumption. Many attempts to define shamanism globally have been made. Joan B. Townsend boils it down by saying, "The entire raison d'être of shamanism is to interact with the spirits for the benefit of those in the material world" (1997:431–432). She suggests the following basic criteria of shamanism: Shamans have direct control over spirits, communicating with them in ecstatic trance (some altered state of consciousness), working to heal their clients' physical, psychological, or emotional illnesses. Shamans can often send their souls on magical flights and can call spirits to a séance where they speak for them.

Since the early days of anthropological writings on religion, people have suggested that shamans represented the first form of religion. This idea was based on the fact that shamans often were found in small-scale band or tribal societies. For example, A. F. C. Wallace proposed a fourfold typology of religions:

> At the most primitive level, *shamanic* religions, containing only shamanic and individualistic cult institutions; *communal* religions, containing communal, shamanic, and individualistic cult institutions; *Olympian* religions, containing an Olympian variety of ecclesiastical institutions, along with the other three; and *monotheistic* religions, with a monotheistic ecclesiastical cult institution, together with communal, shamanic, and individualistic cult institutions. (Wallace, 1966:88, 89)

In support of this idea of shamanism being especially primitive, some Palaeolithic cave paintings in Europe have been read as depicting shamans: human figures with animal masks or heads. Another early line of thought viewed shamans as mentally deranged individuals who had found refuge and a socially acceptable role where their flights of madness or seizures would be seen as communication with or possession by supernatural powers. This view led to the formulation that the scorned schizophrenic in one culture is the celebrated shaman of another.

More recently, these shamanistic ecstasies or trances have been studied not as signs of mental illness but as deliberately achieved altered states of consciousness (Atkinson, 1992). This line of reasoning was particularly stimulated by the drug culture that has burgeoned in North America and Europe since the 1960s. It began as recreational exploration—the "turn on, tune in, drop out" of Timothy Leary—and led many, including anthropologists, to examine seriously the ways that other cultures achieve and then use altered states of consciousness. Not surprisingly, these researchers studied the various kinds of practitioners around the world who represented long traditions of healers. Also not surprisingly, the cultural anthropologists situated in traditional academic institutions have felt great ambivalence about getting too close to personal ecstatic states of shamans.

FOCUS CULTURE

Shamanism on the North Coast of Peru

OVERVIEW

Location: North coast of Peru
Culture: Mestizo (Spanish and local)
Language: Spanish
Religion: Roman Catholic, much influenced by local folk practices
Economy: Cotton, sugar, and fishing

The eastern half of Peru is low Amazon basin rain forest, the western half consists of the high Andes with snow-capped peaks exceeding 20,000 feet in altitude. But in the far west, along the Pacific Coast, runs a narrow coastal strip containing cities, a few rivers, and some of the driest deserts in the world. If the land is inhospitable and unproductive, the sea is not. Indeed, fishing is a major subsistence and commercial activity. Much of the Peruvian population lives in this region. The northernmost part of this coastal strip, around the cities of Trujillo and Chiclayo, just south of the Ecuador border, is famous for its shamans, or *curanderos*.

In southern Peru, in the high country, are the descendents of the Incas, still speaking

Quechua. Even further south, reaching into Boliva, are Aymara speakers. In northern Peru, the people speak Spanish, are Roman Catholic, and are called *mestizos* (mixed Spanish and Indian background). Many of the people of the North Coast are recent arrivals from the Andean region who have come to the cities looking for work.

The past is literally close to the surface in Peru, for the arid conditions have preserved architecture and burials from prehistoric cultures like Moche and Chavin. Not only do these sites provide materials for scientific analysis and museums, but their prehistoric objects are also incorporated into modern shamanic rituals. Near Trujillo lie the remains of the city of Chan Chan, built of adobe centuries ago, but still dissolving into the desert at a very slow pace.

The tradition of the curanderos has its roots both in the Christianity of the Near East and in the prehistoric traditions of the entire Andean region itself. Although no written records exist from the times before the Spanish invasion, these cultures produced some of the world's greatest ceramics. Their clay vessels, molded and painted, are almost ethnographic in themselves, for they depict, in realistic form, individual people, dress, and ritual. Much of the ritual is undecipherable, but there certainly appear to be images of shamans. In fact, the major hallucinogen of modern shamans—the San Pedro cactus—is represented in these prehistoric pots.

Curanderos appear in the early colonial records as the Spanish tried, without success, to suppress practices like shamanism. In recent years, many anthropological, medical, psychiatric, and ethnobotanical studies of curanderos have been published in both English and Spanish. One of the most extensive projects has been carried out by Douglas Sharon and his colleagues from the University of California at Los Angeles (UCLA). Sharon first worked with Eduardo Calderón, a particularly thoughtful and charismatic shaman, about whom Sharon and Richard Cowan made the film *Eduardo the Healer.* In the 1980s, Sharon, Donald Joralemon, and others extended their studies to other curanderos, so we now have detailed and comparative information about the shamans, their belief systems, their rituals, and their patients. Although women of the region are often known as herbalist curers, few, if any, women apparently deal with magic as shamans.

Doing participant observation ethnography of shamans demands much more intensive participation than most other ethnographic research. Sharon interviewed Calderón at length, observed curing rituals, and then became his apprentice. As such, he actively assisted in all-night curing sessions, working with the objects used in curing, ingesting the San Pedro cactus, and inhaling the tobacco juice that is a part of the rituals.

Curanderos use their magic for good, to cure people. The main affliction is called by the general term *dano,* meaning a misfortune or illness sent by a *brujo,* a witch or sorcerer. The line between curandero and brujo is sometimes quite fuzzy. In fact, at least one of the 12 curanderos described in the Joralemon and Sharon book claims that he has made a pact with the devil, but denies that he is actually a brujo (1993:36–47). It seems likely that these widespread beliefs in dano caused by brujos and countered by curanderos is caused by, or at least sustained by, the desperate economic conditions of northern Peru over the centuries. (As the anxiety theory of magic suggests, when human skill is inadequate to overcome the circumstances, people often resort to magic.) In earlier times, the Spanish colonial rule was mainly concerned with extracting labor from the people on plantations and later in mines. Independence was gained in the 1820s, but led to few changes in the rate of peasant exploitation by the central government. In recent years, culminating in the 1980s, when much of the research in shamanism was taking place, inflation in Peru grew at astonishing rates. It is easy to understand how fear of witches and recourse to shamans would be maintained under such desperate conditions where the wealth or good fortune of a few would create great envy among the rest (Sharon, 1978:23–29; Joralemon and Sharon, 1993:10–12).

The major rituals of the curanderos occur during all-night curing sessions (Eduardo performs one in the film). In this session, the curandero uses hallucinogens to achieve a state in which he can communicate with the spirits, and the objects spread out on his mesa facilitate the communication. The entire performance is aimed at removing the dano, the witchcraft, and restoring balance to the victim.

The prime hallucinogen is prepared from a tall, spineless cactus called San Pedro, which is gathered in special ritual ways in the mountains. As noted earlier, San Pedro is shown on pre-Columbian vessels, leaving little doubt that these images depict shamanism very like that practiced today. The *mesa* (Spanish for "table") is the hallmark of all North Coast shamans. Each has his own, albeit with somewhat different objects. Joralemon and Sharon discuss and present photographs of the mesas of the twelve curanderos they studied.

Despite variations, there is a basic pattern for the mesa. It is a piece of cloth about two feet by four feet, placed on the ground. Various objects of magical and symbolic significance are laid out on the mesa or stuck in the ground beside it. The cloth contains two and sometimes three zones. The zone on the left is the Campo Ganadero, "the Field of the Sly Dealer"—that is, Satan. The objects placed on this field have to do with evil. Some collections include ancient items like potsherds and stones from archaeological sites. On the right side of the cloth is the Campo Justiciero, "The Field of the Divine Judge" or "Divine Justice." The objects on this zone include Catholic objects like images of saints and a crucifix. A small zone down the center of the cloth is the Campo Medio, or "Middle Field," dominated by an image of Saint Cyprian.

According to Sharon, the entire mesa represents the opposition of Good (represented by Christ, on the right) and Evil (dominated by Satan on the left), with the mediating middle governed by the transitional figure St. Cyprian, who was supposed to have been a sorcerer until he become a Christian (1978:62ff). The curandero draws on the powers of the right field to combat evil (the dona), while a brujo would use the objects of the left side to cast his spells. Clearly, although the various curanderos have slightly different arrays of objects and interpretations of their meanings, and may even differ in the depths of their understandings, there is a common cultural schema about misfortune, its causes, and its cures that is held by herbalists, curanderos, and brujos as well as by their clients. ♦

Witchcraft: Using the Power for Evil. Sorcerers and witches are common in many cultures and are distinguished from healers and other mediums in that they are forces of evil. A **sorcerer** is generally a person who learns magic rituals and uses them to inflict harm. **Witches,** in contrast, are believed to have psychic powers that are used for harmful purposes. In many cultures where witchcraft is prevalent, witches don't actually exist. They are witches only because of evil actions that are attributed to them. This label may be imposed on someone whose actions are suspect for some reason or who is the object of disapproval in the community. In fact, part of the ritual in many societies is trying to identify witches, who can take many forms. Witchcraft is often used to explain misfortune and bad luck.

Although there are no actual witches, accusations of witchcraft against people are known in many cultures, and witches are often featured in the oral literature and drama. Witches have long played a role in the European imagination in folktales (*Snow White*), Shakespeare (*Macbeth*), and popular fiction (*The Wizard of Oz*). Witchcraft accusations were common in Europe in the 18th century, and of course in Salem, Massachusetts, in the 17th century, depicted in *The Crucible.*

The Balinese worry about witchcraft, protect infants from possible attacks of witches, and even file their incisors and canine teeth down so that they will not look like animals or witches (Lansing, 1995:37). The terrifying witch Rangda appears in the famous Balinese temple dance (shown memorably in Gregory Bateson and Margaret Mead's film from the 1930s, *Trance and Dance in Bali*). People go to balians, spirit mediums, to learn who has been bewitching them or their families.

Strangers or enemies, people "over there," are often thought to be witches. The Ju/'hoansi think that their African neighbors are witches (Lee, 1993:109). The Dani talk about women who sprinkle a white powder on a cooked sweet potato before offering it to you to eat. The result is fatal. When I walked to other areas, I was often warned about "those people." Also, when I probed about the cause of a person's death, we would eventually get to a witch who did it. These people were always women, and they were always people from other regions (even if they lived locally).

How do we account for this widespread idea that there are certain people out there who are manipulating supernatural powers to hurt other people (an idea that is surely not true)?

Clyde Kluckhohn, in his classic study of Navajo witchcraft (1944), showed that Navajo who were accused of witchcraft were usually very rich men living far away. Great personal wealth is a threat to the Navajo notion of equality: People should be sharing, not accumulating. So the witchcraft accusations function as leveling devices, as instruments of social control threatening anyone who goes far beyond the cultural norms. One thinks of the Ju/'hoansi woman N!ai, in the film *N!ai,* from Chapter 10, on gender and sexuality, who had not shared her wealth with the others, so they used gossip to attack her. In that case, the gossip was about sex. Presumably, they would have called her a witch if that weapon had been available to their culture.

In 20th-century U.S. politics, the phrase "witch hunt" has been applied to the investigations and trials of the 1940s and 1950s, when Senator Joseph McCarthy and others accused many prominent Americans, including Hollywood producers, directors, actors, and screenwriters, of being Communists or "Communist sympathizers." Some were, and some were not, but the use and threat of accusations were powerful weapons of social control against those who might be inclined to question the Cold War orthodoxy.

A second function of witchcraft belief is to explain the inexplicable. Evans-Pritchard (1965), writing about Azande witchcraft, gave a mundane example. Why should that particular granary collapse on you just at the moment when you were sitting in its shade? One satisfactory answer is witchcraft. Someone has used supernatural powers to harm you. Even if the obvious physical cause is that the granary's legs were weakened by termites, you question the timing. Why did it collapse just then, while you were there? Witchcraft is a convenient answer. The next step is to figure out whom to accuse of this witchcraft and what you will do about it.

New Age Witches.   While the standard ethnographic literature from many cultures includes imaginary accounts of people who are said to use magic to harm other people and are labeled "witches," there is quite another tradition of actual people who call themselves witches. An American anthropologist, T. M. Luhrmann, spent 14 months doing fieldwork in England on "ritual magic in contemporary England" (the subtitle of her 1989 book). Even though Luhrmann was very open about her research motive, the witches, magicians, kabbalists, and other she encountered were hospitable and forthcoming, and she was initiated into several different sorts of covens and similar groups.

A bewildering array of such occult practitioners, known as **New Age Witches,** exists. While they tend to avoid publicity because of the general public's scorn and ridicule, they have many bookstores, periodicals, and open meetings and fairs. They are definitely not what we could call the witches of the imagination, those cultural schemas of malevolent practitioners common in many societies, including colonial Massachusetts. These modern-day witches are real and do not use their magic to harm. Luhrmann states flatly that "I never encountered anything remotely resembling Satanism," although

> there were rumors of a Satanic cult in California and occasional stories of a cat sacrificed in Highgate cemetery. Indeed magicians seem very concerned about morality. They talk about black magic; they usually tell you that there are black magicians elsewhere and stress that they, by contrast, are very white.
> (Luhrmann, 1989:81)

These English witches and magicians are remarkable for their educated, middle-class normality and for the literary basis of their craft. Although this form of occultism seems to have developed in England only in the 20th century, it avidly searches for directions in older traditions: Egyptian, Nordic, Jewish, and such. Its immediate roots are in 19th-century spiritualism and psychical research.

The New Age witches raise some very different questions than do practitioners of tribal magic. It is sometimes argued that because magic is not scientific, it involves a primitive way of thinking characteristic of those tribal Others. These English magicians, however, are well educated in the Western scientific mode and become occultists only later, as adults. Luhrmann was particularly interested in the

Wikkans, New Age "Witches" in the United States.
(Credit: © Kirk Condyles)

"mercurial complexity of belief." She asked, "Why do people find magic persuasive?" In particular, why do these educated Englishmen and women believe in magic? She found that an important factor was the excitement of learning the secrets of an ordered world, where essential connections between words and acts (remember sympathetic magic) could be manipulated by knowledgeable magicians. Although in their workaday lives, many were scientists of one sort of another, as magicians they were really not interested in that sort of testable truth.

Augury

A much more mundane approach to the use of sacred power by humans is the practice of **augury.** Anyone can practice augury because it involves the examination of common objects or the performance of simple procedures to find answers to basic questions about the past ("Who was the murderer?"), the present ("What is the illness?"), or the future ("In which direction shall we hunt?"). Reading tea leaves, dealing Tarot cards, and using a Ouija board are all examples of the use of augury.

Humans have used augury for millennia. The earliest forms of Chinese writing, from about 4000 B.C., are found on tortoise shells and deer scapulae. Questions were scratched on the shells or bones, which were dropped in the fire, and the heat cracks were then read as the answers. People all over the world have used a variety of sorts of auguries: bones, intestines of animals or birds, poisons, and even dreams (Abbink, 1993; Hoskins, 1993:n8).

Case Study: Scapulamancy in Labrador. Anthropologists and others have long described auguries as part of the religious complex, but in 1957 O. K. Moore suggested how they might function in the ecological system. His example was taken from the Naskapi Indians of Labrador, who based their hunting strategy on the results of **scapulamancy** (holding caribou shoulderblade bones over hot coals and "reading" the cracks and burnt spots). When they were uncertain where to find game, they performed this augury. What is interesting here is that scapulamancy was a last resort, used when their hunting knowledge couldn't help them. Moore points out that humans tend to behave in patterned ways, and presumably even caribou could figure out the hunters' habits and take evasive action. Scapulamancy helps the hunters to outwit their prey by rendering their behavior unpredictable: "It is in essence a very crude way of randomizing human behavior under conditions where avoiding fixed patterns of activity may be an advantage" (Moore, 1957:73).

Case Study: Birdwatching in Borneo. Michael Dove used the same logic to show the ecological role of augury for the Kantu', a horticultural people of West Kalimantan (Indonesian Borneo). The Kantu' read the flights and songs of seven kinds of

The Kantu' augury called "taking omens from the kempang stick," like their bird auguries, foretells events relevant to their swidden horticulture. *(Credit: Dr. Michael Dove)*

forest birds to determine where to plant their gardens. Dove said that because so many variables influence the success of the gardens, it is in the interests of the Kantu' households and villages to randomly diversify their planting. The augury results are arbitrary, based on very complex rules for reading the birds' behavior. Like the Naskapi scapulamancy, the Kantu' augury established true randomization, giving them the best chance of success: "The augural system, through both instrumental and symbolic means, helps to randomize swidden behavior and minimizes a tendency towards systematization" (Dove, 1993:145).

(How about football, Coach? The outrageous suggestion has been made that a football team that used a true random procedure to call its plays would have great success over its logical but befuddled opponents!)

RITUALS

Rites of Passage

In 1908, the Belgian anthropologist Arnold van Gennep introduced the phrase **rites of passage** to describe the formal similarities in the rituals that move a person from one status to another (1908/1960). Many examples of these rituals abound. There are transitions that everyone makes in the course of the life cycle, as well as more individually achieved ones.

The prototypical rite of passage is the boys' initiation, the ceremony that marks the transition from boyhood to manhood. On the basis of reports of Australian Aborigines, van Gennep outlined a series of steps that boys go through in this passage into adulthood. It begins with a rite of separation, in which the boys are removed from the group. They then go through a ritual period of transition (a **liminal period**), which often lasts four days and in which various ritual reversals of ordinary life take place. The late Victor Turner (1964/1967) spoke of this liminal period as "Betwixt and Between" to describe the symbolic ambiguity of the social positions of the boys during this period. They are neither boys nor men, but somewhere in between. The rite of passage concludes with a ritual of reincorporation when the initiates are welcomed back into the community in their new capacity as adults, with new roles and responsibilities. Van Gennep pointed out that this process may be further complicated in some instances when entering and exiting the liminal period entails a three-part maneuver in which the features of the entire rite are replicated (see Figure 12.1).

Although not every boys' initiation follows exactly the same steps, the power of van Gennep's generalized structure is evident in its applicability to many different cultures. When I followed the Dani boys' initiation, I was astonished; it was almost as if they had read van Gennep's book. The boys were removed to a specially built compound called *the Sacred Place* (*wusama*), where they were purged of impurities. They stayed for four days, eating strange foods and doing strange things such as taking baths every morning in the cold dew. Their return to normal life, the reincorporation, was preceded by a special feast of ancient foods, things that had been hunted and gathered in times before the Dani grew sweet potatoes.

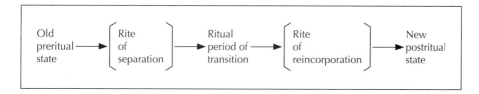

FIGURE 12.1 Rites of passage (after Arnold van Gennep and Victor Turner).

The Nuer boys' initiation ceremony, called *gar,* which we saw in the film *The Nuer,* has many similarities. First (in the rite of separation) the boys are stripped, their iron bracelets are cut off, and their hair (even eyebrows) is shaved. Their foreheads are cut, and they waddle upside down on all fours into the seclusion hut, where they are fed special foods. Evans-Pritchard described the entry and exit:

> On the day of the cutting, and on the day of the passing out of seclusion, sacrifices are made and there is festivity, which includes licentious horseplay and the singing of lewd songs. (Evans-Pritchard, 1940:250)

In the initiation ceremony for Dani boys, the initiates literally pass through arches as they move from boyhood to manhood. *(Credit: Karl G. Heider)*

Not every culture has a clearly defined passage from childhood to adulthood. On the one hand, for both the Ju/'hoansi and the Yanomamo, the rite of passage appears to be less clearly defined, perhaps subsumed into the wedding ceremony. The Balinese, on the other hand, have several important rites of passage for both boys and girls marking different stages of maturity: A three-month ceremony, a 210-day ceremony, a puberty rite, and a tooth-filing ceremony all precede marriage.

For most Americans, there are no real coming-of-age ceremonies, although the Jewish bar/bat mitzvah and both Jewish and Muslim boys' circumcision ceremonies and some Christian confirmation services come close. There has been a great proliferation of other, purely secular, rites of passage. Schools (even kindergarten) celebrate passage to the next level with graduation ceremonies. Voluntary clubs of all sorts hold initiation ceremonies, and debutante dances announce the eligibility for marriage of young women. When the activities of the liminal period get too extreme, they are called *hazing* and often are made illegal (college fraternities make the newspapers this way). But Arnold van Gennep would find that contemporary American rites of passage often fall into quite familiar patterns, with the period of transition marked by strange behavior.

In the bar mitzvah ceremony, the Jewish boy reads from the Torah and demonstrates that he has an adult understanding of his religion. *(Credit: James Gibson)*

Rites of Intensification

At first glance, a funeral seems like a prime example of a rite of passage. What more significant passage could there be than from life to death? If we look at the functions of a funeral, at what it does, however, we see that it is aimed at the survivors. An initiation ceremony, as a rite of passage, is a drama of transformation that the initiate experiences in a deeply personal way. At a funeral, the audience has the experience. This sort of ritual has been termed a **rite of intensification** (Chapple and Coon, 1942) to emphasize the way in which the ceremony can function to dramatize and reaffirm the social network itself. A funeral takes place when the social fabric has been rent by the death of a member, and one of its functions is to mend the gap by bringing people together again. Funerals are often marked by the exchange of gifts, a continuation of the gift exchange cycle that began at the deceased person's earlier rites of passage. A second common element in funerals is commensuality, the ritualized eating together that, like gift giving, reaffirms social ties.

Dani funerals, for example, have three stages, each one bringing together a larger group of people. At the time of a death, the exchanges and feasting during the cremation involve close kin and neighbors. A few years later, the entire confederation holds a memorial feast for the dozen or two people who have died since the last such event. And every five years or so, all funerals of the entire alliance are finally concluded in a single great ceremony.

In Bali, one finds a similar escalating of the social groups involved. Often, in villages, people are simply buried at the time of death. Then, perhaps several years later, the villagers combine their resources to stage a large dramatic cremation for several deceased people. The remains are dug up, placed in carved wooden animal-figure caskets, and cremated. In a huge procession, the ashes are taken to the south coast to be thrown into the ocean.

Other examples of rights of intensification are routine weekly church, synagogue, or mosque services. Of course, it should be noted that many ceremonies combine the functions of passage and integration if they bring numbers of people together to celebrate an individual's passage.

WORLD RELIGIONS AND LOCAL PRACTICES

In recent years, anthropology has increasingly looked beyond the village or the tribal boundaries to see how a local group is related to wider cultural systems. In the study of religions, however, the investigation of world religions as they are practiced in different parts of the world has been slow to develop. John Bowen, who himself has written important analyses of Islam in northern Sumatra, Indonesia (1991, 1993a), has thought about this problem (1993b). In part, Bowen says, it is because of the very fact that they are world religions, with written sources and standardized rituals that transcend local boundaries. Bowen points out that anthropologists have often relied on Robert Redfield's (1956) distinction between the "Great Tradition," the official version of Christianity or Hinduism or Buddhism as located in scripture and theological commentary, and the "Little Tradition," the purely local practices that can be observed in village or tribe. But the distinction between Great and Little Traditions is not firm, for local people often are very knowledgeable about the scriptures and theologies of the Great Tradition.

By **world religions,** we usually refer to those religions that have the most adherents, have most successfully crossed cultural boundaries, and have had the greatest effects on history. They are—in order of size—Christianity, Islam, Hinduism, Buddhism, and Judaism. This list is somewhat Eurocentric, and one might want to expand it to include Sikhs and Confucianism. Nevertheless, each of the first five religions has spread far beyond its culture of origin by means of migration and conversion.

In comparing the local forms of world religions, we notice **syncretism,** the incorporation into a cultural complex of borrowed elements. As the world religions spread and encountered local religions, they often simply absorbed some of the local features. Thus, as Hinduism spread across India and into Southeast Asia, it took on many different local colorings. So the great Hindu texts such as the Mahabharata or the Ramayana are known throughout the Hindu world, but actual practices and beliefs in North India differ from those in South India, and even more from those on Bali. Much the same is true for Islam (and its Koran) in the Middle East, Africa, China, Java, and Kansas: Everywhere the same Koran is recited in Arabic, but local language and local culture make for local differences. Of course, the basic principle of syncretism, that cultures tend to absorb from other cultures, is valid for much more than the sphere of religion.

As religions spread, all the dynamics of culture change that we shall discuss in Chapter 13 come into play. Christians in Ireland, or Hindus in central Java, long cut off from their religious centers, developed their own versions of their religions. As these world religions moved into territories, they often met and absorbed elements of local religions.

Syncretism can be a controversial concept (see especially Stewart and Shaw, 1994; Gellner, 1997). The term implies that somewhere "pure" religions or cultures exist, when in fact it seems more accurate to say that all religions are to some degree syncretic. Syncretism is also at times the center of debate within religions, when reformists attack others as having "lost the faith," having succumbed to syncretism. Conversely, local groups may proudly claim that they have adapted their religion to local customs (see the photograph of a Dani Jesus on page 395). Most of our focus cultures show some sort of syncretism.

SEEING ANTHROPOLOGY

Eduardo the Healer

Written and produced by Douglas G. Sharon and Richard Cowan
Archaeological consultant: Christopher B. Donnan
Ethnographic consultant: Faye K. Sharon
Cinematographer: Robert Primes

Eduardo the Healer is both the story of how Eduardo Calderón became a shamanistic healer, or curandero, and an account of a curing session that Eduardo performed for a client, Asmat. The film is based closely on the ethnographic research of Douglas Sharon, who has writing and production credits.

The short clip opens as Eduardo the curandero is sitting at a table slicing up the San Pedro cactus, preparing for a final curing session with his patient, Luciano Asmat. The film does not go into detail about Asmat's problem but we know from elsewhere (Calderón et al., 1982:9) that he had become too successful too fast and was the subject of "gossip, ostracism, and witchcraft" aimed at him by his resentful neighbors. (This circumstance is not unlike the Navajo pattern of witchcraft belief discussed earlier in this chapter.) Eduardo recounts his life story to his assistants (and the camera), how he attended a Catholic seminary and a fine arts school, worked as a bricklayer, discovered fishing, restored part of the prehistoric site of Chan Chan, and then finally found his true calling as curandero and maker of (fake) prehistoric vessels. He explains how he has studied the prehistoric Moche pottery "like a book" to learn how the Ancients cured people. We see several Moche pots with images of women curanderas holding the sacred San Pedro cactus, together with realistic depictions of people with various maladies.

Eduardo Calderón, the curandero, or spirit medium healer, of northern Peru, with his sacred mesa, the collection of objects that he uses in his ceremonies. *(Credit: Dr. Douglas Sharon/ San Diego Museum of Man)*

The complete film begins with Eduardo in his workshop making replicas of pre-historic Moche pots, pressing clay into molds. At breakfast with his family, he discusses curing. A woman drops by requesting a guinea pig divination to diagnose the cause of her illness. Saying Christian prayers, Eduardo rubs the guinea pig over her body, then kills it and examines the entrails. He proclaims that at least it is not witchcraft. We go with Eduardo into the market (in Trujillo?), where he buys the San Pedro cactus for the evening's ritual from a woman. They reminisce about how she had cured him when he was 17, but now "he is my master." In his house, we see an eclectic display of books—Gandhi, Jung, Dostoyevski, Edgar Allan Poe, Baudelaire, and books on Peruvian archaeology.

The ceremony for Asmat—in the short clip—begins. When it is finished, Eduardo and Asmat agree that it worked—he is getting better, "more tranquil. I'm moving ahead now."

Setup Questions

1. Can you see examples of syncretism—Christian and ancient Peruvian?
2. What is the role of the San Pedro cactus in this ceremony?
3. What do the prehistoric Moche ceramics show?   ♦

HOLLYWOOD-STYLE ANTHROPOLOGY

Witchcraft in Massachusetts: *The Crucible*

The Crucible   1996   123 minutes

Daniel Day-Lewis as John Proctor
Winona Ryder as Abigail
Paul Schofield as Judge Danforth
Joan Allen as Elizabeth Proctor

The village of Salem, Massachusetts Bay Colony, 1690s: The overheated religious atmosphere led some girls to make accusations of witchcraft against their neighbors in order to escape punishment for their own misdeeds. The elders of the colony enthusiastically encouraged the witch hunt. Finally, after 19 adults were executed as witches, the fervor died out.

Arthur Miller's play opened in 1953 as a comment on the anti-Communist "witch hunt" of 1950s America. This film, with screenplay by Miller, is the first American film version. It follows the basic facts of Salem closely.

Setup Questions

1. Are there witches in Salem?
2. Why do so many people join in?
3. Who is accused, and why?

4. What are the various functions of these witchcraft accusations?
5. What is Abigail's defense of herself?
6. What is the contribution of Tabitha, the West Indian woman?   ◆

CHAPTER SUMMARY

- Magic and religion are ways of dealing with the supernatural. This statement is unavoidably ethnocentric, for what is supernatural to one culture may be prosaically natural to another.
- Malinowski's distinction between magic (spells to coerce the supernatural), religion (ways to implore the supernatural), and science (practical ways to effect changes in the natural world) remains much used.
- Malinowski's anxiety theory of magic and religion often works: Where a person's (or a culture's) scientific technology is inadequate to avert danger or failure, people often revert to magic or religion.
- Sympathetic magic relies on ideas that things are connected in certain (nonempirical) ways.
- The law of contagion assumes an identity between things once in contact.
- The law of similarity assumes an identity between similar things.
- The law of opposites assumes an identity between opposites.
- If one does something to or something happens to one member of an identity pair, the other members will be similarly affected.
- Many sorts of sacred powers exist, often taking the form of a soul matter lodged in an individual. Mana is power that can reside in objects as well as humans. When the power is especially strong, it is taboo, or dangerous to the uninitiated.
- Totemism is a general term for various significant associations between humans (groups or individuals) and individuals or species of the natural world. It is commonly a property of unilineal descent groups like clans as well as American schools and colleges.
- Most societies have specialists that have the ability or power to mediate between humans and the supernatural world. Shamans use their powers for good. Sorcerers (which actually exist) and witches (which do not exist but are believed in) use their powers to do harm. (New Age witches do not try to harm others.)
- Rites of passage are rituals celebrating the movement of a person from one status to another (for example, initiation ceremonies); rites of intensification reaffirm the bonds holding a community together (often, as at funerals or after some other loss).

KEY TERMS

animatism	law of contagion	magic
animism	law of opposites	mana
anxiety theory of magic	law of similarity	mascots
augury	liminal period	monotheism

polytheism   science   syncretism
religion   shaman   taboo
rite of intensification   sorcerer   witch
rite of passage   soul matter   Witch, New Age
ritual   supernatural   world religion
scapulamancy   sympathetic magic

QUESTIONS TO THINK ABOUT

- Can you find behavior that supports Malinowski's anxiety theory of magic and religion?
- Would you wear Hitler's sweater?
- Explain Christian and Buddhist relics.
- Do the meanings of "taboo" today have any relation to the original Polynesian meanings?
- Your school most likely has a totem (or "mascot"). How do people think about it? (As merely a joke? Strongly identify with it? Revere it?)
- How closely do the rites of passage that you have been through fit van Gennep's formula?

SUGGESTIONS FOR FURTHER READING

Bowen, John R.
1993   Muslims Through Discourse: Religion and Ritual in Gayo Society. Princeton, NJ: Princeton University Press. *An ethnography of debate over religion carried out by people in highland Sumatra.*
1998   Religions in Practice: An Approach to the Anthropology of Religion. Boston: Allyn and Bacon. *An excellent introduction to the entire subject.*

Bowen, John R. (ed.)
1998   Religion in Culture and Society. Boston: Allyn and Bacon. *A collection of papers.*

Calderón, Eduardo, Richard Cowan, Douglas Sharon, and F. Kaye Sharon
1982   Eduardo el Curandero: The Words of a Peruvian Healer. Richmond, CA: North Atlantic Books. *Verbatim transcript of the tapes the team made of Eduardo, following the film,* Eduardo the Healer.

Spence, Jonathan D.
1996   God's Chinese Son: The Taiping Heavenly Kingdom of Hong Xiuquan. New York: W. W. Norton. *In one of the largest millennial movements ever, between 1845 and 1864 some 20 million Chinese were killed in an attempt to establish a Christian-inspired religion in China.*

White, O. Kendall, and Daryl White (eds.)
1994   Religion in the Contemporary South: Diversity, Community, and Identity. Athens: University of Georgia Press. *A Southern Anthropological Society collection of papers on the wide range of religious activity in the U.S. South.*

CHAPTER 13

Culture Change

A boy swings on a vine in 1956 near the ruins of Angkor Wat (Cambodia), 12th century C.E. *(Credit: Karl G. Heider)*

PRESS WATCH: Headline Anthropology

Forces of Change
  Change Due to Contact Through Trade
  Diffusion
  Modernization
  Innovation: The Internal Dynamics of
    Change
  Change in Language

DOING ANTHROPOLOGY: Nailing Down
    Language Change
FOCUS CULTURE: The Changing Trobriand
    Islands
  Revitalization Movements
Indigenous Rights in a Changing World
    Rights to Resources: Land and Water
    Intellectual Property Rights

381

Transnationalism

SEEING ANTHROPOLOGY: Trobriand Cricket: An Ingenious Response to Colonialism

HOLLYWOOD-STYLE ANTHROPOLOGY: To Change or Not?: *Who Watches the Watchers?*

Chapter Summary

HEADLINE ANTHROPOLOGY

PRESS WATCH

Some of the subjects discussed in this chapter have made their way into current news stories. For example:

◆ A joint Israeli-Palestinian project to create a Sesame Street television show where Israeli and Palestinian puppets live on the same street has fallen victim to the reality of present animosities, but the participants still hope that it can make a difference.
—New York Times, *July 30, 2002.*

◆ Some five million Filipinos live abroad, and their remittances are the second largest source of foreign exchange for the Philippines.
—New York Times, *April 8, 2002.*

◆ Co-op City, in the Bronx, is the largest NORC (naturally occurring retirement community) in the country. Working people who moved there in the late 1960s are now reaching retirement age and slowly transforming the apartment complex into a retirement community.
—New York Times, *August 5, 2002.*

◆ US schools are being swamped by immigrant students who do not know English. "We are now in the largest wave of immigration in the history of the United States," said Dr. Marcelo Suarez-Orozco, Harvard professor of education.
—New York Times, *August 5, 2002.*

Cultures change. All cultures change all the time. But different aspects of cultures change at different rates. And some aspects of cultures can be remarkably stable over long periods of time. As William Faulkner once said, "The past is not dead. It is not even past."

A culture is a complex mix of old and new. Often, archaic traits—those persistent remnants from earlier times—are found embedded in a culture. The meal in the Dani boys' initiation ceremony is made up of wild foods that once were gathered but now are rarely if ever eaten. Long medieval academic gowns and hoods, which were everyday wear in early European universities, can be seen today in American colleges at graduation ceremonies, serving as a silent link to the past. The Dani practice of chopping off girls' fingers as funeral sacrifices simply persisted with increasingly little reason until it was suddenly discarded in the face of Christian missionary pressure.

In the previous chapters, we often looked at cultures as still photographs that capture rich context at one moment in time. We now shift to thinking of culture as a movie film or videotape that allows us to see change. We have discussed the fact that past ethnographies have been written in the mode of the *ethnographic present,* that moment when the ethnographer was doing fieldwork for a few months or a year or two, or some reconstructed time in the past before change began. The fine analysis of action and interaction that this form permits is very valuable. Nevertheless, the model of a culture as a sort of engine chugging along in a dynamic but essentially unvarying equilibrium has its limits. We need another model, that of culture as constantly changing, always somewhat out of equilibrium, always adapting.

Some special terms have been used for this perspective that focuses on change. Studies of **acculturation** examine cultural changes that resulted from extended, direct contact between two or more previously autonomous groups. These types of studies were popular in the mid-20th century, often looking at the adjustments made by native North American cultures to the overwhelming Anglo-American impact. **Ethnohistory** is another approach that combines written historical records with oral history to achieve narration over time. More and more, cultural anthropologists are appreciating the importance of gaining this sort of perspective—a lesson that has long been taught by both historians and archaeologists.

FORCES OF CHANGE

For years, anthropologists assumed that many of the apparently isolated cultures around the world remained fairly stable, experiencing some change, but not as a result of contact with the outside world. The belief was that these "isolated" societies did not trade with the outside world or come into direct contact with it until the forces of colonialism, modernization, and globalization intruded on their worlds. This assumption lies behind the "Star Trek: Next Generation" episode *Who Watches the Watchers?* Now, that assumption is being questioned. It seems more likely that the cultures of the world were tied into regional systems of trade, and even global systems, long before anthropologists thought they were. Now, of course, everyone agrees that there are no isolated cultures. The question is, Can you still study cultures as independent entities, or can you study them only as part of a larger system?

Contemporary anthropologists such as Jonathan Friedman (1994) who have been advocating a global anthropology believe that one cannot ignore the global connections. Social scientists such as Immanuel Wallerstein (1985) have been studying the world system in terms of the economic and political interdependence of nation-states around the world. While Wallerstein was discovering the global connections between state-level societies, anthropologists have been uncovering evidence that small-scale cultures were also hooked into regional systems of exchange. These systems were based primarily on the exchange of economic goods, but along these channels flowed many other sorts of ideas. The Kula Ring has provided an excellent example of this kind of system of exchange, but it is thought to have been a fairly unique example of a regional trading network. The Dani and Ju/'hoansi were initially described as isolated societies, having no contact with the outside world. However, subsequent research has revealed extensive trade between these societies and others in their region that has existed for centuries.

Change Due to Contact through Trade

The Ju/'hoansi, for example, have used iron tools and arrow points and pottery traded from Bantu neighbors for some time. Richard Lee points out, "Such trade is noted in Ju/'hoansi oral histories in which desert products such as furs and ivory were exchanged for iron, (later) tobacco, and possibly agricultural products" (Lee, 1993:20).

Lee's evidence suggests that this influence is relatively recent, but he has been strongly challenged by other anthropologists who think that the Ju/'hoansi have been integrated into the regional system for centuries (see Wilmsen and Denbow, 1990). In any case, both sides agree that by the second half of the 20th century, the Ju/'hoansi were not isolated.

The large Dani population in the Grand Valley is based on intensive sweet potato horticulture, but the sweet potato is a South American plant that was probably introduced in the last few hundred years. Before what has been called "the great sweet potato explosion," it is likely that the Dani were hunters and gatherers, perhaps harvesting sago from sago palms at lower altitudes and only occasionally venturing into the 5,000-foot-high Grand Valley. By the 20th century, all of the New Guinea Highlands were populated, and these cultures were part of a vast trading network. It was quite unorganized, but it connected people from one village to the next, from one valley to the next. By a series of these modest links, even the most isolated settlements had somehow gotten cowries and other ocean shells that moved up from the coast to the most remote mountain valley. Also, evidence suggests that a regional Highlands religious cult focused on stories of a female hero who brought culture artifacts and plants to various groups. The cult is well known for hundreds of miles across Papua New Guinea and probably extends even to the Dani in Irian Jaya (Heider, 1997).

In short, the **world systems** approach, which focuses on intersocietal interactions, seems to provide a more accurate picture of cultures such as the Ju/'hoansi and Dani than do approaches based on assumptions of independence, isolation, and cultures untouched by the rest of the world.

Diffusion

Diffusion refers to the spread of cultural items from one culture to another, often for great distances. When material objects move from one culture to another, as the sweet potato spread from South America, reaching as far as the New Guinea Highlands, or tobacco from the New World reached Europe, there may be little alteration, and things move fairly intact. However, symbolic culture, such as language, beliefs, ritual, and games, often changes in the transmission process. Extreme instances of this trend are called **stimulus diffusion,** in which the ideas from one culture have triggered similar but drastically different versions in another culture. A classic case of stimulus diffusion is the alphabet devised in 1821 by the Cherokee leader Sequoia. Although he could not read English, he understood the principle of writing and had seen English letters. His alphabet used some letters from English (but with different sound values) together with some new letters and served the Cherokee well. There were actually eighty-six characters, some standing for single sounds and some for syllables (Figure 13.1). Books and newspapers were published in Sequoia's alphabet until it was prohibited by the U.S. government.

The seemingly frivolous realm of play offers other examples of cultural diffusion, in which cultures reshape games to conform to cultural norms and patterns. We have seen what happened when, in the 19th century, Japan accepted the American game of baseball, but on its own terms. The rules stayed the same, but the

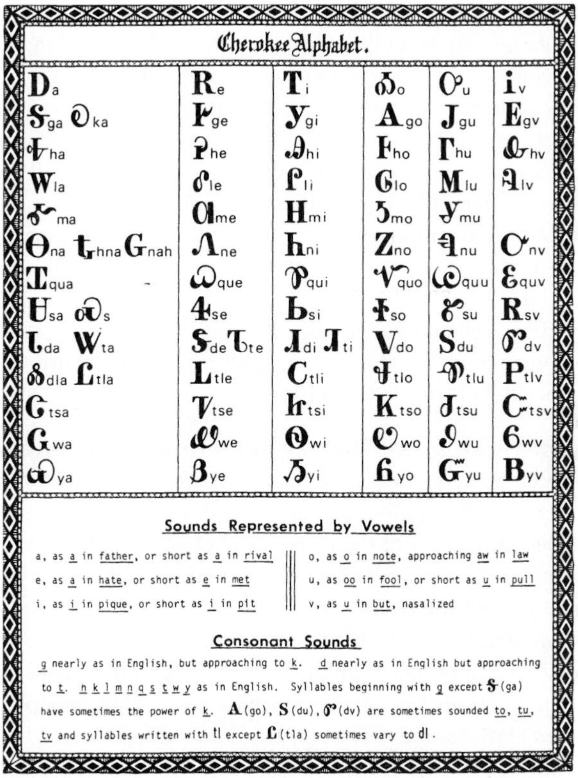

FIGURE 13.1 In the early decades of the 19th century, the great Cherokee leader Sequoia created an alphabet for writing Cherokee. It was inspired by the English alphabet—but how many symbols have the same values as in English? *(Credit: From Holmes and Smith (1992),* Beginning Cherokee, *second edition. Reprinted by permission of the University of Oklahoma Press.)*

institutional structure of the ball clubs as well as the strategy of play changed to reflect the greater Japanese cultural emphasis on groups in contrast to the American cultural emphasis on individualism (for example, no players' strikes, lots more use of sacrifice bunts). The film *Trobriand Cricket* reveals how the Trobriand Islanders reshaped the staid British game of cricket to a more Trobriand form of competition.

The ultimate diffusionists are those who have suggested that the high cultures of Middle America and the Andes were brought from outer space, presumably on the grounds that the Native Americans were incapable of developing such complex monumental cultures on their own.

Modernization

Modernization is a term commonly used to label culture change, particularly when directing attention to (1) the way in which that change is driven by forces of the global political economy and (2) the state of **modernity,** or how the newly emerging forms more closely resemble Western forms ("Western" meaning the European Community, North America, and perhaps Japan). In this sense, the term *modernity* is profoundly ethnocentric. It is also very broad, for it covers the introduction of plastic buckets to the Trobriand Islanders, the establishment of free elections and liberal democracy in Indonesia, the outlawing of female genital mutilation in Africa, and the use of snowmobiles by Inuit and Lapps.

Modernization and modernity are not applied to all instances of culture change. Some sorts of culture change, which do not meet the second requirement mentioned earlier, would not be considered modernization. Revitalization movements—for example, the militant Islamic revolutions in Iran or the Taliban in Afghanistan—would usually be considered retrograde, not modern. (Revitalization movements are discussed in more detail later in this chapter.)

The Yavapai: Finding the Thread of Cultural Consistency. When a relatively isolated culture is suddenly exposed to the forces of modernization and is drawn into a regional or global economic system, cultural change is rapid and dramatic. Yet even in the face of these forces of change, cultures still manage to maintain some elements of their own cultural identity, and in this we see the common threads that connect the traditional with the modern.

The Yavapai Indians of Arizona provide an example of the kind of drastic economic, political, and religious changes that were imposed on most Native American groups as the American continent was settled. This example also shows how a culture makes choices that reflect its traditions even when its traditional lifeways are destroyed.

Until the middle of the 19th century, the Yavapai lived in small bands roaming the high deserts north and east of present-day Phoenix. They were foragers, hunting deer and rabbit, eating the fruits of the giant saguaro cactus, and making bread out of a flour ground from mesquite tree beans. They did not farm and became enemies of the neighboring horticultural Pima. Not only did the Yavapai frequently attack these farmers, who grew corn, beans, and squash in their fields along the Salt River to the South, but they were also disdainful of this sedentary lifestyle.

When Anglos moved west after the Civil War, they soon came into conflict with the Yavapai, whose land was ideal for grazing cattle and was said to conceal gold. The U.S. Army protected the newcomers by rounding up the Yavapai and taking them to the San Carlos Apache Reservation to the east. But the Apache were also old enemies of the Yavapai, and relations got worse when Yavapai scouts helped the army to capture the great Apache leader Geronimo. Finally, San Carlos became unbearable, and the Yavapai slipped away, back to their old homes in central Arizona. The federal government allowed them to stay this time and created a couple of tiny reservations for them.

The Fort McDowell Reservation, on the Verde River near Phoenix, included some of the richest river-bottom land in Arizona. But the Yavapai had no knowledge of farming and retained their traditional contempt for farmers like the Pima. They were given little help or training but were expected to turn into industrious farmers. Not surprisingly, their attempts were discouraging failures. And so it went across the cultural spectrum. Their traditional political system had been informal, consensus being the basis for decision making. Once the Yavapai were on their own reservation, the Bureau of Indian Affairs imposed a formal tribal council with majority rule, and the result was stalemate and frequent violence.

Because of the incongruity of their traditions with the life they were being forced to live, these changes tore at the social fabric that had always held the Yavapai together. In all this chaos, however, they were able to find some degree of control in their rejection of Catholicism and acceptance of Protestantism. In their traditional religion, the culture hero and his grandmother were important. When both Presbyterian and Catholic missionaries tried to convert them, the Yavapai chose the Protestants, with their emphasis on Jesus. The Yavapai explained their rejection of Catholicism on the grounds of cultural congruence. Jesus resembled their

A Yavapai homestead on the Fort McDowell Reservation, 1955. (*Credit: Karl G. Heider*)

culture hero. The importance of Mary in Catholicism had no similarities to their traditions, and they felt more comfortable with Protestantism. In each of these cases in which outsiders pushed change on them—economics, politics, and religion—their traditional cultural pattern became a major factor that determined the success or failure of outside influences (Heider, 1956).

Innovation: The Internal Dynamics of Change

There is so much interaction between cultures and so few really isolated cultures that purely internal change that is unaffected by any outside influences—that is, **innovation**—is difficult to demonstrate. However, in theory, it should happen. The old party game "Rumor" is a model. Someone whispers a sentence to someone else, who passes it on to the next person. After a dozen such transfers, the message turns out to have been significantly altered without any outside influence. It stands to reason that as cultural ideas are passed from parent to child, from older sibling to younger, alterations happen. Also, factors such as boredom, human ingenuity, and children's desire to do things differently than their parents did would seem likely to produce change over time in even the most isolated culture. The problem is, not surprisingly, that we know little about any extremely isolated cultures. There seems to be good evidence that the Dani in the area where I worked had given up cannibalism in the 1930s, at a time when they had no contact with outsiders (see Chapter 3). But we can only speculate about the dynamics of that cultural change. Perhaps it was systemic, an alteration in religious beliefs or in personality. Perhaps it was some historically specific event, such as a period of peace or a period of disease, causing a hiatus in cannibalism, after which it was just not renewed. We do not know.

Change in Language

Working at a much more global and scientific level, some anthropological linguists have studied change in languages. In the 1950s they suggested that all human languages alter their base vocabulary at the same rate over the centuries. According to this assumption, they could measure the differences between the base vocabulary of two related languages and determine the time when the two languages split apart. This approach, called **glottochronology** or **lexicostatistics,** offers some particularly good examples of internally generated change that can be distinguished from the more obvious loan words and other external borrowings.

The working assumption was that about 19% of the base vocabulary—the words for the most common things and events—would be lost in the course of 1,000 years. More importantly, these words would be lost at random, without reference to their importance. Thus, if the speakers of Language A split, with some moving away from the rest, the language of each group would continue changing but in different ways. After 1,000 years, each language, A_1 and A_2, would retain only about 81% of the words of the original language A. However, because they had been changing in different directions, there would be even fewer shared words between Language A_1 and Language A_2. If each had only 81% of the original language, and if both had been changing at the same rate, then the percentage of words that both had in common would be 81% of 81%, or 66% (see Figure 13.2).

For example, the Malagasy language spoken in Madagascar, off the east coast of Africa, certainly seems to be closely related to the Austronesian languages of Indonesia. But when did the Malagasy leave Indonesia? And what are this language's closest relatives in Indonesia? Isidor Dyen (1953/1975) used lexicostatistics to determine that the greatest degree of shared cognates in the basic words occurs between Malagasy and Maanyan, spoken in Borneo (45%). On the basis of the formula that a language loses 19% of the base vocabulary every 1,000 years, Dyen concluded that the two languages began to separate some 1,900 years ago.

There is good evidence for a standard, internal change not only in the vocabularies of languages but also in sounds. There seems to be a constant rate of sound change across languages (Labov, 1994:603). It seems likely that if other areas of culture were as amenable to close analysis as language, it would turn out that the rest of culture was undergoing internally generated change as well.

DOING ANTHROPOLOGY

Nailing Down Language Change

To get a sense of how quickly language is changing, interview someone ten years older or ten years younger than yourself. Try, with that person's help, to find as many words as possible that one of you—but not the other—uses, know, or has heard.   ♦

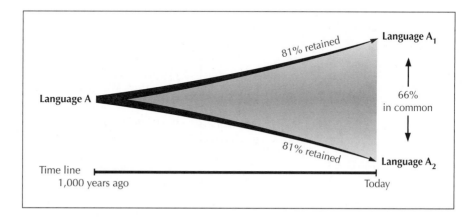

FIGURE 13.2 Lexicostatistics (glottochronology) is based on the principle of constant linguistic change as measured in the basic vocabulary. In this illustration, the speakers of Language A split apart. One thousand years later, there were two languages, A_1 and A_2. Each had retained only 81% of the basic vocabulary of old Language A. But assuming that the losses from each branch were random, then the two modern languages would share only about 66% of basic vocabulary (81% of 81%).

FOCUS CULTURE

The Changing Trobriand Islands

OVERVIEW

Location: A small group of islands in Melanesia, off the eastern tip of New Guinea, part of the nation of Papua New Guinea

Geography: The islands are heavily forested, and temperatures range from the mid-70s to the mid-80s. These small islands are low-lying coral atolls.

Population: 20,000

Language: Trobriand (Kilivila) is an Austronesian language. Some people use *tok pisin* (neo-Melanesian) and English.

Religion: Animism, some Christianity

Economy: Slash-and-burn horticulture, growing yams and other vegetables; some domestic animals; fishing is important.

Sociopolitical Organization: Matrilineal clans with ranked statuses and chiefs. Now, elected representatives serve in the national parliament.

The Trobriand Islands are four inhabited coral atolls (plus many small, uninhabited points of land) lying off the southeastern tip of New Guinea. Together with their neighboring islands, they make up what is called the Massim District. The various societies who resided in the Trobriands carried on extensive trade among themselves. That trade was shaped in great part by the kula system, made famous by Bronislaw Malinowski (1922), discussed by Marcel Mauss in his work *The Gift* (1925), and examined by many others since then. We have already considered the Trobriands in Chapter 7, on exchange, and in Chapter 10, on gender. Here we look at culture change in the Trobriands.

Change has been a constant for the Trobriands. Island-dwelling seafarers living among countless similar groups in the Coral Sea, they visited and were visited for centuries. From the mid-19th century, they were being described by Europeans. By the end of the century, the Trobriands were incorporated into the British colony of New Guinea and played host to Methodist missionaries (both British and Polynesian), colonial administrators, European tra-

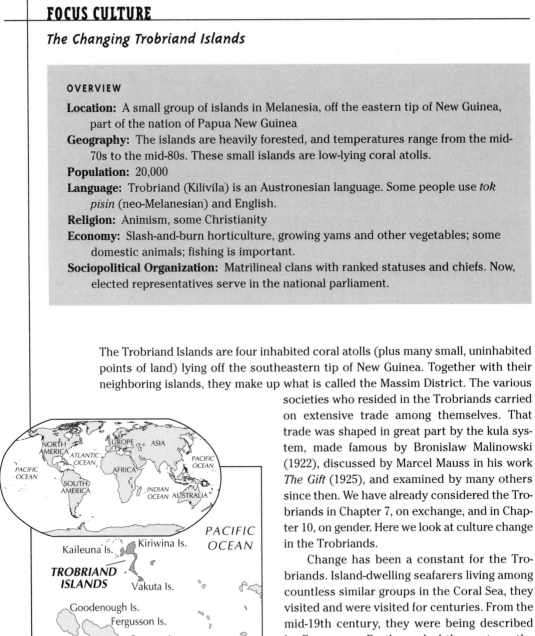

Kaileuna Is.   Kiriwina Is.

TROBRIAND ISLANDS   Vakuta Is.

Goodenough Is.

Fergusson Is.

Sanaroa Is.

Normanby Is.

PAPUA NEW GUINEA   *Coral Sea*

PACIFIC OCEAN

ders, prospectors, and scientific expeditions. Christianity, pacification, and participation in the world economy through copra production and (often unwilling) labor on Australian sugar plantations resulted. What Malinowski observed between 1915 and 1918 was far from a pristine, uncontacted version of Trobriand culture. In fact, from Malinowski's asides in *Argonauts of the Western Pacific* (1922), we get a sense of how many Europeans were present, even though the book contains little discussion of the effect they were having on the Trobrianders. This resolute adherence to an ethnographic present, with little concern for change over time, is a characteristic of most ethnographic accounts of the kula exchange. Nevertheless, changes have certainly occurred (see especially Leach, 1983).

The use of money to buy into kula partnerships has generally failed (but remember Hutchinson's analysis of the gradual substitution of money for cattle in Nuer bride wealth payments, described in Chapter 9). Motor launches and trawlers, now common, have not substantially replaced outrigger canoes in kula voyages. Perhaps the most interesting change is the way that politics in the new nation of Papua New Guinea has taken advantage of the kula networks. Candidates and social movements have used kula partnerships and the competitive feasting patterns to develop and display their power at the ballot box. (This hidden agenda in *Trobriand Cricket* is not revealed until the end of the film.) Curiously, high standing in the Kula Ring has been more influential in national elections than in local elections (Leach, 1983).

Jerry Leach considers that the most important innovation has evolved because of the regular supplying of food and other consumer goods throughout the area by shipping companies. In the past, this sort of trade accompanied the kula voyages under the protection of the kula chiefs. Nevertheless, even with the loss of this trading function, traditional Kula exchanges continue to flourish (Leach, 1983:16).

In the opinion of Gunter Senft, a linguist who studied Kilivila, the Trobriand language, the situation in 1982 when he made his first field trip had changed little in the 64 years since Malinowski's time. In the six years between his first and second visit, however, Senft saw major changes (Senft, 1992). On his first visit, the objects of everyday use had generally been handmade, often with artistic embellishments. By 1989, few Trobrianders were still making them. Instead, people were using store-bought imports made of plastic, glass, or metal. The tourist demand for carvings has resulted in quantities of inferior work and little encouragement for the best art of the master carvers.

As a linguist, Senft was particularly interested in how these changes affected the language. As craft skills were lost, much vocabulary dealing with parts and processes was no longer needed. Artificial dyes replaced homemade dyes, and the folk botanical knowledge involved in their manufacture slipped away. Loan words from English were introduced to refer to many of the new store-bought objects. The linguistic change was not limited to vocabulary. Learning the traditional craft skills often involved a long apprenticeship with a master, a relationship that demanded the use of a formal style of respect talk. Thus the apprentice not only learned the particular craft skill, but also developed skills in the strategies of

Trobriand Island man with canoe. *(Credit: © Tim Laman/Anthro Photo)*

these respect forms. As Senft points out, the move from making artistic utilitarian objects to buying their plastic replacements in stores had some far-reaching implications:

> The changes in the Trobriand Islanders' concept of aesthetics also imply for the young generation a loss in the range of language-use strategies. This loss itself most probably will cause further changes in the Trobriand Islanders' construction of social reality, for up till now a person who mastered the whole range of Trobriand Islanders' rhetoric, versatility and erudition could exercise much political influence in Trobriand Islands society. (Senft, 1992:73)

In short, from a holistic standpoint, we see that plastic buckets from China trigger changes that resonate far beyond mere material culture, affecting Trobriand language as well as Trobriand political behavior.   ◆

Revitalization Movements

A particularly dramatic sort of culture change, which has attracted much anthropological attention, has been labeled **revitalization movements** by Anthony F. C. Wallace and defined as "any conscious, organized effort by members of a society to construct a more satisfying culture" (1966:30).

Particular variations on the theme of revitalization have been called **cargo cults** (in which the emphasis is on material goods that will magically appear), **messianic movements** (in which a leader is designated as a savior), **millenarian movements** (in which a new era is anticipated in which the poor and disadvantaged will be saved), **nativistic** or **revivalistic movements** (in which the traditions of the past are restored), and *new religions.* These movements often are religious and often incorporate magical means. A frequent theme is a restoration of some real or imagined but certainly more satisfactory cultural state of the past. Classic instances are the Ghost Dance of the late-19th-century Indians on the Great Plains and the cargo cults of 20th-century Melanesia.

Wallace suggested that revitalization movements pass through several common stages (1966:158–163):

1. The steady state, in which culture change is relatively slow and nondisruptive,
2. A period of increased individual stress, leading to
3. A period of cultural distortion, in which things begin to fall apart, followed by
4. A period of revitalization, in which a new religious movement arises that promises a return to a good life; it attracts converts, actually making significant changes, and then, as it becomes institutionalized, it results in
5. A new steady state.

Wallace speculated that

all religions and religious productions, such as myths and rituals, come into existence as parts of the program or code of religious revitalization movements. . . . Such a line of thought leads to the view that religious belief and practice always originate in situations of social and cultural stress and are, in fact, an effort on the part of the stress-laden to construct systems of dogma, myth, and ritual which are internally coherent as well as true descriptions of a world system and which thus will serve as guides to efficient action. (Wallace, 1966:30)

Adolf Hitler and his National Socialist party used similar thinking to gain power in Germany in the late 1920s and early 1930s, certainly a time of "increased personal stress" and "cultural distortion," to use Wallace's terms. The Nazis deliberately espoused a return to an idealized Germanic cultural past, a basically medieval time when Germanic culture was supposedly noble and the German race was pure. The attempts to purify German culture now seem slightly ludicrous, but the Holocaust, which was central to Germany's attempt to recreate a pure Aryan race, still casts its shadow of horror.

Often, these movements arose in the aftershocks of Western colonial expansion, when people who had lost their autonomy longed to return to the selectively remembered days before the Europeans arrived. Typically, the movements were led by a charismatic figure.

Case Study: The Ghost Dance.   The **Ghost Dance** first appeared in Nevada in 1889, when a Paiute prophet named Wovoka brought a message of peace and renewal that was directed particularly at Indian cultures (see Kehoe, 1989). This movement quickly spread across the West. It took different forms in different cultures but had a particularly militaristic twist among the Lakota (western Sioux). Its background was certainly a period of "increasing individual stress" and "cultural distortion."

In 1868 the Lakota had signed a treaty with the U.S. government that gave the Lakota a large reservation in South Dakota "in perpetuity." But in 1890 this treaty was abrogated, much of the Lakotas' land taken away, and when the Lakota objected, their government rations were cut drastically. They were more than ripe for an aggressive version of the Ghost Dance.

People believed that if they wore certain sacred white clothing, they could not be hurt by bullets. This protection, along with the return of their ancestors, would help them to drive off the "white man" and bring back the buffalo herds, thereby creating a new steady state in the form of the idealized old Lakota culture. The movement was brought to a bloody end with the assassination of Sitting Bull by the U.S. Army on December 15, 1890, and the massacre of 153 Lakota at Wounded Knee, South Dakota, two weeks later. Although this Ghost Dance movement was presumed to be dead, Alice Kehoe found surviving elements of the movement in Saskatchewan in the 1960s (1989:129ff).

Cargo Cults. Melanesia experienced a characteristic form of revitalization movement called the *cargo cult,* in which, typically, the Europeans would disappear and their material (cargo) would belong to the local people (Lawrence, 1964; Steinbauer, 1971/1979). Cargo cults had been known in Melanesia in the 1930s but were stimulated by the massive movement of personnel and materials during World War II. In the course of the Allied movements northward against Japan, huge numbers of American soldiers with all their supplies would suddenly and inexplicably descend on an island, stay a while, and then leave to follow the action elsewhere. Many different movements sprang up, usually intending to gain a return of all the goods, the Cargo. Often, it was said that the Europeans had hidden the first page of the Bible, in which God had granted all this wealth to the islanders, not the Europeans.

Although the Grand Valley Dani seemed uninterested in such cargo cults, Denise O'Brien found these cults in the Western Dani region (O'Brien and Ploeg, 1964). In this region, people burned their weapons and sacred objects, embraced Christianity, and in some areas built airstrips, where they sat with chunks of wood painted to resemble radios, awaiting the airplanes that would bring them the goods that had been mistakenly diverted to the European missionaries.

Why were the Grand Valley Dani immune to the movement and the Western Dani, seemingly so similar, so eager to accept it? These two groups of Dani did have some shared cultural elements and a similar experience with missionaries and government. However, their economic situations differed dramatically. It seems that the traditional Western Dani were a good deal more marginal economically and under more cultural stress from witches and warfare than were the Grand Valley Dani (Heider, 1975). In Wallace's terms, this fact would be a reasonable explanation.

In the Grand Valley of the Balim, in Irian Jaya Indonesia, a hidden cave that held sacred Dani objects has been turned into a shrine to the Virgin Mary and is a pilgrimage site for Roman Catholics. A statue of the Virgin was placed in the cave, but the Dani objects were not removed. On the approach to the cave, the Stations of the Cross are commemorated by plaques that represent Jesus wearing a Dani penis gourd. *(Credit: Karl G. Heider)*

INDIGENOUS RIGHTS IN A CHANGING WORLD

The term **indigenous peoples** has no precise definition, but has been described by David Maybury-Lewis thus:

> Indigenous peoples normally claim a special tie to their lands and strive to maintain a way of life that is different from that of the mainstream in whichever country they inhabit. Their salient characteristic is that they are dominated by alien rulers and are commonly marginal to the states that claim jurisdiction over them. (Maybury-Lewis, 1999:3)

Until recently, most countries (or national cultures) tended to consider the indigenous tribal cultures and their lands as little more than natural resources to be exploited at will, rather like coal or oil deposits. In the past few years, this sort of thinking has begun to change. More attention is being paid to **indigenous rights.** In 1999, for example, Canada relinquished much of its sovereignty over a large part of the Northern Territories, creating an Inuit territory. In May 1999, Harvard University returned some 2,000 skeletons that had been excavated in the 1920s at the Pecos site to their descendants now living in the Jemez pueblo in New Mexico. The world is changing—slowly.

Rights to Resources: Land and Water

The problem is simply put: "Most of the world's indigenous or cultural communities live on land to which they do not have legal title" (Galaty and Munei, 1999:68).

Land ownership or usage rights tend to be orally transmitted, archived in the collective memories of local people, and marked by vague boundaries. On the whole, recent ethnographic reports on land disputes describe how individual peoples continue to lose the lands they long occupied. The James Bay Cree of Quebec saw much of their hunting territory taken by a mammoth hydroelectric project (Niezen, 1998). In both Brazil and Paraguay, the Guarani forest lands are being cleared and converted into farms and ranches for non-Guarani (Reed, 1997). In Botswana, a large part of Ju/'hoansi foraging territory was turned into the Central Kalahari Game Preserve, and Ju/'hoansi hunting and gathering was prohibited (Hitchcock, 1999). In Tanzania, Maasai pastoralists were brutally removed from the Mkomazi Game Reserve (Tenga, 1999). These examples look much like the age-old practice of ousting indigenous peoples for the benefit of selected members of the national majority. A significant change is involved, however: An increasing number of these dispossessions are clothed in some sort of legal terms, approved by a national court system, and often underwritten by international aid or multinational corporations. These characteristics open the possibility of reversing the process

Today, many Ju/'hoansi have been forced into government resettlement camps and no longer freely hunt and gather in the Kalahari Desert. *(Credit: Documentary Educational Resources)*

by legal appeal and through international public embarrassment. In his analysis of land tenure cases in Tanzania, Ben Lobulu reports on some tentative success in protecting the rights of indigenous people (1999). David Maybury-Lewis, taking the most optimistic position for change, says, "One can take some modest consolation from the sporadic operations of democratic institutions and honest and efficient courts" (1999:3).

Intellectual Property Rights

Intellectual property is a term used to describe native knowledge (see, for example, Brush and Stabinsky, 1996). When such knowledge becomes valuable on the market, the question of ownership arises. For example, when a particular medicinal plant that is known to tribal healers comes into the hands of a multinational drug company, which turns it into a profitable medicine, who gets the profits? What does the company owe to the shaman? As long as the other cultures of the world were considered primitive, there was no incentive to learn from them. Today, with the growing realization of the full implications of technology, this attitude is changing.

Ethnobotany is the study of what different cultures know about the plants in their environment, very much with an eye toward practical applications (see Schultes and von Reis, 1995). Even before the label was used, travelers often brought the botanical discoveries of one culture to another, sometimes with profound effects (rubber, quinine, and potatoes are some of the more famous examples). Today, there are ethnobotanists such as Mark J. Plotkin (1993) who spend years among South American tribes studying local knowledge of the properties of plants. The goal is to find new, more effective medicines, foods, and other useful products before the old wisdom is displaced by modernization and rain forests are clear-cut for cattle ranches.

In Chapter 1, we saw how Stephen Lansing came to appreciate the Balinese's knowledge about their own rice irrigation system and how he tried to bring it to the attention of the outside "experts." In Chapter 6, we saw how both Michael Dove (1988a) and James C. Scott (1998) insisted on the necessity of understanding and appreciating local knowledge before trying to implement change.

Taking it a step further, we see that when this local knowledge involves questions of individual proprietary rights, and those rights have market value, things become more complicated. Michael F. Brown asked, "Can culture be copyrighted?" in an article published in *Current Anthropology* along with 15 responses to the article (1998). These 16 voices (apparently none of them from indigenous peoples) constitute an important step in a debate that is sure to continue well into the 21st century.

The basic question is, What rights do (or should) people have to their own cultures? This issue quickly proliferates into a vast number of specific questions as it affects some of the following situations:

- Ritual secrets collected and published a century ago
- T-shirts with tribal motifs

- Commercial movies (for example, John Ford's *Fort Apache*)
- Film comedies made by outsiders (for example, *The Gods Must Be Crazy*)
- Film comedies made by insiders (for example, *Smoke Signals*)
- Ethnographic films (like those described in this book)
- Use of nonsecret public symbols (for example, the figure of the Buddha or the Christian cross)
- New Age appropriation of tribal rituals
- Tribal images as college mascots

And there are other questions:

- Who, with what sort of bureaucracy, would enforce any rules?
- Who, as an individual or a group, has the actual legal rights (in cultures with more than a very few people)?
- Do huge national cultures (like the United States) or international cultures (like Islam or Christianity) have the same rights as small powerless tribes?
- Given what we know about cultural diffusion and syncretism, how do we decide which parts of a culture belong to it anyway?

You can undoubtedly think of more such vexing examples. The issue is real. Once raised, these questions must be dealt with.

Transnationalism

Anthropology has long looked at the diffusion of objects, games, religions, or the like as they move from one culture to another and as they, in their transits, are transformed. Recently, the phenomenon of **transnationalism,** as embodied in *transmigrants,* has attracted much attention. "Transmigrants are immigrants whose daily lives depend on multiple and constant interconnections across international borders and whose public identities are configured in relationship to more than one nation-state" (Glick Schiller et al., 1995:48; see also Glick Schiller et al., 1992).

Arjun Appadurai has emphasized the sort of rethinking that will be necessary for anthropologists who want to understand transnationalism:

> As groups migrate, regroup in new locations, reconstruct their histories, and reconfigure their ethnic "projects," the *ethno* in ethnography takes on a slippery, nonlocalized quality, to which the descriptive practices of anthropology will have to respond. (Appadurai, 1991:191)

The pattern of immigrants who left their homes behind to seek a new life in another valley or continent is being supplemented by a new pattern of cosmopolitan transnationals who retain their cultural ties to more than one homeland. This picture is not a temporary situation that will go away by itself or that can be removed by turning up the heat under some metaphorical national melting pot. In 1995, in the Dani compound where I lived for two years in the early 1960s, I met two men whom I had known as boys. They told of being on a six-month dance tour of the

United States, where they shook hands with President Bush. Now they are back in the old neighborhood, but surely they have taken the first giant step toward transnationalism.

SEEING ANTHROPOLOGY

Trobriand Cricket: An Ingenious Response to Colonialism

Filmmaker and anthropologist: Jerry W. Leach

Cultures are never totally consistent in the sense that all elements neatly mesh. But we can recognize a certain trend toward **cultural consistency** in the acceptance or rejection of traits. In other words, change is not completely random; the shape of a culture will have some effect on what is accepted or rejected or how borrowed traits are reshaped to match the culture. In some cases, cultural borrowing is voluntary, and it is the borrowed trait that changes more than the culture doing the borrowing. The complex interaction between an introduced trait and the local culture is well demonstrated in *Trobriand Cricket,* in which we see how the Trobrianders chose to adapt the game of cricket to their culture and play it in their way.

A cricket "runner" in a match between "The Aeroplane" and "The Mud Crab" in the Trobriand Islands in July 1971. An early change in Trobriand cricket was to have runners do the running rather than the batsmen. This speeded up play and allowed older men to play. The idea may have been suggested by Polynesian missionaries in the Trobriands. *(Credit: Jerry W. Leach)*

The Trobriand culture illustrates how difficult it is to label people as either "conservative" or "innovative." Methodist missionaries arrived in the Trobriands in 1894, soon followed by Australian government officials, traders, shopkeepers, pearlers, and Sacred Heart Catholics. During World War II, both Australian and American troops were stationed there, and two landing fields were built. All this activity had an effect on Trobriand culture, as we see in the film. Nevertheless, the Trobrianders had a great ability to incorporate outside influence while retaining much of their old culture. What happened to the staid English game of cricket is just one example. As Weiner says,

> In the Trobriand case we recognize how the attempt to achieve a degree of permanence against everything that tends toward destruction is the driving force in the constitution of the social system. (Weiner, 1988:165)

As the subtitle of the film proclaims, *Trobriand Cricket* is "An Ingenious Response to Colonialism." The British introduced cricket to many of their colonies, and Jamaicans, Indians, and Pakistanis are among the world's best cricketers today. In the Trobriand Islands, cricket escaped from its English mold. In the hands of the Trobrianders, it was transformed dramatically to become an enterprise that reflects and supports Trobriand culture, not transplanted English culture.

The film was made by an American anthropologist, Jerry W. Leach. He very carefully constructed it to have the maximum effects on a British audience that knows cricket the way an American audience knows baseball. In his essay on the film (1988), Leach emphasized how virtually every scene shows the ingeniousness of this Trobriand response to colonialism. This film is certainly one of the most deliberately constructed of all of our films.

The short clip is taken from the very beginning of the film. In the opening shots, young men wearing little clothing, but body paint, face paint, and feathers, play a game. An English audience recognizes it immediately as cricket, but as a most exotic form of cricket. A short background sequence on English cricket emphasizes how it has changed over the years, even in England. Next, a history of cricket in the Trobriands explains how missionaries introduced it in 1903 but the sport was eventually taken over by the Trobrianders. They changed it into their own style, incorporating traditional Trobriand elements of war, magic, erotic display and courtship, and ritual competitive feasting and gift exchange.

The complete film continues with more details of magic used in cricket. Each team has special dances and chants. Some dances recall Allied troops marching in World War II; another dance imitates bombers taking off from the air base on the island. The final section of the film follows an actual cricket match. The host team always has to win, although the visitors may claim a moral victory in playing or in dancing. At the close of the day, an elaborate exchange of gifts between hosts and guests takes place. At the end of the film, we learn that one political movement sponsored it, and so not only the cricket match but also the film itself can be considered part of national politics in the nation of Papua New Guinea. The film closes with shots of young Trobriand boys playing cricket, suggesting that the game will continue to evolve in the future.

Setup Questions

1. Pay attention to the first shots. They are intended to shock an English audience. Why?
2. How much has English cricket itself changed over the years?
3. How does English cricket reflect English cultural values?
4. What effects do the team dances have?
5. What is the emotional tone of these events?   ♦

HOLLYWOOD-STYLE ANTHROPOLOGY

To Change or Not?: *Who Watches the Watchers?*

Who Watches the Watchers?   "Star Trek: The Next Generation"   Episode 52   1989
Stardate 43173.5

> Patrick Stewart as Captain Jean-Luc Picard
> Ray Wise as Liko
> Marina Sirtis as Counselor Deanna Troi

Once more we look to "Star Trek" for anthropology. In this episode an anthropological team has been studying some Proto-Vulcan humanoids living in a Bronze Age sort of culture on the planet Mintaka Three. The team's secret observation post had an accident and has lost contact with the *Enterprise,* so a rescue team is beamed down to learn what has happened. A Mintakan man, Liko, is badly hurt and is taken to the starship for medication. This rescue is of course in violation of the Prime Directive ("do not interfere"). When he is returned to his village, he tries to make sense of what he has seen, and Captain Picard and his people must try to undo the damage of his misunderstood knowledge.

Setup Questions

1. Compare the Prime Directive to the American Anthropological Association Code of Ethics.
2. How does Captain Picard explain cultural evolution?
3. How does Captain Picard explain anthropological research?
4. What is suggested about the development of religion?
5. Are the Mintakans really so rational?
6. How might applied anthropology deal with the Mintakans?
7. How much of an ethnography of the Mintakans can you do?   ♦

CHAPTER SUMMARY

- Cultures are always in flux, so it is necessary to describe and account for change even though it is difficult to appreciate at any one particular moment.
- Both the Trobriand Islanders and the Yavapai provide examples of how complex change can be and how some aspects of culture change more readily than others.
- To some extent, change is the result of internal forces, the consequence of individual variation (because cultures are never totally shared), and the outcome of adventurous and imaginative individuals.
- No culture is in complete equilibrium.
- Studies of languages, especially their lexicons, suggest a measurable and constant rate of change.
- No cultures are truly isolated, and much culture change results from interaction between cultures. Trade, intermarriage, refugees, and war all facilitate the exchange of objects and ideas.
- Diffusion is the spread of cultural ideas and objects from one culture to another. Stimulus diffusion is the term used to describe instances when one cultural trait inspires another culture to emulate it with more or less accurate reproduction.
- The many forms of revitalization movements are attempts—often quite drastic—to create new cultures or to restore old cultures, usually in response to major cultural stress.
- Recently, increasing attention has been given to the idea that indigenous peoples are not merely resources to be exploited, but have certain rights that must be respected even by more powerful societies.
- Transnationalism is the result of recent immigrations (usually to Europe or North America) by people who still maintain close ties to their culture and country of origin. A whole new state of biculturalism is emerging.

KEY TERMS

acculturation	indigenous rights	nativistic movement
cargo cult	innovation	revitalization movement
cultural consistency	intellectual property	revivalistic movement
diffusion	lexicostatistics	stimulus diffusion
ethnohistory	messianic movement	transnationalism
Ghost Dance	millenarian movement	world systems
glottochronology	modernity	
indigenous peoples	modernization	

QUESTIONS TO THINK ABOUT

- Many cultural movements (especially religiously oriented ones) that we casually call "conservative" or "fundamentalist" are, in fact, radical agents of revitalization, or change. Is this a paradox?
- To the extent that you know about such movements, do they fit Wallace's scheme?

- Ideas of extraterrestrial contact with Earth have long been with us. What sorts of diffusion are presumed to occur when the aliens contact Earth cultures? (Think of van Däniken, *Star Trek, The X-Files,* and so on.)
- Local festivals celebrating some unusual trait or event seem to be cropping up everywhere (the Okra Fest, the Chitlin Strut, Pioneer Days, and so on). How do you interpret this movement in terms of the ideas in this chapter?
- Why is soccer the most popular game in the world (except in the United States), but cricket almost totally limited to the cultures of the former British empire? What about baseball?

SUGGESTIONS FOR FURTHER READING

Anderson, Benedict
1998   The Spectre of Comparisons: Nationalism, Southeast Asia and the World. London: Verso. *A professor of international studies considers the cultural implications of political change, and vice versa.*

Appadurai, Arjun
1996   Modernity at Large: Cultural Dimensions of Globalization. Minneapolis: University of Minnesota Press. *A professor of anthropology looks at the entire world.*

Errington, Federick K., and Deborah B. Gewertz
1995   Articulating Change in the "Last Unknown." Boulder, CO: Westview. *Two of the most experienced ethnographers of Papua New Guinea continue their tracking of culture change.*

Ong, Aihwa
1999   Flexible Citizenship: The Cultural Logics of Transnationality. Durham, NC: Duke University Press. *The Chinese as transnationals.*

Verdery, Katherine
1995   What Was Socialism? What Comes After? Princeton, NJ: Princeton University Press. *An anthropological approach to understanding change in Eastern Europe.*

Watson, James J. (ed.)
1996   Golden Arches East: McDonalds in East Asia. *How the world's leading hamburger chain emerges in five Asian countries.*

Look at articles in recent issues of Cultural Survival Quarterly.

CHAPTER 14

Medical Anthropology and the Future

Medical
treatment.
Borobudur,
Java, 9th
century C.E.
*(Credit: Karl G.
Heider)*

PRESS WATCH

HEADLINE ANTHROPOLOGY

Some of the subjects discussed in this chapter have made their way into current news stories. For example:

◆ Scientists are examining the effects of the sap of the gugul tree, which has been used for 2000 years by folk healers in India to control weight.

—The State *(Columbia, South Carolina), May 3, 2002.*

◆ A University of South Carolina public health study "proves what public health experts have known for years—if you want to improve health care for poor minorities in rural areas, you must first improve the rural economy."

—The State *(Columbia, South Carolina), June 28, 2002.*

◆ Medical researchers say that the traditional folk treatments for snake bite, namely, use a tourniquet, cut into the flesh around the bite and suck out the poison, immerse the affected area in ice water, and drink stimulants, are all dangerous. (It is best to get the victim immediately to a medical facility for treatment.)

—New York Times, *August 1, 2002.*

◆ In Canada, doughnuts are a symbol of a national spurt in obesity, disturbing health experts. "The trend is mimicking the United States. We're five years behind, but catching up," said Anne Kennedy, president of Canada's National Institute of Nutrition.

—New York Times, *August 5, 2002.*

Where does cultural anthropology go in this new millennium? Most of the concerns of a hundred years ago are still in play for today's anthropology, and many new ones have emerged. In 2002 a special issue of *American Anthropologist* celebrated the one hundredth anniversary of the American Anthropological Association. Ward Goodenough (2002) reviewed anthropology in the 20th century, and Laura Nader, in responding to his article, picked up on themes that will be increasingly important in the future (2002). This dialogue between Goodenough and Nader provides a fine evaluation of the state of the field.

For this last chapter, we look at **medical anthropology,** a broad cover term for various branches of research that together embody many strengths and concerns of anthropology: it is multifield (combining ethnography and biological anthropology), it often uses ethnographic fieldwork—that is, personal immersion that allows anthropologists to reach understandings that might otherwise be inaccessible—and it addresses some of the most intractable problems of our age.

MEDICAL ANTHROPOLOGY

Local Knowledge

Think of aspirin, one of the cheapest, most widely used medicines. It is an analgesic, easing pain; it is a blood thinner, reducing the risk of heart attacks. Long before scientific medicine developed, people in various cultures chewed willow bark to relieve pain. In the 19th-century the Bayer Chemical Company picked up on it, refined it, and marketed it as aspirin.

We have already come across local knowledge in the Balinese rice irrigation system (Chapter 1), in the Dani pig complex (Chapter 6), in Ju/'hoansi hunting (Chapter 6), and in the debate over intellectual property rights (Chapter 13). But research has barely begun to understand the many things that peoples all over the world know about medicines.

Local knowledge refers especially to traditional technical competence developed by the people of a culture as an adaptation to their environment. Rice irrigation systems in Bali or igloos in the arctic are obvious examples. But **folk medicine** is quite different. It usually incorporates complex chemical compounds found in local flora and fauna. It is as if countless brilliant scientists in countless generations of countless cultures were running countless research laboratories, observing and experimenting with everything growing around them. Mark J. Plotkin is an **ethnobotanist** who sounds like the inspiration for Dr. Robert Campbell in *Medicine Man*. He has worked for decades in the Amazon rain forests and has described the immensity of this activity. Taken as a whole, it surely must constitute one of the greatest achievements of human inquiry. But now the plants and animals are going extinct, cultures are changing, and old knowledge is being forgotten as new, "modern" skills are learned.

There has been a shift from denigrating the mumbo jumbo of witch doctors to respecting the knowledge of local experts (see Cox, 2000). Yet, as the possibilities of folk medicines are better appreciated, what of the intellectual rights of local people? How should profits from local medical discoveries be shared between the people and the drug companies that can market their discoveries? Just as **bioprospecting** research is booming, so are the controversies rising from it, such as understanding pain.

Pain—Acute and Chronic

Several anthropologists have been studying acute and chronic pain. We bump into acute pain in the course of our normal lives. The causes are usually obvious, like a stubbed toe, a paper cut, or even a hangover. And the pain usually disappears after a short time, with or without medication. But some pain is persistent, chronic pain that in the United States is responsible for a high percentage of occupational disabilities at an annual cost of billions of dollars each year. Orthodox medicine has been generally ineffective in dealing with chronic pain, and alternative medicines and healing practices are often tried. But pain is experienced. It does not bleed or show up on an x-ray. Since generally neither physicians nor family members can either see or alleviate chronic pain, it is easy for them to lose patience with the sufferer, even to decide that the pain is somehow "all in the mind," and so not real or, even worse, is being faked in order to get insurance money or win a court settlement.

Many people who regularly encounter pain, like medical and dental practitioners, firmly believe that culture shapes the experience of pain, both by giving culture-specific meanings to pain and by providing culture-specific responses to pain. Some research has tried to nail these ideas down, but with questionable success (e.g., Zborowski, 1952; Zola, 1966; Lipton and Marbach, 1984). More recently, medical anthropologists, especially those working with Arthur Kleinman at Harvard, have taken a different approach by looking at "pain as human experience" (M. D. Good et al., 1992). Rather than pain and cultural background (or, more commonly, national heritage), the emphasis has shifted to exploring individual experiences with pain.

Case Study: Camp Pain

Jean E. Jackson is a linguistic anthropologist who has spent most of her career studying a tribe in the Amazon. But for a year she immersed herself in the life of a pain treatment center in the United States that she calls "Camp Pain" (Jackson, 2000). She was concerned with the patients' experiences of chronic pain, how they talked about it, how they tried to make sense of it. It has long been said that pain is so personal that it is beyond the reach of language. President Bill Clinton's line "I can feel your pain" is, then, fatuous. Jackson looks back on her fieldwork as a good experience, but it must have been extremely difficult. However, she gradually won the confidence of both patients and staff. Her ethnography is a rich account of how people talk about their experiences of pain. In contrast to the earlier "culture and pain" studies, she tells us virtually nothing about the culture of any patients or staff and makes no attempt to relate their experiences to their cultural background.

The question of the cultural construction of pain has not disappeared. For example, the film for this chapter, *House of the Spirit,* refers to the Khmer acceptance of pain in healing practices. And in Focus Culture we will discuss how John Marcucci connects the Khmer schemas of pain with their Therevada Buddhist ideas of suffering.

Menopause

We have made great advances in medicine and medical technology, but the best cures in the world will not work if the patients will not take them. I have taught about the anthropology of nonverbal communication at the University of South Carolina School of Medicine, telling the students only partly in jest that if they want to avoid malpractice suits, they must coordinate their nonverbal communication with that of their patients.

More importantly, medical anthropologists have made much progress in looking at health and disease as culturally constructed labels, not necessarily simple biological facts. For example, menopause has become a major concern in the United States, both in the popular press and in medical circles. It would seem to be an ideal example of the biocultural model, for aging is an inevitable part of the human life cycle, and cultures do construct different schemas for understanding aging. Margaret Lock, a medical anthropologist at McGill University who has carried out long-term research

Margaret Lock interviews Japanese women about their understanding of aging and menopause. *(Credit: Margaret Lock, Dept. of Social Sciences Medicine, McGill University, Montreal, Canada)*

in Japan, has shown how complex the problem is (1993). In the course of her field-work, she talked extensively with middle-aged women and medical practitioners, and dug into historical sources and medical statistics.

The problem of comparing cultural ideas about menopause and *konenki* (the current most popular Japanese term) is complicated by the extreme fuzziness of both terms. They are both used to refer to two things: the drop in hormonal levels and subsequent termination of menstruation and, more generally, the multiple aspects of aging in women in their forties and fifties. Japanese are more likely to see menopause in the broader sense and, for example, often suggest that serious effects can be avoided altogether. In the common American schema, menopause is marked by hot flashes and severe night-time sweating. These symptoms are virtually unknown in Japan. Japanese women report various kinds of aches and pains. Whether these differences are innate biologically or the result of culturally determined diet is still an open question.

Whereas Americans understand menopause as a disease, specifically as a hormone-deficiency disease that is to be treated with estrogen supplements, Japanese think of konenki as "a natural transition, one through which both men and women must pass, but during which, because of their biological makeup, women are thought to be more vulnerable than men to physical and emotional difficulties" (Lock, 1993:293). Not surprisingly, given their understandings, Japanese have (so far) been reluctant to use hormone replacement therapy.

What Lock contributes to the public debate in the United States (and, presumably, in Japan) is her insistence on looking at menopause in the context of aging as normal and not pathological. She challenges the cultural mythologies of gender, age, and beauty:

> The first step in piercing these ideologies is, I believe, to listen to the narratives and poetry of women, Japanese and North American, understand the reality of their lives and how these fit into local social worlds that women shape and orchestrate as best they may. Then surely too we must drag other shadowy figures fully into the picture, because men too grow old and die, but we hear so little about the aging male. Only then may we dispel vacuous moralizing cloaked by scientific legitimacy and banish Menopausal Woman to oblivion. (Lock, 1993:387)

Immigrant Health Care

Another area in which anthropologists can be helpful is in designing health care programs for immigrant populations. Immigrants come to the United States with their own belief systems and traditions intact. Because of cultural differences, they might not be able to use the U.S. health care system effectively. It is critical that an awareness of the cultural context be involved in helping immigrants understand the U.S. system.

But it is not simply that immigrants do not understand the medical assumptions and practices in their new homes. The medical establishment often does not understand the culture of the immigrants. Rebecca G. Martinez and her colleagues studied beliefs about cervical cancer held by both physicians and Latina immigrants (Mexican and Salvadoran) in Orange County, California. The physicians considered cervical cancer to be a sexually transmitted disease (STD) caused by viruses transmitted by promiscuous sexual activity. The Latina women understood cervical cancer in much broader terms, attributing it to various sorts of disruptive behavior like abortion and poor hygiene, and including men's behaviors. The disparate understandings impeded both prevention and treatment of cervical cancer. The researchers concluded that

> our results imply that health educators should develop cervical cancer control programs for Latina immigrants that take into consideration the strong moral foundations regulating beliefs about risk factors for this disease. (Martinez et al., 1997:357)

Furthermore, they emphasized the importance of educating the physicians. (Given that the physicians in their sample came from several different cultures, one wonders how much agreement there was among them. Do the world's medical schools create a worldwide physicians' culture that overrides local folk knowledge completely?)

Geri-Ann Galanti is an anthropologist who teaches nurses, and she has put together a sort of handbook, *Caring for Patients from Different Cultures,* subtitled *Case Studies from American Hospitals* (1997). She collected examples of cultural misunderstandings from hundreds of nurses and created a collection that is meant as a practical guide, not a theoretical exploration.

FOCUS CULTURE

The Suffering and Pain of the Khmer

OVERVIEW

Location: On the Mekong River in Southeast Asia
Geography: Fertile plains, flooding in the rainy season
Population: 8,500,000
Language: Mon-Khmer family, Austroasiatic language stock (related to Vietnamese)
Religion: A local variant of Therevada Buddhism
Economy: Wet rice agriculture
Sociopolitical Organization: Strong hierarchical class system, formerly a kingdom, then a communist dictatorship, and now a democratic state

---

No culture has ever suffered as much at the hands of its own people as that of the Khmers of Cambodia. Between 1975 and 1979, the hard-line communist Khmer Rouge controlled the country, called it *Democratic Kampuchea,* and systematically tried to erase much of the traditional culture and those who were the leading bearers of that culture. Intellectuals, artists, Buddhist priests, and white-collar workers of all kinds were driven out of the cities, put to manual labor tasks, and murdered. As many as 3 million people died, of a population of 10 million. This period was well dramatized in the popular film *The Killing Fields.*

The Khmer were one of the old populations of Southeast Asia even before the Thai peoples moved south from China. For some six centuries, from the 9th to the 16th century A.D., the Khmer kingdom centered on Angkor was the major power in mainland Southeast Asia. The Hindu-Buddhist temples of Angkor Wat, Angkor Tom, and many others were built around the 9th and 10th centuries and are still among the world's greatest monuments. The rise of Thai power to the west, Vietnamese power to the east, and finally the French colonial empire in the late 19th century reduced Khmer influence.

In 1954 the French left Indochina, and three independent states were created: Vietnam, Laos, and Cambodia. By 1970, Cambodia, under Prince Norodom Sihanouk, was drawn into the American–Vietnamese war. The prince was deposed, and the Khmer Republic, under Lon Nol, was established. It lasted five years before the communist Khmer Rouge under Pol Pot took over. They in turn were driven out to border refuges by invading Vietnamese forces, and then in 1989, a new state of Cambodia held elections with the help of the United Nations. The story is far from over, and Cambodia remains one of the world's powder kegs, for both the Khmer Rouge and the Vietnamese wait in the wings.

Khmer culture was dominated by Theravada Buddhism, which was the state religion, although there was no formal national religious organization. Nancy Smith-Hefner quotes the common saying, "To be Khmer is to be Buddhist" (1999:16). Ritual life from the greatest ceremonies of the palace and the capital down to the village level were Theravada Buddhist. Monks lived in temples throughout the land and were an important part of the religious and social life. Khmer dance and theater, based on stories from the Hindu epic *The Ramayana*, were lively at both the palace and the village level. Like most Southeast Asian lowland cultures, the Khmer economy was village oriented, based on irrigated rice. Today, the Khmer who still live in Cambodia are slowly rebuilding and restoring their land and their culture. The tens of thousands of Khmer refugees who have migrated to the United States are both learning American culture and remembering Khmer culture.

A marketplace in a Cambodian village. *(Credit: © Gontier/The Image Works)*

Understanding these Khmer refugees taxes the imagination of even the most sympathetic and knowledgeable Americans. It is not simply a matter of setting Khmer culture and values alongside American culture and values to look for matches and mismatches. There is the added factor that the Khmer have experienced genocide and refugee trauma. As some American scholars put it,

> One needs to abandon a view of Khmer refugees as biculturals, people who come from one culture and now live in a second, and exchange it for a perspective that sees war, flight, camp life, and resettlement as a series of distinctive cultural experiences that have far-reaching impact on refugees. "Being Khmer" is a particular and cultural orientation set within a particular context shared only by other Cambodians. An awareness of Khmer culture is not sufficient for an understanding of the varied experiences of Khmer refugees. (Ledgerwood et al., 1994:18, 19)

One of the most problematic points of culture contact for Khmer refugees in the United States is health care, as we see in the film *House of the Spirit.* The two cultures' schemas of health, illness, and the body are very different. This disparity is especially evident in concepts of pain. John Marcucci, who was trained as a medical anthropologist, has described how important pain is for Khmer:

> The sharing of pain . . . is a major element by which the Khmer distinguish their identity and provide a meaning to their existence. (1994:129)

American doctors observe that their Khmer patients rarely express pain, and Marcucci has tried to explain the meanings of pain for Khmer. An underlying tenet of Theravada Buddhism is the general idea that life is suffering. That is, a person's fate is to suffer. In another way of thinking, however, and one based more on spirit beliefs than on Buddhism, much pain is caused by evil spirits. Khmer do not hesitate to visit special healers, the **Krou Khmer,** to be relieved of this spirit-caused pain. The curing treatments often involve the infliction of pain. In one treatment called **cupping,** a small candle is lit on a person's forehead, then covered with a drinking glass. As the flame uses up the oxygen inside the glass, a vacuum sucks the skin up into the glass. A raised dome of skin, red with broken blood vessels, lasts for several days. In **coining,** a heated coin is rubbed hard on the arms or chest, causing painful welts. Alternatively, a small piece of cotton might be set afire on the skin. Intentionally caused pain is not a normal part of American medical practice, and so, not surprisingly, U.S. medical and public health practitioners find these methods abusive, especially when applied to a child.

As usual, generalizations about culture have some exceptions. It is possible to identify schemas of beneficial or morally good pain and suffering in some aspects of Christianity, as well as in physical training regimes where "no pain, no gain" is a slogan. But considering the incredible consumption of over-the-counter and prescription painkillers in the United States, it is fair to make a generalization: For the Khmer, some kinds of pain are good; for Americans, pain is usually bad. Also, for the Khmer, the ultimate purpose of this deliberately inflicted pain is to heal by restoring harmony to the body. ◆

The Anthropology of HIV/AIDS

Ever since the emergence of HIV/AIDS as a worldwide epidemic or pandemic in the early 1980s, anthropologists have been studying various aspects of the disease.

Studying AIDS. Abby Ruddick wrote her Ph.D. dissertation at Brown University on medicine in Bali (1986) and has stayed on in Bali to advise nongovernmental organizations (NGOs) from abroad that are working on public health projects in Indonesia, particularly on HIV/AIDS. To understand how to change behavior that can lead to HIV/AIDS takes an understanding of that behavior in the first place.

One example of how ethnographic fieldwork can contribute to health policy is Stephen Koester's study of the drug scene in Denver (1994, 1996). One way in which HIV/AIDS is spread is through needle sharing among drug users. When hypodermic needles that are used to inject drugs directly into a vein are passed around, they may get contaminated with the HIV virus and infect the next needle user. A major policy question is whether or not public health agencies should provide clean needles to users. Would this **needle exchange** reduce HIV/AIDS transmission, or would it only encourage drug use? A bit of accepted wisdom in health policy circles was the idea that drug users prefer to share needles as a sort of bonding ritual, and so they would not accept free clean needles anyway. This idea had a certain sociological sophistication and was not challenged until Koester and others did fieldwork, looking at people's real behavior and ideas about drug use. It turned out that needle sharing is not some sort of bonding ritual but is a rational strategy to avoid being arrested on antiparaphernalia law violations. Rather than risk carrying a needle, users resort to "shooting galleries" where they can rent a needle, use it, and walk away clean. This study is a simple example and does not solve the problem. But it brings information about the drug culture into policy discussions that were otherwise proceeding on very dubious assumptions about human behavior.

In 1997, Merrill Singer edited an issue of the journal *Medical Anthropology* on "Needle Exchange and AIDS Prevention." Although he recognized the political complications of needle exchange, he concluded by recognizing

> the now substantial, yet far from complete, body of studies that indicate the substantial contribution of needle exchange to AIDS prevention by lowering the frequency of injecting with potentially HIV-contaminated needles while not increasing the frequency of drug use or number of drug users. (Singer, 1997:9)

The linguistic aspects of the HIV/AIDS pandemic in Nepal were discussed by Stacy Leigh Pigg (2001). Nepal was somewhat unusual, for public health campaigns were under way in the late 1980s after the disease was beginning to be understood by scientists but before it had gained much of a foothold in the country. Pigg describes how the Nepalese program went about educating people about the medical and sexual concepts necessary to deal with HIV/AIDS. This became a problem not of simple translation from English, the primary language of AIDS research, to Nepali, the national language. It involved cultural schemas of both beliefs and knowledge in the broadest sense. One problem was how to talk about key concepts like "syndrome," "immune system," and "virus." There were no obvious equivalent words in Nepali. New words could be devised from a Sanskrit base, or the English words could be inserted, with explanations, into Nepali discourse. Even the English word "sex" poses difficulties, not the least of which is the restriction on public discussion of sexuality. So there are real advantages to using English words, which do not have the same restrictions. People feel that English words are more "precise, sanitized, technical, and proper."

This problem of translation is inevitable, for no two languages have precise equivalents, but it is exacerbated by the special technical and cultural circumstances of HIV/AIDS. One partial solution is to bolster the basic information with culturally relevant figurative speech. For example, in Bali men (but no women) carry a kris, a dagger with a straight or multicurved blade. A kris is a symbol of masculinity, and it contains some of the sacred soul matter particular to men. By the 1990s, AIDS-prevention campaigns in Bali promoted the use of condoms with posters picturing a kris with the slogan "Keep your kris in its sheath."

Case Study: HIV/AIDS in Haiti

Paul Farmer is a physician and anthropologist who for the last two decades has split his time between Harvard and a medical clinic in rural Haiti. He has watched HIV/AIDS since its earliest days in Haiti, and his writings put the pandemic into its historical and international context.

In the early 1980s, Haiti had become the symbol of AIDS for North Americans, but this was merely the latest definition of Haiti for Americans. For 200 years Haiti had been a dark, sinister place. From the time of Columbus, the island was exploited by the Spanish and then the French. As the Indian population died off, enslaved Africans were brought in to work the plantations. Serious slave uprisings began in 1791, and by 1804 the Republic of Haiti had become only the second country to free itself from European colonial rule. But the first such country, the United States, still maintained slavery, and the example of Haiti's violent slave revolt terrified the planters of the American South. From the mid-19th century the United States regularly sent warships to protect American interests in Haiti, and from 1915 to 1937 the U.S. Marines occupied Haiti.

Voodoo, with its dark, ecstatic rituals, added to the sinister image of this troublesome land. In the early years of HIV/AIDS, when it was little understood, and when many poor refugees from Haiti were found to be HIV positive, it was easy for North Americans to blame Haitians for the disease.

From the Haitian standpoint, however, AIDS was just the latest indignity foisted on the country from the United States. But a more proximate reason for the illness was explained by Haitian folk beliefs in witchcraft—someone has sent misfortune to another. In his earlier work (e.g., 1992) Paul Farmer emphasized the atmosphere of accusation and counteraccusation that characterized the early days of HIV/AIDS, as well as the historical and cultural contexts from which these accusations were made. In his later work (1999) he concentrates on the effects of poverty. HIV/AIDS cannot be cured, but it can be controlled by massive and very expensive medication that is simply out of reach of most Haitian peasants:

> One can be impressed by the power of modern medicine and yet dejected by our failure to deliver it equitably. . . . Moving along the fault lines of society, HIV continues to entrench itself among the world's poor and marginalized. (Farmer, 1999:264–265)

And so this medical anthropologist, after years of facing the biological, cultural, and historical aspects of HIV/AIDS, winds up with the realization that it is the inequalities built into the transnational social system that will sustain and spread HIV/AIDS among the poor. And once more we see the utility of thinking in terms of a biocultural model, for neither part can be understood alone.

 ## DOING ANTHROPOLOGY

Illness and Culture

There are many news stories about illness in one part of the world or another. Read such a story carefully, and sketch out what seem to be the relevant features of the cultural background. To what extent does the story, as well as the health professionals involved, recognize these cultural features? ◆

FINAL THOUGHTS

There is no such thing as unengaged anthropology. Even the most esoteric information about the most isolated group may come to be important in quite unanticipated ways. At the same time, to an increasing extent, anthropologists are deliberately searching out answers to major human problems like violence, inequality, exploitation, and illness. One of the most powerful lessons of anthropology is **cultural relativity,** an openness to other ways of life, a refusal to demonize others, an insistence that understanding must precede judgment. The anthropologist Michaela di Leonardo has put it well, as a challenge to the new millennium, drawing on the wisdom of the first millennium B.C.E.:

> A self-conscious, historically informed, politically engaged cultural relativism, then, would involve the intellectual process, as in the reception of art, of willful suspension of disbelief for the purpose of gaining access to alternative ways of apprehending and acting in the universe—because they are there, and because we share the earth, and the United States, with culturally varying human populations. Because we are heirs to long, distinctively but not uniquely Western traditions of stigmatizing Others that need to be unraveled if we are to know ourselves properly. Because Western colonialism has affected even those customs we think of as most Other, and vice versa. Because, in the Latin tag, nothing human is alien to us. (di Leonardo, 1998:346)

SEEING ANTHROPOLOGY

House of the Spirit: Perspectives on Cambodian Health Care

Directors: Ellen Bruno and Ellen Kuras
Produced by the American Friends Service Committee

House of the Spirit introduces briefly the recent history of Cambodia and sketches Cambodian culture. Many of the beliefs of Theravada Buddhism are directly relevant to health, particularly the Taoist yin–yang oppositions, the importance of a balance between hot and cold, and a balance of the four elements (wind, water, earth, and fire). Sickness is understood to be the result of falling out of balance, and health care consists of restoring balance, often by calling on traditional practitioners, called *Krou Khmer.*

Much of the film is a visually rather static series of talking heads, but what they are saying is dynamite. Khmer (Cambodians) and Americans in effect carry on a dialog about how to combine the traditional medical care of the Krou Khmer and the modern Western medicine of the M.D.'s. Although neither of the two American physicians ever mentions the word *anthropology,* they are obviously talking about using ethnographic insights to understand the Khmer culture of medicine. Only then can they really help the refugees.

Dr. Denise Rogers says, "We need someone who knows the culture." Dr. Thomas Jones says, "Be sure the communication systems are really working." A Khmer says, "We have to treat not just the disease but the whole person."

The short clip discusses the reluctance of Khmer refugees to use American hospitals or prenatal care services. Khmer expectations of medical practice differ from those of Americans. They resist having blood drawn for tests, they do not continue taking a full course of medication after the immediate symptoms disappear, and so forth. We hear from two American physicians, Dr. Jones and Dr. Rogers, who have great understanding and sympathy for the Khmer and their culture.

The complete film begins with background on Khmer traditional life, especially Buddhism and the belief system relevant to health, a mixture of Theravada Buddhism and Southeast Asian spirit beliefs. When peoples' maladies are caused by bad spirits, they call in specialist healers, Krou Khmer, for diagnosis and treatment. Rubbing a person's skin with a heated coin is a common treatment. Cupping can also be used: a short candle is stood on the forehead and covered with a small glass. The candle creates a vacuum, sucks the skin up into the glass, and creates a red mark (from burst capillaries) that lasts for a week or two. The French introduced their medicine during the colonial period, but after independence in 1953, Cambodian medicine combined Western practices and traditional Khmer healing.

Setup Questions

1. What are the particular problems that physicians need to take into account in working with Khmer patients?

2. How do Khmer schemas about illness, health, and life in general affect their attitudes toward American medical care? (Think of pregnancy, a person's blood supply, use of medicine, and so forth.)
3. What does Dr. Jones mean by "translators"?
4. How does the concept of cultural relativity come into play for these American physicians? Does this concept have any limitations?
5. Compare the Krou Khmer and their cultural setting with Eduardo the healer (in Chapter 12) and his North Coast Peruvian setting. ◆

HOLLYWOOD-STYLE ANTHROPOLOGY

Medical Anthropology and *Medicine Man*

Medicine Man 1992 105 minutes

Sean Connery as Dr. Robert Campbell
Lorraine Bracco as Dr. Rae Crane

Dr. Robert Campbell, brilliant and cranky, has been holed up in a jungle (shot in Mexico) with a tribe (apparently imported Brazilian Indians) for three years, tracking down plants that the people use for medicines and analyzing them for their chemical constituents. Dr. Rae Crane, brilliant and cranky, comes out from the Ashton Foundation headquarters to be his research assistant, to find out what he had been up to, and to bring him back. Sparks fly. He demands that she leave. She refuses: "I'm not a girl. I'm your research assistant." But he has found a cure for cancer in a particular bromelid. Only he used it up saving a woman, and now can't find any more. The rest is predictable—sort of.

Setup Questions

1. How does Dr. Campbell protect the Indians?
2. How does Dr. Campbell explore and use local knowledge?
3. What various ways do the doctors try to (re)discover P37, the magic cure?
4. Is the medicine man a help or a hindrance?
5. What is the most improbable thing in this whole film? ◆

CHAPTER SUMMARY

- Medical anthropology is one prototype of the anthropology of the future because it is cross-disciplinary, it utilizes ethnographic fieldwork, and it addresses critical human problems.
- The local knowledge embodied in the adaptive strategies of various cultures offers important insights into such things as new medicines.
- Bioprospecting for new medicines is both useful and ethnically problematic.

- Acute pain is an example of the combination of biological and cultural processes.
- The cultural component of illness greatly complicates health care delivery across cultural lines, as in the case of Khmer immigrant communities in the United States.
- The pandemic of HIV/AIDS is another example of the biocultural model, where a (biological) illness is greatly exacerbated by cultural, social, and economic factors.

KEY TERMS

bioprospecting	ethnobotany	medical anthropology
coining	folk medicine	multiculturalism
cultural relativity	Krou Khmer	needle exchange
cupping	local knowledge	

QUESTIONS TO THINK ABOUT

- What advantages come from using participant observation to study a problem?
- What, in your opinion, is the most pressing problem today? How can anthropology contribute to solving or at least easing it?
- Do you think that anthropology should continue to gather information that has no practical application?
- (The last was a trick question. Now try this.) Is any knowledge, anthropological or otherwise, totally incapable of being relevant?
- Are you made uneasy when anthropologists write in the popular press or speak in the mass media? Why?
- If you were in charge of training Peace Corps volunteers or other people going to work in a different culture, what are the most important things you would try to get across to them?
- (This is a question from Chapter 1. Try it again now.) Cultural relativity is one of the most important concepts in anthropology, yet at the same time one of the most problematic. Can one be open-minded, willing to understand cultural differences, and yet at the same time consider that some practices, however traditional, are bad?

SUGGESTIONS FOR FURTHER READING

Becker, Elizabeth
1986   When the War Was Over: The Voices of Cambodia's Revolution and Its People. New York: Simon and Schuster.

Chandler, David P.
1991   The Tragedy of Cambodian History: Politics, War, and Revolution. New Haven, CT: Yale University Press.

Fadiman, Anne
1997   The Spirit Catches You and You Fall Down: A Hmong Child, Her American Doctors, and the Collision of Two Cultures. New York: Farrar, Straus Giroux. *The poignant account of a Hmong girl with similar schemas of health and sickness to the Khmer, who received much less cultural understanding than did the Khmer in the film* House of the Spirit.

Greenhalgh, Susan
2001   Under the Medical Gaze: Facts and Fictions of Chronic Pain. Berkeley: University of California Press. *An anthropologist takes a broad critical feminist view of chronic pain, anchored in the experiences of a particular patient.*

Hay, M. Cameron
2001   Remembering to Live: Illness at the Intersection of Anxiety and Knowledge in Rural Indonesia. Ann Arbor: University of Michigan Press. *A medical ethnography of a poor and chronically ill population on the island of Lombok.*

Kleinman, Arthur, Veena Das, and Margaret Lock (eds.)
1997   Social Suffering. Berkeley: University of California Press. *An anthropological view of the pain and suffering attributable to social acts like war, torture, and inequality.*

Lock, Margaret
2002   Twice Dead: Organ Transplants and the Reinvention of Death. Berkeley: University of California Press. *As organ transplants from dead to living become more routine in a technical sense, the definition of death becomes more salient. Lock addresses this virtually intractable problem, comparing the very different attitudes in the United States and Japan.*

Parker, Richard
2001   Sexuality, Culture, and Power in HIV/AIDS Research. Annual Review of Anthropology 30:163–179. *Focuses on the development of anthropological research on HIV/AIDS.*

Schoepf, Brooke G.
2001   International AIDS Research in Anthropology: Taking a Critical Perspective on the Crisis. Annual Review of Anthropology 30:335–361. *Research in the 1990s.*

APPENDIX A
Thinking about Ethnographic Films

In 1970, at the American Anthropological Association meetings in San Diego, Robert Gardner screened *The Nuer* to a large anthropological audience for the first time. Probably everyone in the audience knew the Nuer from Evans-Pritchard's ethnographies. When it was over and the lights came up, we sat stunned. People said, "Evans-Pritchard had never told us that the Nuer were like this!"

A picture is worth a thousand words.

What can that mean? Can one second of a movie (at 24 frames per second) be worth 24,000 words? No. But one could easily use 1,000 words to describe and analyze what is happening in a picture. The title of this book, "*seeing* anthropology," is important, for both the still photographs and the video clips are intended to complement the words of the text in showing how culture works. Just as the words need to be studied, so the images must be thought about carefully. Take the 1879 picture on page 16. You can see at a glance that it refers to Europeans' schemas of their role among humanity. Now spend some time with the picture. Describe and analyze it. What about the faces, clothing, body language, genders, and actions? What do all these details mean? Now try this exercise again: What is the Europeans' image of themselves, of those Others, and of their interrelationships? You can easily use more than 1,000 words to describe this picture. "Seeing anthropology" implies the critical visual analysis of human behavior. The visuals of this textbook—both the still photographs and the video clips—are offered for critical visual analysis.

This appendix is a very brief introduction to ethnographic film, intended to highlight some concepts and some ideas to keep in mind while studying the films. By now, a great deal of literature has focused on ethnographic film. My own book (Heider, 1976b) is a convenient starting place, but there are many more recent publications. For general overviews, there are excellent books by Peter Loizos (1993) and by Ilisa Barbash and Lucien Taylor (1997). There are also books by or about some of the most important ethnographic filmmakers: Jean Rouch (Stoller, 1992); John Marshall (Ruby, 1993); Robert Gardner (T. Cooper, 1995; Kapfer, Petermann, and Thomas, 1990); David and Judith MacDougall (MacDougall, 1998); and Timothy Asch (Lutkehaus, 1995). Here we will touch on a few of the most important issues in ethnographic film. First, though, an abridged history.

As soon as camera and film technology became available, filmmakers looked for subjects. Different exotic peoples, with their costumes and dances, were considered good subject matter. People who were brought from afar to be exhibited in

European expositions were recorded. Explorers and anthropologists went abroad to film Australian Aborigines, Native Americans, and others in their own lands. The first major milestone was in 1922, when Robert Flaherty's *Nanook of the North* was released to tremendous public acclaim.

Anthropologists were slower to see the uses of film in their research. Franz Boas had shot footage of the Kwa Kwaka' Wakw (Kwakiutl) in British Columbia before World War I, but it was not until Gregory Bateson and Margaret Mead did fieldwork in Bali between 1936 and 1939 that major research really incorporated film. Those films were not edited and released until the early 1950s.

The beginning of the modern era of ethnographic filmmaking came in the mid-1940s, with the films of Jean Rouch in France, and in the mid-1950s in the United States, with the films of John Marshall. Marshall began shooting extensive footage of the Ju/'hoansi (!Kung San) of the Kalahari Desert in 1951 and was still at it in the 21st century. The release of *The Hunters* in 1957 opened a productive era for filmmaking in the United States. Jean Rouch made many films in West Africa that are now classics. Rouch first visited West Africa in 1941 and has returned frequently.

The films that we will see range from early footage by John Marshall to decidedly more modern films, often made from a more emic, or native, point of view (for example, the Vietnamese film, *How to Behave (Chuyen Tute),* Chapter 5).

CRITICAL VISUAL ANALYSIS

Words are linear; pictures are nonlinear. That is, words are arranged in sentences that are read in the order intended by the author. Those words refer to one thing at a time. "A well-dressed European man, holding a Bible in his right hand . . . " So could you begin the description of the picture on page 16. When you look at the picture, however, your eye has great freedom to roam around, to notice or ignore details, to make connections, and to interpret meanings. Your reading of the picture is hardly a neat, determined linear act. This idea is even more applicable to films. To complicate things even further, in films there is sometimes a wordy narration that tries to draw attention to only one aspect of the visuals. One skill of critical visual analysis of these films is the ability to see what is happening in the background, or at the sides of the frame, rather than only what the camera has focused on.

Although photographs and film have an apparent veracity, there are at least five ways in which this truthfulness of photographs can be affected:

1. The presence of the camera, or the film crew, can make people self-conscious, altering their usual behavior, perhaps evoking mugging for the camera.
2. The filmmakers can stage scenes, or pose people, to get more effective or more aesthetic shots, in the process altering reality.
3. The very act of photography is extremely selective, pointing the lens in one direction and thus not filming all other possible directions, as well as turning the camera on for only a few moments and so not capturing the rest of the action.

4. Editing, in its acts of including or cutting shots, is selective.
5. Editing, in juxtaposing shots from different times and places (the process called montage), creates an implied unity of action that may not have existed.

And let's not even get into the digital editing possibilities of adding or removing people or things from shots.

ALTERATIONS THROUGH EDITING

Imagine that an anthropologist does fieldwork somewhere. She takes notes and shoots film or video footage. She comes home and prepares a film and a book. For the book, she works over her notes, writes, rewrites, and produces a smoothly flowing manuscript. As she prepares the film, she edits her footage. She throws out some shots, shortens and rearranges other shots. Although she cannot create new footage, the anthropologist can manipulate the original footage—cutting, pasting, and discarding, as well as using narration to cover gaps of shooting and to provide understandings that she has developed late in the game.

In the *Dead Birds* clip (Chapter 3), for example, there are battle sequences edited from footage shot at several different battles. As the narration does not mention this point, only the most attentive observers would pick it up. (I have discussed it in print—see Heider, 1972a, 1976b, 1997.) The narration says that women are making the trip to the brine pool on the day of the battle. It is probably obvious that Robert Gardner, with his camera, was not simultaneously filming both the battle and the salt trek. Both of these constructions of reality seemed reasonable in the early 1960s, when the film was made, for they gave an accurate picture of Dani battles and division of labor. Today, a desire for a different, more literal accuracy might have resulted in different editing.

Another example of creative editing occurs in John Marshall's classic 1957 film about the Ju/'hoansi, *The Hunters* (some shots from it are included in *N!ai*, Marshall's film in Chapter 10). Four men are followed on a long and eventually successful giraffe hunt. The film presents a basically accurate picture of Ju/'hoansi hunting knowledge and techniques. But the hunt itself has been edited together from footage of different men, shot in different years. These conventions of editing have been criticized in recent years. In reality, it would be virtually impossible to make a film that did not, to some extent, use them. Nevertheless, ethnographic film, in so far as it is ethnographic, is held to more scientific standards of truthfulness than other types of film. One solution is to have a study guide of some sort accompany the film to explain the editing decisions. (As models, see Heider, 1972a; Rundstrom, Rundstrom, and Bergum, 1973; Connor, Asch, and Asch, 1986.)

Words can make abstractions and generalizations, but film cannot. Think of trying to visualize "the Nuer have patrilineal clans," or Vietnamese "kindness," or Mayan cargo rankings. Each of these concepts is easy to explain in words but virtually impossible to show in visuals alone. That is, in part, why narration seems so necessary for ethnographic films.

THE VOICE OF THE FILM

In earlier ethnographic films, the voice, or point of view, was that of the filmmaker speaking through the narration. This conceit was not so much a choice as the result of the available technology. There was no way to record sound simultaneously with the visuals ("synch sound"). The machinery was bulky, and the camera made noise that would be picked up by the tape recorder. At best, one could record appropriate sound ("wild sound") and try to match it up with the visuals during the editing process. So, for example, when he was shooting footage for *Dead Birds,* Robert Gardner would ask Michael Rockefeller (our sound man) to record men's feet running on dry ground, or women splashing and chatting at the brine pool. In editing, this wild sound was laid in carefully to give the illusion of synch sound reality. By the early 1970s, it was possible to have real synch sound with 16-mm cameras, but it was still expensive. Most of the footage for *The Nuer* (Chapter 9) was done with older cameras and wild sound. When Robert Gardner visited Hilary Harris on location (Gardner had been filming the Hamar, another group), however, he brought his own camera and filmed several interviews in synch sound.

Later in the 1970s, synch sound equipment became widely available and ethnographic filming began to incorporate it routinely. This technological advance had a major effect on ethnographic filmmaking. Hearing the voices of the people themselves was not just an audio flourish. It changed the very nature of authority on film. Instead of being instructed by the all-knowing narration of the (usually male) outsider, we could listen to the people explain themselves. Even when the conversation was idle chitchat, a sense of greater reality was present. Most of our 15 films convey key ideas and interpretations through such peoples' voices. Of course, outsiders made each of these films—even the Vietnamese film crew of *How to Behave* carefully defines itself as different. Nevertheless, synch sound does much to mitigate the "outsiderness" of film and to give some touch of the native point of view. Even in *Dead Birds* and *Cows of Dolo Ken Paye,* the omniscient narrators at times quote or paraphrase people's comments. (The only exception, alas, is my own film, *Dani Sweet Potatoes.*)

A second important change that synch sound made is to give us not just "the" voice of the people, but multiple, often discordant, voices. The narration style had often simplified matters with statements like "the Dani say . . . " or "the Kpelle believe. . . ." In films that let us hear more than one "voice of the people," we learn that Vietnamese have varied understandings of the concept "kindness" (Chapter 5), that not all Japanese agree about arranged marriages and dominant grandmothers (Chapter 8), and that Malay villagers have many explanations for latah (Chapter 2). This plurality of voices is not trivial, but speaks to the issue of culture as shared (Chapter 2).

HOW VISUAL IS FILM?

None of the films referenced in this book is purely visual. Each has a soundtrack, and each soundtrack carries not only general noise but also words, sentences, and utterances. One—*Dani Sweet Potatoes*—has only words on the soundtrack. At best, the words complement and inform the visuals; at worst, they present information quite unrelated to the visuals and so distract the viewer's attention. For the viewer, it is already a challenge to search shots for complex visual information. If one is being fed data on population density, or some such topic that has little to do with the action on screen, one is distracted from both visual and verbal data.

Ethnographic films do not always use narration. In the 1960s, Asen Balikci and Robert Young made a series of 30-minute films of Netsilik Eskimo life that had only natural sound and no English explanation or translation at all. These films were part of a grade-school curriculum project, and their goal was to show Netsilik technology in such detail that the American schoolchildren could follow and understand the making of an igloo, the creation of a sled, or seal hunting.

FILMING

One way of thinking about behavior is in terms of multiple sets of acts that have beginnings, come to peaks of intensity, and then end. A major challenge of ethnographic filming is to capture these **whole acts.** It takes considerable knowledge of the culture to begin shooting even before an act begins, so as to get its prehistory. Then it takes great patience (and lots of film) to keep shooting as an act winds down and the actors move on to other acts. Anyone can see to shoot the peak moments, but it is the rare photographer who can capture whole acts. Whether the act lasts moments, minutes, hours, days, or years changes the magnitude of the problem but not its basic shape.

Even when shooting whole acts, the filmmaker often **zooms** in for close-up shots. Certainly, there are some moments when close-up detail is needed. I have taken the position that for the most part the lens should be open wider. (This position is not universally applauded—see Hockings, 1997). There are several reasons for using a wide angle.

First, when filming a person, there is a temptation to zoom in on the face. This choice cuts out the rest of the body, and many cultures employ hands and arms to carry important nonverbal information in communication (see Chapter 4). Many or most ethnographic films have been shot by filmmakers from northern Europe or North America, where nonverbal patterns typically emphasize facial communication and the rest of the body is relatively ignored. In filming people of other cultures, these northern Europeans are not aware of the importance of hands and arms and simply do not think to include them in the frame. The principle of **whole bodies** refers to the need, in much communication, to be able to see more than just the face.

A second reason to avoid close-ups in filming communication is that when two people are talking, both are communicating constantly. Perhaps it was Gregory Bateson who said, "Nothing never happens," meaning that no one is ever just sitting there, not communicating. The work of conversation analysts like Charles Goodwin (1981) shows that although two people take turns speaking (with the verbal channel), the person not speaking is still sending messages (through the nonverbal channels) that contribute to the forming of the conversation. Goodwin speaks of "the emergent form of the utterances," meaning that the speaker is constantly reacting to those nonverbal signals being sent by the "listener" and that the two work steadily to shape the utterances. A convention in American fiction films calls for representing a conversation by showing first one person full-frame speaking, then cutting to a full frame of the other answering. This practice does give fine detail of one speaker's face alternating with the other speaker's face, but it completely denies the interactional character of the conversation. The solution is to open the lens wider to include both (or all) speakers at once, thereby capturing the (nonverbal) messages sent by the "listener."

A third reason for using a wide lens is to show the behavioral context, or setting, of an act. Behavior takes place in settings. There are appropriate and inappropriate settings, and settings influence behavior. Thus, especially when looking at unfamiliar cultural behavior, it is important to be able to see it in context.

This argument does not imply that all close-ups are always bad. Sometimes the importance of detail warrants being deprived of the view of the whole body or of the greater context. Ethnographic films rarely show too much context, however, for the zoom lens has a siren song that few photographers can resist—it says, "Zoom me! Zoom me!"

THE FILMMAKER

We have seen that ethnographies are becoming more reflexive, incorporating information about the ethnographer and the effect of the ethnographer on the situation described. The films used in this book show little of such reflexivity. For example, *Dead Birds* gives no hint that the entire Harvard Peabody Expedition was living in the neighborhood and that we were often present, just outside the frame, at many events. *Cows of Dolo Ken Paye* shows a brief glimpse of the anthropologist, James L. Gibbs, Jr., serving for the moment as soundman. Other, more recent films actually show the anthropologist interviewing people. None of these films really deals with the effect that anthropologists may have on the subjects' behavior, however.

A problem for many filmmakers is how to make people sympathetic and understandable when they are doing things bound to disgust the film's audiences. In *Dead Birds,* the killing of a pig at the boy's funeral often turns Americans off and convinces them that the Dani are savage. Never mind that most of those Americans are not vegetarians—they are just not able to watch animals die. As a Nuer man cleans his teeth in the morning in *The Nuer,* the narrator dances away from the fact that he is doing it with cow dung ashes. Surely, these films must at the very least create empathy and understanding across cultures. Must one therefore omit any scene that might have the opposite effect? I made two films about the Dani—*Dani Houses* and *Dani Sweet Potatoes*—to explain the simplicity and sophistication of Dani gardening and architecture. When I showed them to my introductory anthropology class at Andalas University in West Sumatra, Indonesia, I was shocked at the students' reaction. When they saw the films, they roared with scornful laughter, convinced that those people in Irian Jaya were indeed primitive *orang utans* ("people of the forest"). It was a low moment in my teaching career.

THE ETHICS OF "TAKING" PHOTOGRAPHS

"Taking photographs," "shooting film," and "captured on film" are not totally inadvertent metaphors for a process that raises daunting ethical issues. There is inevitably an element of theft and of aggression in filming. One way to avoid the problem is to get "informed consent" from everyone in the film. But even camera-sophisticated Americans cannot be really made aware of all of the possible consequences of appearing in a film. Even if they view the final version of the film, they will not know in advance how audiences will react to them. And what of the people shown in our various film clips? It would have been impossible to obtain truly "informed consent" from each of them, and signed release forms are not the answer.

Speaking as both an anthropologist and a filmmaker, I suggest that there are two possible solutions to this problem. One is to stop making films. The other is to take the greatest care to make films that represent people with understanding and respect, and during the filming to inform and involve them. I choose the second way, even though no magic formula is available for achieving these goals. Nevertheless, these standards allow ethnographic films to be made ethically, doing more good than harm.

SUMMARY

Finally, here are some questions to ask yourself when you watch ethnographic films:

1. Whose voice(s) or point(s) of view does the film present?
2. How much information is carried by the visuals and how much by the sound (talk or narration)?
3. Does the narration complement or distract from the visuals?
4. How visual is the film? Does it show things that would be difficult or impossible to describe in words?
5. What is the balance between close-ups and long shots? What does each contribute?
6. Are whole bodies shown? To what effect? (Is there too much or too little zooming?)

7. Are whole acts shown? To what effect? (Are shots or sequences of shots too short or too long?)
8. Are the anthropologists acknowledged? To what extent?
9. Does the film create empathy? Are there scenes that create antipathy?
10. How does the film establish generalizations or state abstract concepts?
11. Does the film contradict itself? Is this a strength or a weakness?

APPENDIX B

Code of Ethics of the American Anthropological Association

I. PREAMBLE

Anthropological researchers, teachers and practitioners are members of many different communities, each with its own moral rules or codes of ethics. Anthropologists have moral obligations as members of other groups, such as the family, religion, and community as well as the profession. They also have obligations to the scholarly discipline, to the wider society and culture, and to the human species, other species, and the environment. Furthermore, fieldworkers may develop close relationships with persons or animals with whom they work, generating an additional level of ethical considerations.

In a field of such complex involvements and obligations, it is inevitable that misunderstandings, conflicts, and the need to make choices among apparently incompatible values will arise. Anthropologists are responsible for grappling with such difficulties and struggling to resolve them in ways compatible with the principles stated here. The purpose of this Code is to foster discussion and education. The American Anthropological Association (AAA) does not adjudicate claims for unethical behavior.

The principles and guidelines in this Code provide the anthropologist with tools to engage in developing and maintaining an ethical framework for all anthropological work.

II. INTRODUCTION

Anthropology is a multidisciplinary field of science and scholarship, which includes the study of all aspects of humankind—archaeological, biological, linguistic and sociocultural. Anthropology has roots in the natural and social sciences and in the humanities, ranging in approach from basic to applied research and to scholarly interpretation. As the principal organization representing the breadth of anthropology, the American Anthropological Association (AAA) starts from the position that generating and appropriately utilizing knowledge (i.e., publishing, teaching, developing programs, and informing policy) of the peoples of the world, past and present, is a worthy goal; that the generation of anthropological knowledge is a dynamic process using many different and ever-evolving approaches; and that for moral and practical reasons, the generation and utilization of knowledge should be achieved in an ethical manner.

The mission of American Anthropological Association is to advance all aspects of anthropological research and to foster dissemination of anthropological knowledge through publications, teaching, public education, and application. An important part of that mission is to help educate AAA members about ethical obligations and challenges involved in the generation, dissemination, and utilization of anthropological knowledge.

The purpose of this Code is to provide AAA members and other interested persons with guidelines for making ethical choices in the conduct of their anthropological work. Because anthropologists can find themselves in complex situations and subject to more than one code of ethics, the AAA Code of Ethics provides a framework, not an ironclad formula, for making decisions.

Persons using the Code as a guideline for making ethical choices or for teaching are encouraged to seek out illustrative examples and appropriate case studies to enrich their knowledge base.

Anthropologists have a duty to be informed about ethical codes relating to their work, and ought periodically to receive training on current research activities and ethical issues. In addition, departments offering anthropology degrees should include and require ethical training in their curriculums.

No code or set of guidelines can anticipate unique circumstances or direct actions in specific situations. The individual anthropologist must be willing to make carefully considered ethical choices and be prepared to make clear the assumptions, facts and issues on which those choices are based. These guidelines therefore address *general* contexts, priorities and relationships which should be considered in ethical decision making in anthropological work.

III. RESEARCH

In both proposing and carrying out research, anthropological researchers must be open about the purpose(s), potential impacts, and source(s) of support for research projects with funders, colleagues, persons studied or providing information, and with relevant parties affected by the research. Researchers must expect to utilize the results of their work in an appropriate fashion and disseminate the results through appropriate and timely activities. Research fulfilling these expectations is ethical, regardless of the source of funding (public or private) or purpose (i.e., "applied," "basic," "pure," or "proprietary").

Anthropological researchers should be alert to the danger of compromising anthropological ethics as a condition to engage in research, yet also be alert to proper demands of good citizenship or host-guest relations. Active contribution and leadership in seeking to shape public or private sector actions and policies may be as ethically justifiable as inaction, detachment, or noncooperation, depending on circumstances. Similar principles hold for anthropological researchers employed or otherwise affiliated with nonanthropological institutions, public institutions, or private enterprises.

A. Responsibility to people and animals with whom anthropological researchers work and whose lives and cultures they study.

1. Anthropological researchers have primary ethical obligations to the people, species, and materials they study and to the people with whom they work. These obligations can supersede the goal of seeking new knowledge, and can lead to decisions not to undertake or to discontinue a research project when the primary obligation conflicts with other responsibilities, such as those owed to sponsors or clients. These ethical obligations include:

- To avoid harm or wrong, understanding that the development of knowledge can lead to change which may be positive or negative for the people or animals worked with or studied
- To respect the well-being of humans and nonhuman primates
- To work for the long-term conservation of the archaeological, fossil, and historical records
- To consult actively with the affected individuals or group(s), with the goal of establishing a working relationship that can be beneficial to all parties involved

2. Anthropological researchers must do everything in their power to ensure that their research does not harm the safety, dignity, or privacy of the people with whom they work, conduct research, or perform other professional activities. Anthropological researchers working with animals must do everything in their power to ensure that the research does not harm the safety, psychological well-being or survival of the animals or species with which they work.

3. Anthropological researchers must determine in advance whether their hosts/ providers of information wish to remain anonymous or receive recognition, and make every effort to comply with those wishes. Researchers must present to their research participants the possible impacts of the choices, and make clear that despite their best efforts, anonymity may be compromised or recognition fail to materialize.

4. Anthropological researchers should obtain in advance the informed consent of persons being studied, providing information, owning or controlling access to material being studied, or otherwise identified as having interests which might be impacted by the research. It is understood that the degree and breadth of informed consent required will depend on the nature of the project and may be affected by requirements of other codes, laws, and ethics of the country or community in which the research is pursued. Further, it is understood that the informed consent process is dynamic and continuous; the process should be initiated in the project

design and continue through implementation by way of dialogue and negotiation with those studied. Researchers are responsible for identifying and complying with the various informed consent codes, laws and regulations affecting their projects. Informed consent, for the purposes of this code, does not necessarily imply or require a particular written or signed form. It is the quality of the consent, not the format, that is relevant.

5. Anthropological researchers who have developed close and enduring relationships (i.e., covenantal relationships) with either individual persons providing information or with hosts must adhere to the obligations of openness and informed consent, while carefully and respectfully negotiating the limits of the relationship.

6. While anthropologists may gain personally from their work, they must not exploit individuals, groups, animals, or cultural or biological materials. They should recognize their debt to the societies in which they work and their obligation to reciprocate with people studied in appropriate ways.

B. Responsibility to scholarship and science

1. Anthropological researchers must expect to encounter ethical dilemmas at every stage of their work, and must make good-faith efforts to identify potential ethical claims and conflicts in advance when preparing proposals and as projects proceed. A section raising and responding to potential ethical issues should be part of every research proposal.

2. Anthropological researchers bear responsibility for the integrity and reputation of their discipline, of scholarship, and of science. Thus, anthropological researchers are subject to the general moral rules of scientific and scholarly conduct: they should not deceive or knowingly misrepresent (i.e., fabricate evidence, falsify, plagiarize), or attempt to prevent reporting of misconduct, or obstruct the scientific/ scholarly research of others.

3. Anthropological researchers should do all they can to preserve opportunities for future fieldworkers to follow them to the field.

4. Anthropological researchers should utilize the results of their work in an appropriate fashion, and whenever possible disseminate their findings to the scientific and scholarly community.

5. Anthropological researchers should seriously consider all reasonable requests for access to their data and other research materials for purposes of research. They should also make every effort to insure preservation of their fieldwork data for use by posterity.

C. Responsibility to the public

1. Anthropological researchers should make the results of their research appropriately available to sponsors, students, decision makers, and other nonanthropologists. In so doing, they must be truthful; they are not only responsible for the factual content of their statements but also must consider carefully the social and political implications of the information they disseminate. They must do everything in their power to insure that such information is well understood, properly contextualized, and responsibly utilized. They should make clear the empirical bases upon which their reports stand, be candid about their qualifications and philosophical or political biases, and recognize and make clear the limits of anthropological expertise. At the same time, they must be alert to possible harm their information may cause people with whom they work or colleagues.

2. Anthropologists may choose to move beyond disseminating research results to a position of advocacy. This is an individual decision, but not an ethical responsibility.

IV. TEACHING

Responsibility to students and trainees

While adhering to ethical and legal codes governing relations between teachers/mentors and students/trainees at their educational institutions or as members of wider organizations, anthropological teachers should be particularly sensitive to the ways such codes apply in their discipline (for example, when teaching involves close contact with students/trainees in field situations). Among the widely recognized precepts which anthropological teachers, like other teachers/mentors, should follow are:

1. Teachers/mentors should conduct their programs in ways that preclude discrimination on the basis of sex, marital status, "race," social class, political convictions, disability, religion, ethnic background, national origin, sexual orientation, age, or other criteria irrelevant to academic performance.

2. Teachers'/mentors' duties include continually striving to improve their teaching/training techniques; being available and responsive to student/trainee interests; counseling students/trainees realistically regarding career opportunities; conscientiously supervising, encouraging, and supporting students'/trainees' studies; being fair, prompt, and reliable in communicating evaluations; assisting students/trainees in securing research support; and helping students/trainees when they seek professional placement.

3. Teachers/mentors should impress upon students/trainees the ethical challenges involved in every phase of anthropological work; encourage them to reflect upon

this and other codes; encourage dialogue with colleagues on ethical issues; and discourage participation in ethically questionable projects.

4. Teachers/mentors should publicly acknowledge student/trainee assistance in research and preparation of their work; give appropriate credit for coauthorship to students/trainees; encourage publication of worthy student/trainee papers; and compensate students/trainees justly for their participation in all professional activities.

5. Teachers/mentors should beware of the exploitation and serious conflicts of interest which may result if they engage in sexual relations with students/trainees. They must avoid sexual liaisons with students/trainees for whose education and professional training they are in any way responsible.

V. APPLICATION

1. The same ethical guidelines apply to all anthropological work. That is, in both proposing and carrying out research, anthropologists must be open with funders, colleagues, persons studied or providing information, and relevant parties affected by the work about the purpose(s), potential impacts, and source(s) of support for the work. Applied anthropologists must intend and expect to utilize the results of their work appropriately (i.e., publication, teaching, program and policy development) within a reasonable time. In situations in which anthropological knowledge is applied, anthropologists bear the same responsibility to be open and candid about their skills and intentions, and monitor the effects of their work on all persons affected. Anthropologists may be involved in many types of work, frequently affecting individuals and groups with diverse and sometimes conflicting interests. The individual anthropologist must make carefully considered ethical choices and be prepared to make clear the assumptions, facts and issues on which those choices are based.

2. In all dealings with employers, persons hired to pursue anthropological research or apply anthropological knowledge should be honest about their qualifications, capabilities, and aims. Prior to making any professional commitments, they must review the purposes of prospective employers, taking into consideration the employer's past activities and future goals. In working for governmental agencies or private businesses, they should be especially careful not to promise or imply acceptance of conditions contrary to professional ethics or competing commitments.

3. Applied anthropologists, as any anthropologist, should be alert to the danger of compromising anthropological ethics as a condition for engaging in research or practice. They should also be alert to proper demands of hospitality, good citizenship and guest status. Proactive contribution and leadership in shaping public or private sector actions and policies may be as ethically justifiable as inaction, detachment, or noncooperation, depending on circumstances.

VI. EPILOGUE

Anthropological research, teaching, and application, like any human actions, pose choices for which anthropologists individually and collectively bear ethical responsibility. Since anthropologists are members of a variety of groups and subject to a variety of ethical codes, choices must sometimes be made not only between the varied obligations presented in this code but also between those of this code and those incurred in other statuses or roles. This statement does not dictate choice or propose sanctions. Rather, it is designed to promote discussion and provide general guidelines for ethically responsible decisions.

VII. ACKNOWLEDGMENTS

This Code was drafted by the Commission to Review the AAA Statements on Ethics during the period January 1995–March 1997. The Commission members were James Peacock (Chair), Carolyn Fluehr-Lobban, Barbara Frankel, Kathleen Gibson, Janet Levy, and Murray Wax. In addition, the following individuals participated in the Commission meetings: philosopher Bernard Gert, anthropologists Cathleen Crain, Shirley Fiske, David Freyer, Felix Moos, Yolanda Moses, and Niel Tashima; and members of the American Sociological Association Committee on Ethics. Open hearings on the Code were held at the 1995 and 1996 annual meetings of the American Anthropological Association. The Commission solicited comments from all AAA Sections. The first draft of the AAA Code of Ethics was discussed at the May 1995 AAA Section Assembly meeting; the second draft was briefly discussed at the November 1996 meeting of the AAA Section Assembly.

The Final Report of the Commission was published in the September 1995 edition of the *Anthropology Newsletter* and on the AAA web site (http://www.aaanet.org). Drafts of the Code were published in the April 1996 and 1996 annual meeting edition of the *Anthropology Newsletter* and the AAA web site, and comments were solicited from the membership. The Commission considered all comments from the membership in formulating the final draft in February 1997. The Commission gratefully acknowledge the use of some language from the codes of ethics of the National Association for the Practice of Anthropology and the Society for American Archaeology.

GLOSSARY

acculturation: The change that takes place when different cultures interact. The term has been used in many different ways over the last century. Spicer (1968:22) points out that in the 1930s the editor of the *American Anthropologist* wondered if he should even accept articles dealing with acculturated, "hybrid cultures." Today, we are more likely to consider all cultures as changing and SYNCRETIC.

address, term of: A kinship term that is used in talking to that person. (Contrast REFERENCE, TERM OF.)

adjudication: Dispute resolution managed by a judge or other person with power to impose a settlement. (Contrast MEDIATION.)

affine (affinal): An in-law; a person related through one or more marriage links. In parts of the United States, "affines" grade out to mere "connections." (Contrast CONSANGUINE.)

age set (age grade): People not necessarily otherwise related who are born at about the same time and constitute more or less formal groups that cross-cut DESCENT GROUPS. Known especially from East Africa, but vaguer groups like "Generation X" and "Class of 2001" bear some similarities to age sets.

agriculture: Growing crops; usually restricted to use of plows and permanent fields. (Contrast HORTICULTURE.)

allomorph: The different forms of a MORPHEME.

allophone: One of the variant forms of the same PHONEME.

animal husbandry: Raising domestic animals, usually for food or traction (pulling vehicles or plows).

animatism: Beliefs in generalized supernatural powers like MANA that reside in things. (Contrast ANIMISM.)

animism: A very general term covering all sorts of beliefs in spirits, ghosts, and more diffuse supernatural powers.

anthropology: The study of the cultural and biological variations among human groups.

anxiety theory of magic: In those areas where there is much uncertainty and even danger, people will use MAGIC to reduce anxiety (from Bronislaw Malinowski).

applied anthropology: The use of anthropological knowledge to solve practical problems outside the academy.

archaeology: The branch of anthropology that investigates people of the past, usually through excavations of ancient sites.

arranged marriage: Where the primary responsibility for setting up a marriage resides with the groups (clans, families, and so on) of the bride and the groom. (See also GROUPISM. Contrast LOVE MARRIAGE.)

art: The elaboration or ornamentation of an act (like dance) or a thing (like a house) beyond the strictly utilitarian demands.

artifact: Generally anything made by people. Used especially in ARCHAEOLOGY for small objects like tools.

augury: A ritual procedure for learning about past, present, or future.

avunculocal: The practice where the newly married couple lives with an uncle.

balanced reciprocity: The direct or immediate exchange of goods with little or no long-term social consequences.

band: The smallest maximal SOCIAL UNIT, especially characteristic of mobile FORAGERS. (Contrast TRIBE, CHIEFDOM.)

barter: The direct negotiated exchange of goods and services, without the use of money.

berdache: A general term for a socially accepted gender role where a person of one gender (usually male) takes on the dress and activities of the other gender. Best known from the Great Plains of North America.

big man: Informal leader who relies on INFLUENCE, not POWER; especially characteristic of

BAND and TRIBE organizations. (Contrast CHIEF.)

bilateral society: A group that emphasizes both MATRILINEAL and PATRILINEAL descent in its organization of subgroups. (Contrast UNILINEAL.)

biological anthropology: That branch of anthropology which focuses on the human body, including its skeleton, its diseases, and its adaptations and variations.

biological race: The illusion that humans can be subdivided into discrete groups (races) on the basis of physical attributes. It has no scientific basis, but see CULTURAL RACE.

bioprospecting: The ethnobotanical study of a group's local botanical knowledge to find folk medicines that have marketing potential.

bride service: A form of marriage exchange where, after the wedding, the couple lives with the bride's people and the groom works for and with her kin. (Contrast BRIDE WEALTH, DOWRY.)

bride wealth: A form of marriage exchange where the groom (and his kin) give goods to the bride's kin, even as she herself moves in with him. This exchange was sometimes called "bride price" by people who did not see all the complexities of marriage exchange and assumed that he was "buying" her.

Butterworths: A somewhat tongue-in-cheek term for NONVERBAL gestures that people make when they are searching for the right word.

cargo cult: One kind of REVITALIZATION MOVEMENT, best known from Melanesia, where people believe that by performing certain rituals they will receive masses of goods, or cargo.

cargo system: A religious-economic institution of the Chiapas Maya, where men spend great amounts of money and time for the honor and prestige of holding ("carrying") ceremonial offices. (See also LEVELING EFFECT.)

chief: A leader with actual POWER, not just personal INFLUENCE. Characteristic especially of CHIEFDOMS. (Contrast BIG MAN.)

chiefdom: That political organization of a society that allocates real power to the leader or chief.

choreometrics: The study of body movement style especially in dance and work, developed by Alan Lomax.

circumcision: Cutting off the foreskin of a male's penis, often part of initiation rites.

clan: A social group made up of people descended from a common ancestor through the male line (patri-clan) or the female line (matri-clan). Clans are often EXOGAMOUS and are especially common in middle-level, tribal societies.

cline: The steady slope in the measure of an attribute. Humans show physical variation on many attributes (skin color, hair form, and so on) but most variation is clinal. Furthermore, the many clines do not vary together. (See also BIOLOGICAL RACE.)

clitoridectomy: The removal or cutting of a girl's clitoris, usually explained as reducing her sexuality. Euphemistically called "female circumcision." (See also FEMALE GENITAL MUTILATION, INFIBULATION.)

cognatic descent group: A subgroup of a society whose membership is determined by descent through either the female or the male line. (See also BILATERAL SOCIETY. Contrast UNILINEAL DESCENT.)

cognatic society: One which puts relatively equal emphasis on descent through both male and female lines.

cognition: How people think.

coining: A medical practice common in Southeast Asian cultures of alleviating pain by rubbing the body with a heated coin.

colonialism: Where one society wields political, economic, and cultural power over another. Most famously, the 19th-century European empires.

commensuality: Group meals, or feasting, an element in many rituals.

comparative linguistics: Comparing features of different languages to establish their historical relationships and determine language families.

componential analysis: The description of some realm of culture in terms of those dimensions that have meaning for the people themselves.

conflict resolution: The wide range of institutionalized ways, from MEDIATION to ADJUDICA-

TION, that societies have to contain and settle conflict.

consanguine (consanguinal): "Same blood"; a biological relative. (Contrast AFFINE.)

conspicuous consumption: Thorstein Veblen's term for practices that are intended to proclaim the high prestige of the principal through his (usually) profligacy. (See also FOOTBINDING.)

consumption: The third interest of traditional economics (with PRODUCTION and DISTRIBUTION), the use of goods and services.

conversation analysis: The detailed analysis of how people actually speak with each other, with particular attention paid to PARALANGUAGE features.

corporate: Ownership, by a group (like a CLAN), of land, heirlooms, sacred knowledge, and the like.

cousin marriage: In some societies marriage with some cousins is particularly encouraged.

cross-cousin marriage: The marriage of children of opposite-gender siblings. (Contrast PARALLEL COUSIN MARRIAGE.)

cross-cultural studies: Comparison of traits between different cultures.

cultural adaptation: Both the process and the result of changes in a culture made to better interact with and exploit the environmental setting.

cultural anthropology: The study of the cultures of living peoples.

cultural consistency: The assumption that cultures are not composed of random bits of ideas and behaviors, but have some common themes. (See also HOLISM.)

cultural construction: Refers to the particular spin that particular cultures put on such biologically rooted behavior as handedness or language or food patterns.

cultural ecology: The study of how people use cultural knowledge to interact with the natural environment.

cultural evolution: The idea that there are certain general stages of social organization, political organization, economics, art, and the like that human groups move through in regular progression through time.

cultural materialism: The theory that the material facts—the substructural underpinnings of a culture—are of prime importance and will causally shape the superstructural features like religion.

cultural race: The schemas, or cultural ideas, that people have in their minds about how humans are divided into significant and discrete groups based on, especially, physical characteristics, but implicitly including cultural, mental, and moral attitudes also. Although this concept has no biological basis, it does affect behavior. (See also CLINE. Compare BIOLOGICAL RACE.)

cultural relativity: The principle that each culture has its own moral integrity and should not be judged by the standards of other cultures. The extreme view of cultural relativity holds that anything a culture believes in should be accepted, including, presumably, anti-Semitism that leads to the Holocaust, or female genital mutilation, and so forth.

cultural schemas of marriage: The sets of ideas that different cultures have about marriage. (See also SCHEMA.)

cultural themes: Basic organizing principles evident in various cultural practices. (See also GROUPISM, INDIVIDUALISM.)

culture: What this book is all about. A working definition: learned, shared ideas about behavior.

culture of acquisition: The sort of learning common in colleges, where a set of information is to be mastered. (Contrast SITUATED LEARNING.)

culture-neutral terms: Words that can be used to describe behavior in another culture without carrying too many of the meanings over from the first language. (See also ETIC. Contrast EMIC.)

culture-specific terms: Words in one language referring to concepts that are so particular to that culture that they cannot be usefully translated. (See also EMIC. Contrast ETIC.)

cupping: A medical practice for relieving pain by putting a lighted candle inside a mouth-down glass on the body of the sufferer. As the oxygen inside the glass is consumed, skin is sucked in, leaving a raised red mark.

descent group: A social group whose membership is determined by some rule such as descent from a common ancestor through the female line (MATRILINEALITY) or through the male line (PATRILINEALITY). Most such groups are unilineal descent groups, whose rules specify descent through only one line.

descriptive linguistics: Working out the grammar and compiling dictionaries of specific languages.

descriptive morphology: A branch of physical anthropology describing the details of the human body, making racial determinations, and such.

design features: Hockett's phrase for the different attributes of (human) languages that, together, distinguish it from the communication systems of other creatures.

deviance: Behavior that differs significantly from the cultural norm or rule.

diffusion: The movement of cultural ideas from one culture to another, usually with some transformation in the process. Differs from trade, which is simply the movement of objects from one place to another.

discourse analysis: See CONVERSATION ANALYSIS.

display rules: Cultural norms about how emotions should be shown or MASKED.

distribution: One of the basic aspects of economic behavior, the movement of goods and services through some sort of exchange or RECIPROCITY. (See also PRODUCTION and CONSUMPTION.)

division of labor: How work and other activities are allocated to specific sorts of people within a society, according to gender, age, and so forth.

dowry: The marriage exchange in which the bride's kin present goods to the groom and his kin. (Contrast BRIDE WEALTH.)

emblem: A hand gesture that has a specific, agreed-upon concise meaning. (Contrast ILLUSTRATOR.)

emic: Ideas, categories, and explanations of the people themselves. (Contrast ETIC.)

emotions: Certain brief responses (both internal physiological and external behavioral), influenced by cultural norms, to antecedent events.

enculturation: Learning of cultural patterns during childhood. (See also SOCIALIZATION.)

endogamy: The rule that one must marry within one's own group (especially common in societies with classes or castes). (Contrast EXOGAMY.)

environmental determinism: An extreme position of CULTURAL ECOLOGY that holds that cultural traits are the result of the natural environment.

ethical dilemma: In anthropology, usually a situation where one's own personal interests conflict with broader professional standards, or code of ethics.

ethnicity: A person's culture or cultural identity; or a euphemism for "race."

ethnoarchaeology: The attempt, usually by archaeologists, to understand the meanings of the artifacts that they excavate by studying the way contemporary peoples produce and use similar artifacts.

ethnobotany: The study of a group's knowledge about and use of local plants.

ethnocentrism: The use of one's own cultural values, models, or categories to understand and judge another culture.

ethnographic present: A convenient fiction. Describing a culture as it presumably existed before some particular outside intrusion began to modernize it. (See also ACCULTURATION.)

ethnography: That branch of anthropology which studies particular cultures.

ethnohistory: Especially using oral history interviews to elicit the history of people who have not written their own.

ethnology: The anthropological comparisons of cultures.

ethnopsychology: Usually, the folk theories or cultural schemas about psychology (personality, emotion, the self, and so on) that are held by a people.

ethology: The study of nonhuman animal behavior.

etic: The use of culture-neutral, "scientific" terms and categories to describe a culture. (Contrast EMIC.)

evolution: That change (biological or cultural) governed by general principles, proceeding through broad stages.

evolutionary theories: Ways of explaining physical or cultural changes over long periods of time.

exchange: The movement of goods and services between people. (See also DISTRIBUTION, GIFT, and RECIPROCITY.

exogamy: The rule that one must marry outside one's own group (especially common in societies with unilineal descent groups). (Contrast ENDOGAMY.)

explicit function: Referring to cultural behaviors or institutions, the purpose or outcome that is generally known to the people themselves. (Contrast IMPLICIT FUNCTION.)

extended family: Larger than a NUCLEAR FAMILY, extended vertically to three or more generations, perhaps laterally to include cousins, aunts, uncles, living together in a single HOUSEHOLD.

farming: A general term for both AGRICULTURE and HORTICULTURE.

female genital mutilation: Operations performed on girls and young women, including clitoridectomy and infibulation, intended to control their sexuality and sexual activity. Euphemistically called "female circumcision."

female husband: A rare solution to the dilemma of being sonless in a society with great emphasis on maintaining a PATRILINEAGE. A daughter takes on the social role of a male and marries a woman who bears a child in the name of the lineage.

fieldwork: The prototypical research method of anthropology, usually involving living in the midst of a social group. (See also PARTICIPANT OBSERVATION.)

focus groups: A research methodology in which the anthropologist poses questions and stimulates discussions with small groups of informants.

folk ethnography: The cultural schemas that a people have about other cultures. Usually some mix of rank prejudice and actual insight.

folk medicine: The range of substances and practices that a group has developed for health purposes.

food production strategies: How a people use FORAGING, FARMING, PASTORALISM, or, usually, some mix of the three, to get their food.

foodways: All the knowledge and behavior that surrounds the foods of a culture.

footbinding: In Imperial China, upper-class women's feet were warped into uselessness to serve as erotic stimuli and signs of their husband's wealth. (See also CONSPICUOUS CONSUMPTION.)

foraging: The food production strategies of people who live by gathering and hunting foods rather than by farming or herding. (Also HUNTING AND GATHERING).

forms of integration: The various forms of exchange in a society (RECIPROCITY, REDISTRIBUTION, and MARKET) viewed in a HOLISTIC sense.

functional theories: A wide range of explanations for human behavior that focus on the effects, intended or otherwise, of that behavior.

fuzzy categories: A group of things with no precisely bounded definition of membership but usually a clear or core exemplar. You may share in much British CULTURE, but you are either a British citizen or not (SOCIETY).

garbagology: Archaeological research on what people put in their garbage cans on the street.

gardening: Low-tech farming, without plows or tractors, often characterized by shifting, nonpermanent field patterns. Also called HORTICULTURE.

gender: Maleness or femaleness and, in many cultures, another third gender. Used both in biological terms or cultural terms, where it refers to the culturally constructed schemas about gender. (Contrast SEX.)

genealogical method: A first step in field research in a new culture, recording names and kin relationships of all in the group.

generalized reciprocity: Exchange between relatives or others with close social ties, usually involving some time lag between one transaction and its reciprocal. (See also GIFT.)

Ghost Dance: Nineteenth-century Native American REVITALIZATION MOVEMENT spread by STIMULUS DIFFUSION across central North America.

ghost marriage: When a Nuer man dies without having a son to continue his LINEAGE, his kin may formally marry his ghost to a woman who will bear children in his name.

gift: That sort of exchange of goods between people which usually involves a delay between the one gift and the return gift. The people are embedded in a web of social relationships, and the gifts are often said to be "free," but as Marcel

Mauss showed, there are strong obligations to repay gifts.

glottochronology: Measuring change in basic vocabularies of two related languages to determine the length of time since they separated. (See also LEXICOSTATISTICS.)

going native: An outdated term; when an ethnographer slips from a position as interpreter between cultures into total identification with the culture being studied.

groupism: The principle that a person's primary identity is as the member of a social network, as opposed to INDIVIDUALISM.

Heisenberg effect: A concept that anthropology took from physics, referring to the fact that to observe and measure something is also to be intrusive and alter it.

hijra: In India, a ritual role of a person who, through genital operations and behavioral changes, has moved from male to female.

historical particularism: An approach especially associated with Franz Boas, accounting for cultural institutions by detailing the unique historical development, without concern for the general principles involved.

historical theories: A large range of approaches that focus on the origin and development of a trait or institution.

holism: The principle that aspects of a culture are likely to be, to some extent, interrelated, leading to the research principle that it is useful to explore the possible interconnections within a culture.

homogamy: The principle that one should marry someone very much like oneself in terms of social status, education, physical attributes, religion, and so forth.

horticulture: Technologically simple farming, usually carried out with digging sticks or hoes rather than plows.

household: The basic minimal size of an economic and social group living, eating, and sharing together.

house palaver: West African term for MOOT, or local court.

house societies: Societies where basic subgroups are not descent groups but rather the various people, kin and nonkin, who live together in a large house.

hunting and gathering: The food production strategies of FORAGERS, who get their food by hunting, fishing, and gathering wild plants.

hyperstartler: Appearing in any population, those people who have extreme reactions to being startled. In some cultures, culturally elaborated. (See also LATAH.)

illustrator: A hand gesture that accompanies speech but has no independent meaning. (Contrast EMBLEM.)

implicit function: Referring to cultural behaviors or institutions, the purpose or outcome of which is generally not recognized by the people themselves but is identified in the course of anthropological analysis. (Contrast EXPLICIT FUNCTION.)

incest: That sexual intercourse or marriage which is forbidden on the grounds that the two people are too closely related.

indigenous peoples: The original, or earlier, peoples in an area.

indigenous psychology: The culture-specific schemas, theories, explanations, and understandings of mental processes held by a people.

indigenous rights: The realization, emerging slowly in the late 20th century, that even the least powerful societies have rights that must be respected.

individualism: Emphasis on a person as autonomous, independent, not beholden to his or her social groups. (Contrast GROUPISM.)

infibulation: Scarring and sewing together the labia of girls to control their sexuality. (See also CLITORIDECTOMY, FEMALE GENITAL MUTILATION.)

influence: The personal ability to lead, of leaders who lack any real POWER to coerce. (See also BIG MAN.)

innovation: Culture change coming from within. (Contrast DIFFUSION.)

intellectual property: The concept that because a people's cultural knowledge of, say, medicinal plants in their environment may have commercial value, their rights in this knowledge must be respected.

intelligence: A complex bundle of skills and abilities, not necessarily correlated with each other, and very different from the one-dimensional IQ measure.

intensive agriculture: Farming that utilizes plows, tractors, chemical fertilizers, and insecticides, carried out on large permanent fields, often with irrigation. (Contrast HORTICULTURE.)

interactionist theories: Ways of explaining human behavior through focusing on the results of interpersonal interaction.

interpretive theories: Focus on the meanings that people give to behavior and institutions.

kinesics: The study of how the body is used in communication, developed by Ray Birdwhistell and others.

kinship: Relationships between people based on blood ties (CONSANGUINITY) or marriage ties (AFFINITY).

kinship terms: Words used for relatives to designate them (terms of reference) or to address them (terms of address), often expanded metaphorically ("Mother Goose").

Kintampo culture: A prehistoric culture in Ghana, dating from about 3,000 to 3,500 years ago that seems to represent a transitional stage between foraging and full horticulture with domestic animals.

Krou Khmer: A Khmer (Cambodian) spirit medium who heals people.

kula exchange: The great interisland routes along which people of the islands off the eastern tip of New Guinea, including the Trobriand Islanders, circulated valuable shell and coral ornaments.

latah: The Malay cultural elaboration of HYPER-STARTLING, where people (usually dependent, older women) react to a startle with imitative behavior and obscene language.

law: Legislated, proclaimed, explicit rules at the more formal end of the continuum of norms.

law of contagion: Magical belief that objects once in contact can still affect each other.

law of opposites: A principle of magic that opposites have a certain connection and can affect each other.

law of similarity: The principle, common in magic, that similar things have a certain connection, and acts done to one will have an effect on its likeness.

learning: Acquiring knowledge or skills.

legal pluralism: Situations (especially COLONIALISM) in which two or more legal codes coexist.

leveling effect: Cultural institutions that function to reduce the distinctions between rich and poor people through fear (of being accused of being a WITCH) or economic REDISTRIBUTION (like the Chiapas Maya).

levirate: In societies where the continuity of the male line is especially important: when a married man dies without a male heir, his brother or another close kin must marry his widow and produce a son, who will be considered the son of the deceased man. A second function is to provide for widows.

lexicostatistics: The determination of the elapsed time since two related languages diverged by measuring their retention of common basic vocabulary. (See also GLOTTOCHRONOLOGY.)

liminal period: A time, in RITES OF PASSAGE, between leaving the old state and entering the new one, when the initiate is in a sort of symbolic and spiritual "betwixt and between" in Victor Turner's term.

lineage: A unilineal DESCENT GROUP whose members are all descended from the same recent ancestor through males (patrilineage) or females (matrilineage). (A CLAN is usually made up of several lineages.)

linguistic anthropology: That branch of anthropology which is particularly concerned with language, with communication in general, and with how different sorts of communication are related to other aspects of culture.

linguistic determinism: The idea that the structure of a language has a total coercive power to shape perception. More extreme than LINGUISTIC RELATIVISM.)

linguistic relativism: The idea that differences in languages are significantly related to differences in the way people see the world and deal with the world. Sometimes called the Sapir–Whorf hypothesis.

local knowledge: The ideas, knowledge, and skills that a particular cultural group shares; folk science.

love marriage: In societies, or segments of societies, where INDIVIDUALISM outweighs GROUPISM, young people may choose their own spouses and are not forced to rely on their kin to do it for them.

magic: Manipulating the supernatural world through speech and ritual acts. (Contrast RELIGION.)

mana: The supernaturally derived force or power of a particularly important or noble person.

market exchange: Places where exchange takes place using money rather than through BARTER.

marriage: Most commonly, the union of a man and a woman that creates a household, regulates their sexual activity, legitimates their children in a social status, and raises the children. In Linda Stone's words, marriage creates in-laws in that it links two groups together.

mascot: What U.S. schools, colleges, and professional sports teams call their TOTEMS.

masking: The cultural DISPLAY RULE that says one should hide a particular emotion behind the facial expression for another—for example, smile when angry.

material culture: The ARTIFACTS and other objects made and used by people in accord with their cultural schemas.

matriarchy: An old idea that once, somewhere, there was a society in which women held power and ruled, while men were subordinate to them. The ancient Greeks told of the Amazons, a warrior society made up of only women.

matrilineal descent: A rule that membership in a descent group is through one's mother. By extension, such things as inheritance can be matrilineal, through the female line. (Contrast PATRILINEAL DESCENT.)

matrilocal: A rule that the newly married couple live close to the wife's kin. (Contrast PATRILOCAL.)

mechanical solidarity: That minimal DIVISION OF LABOR in which everyone performs pretty much the same tasks. (Contrast ORGANIC SOLIDARITY.)

mediation: Informal dispute settlement in which a third party tries to reconcile the two disputants. (Contrast ADJUDICATION.)

medical anthropology: The anthropological study of ideas and practices of health and illness in different cultures.

medical materialism: The explanation of the foodways, including food prohibitions, of a culture in terms of benefits or dangers of those food items.

mental illness: A vague term for psychological behavior that a particular culture considers DEVIANT.

messianic movement: A REVITALIZATION MOVEMENT that emphasizes the expected appearance of a great leader.

millenarian movement: A REVITALIZATION MOVEMENT that emphasizes a coming transformation on a significant date (like Y2K).

mixed production strategies: The practice, in most groups, of using some combination of subsistence activities to produce food, for example, FORAGING, FARMING, and PASTORALISM.

modernity: A state similar to Western culture.

modernization: An ethnocentric Western notion of culture change that makes other cultures more like us.

moiety: Literally, half; when the entire society is divided into two groups, usually matri-moieties or patri-moieties.

monogamy: The state of an individual with only one spouse or a culture that allows only one spouse at a time.

monotheism: A religious system based on belief in a single high god.

moot: A way of resolving conflict by ADJUDICATION through a local court. (Also known as HOUSE PALAVER.)

morpheme: Like a word or a suffix, a PHONEME or groups of phonemes that conveys meaning.

morphology: The study of the sounds (PHONEMES) or groups of sounds in a language that carry meanings. (See also ALLOMORPH.)

multiculturalism: Where various cultures within a society have at least some political recognition.

multiple intelligences: The idea, propagated by Howard Gardner, that the intelligence of any one person can be considered as made up of several different and not necessarily correlated factors, rather than mapped on a single linear dimension like IQ.

nation: The largest, most formally organized sort of social unit.

national character: A very generalized description of the psychological makeup of an entire nation.

national culture: That which is shared by most of the people of a nation, overarching their regional cultures; usually promoted through radio and television.

nativistic movement: A REVITALIZATION MOVEMENT that emphasizes return to original, "authentic" culture forms.

needle exchange: A controversial public health approach to AIDS/HIV—giving people clean hypodermic needles to keep them from further spreading disease through dirty needles.

negative reciprocity: The distribution of goods without any full reciprocity, usually theft or trickery.

neolocal: That form of postmarriage residence in which the couple is not supposed to live with one set of relatives or another, but can strike out on their own. (Contrast MATRILOCAL, PATRILOCAL.)

non-unilineal descent: When membership in a group is determined by using either PATRILINEAL or MATRILINEAL rules. (See also COGNATIC DESCENT GROUP.)

nonverbal communication: Those channels of communication that involve body movement, hand gestures, use of space and time, and the like, and complement or substitute for language in the narrow sense.

norm: A culturally patterned way of thinking or acting; the cultural rule for behavior. The most formal norms are called LAWS.

nuclear family: Father, mother, and child living in a HOUSEHOLD.

nutritional anthropology: The study of food practices with emphasis on their biological effects.

organic solidarity: That maximal DIVISION OF LABOR in which there are many different, complementary occupations, making people interdependent on the model of the various parts

of the human body. (Contrast MECHANICAL SOLIDARITY.)

othering: The ethnocentric process of demonizing people of other cultures.

paleoanthropology: That branch of anthropology which studies fossil hominids.

paleontology: The study of the past through examination of fossil remains.

paralanguage: Those channels of communication such as intonation, pacing, and the like that are used along with language features in the narrow sense.

parallel cousin marriage: The marriage of children of two siblings of the same gender. (Contrast CROSS-COUSIN MARRIAGE.)

participant observation: A research method in anthropology, taking fieldwork a step further and actually joining in the life and work of the people.

pastoralism: The subsistence mode where a group is primarily engaged in keeping herd animals (cattle, camels, sheep, goats, and so on). Pastoralists either do some farming on the side or live in close contact with farmers.

patriarchy: The principle of male domination in a society. (Contrast MATRIARCHY.)

patrilineal descent: A rule that the membership in a descent group is through one's father. By extension, such things as inheritance can be patrilineal, through the male line. (Contrast MATRILINEAL DESCENT.)

patrilocal: A postmarital residence rule where the couple lives with or close to the husband's kin. (Contrast MATRILOCAL.)

peace: Friendly nonviolent relations between or within social units; the absence of war.

perception: The mental processing of incoming stimuli.

personality: Those various attributes and attitudes that make up a person's individuality.

phoneme: The sound or set of sounds (ALLOPHONES) that make a difference in the meaning of a word (MORPHEME).

phonemic analysis: The set of sounds (ALLOPHONES) that make a difference in the meaning of a word, or MORPHEME. (See also EMIC.)

phonemics: The meaningful classes of sounds in a particular language.

phonetic analysis: The analysis of the physical properties of sounds in a language apart from their phonemic or culture-specific contribution to meaning in any particular language. The ETIC analysis.

phonetics: Defines the spoken sounds in a language in terms of their physical properties.

phonology: The study of the sound system of a language.

phratry: A social organization where two or more clans are associated. (Contrast MOIETY.)

political organization: The structure of a social unit in terms of the allocation of power among individuals, roles, and groups.

polyandry: Where one women has more than one husband at a time. Known mainly from the Himalayas.

polygamy: Where either a man or a woman can have more than one spouse at a time.

polygyny: Where a man can have more than one wife at a time.

polytheism: Belief in more than one god.

postmarital residence: Most societies have rules specifying with which relatives (his, hers, parents', uncles', or new location) the newly married couple should live.

postpartum sexual abstinence: The period after the birth of a child when the parents are not supposed to have sexual relations with each other.

postulates, cultural: Basic principles of a culture on which laws and other norms are based.

potlatch: Ritual feasts where valuables are given away and destroyed in competition for prestige between high-status leaders of societies in the Pacific Northwest.

power: The ability of leaders to coerce obedience from their followers. (See also CHIEFS. Contrast INFLUENCE.)

power differential: The differences between individuals in a social unit in terms of their different abilities to direct the behavior of others.

preferential sororate: Where the culturally ideal marriage of a widower is with the sister of his deceased wife.

primatologist: Someone who studies nonhuman primates (e.g., monkeys and apes).

primitive: An old term with derogatory and racist connotations used for other societies, usually tribal and band societies. In its basic sense of "simple," it could be used for kinds of technologies, for example, but it has been so contaminated by its negative uses that is it rarely employed these days.

production: One of the three main aspects of economics (with DISTRIBUTION and CONSUMPTION). The creation or manufacture of goods.

proxemics: How space and time are used in organizing human interaction, a term especially connected with Edward T. Hall.

psychological anthropology: That branch of anthropology which focuses on cognition, perception, emotion, and the like in a cross-cultural context.

qualitative research: Gathers rich experiential accounts that cannot be precisely measured and compared.

quantitative research: Measures and counts to produce behavioral data that can be tabulated, statistically analyzed, and precisely compared.

questionnaires: a wide range of strict to loosely formulated ways of gathering data through a set of predetermined questions.

race: A pseudoscientific term for a group of people with the same physical attributes. Biologically it doesn't make sense, but culturally people believe and act on their notions of race.

rapport: The relation of trust and friendship that anthropologists try to develop with the people they are studying.

Rashomon effect: The idea that one's fieldwork is affected by personal baggage like one's age, gender, ethnicity, theoretical orientations, and such, and that no ethnographer can be a totally neutral being without attributes.

reciprocity: Distribution of products and services by long-delayed exchange of GIFTS (GENERALIZED RECIPROCITY); BALANCED RECIPROCITY or BARTER; or even NEGATIVE RECIPROCITY.

redistribution: Passing out goods to people, often in exchange for some sort of prestige (a LEVELING EFFECT) (see also CARGO SYSTEM) or pooling and spending, as in taxation.

reference, term of: A kinship term used when talking about someone. (Contrast ADDRESS, TERM OF.)

reflexivity: In an ethnography or an ethnographic film, acknowledging the presence of the researcher/film crew and attempting to evaluate the effect of such intrusion.

religion: A system of beliefs and ritual ways of relating to supernatural beings and forces through beseeching prayers rather than through the formulaic demands of MAGIC.

resistance: How those in subordinate positions manage to thwart the wills of those nominally in power over them.

revitalization movement: An attempt, usually in reaction to outside-caused stress, to make drastic changes, usually with a religious base, in one's culture.

revivalistic movement: A movement whose goal is to return a society or culture to some (often idealized) earlier and better state. (See also REVITALIZATION MOVEMENT.)

rite of intensification: A ceremony whose function is to bring a group together again after some disruptive event.

rite of passage: A ceremony whose function is to dramatize the passage of a person from one status to another (for example, an initiation ceremony that moves a person from boyhood to manhood).

ritual: A stylized act or performance with religious or magical purpose.

Sapir–Whorf hypothesis: Theory based on the ideas of LINGUISTIC RELATIVISM, that the features of a language shape the way in which its speakers perceive and act in the world.

scapulamancy: A form of AUGURY in which the shoulder blade of a large animal is thrown on a fire and the resulting cracks are "read" to foretell the future.

schema: A set of cultural ideas that give coherent meaning to something. An elaboration on the idea of CULTURE.

schemas of romance: The set of ideas that people hold about being in love.

science: In this context, a very tricky term to define nonethnocentrically; a way of dealing with the world without involving the supernatural. (Contrast MAGIC, RELIGION.)

segmentary lineage system: As a LINEAGE grows with new generations, the sublineage branches split off and form independent lineages.

semantic field: A set of words whose referents all lie in the same realm of activity, like kinship terms or color terms.

semantics: The meanings of words.

sex: The cultural constructions and elaborations of action and eroticism around the act of sexual intercourse. (Contrast GENDER.)

sexual dimorphism: When male and female of the same species are strongly different, usually in physical terms.

shaman(ism): A human who can make contact with the supernatural on behalf of other people. Spirit medium.

shifting horticulture: Farming where temporary fields are partially cleared in forest or jungle, planted for a very few crop cycles, then abandoned. (Also known as SLASH-AND-BURN HORTICULTURE.)

sib: A unilineal DESCENT GROUP like a CLAN, but without the clan's territorial limitations.

sign: A signal with a direct, essential relationship to its referent. (A fever is a sign of illness.) (Contrast SYMBOL.)

situated learning: Informal transmission of cultural knowledge with emphasis on in situ, contextualized learning rather than classroom lectures.

situated practice: The learning that takes place in context, as in apprenticeship. (Contrast with CULTURE OF ACQUISITION.)

slash-and-burn horticulture: See SHIFTING HORTICULTURE.

slavery: The ultimate power differential, where one person exercises virtually total control, or ownership, over another.

social anthropology: An especially British form of cultural anthropology, often focusing more on kinship and political relationships than on cultural meanings. In fact, there is little clear line of demarcation between cultural and social anthropology.

social organization: The ways in which a social unit is subdivided into smaller groups whose membership is determined by kinship, age, location, and such criteria.

social structure: See SOCIAL ORGANIZATION.

social unit: A smaller social group within a larger SOCIETY.

socialization: See ENCULTURATION.

society: Organized group of individuals, human or otherwise. (Contrast CULTURE.)

sociolinguistics: The study of how a language is actually used in interactive social settings.

sorcerer: A person who uses magical spells and rituals to (usually) harm someone. (There actually are sorcerers, as distinguished from WITCHES, who are imaginary.)

sororal polygyny: Where the cultural pattern allows or expects a man who has more than one wife to marry sisters.

sororate: When a widower marries the sister of his deceased wife.

soul matter: The belief in many cultures that humans have some sort of vital essence, usually one that departs at death.

specialization: That DIVISION OF LABOR where people do different tasks.

stimulus diffusion: Where ideas passing from one culture to another inspire change, rather than direct movement of goods or importing of teachers.

subculture: A convenient (and nonderogatory) way to refer to various cultural patterns shared by smaller numbers of people within a broader culture.

supernatural: Belief that certain individuals, events, or powers are magical/religious, irrational, or nonscientific. An ultimately ethnocentric judgment.

swastika: The Sanskrit name for one of the oldest and most widespread symbols.

swidden farming: Nonintensive horticulture, also called SHIFTING HORTICULTURE.

symbol: A signal with an indirect, arbitrary relationship to its referent. (A red cross is a symbol of medical help.)

symbolic theories: A wide range of approaches that account for cultural behavior and institutions by focusing on the meanings that they have for the people of that culture.

sympathetic magic: Magical practices based on beliefs of essential mystical connections between things that once were in contact (LAW OF CONTAGION), or that are like each other (LAW OF SIMILARITY), or are opposite to each other (LAW OF OPPOSITES).

syncretism: The incorporation of traits from another culture into the pattern (usually religious) of a culture.

syntax: The grammar of a language.

taboo: The potentially dangerous power of supernatural forces like MANA; now usually meaning "forbidden."

taxation: Where goods or services are collected and then used or redistributed by a central authority.

technology: The tools and techniques of manufacture and production (including both ideas and material objects).

total social phenomenon: Durkheim's phrase for the interconnectedness of institutions with the rest of the culture. (See also HOLISM.)

totemism: The special symbolic and spiritual association between a person or group of persons and a natural phenomenon, individual, or kind.

transgression: The most general term for the violation of a law, custom, or other cultural norm.

transhumance: That form of PASTORALISM in which animals are shifted from one grazing place to another in a yearly cycle.

transnationalism: The condition, especially among contemporary immigrants and refugees, of being firmly rooted in both the culture of origin and the new culture, instead of abandoning the one for the other.

tribe: Middle level in size and complexity of the maximal social organization, in "tribal societies." Lies between BAND and CHIEFDOM.

two-spirit: Recently used term for various alternative genders, especially in Native American cultures.

unclear families: A play on the phrase NUCLEAR FAMILY, referring to the unstandard kin groups resulting from divorce and remarriage and the like.

unilineal descent: Where social groups are subdivided into smaller groups like CLANS on the basis of a single rule of descent; you are either in your mother's group (MATRILINEAL) or your father's group (PATRILINEAL). (Contrast COGNATIC DESCENT GROUP.)

Universal Grammar: The underlying innate, genetically transmitted basic structure of language that allows humans to learn any specific language easily and early.

unobtrusive data collection: The methodology of collecting data that has been left behind by the actors, such that the collection process does not effect the behavior itself.

voluntary associations: Social groups whose members are recruited not through descent rules but through free choice. Many voluntary associations actually hedge, and descent considerations are involved also.

war: Armed conflict between two or more maximal social units.

whole acts: In filming an event, getting the beginning and conclusion as well as the obvious climax.

whole bodies: In filming people, getting what is happening with their entire bodies, and not merely ZOOMING in on their faces.

witch: A person believed to be able to use supernatural powers to harm others.

Witches, New Age: Late-20th-century European and North American practitioners of benevolent magic.

world religions: Those religions that are practiced across cultural boundaries around the world.

world systems: Institutions, especially economic, that cross national boundaries.

zoom: A camera lens that allows one to shift from close-up to wide angle and back. Although at times there is real reason to use it, on the whole zooming is a distracting practice that cuts out much valuable cultural information. Most photographers should leave their zoom lenses at home (or if they are using cameras with built-in zoom lenses, they should exercise great restraint).

BIBLIOGRAPHY

Abbink, J.
    1993   Reading the Entrails: Analysis of an African Divination Discourse. MAN:28(4): 705–726.

Abdullah, Taufik
    1966   Adat and Islam: An Examination of Conflict in Minangkabau. Indonesia 2:1–24.

Acheson, James M.
    1984   The Social Organization of the Maine Lobster Market. Pp. 105–130 in Plattner, Stuart (ed.), Markets and Marketing. Lanham, MD: University Press of America.

Ahearn, Laura
    2001   Invitations to Love: Literacy, Love Letters, and Social Change in Nepal. Ann Arbor: University of Michigan Press.

Altman, Irwin, and Joseph Ginat
    1996   Polygamous Families in Contemporary Society. Cambridge, U.K.: Cambridge University Press.

American Anthropological Association
    1997   Principles of Professional Responsibility. Washington, DC: American Anthropological Association.

American Anthropologist
    1998   AAA Statement on Race. American Anthropologist 100(3): 712–713.

Anderson, Eugene N.
    1988   The Food of China. New Haven, CT: Yale University Press.

Anonymous
    1911   Marriage. Encyclopedia Britannica. Eleventh Edition. Volume 17:753–759.

Appadurai, Arjun
    1991   Global Ethnospaces: Notes and Queries for a Transnational Anthropology. Pp. 191–210 in Fox, Richard G. (ed.), Recapturing Anthropology: Working in the Present. Santa Fe, NM: School of American Research Press.

Appell, George N.
    1978   Ethical Dilemmas in Anthropological Inquiry: A Case Book. Waltham, MA: Crossroads Press.

Applbaum, Kalman D.
    1995   Marriage with the Proper Stranger: Arranged Marriage in Metropolitan Japan. Ethnology 34(1):37–51.

Arensberg, Conrad, and Solon T. Kimball
    1940   Family and Community in Ireland. Cambridge, MA: Harvard University Press.

Arnold, Jeanne E.
    1995   Transportation Innovation and Social Complexity Among Maritime Hunter–Gatherer Societies. American Anthropologist 97(4):733–747.

Atkinson, Jane Monnig
    1989   The Art and Politics of Wana Shamanship. Berkeley: University of California Press.
    1992   Shamanism Today. Pp. 307–330 in Siegel, Bernard J., Alan R. Beals, and Stephen A. Tyler (eds.). Annual Review of Anthropology Vol. 21. Palo Alto, CA: Annual Reviews Inc.

Auge, Marc
    1994/1998   A Sense for the Other: The Timeliness and Relevance of Anthropology. Translated from the French by Amy Jacobs. Stanford, CA: Stanford University Press.

Bachnik, Jane M., and Charles J. Quinn, Jr. (eds.)
    1994   Situated Meaning: Inside and Outside in Japanese Self, Society, and Language. Princeton, NJ: Princeton University Press.

Bailey, Sydney D.
    1972   Prohibitions and Restraints in War. London: Oxford University Press.

Bamberger, Joan
    1974   The Myth of Matriarchy: Why Men Rule in Primitive Society. Pp. 263–280 in Rosaldo, Michelle Zimbalist, and Louise Lamphere (eds.), Women, Culture, and Society. Stanford, CA: Stanford University Press.

Barbash, Ilisa, and Lucien Taylor
    1997   Cross Cultural Filmmaking: A Handbook for Making Documentary and Ethnographic Films and Video. Berkeley: University of California Press.

Barker, Roger G., and Herbert F. Wright
1955   Midwest and Its Children: The Psychological Ecology of an American Town. Evanston, IN: Row, Peterson.

Barkow, Jerome H., Leda Cosmides, and John Tooby (eds.)
1992   The Adapted Mind: Evolutionary Psychology and the Generation of Culture. New York: Oxford University Press.

Barnes, J. A.
1962   African Models in the New Guinea Highlands. MAN 62:5–9.

Barnes, Ruth, and Joanne Eicher (eds.)
1993   Dress and Gender: Making and Meaning in Cultural Contexts. New York: Berg.

Barnouw, Victor
1985   Culture and Personality. Homewood, IL: Dorsey Press.

Bateson, Gregory, and Margaret Mead
1942   Balinese Character: A Photographic Analysis. New York: New York Academy of Sciences.

Bellah, Robert, et al.
1985   Habits of the Heart: Individualism and Commitment in American Life. Berkeley: University of California Press.

Benedict, Ruth
1934   Patterns of Culture. New York: Houghton Mifflin.
1946   The Chrysanthemum and the Sword: Patterns of Japanese Culture. Boston: Houghton Mifflin.

Berlin, Brent
1992   Ethnobiological Classification: Principles of Categorization of Plants and Animals in Traditional Societies. Princeton, NJ: Princeton University Press.

Berlin, Brent, and Paul Kay
1969   Basic Color Terms: Their Universality and Evolution. Berkeley: University of California Press.

Bernard, H. Russell
2000   Social Research Methods: Qualitative and Quantitative Approaches. Thousand Oaks, CA: Sage Publications.

Bernatzik, Hugo Adolf
1938   Die Geister der Gelben Blaetter. Forschungsreisen in Hinterindien. Munich: Verlag F. Bruckmann.

Besnier, Niko
1994   Polynesian Gender Liminality through Time and Space. Pp. 285–328 in Herdt, Gilbert (ed.), Third Sex, Third Gender: Beyond Sexual Dimorphism in Culture and History. New York: Zone Books.

Bestor, Theodore C.
1989   Neighborhood Tokyo. Stanford, CA: Stanford University Press.

Birdwhistell, Ray
1964/1970   Masculinity and Femininity as Display. Pp. 39–46 in Kinesics and Context: Essays on Body Motion Communication. Philadelphia: University of Pennsylvania Press.
1970   Kinesics and Context: Essays on Body Motion Communication. Philadelphia: University of Pennsylvania Press.

Blackwood, Evelyn
1995   Senior Mothers, Model Mothers, and Dutiful Wives: Managing Gender Contradictions in a Minangkabau Village. Pp. 124–158 in Ong, Aihwa, and Michael G. Peletz (eds.), Bewitching Women, Pious Men: Gender and Body Politics in Southeast Asia. Berkeley: University of California Press.

Boas, Franz
1897   The Social Organization and the Secret Societies of the Kwakiutl. Report of U.S. National Museum for 1895. Pp. 311–738. Reprinted 1970, New York: Johnson Reprint Company.

Boddy, Janice
1997   Womb as Oasis: The Symbolic Context of Pharaonic Circumcision in Rural Northern Sudan. Pp. 309–324 in Lancaster, Roger N., and Micaela di Leonardo (eds.), The Gender/Sexuality Reader: Culture, History, Political Economy. New York: Routledge.

Boggs, Stephen T., and Malcolm Naea Chun
1990   Ho'oponopono: A Hawaiian Method of Solving Interpersonal Problems. Pp.122–160 in Watson-Gegeo, Karen, and Geoffrey M. White (eds.), Disentangling: Conflict Discourse in Pacific Societies. Stanford, CA.: Stanford University Press.

Boon, James
1977   The Anthropological Romance of Bali: 1597–1972. Cambridge, England: Cambridge University Press.

Borges, Jorge Luis
   1964   Funes the Memorious. Pp. 59–66 in
      Labyrinths: Selected Stories and Other Writings. New York: New Directions.
Borofsky, Robert (ed.)
   1994   Assessing Cultural Anthropology. New
      York: McGraw-Hill.
Bouquet, Mary
   1993   Reclaiming English Kinship: Portuguese
      Refractions of British Kinship Theory. Manchester, England: Manchester University
      Press.
Bowen, Elenore Smith
   1954/1964   Return to Laughter: An Anthropological Novel. New York: Anchor Books.
Bowen, John R.
   1991   Sumatran Politics and Poetics: Gayo History. New Haven, CT: Yale University Press.
   1993a   Muslims through Discourse: Religion
      and Ritual in Gayo Society. Princeton, NJ:
      Princeton University Press.
   1993b   Discursive Monotheisms. American
      Ethnologist 20(1):185–190.
Brace, C. Loring
   1995   Region Does Not Mean "Race": Reality
      Versus Convention in Forensic Anthropology.
      Journal of Forensic Sciences 40(2): 171–175.
Bramforth, Douglas B.
   1994   Indigenous People, Indigenous Violence:
      Precontact Warfare on the North American
      Great Plains. MAN 29(1):95–115.
Briggs, Charles L.
   1986   Learning How to Ask: A Sociolinguistic
      Appraisal of the Role of the Interview in Social Science Research. Cambridge, U.K.:
      Cambridge University Press.
Briggs, Jean
   1970   Never in Anger: Portrait of an Eskimo
      Family. Cambridge, MA: Harvard University
      Press.
Brown, Donald E.
   1988   The Penis Inserts of Southeast Asia: An
      Annotated Bibliography with an Overview
      and Comparative Perspectives. Berkeley:
      University of California at Berkeley Center
      for Southeast Asia.
Brown, Michael F.
   1997   Thinking About Magic. Pp. 121–136 in
      Glazier, Stephen D. (ed.), Anthropology of

Religion: A Handbook. Westport, CT: Greenwood Press
   1998   Can Culture Be Copyrighted? Cultural
      Anthropology 39(2):193–222.
Brush, Stephen B., and Doreen Stabinsky (eds.)
   1996   Valuing Local Knowledge: Indigenous
      People and Intellectual Property Rights.
      Washington, DC: Island Press.
Burawoy, Michael, et al.
   1991   Ethnography Unbound: Power and Resistance in the Modern Metropolis. Berkeley: University of California Press.
Burton, Richard
   1861/1963   The City of the Saints and Across
      the Rocky Mountains to California. London:
      Longmans, Green, Longman and Roberts.
      1963 edition, edited by Fawn M. Brodie.
      New York: Alfred A. Knopf.
Busbee, Elizabeth R.
   1998   Gendered Language and Lesbian Communication Patterns. Unpublished honors
      thesis. South Carolina College, University of
      South Carolina.

Calderón, Eduardo, Ricard Cowan, Douglas
   Sharon, and F. Kaye Sharon
   1982   Eduardo el Curandero: The words of a
      Peruvian healer. Richmond, CA: North Atlantic Books.
Cancian, Frank
   1965   Economics and Prestige in a Maya Community: The Religious Cargo System in Zinacantan. Stanford, CA: Stanford University
      Press.
   1976   Change and Uncertainty in a Peasant
      Economy: The Maya Corn Farmers of Zinacantan. Stanford, CA: Stanford University
      Press.
Carpenter, Edmund
   1975   Introduction. Pp. 9–27 in Holm, Bill, and
      Bill Reid (eds.), Indian Art of the Northwest
      Coast: A Dialogue on Craftsmanship and
      Aesthetics. Houston: Institute for the Arts,
      Rice University. Seattle: University of Washington Press.
Carsten, Janet, and Stephen Hugh-Jones (eds.)
   1995   About the House: Lévi-Strauss and Beyond. Cambridge, U.K.: Cambridge University Press.

Carucci, Laurence, Michael Brown, and Lynne Pettler
1989   Shared Spaces: Contexts of Interaction in Chicago's Ethnic Communities. New York: AMS Press.

Casey, Joanna
1998   The Ecology of Food Production in West Africa. Pp. 46–70 in Kent, Susan (ed.). Gender in African Prehistory. Walnut Creek: Altamira Press.

Catholic Church
1995   Catechism of the Catholic Church. New York: Doubleday.

Chagnon, Napoleon A.
1992   Yanomamö. Fourth Edition. Fort Worth, TX: Harcourt Brace Jovanovich College Publishers.

Chang, K. C. (ed.)
1977   Food in Chinese Culture: Anthropological and Historical Perspectives. New Haven, CT: Yale University Press.

Chapple, Eliot Dinsmore, and Carleton Stevens Coon
1942   Principles of Anthropology. New York: H. Holt.

Clancy-Smith, Julia, and Frances Gouda (eds.)
1998   Domesticating the Empire: Race, Gender, and Family Life in French and Dutch Colonialism. Charlottesville: University of Virginia Press.

Clavell, James
1975   Shogun: A Novel of Japan. New York: Atheneum.

Coates, Jennifer
1996   Women Talk: Conversation Between Women Friends. Oxford, U.K.: Blackwell Publishers, Inc.

Codere, Helen
1956   The Amiable Side of Kwakiutl Life: The Potlatch and Play Potlatch. American Anthropologist 58:334–351.
1966   Introduction. Kwakiutl Ethnography by Franz Boas. Edited by Helen Codere. Chicago: University of Chicago Press.

Cogan, Daniel
1998   Seeing Power in a College Cafeteria. Pp. 173–185 in Kingsolver, Ann E. (ed.), More Than Class: Studying Power in U.S. Workplaces. Albany: State University of New York Press.

Cohn, Bernard S.
1996   Colonialism and Its Forms of Knowledge: The British in India. Princeton, NJ: Princeton University Press.

Cole, Douglas
1991   The History of the Kwakiutl Potlatch. Pp. 135–176 in Jonaitis, Aldona (ed.), Chiefly Feasts: The Enduring Kwakiutl Potlatch. Seattle: University of Washington Press.

Collier, Jane Fishburne
1988   Marriage and Inequality in Classless Societies. Stanford, CA: Stanford University Press.

Colson, Elizabeth
1974   Introduction. In Ogbu, John. The Next Generation: An Ethnography of Education in an Urban Neighborhood. New York: Academic Press.

Conley, John M., and William M. O'Barr
1990   Rules versus Relationships: The Ethnography of Legal Discourse. Chicago: University of Chicago Press.

Connor, Linda, Patsy Asch, and Timothy Asch
1986   Jero Tapakan: Balinese Healer. Cambridge, U.K.: Cambridge University Press.

Cooper, Frederick, and Ann Laura Stoller (eds.)
1997   Tensions of Empire: Colonial Cultures in a Bourgeois World. Berkeley: University of California Press.

Cooper, Robert
1996   Culture Shock! Thailand. Singapore: Times Books International.

Cooper, Thomas W.
1995   National Rhythms: The Indigenous World of Robert Gardner. New York: Anthology Films Archives.

Cox, Paul A.
2000   Will Tribal Knowledge Survive the Millennium? Science 287(5450):44.

Crichton, Michael
1992   Rising Sun. New York: Ballantine Books.

Cummings, Martha Clark
1994   Lesbian Identity and Negotiation in Discourse. Pp. 144–158 in Bucholtz, Mary, et al. (eds.), Cultural Performances. Proceedings of the Third Berkeley Women and Language Conference. Berkeley Women and Language Group: Berkeley, California.

Dahlberg, Frances (ed.)
  1981   Woman the Gatherer. New Haven, CT: Yale University Press.
Daltabuit, Magali, and Thomas L. Leatherman
  1998   The Biocultural Impact of Tourism on Mayan Communities. Pp. 317–337 in Goodman, Alan H., and Thomas L. Leatherman (eds.), Building a New Biocultural Synthesis: Political Economic Perspectives on Human Biology. Ann Arbor: University of Michigan Press.
Danielsson, Bengt
  1956   Love in the South Seas, translated by F. H. Lyon. New York: Reynal.
Davies, Mel
  1982   Corsets and Conception: Fashion and Demographic Trends in the Nineteenth Century. Comparative Studies in Society and History 24(4):611–641.
deTocqueville, Alexis
  1835, 1840/1969   Democracy in America. New York: Doubleday.
De Vita, Phillip R.
  1990   The Humbled Anthropologist: Tales from the Pacific. Belmont, CA: Wadsworth.
  1992   The Naked Anthropologist: Tales from Around the World. Belmont, CA: Wadsworth.
de Waal, Frans B. M.
  2002   Evolutionary Psychology: the Wheat and the Chaff. Current Directions in Psychological Science 11(6):187–195.
Diamond, Jared
  1997   Guns, Germs, and Steel: The Fates of Human Societies. New York: W. W. Norton.
di Leonardo, Michaela
  1998   Exotics at Home: Anthropologists, Others, American Modernity. Chicago: University of Chicago Press.
Divale, William
  1984   Matrilineal Residence in Pre-literate Society. Ann Arbor: UMI Research Press.
Doi, Takeo
  1971   The Anatomy of Dependence. Tokyo: Kodansha International.
Dorkenoo, Efua
  1994   Cutting the Rose: Female Genital Mutilation: The Practice and Its Prevention. London: Minority Rights Publications.

Douglas, Mary
  1966   The Abominations of Leviticus. Pp. 41–57 in Purity and Danger. London: Routledge and Kegan Paul.
Dove, Michael R.
  1988a   Introduction: Traditional Culture and Development in Contemporary Indonesia. Pp. 1–37 in Dove, Michael R. (ed.), The Real and Imagined Role of Culture in Development: Case Studies from Indonesia. Honolulu: University of Hawaii Press.
  1988b   The Ecology of Intoxication among the Kantu' of West Kalimantan. Pp. 139–182 in Dove, Michael R. (ed.), The Real and Imagined Role of Culture in Development: Case Studies from Indonesia. Honolulu: University of Hawaii Press.
  1993   Uncertainty, Humility, and Adaptation in the Tropical Forest: The Agricultural Augury of the Kantu'. Ethnology 32(2): 145–167.
Dudley, Kathryn Marie
  1999   (Dis)locating the Middle Class. Anthropology Newsletter 40(4):1–4.
Durante, Alessandro
  1994   From Grammar to Politics: Linguistic Anthropology in a Western Samoan Village. Berkeley: University of California Press.
Durkheim, Emile
  1893/1964   The Division of Labor in Society. New York: Macmillan.
  1912   The Elementary Forms of Religious Life. New York: Collier Books.
Durrenberger, E. Paul
  1992   It's All Politics: South Alabama's Seafood Industry. Urbana: University of Illinois Press.
Dyen, Isidore
  1953/1975   Review of Otto Ch. Dahl, Malgache et Maanjan: Une Comparaison Linguistique. Pp. 29–49 in Linguistic Subgrouping and Lexicostatistics. The Hague: Mouton.

Efron, David
  1941/1972   Gesture, Race, and Culture. The Hague: Mouton.
Eggan, Fred
  1950   Social Organization of the Western Pueblos. Chicago: University of Chicago Press.

Eiseman, Fred B., Jr.
  1990   Bali: Sekala and Niskala. Singapore: Periplus.
Ekman, Paul, Robert Levenson, and Wallace V. Friesen
  1983   Autonomic Nervous System Activity Distinguishes among Emotions. Science 221(4616):1208–1210.
Elkin, A. P.
  1938/1964   The Australian Aborigines. Third Edition. Garden City, NY: Anchor Books.
Ember, Melvin, and Carol Ember
  1971   The Conditions Favoring Matrilocal Residence versus Patrilocal Residence. American Anthropologist 73(3):571–594.
Embree, John Fee
  1939   Suye Mura, a Japanese Village. Chicago: University of Chicago Press.
Errington, Shelly
  1989   Meaning and Power in a Southeast Asian Realm. Princeton, NJ: Princeton University Press.
Evans-Pritchard, E. E.
  1940   The Nuer: A Description of the Modes of Livelihood and Political Institutions of a Nilotic People. Oxford, U.K.: Oxford University Press.
  1951   Kinship and Marriage among the Nuer. Oxford, U.K.: Oxford University Press.
  1956   Nuer Religion. Oxford, U.K.: Oxford University Press.
  1965   Witchcraft: Oracles and Magic among the Azande. Oxford, U.K.: Clarendon Press.

Farmer, Paul
  1992   AIDS and Accusation: Haiti and the Geography of Blame. Berkeley: University of California Press.
  1999   Infections and Inequalities: The Modern Plagues. Berkeley: University of California Press.
Farnell, Brenda
  1995   Do You See What I Mean? Plains Indian Sign Talk and the Embodiment of Action. Austin: University of Texas Press.
Ferguson, Leland
  1992   Uncommon Ground: Archaeology and Early African America, 1650–1800. Washington, DC: Smithsonian Institution Press.

Ferguson, R. Brian
  1988   The Anthropology of War: A Bibliography. New York: Harry Frank Guggenheim Foundation.
  1992   A Savage Encounter: Western Contact and the Yanomami War Complex. Pp. 199–227 in Ferguson, R. Brian, and Neil L. Whitehead (eds.), War in the Tribal Zone: Expanding States and Indigenous Warfare. Seattle: University of Washington Press.
  1995   Yanomami Warfare: A Political History. Santa Fe, NM: School of American Research Press.
Finney, Ben
  1994   Voyage of Rediscovery: A Cultural Odyssey through Polynesia. Berkeley: University of California Press.
Firth, Raymond
  1936   We, the Tikopia. New York: American Book Company.
Fisher, Helen
  1999   The First Sex: The Natural Talents of Women and How They Are Changing the World. New York: Random House.
Flinn, Juliana, Leslie Marshall, and Jocelyn Armstrong (eds.)
  1988   Fieldwork and Families: Constructing New Models for Ethnographic Research. Honolulu: University of Hawaii Press.
Fluehr-Lobban, Carolyn
  2003   Darkness in El Dorado: Research Ethics, Then and Now. Pp. 85–104 in Fluehr-Lobban, Carolyn (ed.), Ethics and the Profession of Anthropology. Dialogue for Ethically Conscious Practice (2nd ed.). Walnut Creek, CA: Alta Mira Press.
Fratkin, Elliot
  1997   Pastoralism: Government and Development Issues. Pp. 235–261 in Durham, William H., E. Valentine Daniel, and Bambi B. Schieffelin (eds.), Annual Review of Anthropology. Vol. 26. Palo Alto, CA: Annual Review, Inc.
  1998   Ariaal Pastoralists of Kenya: Surviving Drought and Development in Africa's Arid Lands. Boston: Allyn and Bacon.
Frazer, James
  1922   The Golden Bough: A Study in Magic and Religion. Abridged Edition. New York: Macmillan.

Freeman, Derek
  1983 Margaret Mead and Samoa: The Making and Unmaking of an Anthropological Myth. Cambridge, MA: Harvard University Press.
  1999 The Fateful Hoaxing of Margaret Mead: A Historical Analysis of Her Samoan Research. Boulder, CO: Westview.
Friedl, Ernestine
  1994 Sex the Invisible. American Anthropologist 96(4):833–844.
Friedman, Jonathan
  1994 Cultural Identity and Global Process. London: Sage.
Fry, Douglas P., and Kaj Bjorkqvist (eds.)
  1997 Cultural Variation in Conflict Resolution: Alternatives to Violence. Mahwah, NJ: Lawrence Erlbaum Associates.

Galanti, Geri-Ann
  1997 Caring for Patients from Different Cultures: Case Studies from American Hospitals. Second edition. Philadelphia: University of Pennsylvania Press.
Galaty, John G., and Kimpei Ole Munei
  1999 Maasai Land, Law, and Dispossession. Cultural Survival Quarterly 22(4):68–71.
Gardner, Howard
  1983 Frames of Mind: The Theory of Multiple Intelligences. New York: Basic Books.
  1993 Multiple Intelligences: The Theory in Practice. New York: Basic Books.
Gardner, Robert
  1971 A Chronicle of the Human Experience: Dead Birds. Pp. 430–436 in Jacobs, Lewis (ed.), The Documentary Experience: From Nanook to Woodstock. New York: Hopkinson and Blake.
  1972 On the Making of Dead Birds. Pp. 31–35 in Heider, Karl G. (ed.), The Dani of West Irian: An Ethnographic Companion to the Film Dead Birds. New York: Warner Modular Publications.
Gaulin, Steven J. C., and James S. Boster
  1990 Dowry as Female Competition. American Anthropologist 92(4):994–1005.
Geertz, Clifford
  1972/1973 Deep Play: Notes on the Balinese Cockfight. Pp. 412–453 in The Interpretation of Cultures: Selected Essays by Clifford Geertz. New York: Basic Books.
  1980 Negara: The Theatre State in Nineteenth Century Bali. Princeton, NJ: Princeton University Press.
Geertz, Hildred
  1968 Latah in Java: A Theoretical Paradox. Indonesia 3:93–104.
  1994 Images of Power: Balinese Paintings Made for Gregory Bateson and Margaret Mead. Honolulu: University of Hawaii Press.
Gellner, David
  1997 For Syncretism: The Position of Buddhism in Nepal and Japan Compared. Social Anthropology 5(3):277–291.
Gewertz, Deborah
  1983 Sepik River Societies: A Historical Ethnography of the Chambri and Their Neighbors. New Haven, CT: Yale University Press.
Gibbs, James L., Jr.
  1965 The Kpelle of Liberia. Pp.197–240 in Gibbs, James L., Jr. (ed.), Peoples of Africa. New York: Holt, Rinehart and Winston.
  1969 Law and Personality: Signposts for a New Direction. Pp. 176–207 in Nader, Laura (ed.), Law in Culture and Society. Chicago: Aldine.
Giteau, Madeleine
  1976 The Civilization of Angkor. New York: Rizzoli.
Glick Schiller, Nina, Linda Basch, and Cristina Szanton Blanc (eds.)
  1992 Towards a Transnational Perspective on Migration: Race, Class, Ethnicity and Nationalism Reconsidered. New York: New York Academy of Sciences.
  1995 From Immigrant to Transmigrant: Theorizing Transnational Migration. Anthropological Quarterly 68(1):49–63.
Gmelch, George
  1971 Baseball Magic. Trans-Action 8(8):39–41, 45.
Goldhagen, Daniel Jonah
  1996 Hitler's Willing Executioners: Ordinary Germans and the Holocaust. New York: Knopf.
Goldman, Irving
  1975 The Mouth of Heaven: An Introduction to Kwakiutl Religious Thought. New York: John Wiley and Sons.

Goldstein, Melvyn C.
    1987   When Brothers Share a Wife. Natural
        History 96(3):38–48.
Good, Mary-Jo DelVecchio, Paul E. Brodwin, Byron
    J. Good, and Arthur Kleinman (eds.)
    1992   Pain as Human Experience: An Anthro-
        pological Perspective. Berkeley: University
        of California Press.
Goode, William J.
    1993   World Changes in Divorce Patterns. New
        Haven, CT: Yale University Press.
Goodenough, Ward H.
    1956   Componential Analysis and the Study of
        Meaning. Language 32:195–216.
    2002   Anthropology in the 20th Century and
        Beyond. American Anthropologist
        104(2):423–440.
Goodman, Alan H.
    1995   The Problematics of "Race" in Con-
        temporary Biological Anthropology.
        Pp. 215– 239 in Boaz, N. T., and L. D. Wolfe
        (eds.), Biological Anthropology: The State
        of the Science. Bend, OR: International
        Institute for Human Evolutionary
        Research.
Goodwin, Charles
    1981   Conversational Interaction: Interaction
        Between Speakers and Hearers. New York:
        Academic Press.
    1994   Professional Vision. American Anthro-
        pologist 96(3):606–633.
Goodwin, Charles, and Alessandro Durante
    1992   Rethinking Context: An Introduction.
        Pp. 1–42 in Durante, Alessandro, and
        Charles Goodwin (eds.), Rethinking Con-
        text: Language as an Interactive Phenome-
        non. Cambridge, U.K.: Cambridge University
        Press.
Goodwin, Marjorie H.
    1990   He-Said-She-Said: Talk as Social Organi-
        zation among Black Children. Bloomington:
        Indiana University Press.
Goody, Jack, and S. J. Tambiah
    1973   Bridewealth and Dowry. Cambridge,
        U.K.: Cambridge University Press.
Goulet, Jean-Guy A.
    1996   The "Berdach"/ "Two-Spirit": A Compar-
        ison of Anthropological and Native Con-
        structions of Gendered Identities Among

        Northern Athapaskans. Journal of the Royal
        Anthropological Institute 2(4):683–701.
Gregor, Thomas
    1985   Anxious Pleasures: The Sexual Lives of
        an Amazonian People. Chicago: University
        of Chicago Press.
Gregor, Thomas A., and Daniel R. Gross
    2002   Anthropology and the Search for the
        Enemy Within. Chronicle of Higher Educa-
        tion, July 26.
Gremaux, Rene
    1994   Woman Becomes Man in the Balkans.
        Pp. 241–281 in Herdt, Gilbert (ed.), Third Sex,
        Third Gender: Beyond Sexual Dimorphism in
        Culture and History. New York: Zone Books.
Gruenbaum, Ellen
    1995   Women's Rights and Cultural Self-
        Determination in the Female Genital Mu-
        tilation Controversy. Anthropology
        Newsletter 36(5):14–15.
Guenther, Mathias
    1996   Diversity and Flexibility: The Case of
        the Bushmen of Southern Africa. Pp. 65–86
        in Kent, Susan (ed.), Cultural Diversity
        Among Twentieth Century Foragers. Cam-
        bridge, U.K.: Cambridge University Press.
Guha, Ranajit (ed.)
    1997   A Subaltern Studies Reader. Minneapo-
        lis: University of Minnesota Press.
Gumpertz, John J., and Stephen C. Levinson
    1996a   Introduction: Linguistic Relativity Re-
        examined. Pp. 1–36 in Gumpertz, John J.,
        and Stephen C. Levinson (eds.), Rethinking
        Linguistic Relativity. Cambridge, U.K.: Cam-
        bridge University Press.
Gumpertz, John J., and Stephen C. Levinson (eds.)
    1996b   Rethinking Linguistic Relativity. Cam-
        bridge, U.K.: Cambridge University Press.
Gutmann, Matthew C.
    1996   The Meanings of Macho: Being a Man in
        Mexico City. Berkeley: University of Califor-
        nia Press.
    1997   The Ethnographic (G)ambit: Women and
        the Negotiation of Masculinity in Mexico
        City. American Ethnologist 24(4):833–855.

Hall, Edward
    1959   The Silent Language. Garden City, NY:
        Doubleday.

Hammel, Eugene A.
1972 The Myth of Structural Analysis: Lévi-Strauss and the Three Bears. Addison-Wesley Modular Publications No. 25. Reading, MA: Addison-Wesley.

Hanson, F. Alan
1993 Testing Testing: Social Consequences of the Examined Life. Berkeley: University of California Press.

Harre, Rom, and Robert Finlay-Jones
1986 Emotion Talk across Times. Pp. 220–233 in Harre, Rom (ed.), The Social Construction of Emotions. Oxford, U.K.: Basil Blackwell.

Harrer, Heinrich
1963 Ich komme aus der Steinzeit: Ewiges Eis im Dschungel der Südsee. West Berlin, Germany: Ullstein.

Harris, Marvin
1964 The Nature of Cultural Things. New York: Random House.
1968 The Rise of Anthropological Theory. A History of Theories of Culture. New York: Thomas Y. Crowell.
1979a Cows, Pigs, Wars, and Witches: The Riddles of Culture. New York: Random House.
1979b Cultural Materialism: The Struggle for a Science of Culture. New York: Random House.

Harrison, Faye V.
1998a Introduction: Expanding the Discussion on "Race." American Anthropologist 100(3):609–631.

Harrison, Faye V. (ed.)
1998b Race and Racism. Contemporary Issues Forum: American Anthropologist 100(3).

Heath, Shirley Brice
1983 Ways with Words: Language, Life, and Work in Communities and Classrooms. Cambridge, U.K.: Cambridge University Press.

Heelas, Paul, and Andrew Lock (eds.)
1981 Indigenous Psychologies: The Anthropology of the Self. London: Academic Press.

Heider, Karl G.
1956 Fort McDowell (Yavapai) Acculturation: A Preliminary Report. Unpublished B.A. honors thesis. Department of Anthropology, Harvard University.
1969a Sweet Potato Notes and Lexical Queries. Kroeber Anthropological Society Papers 41:78–86.

1969b Anthropological Models of Incest Laws in the United States. American Anthropologist 71(2):693–701.
1970 The Dugum Dani: A Papuan Culture in the Highlands of West New Guinea. Chicago: Aldine.
1972a The Dani of West Irian: An Ethnographic Companion to the Film Dead Birds. New York: Warner Modular Publications.
1972b The Grand Valley Dani Pig Feast: A Ritual of Passage and Intensification. Oceania 42(3):169–197.
1975 Societal Intensification and Cultural Stress as Determining Factors in the Innovation and Conservatism of Two Dani Cultures. Oceania 46(1):53–67.
1976a Dani Sexuality: A Low Energy System. MAN 11:188–201.
1976b Ethnographic Film. Austin: University of Texas Press.
1980 The Gamecock, the Swamp Fox and the Wizard Owl: The Development of Good Form in an American Totemic Set. Journal of American Folklore 93(36):1–22.
1988 The Rashomon Effect: When Ethnographers Disagree. American Anthropologist 90(1):73–81.
1991 Indonesian Cinema: National Culture on Screen. Honolulu: University of Hawaii Press.
1994 National Cinema, National Culture: The Indonesian Case. Pp. 162–173 in Dissanayake, Wimal (ed.), Colonialism and Nationalism in Asian Cinema. Bloomington: Indiana University Press.
1997 Grand Valley Dani: Peaceful Warriors. Third Edition. Fort Worth, TX: Holt, Rinehart and Winston.

Heider, Karl G., and Carol Hermer
1995 Films for Anthropological Teaching. Eighth Edition. Washington, DC: American Anthropological Association.

Hendrickson, Carol
1995 Weaving Identities: Construction of Dress and Self in a Highland Guatemala Town. Austin: University of Texas Press.

Herdt, Gilbert
1987 The Sambia: Ritual and Gender in New Guinea. Fort Worth, TX: Harcourt Brace Jovanovich.

Herdt, Gilbert (ed.)
    1994 Third Sex, Third Gender: Beyond Sexual Dimorphism in Culture and History. New York: Zone Books.

Herrmann, Gretchen M.
    1997 Gift or Commodity: What Changes Hands in the U.S. Garage Sale? American Ethnologist 24(4):910–930.

Herskovits, Melville J.
    1938 Dahomey, an Ancient West African Kingdom. New York: Augustin.

Hickey, Gerald Cannon
    1964 Village in Vietnam. New Haven, CT: Yale University Press.

Hicks, George
    1973 Appalachian Valley. New York: Holt, Rinehart, and Winston.

Hinton, Alexander Laban
    1996 Agents of Death: Explaining the Cambodian Genocide in Terms of Psychological Dissonance. American Anthropologist 98(4):818–831.
    1998 Why Did You Kill?: The Cambodian Genocide and the Dark Side of Face and Honor. Journal of Asian Studies 57(1):93–122.

Hitchcock, Robert K
    1999 Resource Rights and Resettlement Among the San of Botswana. Culture Survival Quarterly 22(4):51–55.

Hockings, Paul
    1997 Review of Karl G. Heider, Seeing Anthropology. Cultural Anthropology Through Film. Visual Anthropology 10:121–123.

Hockett, Charles
    1960/1977 Logical Considerations in the Study of Animal Communication. Reprinted. Pp.124–162 in The View from Language: Selected Essays 1948–1974. Athens: University of Georgia Press.

Hoebel, E. Adamson
    1954 The Law of Primitive Man: A Study in Comparative Legal Dynamics. Cambridge, MA: Harvard University Press.

Hollan, Douglas Wood, and Jane C. Wellenkamp
    1994 Contentment and Suffering: Culture and Experience in Toraja. New York: Columbia University Press.

Holland, Dorothy C.
    1990 Educated in Romance: Women, Achievement, and College Culture. Chicago: University of Chicago Press.

Holm, Bill, and Bill Reid
    1975 Indian Art of the Northwest Coast: A Dialogue on Craftsmanship and Aesthetics. Houston: Institute for the Arts, Rice University. Seattle: University of Washington Press.

Holmes, Ruth Bradley, and Betty Sharp Smith
    1992 Beginning Cherokee. Norman: University of Oklahoma Press.

Hoskins, Janet
    1989 Why Do Ladies Sing the Blues? Indigo Dyeing, Cloth Production and Gender Symbolism in Kodi. Pp. 141–173 in Weiner, Annette, and Jane Schneider (eds.), Cloth and Human Experience. Washington, DC: Smithsonian Institution Press.
    1993 Violence, Sacrifice, and Divination: Giving and Taking Life in Eastern Indonesia. American Ethnologist 20(1):159–178.

Howe, K. R.
    1984 Where the Waves Fall: A New South Sea Islands History from First Settlement to Colonial Rule. Honolulu: University of Hawaii Press.

Howell, Nancy C.
    1994 Surviving Fieldwork: A 1990 Report of the Advisory Panel on Health and Safety in Fieldwork. Washington, DC: American Anthropological Association.

Howell, Signe, and Roy Willis (eds.)
    1989 Societies at Peace: Anthropological Perspectives. London: Routledge.

Hsu, Francis L. K.
    1983 Rugged Individualism Reconsidered: Essays in Psychological Anthropology. Knoxville: University of Tennessee Press.

Hunt, Geoffrey
    1998 Learning to Hug: An English Anthropologist's Experiences in North America. Pp. 125–136 in De Vita, Philip, and James Armstrong (eds.), Distant Mirrors. Second Edition. Belmont, CA: Wadsworth.

Hutchinson, Sharon E.
    1996 Nuer Dilemmas: Coping with Money, War, and the State. Berkeley: University of California Press.

Ingham, John M.
  1996 Psychological Anthropology Reconsidered. Cambridge, U.K.: Cambridge University Press.
Ivy, Marilyn
  1995 Discourses of the Vanishing: Modernity, Phantasm, Japan. Chicago: University of Chicago Press.

Jacknis, Ira
  1991 George Hunt Collection of Indian Specimens. Pp. 176–225 in Jonaitis, Aldona (ed.), Chiefly Feasts: The Enduring Kwakiutl Potlatch. Seattle: University of Washington Press.
Jackson, Jean E.
  2000 "Camp Pain": Talking with Chronic Pain Patients. Philadelphia: University of Pennsylvania Press.
Jacobs, Sue Thomas
  1994 Two-Spirit People: Native American Gender Identity, Sexuality and Spirituality. Urbana: University of Illinois Press.
James, William
  1910 The Moral Equivalent of War. McClures Magazine, August 1910, and The Popular Science Monthly, October 1910. Reprinted 1967. Pp. 660–671 in John J. McDermott (ed.), The Writings of William James. New York: The Modern Library.
Jamieson, Neil L.
  1993 Understanding Vietnam. Berkeley: University of California Press.
Jankowiak, William R.
  1993 Sex, Death, and Hierarchy in a Chinese City. New York: Columbia University Press.
Jankowiak, William R. (ed.)
  1995 Romantic Passion: A Universal Experience? New York: Columbia University Press.
Jankowiak, William R., and Edward F. Fischer
  1992 A Cross-Cultural Perspective on Romantic Love. Ethnology 31(2):149–155.
Jefferson, Thomas
  1785/1976 Letter to Marquis de Chastellux, Paris, September 2, 1785. Pp. 42–43 in Merrill, Boynton, Jr., Jefferson's Nephews: A Frontier Tragedy. Princeton, NJ: Princeton University Press, 1976.

Joralemon, Donald, and Douglas Sharon
  1993 Sorcery and Shamanism: Curanderos and Clients in Northern Peru. Salt Lake City: University of Utah Press.
Joyner, Charles W.
  1986 Down by the Riverside: A South Carolina Slave Community. Urbana: University of Illinois Press.

Kamen, Henry
  1997 The Spanish Inquisition: A Historical Perspective. New Haven, CT: Yale University Press.
Kammen, Michael
  1972 People of Paradox: An Inquiry Concerning the Origins of American Civilization. New York: Oxford University Press.
Kapfer, Reinhard, Werner Petermann, and Ralph Thomas (eds.)
  1990 Rituale von Leben und Tod: Robert Gardner und seine Filme. Munich: Trickster.
Kaplan, Amy, and Donald E. Pease (eds.)
  1993 Cultures of United States Imperialism. Durham, NC: Duke University Press.
Karston, Peter
  1978 Law, Soldiers, and Combat. Westport, CT: Greenwood Press.
Kay, Paul
  1996 Intra-speaker Relativity. Pp. 77–114 in Gumpertz, John J., and Stephen C. Levinson (eds.), Rethinking Linguistic Relativity. Cambridge, U.K.: Cambridge University Press.
Kehoe, Alice Beck
  1989 The Ghost Dance: Ethnohistory and Revitalization. New York: Holt, Rinehart and Winston.
Keller, Helen
  1902/1958 The Story of My Life. New York: Penguin Books USA Inc.
Kelly, Robert L.
  1995 The Foraging Spectrum: Diversity in Hunter–Gatherer Lifeways. Washington, DC: Smithsonian Institute Press.
Kent, Susan
  1995 Does Sedentarization Promote Gender Inequality?: A Case Study from the Kalahari. Journal of the Royal Anthropological Institute 1(3):513–536.

Kent, Susan (ed.)
1996   Cultural Diversity Among Twentieth-Century Foragers: An African Perspective. Cambridge, U.K.: Cambridge University Press.

Killbride, Phillip
1994   Plural Marriages for Our Time: A Reinvented Option? Westport, CT: Bergin and Garvey.

Kingsolver, Ann E. (ed.)
1998   More Than Class: Studying Power in U.S. Workplaces. Albany: State University of New York Press.

Kluckhohn, Clyde
1944   Navaho Witchcraft. Cambridge, MA: Peabody Museum.

Kluckhohn, Clyde, Henry A. Murray, and David M. Schneider (eds.)
1962   Personality in Nature, Society, and Culture. Second Edition. New York: Alfred A. Knopf.

Koch, Klaus-Friedrich
1974   War and Peace in Jalémó: The Management of Conflict in Highland New Guinea. Cambridge, MA: Harvard University Press.

Koester, Stephen K.
1994   Copping, Running, and Paraphernalia Laws: Contextual Variables and Needle Risk Behavior among Injection Drug Users in Denver. Human Organization 53(3):287–295.
1996   The Process of Drug Injection: Applying Ethnography to the Study of HIV Risk among IDUs. Pp. 133–148 in Rhodes, Tim, and Richard Hartnoll (eds.), AIDS, Drugs and Prevention: Perspectives on Individual and Community Action. London: Routledge.

Koltyk, Jo Ann
1998   New Pioneers in the Heartland: Hmong Life in Wisconsin. Boston: Allyn and Bacon.

Krier, Jennifer
1995   Narrating Herself: Power and Gender in a Minangkabau Woman's Tale of Conflict. Pp. 51–75 in Ong, Aihwa, and Michael G. Peletz (eds.), Bewitching Women, Pious Men: Gender and Body Politics in Southeast Asia. Berkeley: University of California Press.

Kroeber, A. L.
1909/1952   Classificatory Systems of Relationship. Pp. 175–181 in The Nature of Culture. Chicago: University of Chicago Press.

Kroeber, A. L., and Clyde Kluckhohn
1952/1963   Culture: Critical Review of Concepts and Definitions. New York: Vintage Books.

Kuhn, Thomas S.
1970   The Structure of Scientific Revolutions. Second Edition. Chicago: University of Chicago Press.

Labov, William
1994   Principles of Linguistic Change. Oxford, U.K.: Blackwell.

Laderman, Carol
1991   Taming the Wind of Desire: Psychology, Medicine, and Aesthetics in Malay Shamanistic Performance. Berkeley: University of California Press.

Lansing, J. Stephen
1991   Priests and Programmers: Technologies of Power in the Engineered Landscape of Bali. Princeton: Princeton University Press.
1995   The Balinese. Fort Worth, TX: Harcourt Brace College Publishers.

Lave, Jean C.
1990   The Culture of Acquisition and the Practice of Understanding. Pp. 309–327 in Stigler, James W., Richard A. Shweder, and Gilbert Herdt (eds.), Cultural Psychology: Essays on Comparative Human Development. Cambridge, U.K.: Cambridge University Press.
1991   Situated Learning: Legitimate Peripheral Participation. Cambridge, U.K.: Cambridge University Press.

Lawrence, Peter
1964   Road Belong Cargo: A Study of the Cargo Movement in the Southern Madang District, New Guinea. Atlantic Highlands, NJ: Humanities Press.

Layton, Robert
1997   An Introduction to Theory in Anthropology. Cambridge, U.K.: Cambridge University Press.

Leach, Jerry W.
1983   Introduction. Pp. 1–26 in Leach, Jerry W., and Edmund Leach (eds.), The Kula. New

Perspectives on Massim Exchange. Cambridge, U.K.: Cambridge University Press.

1988 Structure and Message in Trobriand Cricket. Pp. 237–251 in Rollwagon, Jack R. (ed.), Anthropological Filmmaking. Chur, Switzerland: Harwood Academic Publishers.

Leap, William L.

1996a Word's Out: Gay Men's English. Minneapolis: University of Minnesota Press.

1996b Study in Gay English: How I Got Here from There. Pp. 128–146 in Lewin, Ellen, and William L. Leap (eds.), Out in the Field: Reflections of Lesbian and Gay Anthropologists. Urbana: University of Illinois Press.

Leavitt, Gregory C.

1990 Sociobiological Explanations of Incest Avoidance: A Critical Review of Evidential Claims. American Anthropologist 92(4):971–993.

Ledgerwood, Judy, Mary Ebihara, and Carol A. Mortland (eds.)

1994 Introduction. Pp. 1–26 in Ebihara, May M., et al. (eds.), Cambodian Culture Since 1975: Homeland and Exile. Ithaca, NY: Cornell University Press.

Lee, Penny

1996 The Whorf Theory Complex. Amsterdam: John Benjamins Publishing Company.

Lee, Richard B.

1979 The !Kung San: Men, Women, and Work in a Foraging Society. Cambridge, U.K.: Cambridge University Press.

1993 The Dobe Ju/'hoansi. Second Edition. Fort Worth, TX: Harcourt Brace College Publishers.

1998 Forward. Pp. ix–xii in Gowdy, John M. (ed.), Limited Wants, Unlimited Means: A Reader on Hunter–Gatherer Economics and the Environment. Washington, DC: Island Press.

Lee, Richard B., and Irvin DeVore (eds.)

1968 Man the Hunter. Chicago: Aldine.

Lefton, Lester

1994 Psychology. Fifth Edition. Boston: Allyn and Bacon.

Lepowsky, Maria

1990 Gender in an Egalitarian Society: A Case Study from the Coral Sea. Pp. 119–223 in Sanday, Peggy Reeves, and Ruth Gallagher

Goodenough (eds.), Beyond the Second Sex: New Directions in the Anthropology of Gender. Philadelphia: University of Pennsylvania Press.

1993 Fruit of the Motherland: Gender in an Egalitarian Society. New York: Columbia University Press.

Lévi-Strauss, Claude

1962/1963 Totemism. Translated by Rodney Needham. Boston: Beacon Press.

1982/1979 The Way of the Masks. Translated from the French by Sylvia Modelski. French edition 1975, 1979. La Voie des Masques. Seattle: University of Washington Press.

Lewin, Ellen

1993 Lesbian Mothers: Accounts of Gender in American Culture. Ithaca, NY: Cornell University Press.

Lieberman, Leonard

1997 "Race" 1997 and 2001: A Race Odyssey. General Anthropology Division. Arlington, VA: American Anthropological Association.

Lightfoot-Klein, Hanny

1989 Prisoners of Ritual: An Odyssey into Female Genital Circumcision. New York: Harrington Park Press.

Linton, Ralph

1924 Totemism and the A.E.F. American Anthropologist 26:296–300.

Lipton, James A., and Joseph J. Marbach

1984 Ethnicity and the Pain Experience. Social Science and Medicine 19(12): 1279–1298.

Livingstone, Frank B.

1962 On the Non-existence of Human Races. Current Anthropology 3:279.

Llewellyn, K. N., and E. Adamson Hoebel

1941 The Cheyenne Way: Conflict and Case Law in Primitive Jurisprudence. Norman: University of Oklahoma Press.

Lobulu, Ben

1999 Dispossession and Land Tenure in Tanzania: What Hope from the Courts? Cultural Survival Quarterly 22(4):64–67.

Lock, Margaret

1993 Encounters with Aging: Mythologies of Menopause in Japan and North America. Berkeley: University of California Press.

Loizos, Peter
    1993   Innovation in Ethnographic Filmmaking.
            From Innocence to Self-Consciousness
            1955–1985. Chicago: University of Chicago
            Press.
Lomax, Alan
    1968   Folk Song Style and Culture. Washing-
            ton, DC: American Association for the Ad-
            vancement of Science.
Long, John Luther
    1898   Madame Butterfly. New York: Century.
Loti, Pierre
    1888   Madame Chrysanthème. Paris: Levy.
Lucy, John A.
    1992a   A Reformulation of the Linguistic Rela-
            tivity Hypothesis. Cambridge, U.K.: Cam-
            bridge University Press.
    1992b   Grammatical Categories and Cogni-
            tion: A Case Study of the Linguistic Relativ-
            ity Hypothesis. Cambridge, U.K.: Cambridge
            University Press.
Luhrmann, T. M.
    1989   Persuasions of the Witch's Craft: Ritual
            Magic in Contemporary England. Cam-
            bridge, MA: Harvard University Press.
Luong, Hy V.
    1992   Revolution in the Village: Tradition
            and Transformation in North Vietnam,
            1925–1988. Honolulu: University of Hawaii
            Press.
Lutkehaus, Nancy (ed.)
    1995   Special Section: Tribute to Timothy Asch.
            Visual Anthropology Review 11(1):2–91.

MacDougall, David
    1998   Transcultural Cinema. Princeton, NJ:
            Princeton University Press.
Malinowski, Bronislaw
    1922   Argonauts of the Western Pacific: An Ac-
            count of Native Enterprise and Adventure
            in the Archipelagos of Melanesian New
            Guinea. New York: Dutton.
    1925/1948   Magic, Science, and Religion.
            Reprinted in Magic, Science, and Other Es-
            says. Garden City, NY: Doubleday Anchor
            Books.
Marcucci, John
    1994   Sharing the Pain: Critical Values and
            Behaviors in Khmer Culture. Pp. 129–140
            in Ebihara, May M., et al. (eds.), Cambo-
            dian Culture Since 1975: Homeland and
            Exile. Ithaca, NY: Cornell University Press.
Maril, Robert Lee
    1995   The Bay Shrimpers of Texas: Rural Fish-
            erman in a Global Economy. Lawrence: Uni-
            versity Press of Kansas.
Marshall, Donald S.
    1971   Sexual Behavior on Mangaia.
            Pp. 103–162 in Marshall, Donald S., and
            Robert C. Suggs (eds.), Human Sexual Be-
            havior. New York: Basic Books.
Martin, Debra L.
    1998   Owning the Sins of the Past: Historical
            Trends, Missed Opportunities, and New Di-
            rections in the Study of Human Remains.
            Pp. 171–190 in Goodman, Alan H., and
            Thomas L. Leatherman (eds.), Building a
            New Biocultural Synthesis: Political and
            Economic Perspective on Human Biology.
            Ann Arbor: University of Michigan Press.
Martinez, Rebecca G., Leo R. Chavez, and F. Allen
Hubbell
    1997   Purity and Passion: Risk and Morality in
            Latina Immigrants and Physicians Beliefs
            about Cervical Cancer. Medical Anthropol-
            ogy 17:337–362.
Masco, Joseph
    1996   Competitive Displays: Negotiating Genea-
            logical Rights to the Potlatch at the American
            Museum of National History. American Anthro-
            pologist 98(4):837–852.
Mauss, Marcel
    1925/1954   The Gift: Forms and Functions of
            Exchange in Archaic Societies. New York:
            Norton.
Maybury-Lewis, David
    1999   The Struggle for Land at the Margins.
            Cultural Survival Quarterly 22(4):3.
McNamara, Robert S.
    1995   In Retrospect: The Tragedy and Lessons
            of Vietnam. New York: Times Books/Random
            House.
McNeill, David
    1992   Hand and Mind: What Gestures Reveal
            about Thought. Chicago: University of
            Chicago Press.
Mead, Margaret
    1928   Coming of Age in Samoa: A Psycho-
            logical Study of Primitive Youth for West-
            ern Civilization. New York: William Morrow.

1930   Social Organization of Manu'a. Honolulu: Bishop Museum.

1935   Sex and Temperament in Three Primitive Societies. New York: Morrow.

1940/1964   War Is Only an Invention—Not a Biological Necessity. Pp. 269–274 in Bramson, Leon, and George W. Goethals (eds.), War: Studies from Psychology Sociology Anthropology. New York: Basic Books.

1968   Alternatives to War. Pp. 215–228 in Fried, Morton, Marvin Harris, and Robert Murphy (eds.), War. The Anthropology of Armed Conflict and Aggression. New York: Doubleday.

Merry, Sally Engle
1990   Getting Justice and Getting Even: Legal Consciousness Among Working-Class Americans. Chicago: University of Chicago Press.

Messenger, John C.
1969   Inis Beag: Isle of Ireland. New York: Holt, Rinehart and Winston.

1971   Sex and Repression in an Irish Folk Community. In Marshall, Donald S., and Robert C. Suggs (eds.), Human Sexual Behavior. New York: Basic Books.

Michener, James A.
1954   Sayonara. New York: Random House.

Miksic, John
1990   Borobudur. Golden Tales of the Buddhas. Singapore: Periplus Editions.

Mintz, Sidney
1961   Pratik: Haitian Personal Economic Relationships. Pp. 54–63 in Proceedings of the 1961 Annual Spring Meeting of the American Anthropological Society. Seattle: University of Washington Press.

1985   Sweetness and Power: The Place of Sugar in Modern History. New York: Viking Penguin Books.

Montagu, Ashley
1978   Learning Non-aggression: The Experience of Non-literate Societies. New York: Oxford University Press.

Moore, Omar Khayam
1957   Divination: A New Perspective. American Anthropologist 59(1):69–74.

Morris, Rosalind C.
1994   New Worlds from Fragments: Film, Ethnography, and the Representation of Northwest Coast Cultures. Boulder, CO: Westview Press.

Murdock, George P.
1948/1965   Waging Baseball on Truk. Pp. 291–293 in Culture and Society: Twenty-Four Essays by George Peter Murdock. Pittsburgh: University of Pittsburgh Press.

1949   Social Structure. New York: Macmillan.

Murphy, Robert F.
1964   Social Distance and the Veil. American Anthropologist 66(6.1):1257–1274.

Myerhoff, Barbara
1979   Number Our Days: Culture and Community Among Elderly Jews in an American Ghetto. New York: Meridian

Myrdal, Gunnar
1944   An American Dilemma: The Negro Problem and Modern Democracy. New York: Harper.

Nader, Laura
1969   Styles of Court Procedure: To Make the Balance. Pp. 69–91 in Nader, Laura (ed.), Law in Culture and Society. Chicago: Aldine.

1972   Up the Anthropologist: Perspectives Gained from Studying Up. Pp. 284–311 in Hymes, Dell (ed.), Reinventing Anthropology. New York: Pantheon Books.

2002   Missing Links: A Commentary on Ward H. Goodenough's Moving Article "Anthropology in the 20th Century and Beyond." American Anthropologist 104.2:441–449.

Nanda, Serena
1990   The Hijras of India. Belmont, CA: Wadsworth.

1994   Hijras: An Alternative Sex and Gender Role in India. Pp. 374–417 in Herdt, Gilbert (ed.), Third Sex, Third Gender: Beyond Sexual Dimorphism in Culture and History. New York: Zone Books.

Narotzky, Susana
1997   New Directions in Economic Anthropology. London: Pluto Press.

Niezen, Ronald
1998   Defending the Land: Sovereignty and Forest Life in James Bay Cree Society. Boston: Allyn and Bacon.

Nigh, Ronald
2002   Maya Medicine in the Biological Gaze: Bioprospecting Research as Herbal Fetishism. Current Anthropology 43(3):464–477.

Nordstrom, Carolyn, and Antonius C. G. M. Robben (eds.)
1995 Fieldwork Under Fire: Contemporary Studies of Violence and Survival. Berkeley: University of California Press.

O'Brien, Denise
1977 Female Husbands in Southern Bantu Societies. In Schlegel, Alice (ed.), Sexual Stratification. New York: Columbia University Press.
O'Brien, Denise, and Anton Ploeg
1964 Acculturation Movements among the Western Dani. American Anthropologist 66(4.2):281–292.
Ochs, Elinor
1992 Indexing Gender. Pp. 336–58 in Durante, Alessandro, and Charles Goodwin (eds.), Rethinking Context: Language as an Interactive Phenomenon. Cambridge, U.K.: Cambridge University Press.
Oetomo, Dede
1991 Patterns of Bisexuality in Indonesia. In Tielman, Rob A. P., et al. (eds.), Bisexuality and HIV/AIDS. Buffalo, NY: Prometheus.
Ogbu, John U.
1974 The Next Generation: An Ethnography of Education in an Urban Neighborhood. New York: Academic Press.
Ong, Aihwa
1987 Spirit of Resistance and Capitalist Discipline: Factory Women in Malaysia. Albany: State University of New York Press.
Opie, Iona and Peter Opie
1959 The Lore and Language of Schoolchildren. Oxford, U.K.: Clarendon Press.
1969 Children's Games in Street and Playground. Oxford, U.K.: Clarendon Press.
Orans, Martin
1996 Not Even Wrong: Margaret Mead, Derek Freeman, and the Samoans. San Francisco, CA: Chandler and Sharp Publications.

Parker, Seymour
1996 Full Brother–Sister Marriages in Roman Egypt: Another Look. Cultural Anthropology 11(3):362–376.
Paul, Robert A.
1994 My Approach to Psychological Anthropology. Pp. 80–102 in Suarez-Orozco, Marcelo M., George Spindler, and Louise

Spindler (eds.), The Making of Psychological Anthropology II. Fort Worth, TX: Harcourt Brace College Publishers.
Peletz, Michael G.
1996 Reason and Passion: Representations of Gender in a Malay Society. Berkeley: University of California Press.
Peltz, Rakhmiel
1998 From Immigrant to Ethnic Culture: American Yiddish in South Philadelphia. Stanford, CA: Stanford University Press.
Pigg, Stacy Leigh
2001 Languages of Sex and AIDS in Nepal: Notes on the Social Production of Commensurability. Cultural Anthropology 16(4):481–541.
Pike, Kenneth L.
1954 Language in Relation to a Unified Theory of the Structure of Human Behavior. The Hague: Mouton.
Pine, Frances
1996 Naming the House and Naming the Land: Kinship and Social Groups in Highland Poland. Journal of the Royal Anthropological Institute 2(3):443–459.
Pinker, Steven
1994 The Language Instinct: How the Mind Creates Language. New York: William Morrow.
Plattner, Stuart (ed.)
1984 Introduction. Pp. vii–xx in Plattner, Stuart (ed.), Markets and Marketing. Lanham, MD: University Press of America.
Plotkin, Mark J.
1993 Tales of a Shaman's Apprentice: An Ethnobotanist Searches for New Medicines in the Amazon Rainforest. New York: Viking.
Polanyi, Karl
1957 Trade and Market in the Early Empires: Economics in History and Theory. Glencoe, IL: Free Press.
1966 Dahomey and the Slave Trade: An Analysis of an Archaic Economy. Seattle: University of Washington Press.
Povinelli, Daniel J., and Jesse M. Bering
2002 The Mentality of Apes Revisited. Current Directions in Psychological Science 11(4):115–121.
Priest, Kersten
1998 Disharmony in the 11:00 A.M. Worship Hour: A Case Study of an Abandoned

Interethnic Church Merger. Unpublished M.A. thesis. Department of Anthropology, University of South Carolina, Columbia.

Pukui, Mary Kawena, E. W. Haertig, and Catherine A. Lee
1972 Nana I Ke Kumu (Look to the Source). Volume I. Honolulu: Hui Hanai.

Quinn, Malcolm
1994 The Swastika: Constructing the Symbol. London: Routledge.

Quinn, Naomi
1987 Convergent Evidence for a Cultural Model of American Marriage. Pp. 173–192 in Holland, Dorothy, and Naomi Quinn (eds.), Cultural Models in Language and Thought. Cambridge, U.K.: Cambridge University Press.

Rappaport, Roy A.
1968 Pigs for the Ancestors. New Haven, CT: Yale University Press.

Redfield, Robert
1956 Peasant Society and Culture. Chicago: University of Chicago Press.

Reed, Richard
1997 Forest Dwellers, Forest Protectors: Indigenous Models for International Development. Boston: Allyn and Bacon.

Reid, Anthony
1988 Southeast Asia in the Age of Commerce, 1450–1680. Volume One: The Lands Below the Winds. New Haven, CT: Yale University Press.

Reid, William
1971 Out of the Silence. New York: Harper and Row.

Rice, Patricia C.
1997 Races or Clines? General Anthropology Division Modules in Teaching Anthropology. Arlington, VA: American Anthropological Association.

Robarchek, Clayton A., and Carole J. Robarchek
1992 Cultures of War and Peace: A Comparative Study of Waorani and Semai. Pp. 189–213 in Silverberg, James, and J. Patrick Gray (eds.), Aggression and Peacefulness in Humans and Other Primates. New York: Oxford University Press.

Robertson, Jennifer
1998 Takarazuka: Sexual Politics and Popular Culture in Modern Japan. Berkeley: University of California Press.

Robinson, Geoffrey
1995 The Dark Side of Paradise: Political Violence in Bali. Ithaca, NY: Cornell University Press.

Rosaldo, Michelle Z.
1980 Knowledge and Passion: Ilongot Notions of Self and Social Life. Cambridge, U.K.: Cambridge University Press.

Rosaldo, Michelle Zimbalist, and Louise Lamphere (eds.)
1974 Women, Culture, and Society. Stanford, CA: Stanford University Press.

Roscoe, Will
1991 The Zuni Man-Woman. Albuquerque: University of New Mexico Press.
1994 How to Become a Berdache: Toward a Unified Analysis of Gender Diversity. Pp. 329–372 in Herdt, Gilbert (ed.), Third Sex, Third Gender: Beyond Sexual Dimorphism in Culture and History. New York: Zone Books.

Rozin, Paul, and Carol Nemeroff
1990 The Laws of Sympathetic Magic. A Psychological Analysis of Similarity and Contagion. Pp. 203–232 in Stigler, James W., Richard A. Shweder, and Gilbert Herdt (eds.), Cultural Psychology: Essays on Comparative Human Development. Cambridge, U.K.: Cambridge University Press.

Ruby, Jay (ed.)
1993 The Cinema of John Marshall. Chur, Switzerland: Harwood Academic Publishers.

Ruddick, Abby
1986 Charmed Lives: Illness, Healing, Power and Gender in a Balinese Village. Unpublished Ph.D. dissertation. Brown University.

Rundstrom, Arnold, Ronald Rundstrom, and Clinton Bergum
1973 Japanese Tea: The Ritual, the Aesthetics, the Way. An Ethnographic Companion to the Film, *The Path.* New York: MSS Information Corp.

Sahlins, Marshall
  1963 Poor Man, Rich Man, Big-Man, Chief. Comparative Studies in Society and History 5:285–303.
  1965 On the Sociology of Primitive Exchange. Pp. 139–236 in Banton, M. (ed.), The Relevance of Models for Social Anthropology. London: Tavistock.
Sanday, Peggy
  1990 Androcentric and Matrifocal Gender Representations in Minangkabau Ideology. Pp. 139–168 in Sanday, Peggy Reeves, and Ruth Gallagher Goodenough (eds.), Beyond the Second Sex: New Directions in the Anthropology of Gender. Philadelphia: University of Pennsylvania Press.
Santos, Bonaventura De Sousa
  1987 Law: A Map of Misreading: Toward a Post-modern Conception of Law. Journal of Law and Society 14(3):279–302.
Scheper-Hughes, Nancy
  1992 Death without Weeping: The Violence of Everyday Life in Brazil. Berkeley: University of California Press.
Scheper-Hughes, Nancy, and Carolyn Sargent (eds.)
  1998 Small Wars: The Cultural Politics of Childhood. Berkeley: University of California Press.
Schieffelin, Bambi, and Eleanor Ochs (eds.)
  1986 Language Socialization Across Culture. Cambridge, U.K.: Cambridge University Press.
Schneider, David M.
  1980 American Kinship: A Cultural Account. Chicago: University of Chicago Press.
Schoeman, Ferdinand
  1992 Privacy and Social Freedom. Cambridge, U.K.: Cambridge University Press.
Schoeman, Ferdinand (ed.)
  1984 Philosophical Dimensions of Privacy: An Anthology. Cambridge, U.K.: Cambridge University Press.
Schultes, R. E., and Siri von Reis (eds.)
  1995 Ethnobotany: Evolution of a Discipline. Portland, OR: Dioscorides Press.
Scott, James C.
  1976 The Moral Economy of the Peasant: Rebellion and Subsistence in Southeast Asia. New Haven, CT: Yale University Press.
  1985 Weapons of the Weak: Everyday Forms of Peasant Resistance. New Haven, CT: Yale University Press.
  1998 Seeing Like a State: How Certain Schemes to Improve the Human Condition Have Failed. New Haven, CT: Yale University Press.
Secoy, Frank Raymond
  1953 Changing Military Patterns on the Great Plains (17th Century Through Early 19th Century). Seattle: University of Washington Press.
Senft, Gunter
  1992 "As Time Goes By . . . " Changes Observed in Trobriand Islanders' Culture and Language, Milne Bay Province, PNG. Pp. 67–89 in Dutton, Tom (ed.), Culture Change, Language Change: Case Studies from Melanesia. Canberra, Australia: ANU. Department of Linguistics, Research School of Pacific Studies.
Shankman, Paul
  1991 Culture Contact, Cultural Ecology, and Dani Warfare. MAN 26(2):299–321.
  1996 The History of Samoan Sexual Conduct and the Mead–Freeman Controversy. American Anthropologist 98(3):555–567.
Sharon, Douglas
  1978 Wizard of the Four Winds: A Shaman's Story. New York: Free Press.
Shaw, Brent D.
  1992 Explaining Incest: Brother–Sister Marriage in Graeco-Roman Egypt. MAN 27(2):267–299.
Sheehan, Elizabeth A.
  1997 Victorian Clitoridectomy: Isaac Baker Brown and His Harmless Operative Procedure. Pp. 325–334 in Lancaster, Roger N., and Micaela di Leonardo (eds.), The Gender/Sexuality Reader: Culture, History, and Political Economy. New York: Routledge.
Sherman, Suzanne
  1993 Lesbian and Gay Marriage: Private Commitments, Public Ceremonies. Philadelphia: Temple University Press.
Shore, Bradd
  1981 Sexuality and Gender in Samoa: Conceptions and Missed Conceptions. Pp. 192–215 in Ortner, Sherry B., and Harriet Whitehead (eds.), Sexual Meanings: The Cultural Con-

struction of Gender and Sexuality. New York: Cambridge University Press.

1982   Sala'ilua: A Samoan Mystery. New York: Columbia University Press.

Shostak, Marjorie
1981   Nisa: The Life and Words of a !Kung Woman. Cambridge, MA: Harvard University Press.

Silverberg, James, and J. Patrick Gray (eds.)
1992   Aggression and Peacefulness in Humans and Other Primates. New York: Oxford University Press.

Simons, Ronald C.
1996   Boo! Culture, Experience, and the Startle Reflex. Oxford, U.K.: Oxford University Press.

Simoons, Frederick J.
1990   Food in China: A Cultural and Historical Inquiry. Boca Raton, FL: CRC Press.

Simpson, Bob
1994   Bringing the "Unclear" Family into Focus: Divorce and Re-marriage in Contemporary Britain. MAN 29(1):831–851.

Singer, Merrill (ed.)
1997   Needle Exchange and AIDS Prevention: Advances and Controversies in Public Health and Social Policy. Medical Anthropology 18:1.

Smith, Robert J.
1978   Kurusu: The Price of Progress in a Japanese Village, 1951–1975. Stanford, CA: Stanford University Press.

Smith-Hefner, Nancy J.
1999   Khmer American: Identity and Moral Education in a Diasporic Community. Berkeley: University of California Press.

Spicer, Edward H.
1968   Acculturation. Pp. 21–27 in Sills, David L. (ed.), International Encyclopedia of the Social Sciences. Vol. 1. New York: Macmillan and Free Press.

Spiro, Melford E.
1958   Children of the Kibbutz. Cambridge, MA: Harvard University Press.

Sponsel, Leslie, and Thomas Gregor (eds.)
1994   The Anthropology of Peace and Nonviolence. Boulder, CO: L. Rienner.
1998   Yanomami: An Arena of Conflict and Aggression in the Amazon. Aggressive Behavior 24:97–122.

Stack, Carol B.
1974   All Our Kin: Strategies for Survival in a Black Community. New York: Harper and Row.

Stanner, W. E. H.
1965   Religion, Totemism and Symbolism. Pp. 207–237 in Berndt, R. M., and C. H. Berndt (eds.), Aboriginal Man in Australia: Essays in Honour of Professor Emeritus A. P. Elkin. Sydney, Australia: Angus and Robertson.

Steinbauer, Friedrich
1971/1979   Melanesian Cargo Cults: New Salvation Movements in the South Pacific. Brisbane, Australia: University of Queensland Press.

Steward, Julian H.
1955   Theory of Culture Change: The Methodology of Multilinear Evolution. Urbana: University of Illinois Press.

Stewart, Charles, and Rosalind Shaw (eds.)
1994   Syncretism/ Anti-syncretism: The Politics of Religious Synthesis. London: Routledge.

Stoller, Paul
1992   The Cinematic Griot: The Ethnography of Jean Rouch. Chicago: University of Chicago Press.

Stone, Linda
1997   Kinship and Gender: An Introduction. Boulder, CO: Westview Press.

Stone-Ferrier, Linda
1989   Spun Virtue, The Lacework of Folly, and the World Wound Upside-Down: Seventeenth Century Dutch Depictions of Female Handwork. Pp. 215–242 in Weiner, Annette, and Jane Schneider (eds.), Cloth and Human Experience. Washington, DC: Smithsonian University Press.

Strathern, Andrew
1992   Let the Bow Go Down. Pp. 229–250 in Ferguson, R. Brian, and Neil L. Whitehead (eds.), War in the Tribal Zone: Expanding States and Indigenous Warfare. Seattle: University of Washington Press.

Suggs, Robert C.
1966   Marquesan Sexual Behavior. New York: Harcourt, Brace and World.

Suttles, Wayne
1991   Streams of Property, Armor of Wealth: The Traditional Kwakiutl Potlatch. Pp. 71–134 in Jonaitis, Aldona (ed.), Chiefly Feasts:

The Enduring Kwakiutl Potlatch. Seattle: University of Washington Press.

Tannen, Deborah
1994 Gender and Discourse. New York: Oxford University Press.
Taylor, Julia
1998 Paper Tangos. Durham, NC: Duke University Press.
Tenga, W. Ringo
1999 Legitimizing Dispossession: The Tanzanian High Court's Decision on the Eviction of Maasai Pastoralists from Mkomazi Game Reserve. Cultural Survival Quarterly 22(4):60–63.
Thomas, Hugh
1997 The Slave Trade: The Story of the Atlantic Slave Trade, 1440–1870. New York: Simon and Schuster.
Tierney, Patrick
2000 Darkness in El Dorado: How Scientists and Journalists Devastated the Amazon. New York: W. W. Norton.
Tonkinson, Robert
1991 The Mardu Aborigines: Living the Dream in Australia's Desert. Second Edition. Fort Worth, TX: Holt, Rinehart and Winston.
Townsend, Joan B.
1957 Shamanism. Pp. 429–469 in Glazier, Stephen O. (ed.), Anthropology of Religion: A Handbook. Westport, CT: Greenwood Press.
Turner, Victor
1964/1967 Betwixt and Between: The Liminal Period in Rites de Passage. Pp. 93–111 in The Forest of Symbols: Aspects of Ndembu Ritual. Ithaca, NY: Cornell University Press.
1979 Introduction to Myerhoff 1979.
Twain, Mark
1884/1979 The Adventures of Huckleberry Finn. New York: Signet.
Tylor, Edward B.
1871/1958 Primitive Culture. London: John Murray. Reprinted Chapters I–X as The Origins of Culture. New York: Harper Torchbook.

van Gennep, Arnold
1908/1960 The Rites of Passage. Chicago: Phoenix Books.

Van Willigen, John, and V. C. Channa
1991 Law, Custom, and Crimes against Women: The Problem of Dowry Death in India. Human Organization 50(4):369–376.
Veblen, Thorstein
1899 The Theory of the Leisure Class. New York: Macmillan.
Vogt, Evon Z.
1970 The Zinacantecos of Mexico: A Modern Maya Way of Life. New York: Holt, Rinehart, and Winston.
1994 Fieldwork Among the Maya: Reflections on the Harvard Chiapas Project. Albuquerque: University of New Mexico Press.

Walens, Stanley
1981 Feasting with Cannibals: An Essay on Kwakiutl Cosmology. Princeton, NJ: Princeton University Press.
Walker, Alice
1992 Possessing the Secret of Joy. New York: Harcourt Brace Jovanovich.
Walker, Alice, and Pratibha Parman
1993 Warrior Marks: Female Genital Mutilation and the Sexual Blinding of Women. New York: Harcourt Brace Jovanovich.
Wallace, Anthony F. C.
1966 Religion: An Anthropological View. New York: Random House.
1969 The Death and Rebirth of the Seneca. New York: Alfred A. Knopf.
Wallerstein, Immanuel M.
1985 The Modern World-System. New York: Academic Press.
Watson, O. Michael
1970 Proxemic Behavior: A Cross-Cultural Study. The Hague: Mouton.
Watson-Gegeo, Karen, and Geoffrey M. White (eds.)
1990 Disentangling: Conflict Discourse in Pacific Societies. Stanford, CA: Stanford University Press.
Webb, Eugene J.
1981 Nonreactive Measures in the Social Sciences. Boston: Houghton Mifflin.
Webster, Gloria Cranmer
1991 The Contemporary Potlatch. Pp. 227–250 in Jonaitis, Aldona (ed.), Chiefly

Feasts: The Enduring Kwakiutl Potlatch. Seattle: University of Washington Press.

Weiner, Annette

1976   Women of Value, Men of Reknown: New Perspectives in Trobriand Exchange. Austin: University of Texas Press.

1988   The Trobrianders of Papua New Guinea. New York: Holt, Rinehart and Winston.

1989   Why Cloth?: Wealth, Gender, and Power in Oceania. Pp. 37–72 in Weiner, Annette B., and Jane Schneider (eds.), Cloth and Human Experience. Washington, DC: Smithsonian Institute Press.

Weiner, Margaret J.

1995   Visible and Invisible Realm: Power, Magic, and Colonial Conquest in Bali. Chicago: University of Chicago Press.

White, Geoffrey M., and John Kirkpatrick (eds.)

1985   Person, Self and Experience: Exploring Pacific Ethnopsychologies. Berkeley: University of California Press.

Whiting, John W. M.

1990   Adolescent Ritual and Identity Conflict. Pp. 357–65 in Stigler, James W., Richard A. Shweder, and Gilbert Herdt (eds.), Cultural Psychology: Essays on Comparative Human Development. Cambridge, U.K.: Cambridge University Press.

Whiting, Robert

1977   The Chrysanthemum and the Bat: Baseball Samurai Style. New York: Dodd, Mead.

Whorf, Benjamin Lee

1956   Language, Thought, and Reality: Selected Writings. Cambridge, MA: Technical Press of MIT.

Widlock, Thomas

1997   Orientation in the Wild: The Shared Cognition of Hai//om Bushpeople. Journal of the Royal Anthropological Institute 3(2):317–332.

Wilmsen, E. N., and J. R. Denbow

1990   Paradigmatic History of San-Speaking Peoples and Current Attempts at Revision. Current Anthropology 31:489–524.

Wilson, Thomas

1986   The Swastika, the Earliest Known Symbol and Its Migrations, with Observations on the Migration of Certain Industries in Prehistorical Times. Washington, DC: U.S. National Museum.

Wolf, Arthur P.

1995   Sexual Attraction and Childhood Association: A Chinese Brief for Eduard Westermarck. Stanford, CA: Stanford University Press.

Wood, J. G.

1879   Uncivilized Races of Men in All Countries of the World: Being a Comprehensive Account of Their Manners and Customs, and of Their Physical, Mental, Moral and Religious Characteristics. Cincinnati, OH: J. A. Brainerd & Company.

Zboroski, Mark

1952   Cultural Components in Responses to Pain. Journal of Social Issues 8(16):16–30.

Zola, Irving Kenneth

1966   Culture and Symptoms—An Analysis of Patients' Presenting Complaints. American Sociological Review 31:615–630.

INDEX